A History of Latin America

Fifth Edition

Benjamin Keen

Professor Emeritus
Northern Illinois University

HOUGHTON MIFFLIN COMPANY   Boston   Toronto

Geneva, Illinois   Palo Alto   Princeton, New Jersey

Cover Designer: Harold Burch, Harold Burch Design, New York City.
Cover Image: Tarsila do Amaral, "Central Railway of Brazil," 1924. Courtesy of
Museu de Arte Contemporânea da Universidade de São Paulo.

Part opener photos: p. 1, Philip Teuscher; p. 179, Reproduccion autorizada por
el Instituto Nacional de Bellas Artes y Literatura/Collection Museo Nacional de
Historia, INAH-SEP; p. 261, Reuters/Bettmann.

Credits continue following index.

Maps by Dick Sanderson; Patty Isaacs, *Parrot Graphics.*

Senior Sponsoring Editor: Jean Woy
Senior Associate Editor: Jeff Greene
Senior Project Editor: Janet Young
Editorial Assistant: Beth Emmons
Senior Production/Design Coordinator: Sarah Ambrose
Senior Manufacturing Coordinator: Priscilla Bailey
Marketing Manager: Pamela Shaffer

Printed in the U.S.A.

Library of Congress Catalog Card Number: 95-76955

ISBN 0-395-74455-5

1 2 3 4 5 6 7 8 9-QM-99 98 97 96 95

such claims "with vitriolic effectiveness" more than a decade earlier. Evans concluded that the dependency approach had established itself as one of the "primary lenses through which scholars, both North American and Latin American, analyze the interaction of classes and the state in the context of an increasingly internationalized economy," and that "it is hard to argue that this approach has been or is likely to be replaced by some new overarching paradigm." Since Evans wrote those words, Latin America has experienced deepening economic and social crises that have given new relevance to the dependency approach.

Writers of the dependency school employ some standard terms that we use in this text: *neocolonialism, neoliberalism,* and *center* and *periphery. Neocolonialism* refers to the dependent condition of countries that enjoy formal political independence. *Neoliberalism* refers to the policies of privatization, austerity, and trade liberalization dictated to dependent countries by the International Monetary Fund and the World Bank as a condition for approval of investment, loans, and debt relief. (The IMF and the World Bank prefer to give such policies the innocuous-sounding name of "structural adjustment programs.") The term *center* is applied to the dominant group of developed capitalist countries, and *periphery* to the underdeveloped or dependent countries.

A word about the organization of this text. In its planning, the decision was made to reject the approach that tries to cover the post-independence history of the twenty Latin American republics in detail, including mention of every general who ever passed through a presidential palace. Most teachers will agree that this approach discourages students by miring them in a bog of tedious facts. Accordingly, it was decided to limit coverage of the national period in the nineteenth century to Mexico, Argentina, Chile, and Brazil, whose history seemed to illustrate best the major issues and trends of the period. In addition to covering these four countries, the survey of the twentieth century broadened to include the central Andean area, with a special concentration on Peru, and Cuba, the scene of a socialist revolu-

tion with continental repercussions. The second edition added a chapter on Central America, where a revolutionary storm, having toppled the U.S.–supported Somoza tyranny in Nicaragua, threatened the rickety structures of oligarchical and military rule in El Salvador and Guatemala. The fourth edition recognized the political and economic importance of the Bolivarian lands of Venezuela and Colombia by including a chapter on the modern history of those countries.

To accommodate alternative course configurations, the present edition of *A History of Latin America* continues to be published in two volumes as well as in a complete version. Volume I includes Latin American history from ancient times to 1910, and Volume II covers Latin American history from Independence to the present. An expanded introduction to Volume II has been added to provide some background for those students who do not take the first half of the course.

The organization of the text has been improved further in this edition. Chapters 6 and 7 in the previous edition, "The Bourbon Reforms and Spanish America" and "Colonial Brazil," are now reversed. This change helps to clarify coverage of these areas. Now the Spanish colonies and Portuguese colony of Brazil are treated first before discussion moves on to the Bourbon reforms and the independence movements.

Lastly, the recent history of all the countries under discussion has been brought up to date, and the rest of the book has been thoroughly revised to reflect current scholarship. Special emphasis is placed on such topics as the impact of neoliberal economic policies and the gathering revolt against them, the effects of the North American Free Trade Agreement, the growing urgency of environmental issues, and the heightened visibility of the women's movement.

The book has also benefited from the careful scrutiny of the fourth edition by colleagues who made valuable suggestions for revision:

Susan Fernandez, University of South Florida
Michael Fry, Fort Lewis College
Thomas Holloway, Cornell University
Evelyn Hu-DeHart, University of Colorado—
    Boulder

Susan Kellogg, University of Houston
Robert M. Levine, University of Miami
Richard W. Slatta, North Carolina State
University

Many but not all of these colleagues' suggestions were adopted; these individuals bear no responsibility for any remaining errors of fact or interpretation. I wish to recall, too, the many students, graduate and undergraduate, who helped me to define my views on Latin American history through the give-and-take of classroom discussion and the reading and discussion of their papers and theses. In particular, I wish to thank two former students, Professors Steven Niblo and Keith Haynes, for sharing with me the findings of their important research on the political economy of the *Porfiriato* and the ideology of the Mexican revolution, respectively.

B.K.

Introduction

The Geographical Background of Latin American History

Latin America, a region of startling physical contrasts, stretches 7,000 miles southward from the Mexican-U.S. border to the tip of Tierra del Fuego on Cape Horn. The widest east-west point, across Peru and Brazil, spans 3,200 miles. This diverse geography has helped produce distinctive development of each Latin American nation.

Latin America has two dominant physical characteristics: enormous mountains and vast river systems. The often snowcapped and sometimes volcanic mountain ranges—the three Sierra Madre ranges in Mexico and the 4,000-mile-long Andes in South America making a western spine from Venezuela to Tierra del Fuego—form the backbone of the landmass. Nearly impassable for most of their length, these mountain ranges boast many peaks of over 22,000 feet. The mountains have presented a formidable barrier to trade and communications in Mexico and the nations of the southern continent. Not only do the mountain ranges separate nations from each other, they divide regions within nations.

The enormous rivers most often lie in lightly populated areas. Three mammoth river systems (the Amazon, the Orinoco, and the Río de la Plata) spread over almost the entire South American continent east of the Andes. The size of the Amazon River Basin and the surrounding tropics—the largest such area in the world—has posed another impediment to the development of transportation and human settlement, although some rivers are navigable for long distances. Only with the advent of modern technology—railroads, telegraph, telephones, automobiles, and airplanes—has geographic isolation been partly overcome, a condition that has helped create markets and forge independent states.

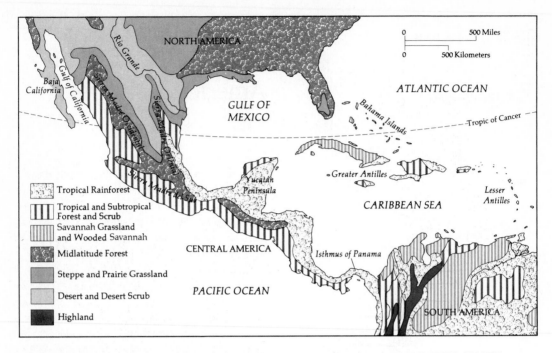

THE MAPS ON THESE TWO PAGES FORM AN OVERALL PICTURE OF THE NATURAL GEOGRAPHIC FEATURES OF LATIN AMERICA: MIDDLE AMERICA (ABOVE) COMPOSED OF MEXICO, CENTRAL AMERICA, AND THE CARIBBEAN REGION; AND SOUTH AMERICA (NEXT PAGE).

Latin America encompasses five climatological regions: high mountains, tropical jungles, deserts, temperate coastal plains, and temperate highlands. The first three are sparsely populated, while the latter two tend to be densely inhabited. With the exception of the Mayan, all the great ancient civilizations arose in the highlands of the Andes and Mexico.

The varied climate and topography of South America, Mexico, and Central America have helped produce this highly uneven distribution of population. Three notable examples, the gargantuan Amazonian region of mostly steamy tropical forests and savannah, the vast desert of Patagonia in southern Argentina, and the northern wastelands of Mexico, support few inhabitants. In contrast to these inhospitable regions, a thin strip along Brazil's coast, the plain along the Río de la Plata estuary in Argentina, and the central plateau of Mexico contain most of the people in these countries. Thus these nations are overpopulated and underpopulated at the same time.

In western South America the heaviest concentration of people is found on the inland plateaus. None of the major cities—Santiago, Chile; Lima, Peru; Quito, Ecuador; and Bogotá and Medellín, Colombia—are ports; there are few good natural harbors on the west coast. In contrast, in eastern South America the major cities—Buenos Aires, Argentina; Montevideo, Uruguay; and São Paulo–Santos, Rio de Janeiro, Bahia, and Recife, Brazil—are situated on the Atlantic coast. The majority of people in Argentina, Brazil, and Uruguay reside on the coastal plains. Mexico City, Guadalajara, and Monterrey, Mexico's largest cities, are inland. Almost all these cities have a population of over one million, with Mexico City, the largest, having over 20 million.

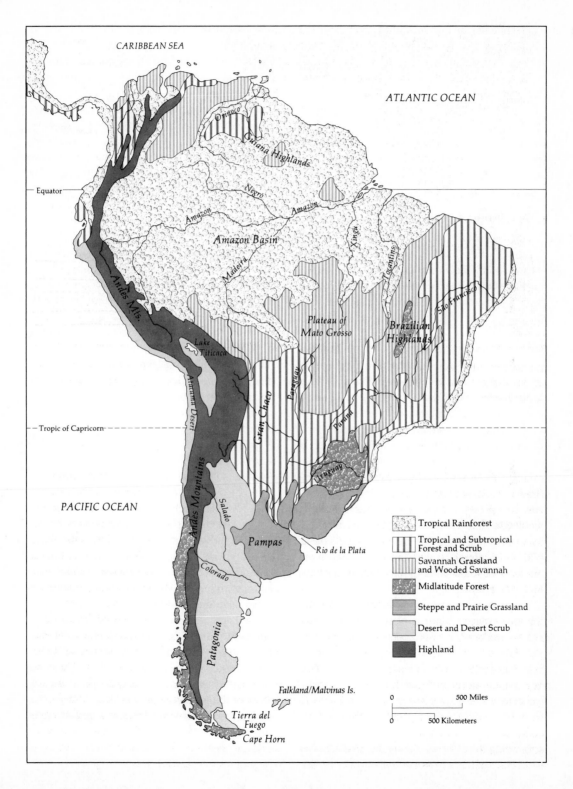

CARIBBEAN SEA

ATLANTIC OCEAN

Orinoco

Guiana Highlands

Equator

Negro

Amazon

Amazon

Amazon Basin

Xingu

Andes Mts.

Madeira

Tocantins

São Francisco

Plateau of
Mato Grosso

Brazilian
Highlands

Lake
Titicaca

Atacama Desert

Gran Chaco

Paraguay

Paraná

Tropic of Capricorn

Uruguay

PACIFIC OCEAN

Andes Mountains

Salado

Pampas

Rio de la Plata

Colorado

Patagonia

Falkland/Malvinas Is.

Tierra del
Fuego

Cape Horn

Tropical Rainforest

Tropical and Subtropical
Forest and Scrub

Savannah Grassland
and Wooded Savannah

Midlatitude Forest

Steppe and Prairie Grassland

Desert and Desert Scrub

Highland

0   500 Miles

0   500 Kilometers

The number of waterways and the amount of rainfall vary greatly from region to region. Mexico has no rivers of importance, while Brazil contains the huge Amazon network. Lack of rain and rivers for irrigation in large areas makes farming impossible. Barely 10 percent of Mexico's land is fertile enough to farm; rainfall is so uncertain in some cultivable areas that drought strikes often and for years at a time. Mexico, with too little water, contrasts with Brazil, with too much. Much of Brazil's vast territory, however, is equally uncultivable as its tropical soils have high acidity and have proved infertile and incapable of sustaining agricultural crops.

On the other hand, Latin America has enormous natural resources for economic development. Mexico and Venezuela rank among the world's largest oil producers. Mexico may have the biggest petroleum reserves of any nation other than Saudi Arabia. Bolivia, Ecuador, Colombia, and Peru also produce oil. Over the centuries, Latin American nations have been leading sources of copper (Mexico and Chile), nitrate (Chile), silver (Peru and Mexico), gold (Brazil), diamonds (Brazil), and tin (Bolivia). Much of the world's coffee is grown on the fertile highlands of Central America, Colombia, and Brazil. Much of the world's cattle have been raised on the plains of northern Mexico, southern Brazil, and central Argentina. Argentina's immense plains, the Pampas, are among the planet's most fertile areas, yielding not only cattle but sheep and wheat as well. Over the past five centuries, the coastal plains of Brazil have produced enormous amounts of sugar. In addition, human ingenuity has converted geographical obstacles into assets. Some extensive river systems have potential for hydroelectric power and provide water for irrigation as well, as has been done in Mexico's arid regions.

The historical record shows that the richness of Latin America's resources has had a significant impact on the economic and political development of Europe and North America. The gold and silver of its New World Empire fueled Spain's wars and diplomacy in Europe for four hundred years. Many scholars trace the origins of the Industrial Revolution in such nations as Great Britain and the Netherlands to resources extracted from Latin America by its colonial masters, Spain and Portugal.

Latin America's resources have affected economic development elsewhere, but how these resources have been developed and by whom and in which ways has profoundly changed the history of the nations in this area. Geography has perhaps narrowed historical alternatives in Latin America, but the decisions of people determined its development. Going back to the colonization by Spain and Portugal, Latin America's history has been marked by exploitation of its peoples and its natural resources. Imperial Spain's policy to drain the lands it conquered of gold, silver, and other resources fixed the pattern for later exploiters. With European dominance came the decisions to subjugate the indigenous peoples and often force them to labor under subhuman conditions in mines and large estates, where many died. In the more recent era, there has been the decision to grow bananas on the coastal plains of Central America instead of corn or other staples of the local diet; this has made export profitable, usually for North American concerns, but this land use has left many, like the Guatemalans, without sufficient food. Meanwhile the uncontrolled expansion of capitalism in the area has led to an ecological crisis, reflected in massive deforestation, severe soil exhaustion, and growing agricultural and industrial pollution. These developments have contributed to rapid depletion of renewable resources, lack of clean water and air, and major epidemics of contagious diseases and other health problems.

The book that follows is a history of the development of Latin America's economy, politics, and society viewed primarily from the perspective of ordinary people, who were exploited and oppressed but who resisted and endured. It is the story of the events and forces that produced the alternatives from which Latin Americans created their world.

Part 1

The Colonial Heritage of Latin America

The number of waterways and the amount of rainfall vary greatly from region to region. Mexico has no rivers of importance, while Brazil contains the huge Amazon network. Lack of rain and rivers for irrigation in large areas makes farming impossible. Barely 10 percent of Mexico's land is fertile enough to farm; rainfall is so uncertain in some cultivable areas that drought strikes often and for years at a time. Mexico, with too little water, contrasts with Brazil, with too much. Much of Brazil's vast territory, however, is equally uncultivable as its tropical soils have high acidity and have proved infertile and incapable of sustaining agricultural crops.

On the other hand, Latin America has enormous natural resources for economic development. Mexico and Venezuela rank among the world's largest oil producers. Mexico may have the biggest petroleum reserves of any nation other than Saudi Arabia. Bolivia, Ecuador, Colombia, and Peru also produce oil. Over the centuries, Latin American nations have been leading sources of copper (Mexico and Chile), nitrate (Chile), silver (Peru and Mexico), gold (Brazil), diamonds (Brazil), and tin (Bolivia). Much of the world's coffee is grown on the fertile highlands of Central America, Colombia, and Brazil. Much of the world's cattle have been raised on the plains of northern Mexico, southern Brazil, and central Argentina. Argentina's immense plains, the Pampas, are among the planet's most fertile areas, yielding not only cattle but sheep and wheat as well. Over the past five centuries, the coastal plains of Brazil have produced enormous amounts of sugar. In addition, human ingenuity has converted geographical obstacles into assets. Some extensive river systems have potential for hydroelectric power and provide water for irrigation as well, as has been done in Mexico's arid regions.

The historical record shows that the richness of Latin America's resources has had a significant impact on the economic and political development of Europe and North America. The gold and silver of its New World Empire fueled Spain's wars and diplomacy in Europe for four hundred years. Many scholars trace the origins of the Industrial Revolution in such nations as Great Britain and the Netherlands to resources extracted from Latin America by its colonial masters, Spain and Portugal.

Latin America's resources have affected economic development elsewhere, but how these resources have been developed and by whom and in which ways has profoundly changed the history of the nations in this area. Geography has perhaps narrowed historical alternatives in Latin America, but the decisions of people determined its development. Going back to the colonization by Spain and Portugal, Latin America's history has been marked by exploitation of its peoples and its natural resources. Imperial Spain's policy to drain the lands it conquered of gold, silver, and other resources fixed the pattern for later exploiters. With European dominance came the decisions to subjugate the indigenous peoples and often force them to labor under subhuman conditions in mines and large estates, where many died. In the more recent era, there has been the decision to grow bananas on the coastal plains of Central America instead of corn or other staples of the local diet; this has made export profitable, usually for North American concerns, but this land use has left many, like the Guatemalans, without sufficient food. Meanwhile the uncontrolled expansion of capitalism in the area has led to an ecological crisis, reflected in massive deforestation, severe soil exhaustion, and growing agricultural and industrial pollution. These developments have contributed to rapid depletion of renewable resources, lack of clean water and air, and major epidemics of contagious diseases and other health problems.

The book that follows is a history of the development of Latin America's economy, politics, and society viewed primarily from the perspective of ordinary people, who were exploited and oppressed but who resisted and endured. It is the story of the events and forces that produced the alternatives from which Latin Americans created their world.

For most North Americans, perhaps, the colonial past is a remote, picturesque time that has little relevance to the way we live now. The situation is very different in Latin America. "Even the casual visitor to Latin America," says the historian Woodrow Borah, "is struck by the survival of institutions and features that are patently colonial." The inventory of colonial survivals includes many articles and practices of everyday life, systems of land use and labor, and a wealth of social relations and attitudes.

Characteristic of the Latin American scene is the coexistence and mingling of colonial and modern elements: the digging stick, the foot plow, and the handloom coexist with the tractor, the conveyor belt, and the computer. In Latin America the colonial past is not a nostalgic memory but a harsh reality. It signifies economic backwardness; political arbitrariness, corruption, and nepotism; a hierarchical social order and attitudes of condescension and contempt on the part of elites toward the masses.

We begin our survey of the colonial period of Latin American history with some account of Ancient America, the name of that long span of time during which the Indians—the first Americans—developed their cultures in virtual isolation from the Old World. The Indian past profoundly influenced the character of the colonial era. By no accident, the chief capitals of the Spanish Empire in America arose in the old Indian heartlands—the Mexican and Peruvian areas—the homes of millions of industrious natives accustomed to performing tribute labor for their ruling classes. The Indians, the Spaniards well knew, were the true wealth of the Indies. Territories that held few Indians failed to attract them or remained marginal in the Spanish colonial scheme of things.

Equally decisive for the character of the colonial period was the Hispanic background. The conquistadors came from a Spain where seven centuries of struggle against the Moslems had made warfare almost a way of life and had created a large *hidalgo* (noble) class that regarded manual labor with contempt. To some the conquest of America appeared to be an extension of the reconquest of Spain from the Moors. "The conquest of Indians," wrote the Spanish chronicler Francisco López de Gómara, "began when the conquest of the Moors had ended, in order

that Spaniards may always war against the infidels." Spain's economic backwardness and immense inequalities of wealth, which sharply limited opportunities for advancement or even a decent livelihood for most Spaniards, help explain the desperate valor of the conquistadors; they also help explain their harshness in dealing with the Indians, and sometimes with each other, and the dog-eat-dog atmosphere of the Conquest. It seems significant that many great captains of the Conquest—Cortés, Pizarro, Valdivia, Balboa—came from the bleak land of Estremadura, Spain's poorest province.

Another factor that may help to explain the peculiarly ferocious, predatory character of the Conquest is the climate of violence that existed in contemporary Spain, a clear legacy of the reconquest and social conditions and values it generated. In his *Spanish Character: Attitudes and Mentalities from the Sixteenth to the Nineteenth Century*, Bartolomé Bennassar notes how widespread and accepted was the incidence of violence in Spain of the sixteenth and seventeenth centuries. According to Bennassar, assassins proliferated, and he illustrates the cheapness of life by the survival of the ancient practice of issuing writs of pardon in return for the payment of blood money—usually a small amount—for the murder of individuals of humble social status. To concede that the historical background had created this climate of violence is not to ascribe to Spaniards a unique capacity for cruelty or deviltry. We know all too well that colonial or imperialist wars and civil wars are replete with atrocities and horrors of every kind. Indeed, what distinguishes Spain among the colonial powers of history is the fact that it produced a minority of men who denounced in the face of the world the crimes of their own countrymen and did all in their power to stop what Bartolomé de Las Casas called "the destruction of the Indies."

From the sixteenth century till now, defenders of Spain's colonial record have charged Las Casas and other accusers with bias and exaggeration, claiming that they created a "Black Legend" of Spanish cruelty and intolerance. In fact, every colonial power has its own Black Legend that is no

4

legend but a dismal reality. The brutality of the Spanish Conquest is matched by that of the genocidal Indian wars the United States waged in the nineteenth century. An American folk hero, General and President Andrew Jackson, supervised the mutilation of some eight hundred Creek Indian corpses, cutting off their noses to count and keep a record of the dead; on another occasion he ordered his troops to kill all the Indian children they could find after killing all the women and men to make sure the group would not survive. The 1899–1902 Filipino revolt against American rule was suppressed with massacres, use of "water torture" to elicit information, and incarceration of civilian populations in concentration camps. General J. Franklin Bell, who took part in that repression, estimated that in Luzon alone over 600,000 people had been killed or died from disease as a result of the war.

On the ruins of the old Indian societies Spain laid the foundations of a new colonial order. Three aspects of that order need to be stressed. One is the predominantly feudal character of its economic structure, social organization, and ideology. That feudal character was most clearly expressed in Spain's Indian policy, which assigned to the Indians the status of a hereditary servile class, obliged to pay tribute in goods, cash, and labor, and engage in unequal trade with their European masters. The same feudal principles assigned separate legal status to Europeans, *castas* (persons of mixed race), and blacks and regulated the conduct and lifestyle of each racial category. These feudal characteristics, admixed with some capitalist elements, formed part of Spain's (and Portugal's) legacy to independent Latin America and help explain the tenacious hold of some anachronistic institutions on the area today.

Another important aspect of the colonial order is that its economy, based in its external relations on the extraction of precious metals and the production of such staples as sugar, cacao, tobacco, and hides, became gradually integrated into the new capitalist order, based on free labor, that arose in northern Europe in the course of the seventeenth and eighteenth centuries. Spain, it-self increasingly dependent economically on the capitalist North, was powerless to prevent the flow of colonial treasure and commodities to its rivals through smuggling, piracy, and foreign takeover of Spanish merchant houses. In the process of insertion into the European capitalist system, the feudal colonial economy acquired some capitalist features. Thus slavery, relatively patriarchal in Europe, acquired a peculiarly brutal character in the Caribbean colonies, with "the civilized horrors of overwork," in the words of Karl Marx, "grafted onto the barbaric horrors of slavery."

Still another important aspect of Spain's colonial order is the ambiguous relationship between the crown and the conquistadors and their descendants. The crown feared the rise of a colonial seigneurial class and sought to rein in the colonists' ambitions; on the other hand, it relied on them for security against internal and external threats, and this disposed the crown to make major concessions to them. Against this background, there developed a continual struggle, sometimes open, sometimes muffled, between the Spanish crown and the conquistadors and their descendants for control of Indian labor and tribute. In that struggle the colonists gradually gained the upper hand.

Spain's decline in the seventeenth century contributed to this shift in the balance of power in favor of the colonists. The emergence in the sixteenth and seventeenth centuries of a hereditary colonial aristocracy rich in land and peons represented a defeat for the crown and for the Indian community whose interests, however feebly, the crown defended. When in the late eighteenth century Spain's kings sought to tighten their control over the colonies, exclude creoles (American-born Spaniards) from high official posts, and institute reforms that sometimes clashed with creole vested interests, it was too late. These policies only alienated a powerful colonial elite whose members already felt a dawning sense of nationality and dreamed of the advantages of a free trade with the outside world.

A parallel development occurred during the same period in the relations between Portugal and Brazil. Between 1810 and 1822, American elites, taking advantage of Spain's and Portugal's distresses, seized power in most of Spanish America and Brazil. These aristocratic rebels wanted no radical social changes or economic diversification; their interests as producers of staples for export to western Europe required the continuance of the system of large estates worked by peons or slaves. As a result, independent Latin America inherited almost intact the colonial legacy of a rigidly stratified society and an externally oriented economy dependent on foreign countries for capital and finished goods.

Chapter 1

Ancient America

A great number of aboriginal groups (Indians), speaking many different languages and having different ways of life, occupied America at the time of its discovery by Columbus. For at least ten thousand years before European discovery, the New World had existed in virtual isolation from the Old. Sporadic and transient contacts between America and Asia no doubt occurred, and some transfer of culture traits, mainly stylistic embellishments, probably took place through trans-Pacific diffusion. But there is no convincing evidence that people or ideas from China, India, or Africa significantly influenced the cultural development of Indian America.

Environment and Culture in Ancient America

During its thousands of years of isolation, America was a unique social laboratory in which the Indians worked out their own destinies, adapting in various ways to their special environments. By 1492 this process had produced results that suggest that the patterns of early human cultural evolution are basically similar the world over. The first Europeans found native groups in much the same stages of cultural development through which parts of the Old World had once passed: Old Stone Age hunters and food gatherers, New Stone Age farmers, and empires as complex as those of Bronze Age Egypt and Mesopotamia.

Racially, the inhabitants of Ancient America were blends of several Asiatic physical types and shared with the modern Indian the typical physical features of dark eyes, straight or wavy black hair, and yellowish or copper skin. Their remote ancestors had probably come from Asia across the Bering Strait in waves of migration that began perhaps as early as forty thousand years ago and continued until about 10,000 B.C. Much controversy, however, surrounds the problem of the approximate date of the first human habitation in America. Some archaeologists argue that no firm evidence exists to refute the traditional view, based on the dating of so-called Folsom stone projectile points found throughout North and South America, that such habitation began about twelve thousand years ago. Revisionists point to the discoveries made in recent decades, especially in Chile and Brazil, that suggest a much earlier occupation.

Two waves of migrations appear to have taken place. The first brought extremely primitive groups who lived by gathering wild fruit, fishing, and hunting small game. A recent archaeological discovery suggests that these primitive hunters and gatherers passed through Peru about twenty-two thousand years ago. The second series of invasions brought big-game hunters who, like their predecessors, spread out through the continent. By 9000 B.C., these Asiatic invaders or their descendants had reached Patagonia, the southern tip of the continent.

This first colonization of America took place in the last part of the great geological epoch known as the Pleistocene, a period of great climatic changes. Glacial ages, during which blankets of ice covered extensive areas of the Old and New Worlds, alternated with periods of thaw, when temperatures rose to approximately present-day levels. Even in ice-free areas, precipitation often increased markedly during the glacial ages, creating lush growth of pastures and woodlands that supported many varieties of game. Consequently, large sections of America in this period were a hunter's paradise. Over its plains and through its forests roamed many large prehistoric beasts. The projectile points of prehistoric hunters have been found near the remains of such animals from one end of America to the other.

Around 9000 B.C., the retreat of the last great glaciation (the Wisconsin), accompanied by drastic climate changes, caused a crisis for the Indian hunting economy. A warmer, drier climate settled over vast areas. Grasslands decreased, and the large animals that had pastured on them gradually died out. The improved techniques of late Pleistocene hunting also may have contributed to the disappearance of these animals. The hunting folk now had to adapt to their changing environment or vanish with the animals that had sustained them.

Southwestern United States, northern Mexico, and other areas offer archaeological evidence of a successful adjustment to the new conditions. The Indians increasingly turned for food to smaller animals, such as deer and jackrabbits, and to edible wild plants, especially seeds, which were ground into a palatable meal. This new way of life eventually led to the development of agriculture. At first, agriculture merely supplemented the older pursuits of hunting and food collecting; its use hardly constituted an "agricultural revolution." The shift from food gathering to food producing was more likely a gradual accumulation of more and more domesticated plants that gradually replaced the wild edible plants. Over an immensely long period, time and energy formerly devoted to hunting and plant collecting were diverted to such agricultural activities as clearing, planting, weeding, gardening, picking, harvesting, and food preparation. But in the long run, agriculture, in the New World as in the Old, had revolutionary effects: people began to lead a more disciplined and sedentary life, the food supply increased, population grew, and division of labor became possible.

In caves in the Mexican highlands, archaeologists have found the wild plants that the Indians gradually domesticated; among the more important are pumpkins, beans, and maize. Domestication of these plants probably occurred between 7000 and 2300 B.C. Among these achievements, none was more significant than the domestication of maize, the mainstay of the great cultures of Ancient America. Manioc (a starchy root cultivated in the tropics as a staple food) and the potato (in Peru) were added to the list of important Indian domesticated plants between 5000 and 1000 B.C.

From its place or places of origin, agriculture swiftly spread over the American continents. By

1492 maize was under cultivation from the northern boundary of present-day United States to Chile. But not all Indian peoples adopted agriculture as a way of life. Some, like the Indians who inhabited the bleak wastes of Tierra del Fuego at the far tip of South America, were forced by severe climatic conditions either to hunt and collect food or starve. Others, like the prosperous, sedentary Indians of the Pacific northwest coast, who lived by waters teeming with fish and forests filled with game, had no reason to abandon their good life in favor of agriculture.

Where agriculture became the principal economic activity, its yield depended on such natural factors as soil fertility and climate and on the farming techniques employed. Forest tribes usually employed the slash-and-burn method of cultivation. Trees and brush were cut down and burned, and maize or other staples were planted in the cleared area with a digging stick. Because this method soon exhausted the soil, the clearing had to be left fallow and a new one made. After this process had gone on long enough, the whole village had to move to a new site or adopt a dispersed pattern of settlement that would allow each family group sufficient land for its needs. Slash-and-burn agriculture thus had a structural weakness that usually sharply limited the cultural development of the Indian peoples who employed it. That a strong controlling authority could at least temporarily overcome the defects of this method is suggested by the success of the Maya: their brilliant civilization arose in a tropical forest environment on a base of slash-and-burn farming directed by a powerful priesthood, but there is now abundant evidence that from very early times this was supplemented by more intensive methods of agriculture.

A more productive agriculture developed in the rugged highlands of Middle America and the Andean altiplano and on the desert coast of Peru. In such arid or semiarid country, favored with a temperate climate and a naturally rich soil, the land could be tilled more easily and its fertility preserved longer with digging-stick methods. Most important, food production could be increased with the aid of irrigation, which led to larger populations and a greater division of labor. The need for cooperation and regulation on irrigation projects favored the rise of strong central governments and the extension of their authority over larger areas. The Aztec and Inca empires arose in natural settings of this kind.

Finally, the vast number of human groups inhabiting the American continents on the eve of the Spanish Conquest can be classified by their subsistence base and the complexity of their social organization into three levels or categories— tribe, chiefdom, and state. These categories correspond to stages in general cultural evolution. The simplest or most primitive, the *band* and *tribal* level, usually correlated with difficult environments (dense forests, plains, or extremely wet, dry, or frigid areas) that sharply limited productivity. The band and tribal level comprises all those small, egalitarian groups based on hunting, fishing, and collecting; on a shifting agriculture; or on a combination of these activities. Hunting and gathering groups were typically nonsedentary, migrating within a given territory in a cyclical pattern according to the seasonal availability of game and edible plants. Groups that supplemented hunting, fishing, and gathering with slash-and-burn agriculture, which usually required making a new clearing after two or three seasons, were semisedentary. The often precarious nature of the subsistence base tended to keep band and tribal population densities low and hinder development of division of labor. The social unit on this level was an autonomous band or a village; a loose association of bands or villages, linked by ties of kinship, real or fictitious, formed a tribe. Social stratification was unknown; all members of the group had access to its hunting and fishing grounds and its land. Village and tribal leaders or chiefs owed their authority to their prowess in battle or other outstanding abilities; the exercise of their authority was limited to the duration of a hunt, a military operation, or some other communal activity.

Typical of these egalitarian societies were many Brazilian tribes of the Amazon basin. A frequent feature of their way of life was constant intertribal warfare whose purpose was to capture prisoners. After being kept for weeks or months the captured warriors were ritually executed and their flesh was cooked and eaten by members of the tribe to gain spiritual strength and perpetuate the tribal feud. The sixteenth-century French philosopher Michel de Montaigne, who read about their customs in travel accounts and met some Brazilian Indians brought to France, was much impressed by their democratic spirit and freedom from the familiar European contrasts of extreme poverty and wealth. He used these impressions to draw an influential literary portrait of the noble savage, the innocent cannibal, who represents a type of moral perfection free from the vices of civilization.

The *chiefdom,* the second category of Indian social organization, represented an intermediate level between primitive tribal societies and more advanced societies featured by social stratification and the state. Most commonly the subsistence base of the chiefdom was intensive farming, which supported a dense population living in large villages. These villages had lost their autonomy and were ruled from an elite center by a paramount chief, who was aided by a hierarchy of subordinate chiefs. Ranking was an important element in chiefdom social organization, but it was defined in kinship terms. Persons were ranked according to their genealogical nearness to the paramount chief, who was often assigned a sacred character and attended by a large retinue of officials and servants. The paramount chief siphoned off the surplus production of the group by requiring tribute payment and forced donations; he used much of this surplus for selective redistribution to officials, retainers, and warriors, thereby enhancing his own power. Warfare between chiefdoms was very common and probably played a decisive role in their origin and expansion through the absorption of neighboring villages. Warfare, leading to the taking of captives who were enslaved and made to labor for their owners, also contributed to the growth of incipient social stratification.

Numerous chiefdoms existed in ancient America on the eve of the Spanish Conquest, with the largest number in the Circum-Caribbean area (in-cluding Panama, Costa Rica, northern Colombia, and Venezuela; and the islands of Hispaniola, Puerto Rico, Jamaica, and Cuba). The Cauca Valley of Colombia alone contained no less than eighty chiefdoms.

The complex, densely populated Chibcha or Muisca chiefdoms, located in the eastern highlands of Colombia, may serve to illustrate this level of social and political integration. They rested on a subsistence base of intensive agriculture and fishing, and hunting was an important supplementary activity. The agricultural techniques most likely included terracing and ridged planting beds (raised above wet basin floors to control moisture) as well as slash-and-burn methods. In addition to maize these chiefdoms cultivated potatoes, *quinoa* (a hardy grain resembling buckwheat), and a wide variety of other plants. The crafts—pottery, weaving, and metallurgy—were highly developed. Their magnificent gold work ranks among the finest such work in ancient America.

At the time of the Spanish Conquest, most of the Muisca territory was dominated by two rival chiefdoms, centered at Bogotá and Tunja respectively; the population of the area has been estimated at about one and a half million. The Muisca lived in large villages of several hundred to several thousand persons. Each village consisted of pole-and-thatch houses and was surrounded by a palisade. The society was divided into commoners and elites, and membership in both sectors entailed differential rights and obligations. Commoners owed tribute in goods and in labor for the support of the chiefs and nobles, who controlled the distribution and consumption of surplus production.

The chiefdom marks the transition to the next and highest stage of organization, sometimes called *civilization* or more simply the *state* level of social and political integration. The dividing line between the two stages, especially in the case of larger and more complex chiefdoms, is difficult to draw, since the state reflected an expansion and deepening of tendencies already present in the chiefdom. There was a growth of division of labor and specialization, indicated by

10

the formation of artisan groups who no longer engaged in farming, the rise of a priesthood in charge of religious and intellectual activities, the rise of a distinct warrior class, and a bureaucracy entrusted with the administration of the state. These changes were accompanied by intensified social stratification and corresponding ideological changes. The kinship ties that in fact or in theory had united the paramount chief and the elite with the commoners became weakened or dissolved, and there arose a true class structure, with a ruling group claiming a separate origin from the commoners whose labor supported it. At the head of the state stood a priest-king or emperor who was sometimes endowed with divine attributes.

The state level of organization required a technological base of high productivity, usually an intensive agriculture that made large use of irrigation, terracing, and other advanced techniques. The state differed from the chiefdom in its larger size and population, the increased exchange of goods between regions, sometimes accompanied by the emergence of a professional merchant class, and the rise of true cities. In addition to being population, administrative, and industrial centers, these cities were cult centers often featured by a monumental architecture not found in chiefdoms. The Aztec, Maya, and Inca societies offer the best-known examples of the state level of organization.

What were the decisive factors in the qualitative leap from the chiefdom to the state in Ancient America? Some regard warfare leading to territorial conquest as the prime mover in this process; others believe that the state arose primarily as a coercive mechanism to resolve internal conflict between economically stratified classes. Others stress the importance of religious ideology in promoting centralized control by elites over populations and their resources. All these factors played a part in the process of state formation.

What appears certain is that, as we noted above, certain environmental conditions are more favorable than others for the formation of early states, especially of their highest form, em-

pire. Indeed, it is more than doubtful that such states could have arisen in such natural settings as the grassy plains of North America, whose hard sod was impervious to Indian digging sticks, or the Amazonian rain forests, usually thought to be unsuitable for farming other than transient slash-and-burn clearings.[1] Specialists often refer to the favored region that combined the necessary environmental conditions for the rise of states and empires as Nuclear America.

Indian Populations in 1492

As a result of researches by anthropologists and historians, information on Ancient America is growing at a rapid rate. Students are more impressed with the complexity of the civilizations of Ancient America and commonly compare them with such advanced Old World cultures as ancient Egypt and Mesopotamia. Recent studies of the population history of Ancient America have contributed to the rising respect for the Indian cultural achievement. If we assume, as many social scientists do, that population density is correlated with a certain technological and cultural level, then a high estimate of the Indian population in 1492 is in some measure a judgment on the old Indian societies and on the colonial societies that arose on their ruins.

The subject of the pre-Conquest population of the Americas, however, has produced sharp, sometimes bitter debate. The first Spanish arrivals in the New World reported very dense populations. Some early estimates of the native population of Hispaniola (modern Haiti and the Dominican Republic) ranged as high as 2 and 4 million. The famous missionary known as Motolinía, who arrived in Mexico in 1524, offered no

---

[1] Archaeologists have recently found evidence at various sites along the shores of the Amazon of complex societies with elaborate pottery, raised fields, and large statues of chiefs. But none of these ancient Amazonian societies appear to have evolved beyond the chiefdom level, and questions remain regarding their origin and the size of their populations.

numbers but wrote that the Indians were as numerous as "the blades of grass in a field." Great densities were also reported for the Inca Empire and Central America. In the twentieth century scholars who assessed these early reports tended to divide into two groups. Some found them generally credible; in the 1920s the American archaeologist H. J. Spinden and the German archaeologist Karl Sapper, taking account of Indian technology and resources, came up with the same overall totals of 40 to 50 millions for the whole New World. Others, like the American anthropologist A. L. Kroeber and the Argentine scholar Angel Rosenblat, concluded that Indian technology could not support the densities cited by the early sources and that the Spaniards had consciously or unconsciously exaggerated the number of Indians they found in order to enhance their own achievements as conquerors or missionaries. Kroeber produced a hemispheric estimate of 8,400,000; Rosenblat raised this figure to 13,385,000.

Beginning in the 1940s, three professors at the University of California, Woodrow Borah, Sherburne Cook, and Lesley B. Simpson, opened a new line of inquiry into the demographic history of Ancient America with a remarkable series of studies focusing on ancient Mexico. Using a variety of Indian and Spanish records and sophisticated statistical methods, the Berkeley school projected backward from a base established from Spanish counts for tribute purposes and arrived at a population figure of 25.3 million for central Mexico on the eve of the Conquest.

Later, Cook and Borah extended their inquiries into other areas. Particularly striking are their conclusions concerning the population of Hispaniola in 1492. Previous estimates of the island's population had ranged from a low of 600,000 to the 3 to 4 million proposed by the sixteenth-century Spanish friar Bartolomé de Las Casas, but those high figures had long been regarded as the exaggerations of a pro-Indian enthusiast. After a careful study of a series of statements and estimates on the aboriginal population of Hispaniola made between 1492 and 1520, Cook and Borah not only confirmed the reliability of Las

Casas's figures but offered even higher probable figures of from 7 to 8 million.

Aside from Borah's suggestion in 1964 that the population of America in 1492 may have been "upwards of 100 million," the Berkeley school did not attempt to estimate the pre-Columbian population of the continent as a whole. A systematic effort of this kind was made by the American anthropologist Henry Dobyns. Assuming that the Indian population was reduced by roughly 95 percent after contact with the Europeans, primarily as a result of new diseases to which the Indians had no acquired immunity, he estimated a pre-Conquest population of between 90 and 112 million; of this figure he assigned 30 million each to central Mexico and Peru.

The findings and methods of the Berkeley school and Dobyns have provoked strong dissent; two notable dissenters from those high findings are William T. Sanders and David Henige. In general, however, the evidence of the last half-century of research in this field quite consistently points to larger populations than were accepted previously. One effort to generalize from this evidence, taking account both of the findings of the Berkeley school and its critics, is that of William T. Denevan (1976), who postulates a total population of 57.3 million—a far cry from Kroeber's 1939 estimate of 8.4 million.

Scholars have also attempted to establish long-range population trends in Ancient America. There is general agreement that on the whole, in Woodrow Borah's words, "American Indians had relatively few diseases and, aside from natural disasters such as floods or droughts causing crop failures, seem to have enjoyed especially good health." Until the Discovery, their isolation protected them from the unified pool of diseases like smallpox, measles, and typhus that had formed in the Old World by the time of the Renaissance. What the long-range perspective may have been, assuming no Discovery, is problematical. In many areas the Indians had developed a system that combined hunting-gathering and shifting slash-and-burn agriculture, often based on the corn-beans-squash triad, that was sustainable, inflicting little damage on the ecosystem.

12   The Taino of the West Indies had developed a sophisticated form of agriculture based on permanent fields of knee-high mounds, called *conucos,* planted in cassava, the sweet potato, and various beans and squashes, that retarded erosion and "gave the highest returns of food in continuous supply by the simplest methods and modest labor." There is little evidence of population pressure on food resources in such areas. On the other hand, historical demographers have found evidence of approaching crisis in the Aztec Empire; Borah gloomily observes: "By the close of the fifteenth century the Indian population of central Mexico was doomed even had there been no European conquests." And scholars are now convinced that population pressure on scant resources may have played a major part in the collapse of the classic Maya civilization of Central America; the evidence includes signs of chronic malnutrition, high infant mortality, and a decline of population from perhaps 12 million to a remnant of about 1.8 million within 150 years. The crisis is linked to deforestation, loss of surface water, and overcultivated, worn-out soils, among other factors.

Nuclear America

Mexico and Peru were the centers of an extensive Indian high culture area that included central and southern Mexico, Central America, and the Andean zone of South America. This is the heartland of Ancient America, the home of its first agricultural civilizations. Evidence of early village life and the basic techniques of civilization—agriculture, pottery, weaving—has been found in almost every part of this territory.

In recent decades, this region has been the scene of major archaeological discoveries. In the Valley of Mexico, in southern Mexico and on its gulf coast, on the high plateau of Bolivia, and in the desert sands of coastal Peru, excavations have uncovered the remains of splendid temples, mighty fortresses, large cities and towns, and pottery and textiles of exquisite artistry. Combining the testimony of the spade with that provided by Indian and Spanish historical accounts, specialists have attempted to reconstruct the history of Nuclear America. The framework for this effort is a sequence of stages based on the technology, social and political organization, religion, and art of a given period. To this sequence of stages specialists commonly assign the names Archaic, Formative or Preclassic, Classic, and Postclassic. This scheme is tentative in detail, with much chronological overlap between stages and considerable variation in the duration of some periods from area to area.

The *Archaic* stage began about nine thousand years ago when a gradual shift from food gathering and hunting to agriculture began in many parts of Nuclear America. This incipient agriculture, however, did not cause revolutionary changes in Indian society. For thousands of years, people continued to live in much the same primitive fashion as before. Social groups were small and probably seminomadic. Weaving was unknown, but a simple pottery appeared in some areas toward the end of the period.

Between 2500 and 1500 B.C., a major cultural advance in various regions of Nuclear America opened the *Formative,* or *Preclassic,* period. Centuries of haphazard experimentation with plants led to the selection of improved, high-yield varieties. These advances ultimately produced an economy solidly based on agriculture and sedentary village life. Maize and other important domesticated plants were brought under careful cultivation; irrigation came into use in some areas; a few animals were domesticated. By the end of the period, pottery and weaving were highly developed. Increased food production enabled villagers to support a class of priests who acted as intermediaries between people and gods. More abundant food also released labor for the construction of ceremonial sites—mounds of earth topped by temples of wood or thatch.

The social unit of the Formative period was a village community composed of one or more kinship groups, but by the end of the period small chiefdoms uniting several villages had appeared. Since land and food were relatively plentiful and populations small, warfare must have been infrequent. Religion centered on the worship of water and fertility gods; human sacrifice was probably absent or rare.

The advances of the Formative period culminated in the *Classic* period, which began around the opening of the Christian era and lasted until approximately A.D. 1000. The term Classic refers to the flowering of material, intellectual, and artistic culture that marked this stage. There was no basic change in technology, but the extension of irrigation works in some areas caused increases in food production and freed manpower for construction and technical tasks. Population also increased, and in some regions genuine cities arose. Architecture, pottery, and weaving reached an impressive level of style. Metallurgy flourished in Peru, as did astronomy, mathematics, and writing in Mesoamerica (central and south Mexico and adjacent upper Central America). The earlier earth mounds gave way to huge stone-faced pyramids, elaborately ornamented and topped by great temples. The construction of palaces and other official buildings nearby made each ceremonial center the administrative capital of a state ruled by a priest-king. Social stratification was already well developed, with the priesthood the main ruling class. However, the growing incidence of warfare in the late Classic period (perhaps caused by population pressure, with greater competition for land and water) brought more recognition and rewards to successful warriors. Religion became an elaborate polytheism served by a large class of priests.

Typical cultures of the Classic period were the Teotihuacán civilization of central Mexico, the Monte Albán culture in southwestern Mexico, and the lowland Maya culture of southern Yucatán and northern Guatemala. The Olmec civilization of the Mexican gulf lowlands displays some Classic features, but falls within the time span usually allotted to the Formative. In Peru the period is best represented by the brilliant Mochica and Nazca civilizations of the coast. The available evidence suggests that the Classic stage was limited to Mesoamerica, the central Andean area (the highlands and coasts of Peru and Bolivia), and the Ecuadorian coast.

The Classic era ended abruptly in both the northern and southern ends of Nuclear America. Shortly before or after A.D. 1000 most of the great Classic centers in Mesoamerica and Peru were abandoned or destroyed by civil war or foreign invasion. Almost certainly, the fall of these civilizations came as the climax of a longer period of decline. Population pressure, soil erosion, and peasant revolts caused by excessive tribute demands are among the explanations that have been advanced for the collapse of the great Classic city-states and kingdoms.

A Time of Troubles, of obscure struggles and migrations of peoples, followed these disasters. Then new civilizations arose on the ruins of the old. The *Postclassic* stage, from about A.D. 1000 to 1500, seems to have repeated on a larger, more complex scale, the rise-and-fall pattern of the previous era. Chronic warfare, reflected in the number of fortifications and fortified communities, and an increased emphasis on urban living were distinguishing features of this stage. Another was the formation of empires through the subjugation of a number of states by one powerful state. The dominant state appropriated a portion of the production of the conquered people, primarily for the benefit of its ruling classes. The Aztec and Inca empires typify this era.

No important advances in technology occurred in the Postclassic period, but in some regions the net of irrigation works was extended. The continuous growth of warfare and the rise of commerce sharpened economic distinctions between nobles and commoners, between rich and poor. The warrior class replaced the priesthood as the main ruling class. Imperialism also influenced the character of religion, enhancing the importance of war gods and human sacrifice. The arts and crafts showed some decline from Classic achievements; there was a tendency toward standardization and mass production of textiles and pottery in some areas.

After reaching a peak of power, the empires displayed the same tendency toward disintegration as their Classic forerunners. The Tiahuanaco civilization and the Inca Empire in Peru may have represented two cycles of empire growth, while the first true Mexican imperial cycle, that of the Aztec conquests, had not ended when the Spaniards conquered America.

14　　Three high civilizations, the Aztecs of Mexico, the Maya of Central America, and the Incas of Peru, have held the center of attention to the virtual exclusion of the others. This partiality is understandable. We know more about these peoples and their ways of life. The Aztec and Inca civilizations still flourished at the coming of the Spaniards, and some conquistadors wrote vivid accounts of what they saw. The colorful story of the Conquest of Mexico and Peru and the unhappy fate of their emperors Moctezuma (Montezuma) and Atahualpa have also served to focus historical and literary attention on the Aztecs and the Incas. Unfortunately, the fame and glamour surrounding these peoples have obscured the achievements of their predecessors, who laid the cultural foundations on which the Maya, Aztecs, and Incas built.

The Aztecs of Mexico

At the opening of the sixteenth century, most of central Mexico, from the fringes of the arid northern plateau southward to the lowlands of Tehuantepec, paid tribute to the Aztecs of the Valley of Mexico. These Aztecs were latecomers in a region that had been the home of highly developed civilizations for almost a thousand years before their arrival.

Pre-Aztec Civilizations

As early as 1000 B.C., the inhabitants of the Valley of Mexico lived in small villages set in the midst of their maize, bean, and squash fields. They cultivated the land with slash-and-burn methods, produced a simple but well-made pottery, and turned out large numbers of small clay figures that suggest a belief in fertility goddessses. By the opening of the Old World's Christian era, small flat-topped mounds appeared, evidence of a more formal religion and directing priesthood.

Much earlier (perhaps spanning the period 1500 to 400 B.C.), arose the precocious and enigmatic Olmec civilization of the gulf coast lowlands, whose influence radiated widely into the central Mexican plateau and Central America. The origins, development, and disappearance of the Olmec culture remain a mystery.

Important elements of the Olmec civilization were its ceremonial centers, monumental stone carving and sculpture, hieroglyphic writing, and probably a calendrical system. The principal Olmec sites are La Venta and Tres Zapotes, in the modern state of Veracruz. Discovery of Olmec culture and evidence of the wide diffusion of its art style have made untenable the older view that Maya civilization was the first in Mesoamerica. It seems likely that Olmec culture was the mother civilization of Mesoamerica.

The technical, artistic, and scientific advances of the Formative period made possible the climactic cultural achievements of the Classic era. In Mexico's central highlands, the Classic period opened in splendor. About the beginning of the Christian era, at Teotihuacán, some twenty-eight miles from Mexico City, arose the mighty pyramids later given the names of the Sun and the Moon, which towered over clusters of imposing temples and other buildings. The stone sculpture used in the decoration of the temples, as well as the marvelous grace and finish of the cement work and the fresco painting, testify to the high development of the arts among the Teotihuacáns. The ancient water god, known to the Aztecs as Tlaloc, seems to have been the chief deity. But the feathered serpent with jaguar fangs, later known as Quetzalcóatl, is also identified with water and fertility and appears prominently in the greatest temple. There is little evidence of war or human sacrifice until a relatively late phase. Priests in benign poses and wearing the symbols of their gods dominate the mural paintings.

This great ceremonial center at Teotihuacán was sacred ground. Probably only the priestly nobility and their servants lived here. Farther out were the residential quarters inhabited by officials, artisans, and merchants. Teotihuacán is estimated to have had a population of at least 50,000. On the outskirts of the city, which covered an area of seven square miles, lived a large rural population that supplied the metropolis

The Olmec culture of the Mexican gulf lowlands produced powerful stone sculpture that featured colossal heads, whose significance is conjectural, like this one found at San Lorenzo, Veracruz.

with its food. It is likely that an intensive agriculture using canal irrigation and terracing on hillslopes formed the economic foundation of the Teotihuacán civilization. Despite the predominantly peaceful aspect of its religion and art, Teotihuacán seems to have been not only a major trading center but also a military state that directly controlled regions as remote as highland Guatemala.

Contemporary with Teotihuacán, but overshadowed by that great city, were other centers of Classic culture in Mesoamerica. To the southwest, at Monte Albán in the rugged mountains of Oaxaca, the Zapotecs erected a great ceremonial center that was also a true city. One of their achievements, probably of Olmec origin, was a complicated system of hieroglyphic writing. In the same period, the Maya Classic civilization flowered in the Petén region of northern Guatemala.

By A.D. 800 the Mesoamerican world had been shaken to its foundations by a crisis that seemed to spread from one Classic center to another. Teotihuacán, Rome of that world, itself perished at the hands of invaders, who burned down the city sometime between A.D. 650 and 800. Toward the latter date, the great ceremonial center at Monte Albán was abandoned. And by A.D. 800 the process of disintegration had reached the Classic Maya heartland of southern Yucatán and northern Guatemala, whose deserted or destroyed centers reverted one by one to the bush.

From this Time of Troubles in Mesoamerica (approximately A.D. 700 to 1000) a new Postclassic order emerged, sometimes appropriately called Militarist. Whereas priests and benign nature gods may have sometimes presided over Mesoamerican societies of the Classic era, warriors and terrible war gods clearly dominated the states that arose on the ruins of the Classic

16

world. In central Mexico the sway of Teotihuacán, probably based above all on cultural and economic supremacy, gave way to strife among new states that warred with one another for land, water, and tribute.

The most important of these, successor to the power of Teotihuacán, was the Toltec "empire," with its capital at Tula, about fifty miles from present-day Mexico City. Lying on the periphery of the Valley of Mexico, Tula may have once been an outpost of Teotihuacán, guarding its frontiers against the hunting tribes of the northern deserts. Following the collapse of Teotihuacán, one such tribe, the Toltecs, swept down from the north, entered the Valley of Mexico, and overwhelmed the pitiful survivors among the Teotihuacán people.

Toltec power and prosperity reached its peak under a ruler named Topiltzin, who moved his capital to Tula in about 980. Apparently renamed Quetzalcóatl in his capacity of high priest of the ancient god worshiped by the Teotihuacáns, Topiltzin-Quetzalcóatl reigned for nineteen years with such splendor that he and his city became legendary. The Song of Quetzalcóatl tells of the wonders of Tula, a true paradise on earth where cotton grew colored and the soil yielded fruit of such size that small ears of corn were used, not as food, but as fuel to heat steam baths. The legends of ancient Mexico celebrate the Toltecs' superhuman powers and talents; they were described as master artisans, as creators of culture. Over this Golden Age presided the great priest-king Quetzalcóatl, who thus revived the glories of Teotihuacán.

Toward the end of Quetzalcóatl's reign, Tula seems to have become the scene of an obscure struggle between two religious traditions. One was associated with the worship of Tezcatlipoca, a Toltec tribal god pictured as an all-powerful and capricious deity who demanded human sacrifice. The other was identified with the cult of the ancient god Quetzalcóatl, who had brought men and women maize, all learning, and the arts. In a version of the Quetzalcóatl legend that may reflect post-Conquest Christian influence, the god demanded of them only the peaceful sacrifice of

jade, snakes, and butterflies. This struggle found fanciful expression in the native legend that tells how the black magic of the enchanter Tezcatlipoca caused the saintly priest-king Quetzalcóatl to fall from grace and drove him into exile from Tula.

Whatever its actual basis, the Quetzalcóatl legend, with its promise that an Indian Redeemer would someday return to reclaim his kingdom, profoundly impressed the people of ancient Mexico and played its part in the destruction of the Aztec Empire. By a singular coincidence, the year in the Aztec cycle of years in which Quetzalcóatl promised to return was the very year in which Cortés landed at Veracruz. Aztec belief in the legend helps to explain the vacillation and contradictory moves of the doomed Moctezuma.

Topiltzin-Quetzalcóatl was succeeded by lesser kings, who vainly struggled to solve the growing problems of the Toltec state. The causes of this crisis are obscure: tremendous droughts may have caused crop failure and famines, perhaps aggravated by Toltec neglect of agriculture in favor of collection of tribute from conquered peoples. A series of revolutions reflected the Toltec economic and social difficulties. The last Toltec king, Huemac, apparently committed suicide about 1174, and the Toltec state disappeared with him. In the following year, a general dispersion or exodus of the Toltecs took place. Tula itself fell into the hands of barbarians in about 1224.

The fall of Tula, situated on the margins of the Valley of Mexico, opened the way for a general invasion of the valley by Nahuatl-speaking northern peoples. These newcomers, called Chichimecs, may be compared to the Germanic invaders who broke into the dying Roman Empire. Like them, the Chichimec leaders respected and tried to absorb the superior culture of the vanquished people. They were eager to intermarry with the surviving Toltec royalty and nobility.

These invaders founded a number of succession-states in the lake country at the bottom of the Valley of Mexico. Legitimately or not, their rulers all claimed the honor of Toltec descent. In artistic and industrial development, the Texco-

A post-Conquest Aztec "map" depicting the migration from their legendary place of origin, Aztlan, to the Valley of Mexico. The map reflects considerable European stylistic influence, but note the characteristic native use of footsteps to show the route the Aztecs followed.

can kingdom, organized in 1260, easily excelled its neighbors. Texcocan civilization reached its climactic moment two centuries later in the reign of King Nezahualcoyotl (1418–1472), distinguished poet, philosopher, and lawgiver, perhaps the most remarkable figure to emerge from the mists of Ancient America.

The Arrival of the Aztecs

Among the last of the Chichimec tribes to arrive in the valley were the Aztecs, or Mexica, the name they gave themselves. The date of their de-

parture from the north was probably about A.D. 1111. Led by four priests and a woman who carried a medicine bundle housing the spirit of their tribal god, Huitzilopochtli, they arrived in the Valley of Mexico in about 1218 after obscure wanderings. The traditional belief that they were basically a hunting and gathering people who were only "half civilized" but had some acquaintance with agriculture, has been questioned by some scholars who hold that by the time of their arrival the Aztecs were typically Mesoamerican in culture, religion, and economic and social organization. Finding the most desirable sites occupied by other tribes, they had to take refuge on marshy lands around Lake Texcoco. Here in 1344 or 1345, they began to build the town of Tenochtitlán. At this time, the Aztec tribe was composed of a small number of kinship, landholding groups called *calpulli.*

The patches of solid ground that formed the Aztec territory were gradually built over with huts of cane and reeds. They were followed later by more ambitious structures of turf, adobe, and light stone. As the population increased, a larger cultivable area became necessary. For this purpose the Aztecs borrowed from their neighbors the technique of making *chinampas*—artificial garden beds formed of masses of earth and rich sediment dredged from the lake bed and held in place by wickerwork. Eventually the roots, striking downward, took firm hold in the lake bottom and created solid ground. On these chinampas the Aztecs grew maize, beans, and other products.

For a long time, the Aztecs were subservient to their powerful neighbors in Azcapotzalco, the dominant power in the lake country in the late fourteenth and early fifteenth centuries. A turning point in Aztec history came in 1428. Led by their war chief Itzcoatl, the Aztecs joined the rebellious city-state of Texcoco and the smaller town of Tlacopan to destroy the tyranny of Azcapotzalco. Their joint victory (1430) led to the rise of a Triple Alliance for the conquest first of the valley, then of much of the Middle American world. Gradually the balance of power shifted to the aggressive Aztec state. Texcoco became a junior partner, and Tlacopan was reduced to a satellite. The strong position of their island fortification and a shrewd policy of forming alliances and sharing the spoils of conquest with strategic mainland towns, which they later came to dominate, help explain Aztec success in gaining control of the Valley of Mexico. In turn, conquest of the valley offered a key to the conquest of Middle America. The valley had the advantages of short internal lines of communication surrounded by easily defensible mountain barriers. Openings to the north, east, west, and south gave Aztec warriors easy access to adjacent valleys.

Conquest of Azcapotzalco gave the Aztecs their first beachhead on the lakeshore. Most of the conquered land and the peasantry living on it were assigned to warrior-nobles who had distinguished themselves in battle. Originally assigned for life, these lands tended to become fiefs held in permanent inheritance. Thus, warfare created new economic and social cleavages within Aztec society. In the process the original kinship basis of the calpulli was eroded and in the Valley of Mexico, at least, it lost most of its autonomy, becoming primarily a social and territorial administrative unit. Composed mostly of *macehualtin* (commoners) who owed tribute, labor, and military service to the Aztec state, the calpulli continued to be led by hereditary elite families who were completely subject to superior Aztec officials whose orders they carried out.

In the Valley of Mexico, and in other highly developed areas, the communal landownership formerly associated with the calpulli also suffered erosion as a result of growing population pressure, forcing some members to leave, internal economic differentiation, and the need to sell or rent communal land in time of famine or some other crisis. Calpulli of the original kinship, landowning type survived better in areas where the process of class stratification and state formation was less pronounced. Over much of central Mexico, however, by the time of the Conquest landlessness and tenant farming appear to have become very widespread, with serflike peasants (*mayeque*) forming perhaps the majority of the Aztec population. These unfree peasants enjoyed only the usufruct of the land and had to render tribute and service to the noble owner. The picture that emerges from recent studies is one of a society "like medieval European society, highly complicated and locally diverse." The growing cleavage between commoners and nobles found ideological reflection in the origin myth that claimed a separate divine origin (from the god Quetzalcóatl) for the Aztec nobility.

Other ideological changes included the elevation of the tribal god Huitzilopochtli to a position of equality with, or supremacy over, the great nature gods traditionally worshiped in the Valley of Mexico, the burning of the ancient picture writings because these books slighted the Aztecs, and the creation of a new history that recognized the Aztec grandeur. A new emphasis was placed on capturing prisoners of war to use as sacrifices on the altars of the Aztec gods in order to assure the continuance of the universe.[2]

The successors of Itzcoatl, sometimes individually, sometimes in alliance with Texcoco, extended Aztec rule over and beyond the Valley of Mexico. By the time Moctezuma II became ruler in 1502, the Triple Alliance was levying tribute on scores of towns, large and small, from the fringes of the arid northern plateau to the lowlands of Tehuantepec, and from the Atlantic to the Pacific. Within this extensive area only a few states or kingdoms, like the fierce Tarascans' state or the city-state of Tlaxcala, retained complete independence. Others, like Cholula, were left at peace in return for their benevolent neutrality or cooperation with the Aztecs. According to some controversial modern estimates, the Aztecs and their allies ruled over a population of perhaps 25 million.

The Aztecs waged war with or without cause. Refusal by a group to pay tribute to the Aztec ruler was sufficient pretext for invasion by the Aztecs. Injuries to the far-ranging Aztec merchants by people of the region they visited sometimes served as motive for invasion. Aztec merchants also prepared the way for conquest by reporting on the resources and defenses of the areas in which they traded; sometimes they acted as spies in hostile territory. If they returned home safely, these valiant merchants were honored by the ruler with amber lip plugs and other gifts. If their enemies discovered them, however, the

consequences were horrid. "They were slain in ambush and served up with chili sauce," says a native account.

Victory in war always had the same results: long lines of captives made the long journey to Tenochtitlán to be offered up on the altars of the gods. In addition, periodic tribute payments of maize, cotton mantles, cacao beans, or other products—depending on the geography and resources of the region—were imposed on the vanquished. Certain lands were also set aside to be cultivated by them for the support of the Aztec crown, priesthood, and state officials or as fiefs given to warriors who had distinguished themselves in battle. A steward or tribute collector, sometimes assisted by a resident garrison, was stationed in the town. For the rest, as a rule the conquered people continued to enjoy autonomy in government, culture, and customs.

Because of its nonintegrated character—reflected in the relative autonomy enjoyed by vanquished peoples and the light Aztec political and military presence in conquered territories—the Aztec empire has traditionally been regarded as an inferior or deficient political organization in comparison with the Inca empire, with its centralized administration, standing armies, massive transfers of populations, and other integrative policies. Recently, however, it has been argued that rather than inferior the Aztec imperial system represented an alternative—but no less efficient—approach to the problem of extracting surplus from tributary peoples at a minimal administrative and military cost. The Aztec army mobilized only for further conquests and the suppression of rebellions. By leaving the defeated regimes in place and avoiding direct territorial control, the Aztec state was spared the expense, inherent in a more integrated empire, of maintaining provincial administrations, standing armies, permanent garrisons, and fortifications.

Aztec Culture and Society

The Aztec capital of Tenochtitlán had a population estimated to be between 150,000 and 200,000. An Indian Venice, the city was an oval island connected to the mainland by three cause-

---

[2] Some social scientists have attempted to explain the Aztec practice of mass human sacrifice and its accompaniment of ritual cannibalism by the lack of protein in the Aztec diet. This theory is contradicted by the variety of animal foods available to the Aztecs and by the fact that neither Indian nor Spanish sources refer to the practice of cannibalism during the great famine that hastened the end of Aztec resistance to the Spanish conquest. For the rest, the sacramental feast, designed to let participants share the grace of the god to whom the prisoner was sacrificed, was simplicity itself, and the captor could not eat of his flesh because of an assumed mystical kinship relationship between the captor and his prisoner.

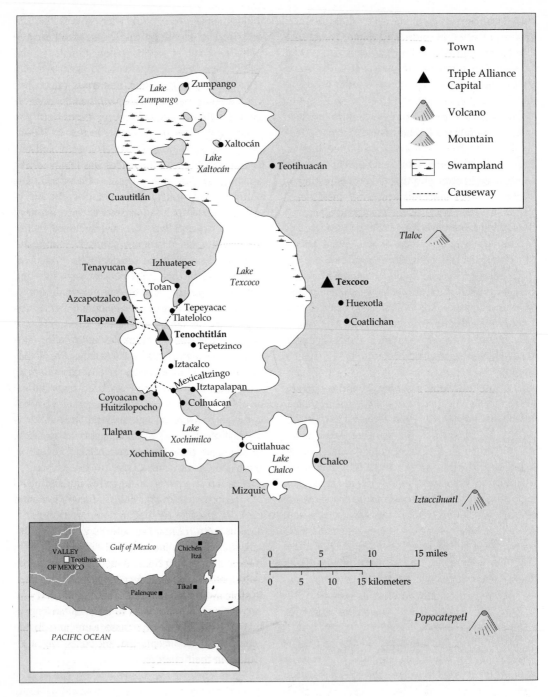

VALLEY OF MEXICO

ways that converged at the center of the city and served as its main arteries of traffic. There were few streets; their place was taken by numerous canals, thronged with canoes and bordered by footpaths giving access to the thousands of houses that lined their sides. An aqueduct in solid masonry brought fresh water from the mountain springs of Chapultepec.

On the outlying chinampas, the Aztec farmers, who paddled their produce to town in tiny dugouts, lived in huts with thatched roofs resting on walls of wattle smeared with mud. Inside each hut were a three-legged *metate* (grinding stone), a few mats that served as beds and seats, some pottery, and little more. The majority of the population—artisans, priests, civil servants, soldiers, and entertainers—lived in more imposing houses. These were sometimes built of adobe, sometimes of a reddish *tezontli* lava, but they were always lime-washed and painted. Far more pretentious than most were the houses of calpulli leaders, merchants, and nobles.

As in housing, Aztec clothing differed according to the individual's economic and social status. For men the essential garments were a loincloth with broad flaps at front and back, usually decorated with fringes and tassels as well as embroidery work, and a blanket about two yards by one in size. This blanket hung under the left arm and was knotted on the right shoulder. Commoners wore plain blankets of maguey fiber or coarse cotton; rich merchants and nobles displayed very elaborate cotton mantles adorned with symbolic designs. Women wore shifts, wraparound skirts of white cotton tied with a narrow belt, and loose, short-sleeved tunics. Both shifts and tunics were decorated with vivid embroidery. Men wore sandals of leather or woven maguey fiber; women went barefoot.

As with dress, so with food: wealth and social position determined its abundance and variety. The fare of the ordinary Aztec consisted of ground maize meal, beans, and vegetables cooked with chili. Meat was rarely seen on the commoner's table, but on festive occasions a dog might be served. It was otherwise with the nobility. A native account of the foods eaten by the lords includes many varieties of tortillas and tamales, roast turkey hen, roast quail, turkey with a sauce of small chilies, tomatoes, and ground squash seeds, venison sprinkled with seeds, many kinds of fish and fruits—and such delicacies as maguey grubs with a sauce of small chilies, winged ants with savory herbs, and rats with sauce. They finished their repast with chocolate, a divine beverage forbidden to commoners.

Education among the Aztecs was highly formal and served the dual purpose of preparing the child for his or her duties in the world and of indoctrinating him or her with the ideals of the tribe. Boys were sent to school at the age of ten or twelve. Sons of commoners, merchants, and artisans attended the *Telpochcalli* (House of Youth), where they received instruction in religion, good usage, and the art of war. The *Calmecac* (Priests' House), a school of higher learning, was reserved in principle for the sons of the nobility, but there is evidence that at least some children of merchants and commoners were admitted. Here, in addition to ordinary training, students received instruction that prepared them to be priests, public officials, and military leaders. The curriculum included what we would today call rhetoric, or a noble manner of speaking, study of religious and philosophical doctrines as revealed in the divine songs of the sacred books, the arts of chronology and astrology, and training in history through study of the *Xiuhamatl* (Books of the Years). The *tlamatinime* (sages) who taught in the Aztec schools were also concerned with the formation of "a true face and heart," the striking Nahuatl metaphor for personality. Self-restraint, moderation, devotion to duty, a stoic awareness that "life is short and filled with hardships, and all comes to an end," an impeccable civility, modesty: these were among the qualities and concepts that the Aztec sages instilled in their charges.

Girls had special schools where they were taught such temple duties as sweeping, offering incense three times during the night, and preparing food for the idols; weaving and other womanly tasks; and general preparation for marriage. Education for the men usually terminated at the

22

age of twenty or twenty-two; for girls, at sixteen or seventeen. These were also the ages at which marriage was contracted.

In a society with such a complex economic and social life, disputes and aggressions inevitably arose and necessitated the development of an elaborate legal code. A hierarchy of courts was topped by two high tribunals that met in the royal palace in Tenochtitlán. The punishments of the Aztecs were severe. Death was the penalty for murder, rebellion, wearing the clothes of the other sex, and adultery; theft was punished by slavery for the first offense, by hanging for the second.

Economic life in Aztec Mexico rested on a base of intensive and extensive agriculture. Intensive irrigation was practiced in areas with reliable water sources; its most notable form was that of the chinampas. Slash-and-burn cultivation, with field rotation, was the rule in other areas, but everywhere maize and beans were the principal crops. In the absence of large domesticated animals to produce manure, night soil was regularly used as fertilizer in chinampa agriculture in the Valley of Mexico. To prevent contamination of the valley's two freshwater lakes by flows of water from the saline ones that were harmful to chinampa agriculture, and to maintain the fairly constant water level that it required, the construction of an elaborate system of dikes, canals, and aqueducts was begun during the reign of King Itzcoatl. This led to the creation of large chinampa areas producing foodstuffs for Tenochtitlán. Productive as they were, however, it is estimated that they accounted for only 5 percent of the city's subsistence needs, and their expansion was limited by the salinity of the remaining lakes. For the balance of its food needs, therefore, Tenochtitlán had to rely on imports obtained by way of tribute and trade. An elaborate, state-controlled trade and transportation network based on regional and metropolitan markets, the *tlameme* (professional carrier) system of portage, and an efficient canoe traffic that linked the entire lake system of the Valley of Mexico funneled a vast quantity of foodstuffs and other bulk goods into Tenochtitlán. Manufactured goods

were then exported from Tenochtitlán to its hinterlands, forming a core-periphery relationship.

The vast scale on which the exchange of goods and services was carried on in the great market of Tenochtitlán aroused the astonishment of the conquistador Cortés, who gave a detailed account of its immense activity. "Each kind of merchandise is sold in its respective street," he wrote, "and they do not mix their kinds of merchandise of any species; thus they preserve perfect order." The Aztecs lacked a unitary system of money, but cacao beans, cotton mantles, quills filled with gold dust, and small copper axes were assigned standardized values and supplemented a barter system of exchange. The Aztecs had no scales; goods were sold by count and measure. The market was patrolled by officials who checked on the fairness of transactions; a merchants' court sat to hear and settle disputes between buyers and sellers.

As the above account implies, by the time of the Conquest division of labor among the Aztecs had progressed to the point where a large class of artisans no longer engaged in agriculture. The artisan class included carpenters, potters, stonemasons, silversmiths, and featherworkers. In the same category belonged such specialists as fishermen, hunters, dancers, and musicians. All these specialists were organized in guilds, each with its guildhall and patron god; their professions were probably hereditary. The artist and the craftsman enjoyed a position of high honor and responsibility in Aztec society. Assigning the origin of all their arts and crafts to the Toltec period, the Aztecs applied the name Toltec to the true or master painter, singer, potter, or sculptor.

Advances in regional division of labor and the growth of the market for luxury goods also led to the emergence of a merchant class, which was organized in a very powerful guild. The wealth of this class and its important military and diplomatic services to the Aztec state made the merchants a third force in Aztec society, ranking only after the warrior nobility and the priesthood. The wealth of the merchants sometimes aroused the distrust and hostility of the Aztec rulers and nobility. Popular animosity toward the merchants is reflected in the words of a native account: "The merchants were those who had plenty, who prospered; the greedy, the well-fed man, the covetous, the niggardly, the miser, who controlled wealth and family . . . the mean, the stingy, the selfish."

The priesthood was the main integrating force in Aztec society. Through its possession of a sacred calendar that regulated the performance of agricultural tasks, it played a key role in the life of the people. The priesthood was also the repository of the accumulated lore and history of the Aztec tribe. By virtue of his special powers of intercession with the gods, his knowledge and wisdom, the priest was called on to intervene in every private or collective crisis of the Aztec. Celibate, austere, continually engaged in the penance of bloodletting, priests wielded an enormous influence over the Aztec people.

The priesthood shared authority and prestige with the nobility, a class that had gained power through war and political centralization. In addition to many warriors, this class consisted of a large bureaucracy made up of tribute collectors, judges, ambassadors, and the like. Such officeholders were rewarded for their services by the revenue from public lands assigned to support them. Their offices were not hereditary. They were, however, normally conferred on sons of fathers who had held the same positions.

The wealth of the warrior nobility consisted chiefly of landed estates. Originally granted for life, these lands eventually became private estates that were handed down from father to son and could be sold or exchanged. The former free peasants on these lands were probably transformed into mayeque, farm workers, or tenant farmers tied to the land. With the expansion of the Aztec Empire, the number of private estates steadily grew.

On the margins of Aztec society was a large class of slaves. Slavery was the punishment for a variety of offenses, including failure to pay debts. Slavery was sometimes assumed by poor people in return for food. Slave owners frequently brought their chattels to the great market at Atzcapotzalco for sale to rich merchants or nobles

for personal service or as sacrificial offerings to the gods.

The Aztec political system on the eve of the Conquest was a mixture of royal despotism and theocracy. Political power was concentrated in a ruling class of priests and nobles, over which presided an absolute ruler resembling an Oriental despot. Originally, the ruler had been chosen by the whole Aztec tribe, assembled for that purpose. Later he was chosen by a tribal council or electoral college dominated by the most important priests, officials, and warriors, including close relatives of the king. The council, in consultation with the kings of Texcoco and Tlacopan, selected the monarch from among the sons, brothers, or nephews of the previous ruler. The new ruler was assisted by a council of four great nobles. At the time of the Conquest the emperor was the luckless Moctezuma II, who succeeded his uncle Ahuitzotl.

Great splendor and intricate ceremonies prevailed in Moctezuma's court. The great nobles of the realm took off their rich ornaments of feather, jade, and gold before entering his presence; barefoot, eyes on the ground, they approached the basketry throne of their king. Moctezuma dined in solitary magnificence, separated by a wooden screen from his servitors and the four great lords with whom he conversed.

This wealth, luxury, and ceremony revealed the great social and economic changes that had taken place in the small, despised Aztec tribe that came to live in the marshes of Lake Texcoco less than two centuries before. The Aztec Empire had reached a peak of pride and power. Yet the Aztec leaders lived in fear; the Aztec chronicles register a deep sense of insecurity. The mounting demands of the Aztec tribute collectors caused revolts on the part of tributary towns. Though repressed, they broke out afresh. The haunted Aztec imagination saw portents of evil on earth and in the troubled air. A child was born with two heads; the volcano Popocatepetl became unusually active; a comet streamed across the sky. The year 1519 approached, the year in which according to Aztec lore the god-king Quetzalcóatl might return to reclaim the realm from which he had

24   been driven centuries before by the forces of evil.

The Maya of Central America

If the Aztecs excelled in war and conquest, the Maya were preeminent in cultural achievement. Certainly, no other Indian group ever demonstrated such extraordinary abilities in architecture, sculpture, painting, mathematics, and astronomy.

The ancient Maya lived in a region comprising portions of modern-day southeastern Mexico, almost all of Guatemala, the western part of Honduras, all of Belize, and the western half of El Salvador. But the Maya civilization attained its highest development in the tropical forest lowland area whose core is the Petén region of Guatemala, at the base of the Yucatán Peninsula. This was the primary center of Maya Classic civilization from about A.D. 250 to 900.[3] The region was rich in wild game and building materials (limestone and fine hardwoods). In almost every other respect it offered immense obstacles to the establishment of a high culture. Clearing the dense forests for planting and controlling weeds were extremely difficult tasks with the primitive implements available. There was no metal, the water supply was uncertain, and communication facilities were poor. Yet it was here that the Maya built some of their largest ceremonial centers.

The contrast between the forbidding environment and the Maya achievement led some specialists to speculate that Maya culture was a transplant from some other, more favorable area. This view has been made obsolete by the discovery of long Preclassic sequences at lowland sites. There is, however, linguistic and archaeological evidence that the lowland Maya were descendants of groups who lived in or near the Olmec area before 1000 B.C. and who brought with them the essential elements of Mesoamerican civilization. In time they developed these elements into their own unique achievements in the sciences, art, and architecture.

Just as puzzling as the rise of the Maya lowland culture in such an inhospitable setting is the dramatic decline that led to a gradual cessation of building activity and eventual abandonment of the ceremonial centers after A.D. 800. Specialists have advanced various explanations for this decline. They include soil exhaustion as a result of slash-and-burn farming, invasion of cornfields by grasslands from the same cause, failure of the water supply, peasant revolts against the ruling priesthood, and the disruptive effects of the fall of Teotihuacán, which had close commercial and political ties with the Maya area. None of these explanations by itself, however, appears completely satisfactory.

Recently a more complex explanation of the Classic Maya collapse has emerged. According to this theory, the cessation of political and commercial contacts with Teotihuacán after about A.D. 550 led to a breakdown of centralized authority—perhaps previously exerted by Tikal, the largest and most important ceremonial center of the southern lowlands—and increased autonomy of local Maya elites. These elites expressed their pride and power by constructing ever more elaborate ceremonial centers, which added to the burdens of commoners. Growing population size and density strained food resources and forced the adoption of more intensive agricultural methods. These, in turn, increased competition for land, which was reflected in the growth of warfare and militarism. Improved agricultural production relieved population pressures for a time and made possible the late Classic flowering (A.D. 600–800), marked by a revival of ceremonial center construction, architecture, and the arts. But renewed population pressures, food shortages, and warfare between regional centers, perhaps aggravated by external attacks, led to a severe cultural and social decline in the last century of the Classic period. The build-up of pressure—so runs the theory—"resulted in a swift and cata-

[3] Recent archaeological discoveries, however, are revolutionizing the dates traditionally assigned to the Maya Classic period. The newly discovered city of Nakbé in the dense tropical forest of northern Guatemala, containing extensive stone monuments and temples, is dated from 600 to 400 B.C., pushing the Classic era back into the time span commonly assigned to the Formative or Preclassic period.

tihuacán was clearly a city. Tikal, in the heart of the Petén, was certainly a metropolitan center with a population of perhaps fifty thousand and a countryside heavily populated over an area of some fifty square miles. There is also evidence of some genuine urbanization in northern Yucatán during the Postclassic period, possibly a result of Toltec influence and the tendency to develop the city or town as a fortified position. Chichén Itzá, an old Classic ceremonial center, was greatly enlarged under Toltec influence, while Mayapan, which succeeded Chichén Itzá as a political and military center, constituted a large urban zone encircled by a great wall.

Awareness of the large size and density of Classic Maya populations, the intensive character of much of their agriculture, and the strict social controls that such complex conditions require has also led to a reassessment of Maya social organization. The older view that the ruling class was a small theocratic elite that ruled over a dispersed peasant population from basically empty ceremonial centers has been abandoned. Increased ability to decipher glyphs on the stelae (carved monuments) periodically erected at Classic Maya centers has contributed to a better understanding of the Maya social order. It was once believed that the content of these inscriptions was exclusively religious and astronomical. In recent decades, however, evidence has accumulated that many of the glyphs carved on stelae, lintels, and other monuments record accessions, wars, and other milestones in the lives of secular rulers. The new interpretation assumes a very complex social order with large distance between the classes. At the apex of the social pyramid stood a hereditary ruler who combined the political, military, and religious leadership of the state. He was surrounded by an aristocracy or nobility, from which were drawn the administrative and executive bureaucracy. Intellectual specialists such as architects, priests, and scribes may have formed another social level. Below them were the numerous artisans required for ceremonial and civil construction—potters, sculptors, stoneworkers, painters, and the like. At the bottom of the social pyramid were the common laborers and peasant farmers who sup-

plied the labor and food that supported this massive superstructure. The weight of their burdens must in time have become crushing, and their discontent may have ignited revolts that brought about the ultimate collapse of the lowland Maya civilization.

Archaeological investigations have thrown new light on Classic Maya family and settlement patterns. The fact that the residential platforms on which most Maya houses rested occur in groups of three or more suggests that the Maya family was extended rather than nuclear. It probably consisted of two or more nuclear families spanning two or more generations with a common ancestor. Male predominance is suggested by the richer furnishings of male graves and the preeminence of men in monumental art, leading to the conclusion that descent was patrilineal, from father to son. Maya dress and diet, like its housing, reflected class distinctions. Maya clothing was much the same as the Aztec: cotton loincloths, leather sandals, and sometimes a mantle knotted about the shoulder for men; and wraparound skirts of cotton and blouses with holes for the head and arms for the women. The same articles of clothing, more ornately decorated, were worn by the upper classes.

Maya Religion and Learning

The great object of Maya religion, as the Spanish bishop Diego de Landa concisely put it, was "that they [the gods] should give them health, life, and sustenance." The principal Maya divinities, like those of the Aztecs, represented those natural forces and objects that most directly affected the material welfare of the people. The supreme god in the Maya pantheon was Itzam Na, a creator god who incorporated in himself the aspects of many other gods; not only creation, but fire, rain, crops, and earth were among his functions or provinces. Other important divinities were the sun god, the moon goddess, the rain god, the maize god, and the much-feared god of death. Like the Aztecs, the Maya believed that a number of worlds had successively appeared and been destroyed; this present world, too, would end in catastrophe.

A Maya bas-relief, dated September 17, 726. Found at a site near Palenque, one of the most impressive Maya ceremonial cities, it shows a priest receiving a jaguar's head from a richly adorned personage.

The Maya view of the afterlife also closely resembled that of the Aztecs. They believed in an Upper World constituted of thirteen layers and an Under World of nine. Over each layer presided a certain god; over the lowest layer of the Under World presided the God of Death, Ah Puch. In common with the Aztecs and other peoples of Middle America, the Maya worshiped and placated the gods with a variety of ritual practices that included fasting, penance by bloodletting, the burning of incense, and human sacrifice. Human sacrifice on a large scale already existed in the late Classic period, marked by growing political turbulence and strife among the lowland

Maya states, but may have increased in the Postclassic period under Toltec influence.

The Maya priests were obsessed with time, to which they assigned an occult or magical content. They developed a calendar that was more accurate than ours in making adjustments in the exact length of the solar year. Maya theologians thought of time as burdens carried on the backs of the gods. At the end of a certain period one god laid down his burden for another god to pick up and continue on the journey of time. A given day or year was lucky or unlucky depending on whether the god-bearer was benevolent or malevolent. Thus, the Maya calendars were primarily divinatory in character; that is, they were used to predict conditions in a particular time period.

Like the Aztecs, the Maya had two almanacs. One was a sacred round of 260 days, corresponding to the pattern of ceremonial life. This calendar was composed of two intermeshing and recurrent cycles of different length: one of thirteen days, recorded as numbers, and the second of twenty days, recorded as names. The name of the fourteenth day-name began with one again. A second cycle was the solar year of 365 days, divided into eighteen "months" of twenty days each, plus a final period of five unlucky days during which all unnecessary activity was banned. Completion of these two cycles coincided every fifty-two years. The Aztecs awaited the end of the fifty-two-year period with great anxiety because they believed that the world might come to an end at this time. A similar belief may have existed among the Maya. Stelae bearing hieroglyphic texts indicating the date and other calendrical data, such as the state of the moon, the position of the planet Venus, and so on, were frequently erected at the end of the fifty-two-year cycle and at other intervals.

The Maya developed the science of mathematics further than any of their Middle American neighbors. Their units were ones, fives, and twenties, with ones designated by dots, fives by bars, and positions for twenty and multiples of twenty. Place-value numeration, based on a sign for zero, was perhaps the greatest intellectual development of Ancient America. In this system, the position of a number determined its value, making it possible for a limited quantity of symbols to express numbers of any size. Its simplicity made it far superior to the contemporary western European arithmetical system, which employed the cumbersome Roman numeration consisting of distinct symbols for each higher unit. It remained for the Arabs to bring their numeration concept to Europe from India, the only other place where it had been invented. Maya mathematics, however, appears to have been applied chiefly to calendrical and astronomical calculation; there is no record of Maya enumeration of people or objects.

Until recently it was believed that Maya hieroglyphic writing, like the mathematics, chiefly served religious and divinatory rather than utilitarian ends. We now have abundant evidence that many of the glyphs carved on the monuments are historical, recording milestones in the lives of Maya rulers. In addition to the inscriptions that appear on stone monuments, lintels, stairways, and other monumental remains, the Maya had great numbers of sacred books or codices, of which only three survive today. These books were painted on folding screens of native paper made of bark. Concerned above all with astronomy, divination, and other related topics, they reveal that Maya astronomers made observations and calculations of truly astounding complexity.

The Maya had no alphabet, properly speaking; that is, the majority of their characters represent ideas or objects rather than sounds. But Maya writing, like the Aztec, had reached the stage of syllabic phonetics through the use of rebus writing, in which the sound of a word is represented by combining pictures or signs of things whose spoken names resemble sounds in the word to be formed. Thus, the Maya word for drought, *kintunyaabil,* was written with four characters, the signs of sun or day (*kin*), stone or 360-day unit of time (*tun*), solar year (*haab*), and the affix *il.* In the 1950s a Russian scholar advanced a theory that Maya writing was truly syllabic and hence could be deciphered by matching the most frequent sound elements in modern Maya to the most frequent signs in the ancient writing, using computers to speed the process of decipherment. The existence of purely phonetic glyphs in the Maya script is now generally accepted by scholars, but they seem to be relatively rare in the deciphered material.

Maya writing was not narrative used to record literature, but the Maya, like the Aztecs, had a large body of myth, legends, poetry, and traditional history that was transmitted orally from generation to generation. Examples of such material are found in the *Popol Vuh,* the so-called Sacred Book of the Quiche Maya of Guatemala. This book deals, among other matters, with the

30

adventures of the heroic twins Hunahpu and Xbalanque, who after many exploits ascended into heaven to become the sun and the moon. It was written in post-Conquest times in the Spanish alphabet by a native who drew on the oral traditions of his people.

In certain types of artistic activity the Maya surpassed all other Middle American peoples. The temples and pyramids at Teotihuacán and Tenochtitlán were often larger than their Maya counterparts but lacked their grace and subtlety. A distinctive feature of Maya architecture was the corbeled vault, or false arch. Other Middle American peoples used horizontal wooden beams to bridge entrances, producing a heavy and squarish impression. The Maya solved the same problem by having the stones on either side of the opening project farther and farther inward, bridging the two sides at the apex by a capstone. Other characteristics of the Maya architectural style were the great façades richly decorated with carved stone and high ornamental roof combs in temples and palaces. Inner walls were frequently covered with paintings, a few of which have survived. The most celebrated of these paintings are the frescoes discovered in 1946 at Bonampak, an isolated site in the tropical forests of the northeastern corner of the Mexican state of Chiapas. They date from about A.D. 800. These frescoes completely cover the inner walls of a small building of three rooms. They tell a story that begins with a ritual dance, goes on to portray an expedition to obtain sacrificial victims, which is followed by a battle scene, and ends with a human sacrifice, ceremonies, and dance. Despite the highly conventionalized and static style, the absence of perspective and shading, and obvious errors in the human figure, there is an effect of realism that is often missing from Aztec or Toltec art.

Students of the Maya have frequently testified to the admirable personal qualities of the people who, with a very limited technology and in a most forbidding environment, created one of the greatest cultural traditions of all time. Bishop Diego de Landa, who burned twenty-seven Maya codices as "works of the devil," nevertheless observed that the Maya were very generous and

hospitable. No one could enter their houses, he wrote, without being offered food and drink.

The Incas of Peru

In the highlands of modern Peru in the mid-fourteenth century, a small tribe rose from obscurity to create by 1500 the mightiest empire of Ancient America. From the time of the discovery and conquest of Peru by Pizarro to the present, the Inca achievements in political and social organization have attracted intense interest. Soon after the Conquest a debate began on the nature of Inca society that has continued almost to the present day. For some it was a "socialist empire"; others viewed it as a forerunner of the "welfare state" of our own time; for still others the Inca realm anticipated the totalitarian tyrannies of the twentieth century. Only recently has more careful study of the evidence, especially the evidence of colonial provincial records of official economic and social inquiries, litigation, wills, and the like, provided a more correct picture of Inca society and banished the traditional labels.

The physical environment of the central Andean area offers a key to the remarkable cultural development of this region. In Peru high mountains rise steeply from the sea, leaving a narrow coastal plain that is a true desert. The Humboldt Current runs north along the coast from the Antarctic, making the ocean much colder than the land; hence the rains fall at sea. But lack of rainfall is compensated for by short rivers that make their precipitous way down from the high snowfields. These rivers create oases at intervals along the coast and provide water for systems of canal irrigation. The aridity of the climate preserves the great natural wealth of the soil, which in areas of heavy rainfall is leached away. The coastal waters of Peru are rich in fish, and its offshore islands, laden in Inca times with millions of tons of guano, made available an inexhaustible source of fertilizer for agriculture.

To be sure, the rugged highlands of modern Peru and Bolivia offer relatively little arable land. But the valleys are fertile and well watered and support a large variety of crops. Maize is grown at lower levels (up to about eleven thousand feet), potatoes and quinoa at higher altitudes. Above the agricultural zone the *puna* (plateau) provides fodder for herds of llamas and alpacas, domesticated members of the camel family, which were important in Inca times as a source of meat and wool. Potentially, this environment offered a basis for large food production and a dense population.

Origins of Inca Culture

Like the Aztecs of ancient Mexico, the Incas of Peru were heirs to a cultural tradition of great antiquity. This tradition had its origin not in the highlands but on the coast. By 2500 B.C., a village life, based chiefly on fishing and food gathering and supplemented by the cultivation of squash, lima beans, and a few other plants, had arisen about the mouths of rivers in the coastal area. Maize, introduced into Peruvian agriculture about 1500 B.C, did not become important until many centuries later.

The transition from the Archaic to the Preclassic period seems to have come later and more suddenly in Peru than in Mesoamerica. After long centuries of the simple village life just described, a strong advance of culture began on the coast about 900 B.C. This advance seems to have been associated with progress in agriculture, especially greater use of maize, and with a movement up the river valleys from the littoral, possibly as a result of population pressure. Between 900 and 500 B.C., a distinctive style in building, art, ceramics, and weaving, known as Chavín (from the name of the site of a great ceremonial center discovered in 1946), spread along the coast and even into the highlands. The most distinctive feature of Chavín is its art style, which features a feline being, presumably a deity, whose cult spread over the area of Chavín influence.

The Classic or Florescent period that emerged in Peru at or shortly before the beginning of the Old World's Christian era reflected further progress in agriculture, notably in the use of irrigation and fertilization. The brilliant culture called Nazca displaced the Chavín along the coast and highlands of southern Peru at this time. Nazca pottery is distinguished by its use of color. Sometimes there are as many as eleven soft pastel shades on one pot. The lovely Nazca textiles display an enormous range of colors.

Even more remarkable was the Mochica culture of the northern Peruvian coast. The Mochica built pyramids and temples, roads and large irrigation canals, and evolved a complex, highly stratified society with a directing priesthood and a powerful priest-king. Metallurgy was well developed, as evidenced by the wide use of copper weapons and tools and the manufacture of alloys of gold, copper, and silver. But as craftsmen and artists the Mochica are best known for their red and black pottery, never surpassed in the perfection of its realistic modeling. The so-called portrait vases, apparently representing actual individuals, mark the acme of Mochica realism. The pottery was also frequently decorated with realistic paintings of the most varied kind, including erotic scenes, which today are collectors' items. The pottery frequently depicts war scenes, suggesting chronic struggles for limited arable land and sources of water. The aggressive Mochica were themselves finally conquered by invaders who ravaged their lands, and a time of turbulence and cultural decline came to northern Peru.

About A.D. 600, the focus of Andean civilization shifted from the coast to the highlands. At the site called Tiahuanaco, just south of Lake Titicaca on the high plateau of Bolivia, there arose a great ceremonial center famed for its megalithic architecture, which was constructed with great stone blocks perfectly fitted together, and for its monumental human statuary. Tiahuanaco seems to have been the capital of a military state that eventually controlled all of southern Peru from Arequipa south to highland Bolivia and Chile. Another people, the Huari, embarked on a career of conquest from their homeland near modern Ayacucho; their territory ultimately included both the coast and highlands as far north as Cajamarca and south to the Tiahuanaco frontier. After a few centuries of domination, the Huari Empire broke up about A.D. 1000. At about the same time the Tiahuanaco sway also came to an end. The disintegration of these empires was followed by

32

a return to political and artistic regionalism in the southern Andean area.

By A.D. 1000, a number of Postclassic states, differing from their predecessors in their greater size, had established their control over large portions of the northern Peruvian coast. Their rise was accompanied by the growth of cities. Each river valley had its own urban center, and an expanded net of irrigation works made support of larger populations possible. The largest of these new states was the Chimu kingdom. Its capital, Chanchan, was an immense city spread over eight square miles, with houses made of great molded adobe bricks grouped into large units or compounds. The Chimu kingdom survived until its conquest by the Inca in the mid-fifteenth century.

Inca Economy and Society

In the highlands, meanwhile, where less settled conditions prevailed, a new power was emerging. The Incas (so called after their own name for the ruling lineage) made a modest appearance in history as one of a number of small tribes that inhabited the Cuzco region in the Andean highlands and struggled with each other for possession of land and water. A strong strategic situation in the Valley of Cuzco and some cultural superiority over their neighbors favored the Incas as they began their career of conquest. Previous empires—Huari, Tiahuanaco, and Chimu—no doubt provided the Incas with instructive precedents for conquest and the consolidation of conquest through a variety of political and socioeconomic techniques. Like other imperialist nations of antiquity, the Incas had a body of myth and legend that ascribed a divine origin to their rulers and gave their warriors a comforting assurance of supernatural favor and protection.

True imperial expansion seems to have begun in the second quarter of the fifteenth century, in the reign of Pachacuti Inca, who was crowned in 1438. Together with his son Topa Inca, also a great conqueror, Pachacuti obtained the submission of many provinces by the skillful use of claims of divine aid, fair promises, threats, and naked force. Reputed to be a great organizer as well as a mighty warrior, Pachacuti is credited with many reforms and innovations, including the establishment of the territorial divisions and elaborate administrative bureaucracy that made the wheels of the Inca Empire go round. By 1527 the boundary markers of the Children of the Sun rested on the modern frontier between Ecuador and Colombia to the north and on the Maule River in Chile to the south. A population of perhaps 9 million people owed allegiance to the emperor. When the Spaniards arrived, the ruler was Atahualpa, who had just won the imperial mantle by defeating his half-brother Huascar.

The Incas maintained their authority with an arsenal of devices that included the spread of their Quechua language (still spoken by five-sixths of the Indians of the central Andean area) as the official language of the empire, the imposition of a unifying state religion, and a shrewd policy of incorporating chieftains of conquered regions into the central bureaucracy. An important factor in the Inca plan of unification was the policy of resettlement, or colonization. This consisted of deporting dissident populations and replacing them with loyal *mitimaes* (colonists) from older provinces of the empire. An excellent network of roads and footpaths linked administrative centers and made it possible to send armies and messengers quickly from one part of the empire to another. Some roads were paved, others were cut into solid rock. Where the land was marshy, the roads passed over causeways; suspension bridges spanned gorges, and pontoon bridges of buoyant reeds were used to cross rivers. The Incas had no system of writing, but they possessed a most efficient means of keeping records in a memory aid called the *quipu,* a stick or cord with a number of knotted strings tied to it. Strings of different colors represented different articles, people, or districts; knots tied in the strings ascended in units representing ones, tens, hundreds, thousands, and so on.

The economic basis of the Inca Empire was its intensive irrigation agriculture capable of supporting without serious strain not only the producers but the large Inca armies, a large admin-

The Chimu, whose extensive kingdom was conquered by the Inca in the mid-twelfth century, are celebrated for their mastery of the metalworker's art, as illustrated by this exquisite effigy vessel in the shape of a deer.

istrative bureaucracy, and many other persons engaged in nonproductive activities. The Incas did not develop this agriculture. By the time of their rise, the original coastal irrigation systems had probably been extended over all suitable areas in coastal and highland Peru. But along with their political and religious institutions, the Incas introduced the advanced practices of irrigation, terracing, and fertilization among conquered peoples of more primitive culture. Terracing was widely used to extend the arable area and to prevent injury to fields and settlements in the narrow Andean valleys from runoff from the steep slopes during the rainy season. Irrigation ditches, sometimes mere trenches, sometimes elaborate stone channels, conducted water to the fields and pastures where it was needed.

Agricultural implements were few and simple. They consisted chiefly of a foot plow, used to break up the ground and dig holes for planting, and a hoe with a bronze blade for general cultivation. As previously noted, the potato and quinoa were staple crops in the higher valleys; maize was the principal crop at lower altitudes; and a wide variety of plants, including cotton, coca, and beans, was cultivated in the lower and hotter valleys. A major function of the Inca state was to regulate the exchange of the products of these multiple environments, primarily through the collection of tribute and its redistribution to various groups in Inca society. The Inca state also promoted self-sufficiency by allowing members of a given community to exploit the resources of different levels of the Andean "vertical" economy.

The basic unit of Inca social organization was the *ayllu,* a kinship group whose members claimed descent from a common ancestor and

34

married within the group. A village community typically consisted of several ayllu. Each ayllu owned certain lands, which were assigned in lots to heads of families. Each family head had the right to use and pass on the land to male descendants but not to sell or otherwise dispose of it. Villagers frequently practiced mutual aid in agricultural tasks, in the construction of dwellings, and in other projects of a private or public nature. The Inca rulers took over this communal principle and utilized it for their own ends in the form of corvée, or unpaid forced labor. In the words of the anthropologist Nathan Wachtel, "the imperial Inca mode of production was based on the ancient communal mode of production which it left in place, while exploiting the principle of reciprocity to legitimate its rule."

Before the Inca conquest, the ayllu were governed by *curacas* (hereditary chiefs) assisted by a council of elders, with a superior curaca or lord (*jatun curaca*) ruling over the whole people or state. Under Inca rule, the kinship basis of ayllu organization was weakened through the planned removal of some of its members and the settlement of strangers in its midst (the system of mitimaes). A varying amount of land was taken from the villages and vested in the Inca state and the state church. In addition to working their own lands and those of their curaca, ayllu members were required to till the Inca state and church lands. The Inca government also used the forced labor of villagers to create new arable land by leveling and terracing slopes. This new land was often turned over as private estates to curacas and Inca military leaders and nobles who had rendered conspicuous service to the Inca state. The Inca himself possessed private estates, and others were owned by the lineages of dead emperors and used to maintain the cult of these former rulers. These private estates were not worked by ayllu members but by a new servile class, the *yanacona*,[4] defined by Spanish sources as "permanent servants"; each ayllu had to contribute a number of such servants or retainers,

who also worked in the Inca temples and palaces and performed personal service.

In addition to agricultural labor, ayllu members had to work on roads, irrigation channels, fortresses, and in the mines, in a system called the *mita*, later adopted by the Spaniards for their own purposes. Another requirement was that villages produce specified quantities of cloth for the state to use in clothing soldiers and retainers. All able-bodied commoners between certain ages were subject to military service. There is no trace of socialism or a welfare state in these arrangements, which favored not the commoners but the Inca dynasty, nobility, priesthood, warriors, and officials. Many of the activities cited as reflecting the benevolence and foresight of the Inca state were actually traditional village and ayllu functions. One such activity was the maintenance of storehouses of grain and cloth by the community for times of crop failure. The Inca state merely took over this principle, as it had taken over the principle of cooperative labor for communal ends, and established storehouses containing the goods produced by the peasants' forced labor on state and church lands. The cloth and grain stored in these warehouses were used primarily to clothe and feed the army, the crown artisans, the conscript labor for public works, and the officials who lived in Cuzco and other towns.

The relations between the Inca and the peasantry were based on the principle of reciprocity, expressed in an elaborate system of gifts and countergifts. The peasantry cultivated the lands of the Inca, worked up his wool and cotton into cloth, and performed various other kinds of labor for him. The Inca, the divine, universal lord, in turn permitted them to cultivate their communal lands and in time of shortages released to the villages the surplus grain in his storehouses. Since the imperial gifts were the products of the peasants' own labor, this "reciprocity" amounted to intensive exploitation of the commoners by the Inca rulers and nobility. We must not underestimate, however, the hold of this ideology, buttressed by a religious world view that regarded the Inca as responsible for defending the order

---

[4] A plural term in Quechua but treated by the Spaniards as singular.

and very existence of the universe, on the Inca peasant mentality.

At the time of the Conquest, a vast gulf separated the regimented and laborious life of the commoners from the luxurious life of the Inca nobility. At the apex of the social pyramid were the Inca and his kinsmen, composed of twelve lineages. Members of these lineages had the privilege of piercing their ears and distending the lobes with large ornaments; hence the name *orejones* (big ears) assigned to the Inca kinsmen by the Spaniards. The orejones were exempt from tribute labor and military service; the same was true of the curacas, who had once been chieftains in their own right, and of a numerous class of specialists—servants, retainers, quipu keepers and other officials, and entertainers. Side by side with the Inca state, which drained off the peasants' surplus production, regulated the exchange of goods between the various regions, and directed vast public works, there arose the incipient feudalism of the Inca nobility and curacas. Their loyalty and services to the Inca were rewarded with rich gifts of land, llamas, and yanacona. Their growing resources enabled them to form their own local clienteles, achieve a certain relative independence of the crown, and play an important role in the disputes over the succession that sometimes followed the emperor's death.

Inca rule over the peasant masses was largely indirect, exercised through local chieftains. It probably did not seriously affect the round of daily life in the villages. The typical peasant house in the highlands was a small hut with walls of fieldstone or adobe and a gable roof thatched with grass. The scanty furniture consisted of a raised sleeping platform, a clay stove, and some clay pots and dishes. A man's clothing consisted of a breechcloth, a sleeveless tunic, and a large cloak over the shoulders with two corners tied in front; the fineness of the cloth used and the ornamentation varied according to social rank. A woman's dress was a wraparound cloth extending from beneath the arms to the ankles, with the top edges drawn over the shoulders and fastened with straight pins. An ornamented sash around the waist and a shoulder mantle completed the woman's apparel. Men adorned themselves with earplugs and bracelets; women wore necklaces and shawl pins.

On the eve of the Spanish Conquest, the Inca state appeared all-powerful. But, like the Aztec Empire, it was rent by deep contradictions. Frequent revolts by conquered peoples were put down with ferocious cruelty. Even the outwardly loyal curacas, former lords of independent states, chafed at the vigilant Inca control and dreamed of regaining their lost freedom.

Inca Religion and Learning

The Inca state religion existed side by side with the much older ancestor cults and the worship of innumerable *huacas* (local objects and places). Chief of the Inca gods was a nameless creator called Viracocha and Pachayachachic (lord and instructor of the world). His cult seems to have been a philosophical religion largely confined to the priesthood and nobility. First in importance after Viracocha was the Sun God, claimed by the Inca royal family as its divine ancestor. Other notable divinities were the Thunder God, who sent the life-giving rain, and the Moon, wife of the Sun, who played a vital role in the regulation of the Inca festival calendar. The Inca idols were housed in numerous temples attended by priests who directed and performed ceremonies that included prayer, sacrifice, confession, and the rite of divination. Another priestly function was the magical cure of disease. The priests were assisted in their religious duties by a class of *mamacuna* (holy women) who had taken vows of permanent chastity. Human sacrifice was performed on very momentous occasions, such as an important victory or some great natural calamity.

Inca art was marked by a high level of technical excellence. The architecture was solid and functional, characterized by massiveness rather than beauty. The stone sculpture, more frequent in the highlands than on the coast, has been described as ponderous and severe. But the tapestries of Inca weavers are among the world's

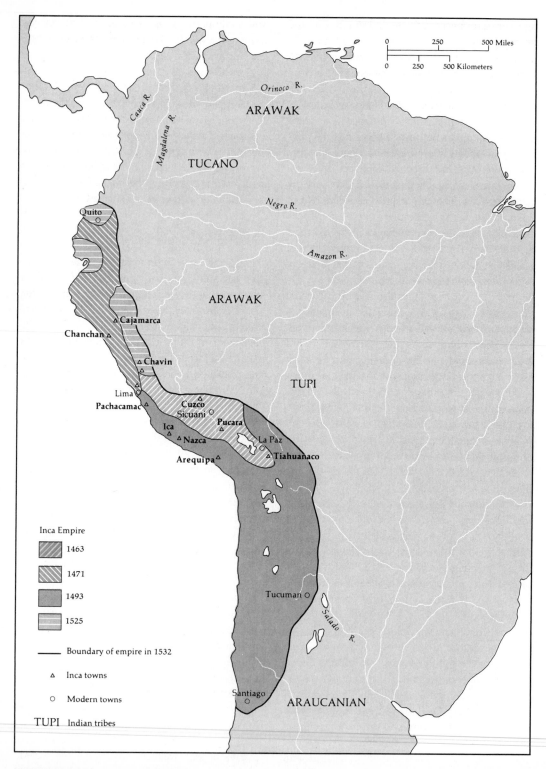

GROWTH OF THE INCA EMPIRE, 1460–1532

textile masterpieces, so fine and intricate is the weaving. Inca metallurgy was also on a high technical and artistic plane. Cuzco, the Inca capital, abounded in gold objects: the imperial palace had gold friezes and panels of gold and silver, and the Temple of the Sun contained a garden with lifelike replicas of plants and animals, all made of hammered gold.

Although the Incas had no system of writing and hence no written literature, narrative poems, prayers, and tales were handed down orally from generation to generation. The Inca hymns and prayers that have been preserved are notable for their lofty thought and beauty of expression. Of the long narrative poems that dealt with Inca mythology, legends, and history, there remain only summaries in Spanish prose.

A melancholy and nostalgic spirit pervades many of the traditional Inca love songs, and the same plaintiveness characterizes the few examples of their music that have come down to us. Based on the five-toned, or pentatonic, scale, this music was performed with an assortment of instruments: flutes, trumpets, and whistles; gongs, bells, and rattles; and several kinds of skin drums and tambourines. The dances that accompanied the music sometimes represented an elementary form of drama.

Spanish conquistadors destroyed Inca political organization and dealt shattering blows to all aspects of Inca civilization, but elements of that culture survive everywhere in the central Andean area. These survivals, tangible and intangible, include the Quechua speech of great numbers of Indians; the numerous Indian communities, or ayllu, still partly based on cooperative principles; the widespread pagan beliefs and rites of the people; and of course the monumental ruins of Sacsahuaman, Ollantaytambo, Machu Picchu, Pisac, and Cuzco itself. Inca civilization also lives in the writings of Peruvian historians, novelists, and statesmen who evoke the vanished Inca greatness and praise the ancient virtues of their people. For many Peruvians, the great technical achievements and social engineering of the Incas, ensuring a modest well-being for all, offer proof of the inherent capacity of their native peoples and a prospect of what the poverty-ridden, strife-torn Peru of today may yet become.

Chapter 2

The Hispanic Background

Conquest was a major theme of Spanish history from very remote times. The prehistoric inhabitants of the peninsula, whose unknown artists produced the marvelous cave paintings of Altamira, were overrun by tribes vaguely called Iberians and by the Celts, who are believed to have come from North Africa and central Europe, respectively, probably before 1000 B.C. New waves of invasion brought the Phoenicians, Greeks, and Carthaginians, commercial nations that established trading posts and cities on the coast but made no effort to dominate the interior. Still later, Spain became a stake of empire in the great struggle for commercial supremacy between Rome and Carthage that ended with the decisive defeat of the latter in 201 B.C. For six centuries thereafter, Rome was the dominant power in the peninsula.

Unlike earlier invaders, the Romans attempted to establish their authority throughout Spain (the name comes from the word *Hispania*, applied by the Romans to the whole peninsula) and to impose their language and institutions on the native peoples. From Latin, made the official language, sprang the various dialects and languages still spoken by the Hispanic peoples. Roman law replaced the customary law of the Celts, Iberians, and other native groups. Native tribal organization was destroyed through forced changes of residence, concentration in towns, and the planting of Roman colonies that served as agencies of pacification and assimilation. Agriculture, mining, and industry developed, and Roman Spain carried on an extensive trade in wheat, wine, and olive oil with Italy. Roman engineers constructed great public roads and aqueducts, some of which are still in use. Roman education and literary culture were brought to Spain, and a number of Spaniards by birth or residence (the satirical poet Martial, the epic poet Lucan, and the philosopher Seneca) made notable contributions to Latin literature.

Early in the fifth century A.D., as a result of the decline of Roman military power, a number of barbarian peoples of Germanic origin invaded Spain. By the last half of the century, one group of invaders, the Visigoths, had gained mastery over most of the peninsula. As a result of long contact with the empire, the Visigoths had already lost part of their barbarism. Their assimilation of Roman culture continued in Spain through contact with the Hispano-Romans. The Visigothic kingdom was Christian; its speech became Latin with a small admixture of Germanic terms; in administration it followed the Roman model. But the succession to the kingship followed Germanic tradition in being elective, a frequent source of great internal strife.

Spain's Medieval Heritage

The divisions among the Goths caused by struggles over kingship played into the hands of the new Muslim power in North Africa. In 711 the Muslims crossed the straits and decisively defeated Roderic, the last Gothic king. Within a few years, all of Spain, aside from the remote region north of the Cantabrian Mountains, had fallen into Muslim hands. But the Muslims' hold on the bleak uplands of Castile was never strong; they preferred the fertile plains and mild climate of southern Spain, which they called Al-Andalus, the land of Andalusia.

The Muslims, heirs to the accumulated cultural wealth of the ancient Mediterranean and Eastern worlds, enriched this heritage with their own magnificent contributions to science, arts, and letters. In the tenth and eleventh centuries, Muslim Spain, with its capital at Córdoba, was an economic and intellectual showplace from which fresh knowledge and ideas flowed into Christian lands. Spanish agriculture gained by the intro-

duction of new irrigation and water-lifting devices and new crops: sugar, saffron, cotton, silk, and citrus fruits. Industry was broadened through the introduction of such products as paper and glass, hitherto unknown to the West. Muslim metalwork, pottery, silk, and leatherwork were esteemed throughout Europe. Many Muslim rulers were patrons of literature and learning; the scholar-king Al-Haquem II built up a library said to have numbered four hundred thousand volumes.

As a rule, the Muslim conquerors did not insist on the conversion of the vanquished Christians, preferring to give them the option of accepting the Islamic faith or paying a special poll tax. The relatively tolerant Muslim rule was favorable to economic and cultural advance. The Jews, who had suffered severe persecution under the Visigoths, enjoyed official protection and made major contributions to medicine, philosophy, and Talmudic studies. The condition of the peasantry probably improved, for the conquerors distributed the vast estates of the Visigothic lords among the serfs, who paid a certain portion of the produce to the Muslim lords and kept the rest for themselves. But in later centuries, these trends were reversed; great landed estates again arose, taxation increased, and severe persecution of Jews and Mozárabes (Christians who had adopted Arab speech and customs) drove many to flee to Christian territory.

Despite its noble achievements, Muslim civilization rested on insecure foundations. The Arab conquerors never fully threw off the tribal form of social organization under which they began their prodigious advance, and the Muslim world was torn by fierce political and religious feuds over control of the empire. In Spain these internal differences were complicated by conflicts between the Arabs and the North African Berbers, recent converts to Islam who were more fanatically devout than were their teachers. By the mid-eleventh century, the caliphate of Córdoba had broken into a large number of *taifas* (states) that constantly warred with each other. These discords enabled the petty Christian kingdoms that had arisen in the north to survive, grow

40

strong, and eventually launch a general advance against the Muslims. In the west, Portugal, having achieved independence from Castile by the mid-twelfth century, attained its historic boundaries two centuries later. In the center, the joint realm of León and Castile pressed its advance; to the east, the kingdom of Aragon steadily expanded at the expense of the disunited Muslim states.

The Reconquest began as a struggle of Christian kings and nobles to regain their lost lands and serfs; only later did it assume the character of a crusade. Early in the ninth century, the tomb of St. James, supposedly found in northwest Spain, became the center of the famous pilgrimage of Santiago de Compostela and gave Spain a warrior patron saint who figured prominently in the Reconquest and the conquest of the New World. But the career of the famous Cid (Ruy Díaz de Vivar), to whom the Arabic title of "lord" was given by his Muslim soldiers, illustrates the absence of religious fanaticism in the first stage of the struggle. True to the ideals of his time, the Cid placed feudal above religious loyalties, and as a vassal of the Muslim kings of Saragossa and Valencia fought Moorish and Christian foes alike. When he captured Valencia for himself in 1094, he allowed the Muslims to worship freely and retain their property, requiring only the payment of tributes authorized by the Koran.

The Muslims vainly sought to check the Christian advance by calling on newly converted, fanatically religious Berber tribes in North Africa to come to their aid. The Christian victory at Las Navas de Tolosa (1212) in Andalusia over a large Berber army marked a turning point in the Reconquest. Ferdinand III of Castile captured Córdoba, the jewel of Muslim Spain, in 1236; the surrender of Seville in 1248 gave him control of the mouth of the Guadalquivir River and communication with the sea. By the time of Ferdinand's death in 1252, the Muslim territory in Spain had been reduced to the small kingdom of Granada. The strength of its position, protected by steep mountains and impassable gorges, and the divisions that arose within the Christian camp gave Granada two and a half more centuries of independent life.

Castile

Castile, the largest and most powerful of the Spanish kingdoms, played the leading role in the Reconquest. The great movement left an enduring stamp on the Castilian character. Centuries of struggle against the Moor made war almost a Castilian way of life and created a large class of warrior-nobles who regarded manual labor with contempt. In the Castilian scale of values, the military virtues of courage, endurance, and honor took the first place. Not only the nobles but the commoners accepted these values. The lure of plunder, land, and other rewards drew many peasants and artisans into the armies of the Reconquest and diffused militarist and aristocratic ideals throughout Castilian society. To these ideals the crusading spirit of the Reconquest, especially in its later phase, added a strong sense of religious superiority and mission.

The Reconquest also helped to shape the character of the Castilian economy. As the Muslims fell back, vast tracts of land came into the possession of the crown. The kings assigned the lion's share of this land to the nobility, the church, and the three military orders of Calatrava, Alcántara, and Santiago. As a result, Castile, especially the area from Toledo south (New Castile), became a region of enormous estates and a very wealthy, powerful aristocracy.

The Reconquest also insured the supremacy of sheep raising over agriculture in Castile. In a time of constant warfare, of raids and counterraids, the mobile sheep was a more secure and valuable form of property than land. With the advance of the Christian frontier, much new territory—frequently too arid for easy agricultural use—was opened to the sheep industry. The introduction of the merino sheep into Spain from North Africa around 1300, coinciding with a sharply increased demand in northern Europe for Spanish wool, gave a marked stimulus to sheep raising. By the late thirteenth century, there had arisen a powerful organization of sheep raisers, the *Mesta*. In return for large subsidies to the crown, this organization received extensive privileges, including the right to move great flocks of sheep across

Spain from summer pastures in the north to winter pastures in the south, with frequent injury to the farmlands and woods in their path. The great nobles dominated the sheep industry as well as agriculture. Their large rents and the profits from the sale of their wool gave them an economic, social, and military power that threatened the supremacy of the king.

The Castilian towns represented the only counterpoise to this power. The advance of the Reconquest and the need to consolidate its gains promoted municipal growth. To attract settlers to the newly conquered territory, the king gave generous *fueros* (charters of liberties) to the towns that sprang up one after another. These charters endowed the towns with administrative autonomy and vast areas of land that extended their jurisdiction into the surrounding countryside. The towns were governed by elected judicial officials known as *alcaldes* and by members of the town council, called *regidores*. The economic expansion of the thirteenth and fourteenth centuries and the growth of the wool trade, above all, made the Castilian towns bustling centers of industry and commerce. The wealth of the towns gave them a peculiar importance in the meetings of the consultative body, or parliament, known as the Cortes. Since the nobles and the clergy were exempt from taxes, the towns' deputies had to vote the money needed by the king. Their price for voting it became the redress of grievances presented in the form of petitions that royal approval transformed into laws.

The Castilian towns had their time of splendor, but in the last analysis the middle class remained small and weak; it was overshadowed by the enormous power of the great nobles. Aware of their weakness, the towns joined their forces in *hermandades,* military associations that resisted the aggressions of the nobles and sometimes of the king. But the posture of the towns was essentially defensive. Without the aid of the king, they could not hope to impose their will on the aristocracy.

As the Muslim power waned, the great nobles turned from fighting the infidel to battling the king, the towns, and each other. In the course of the fourteenth and fifteenth centuries, gained the upper hand in their struggle w. king, usurping royal lands and revenues anu often transforming the monarch into their pawn. The degradation of the crown reached its lowest point in the reign of Henry IV (1454–1474), when there was an almost total breakdown of central government and public order. Beneath this anarchy, however, the continued expansion of economic life inspired a growing demand for a strong monarchy capable of establishing peace and order.

Aragon

The medieval history of the smaller, less populous kingdom of Aragon differed in important ways from that of Castile. The king of Aragon ruled over three states: Aragon, Valencia, and Catalonia, each regarded as a separate *reino* (kingdom), each having its own Cortes. The upland state of Aragon was the poorest, most backward of the three. Valencia was the home of a large Moorish peasant population subject to a Christian landowning nobility. The dominant role in the union was played by Catalonia and its great city of Barcelona, which had given Aragon its dynasty and most of its revenues. A thriving industry and powerful fleets had made Barcelona the center of a commercial empire based on the export of textiles. Catalan arms had also won Sardinia and Sicily for the crown of Aragon. In Aragon, therefore, the ruling class was not the landed nobility, which was relatively poor, but the commercial and industrial oligarchy of Barcelona. The constitutional system of Aragon reflected the supremacy of this class by giving legislative power to the Cortes of Catalonia and by providing special watchdog committees of the Cortes, which guarded against any infringement of the rights and liberties of the subjects.

In the fourteenth and fifteenth centuries, the prosperity of Barcelona was undermined by the ravages of the Black Death, agrarian unrest in the Catalan countryside, struggles between the merchant oligarchy and popular elements in Barcelona, and above all by the loss of traditional

Catalan markets to Genoese competitors. This economic decline sharpened Catalan internal struggles, in which the crown joined on the side of the popular elements. The result was the civil war of 1462–1472, which ended in a qualified victory for the king, John II, but which completed the ruin of Catalonia. The weakness of Aragon on the eve of its union with Castile insured Castilian leadership of the coming new Spain.

The chain of events leading to Spanish unity began with the secret marriage in 1469 of Isabella, sister of Henry IV of Castile, and Ferdinand, son of John II of Aragon. This match was the fruit of complex intrigues in which the personal ambitions of the young couple, the hostility of many Castilian nobles to their king, and the desire of John II to add Castile to his son Ferdinand's heritage all played their part. On the death of Henry IV in 1474, Isabella proclaimed herself queen of Castile with the support of a powerful faction of Castilian nobles and towns that declared that Henry's daughter Juana was illegitimate. This claim led to a dynastic war in which Portugal supported Juana. By 1479 the struggle had ended in Isabella's favor. In the same year, John II died and Ferdinand succeeded to his dominions. Ferdinand and Isabella now became joint rulers of Aragon and Castile, but the terms of their marriage contract carefully subordinated Ferdinand to Isabella in the government of Castile and excluded Isabella from the administration of Aragon. The process of Spanish unification, however, had begun. Under the leadership of Castile, Spain embarked on a remarkable career of domestic progress and imperial expansion.

The Spain of Ferdinand and Isabella

Restoration of Order

The young monarchs faced an urgent problem of restoring peace and order in their respective kingdoms. Catalonia was still troubled by struggles between feudal lords and serfs determined to end their legal servitude. Ferdinand intervened to bring about a solution relatively favorable to the peasantry. His ruling of Guadalupe (1486) ended serfdom in Catalonia and enabled fifty thousand peasants to become small landowners. But he made no effort to reform Aragon's archaic constitutional system, which set strict limits on the royal power. As a result, Castile and Aragon, despite their newfound unity, continued to move along divergent political courses.

The task of restoring order was greater in Castile. The age of anarchy under Henry IV had transformed cities into battlefields and parts of the countryside into a desert. To eradicate the evils of banditry and feudal violence, Isabella counted above all on the support of the towns and the middle classes. The Cortes of Madrigal (1476) forged a solid alliance between the crown and the towns for the suppression of disorder. Their instrument was the *Santa Hermandad,* a police force paid for and manned principally by the towns but under the direct control of the crown. The efficiency of this force and the severe and prompt punishments meted out by its tribunals gradually restored peace in Castile.

But Isabella's program went beyond this immediate goal. She proposed to bend to the royal will all the great institutions of medieval Castile: the nobility, the church, and the towns themselves. The Cortes of Toledo of 1480 reduced the power of the grandees (nobles of the first rank) in various ways. An Act of Resumption compelled them to return to the crown about half the revenues they had usurped since 1464. Another reform reorganized the Council of Castile, the central governing agency of the kingdom. This reform reduced the grandees who had dominated the old royal council to holders of empty dignities. It vested effective responsibility and power in *letrados* (officials usually possessed of legal training), who were drawn from the lower nobility, the middle class, and *conversos* (converted Jews). The same end of curbing aristocratic power was served by the establishment of a hierarchy of courts and magistrates that ascended from the *corregidor* (the royal officer who watched over the affairs of a municipality)

Isabella and Ferdinand transformed Spain into one of the strongest European kingdoms of the fifteenth century.

through the *cancillerías* (the high law courts of Castile) up to the Council of Castile, the highest court as well as the supreme administrative body of the country. At all levels, the crown asserted its judicial primacy, including the right of intervention in the feudal jurisdiction of the nobility.

The vast wealth of the military orders made them veritable states within the Castilian state. The crown determined to weaken their power by securing for itself control of these orders. When the grand mastership of Santiago fell vacant in 1476, Isabella personally appeared before the dignitaries of the order to insist that they confer the headship on her husband; they meekly assented. When the grand masterships of Calatrava and Alcántara fell vacant, they too were duly conferred on Ferdinand. By these moves, the crown gained new sources of revenue and patronage.

The towns had served the crown well in the struggle against anarchy, but in the past two centuries their democratic traditions had declined, and many had fallen under the control of selfish oligarchies. Some, like Seville, had become battlefields of aristocratic factions. These disorders provided Isabella with pretexts for resuming the policy, initiated by some of her predecessors, of intervening in municipal affairs by introducing corregidores into the towns. These officials combined administrative and judicial functions and steadily usurped the roles of the alcaldes and regidores. Ferdinand and Isabella also carried forward another practice begun by their predecessors. The offices of alcalde and regidor in towns with royal charters were made appointive by the crown instead of elective by the householders. *Villas de señorío* (towns under noble or ecclesiastical jurisdiction) were permitted to function under the traditional system, but with the right of royal intervention if necessary.

44

The taming of the towns was accompanied by a decline in the importance of the Cortes. An important factor in this decline was the large increase in revenues from royal taxes, such as the *alcabala* (sales tax), which freed the crown from excessive dependence on the grants of the Cortes. The increased supervision of the crown over the municipalities also decreased the likelihood of resistance by their deputies in the Cortes to royal demands. The sovereigns summoned the Castilian Cortes only when they needed money. When the treasury was full or when peace prevailed they ignored them.

Religious and Economic Reforms

In their march toward absolute power, the monarchs did not hesitate to challenge the church. Under their pressure, the weak popes of this period yielded to them the right of *patronato* (the right of appointment to all major ecclesiastical benefices in the Spanish realms). Although, unlike Henry VIII of England, Ferdinand and Isabella never despoiled the church of its vast landed possessions, they did drain off for themselves a part of the ecclesiastical wealth by taking one-third of all the tithes paid to the Castilian church and the proceeds from the sale of indulgences.

To ensure the loyalty of the church, to make it an effective instrument of royal policy, the sovereigns had to purge it of abuses that included plural benefices, absenteeism, and concubinage. The pious Isabella found a strong ally in the work of reform in a dissident faction of the regular clergy (those belonging to a monastic order or religious community). This group, who called themselves Observants, protested against the worldliness of their colleagues and demanded a return to the strict simplicity of the primitive church. The struggle for reform began within the Franciscan order under the leadership of the ascetic Francisco Jiménez de Cisneros, whom Isabella appointed archbishop of Toledo in 1495, and spread to the other orders. It grew so heated that four hundred Andalusian friars preferred moving to North Africa and becoming Muslims, rather than accept the new rule. The dispute ended in the complete victory of the Observants over their more easygoing brethren.

Isabella was less successful in efforts to reform the secular (or nonmonastic) clergy, but here too an improvement took place. The great ecclesiastical offices ceased to be a monopoly of the aristocracy. Isabella preferred to select prelates from the lower nobility and the middle class, taking account of the morals and learning of the candidates. The Isabelline religious reform had a special meaning for the New World: it insured that the Faith would be carried to the Indies by an elite force of clergy often distinguished for their zeal, humanity, and learning.

The sovereigns also gave attention to the need for economic reform. They attempted to promote Castilian industry and commerce by protectionist measures. They forbade the export of gold and silver, sporadically barred the import of cloth that competed with native products, and encouraged Italian and Flemish artisans to settle in Spain. They promulgated navigation acts that gave preference to domestic shipping and subsidies to domestic shipbuilding. They suppressed all the internal tolls that had been established in Castile since 1464 and made an effort to standardize weights and measures. Under Isabella's predecessors, a serious depreciation of the currency had taken place. To restore the credit of the coinage, Isabella suppressed all private mints and struck an excellent money that equaled foreign coins in value. All these measures contributed to an economic expansion and consequently to a rapid increase of crown revenues, from 885,000 *reales* in 1474 to 26,283,334 *reales* in 1504.

Despite their basically pragmatic outlook, the sovereigns had broad intellectual and artistic interests. To their court they summoned Italian humanists like Alessandro Geraldini, Lucio Marineo Siculo, and Peter Martyr de Anghera to tutor their children and the sons of the greatest houses of Spain. Enlightened prelates like Archbishop Jiménez de Cisneros founded new schools and universities to rival the famed University of Salamanca. Spain herself produced some distinguished practitioners of the new learning, such as Antonio de Nebrija, grammarian, historian, and lexicographer, who in 1492 published and presented to Isabella a Castilian grammar—the first grammar of any modern European language. The vitality of the Castilian language and life found expression in a realistic masterpiece, the novel *La Celestina* (1499) by Fernando de Rojas. Meanwhile, Spanish architecture and sculpture developed its own style, known as plateresque, an ornamental blend of Moorish arabesques, flowers, foliage, and Renaissance motifs.

Foreign Policy

The restoration of domestic peace enabled the sovereigns to turn their attention to questions of foreign policy. For the Castilian Isabella, the conquest of Granada came first. Hardly had their authority been firmly restored when the sovereigns demanded of the Granadan ruler the tribute paid by his predecessors to Castile. Abdul Hassan replied that his mints now coined steel, not gold. The wealth of the Granadan kingdom and its mountainous terrain enabled the Moors to hold out for ten years. But the superior Spanish military power, especially the formidable new arm of artillery, finally broke the Muslim resistance. In January 1492, Granada surrendered to Ferdinand and Isabella, on whom Pope Alexander VI bestowed the title "The Catholic Sovereigns" in honor of their crusading piety.

Whereas Isabella's heart was set on the conquest of Granada, Ferdinand, heir to Aragon's Mediterranean empire and the traditional rivalry between France and Aragon, looked eastward to Aragon's borders with France and to Italy. He achieved most of his goals after Isabella's death in 1504. Employing an adroit blend of war and diplomacy, he obtained the return of two Aragonese provinces lost to France by previous rulers, the incorporation of the kingdom of Naples into the Aragonese empire, and the checkmating of French designs in Italy. In the course of Ferdinand's Italian wars, his commanders, especially the "Great Captain," Gonzalo de Córdoba, created a new-style Spanish army armed with great firepower and strong offensive and defensive weapons. The new system, first tested in Italy, established Spain's military supremacy in Europe.

Before his death, Ferdinand rounded out his conquests with the acquisition of Navarre (1512), which gave Spain a strongly defensible frontier with France.

The Catholic Sovereigns rendered major services to the Spanish people. They tamed the arrogant nobility, defeated the Moors, and united the Spanish kingdoms in the pursuit of common goals. They encouraged the growth of trade and industry and showed themselves to be intelligent patrons of learning and the arts. Their prudent diplomacy gave Spain a place among the first powers of Europe. In the same period, America was discovered under Castilian auspices, the Caribbean became a Spanish lake, and Spanish explorers and adventurers, by the end of the reign, were at the approaches to the great Indian empires of Mexico and Peru. Small wonder that monarchs who presided over such victories became for succeeding generations of Spaniards the objects of a national cult and legend.

Reappraisal of Ferdinand and Isabella's Policies

For modern historians, the fame of the Catholic Sovereigns has lost some of its luster. These historians charge Ferdinand and Isabella with mistaken policies that nullified much of the sound part of their work. One of these errors was a definite bias in favor of the economic and social interests of the aristocracy. If the nobility lost most of its political power under Ferdinand and Isabella, nothing of the kind happened in the economic sphere. Concentration of land in noble hands actually increased during their reign. The Cortes of 1480, which forced the nobility to surrender about half the lands and revenues usurped from the crown since 1464, explicitly authorized the nobles to retain the vast holdings acquired prior to that date. A policy of assigning a lion's share of the territory reconquered from the Muslims to the grandees also favored the growth of land monopoly. After the War of Granada, moreover, the great nobles used their private armies and increased political influence to expand their territories and seigneurial control. This "aristocratic offensive" met with little

Bay of Biscay

FRANCE

Coruña · Oviedo · Santander

KINGDOM OF GALICIA

PRINCIPALITY OF ASTURIAS

Santiago de Compostela · León · Bilbao · Pamplona

ROUSSILLON CERDAÑA

Perpignan

Burgos

PRINCIPALITY OF CATALONIA

Braganza · Valladolid · Saragossa · Barcelona

Oporto · *Duero R.* · *Ebro R.* · Tarragona

Viseu · Medina del Campo · Segovia · Molina

Salamanca · Guadalajara

Coimbra · Avila · Madrid

Toledo

KINGDOM OF VALENCIA

Minorca

Tagus R.

Majorca

Cintra · Crato · Alcantara

Lisbon · Badajóz · *Guadiana R.*

Valencia

Iviza

Formentera

ESTREMADURA

Calatrava

KINGDOM OF CÓRDOBA · **KINGDOM OF JAÉN**

Córdoba · Baeza · Alicante

SPANISH ALGARVE · **ANDALUSIA** · *Guadalquivir R.* · Jaén · **KINGDOM OF MURCIA** · Murcia

Cartagena

MEDITERRANEAN SEA

Cape St. Vincent · Tavira · Huelva · Seville · Granada · Almeriá

ALGARVE

Jerez de la Fontera · Málaga

Palos de la Fontera · Cádiz

San Lúcar de Bàrrameda · Algeciras · Gibraltar

ATLANTIC OCEAN

MOROCCO

	Kingdom of Castile and León with its dependencies
	Kingdom of Aragón with its dependencies
	Kingdom of Navarre
	Kingdom of Portugal
	Kingdom of Granada

0 ——— 100 ——— 200 Miles

0 ——— 100 ——— 200 Kilometers

SPAIN IN THE TIME OF CHRISTOPHER COLUMBUS

resistance from the crown. As a result, about 2 or 3 percent of the population owned 95 percent of the land by 1500.

This land monopoly reduced the great majority of the Castilian peasants to the condition of tenants heavily burdened by rents, seigneurial dues, tithes, and taxes. True, serfdom in the strict sense had apparently disappeared from most parts of Castile by 1480; the Castilian peasant was legally free to leave his village and move elsewhere at will. But since the nobility owned virtually all the land, the peasant's liberty was, as the Spanish historian Jaime Vicens Vives puts it, the liberty "to die of hunger."

The royal policy of favoring sheep raising over agriculture was equally harmful to long-range Spanish economic interests. Like their predecessors, the Sovereigns were influenced by the taxes and export duties paid by the sheep farmers and by the inflow of gold in payment for Spanish wool. As a result, they granted extensive privileges to the sheep raisers' guild, the Mesta. The climax of these favors was a 1501 law that reserved in perpetuity for pasture all land on which the migrant flocks had ever pastured. This measure barred vast tracts of land in Andalusia and Estremadura from being used for agriculture. The privilege granted the shepherds to cut branches from trees for fuel or to make fences and to trim or even fell trees whenever pasturage was scarce, together with the practice of burning the trees in autumn to produce better spring pasturage, contributed heavily to deforestation and soil erosion. Moreover, the overflow of sheep from their legal passage caused much damage to crops and soil. In a time of growing population, these policies and conditions inevitably produced serious food deficits. Chronic shortages climaxed in a devastating food crisis in the early sixteenth century.

Modern historians also question the traditional view that Spanish industry made spectacular advances under the Catholic Sovereigns. These historians claim that the only true industries of the period were the iron industry of the Basque provinces and the cloth industry of the Castilian central zone, which received a strong stimulus from the discovery of America and the opening of American markets. The resulting industrial prosperity lasted until shortly after the middle of the sixteenth century. But the level of industrial production never reached that of England, the Low Countries, and Italy. The abject poverty of the peasantry, which composed 80 percent of the population, sharply limited the effective market for manufactured goods. Shortages of capital and skilled labor also acted as a brake on industrial expansion. Other obstacles to industrial growth were the excessive costs of transport by mule train and oxcarts across the rugged peninsula and the customs barriers that continued to separate the Spanish kingdoms. Nor were the paternalistic measures of the sovereigns invariably helpful to industry. Through Ferdinand's influence, a guild system modeled on the rigid Catalan model was introduced into the Castilian towns. In this the Sovereigns did Castilian industry no service, for they fastened the straitjacket of guild organization on it precisely at the time when the discovery and colonization of America, the influx of American gold and silver, and the resulting economic upsurge challenged Spanish

industry to transform its techniques, lower costs, increase output and quality, and thereby establish Spanish economic as well as political supremacy in Europe.

No policy of the Sovereigns has come under harsher attack than their anti-Semitic measures. During the early Middle Ages, the Jews formed an influential and prosperous group in Spanish society. Down to the close of the thirteenth century, a relatively tolerant spirit prevailed in Christian Spain. Relations among Jews, Christians, and Muslims were so close and neighborly as to provoke protests by the church. In the fourteenth century, these relations began to deteriorate. Efforts by the clergy to arouse hatred of the Jews

Religious intolerance reached a peak during the reigns of Ferdinand and Isabella. In 1492, the Sovereigns ordered all Jews who refused to be baptized to leave Spain. In the picture below, a Jew kneeling before wealthy religious and secular authorities submits to an interrogation.

48

and popular resentment of such specialized Jewish economic activities as usury and tax farming, which caused severe hardship for peasants and other groups, contributed to this process. The rise of anti-Semitism led to the adoption of repressive legislation by the crown and to a wave of attacks on Jewish communities. To save their lives, many Jews accepted baptism; they came to form a very numerous class of conversos.

The converts soon achieved a marked prosperity and influence as tax farmers, court physicians, counselors, and lawyers. Wealthy, unhampered by feudal traditions, intellectually curious, intensely ambitious, the conversos incurred the hostility not only of peasants but of the church and of many nobles and burghers. Whether heretics or not, they posed a threat to the feudal order based on landed wealth, hereditary status, and religious orthodoxy. The envy and hostility they aroused help to explain why the Sovereigns, who had surrounded themselves with Jewish and converso advisers, and one of whom (Ferdinand) had Jewish blood in his veins, established the Inquisition and expelled the Jews from Spain. When the crown had tamed the nobility and the towns, when it had acquired large new sources of revenue, its dependence on the Jews and conversos was reduced; these groups became dispensable. The sacrifice of the Jews and conversos sealed the alliance between the absolute monarchy and the church and nobility.

The conversos first felt the blows of religious persecution with the establishment of the Spanish Inquisition in Castile in 1478. The task of this tribunal was to detect, try, and punish heresy, and its special target was the mass of conversos, many of whom were suspected of secretly adhering to Judaism. As a result of the Inquisition's activities, some two thousand conversos were burned at the stake; a hundred and twenty thousand fled abroad. As certain Spanish towns pointed out in memorials protesting the establishment of the Inquisition, the purge had a disastrous effect on the Spanish economy by causing this great flight of the conversos and their capital.

The Jews had a breathing space of twelve years during the costly War of Granada, for they were among the largest contributors to the royal finances. The surrender of Granada, however, brought near a decision on the fate of the Jews. The conquest of a rich territory and an industrious Moorish population, ending the drain of the war, meant that the Jews were no longer financially indispensable. After some hesitation, the Sovereigns yielded to anti-Semitic pressure and, on March 30, 1492, signed the edict giving the Jews the choice of conversion or expulsion.

The destruction or flight of many conversos and the expulsion of the Jews certainly contributed to the dreary picture presented by the Spanish economy at the close of the sixteenth century. The purge of the conversos eliminated from Spanish life its most vital merchant and artisan elements, the groups that in England and Holland were preparing the ground for the Industrial Revolution. The flight of converso artisans dealt Spanish industry a heavy blow and was directly responsible for royal edicts (1484) inviting foreign artisans to settle in Castile with exemption from taxes for ten years.

The anti-Semitic policies of the Sovereigns also harmed Spanish science and thought in general. The Inquisition helped to blight the spirit of free inquiry and discussion in Spain at a time when the Renaissance was giving an extraordinary impulse to the play of European intellect in all fields. The Sovereigns, who laid the foundations of Spain's greatness in so short a time, bear much of the responsibility for its premature decline. But the contradictions in their policies, the incorrect decisions that nullified much of the sound part of their work, resulted from more than personal errors of judgment; they reflected the structural weakness and backwardness of Spanish society as it emerged from seven centuries of struggle against the Moor.

The Hapsburg Era: Triumph and Tragedy

Isabella's death in 1504 placed all of the Iberian Peninsula except Portugal under the rule of Ferdinand. Isabella's will had named her daughter

Juana as successor, with the provision that Ferdinand should govern in case Juana proved unable. Since Juana's growing mental instability made her unfit to govern, Ferdinand assumed the regency. Juana's husband, Philip the Handsome of Burgundy, supported by a number of Castilian nobles, challenged Ferdinand's right to rule Castile, but Philip's sudden death in 1506 left Ferdinand undisputed master of Spain. Ferdinand himself died in 1516. To the Spanish throne ascended his grandson Charles, eldest son of Juana and Philip. Through his maternal grandparents, Charles inherited Spain, Naples and Sicily, and the Spanish possessions in Africa and America. Through his paternal grandparents, Marie of Burgundy and the Holy Roman emperor Maximilian, he inherited the territories of the house of Burgundy, which included the rich Netherlands, and the German possessions of the house of Hapsburg.

The Reign of Charles V

A solemn youth with the characteristic jutting underjaw of the Hapsburgs, Charles (first of that name in Spain and fifth in the Holy Roman Empire) had been born and reared in Flanders and knew no Spanish. Ferdinand had hoped that his younger grandson of the same name, who had been educated in Spain, would succeed him on the throne, but on his deathbed the old king had reluctantly consented to rescind his previous will and name Charles his heir. As the result of the accession of Charles to the throne of Spain, the course of Spanish history underwent a decisive change.

The Catholic Sovereigns, whatever their errors, had attempted to foster Spain's economic development and its partial unity; their prudent diplomacy set for itself limited goals. They had advanced toward absolute monarchy discreetly, respecting both the sensitivities of their peoples and those traditions that did not stand in the way of their designs. Charles, reared at the court of Burgundy in a spirit of royal absolutism, had a different notion of kingship. On his arrival in Spain he immediately alienated his subjects by his haughty manner and by the greed of his Flem-

ish courtiers, whom he placed in all key positions. He aroused even greater resentment by attempting to make the Castilians pay the bill for his election as Holy Roman emperor to succeed his grandfather Maximilian. Having achieved his ambition by expending immense sums of money, which placed him deeply in debt to the German banking house of Fugger, Charles hurried off to Germany.

For Castilians the election appeared to mean an absentee king and heavier tax burdens. Popular wrath burst forth in the revolt of the Castilian towns, or communes, in 1520–1521. The revolt of the *Comuneros* has been called the first bourgeois revolution in Europe, but it began as an essentially conservative movement: the rebels demanded that Charles return to Spain and make his residence there, that the drain of money abroad end, that no more foreigners be appointed to offices in Spain. Many nobles supported the rebellion at this stage, although the grandees remained neutral or hostile. But the leadership of the revolution soon fell into more radical hands. Simultaneously, there arose in Valencia a revolt of the artisans and middle classes against the great landowners. As a result of these developments, the Comunero movement lost almost all aristocratic support. In April 1521 the Comunero army suffered a total defeat, and the revolt began to fall apart. In July 1522, Charles was able to return to Spain, with four thousand German troops at his side. The last effort of the Spanish people to turn the political clock back, to prevent the final success of the centralizing and absolutist policies initiated by the Catholic Sovereigns, had failed.

For a time, at least, the dazzling successes of Charles V in the New and the Old Worlds reconciled the Spanish people to the new course. Spaniards rejoiced over the conquests of Cortés and Pizarro and the victories of the invincible Spanish infantry in Europe. They set to dreaming of El Dorados, universal empires, and a universal church. The poet Hernando de Acuña gave voice to Spain's exalted mood:

One Fold, one Shepherd only on the earth . . .
One Monarch, one Empire, and one Sword.

50

War dominated Charles's reign: war against France, against the Protestant princes of Germany, against the Turks, even against the pope, whose holdings in central Italy were threatened by Spanish expansionism. Actually, only one of these wars vitally concerned Spain's national interests: the struggle with the Turkish Empire, whose growing naval power endangered Aragon's possessions in Italy and Sicily and even threatened Spain's coasts with attack. Yet Charles, absorbed in the Protestant problem and his rivalry with France, pursued this struggle against the infidel less consistently than the others; in the end, it declined to a mere holding operation.

The impressive victories of Spanish arms on land and sea had few tangible results, for Charles, embroiled in too many quarters, could not take full advantage of his successes. In 1556 Charles renounced the Spanish throne in favor of his son Philip. Charles had failed in all his major objectives. The Protestant heresy still flourished in the north; the Turks remained solidly entrenched in North Africa, and their piratical fleets prowled the Mediterranean. Charles's project of placing his son Philip on the imperial throne had broken on the opposition of German princes, Protestant and Catholic, and of Charles's own brother Ferdinand, who wished to make the title of Holy Roman emperor hereditary in his own line. Charles's other dream of bringing England into the empire by marrying Philip to Mary Tudor collapsed when Mary died in 1558.

Meanwhile, Spaniards groaned under a crushing burden of debts and taxes, with Castile bearing the main part of the load. German and Italian merchant-princes and bankers, to whom an ever-increasing part of the royal revenue was pledged for loans, took over important segments of the Spanish economy. The Fuggers assumed the administration of the estates of the military orders and the exploitation of the mercury mines of Almadén. Their rivals, the Welsers, took over the Galician mines and received the American province of Venezuela as a fief whose Indians they barbarously exploited. To find money for his fantastically expensive foreign enterprises, Charles resorted to extraordinary measures: he extracted ever larger grants from the Cortes of Castile and Aragon; he multiplied royal taxes; he appropriated remittances of American treasure to private individuals, compensating the victims with *juros* (bonds). When his son Philip came to the throne in 1556, Spain was bankrupt.

The Reign of Philip II and the Remaining Hapsburgs

The reign of Philip (1556–1598) continued in all essential respects the policies of his father, with the same general results. Spain won brilliant military victories, which Philip failed to follow up from lack of funds or because some new crisis diverted his attention to another quarter. His hopes of dominating France by playing on the divisions between Huguenots and Catholics were frustrated when the Protestant Henry of Navarre entered the Catholic church, a move that united France behind Henry and forced Philip to sign a peace with him. The war against the Turks produced the great sea victory of Lepanto (1571), which broke the Turkish naval power, but when Philip's reign ended, the Turks remained in control of most of North Africa. In the prosperous Netherlands, the richest jewel in his imperial crown, Philip's policies of religious repression and absolutism provoked a great revolt that continued throughout his reign and imposed a terrible drain on the Spanish treasury. War with England flowed from the accession of the Protestant Elizabeth to the throne, from her unofficial support to the Dutch rebels, and from the encroachments of English corsairs and smugglers in American waters.

The crushing defeat of the Invincible Armada in 1588 dealt a heavy blow to Spain's self-confidence and virtually sealed the doom of Philip's crusade against the heretical north. Philip succeeded in another enterprise, the annexation of Portugal (1580), which gave Spain considerably more naval strength and a long Atlantic seaboard to use in a struggle against the Protestant north. But Philip failed to exploit these strategic opportunities, and Portugal, whose colonies and ships now became fair game for Dutch and

English seafarers, grew increasingly discontent with a union whose disadvantages exceeded its gains.

At his death in 1598, Philip II left a Spain in which the forces of disintegration were at work but which was still powerful enough militarily and territorially to be feared and respected. Under his successors, Spain entered a rapid decline. This decline first became visible in the area of diplomacy and war. The truce of 1609 with the Dutch, which tacitly recognized Dutch independence, was an early sign of waning Spanish power. The defeat of the famous Spanish infantry at the battle of Rocroi (1643) revealed the obsolescence of Spanish military organization and tactics and marked the end of Spanish military preponderance on the Continent. By the third quarter of the century, Spain, reduced to the defensive, had been compelled to sign a series of humiliating treaties by which she lost the Dutch Netherlands, part of Flanders, Luxembourg, and a string of lesser possessions.

The crisis existed at home as well as abroad. Efforts to make other Spanish kingdoms bear part of the burdens of the wars in which Castile had been so long engaged caused resentment and resistance. The able but imprudent favorite of Philip IV, Count Olivares, aroused a storm by his efforts to billet troops in Catalonia and otherwise make Catalonia contribute to the Castilian war effort at the expense of the ancient fueros, or privileges, of the principality. In 1640 a formidable revolt broke out; it continued for twelve years and shattered the economy of Catalonia. In the same year, Portugal, weary of a union that brought more losses than gains, successfully revolted against Spanish rule. Lesser insurrections took place in Biscay, Andalusia, Sicily, and Naples.

A decline in the quality of Spain's rulers no doubt contributed to this political decline. Philip II, "a glorious failure," had worked diligently to achieve his goals of Spanish predominance in Europe and the liquidation of Protestantism. His successors, Philip III (1598–1621) and Philip IV (1621–1665), were weak and incompetent kings who preferred to leave the work of government in the hands of favorites. The last Hapsburg king of Spain, Charles II (1665–1700), was a pathetic imbecile, totally incapable of ruling.

The Waning Economy and Society

The quality of the rulers of Spain had less to do with its decay than the crumbling of the economic foundations on which the empire rested. By the 1590s, the Castilian economy had begun to crack under the strain of costly Hapsburg adventures in foreign policy. Philip II several times resorted to bankruptcy to evade payments of debts to foreign bankers. His successors, lacking Philip's resources, were driven to currency inflation, which caused a flight of gold and silver abroad, until the national currency consisted largely of copper. But the development that contributed most to the Spanish economic crisis was a drastic decline in the inflow of American treasure in the middle decades of the seventeenth century, from about 135 million pesos in the decade from 1591 to 1600 to 19 million pesos in the decade from 1651 to 1660 (the complex causes of this decline will be discussed in Chapter 4).

By the end of the first quarter of the seventeenth century, signs of economic decline were on every hand. In the reign of Charles V, Seville had sixteen thousand looms producing silk and wool; at the death of Philip III in 1621, only four hundred remained. Toledo had fifty woolen manufacturing establishments in the sixteenth century; it had thirteen in 1665. The plight of agriculture was shown by a chronic shortage of foodstuffs, sometimes approaching famine conditions, and by the exodus of peasants from the countryside. Castile became a land of deserted villages. In the period from 1600 to 1700, Spain also suffered an absolute loss of population, from about 8 million to 6 million. The ravages of epidemics, aggravated by near-famine conditions; the expulsion of the Moriscos, or converted Moors, between 1609 and 1614; and emigration to the Indies contributed to this heavy loss.

The economic decline caused a contraction of Spain's artisan and merchant class, strengthened the domination of aristocratic values, and fos-

52   tered the growth of parasitism. In the seventeenth century, ambitious young Spaniards looked above all to the church and the court for an assured living. In 1626, Spain had nine thousand monasteries; at the end of the century, there were about 200,000 monks and priests in a population of 6 million. The nobility formed another very large unproductive class. At the end of the century, according to one calculation, Spain had four times as many nobles as France with its much larger population. The highest rung of the ladder of nobility was occupied by a small number of grandees—counts, dukes, marquis—who possessed enormous wealth and immense prerogatives; the lowest was occupied by a great number of hidalgos, petty nobles whose sole capital often was their honor and the precious letters patent that attested to their rank and their superiority over base *pecheros* (taxpayers), peasants, artisans, and burghers. The noble contempt for labor infected all classes. The number of vagabonds steadily grew; meanwhile, agriculture lacked enough laborers to till the land.

Literary and Artistic Developments

Spreading into all areas of Spanish life, the *decadencia* (decadence) inspired moods of pessimism, fatalism, and cynicism. Spanish society presented extreme contrasts: great wealth and abject poverty, displays of fanatical piety and scandalous manners, desperate efforts to revive the imperial glories of a past age by kings who sometimes lacked the cash to pay their servants and supply the royal table. The paradoxes of Spanish life, the contrast between the ideal and the real, stimulated the Spanish literary imagination. In this time, so sterile in other respects, Spain enjoyed a Golden Age of letters. As early as 1554, the unknown author of *Lazarillo de Tormes,* first of the picaresque novels, captured the seamy reality of a Spanish world teeming with rogues and vagabonds. Its hero relates his adventures under a succession of masters—a blind beggar, a stingy priest, a hungry hidalgo; he finally attains his highest hope, a sinecure as a town crier, secured for him by a priest whose mistress he had married.

The picaresque genre reached its climax in the *Guzmán de Alfarache* of Mateo de Alemán (1599), with its note of somber pessimism: "All steal, all lie. . . . You will not find a soul who is man unto man." The cleavage in the Spanish soul, the conflict between the ideal and the real, acquired a universal meaning and symbolism in the *Don Quijote* (1605) of Miguel Cervantes de Saavedra. The corrosive satires of Francisco Quevedo (1580–1645) gave voice to the despair of many seventeenth-century intellectuals. "There are many things here," wrote Quevedo, "that seem to exist and have their being, and yet they are nothing more than a name and an appearance."

By contrast, Spanish drama of the Golden Age only faintly reflected the national crisis. The plays of Lope de Vega (1562–1645) are rich in invention, sparkling dialogue, and melodious verse; his gallant hidalgos, courageous and clever heroines, and dignified peasants evoke the best traditions of Spain's past with a curious disregard for the dismal present. The dramas of Calderón de la Barca (1600–1681), however, suggest the defeatist temper of late seventeenth-century Spain by their tragic view of life and their stress on the illusory nature of reality: *"La vida es sueño, y los sueños sueño son"* ("Life is a dream, and our dreams are part of a dream").

Spanish painting of the Golden Age, like the literature, mirrors the transition from the confident and exalted mood of the early sixteenth century to the disillusioned spirit of the late seventeenth century. The great age of painting began with El Greco (1541–1616), whose work blends naturalism, deliberate distortion, and intense emotion to convey the somber religious passion of the Spain of Philip II. Yet some of El Greco's portraits are done with a magnificent realism. The mysticism of El Greco is completely absent from the canvases of Diego Velázquez (1599–1660). With a sovereign mastery of light, coloring, and movement, Velázquez captured for all time the palace life of two Spanish kings, presenting with the same detachment the princes and princesses and the dwarfs and buffoons of the court.

As we shall see in Chapter 5, the seventeenth-century Spanish decadencia profoundly influenced the relations between Spain and its American col-

Diego Velázquez's portrait *Las Meniñas* (*The Maids of Honor*) is a culminating work of the Spanish seventeenth-century school of painting. Note the utter detachment with which Velázquez treats the members of the Royal Family, the ladies-in-waiting, and two dwarfs, making no effort to enhance the dignity or beauty of one at the expense of the other.

onies. The loosening of economic and political ties between the mother country and the colonies, along with growing colonial self-sufficiency and self-consciousness, produced a shift in the balance of forces in favor of the colonists—a change that Spain's best efforts could not reverse.

The death of the wretched Charles II in 1700 brought the Hapsburg era to its end. Even before that symbolic death there had been some signs of a Spanish demographic and economic revival, notably in Catalonia, which by the 1670s had made a strong recovery from the depths of the great depression. Under a new foreign dynasty, the Bourbons, who were supported by all the progressive elements in Spanish society, Spain was about to begin a remarkable, many-sided effort at national reconstruction.

Chapter 3

The Conquest of America

The European discovery of America resulted from efforts to find a sea road to the East that would break the monopoly of Egypt and Venice over the lucrative trade in spices and other Oriental products. The drain of their scanty stock of gold and silver into the pockets of Italian and Levantine middlemen had grown increasingly intolerable to the merchants and monarchs of western Europe. Portugal took a decisive lead in the race to find a waterway to the land of spices. It had important advantages over its rivals: a long Atlantic seaboard with excellent harbors, a large class of fishermen and sailors, and an aristocracy that early learned to supplement its meager revenue from the land with income from trade and shipbuilding. Earlier than any other European country, Portugal became a unified nation-state under an able dynasty, the house of Avis, which formed a firm alliance with the merchant class and took a personal interest in the expansion of commerce. This fact helps explain Portugal's head start in the work of discovery. The Portuguese victory of Aljubarrota (1385), gained with English support, ended for a time Castile's efforts to absorb its smaller neighbor and released Portuguese energies for an ambitious program of overseas expansion.

The Great Voyages

Exploration Under Prince Henry

The famous Prince Henry (1394–1460) initiated the Portuguese era of exploration and discovery. Henry, somewhat misleadingly known as "the Navigator" since he never sailed beyond sight of land, united a medieval crusading spirit with the more modern desire to penetrate the secrets of unknown lands and seas and reap the profits of expanded trade. In 1415, Henry participated in the capture of the Moroccan seaport of Ceuta, a great Muslim trading center from which caravans crossed the desert to Timbuktu, returning with ivory and gold obtained by barter from the blacks of the Niger basin. Possession of the African beachhead of Ceuta opened up large prospects for the Portuguese. By penetrating to the sources of Ceuta gold, they could relieve a serious Portuguese shortage of the precious metal; Henry also hoped to reach the land of the fabled Christian ruler Prester John. Prester John was already identified with the emperor of Abyssinia, but no one knew how far his empire extended. An alliance with this ruler, it was hoped, would encircle the Muslims in North Africa with a powerful league of Christian states.

Efforts to expand the Moroccan beachhead, however, made little progress. If the Portuguese could not penetrate the Muslim barrier that separated them from the southern sources of gold and the kingdom of Prester John, could they not reach these goals by sea? In 1419, Henry set up a headquarters at Sagres on Cape St. Vincent, the rocky tip of southwest Portugal. Here he assembled a group of expert seamen and scientists. At the nearby port of Lagos, he began the construction of stronger and larger ships, equipped with the compass and the improved astrolabe. Beginning in 1420, he sent ship after ship to explore the western coast of Africa. Each captain was required to enter in his log data concerning currents, winds, and calms and to sketch the coastline. An eminent converso map maker, Jehuda Crespes, used these data to produce ever more detailed and accurate charts.

The first decade of exploration resulted in the discovery of the Madeiras and the Azores. But progress southward was slow; the imaginary barriers of a flaming torrid zone and a green sea of darkness made sailors excessively cautious. Passage in 1434 around Cape Bojador, the first major landmark on the West African coast, proved these fears groundless. Before Henry's death in 1460, the Portuguese had pushed as far as the Gulf of Guinea and had begun a lucrative trade in

gold dust and slaves captured in raids or bought from coastal chiefs. Henry's death brought a slackening in the pace of exploration. But the advance down the African coast continued, under private auspices and as an adjunct to the slave trade, the first bitter fruit of European overseas expansion. In 1469 a wealthy merchant, Fernão Gomes, secured a monopoly of the trade to Guinea (the name then given to the whole African coast), on condition that he explore farther south at the rate of a hundred miles a year. Complying with his pledge, Gomes sent his ships eastward along the Gold, Ivory, and Slave coasts and then southward almost to the mouth of the Congo.

The Sea Route to the East

Under the energetic John II, who came to the throne in 1481, the crown resumed control and direction of the African enterprise. At Mina, on the Gold Coast, John established a fort that became a center of trade in slaves, ivory, gold dust, and a coarse black pepper, as well as a base for further exploration. If Henry had dreamed of finding gold and Prester John, the project of reaching India by rounding Africa was now uppermost in John's mind. In 1483 an expedition commanded by Diogo Cão discovered the mouth of the Congo River and sailed partway up the mighty stream. On a second voyage in 1484, Cão pushed as far south as Cape Cross in southwest Africa. The Portuguese monarch sensed that victory was near. In 1487 a fleet headed by Bartholomeu Dias left Lisbon with orders to pass the farthest point reached by Cão and if possible sail round the tip of Africa. After he had cruised farther south than any captain before him, a providential gale blew Dias's ships in a wide sweep around the Cape of Good Hope and to a landfall on the coast of East Africa. He had solved the problem of a sea road to the Indies and returned to Lisbon to report his success to King John.

The route to the East lay open. But domestic and foreign problems distracted John's attention from the Indian enterprise. He died in 1495 without having sent the expedition for which he had made elaborate preparations. His successor, Manuel I, known as the Fortunate, carried out

56 John's plan. In 1497 a fleet of four ships, commanded by the tough, surly nobleman Vasco da Gama, sailed from Lisbon on a voyage that inaugurated the age of European imperialism in Asia. After rounding the Cape, da Gama sailed into the Indian Ocean and up the coast of East Africa. At Malinda, in modern Kenya, he took on an Arab pilot who guided the fleet to Calicut, the great spice trade center on the west coast of India. Received with hostility by the dominant Arab traders and with indifference by the local Indian potentate, who scorned his petty gifts, the persistent da Gama managed to load his holds with a cargo of pepper and cinnamon and returned to Lisbon in 1499 with two of the four ships with which he had begun his voyage. A new fleet, commanded by Pedro Álvares Cabral, was quickly outfitted and sent to India. Swinging far west in the south Atlantic, Cabral made a landfall on the coast of Brazil in early 1500 and sent one ship back to Lisbon to report his discovery before continuing to India. He returned to Portugal with a cargo of spices and a story of severe fighting with Arab merchants determined to resist the Portuguese intruders.

The great soldier and administrator Afonso de Albuquerque, who set out in 1509, completed the work begun by da Gama. He understood that in order to squeeze out the Egyptian and Venetian competition and gain a total monopoly of the spice trade he must conquer key points on the trade routes of the Indian Ocean. Capture of Malacca on the Malay Peninsula gave the Portuguese control of the strait through which East Indian spices entered the Indian Ocean. Capture of Muscat and Ormuz barred entrance to the Persian Gulf and closed that route to Europe to other nations' ships. The Portuguese strategy was not completely successful, but it diverted to Lisbon the greater part of the spice supply.

For a time, Portugal basked in the sun of an unprecedented prosperity. But the strain of maintaining its vast Eastern defense establishment was too great for Portugal's limited manpower and financial resources, and expenses began to outrun revenues. To make matters worse, under Spanish pressure King Manuel decreed the expulsion of all unbaptized Jews in 1496. As a result, Portugal lost the only native group financially capable of exploiting the investment opportunities offered by the Portuguese triumph in the East. Florentine and German bankers quickly moved in and diverted most of the profits of the Eastern spice trade abroad. Lisbon soon became a mere depot. Cargoes arriving there from the East were shipped almost at once to Antwerp or Amsterdam, better situated as centers of distribution to European customers. In time, Dutch and English rivals snatched most of the Asiatic colonies from Portugal's failing hands.

Advance into the Atlantic

Certain groups of islands lying in the eastern Atlantic—the Canaries, Madeiras, Azores, and Cape Verdes—early attracted the attention of Portugal and Spain. These islands played a strategic role in the discovery and colonization of America, providing steppingstones and staging areas for the crossing to America, and their conquest, colonization, and economic organization set the pattern for Iberian colonial policies in the New World. Italian (especially Genoese) merchants and bankers contributed much of the capital and technical skills needed for the economic organization of these islands.

The Madeira island group, colonized in 1425, became the most important Portuguese colony in the eastern Atlantic. Madeira's soil and climate were suitable for growing sugar, the most lucrative cash crop of the time, and with Genoese financial and technical aid sugar production was established in Madeira, using first slaves from the Canary Islands and later African slaves. By 1460 Madeira had its first sugar mill; by 1478 it was the largest sugar producer in the Western world. The Portuguese were to apply the same successful formula—the combination of sugar and African slave labor—in their colonization of Brazil.

The Canaries had been known to Europeans since the early fourteenth century, but their definitive conquest by Castile began in 1402. The islanders (Guanches), a herding and farming people organized in mutually hostile tribes, resisted fiercely, and the conquest was not complete until about 1497. Less than two centuries after the conquest of the Canaries began, the Guanches, who once may have numbered between 50,000 and 100,000, were extinct, chiefly as a result of mistreatment and disease. The conquest of the Canaries foretold similar developments in the Caribbean.

Like the Madeiras, the Canaries became a laboratory for testing political and economic institutions later transferred to the Indies. Although the lordship of the islands was vested in the crown, the monarchs made agreements (*capitulaciones*) with individual captains (*adelantados*) who were authorized to conquer specific regions and granted large governing powers and other privileges. These agreements resembled the contracts made with military leaders during the Reconquista and with Columbus, Francisco Pizzaro, and other great captains during the conquest of America.

Like the Madeiras, too, the Canaries became a testing ground for a plantation system based on sugar and slave labor. By the early sixteenth century, there were twenty-nine sugar mills in operation. The character of the Canaries as a way station between Europe and America for sugar production is indicated by the fact that cuttings for the planting of sugar cane and sugar-processing techniques were transferred from the Canaries to the Caribbean soon after its discovery and conquest.

The Voyages of Columbus

The search for a sea road to the Indies inspired more than one solution. If some believed that the route around Africa offered the answer to the Eastern riddle, others favored sailing due west across the Atlantic. This view had the support of an eminent authority, the Florentine scientist Paolo Toscanelli, who in 1474 advised the Portuguese to try the western route as "shorter than the one which you are pursuing by way of Guinea." His letter came to the attention of an obscure Italian seafarer, Christopher Columbus, who had been reflecting on the problem, and

helped confirm his belief that such a passage from Europe to Cipangu (Japan) and Cathay (China) would be easy. This conception rested on a gross underestimate of the earth's circumference and an equal overestimate of the size and eastward extension of Asia. Since all educated Europeans believed the world was round, that question never entered into the dispute between Columbus and his opponents. The main issue was the extent of the ocean between Europe and Asia, and on this point the opposition was right.

For Columbus the idea of reaching the East by sailing west acquired all the force of an obsession. A figure of transition from the dying Middle Ages to the world of capitalism and science, a curious combination of mystic and practical man, Columbus became convinced that God himself had revealed to him "that it was feasible to sail from here to the Indies, and placed in me a burning desire to carry out this plan."

About 1484, Columbus, who then resided in Lisbon, offered to make a western voyage of discovery for John II, but a committee of experts who listened to his proposal advised the king to turn it down. Undismayed by his rebuff, Columbus next turned to Castile. After eight years of discouraging delays and negotiation, Isabella—in a last-minute change of mind—agreed to support the "Enterprise of the Indies." The capitulación (contract) made by the queen with Columbus named him admiral, viceroy, and governor of the lands he should discover and promised him a generous share in the profits of the venture.

On August 3, 1492, Columbus sailed from Palos with three small ships, the *Pinta,* the *Santa María,* and the *Niña,* manned not by the jailbirds of legend but by experienced crews under competent officers. The voyage was remarkably prosperous, with fair winds the whole way out. But the great distance beyond sight of land began to worry some of the men, and by the end of September there was grumbling aboard the *Santa María,* Columbus's flagship. According to Columbus's son Ferdinand, some sailors proposed to heave the admiral overboard and return to Spain with the report that he had fallen in while watching the stars. Columbus managed to calm his men, and soon floating gulfweed and bosun birds gave signs of land. On October 12, they made landfall at an island in the Bahamas that Columbus named San Salvador.

Cruising southward through the Bahamas, Columbus came to the northeast coast of Cuba, which he took for part of Cathay. An embassy sent to find the Great Khan failed in its mission but returned with reports of a hospitable reception by natives who introduced the Spaniards to the use of "certain herbs the smoke of which they inhale," an early reference to tobacco. Next Columbus sailed eastward to explore the northern coast of an island (present-day Dominican Republic and Haiti) he named Española (Hispaniola). Here the Spaniards were cheered by the discovery of some alluvial gold and gold ornaments, which the natives bartered for Spanish trinkets.

From Hispaniola, on whose coast Columbus lost his flagship, he returned to Spain to report his supposed discovery of the Indies. The Sovereigns received him with signal honors and ordered him to prepare immediately a second expedition to follow up his discovery. In response to Portuguese charges of encroachment on an area in the Atlantic reserved to Portugal by a previous treaty with Castile, Ferdinand and Isabella appealed for help to Pope Alexander VI, himself a Spaniard. The pontiff complied by issuing a series of bulls in 1493 that assigned to Castile all lands discovered or to be discovered by Columbus and drew a line from north to south a hundred leagues west of the Azores and Cape Verdes; west of this line was to be a Spanish sphere of exploration. To John II this demarcation line seemed to threaten Portuguese interests in the south Atlantic and the promising route around Africa to the East. Yielding to Portuguese pressure, Ferdinand and Isabella signed in 1494 the Treaty of Tordesillas, which established a boundary 270 leagues farther west. Portugal obtained exclusive rights of discovery and conquest east of this line; Castile gained the same rights to the west.

Columbus returned to Hispaniola at the end of 1493 with a fleet of seventeen ships carrying twelve hundred people, most of them artisans

and peasants, with a sprinkling of "caballeros, hidalgos, and other men of worth, drawn by the fame of gold and the other wonders of that land." The settlers soon gave themselves up to gold hunting and preying on the Indians. A foreigner of obscure origins, Columbus lacked the powers and personal qualities needed to control this turbulent mass of fortune hunters.

After founding the town of Isabella on the north coast of Hispaniola, Columbus sailed again in quest of Cathay. He coasted down the southern shore of Cuba almost to its western end. The great length of the island convinced him that he had reached the Asiatic mainland. To extinguish all doubts he made his officers and crews take solemn oath, "on pain of a hundred lashes and having the tongue slit if they ever gainsaid the same," that Cuba was the mainland of Asia. In 1496 he returned to Spain to report his discoveries and answer charges sent by disgruntled settlers to the court. He left behind his brother Bartholomew, who removed the settlement from Isabella to a healthier site on the south shore, naming the new town Santo Domingo.

The first two voyages had not paid their way, but the sovereigns still had faith in Columbus and outfitted a third fleet in 1498. On this voyage he discovered Trinidad and the mouths of the Orinoco. The mighty current of sweet water discharged by the great river made Columbus conclude that he was on the shores of a continent, but his crotchety mysticism also suggested that the Orinoco was one of the four rivers of Paradise and had its source in the Garden of Eden.

Columbus arrived in Hispaniola to find chaos. The intolerable demands of the greedy Castilian adventurers had provoked the peaceable Taino Indians to the point of war. The Spaniards, disappointed in their hopes of quick wealth, blamed the Columbus brothers for their misfortunes and rose in revolt under a leader named Roldán. To appease the rebels Columbus had to issue pardons and grant land and Indian slaves. Meanwhile, acting on a stream of complaints against Columbus, the sovereigns had sent out an agent, Francisco de Bobadilla, to supersede Columbus and investigate the charges against the discoverer. Arriving at the island, the irascible Bobadilla seized Columbus and his brother and sent them to Spain in chains. Although Isabella immediately disavowed Bobadilla's arbitrary actions, Columbus never again exercised the functions of viceroy and governor in the New World.

Still gripped by his great illusion, Columbus continued to dream of finding a western way to the land of spices. He was allowed to make one more voyage, the most difficult and disastrous of all. He was now convinced that between the mainland he had recently discovered and the Malay Peninsula shown on ancient maps there must be a strait that would lead into the Indian Ocean. In 1502 he sailed in search of this strait and a route to southern Asia. From Hispaniola, where he was not permitted to land, he crossed the Caribbean to the coast of Central America and followed it south to the Isthmus of Panama. Here he believed he was ten days' journey from the Ganges River. In Panama he found some gold, but the hoped-for strait continued to elude him. He finally departed for Hispaniola with his two remaining ships but was forced to beach the worm-riddled craft on Jamaica, where he and his men were marooned for a year awaiting the arrival of a relief ship. In November 1504 Columbus returned to Europe. Broken in health, convinced of the ingratitude of princes, he died in 1506 a rich but embittered man.

The Discovery of America in Historical Perspective

The approach of the five hundredth anniversary of the discovery of America in 1992 produced an outpouring of writings seeking to throw new light on that momentous event. There has long been agreement that the Discovery had prodigious consequences, but also dispute as to whether they should cause jubilation or regret. The Spanish chronicler Francisco López de Gómara, filled with imperialist pride, had no doubts on that score. "The greatest event since the creation of the world (excluding the incarnation of Him who created it)," he wrote in 1552, "is the discovery of the Indies." But the radical Italian philosopher Giordano Bruno, who was burned for heresy in 1600, strongly dissented, assailing Columbus as

one of those "audacious navigators" who only "disturbed the peace of others . . . increased the vices of nations, spread fresh follies by violence, and . . . taught men a new art and means of tyranny and assassination among themselves."

Until recently, however, few Europeans and Americans questioned the splendor and value of Columbus's achievement. In the nineteenth century the Discovery came to be viewed as a harbinger and cause of the great movement of Western economic expansion and domination of the globe that was then under way. Celebrations of the Discovery were especially exuberant in the United States, where a mystic link was seen between that event and the spectacular rise of the great republic of the West. In this period Columbus was transformed into an almost mythic hero, a larger-than-life figure who overcame all the obstacles placed in his path by prejudiced and ignorant adversaries in order to complete his providential task.

Until well into the twentieth century this view of the Discovery as an event that should inspire unalloyed pride and satisfaction was rarely challenged. Only the immense political and economic changes caused by World War II and the anticolonial revolutions unleashed by the conflict led to a new way of looking at the Discovery and its repercussions. That new frame of reference is commonly known as "the Vision of the Vanquished" because it takes as its point of departure the impact of the Discovery not on Europe but on the peoples and cultures of the Americas. Awareness of the ethnocentric, Eurocentric connotations of the term "discovery" has even led many scholars to replace it with the more neutral term "encounter" (*encuentro* in Spanish). America, after all, was not an empty continent when the first Europeans arrived; its true "discoverers" were the people who had crossed over from Asia by way of the Bering Strait many thousands of years before. But the word "encounter," with its suggestion of a peaceful meeting of peoples and cultures, hardly fits the grim reality of the European invasion of Indian America, so we shall continue to use "discovery" for lack of a better word.

"The Vision of the Vanquished" initiated a more balanced assessment of the discovery of

60   America and its consequences. Such an assessment begins by noting that, for the native peoples of America, the Discovery and its sequel of the Conquest were an unmitigated disaster. The combination of new diseases to which the Indians had no acquired immunity, their brutal exploitation, and the resulting social disorganization and loss of will to live led to perhaps the greatest demographic catastrophe in recorded history, with an estimated loss of between 90 and 95 percent of the native population between 1492 and 1575. The Discovery and the Conquest also cut short the independent development of brilliant civilizations like the Aztec and Inca empires, which, many scholars believe, had not exhausted their possibilities for further cultural advance and flowering. Finally, the Discovery initiated a process of ecological devastation in the New World through the introduction of European animals, plants, and agricultural practices that transformed long-stable ecosystems. Columbus began the process on Hispaniola by introducing the extensive Spanish system of farming with plows and cattle ranching, producing rapid soil erosion and deforestation. The process begun by Columbus continues to this day, as evidenced by the rapid destruction of Latin America's rain forests. This too is part of the "Columbian legacy."

The impact of the Discovery on Europe and its long-term development was much more positive. That impact, as noted long ago by Adam Smith and Karl Marx, is clearest in the realm of economics. Historians may debate the impact of American precious metals on Europe's sixteenth-century "price revolution" or the contribution of the slave trade to the "primitive accumulation" of capital in Europe. It is beyond dispute, however, that the combination of these and other events flowing from the discovery of America gave an immense stimulus to Europe's economic modernization and the rise of capitalism, which in turn hastened and facilitated its domination of the rest of the globe.

The intellectual impact of the Discovery on Europe is more difficult to measure, but it seems indisputable that the expansion of geographical horizons produced by the discovery of America was accompanied by an expansion of mental horizons and the rise of new ways of viewing the world that significantly contributed to intellectual progress. One of the first casualties of the great geographic discoveries was the authority of the ancients and even of the church fathers. Thus the Spanish friar Bartolomé de Las Casas (1484–1566), writing on the traditional belief in uninhabitable zones, in one paragraph managed to demolish the authority of Saint Augustine and the ancients, who, "after all, did not know very much." In the writings of Las Casas and other chroniclers who had actually traveled in America, such phrases as "I can testify from personal experience" or "This I saw with my own eyes" replace the medieval citing of authority as decisive proofs of truthful reporting of the facts.

The discovery of America and its peoples also produced disputes about the origins and nature of the Indians that led to the founding of anthropology. The desire to prove the essential humanity and equality of the Indians inspired some sixteenth-century Spanish missionaries to make profound investigations of Indian culture. One of the greatest of these friar-anthropologists was, again, Bartolomé de Las Casas, one of whose works is an immense accumulation of ethnographic data used to demonstrate that the Indians fully met the requirements laid down by Aristotle for the good life. Las Casas, resting his case above all on experience and observation, offered an environmentalist explanation of cultural differences and regarded with scientific detachment such deviations from European standards as Indian human sacrifices and ritual cannibalism.

Reflection on the apparent novelty and strangeness of some Indian ways, and the effort of pro-Indian friar-anthropologists to understand and explain those ways, also led to the development of a cultural relativism that, like the rejection of authority, represented a sharp break with the past. Las Casas, for example, subjected the term "barbarian" to a careful semantic analysis that robbed it, as applied to advanced Indian cultures like the Aztec or the Inca, of most of its sting. Michel de Montaigne, who avidly read accounts of Indian customs, observed in his famous essay on the Brazilian Indians, "Of Cannibals": "I think there is nothing barbarous and savage in this nation, from what I have been told, except that each man calls barbarian whatever is not his own practice."

The discovery of America and its peoples also inspired some Europeans, troubled by the follies and social injustices of Renaissance Europe, to propose radical new schemes of political and economic organization. In 1516, for example, Thomas More published *Utopia,* portraying a pagan, socialist society whose institutions were governed by justice and reason, so unlike the states of contemporary Europe, which More described as a "conspiracy of the rich" against the poor. More's narrator, who tells about the Utopians and their institutions, claims to be a sailor who made three voyages with Amerigo Vespucci. The principal source of More's ideas about the evils of private property and the benefits of popular government appears to be a key passage about Indian customs and beliefs in Vespucci's *Second Letter*:

Having no laws and no religious doctrine, they live according to nature. They understand nothing of the immortality of the soul. There is no possession of private property among them, for everything is in common. They have no king, nor do they obey anyone. Each is his own master. There is no administration of justice, which is unnecessary to them. . . .

But if the Discovery had a beneficial impact on European intellectual life, reflected in the new rejection of authority, the growth of cultural relativism, and the impulse it gave to unorthodox social and political thought, it also reinforced the negative European attitudes of racism and ethnocentrism. The great Flemish map maker Abraham Ortelius gave clear expression to these attitudes in his 1579 world atlas. To the map of Europe Ortelius attached a note proclaiming Europe's historic mission of world conquest, in process of fulfillment by Spain and Portugal, "who between them dominate the four parts of the globe." Ortelius declared that Europeans had always surpassed all other peoples in intelligence

and physical dexterity, thus qualifying them to govern the other parts of the globe.

The broad vision of Las Casas, who proclaimed that "all mankind is one," and of Montaigne, who furiously denounced European wars and atrocities against the Indians and proposed a "brotherly fellowship and understanding" as the proper relationship between Europeans and the peoples of the New World, was not typical of contemporary thinking on the subject. Colonial rivals might condemn Spanish behavior toward the Indians, but they usually agreed in regarding them as tainted with vices, and as "poor barbarians."

The perspective of "The Vision of the Vanquished" and new approaches in historical research combine to give us a better understanding of the man Columbus and his dealings with the people he wrongly called "Indians." A curious blend of medieval mystic and modern entrepreneur, Columbus revealed the contradictions in his thought by his comment on gold: "O, most excellent gold! Who has gold has a treasure with which he gets what he wants, imposes his will on the world, and even helps souls to paradise." In *Conquest of America,* Tźvetan Todorov subjects the ideology of Columbus (which represented the ideology of the European invaders) to a careful and subtle dissection that reveals other contradictions. Sometimes Columbus views the Indians as "noble savages"; sometimes, according to the occasion, he sees them as "filthy dogs." Todorov explains that both myths rest on a common base: scorn for the Indians and refusal to admit them as human beings with the same rights as himself. In the last analysis, Columbus regards the Indians not as human beings but as objects. This is well illustrated by a letter he wrote to the Spanish monarchs in September 1498:

We can send from here in the name of the Holy Trinity, all the slaves and brazilwood that can be sold. If my information is correct, one could sell 4000 slaves that would bring at least twenty millions. . . . And I believe that my information is correct, for in Castile and Aragon and Italy and Sicily and the islands of Portugal and Aragon and the Canary Islands they use up many slaves, and the number of slaves coming from Guinea is diminishing. . . . And although the Indian slaves tend to die off now, this will not always be the case, for the same thing used to happen with the slaves from Africa and the Canary Islands.

In fact, Columbus early on conceived the idea of supplementing the search for a western route to the Indies and for gold with the enslavement of Indians and their sale in Castile. To make the idea more palatable to the Spanish monarchs, he proposed to limit the slave hunting to a supposed "cannibal" people, the Caribs. When the Indians of Hispaniola rose in revolt against their intolerable treatment, it provided another legal justification for their enslavement. Between 1494 and 1500 Columbus sent some 2,000 Indians to the slave markets of Castile. Contrary to legend, Queen Isabella approved of the majority of these shipments.

Columbus, of course, viewed Indian slavery from the background of a merchant adventurer who was very familiar with the conduct of Portugal's African slave trade, in which other Genoese merchants were deeply involved. He lived at a time when slavery, under certain conditions, was almost universally regarded as licit and proper. His callous lack of concern for the life and death of the Indians he enslaved does not make him a monster. If he ardently desired gold, it was not from vulgar greed alone. To be sure, as the Spanish scholar Juan Gil observes, he was "fascinated by the tinkle of maravedis."[1] He bargained hard with the Spanish monarchs for the highest possible share of profits from his discoveries, and despite his lamentation in his last years about his poverty and even the lack of a roof over his head, he died a millionaire. But there was another side to Columbus. He viewed gold as a means of promoting the universal triumph of Christianity, urged his royal masters to use the revenues from the Indies for a crusade to wrest the Holy Land from Muslim hands, and offered himself to head the crusader host. There was a constant tension in Columbus between the medieval mystic who believed the world would end in 155 years and the Renaissance man filled

[1] A Spanish coin.

with a drive to achieve power, titles, wealth, and fame.

To assess the significance of Columbus's achievement properly, it must be understood that he was the instrument of historical forces of which he was unaware, forces of transition from the dying Middle Ages to the rising world of capitalism, whose success required the conquest of the world and the creation of a world market. That process in turn required an ideological justification, a proud conviction of the superiority of white Europeans over all other peoples and races. Columbus's work in the Caribbean represents the first tragic application of that ideology in the New World. If not the father of imperialism, he was at least one of its fathers, and bears part of the responsibility for the devastating effects of that system of domination.

Balboa and Magellan

Other explorers followed in the wake of Columbus's ships and gradually made known the immense extent of the mainland coast of South America. In 1499 Alonso de Ojeda, accompanied by the pilot Juan de la Cosa and the Florentine Amerigo Vespucci, sailed to the mouths of the Orinoco and explored the coast of Venezuela. Vespucci took part in another voyage in 1501–1502 under the flag of Portugal. This expedition, sent to follow up the discovery of Brazil by Pedro Álvares Cabral in 1500, explored the Brazilian coast from Salvador da Bahia to Rio de Janeiro before turning back. Vespucci's letters to his patrons, Giovanni and Lorenzo de' Medici, reveal an urbane, cultivated Renaissance figure with a flair for lively and realistic description of the fauna, flora, and inhabitants of the New World. His letters were published and circulated widely in the early 1500s. One (whose authenticity is disputed) told of a nonexistent voyage in 1497 and gave him the fame of being the first European to set foot on the South American continent. A German geographer, Martin Waldseemuller, decided to honor Vespucci by assigning the name America to the area of Brazil in a map of the newly discovered lands. The name caught on and presently was applied to the whole of the New World.

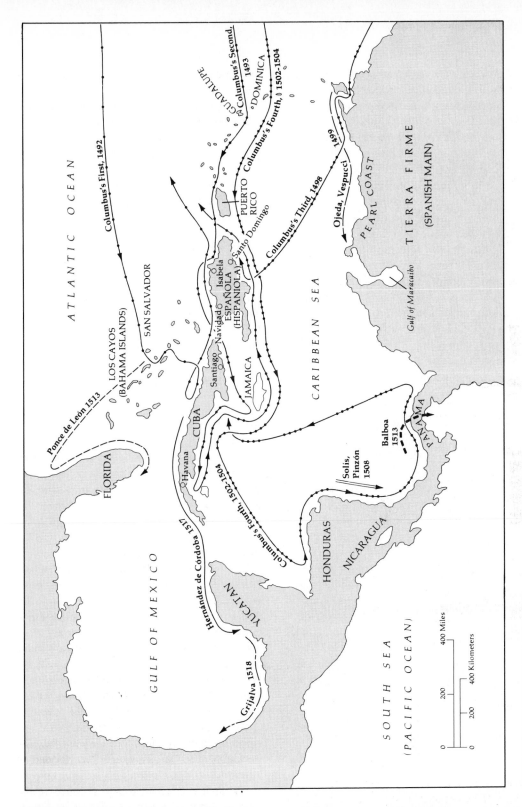

EARLY SPANISH VOYAGES IN THE CARIBBEAN

63

A growing shortage of Indian labor and the general lack of economic opportunities for new settlers on Hispaniola incited Spanish slave hunters and adventurers to explore and conquer the remaining Greater Antilles. Puerto Rico, Jamaica, and Cuba were occupied between 1509 and 1511. In the same period, efforts to found colonies on the coast of northern Colombia and Panama failed disastrously, and the remnants of two expeditions were united under the energetic leadership of the conquistador Vasco Núñez de Balboa to form the new settlement of Darien on the Isthmus of Panama. Moved by Indian tales of a great sea, south of which lay a land overflowing with gold, Balboa led an expedition across the forests and mountains of Panama to the shores of the Pacific. He might have gone on to discover the Inca Empire of Peru if he had not aroused the jealousy of his terrible father-in-law, the "two-legged tiger," Pedrarias Dávila, sent out by Charles V in 1514 as governor of the isthmus. Charged with treason and desertion, the discoverer of the Pacific was tried, condemned, and beheaded in 1519.

The discovery of the "South Sea" confirmed Columbus's reports on his fourth voyage of a narrow isthmus beyond which lay a sea that led to India. Although further exploration was required to dispel the lingering belief that the whole American landmass was a peninsula projecting from southeast Asia, the work of discovery after 1513 centered on the search for a waterway to the East through or around the American continent. Ferdinand Magellan, a Portuguese who had fought in India and the East Indies, was convinced that a short passage to the East existed south of Brazil. Failing to interest the Portuguese king in his project, Magellan turned to Spain, with greater success. The resulting voyage of circumnavigation of the globe, 1519–1522, the first in history, represented an immense navigational feat and greatly increased Europe's stock of geographical knowledge. But, aside from the acquisition of the Philippines for Spain, Magellan's exploit had little practical value, for his new route to the East was too long to have commercial significance. The net result was to enhance the value of America in Spanish eyes. Disillusioned with the dream of easy access to the riches of the East, Spain turned with concentrated energy to the task of extending her American conquests and to the exploitation of the human and natural resources of the New World.

The Conquest of Mexico

Early Contact with Moctezuma

A disturbing report reached the Aztec capital of Tenochtitlán in 1518. Up from the coast of the Gulf of Mexico hurried the tribute collector Pinotl to inform King Moctezuma of the approach from the sea of winged towers bearing men with white faces and heavy beards. Pinotl had communicated with these men by signs and had exchanged gifts with their leader. Before departing, the mysterious visitors had promised (so Pinotl interpreted their gestures) to return soon and visit Moctezuma in his city in the mountains.

Indian accounts agree that the news filled Moctezuma with dismay. Could the leader of these strangers be the redeemer-god Quetzalcóatl, returning to reclaim his lost kingdom? According to one Aztec source, Moctezuma exclaimed: "He has appeared! He has come back! He will come here, to the place of his throne and canopy, for that is what he promised when he departed!"

The "winged towers" were the ships of the Spanish captain Juan de Grijalva, sent by Governor Diego Velázquez of Cuba to explore the coasts whose existence the slave-hunting expedition of Francisco Hernández de Córdoba (1517) had already made known. Córdoba had discovered the peninsula of Yucatán, inhabited by Maya Indians whose cotton cloaks and brilliant plumes, stone pyramids, temples, and gold ornaments revealed a native culture far more advanced than any the Spaniards had hitherto encountered. Córdoba met with disastrous defeat at the hands of the Maya and returned to Cuba to die of his wounds. He brought back enough gold and other signs of Indian wealth, however, to encourage Velázquez to outfit a new venture, which he entrusted to his kinsman Juan de Grijalva.

Grijalva sailed from Santiago in April 1518, touched at the island of Cozumel on the northeastern corner of Yucatán, then coasted down the peninsula, following Córdoba's route. In June they reached the limits of Moctezuma's empire. At a river that Grijalva named Banderas they were greeted by natives waving white flags and inviting them by signs to draw near. Here Grijalva's flagship was boarded by the Aztec official Pinotl, whose report was to cause so much consternation in Tenochtitlán. A lively trade developed, with Indians bartering gold for Spanish green beads. Grijalva was now convinced that he had come to a wealthy kingdom filled with many large towns. Near the present port of Veracruz, Grijalva sent Pedro de Alvarado back to Cuba with the gold that had been gained by barter. Alvarado was to report to Velázquez what had been accomplished, request authority to found a colony, and seek reinforcements. Grijalva himself sailed on with three other ships, perhaps as far as the river Pánuco, which marked the northern limits of the Aztec Empire. Then he turned back and retraced his course, arriving in Cuba in November 1518.

Cortés-Quetzalcóatl[2]

Velázquez was already planning a third expedition to conquer the Mexican mainland. He passed

[2] In relating the conquest of Mexico, I have often given the Aztec version of events, with all its fantastic elements, as told in the *Florentine Codex,* compiled by the great missionary-scholar Bernardino de Sahagún, because it offers a remarkable insight into the Aztec mentality and reaction to the Conquest. In that version the legend that foretold the return of the god-king Quetzalcóatl plays a prominent role; initially, at least, the conquistador Cortés appears to have been identified with the god himself or with his emissary. Recently, however, some skeptical scholars have suggested that the legend is a post-Conquest native rationalization of the Aztec defeat or a combined Spanish-Indian creation, or even a pure invention of Cortés, who twice cites a version of the legend as told by Moctezuma. This skeptical point of view strikes me as ahistorical. History records numerous legends prophesying the return of redeemer-gods or kings. If medieval Germans could believe in the return of the emperor Frederick Barbarossa, if Renaissance Portuguese could believe in the return of King Sebastian, why could not the Aztecs believe in the return of the god-king Quetzalcóatl?

over Grijalva and chose as leader of the expedition the thirty-four-year-old Fernando Cortés, a native of Medellín in the Spanish province of Estremadura. Cortés was born in 1485 into an hidalgo family of modest means. At the age of fourteen he went to Salamanca, seat of a great Spanish university, to prepare for the study of law, but left some years later, determined on a military career. He had to choose between Italy, the great battlefield of Europe, where Spanish arms were winning fame under the great captain Gonzalo de Córdoba, and the Indies, land of gold, Amazons, and El Dorados. In 1504, aged nineteen, he embarked for Hispaniola.

Soon after arriving on the island he participated in his first military exploit, the suppression of a revolt of Indians made desperate by Spanish mistreatment. His reward was an *encomienda* (a grant of Indian tribute and labor). In 1511 he served under Velázquez in the easy conquest of Cuba. The following year he was appointed alcalde of the newly founded town of Santiago in Cuba. In 1518 he persuaded Velázquez to give him command of the new expedition to the Mexican mainland. At the last moment the distrustful governor decided to recall him, but Cortés simply disregarded Velázquez's messages. In February 1519, he sailed from Cuba with a force of some six hundred men. Because Velázquez had not completed negotiations with the emperor Charles for an agreement authorizing the conquest and settlement of the mainland, Cortés's instructions permitted him only to trade and explore.

Cortés's fleet first touched land at the island of Cozumel, where they rescued a Spanish castaway, Jerónimo de Aguilar, who had lived among the Maya for eight years. In March 1519 Cortés landed on the coast of Tabasco, defeated local Indians in a sharp skirmish, and secured from them along with pledges of friendship the Mexican girl Malinche, who was to serve him as interpreter, adviser, and mistress. In April he dropped anchor near the site of modern Veracruz. He had contrived a way to free himself from Velázquez's irksome authority. In apparent deference to the wishes of a majority of his followers, who claimed that conquest and settlement would

1. Spanish firearms and cannon, though primitive by modern standards, gave the invaders a decided superiority over Indians armed with bows and arrows, wooden lances and darts, slings, Inca war clubs with stone or bronze heads, and Aztec wooden swords tipped with obsidian points. Even more decisive for the Spanish was the horse, an animal unknown to the Indians, who at least initially regarded it with awe. The Spanish cavalryman, armed with lance and sword, clad in armor and chain mail, had a striking force comparable to that of the modern tank. Time and time again, a small Spanish squadron of cavalry routed a much larger number of Indian warriors.

2. Diseases, notably smallpox, unwittingly introduced by the invaders became effective Spanish allies. To give one instance, smallpox raged in Tenochtitlán during the Spanish siege of the city, killing King Cuitlahuac and many Aztec soldiers and civilians, and thereby contributed to its fall.

3. The Spaniards were Renaissance men with a basically secular outlook, while the Indians represented a much more archaic worldview in which ritual and magic played a large role. Certainly the conquistadors were in part inspired by religious zeal. For the Spanish, however, war was basically a science or art based on centuries of European study and practice of military strategy and tactics. For the Aztecs and the Incas, war had a large religious component. The Aztec method of waging war, for example, emphasized capturing Spaniards and dragging them off to be sacrificed to the Indian gods instead of killing them on the spot. Indian warfare also included elaborate ceremonies and conventions that required giving proper notice to a people targeted for attack. The Spaniards did not limit themselves with such conventions.[3]

4. Internal division was a major factor in the swift collapse of the Indian empires. Hatred of the Aztecs by tributary peoples or unvanquished peoples like the Tlaxcalans explains why Indian auxiliaries formed a majority of Cortés's forces during the last struggle for Tenochtitlán. In what is now Peru, the conflict between two claimants of the Inca throne and their followers played directly into Pizarro's hands. Also, the Inca Empire was a mosaic of states, some quite recently incorporated into the empire, and the former lords or curacas of these states, eager to regain their independence, rallied to the Spanish side. All too late, these Indians discovered that they had exchanged one oppressor for a worse one.

Thus, the sophisticated, highly organized Indian empires fell to the Spaniards because of their superior armament, the decimating diseases that they brought, the differing worldviews of the two peoples, and the internal divisions within the empires themselves.

The Quest for El Dorado

Exploration in North America

From its original base in the West Indies and from the two new centers of Mexico and Peru, the great movement of Spanish exploration radiated in all directions. While Spanish ships were launched on the waters of the Pacific to search for the Spice Islands, land expeditions roamed the interior of North and South America in quest of new golden kingdoms.

The North American mainland early attracted the attention of Spanish gold hunters and slave hunters based in the West Indies. In 1513 Ponce de León, governor of Puerto Rico, sailed west and discovered a subtropical land to which he gave the name La Florida. His subsequent efforts to colonize the region ended with his death at the hands of Indians. In the 1520s another expedition, ineptly led by Pánfilo de Narváez, met with disaster in the vast, indefinite expanse of La Florida. Only four survivors of the venture, among them its future chronicler, the honest and humane Alvar Núñez Cabeza de Vaca, reached Mexico safely after a great, circuitous trek over the

---

[3] One exception was the *Requerimiento,* or Requirement, a document designed to satisfy Spanish royal conscience. It contained Spanish demands that must be read to and rejected by Indians before making war on them. For the farcical use of this document, see Chapter 4.

plains of Texas. In the last stages of his journey, Núñez was followed by thousands of adoring Indians, "clouds of witnesses" to his reputation as a medicine man of great powers.

Núñez's tales of adventure, with their hints of populous cities just beyond the horizon, inspired the conquistador Hernando de Soto, a veteran of the conquest of Peru, to try his fortune in La Florida. In 1542, after three years of unprofitable wanderings and struggles with Indians in the great area between modern-day South Carolina and Arkansas, the discoverer of the Mississippi died in the wilderness of a fever.

The strange tales told by Núñez and his three companions on their arrival in Mexico in 1536, and the even stranger story told by a certain Fray Marcos, who claimed to have seen in the far north one of the Seven Cities of the mythical golden realm of Cibola (from a great distance, it was true), persuaded Viceroy Antonio de Mendoza in 1540 to send an expedition northward commanded by Francisco Vásquez de Coronado. For two years, Spanish knights in armor pursued the elusive realm of gold through the future states of Arizona, New Mexico, Colorado, Oklahoma, Kansas, and possibly Nebraska. Disillusioned by the humble reality of the Zuñi pueblos of Arizona, the apparent source of the Cibola myth, Coronado went on to discover the Grand Canyon of the Colorado and then pushed east in search of still another El Dorado, this time called Quivira. Intruders who left no trace of their passage, the Spaniards were repelled by the immensity of the great plains and returned home bitterly disappointed with their failure to find treasure.

Further Exploration in South America

The golden will-o'-the-wisp that lured Spanish knights into the deserts of the Southwest also beckoned to them from South America's jungles and mountains. From the town of Santa Marta, founded in 1525 on the coast of modern Colombia, an expedition led by Gonzalo Jiménez de Quesada set out in 1536 on a difficult journey up the Magdalena River in search of gold and a passage to the Pacific. They suffered incredible hard-

ships before they finally emerged onto the high plateau east of the Magdalena inhabited by the Chibcha. These Indians were primarily farmers, were skillful in casting gold and copper ornaments, lived in palisaded towns, and were ruled by a chieftain called the Zipa. After defeating them in battle, Jiménez de Quesada founded in 1538 the town of Santa Fé de Bogatá, future capital of the province of New Granada. The immense treasure in gold and emeralds looted from the Chibcha fired Spanish imaginations and inspired fantasies about yet other golden kingdoms. The most famous of these legends was that of El Dorado (the Golden Man).

The dream of spices also played its part in inspiring the saga of Spanish exploration and conquest. Attracted by accounts of an eastern land where cinnamon trees grew in profusion, Gonzalo Pizarro led an expedition in 1539 from Quito in modern Ecuador across the Andes and down the forested eastern slopes of the mountains. Cinnamon was found, but in disappointingly small quantities. Lured on by the customary Indian tall tales of rich kingdoms somewhere beyond the horizon, designed to trick the intruders into moving on, the treasure hunters plunged deep into the wilderness. Gonzalo's lieutenant, Francisco de Orellana, sent with a party down a certain stream in search of food, found the current too strong to return and went on to enter a great river whose course he followed in two makeshift boats for a distance of eighteen hundred leagues, eventually emerging from its mouth to reach Spanish settlements in Venezuela. Meanwhile, the disgruntled Pizarro and his men made their way back home as best they could. On the banks of the great river, Orellana fought Indians whose women joined the battle. For this reason, he gave the river its Spanish name of Amazonas, an illustration of the myth-making process among the Spaniards of the Conquest.

Among others who pursued phantom kingdoms in the wilderness of the Amazon and Orinoco river systems was Sir Walter Raleigh, wise in other things but naive and credulous about El Dorado. Raleigh staked and lost his head on his promise to find a gold mine for King James of

74

Colorado R.

Mississippi R.

**De Soto
1539-1542**

ATLANTIC OCEAN

Rio Grande

Coronado 1540-1542

**Cabeza de Vaca
1528-1536**

MEXICO

**Cortés
1519**

Mexico City

**Alvarado and others
1522-1528**

**Jiménez de Quesada
1536-1538**

○ Bogotá

**Belalcazar
1533-1538**

Quito ○

Orellana 1541-42

Amazon R.

Pizarro 1531-1533

PERU   Cuzco ○

Cabeza de Vaca 1540

**Almagro
1535-1537**

PACIFIC OCEAN

TORDESILLAS LINE 1494

**Cabot
1525**

**Valdivia
1540-1553**

0   500   1000 Miles

0   500   1000 Kilometers

EARLY SPANISH OVERLAND EXPEDITIONS

England. His description of the "Rich and Beautiful Empire of Guiana" incorporated just about all the elements of the legend of El Dorado, including the themes of lost Inca treasure, the Golden Man who was anointed with gold dust, which he washed off in a sacred lake, and a warlike tribe of women.

In the southern reaches of the continent, which possessed little gold or silver, new agricultural and pastoral settlements arose. In 1537 Pizarro's comrade and rival, Diego de Almagro, made a fruitless march across the rugged Andean altiplano and the sun-baked Chilean desert in search of gold. He returned, bitterly disappointed, to a final confrontation with Pizarro. Two years later, Pizarro authorized Pedro de Valdivia to undertake the conquest of the lands to the south of Peru. After crossing the desert of northern Chile, Valdivia reached the fertile Central Valley and founded there the town of Santiago. In constant struggle with the Araucanian Indians, Valdivia laid the foundations of an agricultural colony based on the servile labor of other, more pacific Indians. He was captured and killed by the Araucanians during an expedition southward in 1553.

In the same period (1536), the town of Buenos Aires was founded on the estuary of the Rio de la Plata by the adelantado Pedro de Mendoza, who brought twenty-five hundred colonists in fourteen ships. But Buenos Aires was soon abandoned by its famished inhabitants, who moved almost a thousand miles upstream to the newly founded town of Asunción in Paraguay, where a genial climate, an abundance of food, and a multitude of docile Guarani Indians created more favorable conditions for Spanish settlement. Asunción became the capital of Paraguay and all the Spanish territory in southeastern South America. Not until 1580 was Buenos Aires permanently resettled by colonists coming from Asunción.

The Conquistadors

What sort of men were the conquistadors? The conquest of America attracted a wide variety of types. There was a sprinkling of professional soldiers, some with backgrounds of service in the Italian wars and some with pasts that they preferred to forget. The old conquistador Gonzalo Fernández de Oviedo had such men in mind when he warned the organizers of expeditions against "fine-feathered birds and great talkers" who "will either slay you or sell you or forsake you when they find that you promised them more in Spain than you can produce." In one of his *Exemplary Tales,* Cervantes describes the Indies as "the refuge and shelter of the desperate men of Spain, sanctuary of rebels, safe-conduct of homicides." No doubt men of this type contributed more than their share of the atrocities that stained the Spanish Conquest. But the background of the conquistadors was extremely varied, running the whole gamut of the Spanish social spectrum. The majority were commoners, but there were many marginal hidalgos, poor gentlemen who wished to improve their fortunes. Of the 168 men who captured Atahualpa at Cajamarca in 1532, 38 were hidalgos and 91 plebeians, with the background of the rest unknown or uncertain. According to James Lockhart, who has studied the men of Cajamarca, 51 members of the group were definitely literate and about 76 "almost certainly functioning literates." The group included 19 artisans, 12 notaries or clerks, and 13 "men of affairs."

Of the Spanish kingdoms, Castile provided the largest contingent, with natives of Andalusia predominating in the first, or Caribbean, phase of the Conquest; men from Estremadura, the poorest region of Spain, made up the largest single group in the second, or mainland, phase. Cortés, Pizarro, Almagro, Valdivia, Balboa, Orellana, and other famous conquistadors all came from Estremadura. Foreigners were not absent from the Conquest. Oviedo, in an attempt to clear Spaniards of sole responsibility for the crimes committed in the Indies, assures us that men had come there from every part of Christendom: there were Italians, Germans, Scots, Englishmen, Frenchmen, Hungarians, Poles, Greeks, Portuguese, and men "from all the other nations of Asia, Africa, and Europe."

By the 1520s an institution inherited from the Spanish *Reconquista,* the *compaña* (warrior band), whose members shared in the profits of conquest according to certain rules, had become the principal instrument of Spanish expansion in the New World. At its head stood a military leader who usually possessed a royal capitulación, which vested him with the title of adelantado and with the governorship of the territory to be conquered. Sometimes these men were wealthy in their own right and contributed large sums or incurred enormous debts to finance the expedition. Italian, German, and Spanish merchant capitalists and royal officials grown wealthy through the Indian slave trade or other means provided much of the capital needed to fit out ships, acquire horses and slaves, and supply arms and food.

The warrior band was in principle a military democracy, with the distribution of spoils carried out by a committee elected from among the entire company. After subtracting the quinto and the common debts, the remaining booty was divided into equal shares. In the distribution of Atahualpa's treasure, there were 217 such shares, each worth 5,345 gold pesos, a tidy sum for that time. Distribution was made in accordance with the individual's rank and contribution to the enterprise. The norm was one share for a *peón* or foot soldier, two for a *caballero* or horseman (one for the rider, another for the horse), and more for a captain.

Despite its democratic aspect, the captains, large investors, and royal officials dominated the enterprise of conquest and took the lion's share for themselves. Some of the men were servants or slaves of the captains and investors, and their shares went entirely or in part to their employers or masters; in other cases, conquistadors had borrowed or bought on credit to outfit themselves, and the greater part of their earnings went to their creditors. Contemporary accounts complain of the predatory ways of some captains, who sold supplies to their men in time of need at profiteering prices. At a later stage of each conquest came the distribution of encomiendas. Craftsmen and other plebeians received encomiendas after the conquest of Mexico and Peru; later, however, only the leaders and hidalgo members of expeditions were rewarded with such grants.

Bravery, tenacity, and an incredible capacity for enduring hardships were among the conspicuous virtues of the conquistador. The legendary Castilian austerity prepared the conquistador for the difficulties he encountered in the New World. The Spanish common soldier of the War of Granada ate only once a day, fortifying himself occasionally with swigs of the thin, sharply bitter wine he carried in a leather bottle. His single meal was a salad of onions, garlic, cucumbers, and peppers chopped very finely and mixed with bread crumbs, olive oil, vinegar, and water. Soldiers with such traditions were capable of marching a day's journey on a handful of toasted corn.

It would be folly to deny that many conquistadors were hard, ruthless men, hard in dealing with each other and harder still with the Indians. We do not have to rely on the testimony of defenders of the Indians like Bartolomé de Las Casas. The conquistador and chronicler Gonzalo Fernández de Oviedo, an ardent imperialist who shared the typical contempt of the colonists for the Indian, told horror stories resembling those of Las Casas and wrote that some conquistadors could more accurately be called "depopulators or destroyers of the new lands." The harshness of the conquistador reflected the conditions that formed his character: the climate of violence of Spain as it emerged from seven centuries of warfare against the Moor, the desperate struggle of most Spaniards to survive in a society divided by great inequalities of wealth, and the brutalizing effects of a colonial war.

It would be wrong, however, to conclude that all conquistadors fitted this negative pattern. Some were transformed by their experiences, were taught humility and respect for Indian values, or even came to concede the moral superiority of the Indian over the Spaniard. This was the lesson that Alvar Núñez Cabeza de Vaca learned in the course of his immense eight-year trek from the Gulf Coast of Texas to Mexico, which he survived thanks to the generosity of the Indians. In his account of his adventures the roles of the Indians and the Spaniards are reversed: the Spaniards are presented as savages and the Indians as humane and civilized. Another conquistador, Pedro Cieza de León, the "prince of chroniclers," had high praise for Inca civilization, criticized the cruelties of the Conquest, and clearly sympathized with the ideas of Las Casas. Yet another conquistador, Alonso de Ercilla, author of the finest Spanish epic poem of the sixteenth century, *La Araucana,* dealing with the struggle of the Araucanian Indians of Chile against the Spaniards, reverses the customary roles: he praises and even glorifies the Indians, who appear throughout the poem as a heroic people determined to be free, while the victorious Spaniards are portrayed as cowardly, greedy, and selfish.

A fierce nationalism and a religious fanaticism—more often manifested in a brutal contempt for the Indian than in a desire for his or her conversion—were essential elements in the psychological make-up of the conquistador. Add to these traits the quality of romanticism. The Reconquest, filled with a thousand combats, raids, and ambushes, had heated the Spanish imagination to an incandescent pitch. Spanish romanticism found expression in a rich literature of romances, popular ballads that celebrated the exploits of the frontier wars against the Moors and that were frequently on the lips of the conquistadors. The literate soldiers of the Conquest were also influenced by their reading of classic literature, especially of the romances of chivalry with their prodigious line of perfect knights and their mythical islands, Amazons, and giants, which the fantasy of the conquistadors placed in one or another part of the Indies. The conquistador was romantically conscious of his historical role. Some of Cortés's soldiers boasted to him that neither the Romans nor Alexander had ever performed deeds equal to theirs, to which Cortés replied that "far more will be said in future history books about our exploits than has ever been said about those of the past."

Of the trinity of motives (God, Gold, and Glory) commonly assigned to the Spanish conquistador, the second was certainly uppermost in the minds of most. "Do not say that you are going to the Indies to serve the king and to employ your time as a brave man and an hidalgo should," observed Oviedo in an open letter to would-be conquerors, "for you know the truth is just the opposite: you are going solely because you want to have a larger fortune than your father and your neighbors." Pizarro put it even more plainly in his reply to a priest who urged the need for spreading the Faith among the Indians. "I have not come for any such reasons. I have come to take away from them their gold." The conquistador and chronicler of the conquest of Mexico, Bernal Díaz del Castillo, ingenuously declared that the conquerors died "in the service of God and of His Majesty, and to give light to those who sat in darkness— and also to acquire that gold which most men covet." But the worthy Bernal wrote with the self-serving end of gaining additional rewards for his "great and notable service" to the king, and his book was meant for their grave worships, the members of the Royal Council of the Indies.

Most conquistadors dreamed of eventually returning to Spain with enough money to found a family and live in a style that would earn them the respect and admiration of their neighbors. Only a minority, chiefly large merchants and *encomenderos,* acquired the capital needed to fulfill this ambition, and not all of them returned to Spain. The majority, lacking encomiendas or other sources of wealth, remained and often formed ties of dependency with more powerful Spaniards, usually encomenderos whose service they entered as artisans, military retainers, or overseers of their encomiendas or other enterprises. After 1535, as more and more would-be conquistadors came to the Indies while the opportunities for joining profitable conquests diminished, the problem of a large number of unemployed and turbulent Spaniards, many of whom wandered about, robbing and abusing the Indians, caused serious concern to royal officials and to the crown itself.

Most conquistadors and other early Spanish settlers in the Indies were single young males, with a sprinkling of married men who had left their wives at home while they sought their fortunes. Aside from an occasional mistress or camp follower, few Spanish women accompanied the expeditions. Once the fighting had stopped, however, a small stream of Spanish women began to cross the Atlantic. Some were wives coming to rejoin their husbands (there were laws, generally unenforced, requiring that a married man must have his wife come to live with him or be deported to Spain); others were mothers, sisters, or nieces of the settlers. Marriages with Indian women were not uncommon; even hidalgos were happy at the opportunity to marry a wealthy Indian noblewoman like Moctezuma's daughter, Tecuixpo (Isabel Moctezuma), who was wed to three Spanish husbands in turn. After mid-century, however, most Spaniards of all social levels tended to marry Spanish women, either immigrants or those born in the Indies. By the last quarter of the century, the Spanish family and household, based on strong clan and regional loyalties, had been reconstituted in the Indies.

Of the thousands of bold captains and their followers who rode or marched under the banner of Castile to the conquest of America, few lived to enjoy in peace and prosperity the fruits of their valor, their sufferings, and their cruelties. "I do not like the title of adelantado," wrote Oviedo, "for actually that honor and title is an evil omen in the Indies, and many who bore it have come to an evil end." Of those who survived the battles and the marches, a few received the lion's share of spoils, land, and Indians; the majority remained in modest or worse circumstances, and frequently in debt. The conflict between the haves and the have-nots among the conquerors contributed significantly to the explosive, tension-ridden state of affairs in the Indies in the decades following the Conquest.

Lope de Aguirre: An Underdog of the Conquest

That conflict was a major ingredient in the devil's brew of passions that produced three decades of murderous civil wars and revolts among the Spaniards in Peru following the fall of the Inca empire. The defeat of the great revolt of Gonzalo Pizarro in 1548 brought no lasting peace to Peru, for it left seething with discontent the many adventurers who had flocked from all parts of the Indies to join the struggle against Pizarro. These men had hoped to be fittingly rewarded for their services to the crown. Instead Pizarro's wily conqueror, La Gasca, added to the encomiendas of the rich and powerful friends who had abandoned Pizarro and come over to the royal side. The sense of betrayal felt by many rank-and-file conquistadors was expressed by Pero López, who charged that La Gasca had left "all His Majesty's servants poor, while he let many of His Majesty's foes keep all they had and even gave them much more."

The Viceroy Cañete clearly defined the economic essence of the problem in a letter that he wrote to Emperor Charles V in 1551; he reported that there were only 480 encomiendas in Peru, whereas the number of Spaniards was 8,000. Including the jobs that the colonial administration could provide, only 1,000 Spaniards could "have food to eat." Cañete's only solution to rid Peru of the plague of unemployed conquistadors was to send them off on new conquests, "for it is well known that they will not work or dig or plow, and they say that they did not come to these parts to do such things." The emperor agreed; permission for new conquests, he wrote the viceroy in December 1555, would serve "to rid and cleanse the country of the idle and licentious men who are there at present and who would leave to engage in that business. . . ." Accordingly, Charles revoked a decree of 1549, issued at the urging of Las Casas, which prohibited new Indian conquests.

The career of the famous Lope de Aguirre, "the Wanderer," casts a vivid light on the psychology and mentality of the disinherited conquistador host. A veteran conquistador, Aguirre was fifty, lame in one leg as a result of wounds, and had spent a quarter-century in a fruitless search for fortune in the Indies when the rumor of a new El Dorado in the heart of the Amazon wilderness caused feverish excitement in Peru. Whether or not the legendary realm existed, it provided a convenient means of solving a potentially explosive social problem. In 1559 Viceroy Andrés Hurtado de Mendoza authorized Pedro de Ursúa to lead an expedition to search for the province of "Omagua and Dorado." Lope de Aguirre, accompanied by his young mestiza daughter, formed part of the expedition when it sailed down the Huallaga River, a tributary of the Amazon, in quest of the new golden realm. Ursúa proved to be a poor leader and unrest, aggravated by intolerable heat, disease, and lack of food, soon grew into a mutiny whose ringleader was Lope de Aguirre. Ursúa was murdered and, although the rebels raised a Spanish noble named Fernando de Guzmán to be their figurehead "prince," Aguirre soon became the expedition's undisputed leader.

He had devised an audacious new plan that had nothing to do with the quest for El Dorado. It called for the conquest of Peru, removal of its present rulers, and rewards for old conquistadors like himself

for the labors we have had in conquering and pacifying the native Indians of those kingdoms. For although we won those Indians with our persons and effort, spilling our blood, at our expense, we were not rewarded. . . . Instead the Viceroy exiled us with deception and falsehood, saying that we were coming to the best and most populous land in the world, when it is in fact bad and uninhabitable. . . .

Having constructed two large boats on the banks of the Amazon, the expedition sailed off down the great river, bound for the conquest of Peru. Aguirre's distrust of Guzmán soon led to the killing of the "lord and Prince of Peru," his mistress, and followers. By the time Aguirre and his men entered the Atlantic in July 1561 other killings had reduced the number of Spaniards from 370 to 230. Sailing past the shores of Guiana, they reached the island of Margarita off the Venezuelan coast on July 21. Having seized the island and killed its governor, Aguirre first planned to sail for Panama, capture Nombre de Dios (later Portobelo), and raise an army of discontented soldiers for an invasion of Peru. Finding this plan impracticable, he decided to sail to the mainland and advance over the northern Andes toward Peru. In September he landed on the coast of Venezuela, captured the town of Valencia, and proclaimed a "cruel war of fire and sword" against King Philip II of Spain. But by now the

alarm had gone out in all directions and overwhelming royal forces were moving against him. His small army, already much diminished by his summary executions of suspected traitors, began to melt away as a result of growing desertions. On October 27, 1561, after a number of his most trusted followers had fled to the royalist camp, Aguirre ran his sixteen-year-old daughter through with his sword to save her, he said, from going through life as the daughter of a rebel. Shortly after he was killed by arquebus shots fired by two of his former soldiers.

Some weeks before his death, Aguirre had written a remarkable letter to King Philip. Although it offers a conquistador's vision of the Conquest and the world it created, it is not the vision of the great captains in the heroic mold of Cortés. It is the vision of the underdogs of the Conquest, bitter over their betrayal by the great captains, the viceroys, cunning letrados (officials with legal training) or judges like La Gasca, and their king. Aguirre insists that he is of Old Christian descent and of noble blood, but admits that he was born of "middling parents," an admission that he was probably one of the many poor hidalgos who came to the Indies in search of fame and fortune.

Aguirre mingles an account of the services that he and his comrades had rendered to the crown in the Indies with fierce attacks on the king's ingratitude and the great injustices that they had suffered at the hands of his corrupt and greedy ministers:

Consider, King and Lord, that you cannot justly take any profits from this land, where you risked nothing, until you have properly rewarded those who labored and sweated there in your service. . . . Few kings go to hell, because there are so few of you, but if there were many none would go to heaven. I hold it for certain that even in hell you would be worse than Lucifer, for your whole ambition is to quench your insatiable thirst for human blood.

Despite this blasphemously revolutionary sentiment, Aguirre expressed the horror that he and his comrades felt for the Lutheran heresy and assured the king that, sinners though they were,

80

they accepted completely the teachings of the Holy Mother Church of Rome. But Aguirre denounced the scandalous dissolution and pride of the friars in the Indies. "Their whole way of life here is to acquire material goods and sell the sacraments of the church for a price. They are enemies of the poor—ambitious, gluttonous, and proud—so that even the meanest friar seeks to govern and rule these lands." Mockingly, Aguirre wrote that the life the friars led was very bitter and burdensome; by way of penance each had a dozen Indian girls working in his kitchen and as many boys employed in fishing, hunting partridges, and gathering fruit.

Aguirre was also harsh in his comments on the royal officials in Peru. He noted that each royal *oidor* (judge) received an annual salary of 4,000 pesos plus 8,000 pesos of expenses, yet at the end of three years of service each had saved 60,000 pesos and acquired estates and other possessions to boot. Moreover, they were so proud that "whenever we run into them they want us to

drop on our knees and worship them like Nebuchadnezzar." Aguirre advised the king not to entrust the discharge of his royal conscience to these judges, for they spent all their time planning marriages for their children, and their common refrain was, "To the left and to the right, I claim all in my sight."

Aguirre closed his revealing letter by wishing King Philip good fortune in his struggle against the Turks and the French and all others "who wish to make war on you in those parts. In these, God grant that we may obtain with our arms the reward rightfully due us, but which you have denied." He signed himself, "son of your loyal Basque vassals and rebel till death against you for your ingratitude, Lope de Aguirre, the Wanderer."[4]

[4] I am grateful to Professor Thomas Holloway of the History Department of Cornell University for calling my attention to the peculiar interest of the Aguirre episode and for allowing me to use his translation of Aguirre's letter to Philip II.

Chapter 4

The Economic Foundations of Colonial Life

From the first days of the Conquest, the Spanish government faced a problem of harmonizing the demand of the conquistadors for cheap Indian labor, which they frequently employed in a wasteful and destructive manner, with the crown's interest in the preservation of a large, tribute-paying Indian population. The first decades of colonial experience demonstrated that the Indians, left to the tender mercies of the colonists, might either become an extinct race, as actually happened on the once densely populated island of Hispaniola, or rise in revolts threatening the very existence of the Spanish Empire in America. The crown naturally regarded these alternatives with distaste.

The Indian question had other facets. There was a political issue, for excessive concentration of land and Indians in the hands of colonists might lead to the rise of a class of feudal lords independent of royal authority, a development the Spanish kings were determined to prevent. The church also had a major interest in the Indian problem. If the Indians died out as a result of Spanish mistreatment, the great task of saving pagan souls would remain incomplete and the good name of the church would suffer. Besides, who then would build churches and monasteries and support the servants of God in the Indies?

The dispute over Indian policy immediately assumed the dramatic outward form of a struggle of ideas. For reasons deeply rooted in Spain's medieval past, Spanish thought of the sixteenth century had a strongly legalistic and scholastic character. At a time when scholasticism[1] was dying in

---

[1] A system of theological and philosophical doctrine and inquiry that predominated in the Middle Ages. It was based chiefly on the authority of the church fathers and of Aristotle and his commentators.

other Western lands, it retained great vitality in Spain as a philosophic method and as an instrument for the solution of private and public problems. The need "to discharge the royal conscience," to make the royal actions conform to the natural and divine law, helps explain Spanish preoccupation with the doctrinal foundations of Indian policy. What was the nature of the Indians? What was their cultural level? Were they the slaves by nature described by Aristotle, a race of subhumans who might properly be conquered and made to serve the Spaniards? What rights and obligations did the papal donation of America to the Spanish monarchs confer on them? Summoned by the monarchs to answer these and similar questions, jurists and theologians waged a battle of books in which they bombarded each other with citations from Aristotle, the church fathers, and medieval philosophers. Less frequently, they supported their positions with materials based on direct observation or written accounts of Indian life.

Tribute and Labor in the Spanish Colonies

Behind the subtle disputations over Spain's obligations to the Indians, however, went on a complex struggle over the question of who should control Indian labor and tribute, the foundations of the Spanish Empire in America. The main parties to this struggle were the crown, the church, and the colonists.

The Encomienda and Slavery

Hispaniola was the first testing ground of Spain's Indian policy. The situation created on the island by the arrival of Columbus's second expedition has been aptly summed up by Samuel Eliot Morison in the phrase "Hell on Hispaniola." Eager to prove to the crown the value of his discoveries, Columbus compelled the natives to bring in a daily tribute of gold dust. When the hard-pressed Indians revolted, they were hunted down, and

hundreds were sent to Spain as slaves. Later, yielding to the demands of rebellious settlers, Columbus distributed the Indians among them, with the grantees enjoying the right to use the forced labor of the natives.

This temporary arrangement, formalized in the administration of Governor Nicolás de Ovando and sanctioned by the crown, became the encomienda. This system, which had its origin in the Spanish medieval practice of granting jurisdiction over lands and people captured from the Moors to leading warriors, consisted in the assignment to a colonist of a group of Indians who were to serve him with tribute and labor. He in turn assumed the obligation of protecting his Indians, paying for the support of a parish priest, and helping defend the colony. In practice, the encomienda in the West Indies proved a hideous slavery. Basically as a result of this mistreatment and the disorganization of Indian society, the Indian population of Hispaniola dwindled from several million to 29,000 within two decades. This decline was not the result of epidemic disease, for there is no record of any epidemic among the Indians of the Antilles before 1518.

The first voices raised against this state of affairs were those of a company of Dominican friars who arrived in Hispaniola in 1510. Their spokesman was Father Antón Montesino, who on Advent Sunday, 1511, ascended the church pulpit to threaten the Spaniards of the island with damnation for their offenses against the natives. The angry colonists and the Dominicans soon carried their dispute to the court. King Ferdinand responded by approving a code of Spanish-Indian relations, the Laws of Burgos (1512–1513), which did little more than sanction and regularize the existing situation.

The agitation the Dominicans began raised the larger question of the legality of Spain's claim to the Indies. To satisfy the royal conscience, a distinguished jurist, Dr. Juan López de Palacios Rubios, drew up a document, the *Requerimiento,* which the conquistadors were supposed to read to the Indians before making war on them. This curious manifesto called on the natives to acknowledge the supremacy of the church and the

A post-Conquest Indian codex presents a fanciful version of Spanish conquistadors attempting to wade ashore on the Mexican coast and battling Aztec warriors.

pope and the sovereignty of the Spanish monarchs over their lands by virtue of the papal donation of 1493, on pain of suffering war and enslavement. Not until they had rejected those demands, which were to be made known to them by interpreters, could war be legally waged against them. Some conquistadors took the Requirement lightly, mumbling it into their beards before an attack or reading it to captured Indians after a raid; the chronicler Oviedo relates that Palacios Rubios himself laughed heartily when told of the strange use these captains made of the document.

Bartolomé de Las Casas, the former encomendero who had repented of his ways and later turned friar, now joined the struggle against Indian slavery and the doctrines of Palacios Rubios. Of the Requirement, Las Casas said that on reading it he could not decide whether to laugh or weep. Las Casas argued that the papal grant of America to the crown of Castile had been made solely for the purpose of conversion; it gave the Spanish crown no temporal power or possession in the Indies. The Indians had rightful possession of their lands by natural law and the law of nations. All Spanish wars and conquests in the New World were illegal. Spain must bring Christianity to the Indians by the only method "that is proper and natural to men . . . namely, love and gentleness and kindness."

Las Casas hoped for a peaceful colonization of the New World by Spanish farmers who would live side by side with the Indians, teach them to farm and live in a civilized way, and gradually bring into being an ideal Christian community. A series of disillusioning experiences, including the destruction of an experiment along those lines on the coast of Venezuela (1521) by Indians who had suffered from the raids of Spanish slave hunters, turned Las Casas's mind toward more radical solutions. His final program called for the suppression of all encomiendas, liberation of the Indians from all forms of servitude except a small voluntary tribute to the crown in recompense for its gift of Christianity, and the restoration of the ancient Indian states and rulers, the rightful owners of those lands. Over these states the Spanish king would preside as "Emperor over many kings" in order to fulfill his sacred mission of bringing the Indians to the Catholic faith and the Christian way of life. The instruments of that mission should be friars, who would enjoy special jurisdiction over the Indians and protect them from the corrupting influence of lay Spaniards. Although Las Casas's proposals appeared radical, they in fact served the royal aim of curbing the power of the conquistadors and preventing the rise of a powerful colonial feudalism in the New World. Not humanitarianism but self-interest, above all, explains the partial official support that Las Casas's reform efforts received in the reign of Charles V (1516–1556).

The question of Indian policy became crucial with the discovery and conquest of the rich, populous empires of Mexico and Peru. The most elementary interests of the crown demanded that the West Indian catastrophe should not be repeated in the newly conquered lands. In 1523, Las Casas appeared to have won a major victory. King Charles sent Cortés an order forbidding the establishment of encomiendas in New Spain (the name given to the former Aztec Empire), because "God created the Indians free and not subject." Cortés, who had already assigned encomiendas to himself and his comrades, did not enforce the order. Backed by the strength and needs of his hard-bitten soldiers, he argued so persuasively for the encomienda system as necessary for the welfare and security of the colony that the royal order was revoked. Encomienda tribute and labor continued to be the main source of income for the colonists until the middle of the sixteenth century. The labor of encomienda Indians was supplemented by that of Indian slaves captured in wars or obtained from Indian slave owners.

The New Laws of the Indies and the Encomienda

Despite its retreat in the face of Cortés's disobedience, the crown renewed its efforts to bring Indian tribute and labor under royal control. Cautiously, it moved to curb the power of the conquistadors. The second audiencia (high court) of New Spain was established in 1531–1532 after a stormy period of rule by the first "gangster" audiencia, which devoted itself to despoiling Cortés and mercilessly oppressing the Indians. Taking the first steps in the regulation of Indian tribute and labor, the second audiencia moderated the tribute paid by many Indian towns, provided for registration of tribute assessments, and forbade, in principle, the use of Indians as carriers without their consent. The climax of royal intervention came with proclamation of the New Laws of the Indies (1542). These laws appeared to doom the encomienda. They prohibited the enslavement of Indians, ordered the release of slaves to whom legal title could not be proved, barred compulsory personal service by the Indians, regulated tribute, and declared that existing encomiendas were to lapse on the death of the holder.

In Peru the New Laws provoked a great revolt; in New Spain they caused a storm of protest by the encomenderos and a large part of the clergy. Under this pressure the crown again retreated. The laws forbidding Indian slavery and forced labor were reaffirmed, but the right of inheritance by the heir of an encomendero was recognized and even extended by stages to a third, fourth, and sometimes even a fifth life. Thereafter, or earlier in the absence of an heir, the encomienda reverted to the crown. In the natural course of events, the number of encomiendas steadily diminished and that of crown towns increased.

By about 1560 the encomienda had been partially "tamed." Royal intervention had curbed the power of the encomenderos and partially stabilized the tribute and labor situation, at least in areas near the colonial capitals. Tribute was now assessed in most places by the audiencias, which made a continuing effort to adjust it to the fluctuations of population and harvests on appeal from the Indians. The institution of *visita* and *cuenta* was employed to make such adjustments. The visita (inspection of an Indian town) yielded information concerning its resources or capacity to pay, which was needed to determine its per capita quota. The cuenta (count), made at the same time, gave the number of tribute payers. About 1560 the annual tribute paid to the king or to an encomendero by each married tributary Indian in New Spain was usually one silver peso and four-fifths of a bushel of maize or its equivalent in other produce.

This mechanism of assessment and copious protective legislation did not bring significant or enduring relief to the Indians. Padding of population counts and other abuses by encomenderos and other interested parties were common. More important, recounts and reassessments consistently lagged behind the rapidly shrinking number of tribute payers, with the result that the survivors had to bear the tribute burdens of those who had died or fled. Moreover, from the accession to the throne of Philip II (1556), the dominant motive of Spain's Indian policy became the increase of royal revenues in order to relieve the crown's desperate financial crisis. Indian groups hitherto exempt from tribute lost their favored status, and the tribute quota was progressively raised. As a result of these measures and the gradual reversion of encomiendas to the crown, the amount of royal tribute collected annually in New Spain rose from about 100,000 pesos to well over 1 million pesos between 1550 and the close of the eighteenth century. (These figures do not take account of the impact on the tribute's value due to the considerable rise in prices during the same period.)

For the colonists, however, the encomienda steadily declined in economic value. They lost the right to demand labor from their tributaries (1549); they also lost their fight to make the encomienda perpetual. The heaviest blow of all to the encomendero class was the catastrophic decline of the Indian population in the second half of the sixteenth century. In central Mexico, the Indian population dropped from perhaps 25 million in 1519 to slightly over 1 million in 1605. On the central coast of Peru, the tributary population seems to have fallen by 1575 to 4 percent of what it had been before the Conquest. For reasons that remain unclear, the rates of population decline in both Mexico and Peru appear to have been considerably higher on the coast than in the highlands. Disease, especially diseases of European origin against which the Indians had no acquired immunity, such as measles, smallpox, typhus, and malaria, was the major direct cause of this demographic disaster. But overwork, malnutrition, severe social disorganization, and the resulting loss of will to live underlay the terrible mortality associated with the great epidemics and even with epidemic-free years. In Peru the great civil wars and disorders of the period from 1535 to 1550 undoubtedly contributed materially to Indian depopulation.

As the number of their tributaries fell, the encomenderos' income from tribute dropped proportionately, while their expenses, which included the maintenance of a steward to collect tribute, support of a parish priest, and heavy taxes, remained steady or even increased. As a result, many encomenderos, as well as other Spaniards without encomiendas, began to engage in the more lucrative pursuits of agriculture, stock raising, and mining. The decline of the Indian population, sharply reducing the flow of foodstuffs and metals, stimulated a rapid growth of *haciendas* (Spanish estates) producing grain and meat.

Thus, in central Mexico by the 1570s, and in the northern and central Andean highlands by the end of the sixteenth century, the encomienda had lost its original character of an institution based on the use of Indian labor without payment. Its importance as a source of revenue to Spanish colonists had greatly diminished, and it had been placed in the way of extinction through the progressive reversion of individual encomiendas to the crown. These changes, however, did not take place everywhere. In areas that lacked precious metals or where Indian agricultural productivity was low, and where consequently there was little danger of the colonists acquiring excessive power, the crown permitted encomenderos to continue exploiting the forced labor of the Indians. This was the case in Chile, where the encomienda based on personal service continued until 1791; in Venezuela, where it survived until the 1680s; and in Paraguay, where it still existed in the early 1800s. The crown also allowed the encomienda as a labor system to continue in such areas of New Spain as Oaxaca and Yucatán.

The Repartimiento, Yanaconaje, and Free Labor

In the key areas of central Mexico and the Andean highlands, however, a new system, the *repartimiento,* replaced forced labor under the encomienda after 1550. Under this system, all adult male Indians had to give a certain amount of their time in rotation throughout the year to work in Spanish mines and workshops, on farms and ranches, and on public works. By this means, the crown sought to regulate the use of an ever-diminishing pool of Indian labor and give access to such labor to both encomenderos and the growing number of Spaniards without encomiendas. The Indians received a token wage for their work, but the repartimiento, like the encomienda, was essentially disguised slavery. Indians who avoided service and community leaders who failed to provide the required quotas were imprisoned, fined, and physically punished.

In Peru, where the condition of the Indians seems to have been generally worse than in New Spain, the repartimiento (here known as the *mita*) produced especially disastrous effects. Under this system, developed by Viceroy Francisco de Toledo in the 1570s, all able-bodied Indian men in the provinces subject to the mita were required to work for six-month periods, one year in seven, at Potosí or other mining centers, or were assigned to other Spanish employers. The silver mines of Potosí and the Huancavelica mercury mine were notorious deathtraps for Indian laborers under the mita. In Peru and Bolivia, the

mita remained an important source of labor in mining and agriculture to the end of the colonial period.

In the Andean area, the repartimiento was supplemented by another institution taken over from Inca society—the system of *yanaconas,* Indians who were separated from their communities and served Spaniards as personal servants or were attached to their estates. Like European serfs, the yanaconas were transferred from one landowner to another together with the estate. It is estimated that by the end of the sixteenth century the number of yanaconas on Spanish haciendas was almost equal to the number of Indians who lived in their own communities.

Although the repartimiento offered a temporary solution for the critical labor problem, many Spanish employers found it unsatisfactory, for it did not provide a dependable and continuing supply of labor. From an early date, mine owners and *hacendados* in New Spain turned increasingly to the use of free or contractual Indian wage labor. The heavy weight of tribute and repartimiento obligations on a diminishing native population and Spanish usurpation of Indian communal lands induced many Indians to accept an hacendado's invitation to become farm laborers working for wages, mostly paid in kind. Some traveled back and forth to work from their communities; others became resident peons on the haciendas. Other Indians were drawn to the northern silver mines by the lure of relatively high wages.

By 1630, when the crown abolished the agricultural repartimiento in central Mexico, the move provoked little or no protest, for most landowners relied on free labor. The mining repartimiento continued longer in New Spain. It was still employed intermittently in the eighteenth century but had little importance, for the mines of New Spain operated mainly with contractual labor. In Peru and Bolivia, where the mita, supplemented by *yanaconaje,* was the dominant labor system, providing a mass of cheap workers for the high-cost silver mines, free labor was less important. However, there were as many as forty thousand free Indian miners (known as *mingas*) employed at the Potosí mines in the seventeenth century.[2]

From the first, this so-called free labor was often associated with debt servitude. The second half of the seventeenth century saw the growth of the system of *repartimiento* or *repartimiento de mercancías*,[3] the compulsory purchase by Indians of goods from district governors (corregidores, alcaldes mayores). In combination with their other burdens, repartimiento was a powerful inducement for Indians to accept advances of cash and goods from Spanish hacendados; the tribute payment was usually included in the reckoning. An Indian so indebted had to work for his employer until the debt was paid. Despite its later evil reputation, peonage, whether or not enforced by debts, had definite advantages for many Indians. It usually freed them from the recurrent tribute and repartimiento burdens of the Indian community and often gave some security in the form of a plot of land the Indian could work for himself and his family. But if the hacienda offered some Indians escape from their intolerable conditions, it aggravated the difficulties of those who remained on their ancestral lands. The hacienda expanded by legal or illegal means at the expense of the Indian pueblo, absorbing whole towns and leaving others without enough land for their people when the long population decline finally ended in the first half of the seventeenth century and a slow recovery began. The hacienda also lured laborers from the pueblo, making it difficult for the Indian town to meet its tribute and repartimiento obligations. Between the two *repúblicas* (commonwealths), the *república de indios* and the *república de españoles*, as Spanish documents frequently called them, stretched a gulf of hostility and distrust.

The importance of debt servitude as a means of securing and holding labor seems to have varied according to the availability of free labor. It was used extensively in northern Mexico, where such labor was scarce, but appears to have been less important in central Mexico, where it was more abundant. Some recent studies stress that debt peonage was "more of an inducement than a bond," with the size of advances reflecting the bargaining power of labor in dealing with employers and that hacendados sometimes made no special effort to recover their peons who had fled without repayment of loans. But the evidence for such relative lack of concern about fugitive peons comes chiefly from late-eighteenth-century Mexico, when labor was increasingly abundant. For earlier, labor-scarce periods, there is much evidence of strenuous efforts to compel Indians to remain on estates until their debts had been paid off. Indeed, hacendados and officials sometimes likened Mexican peons to European serfs who were bound to their estates, with the right to their services passing with the transfer of the land from one owner to another.

Widely used in agriculture and mining, debt servitude assumed its harshest form in the numerous *obrajes* (workshops) producing cloth and other goods that sprang up in many areas in the sixteenth and seventeenth centuries. Convict labor, assigned to employers by Spanish judges, was early supplemented by the "free" labor of Indians who were ensnared by a variety of devices. Indians were often tempted into these workshops by an offer of liquor or a small sum of money and, once inside the gates, were never let out again. "In this way," wrote a seventeenth-century observer, "they have gathered in and duped many married Indians with families, who have passed into oblivion here for twenty years, or longer, or their whole lives, without their wives or children knowing anything about them; for even if they want to get out, they cannot, thanks to the great watchfulness with which the doormen guard the exits."

[2] In the early seventeenth century the growing shortage of Indian labor, due to the ravages of epidemic disease and the flight of Indians from communities subject to the mita, gave rise to a system whereby the delivery of mita labor was replaced by deliveries of silver collected from Indian communities and raised through the operation of economic enterprises supervised by the curacas. Mine owners used this silver to cover minga costs and to hire minga substitutes for mita labor (*mitayos*) not received in person.

[3] The term *repartimiento* was also applied to the periodic conscription of Indians for labor useful to the Spanish community.

Black Slavery

Side by side with the disguised slavery of repartimiento and debt servitude existed black slavery. For a variety of reasons, including the fact that Spaniards and Portuguese were accustomed to the holding of black slaves, the tradition that blacks were descendants of the biblical Ham and bore his curse, and the belief that they were better able to support the hardships of plantation labor, Spanish defenders of the Indian did not display the same zeal on behalf of the enslaved Africans.

In fact, the rapid development of sugar cane agriculture in the West Indies in the early 1500s brought an insistent demand for black slave labor to replace the vanishing Indians. There arose a lucrative slave trade, chiefly carried on by foreigners under a system of *asiento* (contract between an individual or company and the Spanish crown). The high cost of slaves tended to limit their use to the more profitable plantation cultures or to domestic service in the homes of the wealthy. Large numbers lived on the coasts of Venezuela and Colombia, where they were employed in the production of such crops as cacao, sugar, and tobacco, and in the coastal valleys of Peru, where they labored on sugar and cotton plantations, but smaller concentrations were found in every part of the Indies. In Chapter 5, we shall consider the much disputed question whether African slavery in Hispanic America was "milder" than in other European colonies.

In summary, all colonial labor systems rested in varying degrees on servitude and coercion. Although contractual labor gradually emerged as the theoretical norm, all the labor systems just described coexisted throughout the colonial period. Indian slavery, for example, was abolished in 1542, but Indian wars and enslavement continued in frontier areas on various pretexts into the eighteenth century. Which labor system dominated at a given time and place depended on such factors as the area's natural resources, the number of Europeans in the area and the character of their economic activities, the size and cultural level of its Indian population, and the crown's economic and political interests. Finally,

it should be noted that in the course of the sixteenth and seventeenth centuries the labor pool was gradually expanded by the addition of mestizos (mixtures of Indians and whites), free blacks and mulattos, and poor whites. Since most of these people were exempt from encomienda and repartimiento obligations, they usually worked for wages and enjoyed freedom of movement, but like the Indians were subject to control through debts. In Chapter 6, we will discuss eighteenth-century changes in the labor system.

The Colonial Economy

The Conquest disrupted the traditional subsistence-and-tribute economy of the Indians. War and disease took a heavy toll of lives, to the detriment of production; in some areas the complex irrigation networks established and maintained by Indian centralized authorities were destroyed or fell into ruin. The Conquest also transformed the character and tempo of Indian economic activity. When the frenzied scramble for treasure had ended with the exhaustion of the available gold and silver objects, the encomienda became the principal instrument for the extraction of wealth from the vanquished. The peoples of the Aztec and Inca empires were accustomed to paying tribute in labor and commodities to their rulers and nobility. But the tribute demands of the old ruling classes, although apparently increasing on the eve of the Conquest, had been limited by custom and by the capacity of Indian ruling groups to utilize tribute goods. The greater part of such tribute was destined for consumption or display, not for trade. The demands of the new Spanish masters, on the other hand, were unlimited. Gold and silver were the great objects; if these could not be obtained directly, the encomenderos proposed to obtain them by sale in local or distant markets of the tribute goods produced by their Indians. Driven by visions of infinite wealth, the Spaniards took no account of what the Indians had formerly given in tribute and exploited them mercilessly. A compassionate missionary, writing in 1554, complained that before the Conquest the Indians in his part of Mexico

never used to give such large loads of mantas [*pieces of cotton cloth*], *nor had they ever heard of beds, fine cotton fabrics, wax, or a thousand other fripperies like bed sheets, tablecloths, shirts, and skirts. All they used to do was cultivate the fields of their lords, build their houses, repair the temples, and give of the produce of their fields when their lords asked for it.*

Cortés as a Businessman

The business career of Hernando Cortés illustrates the large variety and scale of the economic activities of some encomenderos. By 1528 Cortés was already worth 500,000 gold pesos. Part of this wealth represented his share of the loot taken in Tenochtitlán and other places during and immediately after the Conquest. But his chief source of income was his encomienda holdings. To himself he assigned the richest tribute areas in the former Aztec Empire. At the time of his death in 1547, although many of his encomiendas had been drastically reduced and tribute assessments lowered, he was still receiving 30,000 gold pesos annually from this source. He received large quantities of gold dust, textiles, maize, poultry, and other products from encomienda towns. The pueblo of Cuernavaca (near Mexico City) alone gave as part of its annual tribute cloth worth 5,000 gold pesos. Cortés's agents sold the tribute cloth and other products to traders who retailed them in Mexico City and other Spanish towns. Cortés had his own extensive real estate holdings in Mexico City. On or near the central square he erected shops, some of which he used for his own trading interests, others of which he rented out.

Cortés was an empire builder in the economic as well as political sense of the word. He invested the capital he acquired from encomienda tribute and labor in many enterprises. Mining attracted his special attention. In the Oaxaca and Michoacán districts, he had gangs of Indian slaves, more than a thousand in each, panning gold; many of these slaves died from hard labor and inadequate

food. In 1529 these mining areas brought him 12,000 pesos in gold annually. In addition to his own mining properties, Cortés held others, such as silver mines in the Taxco area of Mexico, in partnerships. In such cases, his investment usually consisted of goods, livestock, or the labor of his encomienda Indians or his Indian and black slaves.

After encomienda tribute, agriculture and stock raising were Cortés's largest sources of income. He had large landholdings in various parts of Mexico, some acquired by royal grant, others usurped from Indians. He employed encomienda labor to grow maize on his land. His fields in the vicinity of Oaxaca alone produced ten to fifteen thousand bushels a year. Part of this grain he sold in the Spanish towns and at the mines, part went to feed his gangs of slaves at the gold washings and his Indian carriers. Cortés also raised great numbers of cattle and hogs, which were butchered in his own slaughterhouses. Near Tehuantepec he had herds of more than ten thousand wild cattle, which supplied hides and tallow for export to Panama and Peru.

The restless Cortés also pioneered in the development of the Mexican sugar industry. By 1547 his plantations were producing more than three hundred thousand pounds of sugar annually, most of which was sold to agents of European merchants for export. If he was not the first to experiment with silk raising in New Spain, as he claimed, he certainly went into the business on a large scale, laying out thousands of mulberry trees with the labor of Indians paid in cash or cacao beans. In this venture, however, he suffered heavy losses. Nonetheless, the variety and extent of Cortés's business interests suggest how misleading is the familiar portrait of the conquistador as a purely feudal type devoted only to war and plunder, disdainful of all trade and industry.

The Growth of the Haciendas

Among the first generation of colonists, large-scale enterprises such as those of Cortés were rare. The typical encomendero was content to occupy a relatively small land grant and draw

90

tribute from his Indians, who continued to live and work in large numbers on their ancestral lands. The major shift from reliance on encomienda tribute to the development of Spanish commercial agriculture and stock raising came after 1550 in response to the massive Indian population decline and the crown's restrictive legislation, which combined to deprive the encomienda of much of its economic value. Acute food shortages in the Spanish towns created new economic opportunities for Spanish farmers and ranchers. Simultaneously, the reduction of Indian populations left vacant large expanses of Indian land, which Spanish colonists hastened to occupy for wheat raising or, more commonly, as sheep or cattle ranges.

By the end of the sixteenth century, the Spanish-owned hacienda was responsible for the bulk of agricultural commercial production and pressed ever more aggressively on the shrinking Indian sector of the colonial economy. Spanish colonists used various methods to "free" land from Indian occupation: purchase, usurpation, and *congregación* (forced concentration of Indians in new communities, ostensibly to facilitate control and Christianization). Although Spain's declared policy was to protect Indian community land, the numerous laws forbidding encroachment on such land failed to halt the advance of the hacienda. The power of the hacendados, whose ranks included high royal officials, churchmen, and wealthy merchants, usually carried all before it.

In the seventeenth century, the crown, facing an acute, chronic economic crisis, actually encouraged usurpation of Indian lands by adopting the device of *composición* (settlement), which legalized the defective title of the usurper through payment of a fee to the king. Not only Indian communities but communities of Spanish or mestizo small farmers saw their lands devoured by the advancing hacienda. A striking feature of this process was that land was sometimes primarily acquired not for use but to obtain Indian day laborers and peons by depriving them of their fields or to eliminate competition by Indian or other small producers. The establishment of a *mayorazgo* (entailed estate) assured the perpe-

tuation of the consolidated property in the hands of the owner's descendants, but this feudal device required approval by the crown and payment of a large fee and benefited only a small number of very wealthy families.

A more common strategy for consolidation and preservation of holdings was marriage within the extended family, often between cousins. In the majority of cases, however, this and other strategies for ensuring the longevity of family estates were less than successful. Spanish inheritance laws requiring the equal division of estates among heirs, economic downturns, and lack of investment capital as a result of large expenditures for conspicuous consumption and donations to the church were some of the factors that made for an unstable landed elite and a high turnover rate in estate ownership. Historian Susan Ramirez studied the collective biography of colonial elite families who lived in north coastal Peru over a period of three hundred years. She found that, contrary to tradition, this elite was "unstable, open, and in constant flux," with most families lasting no more than two or three generations. The historian Lucas Alamán, himself a member of Mexico's former colonial elite, alluded to this instability at the top, citing the Mexican proverb that said, "The father a merchant, the son a gentleman, the grandson a beggar."

The tempo of land concentration varied from region to region according to its resources and proximity to markets. In the Valley of Mexico, for example, the bulk of the land was held by great haciendas by the end of the colonial period. Indian commoners and chiefs, on the other hand, retained much of the land in the province of Oaxaca, which had limited markets for its crops. Recent studies of the colonial hacienda stress the large variations in hacienda size and productivity from one region to another. This variety in size and productivity reflects the great regional divergencies in productive potential—determined by proximity to water and quality of soil—and in access to labor and markets, among other variables, in the vast Spanish Empire in America.

Despite the long-term trend toward land concentration, there gradually arose a class of white and mixed-blood small farmers of uncertain size.

In Mexico such small farmers, typically mestizos, came to be known as *rancheros* and they were interspersed among the Indian villages and commercial estates of the central and southern highlands. Some were former majordomos or foremen of large landowners from whom they rented or leased unused portions of their estates, generally raising products for sale in local markets. Their limited resources and dependence on large landowners made their situation precarious; in prosperous times of rising land values their small properties were often swallowed up by their wealthy neighbors. A less frequent occurrence, successful rancheros might expand their holdings and themselves join the ranks of the landed elite.

Spanish Agriculture in the New World

Spanish agriculture differed from Indian land use in significant ways. First, it was extensive, cultivating large tracts with plows and draft animals, in contrast with the intensive Indian digging-stick agriculture. Second, Spanish agriculture was predominantly commercial, producing commodities for sale in local or distant markets, in contrast with the subsistence character of traditional Indian agriculture. Through the need to pay tribute and other obligations in cash, the Indian farmer came under increasing pressure to produce for the market. But, as a rule, the hacendado's superior resources made it difficult for the Indian farmer to compete except in times of abundant harvests, and he tended to fall back to the level of subsistence agriculture, whose meager yield he sometimes supplemented by labor for the local hacendado.

Spanish colonial agriculture early produced wheat on a large scale for sale in urban centers like Mexico City, Lima, Veracruz, and Cartagena; maize was also grown on haciendas for the sizable Indian consumers' market in Mexico City and Lima. Sugar, like wheat, was one of Europe's agricultural gifts to America. Spaniards brought it from the Canary Islands to Hispaniola, where it soon became the foundation of the island's prosperity. By 1550 more than twenty sugar mills processed cane into sugar, which was shipped in great quantities to Spain. "The sugar industry is the principal industry of those islands," wrote José de Acosta at the end of the sixteenth century, "such a taste have men developed for sweets." From the West Indies sugar quickly spread to Mexico and Peru. Sugar refining, with its large capital outlays for equipment and black slaves, was, after silver mining, the largest-scale enterprise in the Indies.

In the irrigated coastal valleys of Peru, wine and olives, as well as sugar, were produced in quantity. The silk industry had a brief period of prosperity in Mexico, but soon declined in the face of labor shortages and competition from Chinese silk brought in the Manila galleons from the Philippines to the port of Acapulco. Spain's sporadic efforts to discourage the production of wine, olives, and silk, regarded as interfering with Spanish exports of the same products, seem to have had little effect. Other products cultivated by the Spaniards on an extensive plantation basis included tobacco, cacao, and indigo. A unique Mexican and Central American export, highly valued by the European cloth industry, was cochineal, a blood-red dye made from the dried bodies of insects parasitic on the nopal cactus.

Spain made a major contribution to American economic life with the introduction of various domestic animals—chickens, mules, horses, cattle, pigs, and sheep. The mules and horses revolutionized transport, gradually eliminating the familiar spectacle of long lines of Indian carriers loaded down with burdens. Horses and mules became vital to the mining industry for hauling and for turning machinery. Cattle and smaller domesticated animals greatly enlarged the food resources of the continent. Meat was indispensable to the mining industry, for only a meat diet could sustain the hard work of the miners. "If the mines have been worked at all," wrote a Spanish judge in 1606, "it is thanks to the plentiful and cheap supply of livestock." Indians quickly introduced meat into their diet; writing of the Valley of Mexico, Charles Gibson observes: "By 1598 it could be said that the Indian taste for meat had become fixed and unalterable." In addition to meat, cattle provided hides for export to Spain and other

European centers of leather manufacture, as well as hides and tallow (used for lighting) for the domestic market, especially in the mining areas. Sheep raisers found a large market for their wool in the textile workshops that arose in many parts of the colonies.

In a densely settled region like central Mexico, the explosive increase of Spanish cattle and sheep had catastrophic consequences. A horde of animals swarmed over the land, often invading not only the land vacated by the dwindling Indian population but the reserves of land needed by the Indian system of field rotation. Cattle trampled the Indian crops, causing untold damage; torrential rains caused massive erosion on valley slopes close-cropped by sheep. By the end of the sixteenth century, however, the Mexican cattle industry had become stabilized. Exhaustion of virgin pasturelands, mass slaughter of cattle for their hides and tallow, and official efforts to halt grazing on Indian harvest lands had produced a marked reduction in the herds. The problem further abated in the seventeenth century as a result of the cumulative transfer of Indian lands in the central valley to Spaniards who established haciendas growing pulque (a fermented drink made from maguey that was very popular with the natives) and wheat. Gradually, the cattle ranches and sheep herds moved to new, permanent grazing grounds in the sparsely settled, semiarid north.

An equally rapid increase of horses, mules, and cattle took place in the vast, rich pampas (grasslands) of the Río de la Plata (modern Argentina). Their increase in this area of almost infinite pasturage soon outstripped potential demand and utilization, and herds of wild cattle became a common phenomenon in La Plata as in other parts of Spanish America. Barred by Spanish law from seaborne trade with the outside world, the inhabitants of this remote province, lacking precious metals or abundant Indian labor, relieved their poverty by illegal commerce with Dutch and other foreign traders, who carried their hides and tallow to Europe. In addition, they also sent mules and horses, hides and tallow to the mining regions of Upper Peru (Bolivia).

Another center of the cattle industry was the West Indies. José de Acosta wrote in about 1590 that

the cattle have multiplied so greatly in Santo Domingo, and in other islands of that region that they wander by the thousands through the forests and fields, all masterless. They hunt these beasts only for their hides; whites and Negroes go out on horseback, equipped with a kind of hooked knife, to chase the cattle, and any animal that falls to their knives is theirs. They kill it and carry the hide home, leaving the flesh to rot; no one wants it, since meat is so plentiful.

Colonial Mining and Industry

Mining, as the principal source of royal revenue in the form of the quinto, or royal fifth of all gold, silver, or other precious metals obtained in the Indies, received the special attention and protection of the crown. Silver, rather than gold, was the principal product of the American mines. Spain's proudest possession in the New World was the great silver mine of Potosí in Upper Peru, whose flow of treasure attained gigantic proportions between 1579 and 1635. Potosí was discovered in 1545; the rich Mexican silver mines of Zacatecas and Guanajuato were opened up in 1548 and 1558. In the same period, important gold placers (sand or gravel deposits containing eroded particles of the ore) were found in central Chile and in the interior of New Granada (Colombia). The introduction of the patio process for separating the silver from the ore with mercury (1556) gave a great stimulus to silver mining. The chief source of mercury for Potosí silver was the Huancavelica mine in Peru, where labor was "a thing of horror"; Mexican silver was chiefly processed with mercury from the Almadén mine in Spain. As in other times and places, the mining industry brought prosperity to a few, failure or small success to the great majority.

Lack of capital to finance technical improvements required by the increasing depth of mines, flooding, and similar problems, combined with

A scene from Gonzalo Fernández de Oviedo's 1535 *History of the Indies,* showing Indians panning for gold.

shortages and the high cost of mercury (a crown monopoly), caused a precipitous decline of silver production in the viceroyalty of Peru after 1650. In Mexico production levels fluctuated, with output declining in some old centers and rising in new ones, but here the long-range trend for the seventeenth century seems to have been upward. (An older view claimed that an acute labor shortage caused by the catastrophic fall of the Indian population was the root cause of a supposed decline in silver production in New Spain, but it now appears that mine owners in general had little difficulty in filling their labor needs.) As silver production fell, colonial agriculture and stock raising, which had expanded to satisfy the demands of the mining centers for grain, meat, hides, tallow, and work animals, also entered a period of contraction. There was a shift from large-scale commercial enterprise to an emphasis on self-sufficiency. A simultaneous crisis of the European economy reduced the demand for such colonial staples as hides, sugar, and indigo. The decline of silver mining aggravated the chronic colonial problem of coin shortage and unreliability, leading to increased resort to barter and substitute money on the local level and adding to the difficulties of long-distance trade.

The colonial depression was far from total, however, for the economic picture is a mixed one. It has been argued, for example, that the spectacular decline in silver remittances to Castile, cited in support of the thesis of a colonial seventeenth-century economic crisis, was caused in part by a growing colonial self-sufficiency that reduced dependence on European goods. By the start of the seventeenth century, Mexico, Peru, and Chile had become self-sufficient in grains and partly so in wine, olive oil, ironware, and furniture. This growing self-sufficiency coincided with a decay of Spanish industry that sharply curtailed the mother country's exports to the Indies.

In New Spain, proceeds from the alcabala, a significant indicator of the state of the economy, increased until 1638 and declined only slightly thereafter. Although trade with Seville declined, the same was not generally true of interprovincial trade; in the 1620s a vigorous trade in cacao, Venezuela's principal export, developed between that colony and Mexico. Trade also flourished between Chile and Peru. On balance, however, the description of the colonial seventeenth century as a century of depression is probably correct. It also seems likely that the reduced tempo of economic activity in mining and agriculture lessened

94

the worst exploitation of Indian labor and helped initiate the slow Indian population recovery that was under way by the last quarter of the seventeenth century.

The Spaniards found a flourishing handicrafts industry in the advanced culture areas of Mexico, Central America, and Peru. Throughout the colonial period, the majority of the natives continued to supply most of their own needs for pottery, clothing, and household goods. In the Spanish towns, craft guilds modeled on those of Spain arose in response to the high prices for all Spanish imported goods. To avoid competition from Indian, black, and mestizo artisans, who quickly learned the Spanish crafts, they were incorporated into the Spanish-controlled guilds but were barred from becoming masters. The chronic shortage of skilled labor, however, soon made all such racial restrictions a dead letter. These guilds attempted to maintain careful control over the quantity and quality of production in industries serving the needs of the colonial upper class.

The period up to about 1630 saw a steady growth of factory-type establishments, the previously mentioned obrajes, many of which produced cheap cotton and woolen goods for popular consumption. Most of these enterprises were privately owned, but some were operated by Indian communities to meet their tribute payments. A number of towns in New Spain (Mexico City, Puebla, Tlaxcala, among others) were centers of this textile industry. Other primitive factories produced such articles as soap, chinaware, and leather. The seventeenth-century depression seems to have blighted the once-flourishing textile industry of New Spain but does not appear to have had the same harmful effects elsewhere. To some extent, the depression, by reducing the capacity to purchase foreign imports, may have promoted the growth of colonial industry. The population increase of the late seventeenth century may have also stimulated the growth of manufacturing. There is little evidence that sporadic Spanish legislative efforts to restrict the growth of colonial manufacturers achieved their purpose.

Commerce, Smuggling, and Piracy

The Colonial Commercial System

Spain's colonial commercial system was restrictive, exclusive, and regimented in character, in conformity with the mercantilist standards of that day. Control over all colonial trade, under the Royal Council of the Indies, was vested in the Casa de Contratación (House of Trade), established in 1503 in Seville. This agency licensed and supervised all ships, passengers, crews, and goods passing to and from the Indies. It also collected import and export duties and the royal share of all precious metals and stones brought from the Indies, licensed all pilots, and maintained a *padrón real* (standard chart) to which all charts issued to ships in the Indies trade had to conform. It even operated a school of navigation that trained the pilots and officers needed to sail the ships in the transatlantic trade.

Commerce with the colonies was restricted until the eighteenth century to the wealthier merchants of Seville and Cádiz, who were organized in a guild that exercised great influence in all matters relating to colonial trade. With the aim of preventing contraband trade and safeguarding the Seville monopoly, trade was concentrated in three American ports, Veracruz in New Spain, Cartagena in New Granada, and Nombre de Dios on the Isthmus of Panama. The Seville merchant oligarchy and corresponding merchant groups in the Indies, particularly the merchant guilds in Mexico City and Lima, deliberately kept the colonial markets understocked. In general they played into each other's hands at the expense of the colonists, who were forced to pay exorbitant prices for all European goods acquired through legal channels. Inevitably, the system generated colonial discontent and stimulated the growth of contraband trade.

With the object of enforcing the closed-port policy and protecting merchant vessels against foreign attack, a fleet system was developed and made obligatory in the sixteenth century. As perfected about the middle of the century, it called for the annual sailing under armed convoy of two fleets, each numbering fifty or more ships, one sailing in the spring for Veracruz and taking with it ships bound for Honduras and the West Indies, the other sailing in August for Panama and convoying ships for Cartagena and other ports on the northern coast of South America. Veracruz supplied Mexico and most of Central America; from Portobelo goods were carried across the isthmus and shipped to Lima, the distribution point for Spanish goods to places as distant as Chile and Buenos Aires. Having loaded their returns of silver and colonial produce, the fleets were to rendezvous at Havana and sail for Spain in the spring, before the onset of the hurricane season. In the seventeenth century, as a result of Spain's economic decadence and the growing volume of contraband trade, fleet sailings became increasingly irregular.

Danger and difficulty attended the long voyage to the Indies from the time a ship left Seville to thread its careful way down the shoal-ridden Guadalquivir to the Mediterranean. Hunger and thirst, seasickness and scurvy at sea, and yellow fever and malaria in tropical harbors like Veracruz and Portobelo were familiar afflictions. Storms at sea took a heavy toll of ships; foreign pirates and privateers posed a chronic threat. Gluts of goods in the colonial markets as a result of competition from foreign smugglers, and frequent confiscation of silver by the crown, with tardy or inadequate compensation, often reduced merchants' profits to the vanishing point. But the heaviest damage to Spanish commercial interests stemmed from the activities of foreign smugglers and pirates, who seized the opportunity presented by Spain's growing economic and military weakness.

Spanish industry, handicapped by its guild organization and technical backwardness, could not supply the colonies with cheap and abundant manufactures in return for colonial foodstuffs and raw materials, as required by the implied terms of the mercantilist bargain. Indeed, it was not in the interest of the merchant monopolists of Seville and Cádiz, who throve on a regime of scarcity and high prices, to permit an abundant flow of manufactures to the colonies. Prices to the colonial consumer were also raised by a multitude of taxes: the *avería* (convoy tax), the *almojarifazgo* (import duty), and the alcabala. Inevitably, the manufacturers and merchants of the advanced industrial nations of northern Europe sought to enter by force or guile into the large and unsatisfied Spanish-American markets. The ambitious monarchs of those lands scoffed at Spain's claim of dominion over all the Western Hemisphere except that portion that belonged to Portugal; they defied Spanish edicts forbidding foreigners to navigate American waters or trade on American coasts on pain of destruction of ships and crews. The ironic query said to have been addressed by Francis I of France to the kings of Spain and Portugal summed up the foreign viewpoint: "Show me, I pray you, the will of our father Adam, that I may see if he has really made you his only universal heirs."

The English Threat and Sir Francis Drake

England soon emerged as the principal threat to Spain's empire in America. The accumulation of capital and development of manufacturing under the fostering care of the Tudor kings produced an explosion of English commercial energies in the reign of Queen Elizabeth I. The Old World did not provide sufficient outlets for these erupting energies, and England's merchant adventurers eagerly turned to America. The historic slave-trading voyage of John Hawkins to the West Indies in 1562 opened England's drive to break into the closed Spanish-American markets. Half honest trader, half corsair, Hawkins came to the Indies heavily armed and ready to compel the colonists to trade with him at cannon point, but he showed himself scrupulously honest in his business dealings with the Spaniards, even to the point of paying the royal license and customs dues. Hawkins owed the success of his first two American voyages to the needs of the Spanish settlers, who were ready to trade with a Lutheran heretic or the devil himself to satisfy their desperate need for slave labor and European wares.

To cover up these violations of Spanish law, the venal local officials made a thin pretense of resistance. But by 1567 the pretense had worn too thin, the Spanish government had taken alarm, and angry orders went out to drive the English smugglers away. Stiffening Spanish resistance culminated in the near-destruction of Hawkins's trading fleet by a Spanish naval force at Veracruz in 1568.

Only two of the English ships managed to get away; one was commanded by Hawkins, the other by his cousin, Francis Drake. Four years later, Drake left England with four small ships, bound for the Isthmus of Panama. In actions marked by audacity and careful planning, he stormed and plundered the town of Nombre de Dios, escaping at dawn. Later, he made the most lucrative haul in the history of piracy by capturing the pack train carrying Peruvian silver from the Pacific side of the isthmus to Nombre de Dios. In 1577, Drake set sail again on an expedition that had the secret sponsorship and support of Queen Elizabeth. Its objects were to "singe the King of Spain's beard" by seizing his treasure ships and ravaging his colonial towns; to explore the whole Pacific coast of America, taking possession of the regions beyond the limits of Spanish occupation; and to display English maritime prowess by means of a second circumnavigation of the globe. The expedition of 1577 led by Francis Drake achieved these goals. In the 1580s, Drake made other voyages of reprisal against Cartagena, St. Augustine, and Santo Domingo. It is small wonder that the name of Drake became a word of fear to the inhabitants of colonial coastal towns.

Inroads by Other Europeans

In the seventeenth century, piracy and smuggling were supplemented by efforts to found colonies, not only on the mainland of North America but in the forbidden waters of the Spanish Main. The Dutch, intermittently at war with Spain since 1576, launched a formidable military and commercial offensive against the Spanish West Indies. Their principal instrument was the Dutch West India Company, organized in 1621. A brilliant admiral, Piet Heyn, captured the whole homebound Veracruz treasure fleet off the coast of Cuba in 1628. That victory brought a dividend of 50 percent to the company's shareholders and financed a new company offensive against Brazil that resulted in Dutch occupation of the rich sugar-producing Brazilian northeast for a quarter-century (1630–1654).

Dutch capture of Curaçao, hard off the coast of Venezuela (1634), gave them an invaluable smuggling base and emboldened the French and English to seize both unoccupied and occupied Spanish islands—Barbados and St. Kitts, Martinique and Guadeloupe. In 1655 an English Puritan fleet, defeated in an effort to capture Santo Domingo, turned on Jamaica and easily captured the thinly settled island. In the same period, French corsairs based in the pirate lair of Tortuga began to settle the adjacent northwest corner of Hispaniola, virtually abandoned by Spaniards since 1605. By 1665 this region had become the French colony of St. Domingue, with a governor appointed by the trading Compagnie des Indes.

The Effects of Pirates and Smugglers on Spanish Prosperity

In this period, piracy in the West Indies became a highly organized, large-scale activity often enjoying the open or covert protection of the English governors of Jamaica and the French governors of St. Domingue. Two leading figures in this unsavory business were the ferocious French pirate L'Olonnois and the equally unscrupulous English buccaneer Henry Morgan. Romantic literature has cast a false glamour about these gangsters of the sea. Unlike the nationalistic and fervently Protestant Drake, the typical pirate captain of the seventeenth century was quite free of patriotic or religious zeal and plied his trade in the calculating spirit of a businessman engaged in a likely speculation.

Piracy entered on a decline following the signing of the Treaty of Madrid in 1670 between England and Spain, by which the British government agreed to aid in the suppression of the corsairs in return for Spanish recognition of its sovereignty over the British and West Indian islands. French buccaneers, however, continued active until the signing of the Treaty of Ryswick in 1697, by which Spain formally recognized French possession of St. Domingue.

The injury inflicted on Spanish prosperity and prestige by pirates and privateers, great as it was, was dwarfed by the losses caused by the less spectacular operations of foreign smugglers. Contraband trade steadily increased in the course of the sixteenth and seventeenth centuries. European establishments in Jamaica, St. Domingue, and the Lesser Antilles became so many bases for contraband trade with the Spanish colonies. Buenos Aires was another funnel through which Dutch and other foreign traders poured immense quantities of goods that reached markets as distant as Peru. By the end of the seventeenth century, French companies operating behind the façades of Spanish merchant houses in Seville and Cádiz dominated even the legal trade with the Indies.

A shrewd English observer put his finger on the major source of Spain's misfortunes: her economic weakness. The Spaniards, he remarked, were said to be stewards for the rest of Europe:

Their galleons bring the silver into Spain, but neither wisdom nor power can keep it there; it runs out as fast as it comes in, nay, and faster. . . . At first sight this seems to be strange and incredible; but when we come to examine it, the mystery is by no means impenetrable. The silver and rich commodities which come from the Indies come not for nothing (the king's duties excepted) and very little of the goods or manufactures for which they come, belong to the subjects of the crown of Spain. It is evident, therefore, that the Spanish merchants are but factors, and that the greatest part of the returns from the West Indies belong to those foreigners for whom they negotiate.

Spanish economists of the seventeenth century understood the causes of Spain's plight. Their writings offered sound criticisms of the existing state of affairs and constructive proposals for reform. But their arguments were powerless to change the course of Spanish policy, dictated by small mercantile and aristocratic cliques whose special interests and privileges were wholly incompatible with the cause of reform.

The Framework of the Colonial Economy

Was the colonial economy capitalist, feudal, or something in between? Scholars have hotly debated this issue. Some, who believe that production for the market is the defining feature of capitalism, argue that Latin America has been capitalist since the Discovery.[4] Others deny the relevance of the concepts of feudalism and capitalism, taken from a European context, to a unique colonial reality. Most students, however, will admit the presence of capitalist, feudal, and even more archaic elements, such as the pre-Columbian Indian communities based on communal land tenure, in the colonial economy. Spain tried, though not consistently, to preserve and protect that ancient corporate landowning system because it gave the crown direct control over Indian labor and tribute, which it could then allocate to the colonial elite in accord with its own policies and interests. That collective landowning system suffered severe erosion in the course of the colonial period due to the expansion of the Spanish agricultural sector but at its close still maintained a large presence in many areas.

The feudal or semifeudal elements in the colonial economy included labor systems based in varying degrees on servitude and coercion, the nonmonetary character of many economic transactions, and the technical backwardness of industry and agriculture, which reflected the very low level of investment in production in contrast with the high levels of expenditure for conspicuous consumption, the church, and charity. Regulations such as those that forbade Indians to wear European clothes or own land privately that seriously hampered the development of a market economy may also be called feudal.

[4] A leading exponent of the "Latin America-has-been-capitalist-all-along" view is André Gunder Frank; see Frank's *Capitalism and Underdevelopment in Latin America* (1969). That view has come under heavy fire from scholars who define capitalism, first and foremost, as a mode of production based on wage labor that has lost its own means of production. See, for example, Colin Mooers, *The Making of Bourgeois Europe* (1991), pp. 5–17.

This predominantly feudal character of the colonial economy reflected Spain's own backwardness. Indeed, in the course of the colonial period Spain became in certain ways more feudal, more seigneurial. Part of the reason is that most of the wealth that flowed from the Indies to Spain went to pay for costly wars and diplomacy, support a parasitic nobility, and import goods from northern Europe, leaving little for development. Spain's dependence on colonial tribute and colonial trade monopoly inevitably strengthened the dominant aristocratic ideology and discouraged the rise of a dynamic entrepreneurial class. In fact, the passion for noble titles infected many members of the small middle class, who hastened to abandon their trades and invest their wealth in a mayorazgo (an entailed estate). If the nobility had lost their feudal power to the crown on the national level, they were compensated, says John Lynch, "by the extension of their economic power, a process in which the crown itself was a willing ally," and they retained their feudal powers in their own districts, where they levied feudal dues, appointed local officials, and meted out justice. Indeed, under the last, weak Hapsburg kings, the nobility regained much of their old political power. "By the late seventeenth century," writes Henry Kamen, "Spain was probably the only west European country to be completely and unquestionably under the control of the titled aristocracy." This aristocratic hegemony was a recipe for economic decay and collapse. We shall see that Spanish efforts in the eighteenth century to reverse these trends were too little and too late.

The colonial economy also contained some capitalist elements. Although based on such noncapitalist labor systems as slavery and debt peonage, the gold and silver mines and the haciendas, ranches, and plantations producing sugar, hides, cochineal, indigo, and other commodities for external markets were fully integrated into the expanding world market. These enterprises reflected the price fluctuations and other vicissitudes of that market and promoted the accumulation of capital, not in Spain, but in England and other lands of rising capitalism. Some capitalist shoots appeared in the colonies as well, notably in the great mining centers, sugar mills, and workshops that were marked by some development of free labor and division of labor.

But the development of colonial capitalism remained embryonic, stunted by the overwhelming weight of feudal relationships and attitudes and the continuous siphoning off of wealth to Spain, itself an economic satellite of the more advanced capitalist countries of northwest Europe. The double character of the colonial plantation—often self-sufficient and nonmonetary in its internal relations but oriented externally toward European markets—reflected the dualism of the colonial economy.

Chapter 5

State, Church, and Society

The political organization of the Spanish Empire in America reflected the centralized, absolutist regime by which Spain itself was governed. By the time of the discovery and conquest of America, Castilian parliamentary institutions and municipal rights and exemptions had lost most of their former vitality. The process of centralization begun by the Catholic Sovereigns reached its climax under the first two Hapsburgs. In Castile there arose a ponderous administrative bureaucracy capped by a series of royal councils appointed by and directly responsible to the king. Aragon, which stubbornly resisted royal encroachments on its fueros (charters of liberties), retained a large measure of autonomy until the eighteenth century. Even in Castile, however, Hapsburg absolutism left largely intact the formal and informal power of the great lords over their peasantry. In Aragon, in whose soil feudal relations were more deeply rooted, the arrogant nobility claimed a broad seigneurial jurisdiction, including the right of life and death over its serfs, as late as the last decades of the seventeenth century. This contrast between the formal concentration of authority in the hands of royal officials and the actual exercise of supreme power on the local level by great landowners was to characterize the political structure of Spanish America as well.

Political Institutions of the Spanish Empire

Formation of Colonial Administration

The pattern of Spain's administration of its colonies was formed in the critical period between

1492 and 1550. The final result reflected the steady growth of centralized rule in Spain itself and the application of a trial-and-error method to the problems of colonial government. To Columbus, Cortés, Pizarro, and other great expeditionary leaders, the Spanish kings granted sweeping political powers that made these men almost sovereign in the territories they had won or proposed to subdue. But once the importance of these conquests was revealed, royal jealousy of the great conquistadors was quick to show itself. Their authority was soon revoked or strictly limited, and the institutions that had been employed in Spain to achieve centralized political control were transferred to America for the same end. By the mid-sixteenth century, the political organization of the Indies had assumed the definitive form it was to retain, with slight variations, until late in the eighteenth century.

The Council of the Indies, originally a standing committee of the all-powerful Council of Castile but chartered in 1524 as a separate agency, stood at the head of the Spanish imperial administration almost to the end of the colonial period. Although great nobles and court favorites were appointed to the council, especially in the seventeenth century, its membership consisted predominantly of lawyers. Under the king, whose active participation in its work varied from monarch to monarch, it was the supreme legislative, judicial, and executive institution of government. One of its most important functions was the nomination to the king of all high colonial officials. It also framed a vast body of legislation for the Indies—the famous Laws of the Indies (1681)—which combined decrees of the most important kind with others of a very trivial character. Although the council was frequently staffed by conscientious and highly capable officials in the early Hapsburg period, the quality of its personnel tended to decline under the inept princes of the seventeenth century. Nonetheless, historians owe the council a particular debt for its initiative in seeking to obtain detailed information on the history, geography, resources, and population of all the colonies. The *relaciones* (reports) that incorporated this information represent a rich mine of materials for students of colonial Spanish America.

The Royal Agents

The principal royal agents in the colonies were the viceroys, the captains general, and the audiencias. The viceroys and captains general had essentially the same functions, differing only in the greater importance and extent of the territory assigned to the jurisdiction of the former. Each was the supreme civil and military officer in his realm, having in his charge such vital matters as the maintenance and increase of the royal revenues, defense, Indian welfare, and a multitude of other responsibilities. At the end of the Hapsburg era, in 1700, there were two great American viceroyalties. The viceroyalty of New Spain, with its capital at Mexico City, included all the Spanish possessions north of the Isthmus of Panama; that of Peru, with its capital at Lima, embraced all of Spanish South America except for the coast of Venezuela. Captains general, theoretically subordinate to the viceroys but in practice virtually independent of them, governed large subdivisions of these vast territories. Other subdivisions, called *presidencias,* were governed by audiencias. Their judge-presidents acted as governors, but military authority was usually reserved to the viceroy. Overlapping and shifting of jurisdiction was common throughout the colonial period and formed the subject of frequent disputes among royal officials.

A colonial viceroy, regarded as the very image of his royal master, enjoyed an immense delegated authority, which was augmented by the distance that separated him from Spain and by the frequently spineless or venal nature of lesser officials. He might be a lawyer or even a priest by background but was most commonly a representative of one of the great noble and wealthy houses of Spain. A court modeled on that of Castile, a numerous retinue, and the constant display of pomp and circumstance bore witness to his exalted status. In theory, his freedom of action was limited by the laws and instructions issued by the Council of the Indies, but a sensible

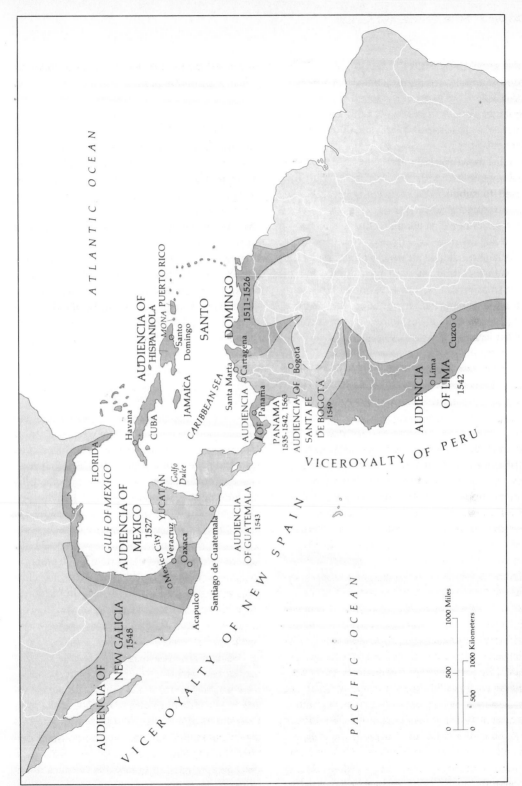

ATLANTIC OCEAN

AUDIENCIA OF HISPANIOLA

MONA PUERTO RICO

Santo Domingo

SANTO DOMINGO 1511–1526

Cuzco

JAMAICA

CARIBBEAN SEA

Cartagena

AUDIENCIA OF Bogotá

Lima

AUDIENCIA OF LIMA 1542

Havana

CUBA

Santa Marta

AUDIENCIA OF PANAMA

PANAMA 1535–1542, 1563

AUDIENCIA OF SANTA FE DE BOGOTA 1549

VICEROYALTY OF PERU

FLORIDA

GULF OF MEXICO

AUDIENCIA OF MEXICO 1527

YUCATAN

Golfo Dulce

Veracruz

Mexico City

Oaxaca

Santiago de Guatemala

AUDIENCIA OF GUATEMALA 1543

VICEROYALTY OF NEW SPAIN

AUDIENCIA OF NEW GALICIA 1548

Acapulco

PACIFIC OCEAN

| 0 | 500 | 1000 Miles |
| 0 | 500 | 1000 Kilometers |

VICEROYALTIES AND AUDIENCIAS IN SIXTEENTH-CENTURY SPANISH AMERICA recognition of the need to adapt the laws to existing circumstances gave him a vast discretionary power. The viceroy employed the formula *obedezco pero no cumplo*—"I obey but do not carry out"—to set aside unrealistic or unenforceable legislation.

The sixteenth century saw some able and even distinguished viceroys in the New World. The viceroy Francisco de Toledo (1569–1581), the "supreme organizer of Peru," was certainly an energetic, hardworking administrator who consolidated Spanish rule and imposed royal authority in Peru. His Indian resettlement program and his institution of *mita,* the system of forced Indian labor in the mines, however, profoundly disrupted Indian social organization and took a heavy toll of Indian lives. In New Spain, such capable officials as Antonio de Mendoza (1530–1550) and his successor, Luis de Velasco (1550–1564), wrestled with the problems left by the Conquest. They strove to curb the power of the conquistadors and to promote economic advance; sometimes they also tried, to a limited degree, to protect the interests of the Indians. But the predatory spirit of the colonists, royal distrust of excessive initiative on the part of high colonial officials, and opposition from other sectors of the official bureaucracy largely thwarted their efforts. In the seventeenth century, in an atmosphere of growing financial crisis, corruption, and cynicism at the Spanish court, the quality of the viceroys inevitably declined. In 1695, by way of illustration, the viceroyships of Peru and Mexico were. in effect, sold to the highest bidders.

Each viceroy or captain general was assisted in the performance of his duties by an audiencia, which was the highest court of appeal in its district and also served as the viceroy's council of state. The joint decisions of viceroy and audiencia, taken in administrative sessions, had the force of law, giving the audiencia a legislative character roughly comparable to that of the Council of the Indies in relation to the king. Although the viceroy had supreme executive and administrative power and was not legally obliged to heed the advice of the audiencia, its immense prestige and its right to correspond directly with the Council of the Indies made it a potential and actual check on the viceregal authority. The crown, ever distrustful of its colonial officers, thus developed a system of checks and balances that assured ample deliberation and consultation on all important questions but that also encouraged indecision and delay.

In addition to hearing appellate cases and holding consultative meetings with their viceroy or captain general, oidores were required to make regular tours of inspection of their respective provinces with the object of making a searching inquiry into economic and social conditions, treatment of the Indians, and other matters of interest to the crown. Although viceroys and oidores were well paid by colonial standards, the style of life their positions demanded was expensive, and the viceroy or oidor who did not take advantage of his office to enrich himself could expect to return to Spain poor.

Provincial Administration

Provincial administration in the Indies was entrusted to royal officials who governed districts of varying size and importance from their chief towns and who usually held the title of corregidor or alcalde mayor. Some were appointed by the viceroy (from whom they often bought their jobs), others by the crown. They possessed supreme judicial and political authority in their districts and represented the royal interest in the *cabildos* (town councils). Certain civil and criminal cases could be appealed from the municipal magistrates to the corregidor, and from him to the audiencia. If not trained as a lawyer, the corregidor was assisted by an *asesor* (legal counsel) in the trial of judicial cases.

Corregidores were of two kinds. Some presided over Spanish towns; others, *corregidores de indios,* administered Indian pueblos, or towns, which paid tribute to the crown. One of the principal duties of the corregidor de indios, who was usually appointed for three years, was to protect the natives from fraudulent or extortionate practices on the part of the whites, but there is ample testimony that the corregidor was himself the worst offender in this respect. Indian *caciques* (chiefs) often were his accomplices in these ex-

COREGIDORDEMINAS
COMOLOCASTIGACRV

Scenes showing mistreatment of Indians by a corregidor, from *La Nueva Crónica* (*The New Chronicle*) of the seventeenth-century Indian noble Felipe Waman Puma de Ayala, illustrated by the author.

tortions. Perhaps the worst abuses of his authority arose in connection with the practice of repartimiento or repartimiento de mercancías, the mandatory purchase of goods from the corregidor by the Indians of his district. Ostensibly designed to protect the Indians from the frauds or wiles of private Spanish traders, the corregidor's exclusive right to trade with the Indians became an instrument for his own speedy enrichment at the expense of the natives.

The crown employed an arsenal of regulations to insure good and honest performance on the part of public officials. Viceroys and oidores were forbidden to engage in trade or hold land within their jurisdictions or to accept gifts or fees; even their social life was hedged about with many restrictions. All royal officials, from the viceroy down, faced a *residencia* (judicial review) of their conduct at the end of their term of office. This took the form of a public hearing at which all who chose could appear before the judge of residence to present charges or testify for or against the official in question. At the end of the process, the judge found the official guilty or innocent of part or all of the charges and handed down a sentence that could be appealed to the Council of the Indies. Another device, the visita, was an investigation of official conduct, usually made unannounced by a *visitador* specially appointed for this purpose by the crown or, in the case of lesser officials, by the viceroy in consultation with the audiencia. As a rule, the visita was no more effective than the residencia in preventing or punishing official misdeeds.

The only political institution in the Indies that satisfied to some degree local aspirations for self-rule was the town council, known as the cabildo or *ayuntamiento*. Any suggestion, however, that the cabildo had some kind of democratic character has no basis in fact. At an early date, the crown assumed the right to appoint the regidores and alcaldes. Under Philip II and his successors, it became the established practice for the king to sell these posts to the highest bidder, with a right of resale or bequest, on condition that a certain portion of the value be paid to the crown as a tax at each transfer. In some towns, however, cabildo members elected their successors.

Throughout the colonial period, the municipal councils were closed, self-perpetuating oligarchies of rich landowners, mine owners, and merchants, who "ran the council as an exclusive club." These men frequently received no salaries for their duties and used their positions to distribute municipal lands to themselves, assign themselves Indian labor, and in general serve the narrow interests of their class. Their official tasks included supervision of local markets, distribution of town lands, and local taxation. They also elected the alcaldes, who administered justice as courts of first instance. Vigilantly supervised by the provincial governor, or corregidor, who frequently intervened in its affairs, the cabildo soon lost such autonomy as it may have possessed in the early days. Yet, despite its undemocratic character, inefficiency, and waning prestige and

104

autonomy, the cabildo was not without potential significance. As the only political institution in which the creoles (American-born Spaniards) were largely represented, it was destined to play an important part in the coming of the nineteenth-century wars of independence.

The officials and agencies just described represented only a small part of the apparatus of colonial government. A large number of secretaries (*escribanos*) attended to the paperwork of the various departments. As a rule, they collected no salaries but were reimbursed by fees for their services. There was a multitude of police officers, collectors of the royal fifth, alcaldes with special jurisdiction, and the like. Under Charles V control of such offices often lay in the hands of high Spanish officials, who sold them to persons who proposed to go to the Indies to exploit their fee-earning possibilities. Beginning with Philip II, many of these offices were withdrawn from private patronage and sold directly by the crown, usually to the highest bidder. In the second half of the seventeenth century, the sale of offices by the crown or the viceroy spread from fee-earning positions to higher, salaried posts. As a rule, the beneficiaries of such transactions sought to return to Spain rich, having made the highest possible profit on their investment. Consequently, corruption in this period became structural in government. Colonial officials, high and low, abused their trusts in innumerable and ingenious ways.

If the royal authority was more or less supreme in the capitals and the surrounding countryside, the same was not true of more distant and isolated regions. In such areas, the royal authority was very remote, and the power of the great landowners was virtually absolute. On their large, self-sufficient estates, they dispensed justice in the manner of feudal lords, holding court and imprisoning peons in their own jails; they raised and maintained their own private armies; and they generally acted as monarchs of all they surveyed. Sometimes these powerful individuals combined their de facto military and judicial power with an official title, which made them representatives of the crown in their vicinities. Spain's growing economic and political weakness

in the late seventeenth century, which loosened the ties between the mother country and her colonies, favored this decentralization of power. The contrast between the nominal concentration of power in the central government and the effective supremacy of great landowners on the local level was one of the legacies of the colonial period to independent Latin America; to this day it remains a characteristic of the political life of many Latin American republics.

Ineffectiveness of Much Spanish Colonial Law

The frequent nonobservance of Spanish colonial law was a fact of colonial political life. In considerable part, this situation reflected the dilemma of royal officials faced with the task of enforcing laws bitterly opposed by powerful colonial elites with whom they generally had close social and economic ties. This dilemma found its most acute expression in the clash between the crown's protective Indian legislation, which reflected its awareness that the conservation of the Indians—the real wealth of the Indies—was clearly in the royal interest, and the drive of colonial elites for maximum profits. The result was that the protective Indian laws were systematically flouted. The crown often closed its eyes to the violations, not only because it wished to avoid confrontation with powerful colonial elites but because those laws sometimes collided with the crown's own narrow, short-range interests (its need for revenue to finance wars and diplomacy and to support a parasitic nobility).

Hence the contradiction between that protective legislation, so often cited by defenders of Spain's work in America, and the reality of Indian life and labor in the colonies. In a report to Philip II, Alonso de Zorita, a judge who retired to an honorable poverty in 1566 after nineteen years of administrative activity in the Indies, wrote:

The wishes of Your Majesty and his Royal Council are well known and are made very plain in the laws that are issued every day in favor of the poor Indians and for their increase and preservation. But these laws are obeyed and not enforced, wherefore there is no end to the destruction of the

Indians, nor does anyone care what Your Majesty decrees.

But not all colonial legislation was so laxly enforced. There was a considerable body of exploitative or discriminatory Indian laws that was in general vigorously enforced, including laws requiring the Indians to pay tribute and perform forced labor for token wages, permitting the forced sale of goods to them at fixed prices, and limiting Indian landownership to a low maximum figure while allowing the indefinite growth of Spanish estates.

How can the longevity of Spanish rule over its American colonies, so distant from a European country that grew steadily weaker in the course of the seventeenth century, be explained? The answer does not lie in Spain's military power since Spain maintained few troops in the Indies until the eighteenth century. Much of the durability of Spanish rule seems to lie in a royal policy of making the large concessions needed to gain and maintain the loyalty of colonial elites. The political apparatus of viceroys, audiencias, corregidores, and the like played a decisive role in implementing this royal program. The frequent failure to enforce Indian protective legislation, the strict enforcement of the exploitative laws, the composiciones (settlements that legalized usurpation of Indian lands through payment of a fee to the king), and the toleration of great abuses by colonial oligarchs are illustrations of the policy. To be sure, alongside this unwritten pact between the crown and the colonial elite for sharing power and the fruits of exploitation of the Indian, black, and mixed-blood people in the Indies went a royal effort to restrain the colonists' power and ambitions. Until the eighteenth century, however, this effort did not go far enough to threaten the existing arrangements.

The Church in the Indies

The Spanish church emerged from the long centuries of struggle against the Muslims with immense wealth and an authority second only to that of the crown. The Catholic Sovereigns, Ferdinand and Isabella, particularly favored the clergy and the spread of its influence as a means of achieving national unity and royal absolutism. The Spanish Inquisition, which they founded, had political as well as religious uses, and under their great-grandson, Philip II, it became the strongest support of an omnipotent crown. While the Spanish towns sank into political and then into economic decadence, and the great nobles were reduced to the position of a courtier class aspiring for favors from the crown, the church steadily gained in wealth and influence. Under the last Hapsburgs, it threatened the supremacy of its royal master. It remained for the enlightened Bourbon kings of the eighteenth century to curb in some measure the excessive power of the church.

Royal control over ecclesiastical affairs, both in Spain and the Indies, was solidly founded on the institution of the *patronato real* (royal patronage). As applied to the colonies, this consisted of the absolute right of the Spanish kings to nominate all church officials, collect tithes, and found churches and monasteries in America. Under diplomatic pressure from King Ferdinand, Pope Julius II had accorded this extraordinary privilege to Spain's rulers in 1508, ostensibly to assist in converting New World heathen. The Spanish monarchs regarded the patronato as their most cherished privilege and reacted sharply to all encroachments on it.

The Spiritual Conquest of America

Beginning with Columbus's second voyage, one or more clergymen accompanied every expedition that sailed for the Indies, and they came in swelling numbers to the conquered territories. The friars formed the spearhead of the second religious invasion that followed on the heels of the Conquest. The friars who came to America in the first decades after the Conquest were, on the whole, an elite group. They were products of one of the periodic revivals of asceticism and discipline in the medieval church, especially of the reform of the orders instituted in Spain by the Catholic Sovereigns and carried out with

106 implacable energy by Cardinal Cisneros. This vanguard group of clergy frequently combined with missionary zeal a sensitive social conscience and a love of learning. The missionaries were frequently impressed by the admirable qualities of the Indians, by their simplicity and freedom from the greed and ambitions of Europeans, by the plasticity of the Indian character. Wrote Vasco de Quiroga, royal judge and later bishop of the province of Michoacán in Mexico:

Anything may be done with these people, they are most docile, and, proceeding with due diligence, may easily be taught Christian doctrine. They possess innately the instincts of humility and obedience, and the Christian impulses of poverty, nakedness, and contempt for the things of this world, going barefoot and bareheaded with the hair long like apostles; in fine, with very tractable minds void of error and ready for impression.

Millenarian[1] and utopian ideals strongly influenced many members of the reformed clergy who came to the Indies in the first decades after the Conquest. Inspired by the vision of a multitude of Indian souls waiting to be saved, they dreamed of a fruitful fusion of Indian and Spanish cultures under the sign of a Christianity returned to its original purity. Such men as Juan de Zumárraga, first bishop and archbishop of Mexico, Vasco de Quiroga, and Bartolomé de Las Casas were profoundly influenced by the humanist, reformist ideas of Erasmus and by Thomas More's *Utopia.* Indeed, Quiroga proposed to the Spanish crown that Indian cities be established and organized on the lines of More's ideal commonwealth, in which the Indians' natural virtues would be preserved and perfected by training in the Christian religion and culture. When the crown ignored his proposals, Quiroga used his own resources to found the pueblos or refuges of Santa Fe in Michoacán. In these communities Quiroga established collec-

tive ownership of property, systematic alternation between agricultural and craft labor, the six-hour working day, work for women, the distribution of the fruits of collective labor according to need, and the shunning of luxuries and of all occupations that were not useful. Quiroga's dream of establishing islands of charity and cooperative life in a sea of exploitive encomiendas and haciendas was doomed to eventual failure, but to this day the Indians of Michoacán revere the name and memory of "Tata Vasco."

The pro-Indian attitudes of the reformist clergy inevitably placed them on a collision course with the encomenderos and other lay Spaniards who sought the unchecked exploitation of the Indians and commonly described the natives as "dogs" (*perros*). To be sure, not all the religious saw eye to eye on the issue of Indian policy. Some, like the famous Franciscan Toribio de Benavente (better known by his Indian name of Motolinía), may be called "realists" or "moderates." These clergy believed that the encomienda, carefully regulated to safeguard Indian welfare, was necessary for the prosperity and security of the Indies. Others, mostly Dominicans whose leader and spokesman was Bartolomé de Las Casas, believed that the encomienda was incompatible with Indian welfare and must be put in the way of extinction.

As we have seen, during the reign of Charles V—who feared the rise of a colonial feudalism based on the encomienda—the Lascasian wing of the clergy won certain victories, capped by the passage of the New Laws of the Indies (1542). By their militant efforts to secure the enforcement of these laws, Las Casas and his disciples incurred the mortal enmity of the encomenderos. Las Casas was repeatedly threatened. The Dominican bishop Antonio de Valdivieso of Nicaragua, who had tried to enforce the abolition of Indian slavery by the New Laws, was assassinated in 1550 by a group of men led by the governor's son. These and other courageous defenders of the Indian, like Bishop Juan del Valle in Colombia and Fray Domingo de Santo Tomás in Peru, may be regarded as forerunners of today's progressive current in the Catholic church. The ideology of

[1] Millenarianism is the medieval doctrine, based on a prophecy in the Book of Revelation and widely held by the reformed clergy, that Christ would return to earth to reign for a thousand years of peace and righteousness, to be followed by the Last Judgment at the end of the world.

Bartolomé de Las Casas condemned the racist attitudes of the conquistadors and defended Indian culture against the scorn of Europeans. His teachings emphasized the dignity of all people.

Las Casas, with its demand that the Spaniards "cease to be *caballeros* by grace of the blood and sweat of the wretched and oppressed," seems to anticipate today's Latin American liberation theology and its "preferential option for the poor."

Despite the partial victories won by Las Casas during the reign of Charles V, the Indianist movement entered on a decline when Philip II took the throne in 1556. Denial of absolution to Spaniards who had violated the laws protecting Indians—an important weapon employed by Las Casas and other pro-Indian clergy—was forbidden by various royal decrees. The church was instructed to concern itself only with questions of worship and preaching, leaving problems in the economic and social relations between Spaniards and Indians to the civil authorities. Since those authorities as a rule were ready to comply with the wishes of encomenderos, great landowners, and other ruling class groups, the descendants of the conquistadors finally obtained the direct, unchallenged dominion over the Indian for which their forebears had struggled. The encomienda (although in decline), the repartimiento or mita, and even slavery (legalized on various pretexts) remained the basic institutions in Spanish-Indian relations. The new anti-Indian political climate was marked by a growing belief in Indian constitutional inferiority, based on the Aristotelian theory of natural slavery, a theory that Las Casas and virtually all other Spanish theologians had previously condemned.

The first missionaries in the Indies did not regard their defense of the Indians against enslavement and exploitation as separate from their primary task of conversion; they reasoned that for conversion to be effective the natives must survive the shock of Conquest, multiply, and live better under the new religion than the old one. Despite the clandestine opposition of surviving pagan priests and some native nobility, the friars converted prodigious numbers of natives, who, willingly or unwillingly, accepted the new and more powerful divinities of the invaders. In Mexico, the Franciscans claimed to have converted more than a million Indians by 1531; the energetic Motolinía asserted that he had converted more than fifteen hundred in one day! Where persuasion failed, pressures of various kinds, including force, were used to obtain conversions. Natives who had been baptized and relapsed into idolatry were charged with heresy and punished, some nobles being hanged or burned at the stake. In order to facilitate the missionary effort, the friars studied the native languages and wrote grammars and vocabularies that are still of value to scholars.

The religious, especially the Franciscans, also assigned a special importance to the establishment of schools in which Indian upper-class youth might receive instruction in the humanities, including Latin, logic, and philosophy, as well as Christian doctrine. The most notable of these centers was the Franciscan Colegio de Santa Cruz in Mexico. Before it entered on a decline in the 1560s as a result of lay hostility or disinterest and the waning fervor of the friars themselves, the school had produced a harvest

The Spanish friars adapted the Aztec system of pictographic writing to make the meaning of the Christian religion clear to the Indians. The bird stands for the Holy Ghost, the figure on the cross for Christ.

of graduates who often combined enthusiasm for European culture with admiration for their own pagan past. These men were invaluable to the missionaries in their effort to reconstruct the history, religion, and social institutions of the ancient Indian civilizations.

Although some of the early friars undertook to destroy all relics of the pagan past—idols, temples, picture writings—the second generation of missionaries became convinced that paganism could not be successfully combated without a thorough study and understanding of the old pre-Conquest Indian way of life. In Mexico there arose a genuine school of ethnography devoted to making an inventory of the rich content of Indian culture. If the primary and avowed motive of this effort was to arm the missionary with the knowledge he needed to discover the concealed presence of pagan rites and practices, intellectual curiosity and delight in the discovery of the material, artistic, and social achievements of the vanished Indian empires also played a part.

The work of conversion, by the subsequent admission of the missionaries themselves, was less than wholly successful. In Mexico, concludes historian Louise M. Burkhart, the Aztecs "were able to become just Christian enough to get by in the colonial social and political setting without compromising their basic ideological and moral orientation." Here the result of the missionary effort was generally a fusion in Indian minds of old and new religious ideas, in which the cult of the Virgin Mary sometimes merged with the worship of pagan divinities. Writing half a century after the conquest of Mexico, the Dominican Diego Durán saw a persistence of paganism in every aspect of Indian life, "in their dances, in their markets, in their baths, in the songs which mourn the loss of their ancient gods." In the same period, the great scholar-missionary Sahagún complained that the Indians continued to celebrate their ancient festivals, in which they sang songs and danced dances with concealed pagan meanings. In Peru the work of conversion was even less successful. "If the Indians admitted the existence of a Christian god," writes Nathan Wachtel, "they considered his influence to be limited to the Spanish world, and looked themselves for protection to their own gods." To this day, Indians in lands like Guatemala and Peru perform ceremonies from the Maya and Inca period.

The friars had to battle not only the Indian tendency toward backsliding but divisions within their own camp. Violent disputes arose among the orders over the degree of prebaptismal instruction required by Indian converts, with the Dominicans and Augustinians demanding stiffer standards than the Franciscans. Other disputes arose as to which order should have jurisdiction over a particular area or pueblo. A more serious conflict arose between the secular and the regular clergy. The pastoral and sacramental duties performed by the regular clergy in America were normally entrusted only to parish priests. Special papal legislation (1522) had been required to grant these functions to the regulars, a concession made necessary by the small number of seculars who came to the Indies in the early years. But after mid-century their number increased, and the bishops increasingly sought to create new parishes manned by seculars. These seculars were intended to replace the regulars in the spiritual direction of Indian converts. The friars resisted by every means at their disposal, but they fought a losing battle. The secular clergy had various advantages in their favor. One was a ruling of the Council of Trent that only clergy under episcopal authority could have parochial jurisdiction. Another was the preference accorded to the episcopal hierarchy by Philip II, who disliked the excessive independence of spirit shown by members of the orders in disputes over Indian policy and other matters.

In 1574 the seculars gained a decisive victory through the issuance of a royal edict giving each bishop virtual control over the number of friars in his diocese and their assignment to parishes. A subsequent decree (1583) stated the principle that secular clergy were to be preferred over friars in all appointments to parishes. But these rulings did not settle this and related questions; from first to last the colonies were a scene of unedifying strife among the clergy over their fields of jurisdiction.

Another source of division within the church was rivalry between American-born and peninsular clergy for control of the higher positions, especially in the orders. Threatened with loss of those positions in provincial elections by the growing creole majority in the seventeenth century, the peninsulars sought and obtained decrees making mandatory alternation of offices between themselves and creoles.

The Moral Decline of the Clergy and the Missionary Impulse

To the factors contributing to the decline of the intellectual and spiritual influence of the orders one must add the gradual loss of a sense of mission and of morale among the regular clergy. Apostolic fervor inevitably declined as the work of conversion in the central areas of the empire approached completion; many of the later arrivals among the clergy preferred a life of ease and profit to one of austerity and service. By the last decades of the sixteenth century, there were frequent complaints against the excessive number

of monasteries and their wealth. The principal sources of this wealth were legacies and other gifts from rich donors—for a rich man not to provide for the church in his will was a matter of scandal. A common procedure used to endow churches, convents, or other religious institutions was to assume a mortgage (*censo*) on the landowner's estate for a fixed amount on which he or she agreed to pay the beneficiary an annual interest of 5 percent. This method of expressing piety was so widely used that in New Spain "at the end of the eighteenth century it was said that there was no hacienda which was not burdened with one or more censos." Another procedure, which served both the donor's piety and family interest, consisted in establishing a chantry to celebrate in perpetuity memorial masses for his or her soul. By designating a family member as chaplain, the donor ensured that control of the income from the endowment would remain in the family. These procedures, continually draining money from the income of estates, writes Mexican historian Enrique Florescano, "helped to destabilize the already precarious haciendas and ranches . . . leaving the religious institutions, in effect, as the real landowners and beneficiaries of rural income."

The resources the church acquired became inalienable in the form of mortmain, or perpetual ownership. When invested in land and mortgages, this wealth brought in more wealth. The enormous economic power of the church gave it a marked advantage over competitors and enabled it to take advantage of weaker lay property owners, especially in time of recession. The last important order to arrive in Spanish America, the Society of Jesus (1572), was also the most fortunate in the number of rich benefactors and the most efficient in running its numerous enterprises, which, it should be said in its favor, were largely used to support its excellent system of *colegios* (secondary schools) and its missions.

Inevitably, this concern with the accumulation of material wealth weakened the ties between the clergy and the humble Indian and mixed-blood masses whose spiritual life they were supposed to direct. As early as the 1570s, there were many complaints of excessive ecclesiastical fees and

110

clerical exploitation of Indian labor. A viceroy of New Spain, the Marqués de Monteclaros, assured King Philip III in 1607 that the Indians suffered the heaviest oppression at the hands of the friars and that one Indian paid more tribute to his parish priest than twenty paid to His Majesty. Hand in hand with a growing materialism went an increasing laxity of morals. Concubinage became so common among the clergy of the later colonial period that it seems to have attracted little official notice or rebuke. By the last decades of the colonial period, the morals of the clergy had declined to a condition that the Mexican historian Lucas Alamán, himself a leader of the clerical party in the period of independence, could only describe as scandalous. From this charge one must in general exclude the Jesuits, noted for their high moral standards and strict discipline; and of course men of excellent character and social conscience were to be found among both the secular and regular clergy.

The missionary impulse of the first friars survived longest on the frontier, "the rim of Christendom." Franciscans first penetrated the great northern interior of New Spain, peopled by hostile Chichimecs, "wild Indians." Franciscans accompanied the Oñate expedition of 1598 into New Mexico and dominated the mission field there until the end of the colonial period; they were also found in such distant outposts of Spanish power as Florida and Georgia. After the expulsion of the Jesuits from the Indies in 1767, the Franciscans took their place directing missionary work among the Indians of California. In addition to their pioneering efforts in California, the early Jesuits were active in the conversion and pacification of the Chichimecs of the north central plateau of Mexico and had exclusive charge of the conversion of the Indian tribes of the northwest coast of Mexico.

The mission was one of three closely linked institutions—the other two being the *presidio* (garrison) and the civil settlement—designed to serve the ends of Spanish imperial expansion and defense on the northern frontier. The mission, it was hoped, would gather the Indian converts into self-contained religious communities, train them

to till the land, herd cattle, and practice various crafts until they became fully Christianized and Hispanicized. The presidios would provide military protection for the neighboring missions and insure a cooperative attitude on the part of the Indian novices. Finally, attracted by the lure of free land, Spaniards of modest means would throng into the area, forming civil settlements that would become bustling centers of life and trade. By all these means, the frontier would be pushed back, pacified, and maintained against foreign encroachment.

This three-pronged attack on the wilderness was not very successful. Romantic literature has created a myth of an idyllic mission society in the American Southwest that does not correspond to reality. Certain tribes on the northern frontier, such as the powerful Apaches of Arizona, New Mexico, and Texas and the Comanches of Texas, never were reduced to mission life. The missionaries had greater success among such sedentary tribes as the Pueblo Indians of New Mexico, the Pima and Opata of Sonora in northwest Mexico, and the Hasinai of east Texas. Even among these peaceful tribes, however, Indian revolts and desertions were frequent. In 1680 the supposedly Christianized Pueblo Indians of New Mexico revolted, slaughtered the friars, and maintained a long, tenacious resistance against Spanish efforts at reconquest. The rise of native leaders who proclaimed that the old gods and way of life were best often sparked wholesale desertions. Mistreatment by soldiers in nearby presidios and the terror inspired by Apache and Comanche raiding parties also provoked frequent flight by mission Indians.

The authoritarian paternalism of the fathers, enforced by the use of stocks, prisons, and whipping posts, produced cultural change in the desired directions, but at the cost of reduced vitality on the part of the Indians affected. One indication of the maiming effect of mission life was the reduced birthrate among the neophytes. Spanish census records show that the mission Indian birthrate in 1783 in Texas was far below that among the Spanish inhabitants of the province. This and desertions made necessary constant recruitment of converts, but the presence of hovering Apache and Comanche bands, mounted on swift horses introduced by the Spaniards, made this hazardous. An indication of the failure of the mission enterprise was the unwillingness of the Spanish government in the late eighteenth century to finance the search for converts.

The civil settlements proved no more successful. By the end of the colonial period, there were only a few scattered towns on the northern frontier, and the continuous raids made life and property so insecure that in New Mexico settlers who petitioned for permission to leave outnumbered recruits coming to the area. Ultimately, the whole task of defending and civilizing the future American Southwest fell on a chain of presidios stretching approximately along the present border between the United States and Mexico. Successive reverses in the open field compelled the Spanish troops to take refuge behind the security of the high presidio walls. In the end Spain was forced to adopt a policy of neutralizing the Apaches and Comanches by periodic distribution of gifts to these warlike tribes. When the outbreak of the wars of independence stopped the flow of gifts, the hostile Indians again took to the warpath, driving by the useless line of presidios into the interior of Mexico.

The most notable instance of successful missionary effort, at least from an economic point of view, was that of the Jesuit establishments in Paraguay, where, favored by a genial climate and fertile soil, the Jesuits established more than thirty missions; these formed the principal field of Jesuit activity in America. Strict discipline, centralized organization, and absolute control over the labor of thousands of docile Indians producing large surpluses enabled the Jesuits to turn their missions into a highly profitable business enterprise. Great quantities of such goods as cotton, tobacco, and hides were shipped down the Paraná River to Buenos Aires for export to Europe. Rather than "Christian socialism," the Jesuit mission system could more correctly be described as "theocratic capitalism."

To protect the missions against slave raiders from the Portuguese colony of São Paulo, the fathers created a native militia armed with European weapons. Every effort was made to limit contact with the outside world. The life of the Indians was rigidly regimented in dress, housing, and the routines of work, play, and rest. The self-imposed isolation of the Jesuit mission empire aroused the curiosity of eighteenth-century European philosophers and literati; Voltaire gave an ironic and fanciful description of it in his witty satire *Candide*.

Jesuit rule in Paraguay and Jesuit mission activity everywhere in the colonies ended when a royal decree expelled the order from the colonies in 1767. Among the motives for this action were the conflict between the nationalistic church policy of the Bourbons and Jesuit emphasis on papal supremacy, suspicions of Jesuit meddling in state affairs generally, and the belief that the Jesuit mission system constituted a state within a state. The expulsion of the Jesuits from Paraguay resulted in intensified exploitation of the Indians by Spanish officials and landowners and in a shedding by the Indians of much of the thin veneer of European culture imposed on them by the missionaries. Within a generation the previously thriving Jesuit villages were in ruins.

The Inquisition in the New World

The Inquisition formally entered the Indies with the establishment by Philip II of tribunals of the Holy Office in Mexico and Lima in 1569. Prior to that time, its functions were performed by clergy who were vested with or assumed inquisitorial powers. Its great privileges, its independence of other courts, and the dread with which the charge of heresy was generally regarded by Spaniards made the Inquisition an effective check on "dangerous thoughts," whether religious, political, or philosophical. The great mass of cases tried by its tribunals, however, had to do with offenses against morality or minor deviations from orthodox religious conduct, such as blasphemy.

Spain's rulers, beginning with Queen Isabella, forbade Jews, Muslims, conversos (New Christians), and persons penanced by the Inquisition from going to the Indies. Many conversos, however, hoping to improve their fortunes and escape the climate of suspicion and hostility that surrounded them in Spain, managed to settle in the Indies, coming as seamen, as servants of licensed passengers, or sometimes even with licenses purchased from the crown. Some attained positions of wealth and authority. Toward the end of the sixteenth century, many conversos settled in New Spain and Peru. Many came from Portugal, where there was a strong revival of Inquisitorial activity following the country's annexation by Spain (1580). One who came to New Spain was Luis de Carvajal, who rose to be captain general and governor of the northern kingdom of New León, which he discovered. Carvajal was a sincere Catholic, but his son and other relatives were fervent practicing Jews, mystics who urged other members of the large converso community of New Spain to return to Judaism. They were denounced to the Inquisition, which tried and condemned them to death as relapsed heretics. The sentences were carried out at a great auto-da-fé (public sentencing) in Mexico City in 1595. In 1635 the Lima Inquisition struck at the converso community of the city. Some were sent to the stake; all suffered confiscation of goods. It suggests the wealth of the Lima conversos, mostly rich merchants, that the Lima office of the Inquisition, having confiscated their property, "emerged as the wealthiest in the world."

As in Spain, the Inquisition in the Indies relied largely on denunciations by informers and employed torture to secure confessions. As in Spain, the damage done by the Inquisition was not limited to the snuffing out of lives and the confiscation of property but included the creation of an atmosphere of fear, distrust, and rigid intellectual conformity. The great poetess Sor Juana Inés de la Cruz alludes to this repressive atmosphere when she mentions her difficulties with "a very saintly and guileless prelate who believed that study was a matter for the Inquisition." Indians, originally subject to the jurisdiction of inquisitors, were later removed from their control as recent converts of limited mental capacity and hence not fully responsible for their deviations from the Faith, but were subject to trial and punishment by an episcopal inquisition.

The Structure of Class and Caste

The social order that arose in the Indies on the ruins of the old Indian societies was based, like that of Spain, on aristocratic or feudal principles. Race, occupation, and religion were the formal criteria that determined an individual's social status. All mechanical labor was regarded as degrading, but large-scale trade (as opposed to retail trade) was compatible with nobility, at least in the Indies. Great emphasis was placed on *limpieza de sangre* (purity of blood), meaning above all descent from "Old Christians," without mixture of converso or Morisco (Muslim) blood. Proofs of such descent were jealously guarded and sometimes manufactured.

The various races and racial mixtures were carefully distinguished and graded in a kind of hierarchy of rank. A trace of black blood legally sufficed to deprive an individual of the right to hold public office or enter the professions, as well as depriving him of the other rights and privileges of white men. The same taint attached to the great mass of mestizos (mixtures of Indians and Spaniards). True, the Laws of the Indies assigned perfect legal equality with whites to mestizos of legitimate birth, but to the very end of the colonial period the charters of certain colonial guilds and schools excluded all mestizos, without distinction.

The lack of solid demographic information and major disagreements among historians regarding the size of pre-Conquest populations make estimates of Spanish America's population in 1650, and of the relative numerical strength of the racial groups composing that population, conjectural. It appears, however, that by that date, or even earlier, the long decline of the Indian population had ended and a slow recovery had begun. It also appears that the European element in the population was growing more rapidly than the Indian. But the groups growing most rapidly were the *castas*, the mixtures resulting from the union of whites and Indians (mestizos) and of whites and blacks (mulattos). The great majority of these mixed-bloods were born out of wedlock.

As noted above, Spanish law and opinion ranked all these racial groups in a descending order of worth and privilege, with Europeans on top and Indians, blacks, and mixtures assigned to lower levels in the social pyramid. This formal ranking did not necessarily correspond to the actual standing of individuals of different racial makeup in society, but it provided the colonial ruling groups with an ideological justification for their rule. It also created a conflict society par excellence, pitting Indians against blacks, caste against caste, inflating poor whites with a sense of their superiority over all colored groups, which hindered forging the unity of the exploited masses and thus served to maintain an oppressive social order.

The White Ruling Class

In practice, racial lines were not very strictly drawn. In the Indies, a white skin was a symbol of social superiority, roughly the equivalent of *hidalguía,* a title of nobility in Spain, but it had no cash value. Not all whites belonged to the privileged economic group. Colonial records testify to the existence of a large class of "poor whites"—vagabonds, beggars, or worse—who disdained work and frequently preyed on the Indians. A Spaniard of this group, compelled by poverty to choose his mate from the colored races, generally doomed his descendants to an inferior economic and social status. But the mestizo or mulatto son of a wealthy Spanish landowner or merchant, if acknowledged and made his legal heir, could pass into the colonial aristocracy. If traces of Indian or black descent were too strong, the father might reach an understanding with the parish priest, who had charge of baptismal certificates; it was also possible for a wealthy mestizo or mulatto to purchase from the crown a document establishing his legal whiteness. Wealth, not gentle birth or racial purity, was the distinguishing characteristic of the colonial aristocracy. Granted this fact, it remains true that the apex of the colonial pyramid was composed overwhelmingly of whites.

This white ruling class was itself divided by group jealousies and hostilities. The Spaniards brought to the New World their regional rivalries and feuds—between Old Castilians and Andalusians, between Castilians and Basques—and in the anarchic, heated atmosphere of the Indies these rivalries often exploded into brawls or even pitched battles. But the most abiding cleavage within the upper class was the division between the Spaniards born in the colonies, called creoles, and the European-born Spaniards, called peninsulars or referred to by such disparaging nicknames as *gachupín* or *chapetón* (tenderfoot). Legally, creoles and peninsulars were equal; indeed Spanish law called for preference to be given in the filling of offices to the descendants of conquistadors and early settlers. In practice, the creoles suffered from a system of discrimination that during most of the colonial period virtually denied them employment in high church and government posts and large-scale commerce. The preference shown for peninsulars over natives sprang from various causes, among them the greater access of Spaniards to the court, the fountainhead of all favors, and royal distrust of the creoles. By the second half of the sixteenth century, the sons or grandsons of conquistadors were complaining of the partiality of the crown and its officials for unworthy newcomers from Spain. The creoles viewed with envenomed spite these Johnny-come-latelies, who often won out in the scramble for *corregimientos* and other government jobs. A Mexican poet, Francisco de Terrazas, expressed the creole complaint in rhyme:

Spain: to us a harsh stepmother you have been,
A mild and loving mother to the stranger,
On him you lavish all your treasures dear,
With us you only share your cares and danger.[2]

The resulting cleavage in the colonial upper class grew wider with the passage of time. Both groups developed an arsenal of arguments to defend their positions. Peninsulars often justified their privileged status by reference to the alleged indolence, incapacity, and frivolity of the creoles,

[2] Francisco de Terrazas, *Poesías,* ed. Antonio Castro Leal (Mexico, 1941), p. 87. From *The Aztec Image in Western Thought* by Benjamin Keen, p. 90. Copyright © 1971 by Rutgers University, the State University of New Jersey. Reprinted by permission of Rutgers University Press.

which they sometimes solemnly attributed to the American climate or other environmental conditions. The creoles responded in kind by describing the Europeans as mean and grasping parvenus. The growing wealth of the creoles from mines, plantations, and cattle ranches only sharpened their resentment at the discrimination from which they suffered. The split within the colonial upper class must be regarded as a major cause of the creole wars of independence.

The Mestizo: An Ambiguous Status

The mestizo arose from a process of racial mixture that began in the first days of the Conquest. In the post-Conquest period, when white women were scarce, the crown and the church viewed Indian-white marriages with some favor; mixed marriages were not uncommon in those years. But this attitude soon changed as the crown, for its own reasons, adopted a policy of systematic segregation of the Indians from the white community. By the first quarter of the seventeenth century, the authoritative writer on Spain's colonial legislation, Juan Solórzano Pereira, could write: "Few Spaniards of honorable position will marry Indian or Negro women." Consequently, the great mass of mestizos had their origin in irregular unions between Spaniards and Indian women. The stigma of illegitimacy, unredeemed by wealth, doomed the majority to the social depths. Some became peons, resembling the Indian in their way of life; others swelled the numerous class of vagabonds; still others enrolled in the colonial militia. Mestizos also contributed to the formation of the rancheros (small farmers) and formed part of the lower middle class of artisans, overseers, and shopkeepers. Without roots in either Indian or Spanish society, scorned and distrusted by both, small wonder that the lower-class mestizo acquired a reputation for violence and instability.

The Indians: A Separate Nation

By contrast with the mestizo, no ambiguity marked the position of the Indian in Spanish law and practice. The Indians constituted a separate nation, the *república de indios*, which also con-stituted a hereditary tribute-paying caste. The descendants of the Indian rulers and hereditary nobility, however, received special consideration, partly from Spanish respect for the concept of *señor natural* (the natural or legitimate lord), partly because they played a useful role as intermediaries between the Spanish rulers and Indian tribute payers. The Indian nobles were allowed to retain all or part of their patrimonial estates and enjoyed such special privileges as the right to ride horses, wear European dress, and carry arms.

There is ample evidence that members of the Indian aristocracy were among the worst exploiters of their own race. Their role as collectors of Indian tribute for the Spaniards offered large opportunities for enrichment at the expense of the commoners. They also usurped communal lands, imposed excessive rents on their Indian tenants, and forced the commoners to labor for them. In part, as Charles Gibson points out, these inordinate demands represented a "response to strain, an effort to maintain position and security" in the face of Spanish encroachments on the lands and prerequisites of the native nobility.

By the end of the sixteenth century, the Indian aristocracy was in full decline. One cause of this decline was Spanish invasion of their lands, to which the Indian nobles responded with costly but often futile litigation. Another cause of their downfall was their responsibility for the collection of tribute from the commoners. When the number of tribute payers in a town declined because of an epidemic or other circumstances, the Indian governor had to make up the arrears on the town's fixed quota or go to jail. In order to make good the deficit, he might have to sell or mortgage his lands. However, at the end of the colonial period, especially in the Andean area, there remained a minority of Indian nobles who had grown wealthy through trade, stock raising, or agriculture, and who enjoyed high social position. Perhaps typical of this small class of wealthy Indian or mestizo nobles was the famous late-eighteenth-century Peruvian cacique José Gabriel Condorcanqui (Tupac Amaru). Lillian Fisher writes that he lived like a Spanish nobleman, wearing "a long coat and knee-breeches of black velvet, a waistcoat of gold tissue worth seventy or eighty *duros* (dollars), embroidered linen, silk stockings, gold buckles at his knees and on his shoes, and a Spanish beaver hat valued at twenty-five duros. He kept his hair curled in ringlets that extended nearly down to his waist." His source of wealth included the ownership of 350 mules, which he used to transport mercury and other goods to Potosí and other places, and a large cacao estate.

By contrast with the privileged treatment accorded to the Indian hereditary nobility, Indian commoners suffered under crushing burdens of tribute, labor, and ecclesiastical fees. Viewed as a constitutionally inferior race and hence as perpetual wards of the Spanish state, they repaid the Spanish tutelage with the obligation to pay tribute and give forced labor. *Gente sin razón* ("people of weak minds") was a phrase commonly applied to the Indians in colonial documents. Their juridical inferiority and status as wards found expression in laws (universally disregarded) forbidding them to make binding contracts or to contract debts in excess of five pesos and in efforts to minimize contact between Indians and other racial groups. These and many other restrictions on Indian activity had an ostensible protective character. But an enlightened Mexican prelate, Bishop Manuel Abad y Queipo, pointed out that these so-called privileges

do them little good and in most respects injure them greatly. Shut up in a narrow space of six hundred rods, assigned by law to the Indian towns, they possess no individual property and are obliged to work the communal lands. . . . Forbidden by law to commingle with the other castes, they are deprived of the instruction and assistance that they should receive from contact with these and other people. They are isolated by their language, and by a useless, tyrannical form of government.

He concluded that the ostensible privileges of the Indians were "an offensive weapon employed by the white class against the Indians, and never serve to defend the latter."

Most of the Indians lived in their own towns, some of pre-Hispanic origin, others created by a process of resettlement of dispersed Indian populations in new towns called "reductions" or "congregations." To serve the ends of Spanish control and tribute collection, the Indian towns were reorganized on the peninsular model, with municipal governments patterned on those of Spanish towns. The Indian cabildo had its regidores, its alcaldes who tried minor cases, and its *gobernador* (governor), who was responsible for the collection and delivery of tribute to the corregidor or the encomendero. These offices as a rule became hereditary in certain aristocratic families.

The Indian town typically was composed of one or more neighborhood or kinship groups (calpulli in Mexico, ayllu in the Andean region), each with its hereditary elders who represented their community in intergroup disputes, acted as intermediaries in arranging marriages, supervised the allotment of land to the group's members, and otherwise served their communities. A certain degree of Hispanicization of Indian commoners took place, reflected above all in religion but also in the adoption of various tools and articles of dress and food. But the barriers erected by Spain between the two communities and the fixed hostility with which they regarded each other prevented any thoroughgoing acculturation. In response to the aggressions and injustices inflicted on it by the white world, the Indian community drew into itself and fought stubbornly not only to preserve its land but its cultural identity, speech, social organization, and traditional dances and songs. After the kinship group, the most important Indian instrumentality for the maintenance of collective identity and security was the *cofradía* (religious brotherhood), whose members were responsible for the maintenance of certain cult activities.

The Conquest and its aftermath inflicted not only heavy material damage on Indian society but serious psychological injury as well. Spanish accounts frequently cite the lament of Indian elders over the loss of the severe discipline, strong family ties, and high moral standards of the pre-Conquest regimes. The Spanish judge Zorita quoted approvingly the remark of an Indian elder that with the coming of the Spaniards to Mexico

116   "all was turned upside down . . . liars, perjurers, and adulterers are no longer punished as they once were because the *principales* (nobles) have lost the power to chastise delinquents. This, say the Indians, is the reason why there are so many lies, disorders, and sinful women." A symptom as well as cause of Indian social disorganization was widespread alcoholism.

Blacks, Mulattos, Zambos: The Lowest Class

Blacks, mulattos, and *zambos* (mixtures of Indians and blacks) occupied the bottom rungs of the colonial social ladder. By the end of the sixteenth century some 75,000 African slaves had been introduced into the Spanish colonies under the system of asiento. The infamous Middle Passage (the journey of slaves across the Atlantic) was a thing of horror; the Jesuit Alonso de Sandoval, who had charge of conversion of slaves and who wrote a book on the subject, left this harrowing description of the arrival of a cargo of slaves in the port of Cartagena in New Granada:

They arrive looking like skeletons; they are led ashore, completely naked, and are shut up in a large court or enclosure . . . and it is a great pity to see so many sick and needy people, denied all care or assistance, for as a rule they are left to lie on the ground, naked and without shelter. . . . I recall that I once saw two of them, already dead, lying on the ground on their backs like animals, their mouths open and full of flies, their arms crossed as if making the sign of the cross . . . and I was astounded to see them dead as a result of such great inhumanity.

By the end of the eighteenth century some 9.5 million slaves had been brought to the Americas. Especially dense concentrations were found in Brazil and in the Caribbean area, which were dominated by plantation economies. Historians have hotly disputed the relative mildness or severity of Latin American black slavery. Recent studies generally support the view that the tempo of economic activity was decisive in determining the intensity of slave exploitation and the harshness of plantation discipline. Certainly manumission of slaves was more frequent in the Hispanic than in the English, Dutch, or French colonies, but it is likely that the unprofitability of slavery under certain conditions contributed more than cultural traditions to this result. Whatever the reasons, by the close of the colonial period slaves formed a minority of the total black and mulatto population. Whatever their treatment, slaves retained the aspiration for freedom. Fear of slave revolts haunted the white ruling class, and slaves frequently fled from their masters. Some of them formed independent communities in remote jungles or mountains that successfully resisted Spanish punitive expeditions.

This stubborn attachment of the black slaves to freedom, reflected in frequent revolts, flights, and other forms of resistance, suggests that the debate over the relative mildness or severity of black slavery in Latin America evades the main issue: the dehumanizing character of even the "mildest" slavery. Brought from Africa by force and violence, cut off from their kindred and peoples, the uprooted slaves were subjected in their new environment to severe deculturation. For reasons of security, slaveowners preferred to purchase slaves of diverse tribal origins, language, and religious beliefs and deliberately promoted tribal disunity among them. The economic interest of the planters dictated that the great majority of the imported slaves should be young, between the ages of fifteen and twenty. This contributed to the process of deculturation, for very few aged blacks, the repositories of tribal lore and traditions in African societies, came in the slaveships. The scarcity of women (the proportion of females in the slave population on Cuban plantations between 1746 and 1822 ranged between 9 and 15 percent) distorted the lives of the slaves, creating a climate of intense sexual repression and family instability. The church might insist on the right of the slave to proper Christian marriage and the sanctity of the marriage, but not until the nineteenth century was the separate sale of husbands, wives, and children forbidden in the Spanish colonies. The right of the master to sell or remove members of the slave's family and his free sexual access to slave women made difficult if not impossible a normal family life for slaves. The world of the slave plantation, resembling a prison rather than a society, left to independent Latin America a bitter heritage of racism, discrimination, and backwardness, problems that in most Latin American countries still await full solution.

Because of harsh treatment, poor living conditions, and the small number of women in the slave population, its rate of reproduction was very low. Miscegenation between white masters and slave women, on the other hand, produced a steady growth of the mulatto population. As noted above, by the end of the colonial period, for a variety of reasons, slaves formed a minority of the total black and mulatto population. Free blacks and mulattos made important contributions to the colonial economy, both in agriculture and as artisans of all kinds. Free blacks and mulattos, like Indians, were required to pay tribute.

Life in the City and on the Hacienda

In addition to the Indian communities, social life in the Spanish colonies had two major centers: the colonial city and the hacienda, or large landed estate. Unlike its European counterpart, the colonial city as a rule did not arise spontaneously as a center of trade or industry but developed in planned fashion to serve the ends of Spanish settlement and administration of the surrounding area. Sometimes it was founded on the ruins of an Indian capital, as in the case of Mexico City. More often it was founded on a site chosen for its strategic or other advantages, as in the case of Lima. By contrast with the usually anarchical layout of Spanish cities, the colonial town typically followed the gridiron plan, with a large central plaza flanked by the cathedral, the governor's *palacio,* and other public buildings. From this central square originated long, wide, and straight streets that intersected to produce uniform, rectangular blocks. This passion for regularity reflected both the influence of Renaissance neoclassical works on architecture and the regulatory zeal of the crown. In sharp contrast to

the carefully planned nucleus of the colonial city was the disorderly layout of the surrounding native *barrios,* slum districts inhabited by a large Indian and mestizo population that provided the Spanish city with cheap labor and combustible material for the riots that shook the cities in times of famine or other troubles.

Into the capitals flowed most of the wealth produced by the mines, plantations, and cattle ranches of the surrounding area. In these cities, in houses whose size and proximity to the center reflected the relative wealth and social position of their owners, lived the rich mine owners and landowners of the colonies. They displayed their wealth by the magnificence of their homes, furnishings, dress, and carriages, and by the multitude of their servants and slaves. By the end of the sixteenth century, Mexico City had already acquired fame for the beauty of its women, horses, and streets, and riches of its shops, and the reckless spending, gaming, and generosity of its aristocracy. The poet Bernardo de Balbuena, in a long poem devoted to "La Grandeza Mexicana" ("The Grandeur of Mexico City"), wrote of

That lavish giving of every ilk,
Without a care how great the cost
Of pearls, of gold, of silver, and of silk.

By the close of the seventeenth century, Mexico City had a population estimated to number 200,000.

Lima, founded in 1534, proud capital of the viceroyalty of Peru, and Potosí, the great Peruvian mining center whose wealth became legendary, were two other major colonial cities. By 1650, when its wealth had already begun to decline, Potosí, with a population of 160,000 inhabitants, was the largest city in South America.

Before the eighteenth century, when changes in government and manners brought a greater stability, violence was prevalent in the colonial city. Duels, assassinations, even pitched battles between different Spanish factions were events frequently mentioned in official records and private diaries. From time to time, the misery of the masses in the native and mixed-blood wards exploded in terrifying upheavals. In 1624 the

120 their own sins and those of their neighbors. Martí's detailed record of these reports and his own investigations and judgments give an impression of sexuality run rampant. "Over fifteen hundred individuals stood accused, primarily of sexual misdeeds," writes Kathy Waldron; "nearly ten percent of the clerics in the province came under attack; and even the governor of Maracaibo was denounced. The accusations included adultery, fornication, concubinage, incest, rape, bigamy, prostitution, lust, homosexuality, bestiality, abortion, and infanticide."

The economic, social, and physical subordination of colonial women to men (prevailing church doctrine accepted a husband's right to beat disobedient or erring wives, but in moderation) is an undisputed fact. But male domination was to some extent limited by the Hispanic property law, which required equal division of estates among heirs and gave women the right to control their dowries and inheritances during and beyond marriage. We know that some colonial women operated as entrepreneurs independently of their husbands; women were often appointed executors of their husbands' wills and frequently managed a husband's business after his death. Two specialists in the field, Asunción Lavrín and Edith Couturier, concluded that colonial women enjoyed more economic independence than had been supposed, "that there was repression; but repression was not the whole reality, and that it did not wholly impair women's ability of expression."

Conventual life provided an especially important means for achieving self-expression and freedom from male domination and sexual exploitation for elite and middle-class women. It was common for one or more daughters of an elite family to enter a convent; in the seventeenth century thirteen Lima convents held more than 20 percent of the city's women. The convents were self-governing institutions that gave women an opportunity to display their capacity for leadership in administration, management of resources (like other church bodies, convents invested their wealth in mortgages on urban and rural properties), and sometimes in politicking, for convents could be the scenes of stormy factional struggle for control. The convent represented a heaven-sent opportunity for a young woman like Sor Juana Inés de la Cruz, who was of a modest family background and who had no particular religious vocation. Her intellectual brilliance made it difficult for her to find a suitable marriage partner, and in any case she lacked the dowry to attract such a man. The convent, though, offered Sor Juana a way to escape the traps of sexual exploitation and cultivate her immense talents. A recent study of Hispanic women in colonial Peru by Luis Martín describes the Peruvian nunnery as "a fortress of women, a true island of women, where . . . women could protect themselves from the corroding and dehumanizing forces of Don Juanism." But a caveat is in order; the subjects of Martín's book are mostly upper-class Hispanic women, surrounded by slaves and servants, who often scorned and sometimes abused their black and Indian sisters.

Unfortunately, little as yet is known of the affairs of non-Hispanic women of the lower classes. What little is known suggests, paradoxically, that early post-Conquest society provided more opportunities for Indian females than for Indian males. The scarcity of white women forced Spaniards to take available Indian women as their mates, "allowing them to fill roles and positions that would ordinarily have been reserved for white women." Their positions in household work, sewing, and small-scale trade placed them in closer contact with Spanish society and helped strengthen their economic and social situation. With the arrival of growing numbers of white women by the late sixteenth century, however, the opportunities and mobility of Indian women became more limited.

Chapter 6

Colonial Brazil

Brazil's existence was unknown in Europe when
the Treaty of Tordesillas (1494) between Spain
and Portugal, fixing the dividing line between the
overseas possessions of the two powers 370
leagues west of the Cape Verde Islands, assigned
a large stretch of the coastline of South America
to the Portuguese zone of exploration and settlement (see map on page 74). In 1500, Pedro Álvares Cabral sailed with a large fleet to follow up
Vasco da Gama's great voyage to India. He was,
according to one explanation, driven by a storm
farther west than he had intended and therefore
made landfall on the Brazilian coast on April 22.
Some historians speculate that he purposely
changed course to investigate reports of land to
the west or to verify a previous discovery. Whatever the reason for his westward course, Cabral
promptly claimed the land for his country and
sent a ship to report his discovery to the king.

The Beginning of Colonial Brazil

Portugal's limited resources, already committed
to the exploitation of the wealth of Africa and the
Far East, made it impossible to undertake a full-
scale colonization of Brazil. But Portugal did not
entirely neglect its new possession. Royal expeditions established the presence of a valuable
dyewood, called brazilwood, that grew abun-
dantly on the coast between the present states of
Pernambuco and São Paulo. Merchant capitalists
soon obtained concessions to engage in the brazilwood trade and established a scattering of
trading posts where European trinkets and other
goods were exchanged with the Indians for brazil
logs and other exotic commodities. A small
trickle of settlers began—some castaways,

ATLANTIC OCEAN

GRÃO PARÁ

Negro R.

Solimões R.

Amazonas R.

Ilha
Marajó

Belem

São Luis
Maranhão

MARANHÃO

Fortaleza

CEARÁ

RIO
GRANDE DO
NORTE

Natal

PIAUÍ

PARAÍBA

Olinda

PERNAMBUCO

Recife

ALAGOAS

SERGIPE

BAHIA

Salvador

Xingu R.

Araguaia R.

São Francisco R.

MATO GROSSO

GOIÁS

Cuiabá R.

Santa Cruz

Pôrto Seguro

MINAS GERAIS

Vila Rica do
Ouro Preto

ESPÍRITO SANTO

Tietê R.

Paraná R.

SÃO PAULO

RIO DE JANEIRO

São Paulo

Rio de Janeiro

Paraguay R.

São Vicente

Santos

PARANÁ

SANTA CATARINA

Ilha Santa Catarina

Paraná R.

Uruguay R.

Treaty boundary 1777

RIO GRANDE DO SUL

Colônia do Sacramento

| | 600 miles |
| 0 | |

| | 600 kilometers |
| 0 | |

COLONIAL BRAZIL

others *degredados* (criminals exiled from Portugal to distant parts of the empire). These exiles were often well received by the local Indians and lived to sire a large number of mixed-bloods who gave valuable assistance to Portuguese colonization. Meanwhile, French merchant ships, also drawn by the lure of brazilwood, began to appear on the Brazilian coast. Alarmed by the presence of these interlopers, King João III sent in 1530 an expedition under Martim Affonso de Sousa to drive away the intruders and to establish permanent settlements in Brazil. In 1532 the first Portuguese town in Brazil, named São Vicente, was founded near the present port of Santos.

The Captaincy System

The limited resources of the Portuguese crown, combined with its heavy commitments in the spice-rich East, forced the king to assign to private individuals the major responsibility for the colonization of Brazil. This responsibility took the form of the captaincy system, already used by Portugal in Madeira, the Azores, and the Cape Verde Islands. The Brazilian coastline was divided into fifteen parallel strips extending inland to the uncertain line of Tordesillas. These strips were granted as hereditary captaincies to a dozen individuals, each of whom agreed to colonize, develop, and defend his captaincy or captaincies at his own expense. The captaincy system represented a curious fusion of feudal and commercial elements. The grantee or donatory was not only a vassal owing allegiance to his lord the king, but a businessman who hoped to derive large profits from his own estates and from taxes obtained from the colonists to whom he had given land. This fusion of feudal and commercial elements characterized the entire Portuguese colonial enterprise in Brazil from the first.

Few of the captaincies proved successful from either the economic or political point of view, since few donatories possessed the combination of investment capital and administrative ability required to attract settlers and defend their captaincies against Indian attacks and foreign intruders. One of the most successful was Duarte Coelho, a veteran of the India enterprise who was granted the captaincy of Pernambuco. His heavy investment in the colony paid off so well that by 1575 his son was the richest man in Brazil, collecting large amounts in quitrents (rents paid in lieu of feudal services) from the fifty sugar mills of the province and himself exporting more than fifty shiploads of sugar a year.

By the mid-sixteenth century, sugar had replaced brazilwood as the foundation of the Brazilian economy. Favored by its soil and climate, the northeast (the provinces of Pernambuco and Bahia) became the seat of a sugar-cane civilization characterized by three features: the *fazenda* (large estate), monoculture, and slave labor. There soon arose a class of large landholders whose extensive plantations and wealth marked them off from their less affluent neighbors. Only the largest planters could afford to erect the *engenhos* (mills) needed to process the sugar before export. Small farmers had to bring their sugar to the millowner for grinding, paying one-fourth to one-third of the harvest for the privilege. Since Europe's apparently insatiable demand for sugar yielded quick and large profits, planters had no incentive to diversify crops, and food agriculture was largely limited to small farms. Although the basic techniques of sugar making remained relatively unchanged from the late sixteenth to the late eighteenth centuries, the reputation of the Brazilian sugar industry for being traditional and backward appears unjustified. In the seventeenth century the Brazilian system was considered a model, and other powers sought to copy it. Not until the mid-eighteenth century, when declining demand and prices for Brazilian sugar produced a crisis, and Brazil's Caribbean rivals developed some new techniques, did that reputation for backwardness arise, and even then, according to historian Stuart Schwartz, "the charge was undeserved."

Portugal's Indian Policy

The problem of labor was first met by raids on Indian villages, the raiders returning with trains of captives who were sold to planters and other employers of labor. These aggressions were the primary cause of the chronic warfare between

124

Soldiers of mixed racial background, like the mulatto soldier shown in this picture, played a large role in expeditions into the Brazilian interior in search of gold, Indian slaves, and runaway black slaves.

the Indians and the Portuguese. But Indian labor was unsatisfactory from an economic point of view, since the natives lacked any tradition of organized work of the kind required by plantation agriculture, were especially susceptible to Old World diseases to which they had no acquired immunity, and offered many forms of resistance, ranging from attempts at escape to suicide. (In this last respect, of course, their response did not differ from that of the African slaves who gradually replaced them.)

As a result, after 1550, planters turned increasingly to the use of black slave labor imported from Africa. But the supply of black slaves was often cut off or sharply reduced by the activity of Dutch pirates and other foreign foes, and Brazilian slave hunters continued to find a market for their wares throughout the colonial period. The most celebrated slave hunters were the *bandeirantes* (from the word *bandeira* meaning "banner"

or "military company") from the upland settlement of São Paulo. Unable to compete in sugar production with the more favorably situated plantation areas of the northeast, these men, who were themselves part Indian in most cases, made slave raiding in the interior their principal occupation. The eternal hope of finding gold or silver in the mysterious interior gave added incentive to their expeditions. As the Indians near the coast dwindled in numbers or fled before the invaders, the bandeirantes pushed even deeper south and west, expanding the frontiers of Brazil in the process.

The Brazilian Indians did not accept the loss of land and liberty without a struggle, but their resistance was handicapped by the fatal tendency of tribes to war against each other, a situation the Portuguese utilized for their own advantage. Forced to retreat into the interior by the superior arms and organization of the whites, the natives often returned to make destructive forays on isolated Portuguese communities. As late as the first part of the nineteenth century, stretches of the Brazilian shore were made uninhabitable by the raids of Indians who lurked in the forests and mountains back of the coast.

But the unequal struggle at last ended here, as in the Spanish colonies, in the total defeat of the natives. Overwork, loss of the will to live, and the ravages of European diseases caused very heavy loss of life among the enslaved Indians. Punitive expeditions against tribes that resisted enslavement or gave some other pretext for sanctions also caused depopulation. The Jesuit father Antônio Vieira, whose denunciations of Portuguese cruelty recall the accusations of Las Casas about the Spanish, claimed that Portuguese mistreatment of Indians had caused the loss of more than 2 million lives in Amazonia in forty years. A distinguished English historian, Charles R. Boxer, considers this claim exaggerated but concedes that the Portuguese "often exterminated whole tribes in a singularly barbarous way."

Almost the only voices raised in protest against the enslavement and mistreatment of Indians were those of the Jesuit missionaries. The first fathers, led by Manoel da Nóbrega, came in

1549 with the captain general Tomé de Sousa. Four years later, another celebrated missionary, José de Anchieta, arrived in Brazil. Far to the south, on the plains of Piratininga, Nóbrega and Anchieta established a colegio or school for Portuguese, mixed-blood, and Indian children that became a model institution of its kind. Around this settlement gradually arose the town of São Paulo, an important point of departure into the interior for "adventurers in search of gold and missionaries in search of souls."

The Jesuits followed a program for the settlement of their Indian converts in *aldeias* (villages) where they lived under the care of the priests, completely segregated from the harmful influence of the white colonists. This program provoked many clashes with the slave hunters and the planters, who had very different ends in view. In an angry protest to the *Mesa da Consciência,* a royal council entrusted with responsibility for the religious affairs of the colony, the planters sought to turn the tables on the Jesuits by claiming that the Indians in the Jesuit villages were "true slaves, who labored as such not only in the colegios but on the so-called Indian lands, which in the end became the estates and sugar mills of the Jesuit fathers."

The clash of interests between the planters and slave hunters and the Jesuit missionaries reached a climax about the middle of the seventeenth century, an era of great activity on the part of the bandeirantes of São Paulo. In various parts of Brazil, the landowners rose in revolt, expelled the Jesuits, and defied royal edicts proclaiming the freedom of the Indians. In 1653 Vieira, a priest of extraordinary oratorical and literary powers, arrived in Brazil with full authority from the king to settle the Indian question as he saw fit. During Lent, Vieira preached a famous sermon to the people of Maranhão in which he denounced Indian slavery in terms comparable to those used by Father Montesinos on Santo Domingo in 1511. The force of Vieira's tremendous blast was weakened by his suggestion that Indian slavery should be continued under certain conditions and by the well-known fact that the Jesuit order itself had both Indian and black slaves. Yet there can be no doubt that the condition of the Indians in the Jesuit mission villages was superior to that of the Indian slaves in the Portuguese towns and plantations. A stronger argument against Jesuit practices is the fact that the system of segregation, however benevolent in intent, represented an arbitrary and mechanical imposition of alien cultural patterns on the Indian population and that it hindered rather than facilitated true social integration of the Indian.

The crown, generally sympathetic to the Jesuit position but under strong pressure from the planter class, pursued for two centuries a policy of compromise that satisfied neither Jesuits nor planters. A decisive turn came during the reform ministry of the marquis de Pombal (1750–1777), who expelled the Jesuits from Portugal and Brazil and secularized their missions. His legislation, forbidding Indian raids and enslavement, accepted the Jesuit thesis of Indian freedom; he also accepted the need for preparing the natives for civilized life and even the principle of concentrating the Indians in communities under the care of administrators responsible for their education and welfare. But his policy did not segregate the Indians from the Portuguese community; it made them available for use as paid workers by the colonists and actually encouraged contact and mingling between the two races, including interracial marriage. Meanwhile, the growth of the African slave trade, also encouraged by Pombal, diminished the demand for Indian labor and thus brought a greater measure of peace to the Indians. Whether Pombal's reform legislation significantly improved the material condition of the Indian population is doubtful, but it contributed to the absorption of the Indians into the colonial population and ultimately into the Brazilian nation. The decisive factor here was race mixture, which increased as a result of the passing of the Jesuit temporal power.

The French and Dutch Challenges

The dyewood, the sugar, and the tobacco of Brazil early attracted the attention of foreign powers. The French were the first to challenge

Portuguese control of the colony. With the aid of Indian allies, they made sporadic efforts to entrench themselves on the coast and in 1555 founded Rio de Janeiro as the capital of what they called Antarctic France. One cultural by-product of French contact with the Indians was the creation of a French image of the Brazilian Indian as a "noble savage," immortalized by the sixteenth-century French philosopher Montaigne in his essay "On Cannibals." But the French offensive in Brazil was weakened by Catholic-Huguenot strife at home, and in 1567 the Portuguese commander Mem de Sá ousted the French and occupied the settlement of Rio de Janeiro.

A more serious threat to Portuguese sovereignty over Brazil was posed by the Dutch, whose West India Company seized and occupied for a quarter of a century (1630–1654) the richest sugar-growing portions of the Brazilian coast. Under the administration of Prince Maurice of Nassau (1637–1644), Dutch Brazil, with its capital at Recife, became the site of brilliant scientific and artistic activity. The Portuguese struggle against the Dutch became an incipient struggle for independence, uniting elements of all races from various parts of Brazil. These motley forces won victories over the Dutch at the first and second battles of Guararapes (1648–1649). Weakened by tenacious Brazilian resistance and a simultaneous war with England, the Dutch withdrew from Pernambuco in 1654. But they took with them the lessons they had learned in the production of sugar and tobacco, and their capital, and transferred both to the West Indies. Soon the plantations and refineries of Barbados and other Caribbean islands gave serious competition to Brazilian sugar in the world market, with a resulting fall of prices. By the last decade of the seventeenth century, the Brazilian sugar industry had entered a long period of stagnation.

The Mineral Cycle, the Cattle Industry, and the Commercial System

In this time of gloom, news of the discovery of gold in the southwestern region later known as Minas Gerais reached the coast in 1695. This discovery opened a new economic cycle, led to the first effective settlement of the interior, and initiated a major shift in Brazil's center of economic and political gravity from north to south. Large numbers of colonists from Bahia, Pernambuco, and Rio de Janeiro, accompanied by their slaves and servants, swarmed into the mining area. Their exodus from the older regions caused an acute shortage of field hands that continued until the gold boom had run its course by the middle of the eighteenth century. The crown tried to stem the exodus by legislation and by policing the trails that led to the mining area, but its efforts were in vain. For two decades (1700–1720), it had no success in asserting royal authority and collecting the royal fifth in the gold fields. Violence between rival groups, especially pioneers from São Paulo and European-born newcomers, reached the scale of civil war in 1708. The mutual weakening of the two sides as a result of these struggles finally enabled the crown to restore order.

In 1710 a new captaincy of "São Paulo and the Mines of Gold" was established; in 1720 it was divided into "São Paulo" and "Minas Gerais." In 1729, wild excitement was caused by the discovery that certain stones found in the area, hitherto thought to be crystals, were in reality diamonds; many adventurers with their slaves turned from gold to diamond washing. The great increase in the supply of diamonds to Europe upset the market, causing a serious fall in price. As a result, the Portuguese government instituted a regime of drastic control over the *Diamantina* (Diamond District) to limit mining and prevent smuggling and thus maintain prices; this regime effectively isolated the district from the outside world.

Like its predecessor, the mineral cycle was marked by rapid and superficial exploitation of the new sources of wealth, followed by an equally swift decline. Mining revenue peaked about 1760, and thereafter both the river gold washings of Minas Gerais and the Diamond District suffered a progressive exhaustion of deposits. By 1809 the English traveler John Mawe could describe the gold-mining center of Villa Rica as a town that "scarcely retains a shadow of its former splendor."

Yet the mineral cycle left a permanent mark on the Brazilian landscape in the form of new centers of settlement in the southwest, not only in Minas Gerais but in the future provinces of Goias and Matto Grosso, Brazil's Far West, which was penetrated by pioneers in search of gold. If the mining camps became deserted, the new towns survived, although with diminished vitality. The decline of the mining industry also spurred efforts to promote the agricultural and pastoral wealth of the region. The shift of the center of economic and political gravity southward from Pernambuco and Bahia to Minas Gerais and Rio de Janeiro was formally recognized in 1763, when Rio de Janeiro became the seat of the viceregal capital.

As the provinces of Minas Gerais and Goias sank into decay, the northeast experienced a partial revival based on increasing European demand for sugar, cotton, and other semitropical products. Between 1750 and 1800, Brazilian cotton production made significant progress but then declined as rapidly as a result of competition from the more efficient cotton growers of the United States. The beginnings of the coffee industry, future giant of the Brazilian economy, also date from the late colonial period.

Cattle raising also made its contribution to the advance of the Brazilian frontier and the growing importance of the south. The intensive agriculture of the coast and the concentration of population in coastal cities like Bahia and Pernambuco created a demand for fresh meat that gave an initial impulse to cattle raising. Since the expansion of plantation agriculture in the coastal zone did not leave enough land for grazing, the cattle industry inevitably had to move inland.

By the second half of the seventeenth century, the penetration of the distant São Francisco Valley from Bahia and Pernambuco was well under way. Powerful cattlemen, with their herds of cattle, their *vaqueiros* (cowboys), and their slaves, entered the *sertão* (backcountry), drove out the Indians, and established fortified ranches and villages for their retainers. Such occupation was legitimized before or after the fact by the official grant of a huge tract of land, a virtual feudal domain, to the cattle baron in question, whose word became law on his estate. The landowner's cattle provided meat for the coastal cities and mining camps, draft animals for the plantations, and hides for export to Europe.

The cattle industry later expanded into the extreme southern region of Rio Grande do Sul, which was colonized by the government in the interests of defense against Spanish expansionist designs. Here too vast land grants were made. The counterpart of the vaqueiro in the south was the *gaúcho.* Like the vaqueiro, the gaúcho was an expert horseman, but he reflected the blend of cultures in the Río de la Plata in his speech, a mixture of Portuguese, Spanish, and Indian dialects; in his dress, the loose, baggy trousers of the Argentine cowboy; and in his chief implement, the *bolas,* balls of stone attached to a rawhide rope, a loan from the pampas Indians, which was used for entangling and bringing down animals.

Portugal, like Spain (with which it was loosely united, 1580–1640), pursued a mercantilist commercial policy, though not as consistently or rigorously. During the period of Spanish domination, Brazil's commerce was firmly restricted to Portuguese nationals and ships. The Dutch, who had been the principal carriers of Brazilian sugar and tobacco to European markets, responded with extensive smuggling and a direct attack on the richest sugar-growing area of Brazil.

Following the successful Portuguese revolt against Spain, the Methuen treaty (1703) was made with England, Portugal's protector and ally. By this treaty, British merchants were permitted to trade between Portuguese and Brazilian ports. But English ships frequently neglected the formality of touching at Lisbon and plied a direct contraband trade with the colony. Since Portuguese industry was incapable of supplying the colonists with the required quantity and quality of manufactured goods, a large proportion of the outward-bound cargoes consisted of foreign textiles and other products, of which England provided the lion's share. Thus, Portugal, mistress of Brazil, itself became a colony of Dutch and English merchants with offices in Lisbon.

In the eighteenth century, during the reign of Dom José I (1750–1777), his prime minister, the

128   marquis de Pombal, an able representative of the ideology of enlightened despotism, launched an administrative and economic reform of the Portuguese Empire that bears comparison with the Bourbon reforms in Spain and Spanish America that were taking place at the same time. Pombal's design was to nationalize Portuguese-Brazilian trade by creating a Portuguese merchant class with enough capital to compete with British merchants and a national industry whose production could dislodge English goods from the Brazilian market. The program required an active state intervention in the imperial economy through the creation of a Board of Trade, which subsidized merchant-financiers with lucrative concessions in Portugal and Brazil; the formation of companies that were granted monopolies over trade with particular regions of Brazil and were expected to develop the economies of those regions; and the institution of a policy of import substitution through state assistance to old and new industries. Despite mistakes, failures, and a partial retreat from Pombal's program after he was forced out of office in 1777, the Pombaline reform achieved at least partial success in its effort to reconquer Brazilian markets for Portugal. Between 1796 and 1802, 30 percent of all the goods shipped to Brazil consisted of Portuguese manufactures, especially cotton cloth. But the flight of the Portuguese royal family from Lisbon to Brazil in 1808 as a result of Napoleon's invasion of Portugal, followed two years later by the signing of a treaty with England that gave the British all the trade privileges they requested, effectively "dismantled the protective edifice so painfully put together since 1750." Britain once again enjoyed a virtual monopoly of trade with Brazil.

Government and Church

The donatory system of government first established in Brazil by the Portuguese crown soon proved unsatisfactory. There was a glaring contradiction between the vast powers granted to the donatories and the authority of the monarch; moreover, few donatories were able to cope with the tasks of defense and colonization for which they had been made responsible. The result was a governmental reform. In 1549 Tomé de Sousa was sent out as governor general to head a central colonial administration for Brazil. Bahia, situated about midway between the flourishing settlements of Pernambuco and São Vicente, became his capital. Gradually, the hereditary rights and privileges of the donatories were revoked, as they were replaced by governors appointed by the king. As the colony expanded, new captaincies were created. In 1763, as previously noted, the governor of Rio de Janeiro replaced his colleague at Bahia as head of the colonial administration, with the title of viceroy. In practice, however, his authority over the other governors was negligible.

The Administrators and Their Deficiencies

The government of Portuguese Brazil broadly resembled that of the Spanish colonies in its spirit, structure, and vices. One notable difference, however, was the much smaller scale of the Portuguese administration. The differing economies of the two empires help to explain this divergence. The Spanish Indies had a relatively diversified economy that served local and regional, as well as overseas, markets and a large Indian population that was an important source of labor and royal tribute. Combined with a Spanish population that numbered 300,000 in 1600 (when only 30,000 Portuguese lived in Brazil), these conditions created an economic base for the rise of hundreds of towns and the need for a numerous officialdom charged with the regulation of Indian labor, the collection of Indian tribute, and many other fiscal and administrative duties. In Portuguese America, on the other hand, the establishment of an elaborate bureaucracy was rendered unnecessary by several factors: the overwhelming importance of exports, especially of sugar, which could be taxed when it was unloaded in Lisbon; the economic and social dominance of the plantation, which made for a weak development of urban life; and the minor role of the Indian population as a source of labor and royal revenue.

During the union of Portugal and Spain, the colonial policies of the two countries were aligned by the creation in 1604 of the *Conselho de India,* whose functions resembled those of the Spanish Council of the Indies. In 1736 the functions of the conselho were assumed by a newly created ministry of *Marinha e Ultramar* (Marine and Overseas). Under the king, this body framed laws for Brazil, appointed governors, and supervised their conduct. The governor, captain general, or viceroy combined in himself military, administrative, and even some judicial duties. His power tended to be absolute but was tempered by certain factors: the constant intervention of the home government, which bound him with precise, strict, and detailed instructions; the counterweights of other authorities, especially the *relações* (high courts), which were both administrative and judicial bodies; and the existence of special administrative organs, such as the intendancies created in the gold and diamond districts, which were completely independent of the governor. Thus in Brazil, as in the Spanish colonies, there operated a system of checks and balances through overlapping functions and the oversight of some officials by others with similar or competing authority, a system that reflected above all the distrust felt by the home government for its agents. Other factors that tended to diminish the authority of the governor were the vastness of the country, the scattered population, the lack of social stability, and the existence of enormous landholdings in which the feudal power of the great planters and cattle barons was virtually unchallenged.

The most important institution of local government was the *Senado da Câmara* (municipal council). The influence of this body varied with the size of the city. Whether elected by a restricted property-owning electorate or chosen by the crown, its membership represented the ruling class of merchants, planters, and professional men. Elections were often marked by struggles for control by rival factions, planters and creoles on one side, merchants and peninsulars on the other. The authority of the câmara extended over its entire *comarca* (district), which often was very large. But its power was limited by the frequent intervention of the *ouvidor,* who usually combined his judicial functions with the administrative duties of corregedor. Generally speaking, the greater the size and wealth of the city, and the farther it was from the viceregal capital, the greater its powers.

Both the crown and the municipal councils levied numerous taxes, whose collection was usually farmed out to private collectors. In return for making a fixed payment to the treasury, these men collected the taxes for the crown and could keep the surplus once the set quota had been met. The system, of course, encouraged fraud and extortion of every kind. Another crippling burden on the population was tithes, which came to 10 percent of the total product, originally payable in kind but later only in cash. Tithes, writes the Brazilian historian Caio Prado Júnior, "ran neck and neck with conscription as one of the great scourges inflicted on the population by the colonial administration."

The besetting vices of Spanish colonial administration—inefficiency, bureaucratic attitudes, slowness, and corruption—were equally prominent in the Portuguese colonial system. Justice was not only costly but incredibly slow and complicated. Cases brought before lower courts ascended the ladder of the higher tribunals: ouvidor, relação, and on up to the crown Board of Appeals, taking as long as ten to fifteen years for resolution.

Over vast areas of the colony, however, administration and courts were virtually nonexistent. Away from the few large towns, local government often meant the rule of great landowners, who joined to their personal influence the authority of office, for it was from their ranks that the royal governors invariably appointed the *capitães móres* (district militia officers). Armed with unlimited power to enlist, command, arrest, and punish, the capitão mór became a popular symbol of despotism and oppression. Sometimes these men used the local militia as feudal levies

130   for war against a rival family; boundary questions and questions of honor were often settled by duels or pitched battles between retainers of rival clans. The feudalism that still dominates much of the Brazilian backcountry may be traced back to these colonial origins.

Corruption pervaded the administrative apparatus from top to bottom. The miserably paid officials prostituted their trusts in innumerable ways: embezzlement, graft, and bribery were well-nigh universal. Antônio Vieira referred to this universal corruption when he conjugated the verb *rapio* (I steal) in all its inflections in his sermon on the "Good Thief."

Some improvement, at least on the higher levels of administration, took place under the auspices of the extremely able and energetic marquis de Pombal. The same tendency toward centralization that characterized Bourbon colonial policy appeared in Portuguese policy in this period. Pombal abolished the remaining hereditary captaincies, restricted the special privileges of the municipalities, and increased the power of the viceroy. In a mercantilist spirit, he sought to promote the economic advance of Brazil with a view to promoting the reconstruction of Portugal, whose condition was truly forlorn.

Typical of the enlightened viceroys of the Pombaline period was the marquis de Lavradio (1769–1779), whose achievements included the transfer of coffee from Pará into São Paulo, in whose fertile red soil it was to flourish mightily. How little changed, however, the administration of Brazil was by the Pombaline reform is suggested by Lavradio's letter of instructions to his successor, in which he gloomily observed that

> *as the salaries of these magistrates [the judges] are small . . . they seek to multiply their emoluments by litigation and discord, which they foment, and not only keep the people unquiet, but put them to heavy expenses, and divert them from their occupations, with the end of promoting their own vile interest and that of their subalterns, who are the principal concocters of these disorders.*

During the twelve years he had governed in Brazil, wrote the viceroy, he had never found one useful establishment instituted by any of these magistrates.

The Church and the State

In Brazil, as in the Spanish colonies, church and state were intimately united. By comparison with the Spanish monarchs, however, the Portuguese kings seemed almost niggardly in their dealings with the church. But their control over its affairs, exercised through the *padroado*—the ecclesiastical patronage granted by the pope to the Portuguese king in his realm and overseas possessions—was as absolute. The king exercised his power through a special board, the *Mesa da Consciência e Ordens* (Board of Conscience and Orders). Rome, however, long maintained a strong indirect influence through the agency of the Jesuits, who were very influential in the Portuguese court until they were expelled from Portugal and Brazil in 1759.

With some honorable exceptions, notably that of the entire Jesuit order, the tone of clerical morality and conduct in Brazil was deplorably low. The clergy were often criticized for their extortionate fees and for the negligence they displayed in the performance of their spiritual duties. Occasionally, priests combined those duties with more mundane activities. Many were planters; others carried on a variety of businesses. One high-ranking crown official summed up his impressions of the clergy in the statement "All they want is money, and they care not a jot for their good name."

Yet the church and the clergy made their own contributions to the life of colonial Brazil. The clergy provided such educational and humanitarian establishments as existed in the colony. From its ranks—which were open to talent and even admitted individuals of mixed blood despite the formal requirement of a special dispensation—came most of the few distinguished names in Brazilian colonial science, learning, and literature. Among them, Jesuit writers again occupy a prominent place. But the cultural poverty of colonial Brazil is suggested by the fact that throughout the colonial period there was not a single university or even a printing press.

Masters and Slaves

Race mixture played a decisive role in the formation of the Brazilian people. The scarcity of white women in the colony, the freedom of the Portuguese from puritanical attitudes, and the despotic power of the great planters over their Indian and black slave women all gave impetus to miscegenation. Of the three possible race combinations—white-black, white-Indian, black-Indian—the first was the most common. The immense majority of these unions were outside wedlock. In 1755 the marquis de Pombal, pursuing the goals of population growth and strengthening of Brazil's borders, issued an order encouraging marriages between Portuguese and Indians and proclaiming the descendants of such union eligible to positions of honor and dignity, but this favor was not extended to white-black unions.

Color, Class, and Slavery

In principle, color lines were strictly drawn. A "pure" white wife or husband, for example, was indispensable to a member of the upper class. But the enormous number of mixed unions outside wedlock and the resulting large progeny, some of whom, at least, were regarded with affection by white fathers and provided with some education and property, inevitably led to blurring of color lines and a fairly frequent phenomenon of "passing." There was a tendency to classify individuals racially, if their color was not too dark, on the basis of social and economic position rather than on their physical appearance. The English traveler Henry Koster alludes to this "polite fiction" in his anecdote concerning a certain great personage, a capitão mór, whom Koster suspected of being a mulatto. In response to his question, his servant replied, "He was, but is not

A scene of Brazilian slavery. New arrivals from Africa wait in a slave dealer's establishment while the seated proprietor negotiates the sale of a child to a prospective customer.

Portuguese exporters, collect large amounts of delinquent taxes, and impose a new head tax. A conspiracy to revolt and establish a republic on the American model was hatched in 1788–1789 by a group of dissidents, most of whom were highly placed members of the colonial elite. The only leading conspirator who was not a member of the aristocracy was José da Silva Xavier, a military officer of low rank who practiced the part-time profession of "Toothpuller," whence the name of *Tiradentes* by which he is known in Brazilian history. An enthusiast for the American Revolution, Silva Xavier apparently possessed copies of the Declaration of Independence and American state constitutions. When the conspiracy was discovered, all the principal conspirators were condemned to death, but the sentences were commuted to exile for all but the plebeian Silva Xavier. His barbarous execution, which he faced with great courage, made him a martyr as well as a precursor of Brazilian independence.

Chapter 7

The Bourbon Reforms and Spanish America

The death of the sickly Charles II in November 1700 marked the end of an era in Spanish history and the beginning of a new and better day, although the signs under which the new day began were far from hopeful. On his deathbed the unhappy Charles, more kingly in his dying than he had ever been before, fought desperately to prevent the triumph of an intrigue for the partition of the Spanish dominions among three claimants of that inheritance, the prince of Bavaria, the archduke Charles of Austria, and Louis XIV's grandson, Philip of Anjou. In one of his last acts, Charles signed a will naming the French Philip, who became Philip V, successor to all his dominions.

English fears at the prospect of a union of France and Spain under a single ruler precipitated the War of the Spanish Succession (1702–1713). The war ended with the Treaty of Utrecht (1713), which granted to Great Britain Gibraltar and Minorca, major trade concessions in the Spanish Indies, and a guarantee against a union of the French and Spanish thrones under Philip. Another peace treaty, concluded the following year, gave the Spanish Netherlands and Spain's Italian possessions to Austria.

Reform and Recovery

Spain's humiliating losses deepened the prevailing sense of pessimism and defeatism, but there were compensations: the shock of defeat in the succession war drove home the need for sweeping reform of Spanish institutions; the loss of the Netherlands and the Italian possessions left Spain

136

with a more manageable, more truly Spanish empire, consisting of the kingdoms of Castile and Aragon and the Indies.

The War of the Spanish Succession also brought a forcible solution of the Aragonese problem, which had long plagued the Hapsburg monarchy. Fearing the authoritarian tendencies of the new Bourbon dynasty and recalling the injuries suffered at French hands during the seventeenth century, the Catalans rose in support of the Austrian claimant in 1705; Aragon and Valencia also invited and received the support of English and Austrian troops. But Aragon and Valencia fell to Philip V's armies in 1707 and suffered immediate loss of their fueros as punishment for supporting the wrong side. The Catalans, abandoned by Great Britain when it signed the peace of Utrecht in 1713, held out until September 1714, when Barcelona surrendered to the Bourbon forces. The fall of the city was followed by the destruction of Catalan liberties and autonomy, with the province being placed under a captain general who governed with the aid of a royal audiencia. The new regime made a systematic but unsuccessful effort to extinguish the Catalan language and nationality.

The Bourbon Reforms

The return of peace permitted the new dynasty to turn its attention to implementing a program of reform inspired by the French model. The reform and ensuing revival of Spain is associated with three princes of the House of Bourbon: Philip V (1700–1746) and his two sons, Ferdinand VI (1746–1759) and Charles III (1759–1788). Under the aegis of "enlightened despotism," the Bourbon kings attempted nothing less than a total overhaul of existing political and economic structures, a total renovation of the national life. Only such sweeping reform could close the gap that separated Spain from the foremost European powers and arm the country with the weapons—a powerful industry, a prosperous agriculture, a strong middle class—it needed to prevent its defeat by England and her allies in the struggle for empire that dominated the eighteenth century.

The movement for reform, although carried out within the framework of royal absolutism and Catholic orthodoxy, inevitably provoked the hostility of reactionary elements within the church and the nobility. As a result, the Bourbons, although supported by such liberal grandees as the count of Floridablanca and the count of Aranda, recruited many of their principal ministers and officials from the ranks of the lesser nobility and the small middle class. These men were strongly influenced by the rationalist spirit of the French Encyclopedists,[1] although they rejected French anticlericalism and deism. They were characteristic of the Spanish Enlightenment in their rigid orthodoxy in religion and politics combined with enthusiastic pursuit of useful knowledge, criticism of defects in the church and clergy, and belief in the power of informed reason to improve society by reorganizing it along more rational lines.

The work of national reconstruction began under Philip V but reached its climax under Charles III. This great reformer-king attempted to revive Spanish industry by removing the stigma attached to manual labor, establishing state-owned textile factories, inviting foreign technical experts into Spain, and encouraging technical education. He aided agriculture by curbing the privileges of the Mesta, or stockbreeders' corporation, and by settling colonies of Spanish and foreign peasants in abandoned regions of the peninsula. He continued and expanded the efforts of his predecessors to encourage shipbuilding and foster trade and communication by the building of roads and canals. Clerical influence declined as a result of the expulsion of the Jesuits in 1767 and of decrees restricting the authority of the Inquisition. Under the cleansing influence of able and honest ministers, a new spirit of austerity and service began to appear among public officials.

But the extent of the changes that took place in Spanish economic and social life under the Bourbons must not be exaggerated. The crown, linked by a thousand bonds to the feudal nobility

---

[1] Writers of the famous *Encyclopédie* (1751–1780), who were identified with the Enlightenment and advocated deism and a rationalist world outlook.

and church, never touched the foundation of the old order, the land monopoly of the nobility, with its corollaries of mass poverty and archaic agricultural methods. As a result of these weaknesses, added to the lack of capital for industrial development and the debility of the Spanish middle class, Spain, despite marked advances in population and production, remained at the close of the era a second- or third-class power by comparison with Great Britain, France, or Holland.

The outbreak of the French Revolution, which followed by a few months the death of Charles III in December 1788, brought the reform era effectively to a halt. Frightened by the overthrow of the French monarchy and the execution of his royal kinsman, Charles IV and his ministers turned sharply to the right. The leading reformers were banished or imprisoned, and the importation of French rationalist and revolutionary literature was forbidden. Yet the clock could not be and was not entirely turned back, either in Spain or in the colonies. It was under the corrupt government of Charles IV, for example, that the expedition of Francisco Xavier Balmis sailed from Spain (1803) to carry the procedure of vaccination to the Spanish dominions in America and Asia, an act that probably saved innumerable lives.

In the field of colonial reform, the Bourbons moved slowly and cautiously, as was natural in view of the powerful vested interests identified with the old order of things. There was never any thought of giving a greater measure of self-government to the colonists or of permitting them to trade more freely with the non-Spanish world. On the contrary, the Bourbons centralized colonial administration still further, with a view to making it more efficient. In addition, their commercial reforms were designed to diminish smuggling and strengthen the exclusive commercial ties between Spain and her colonies, to "reconquer" the colonies economically for Spain.

Revival of Colonial Commerce and Breakdown of Trading Monopoly

The first Bourbon, Philip V, concentrated his efforts on an attempt to reduce smuggling and to revive the fleet system, which had fallen into decay in the late seventeenth century. With the Treaty of Utrecht, the English merchant class had scored an impressive victory in the shape of the asiento; the South Sea Company was granted the exclusive right to supply slaves to Spanish America, with the additional right of sending a shipload of merchandise to Portobelo every year. It was well known that the slave ships carried contraband merchandise, as did the provision ships that accompanied the annual ship and reloaded her with goods. Buenos Aires, where the South Sea Company maintained a trading post, was another funnel through which English traders poured large quantities of contraband goods that penetrated as far as Peru.

The Spanish government sought to check smuggling in the Caribbean by commissioning *guardacostas* (private warships), which prowled the main lanes of trade in search of ships loaded with contraband. The depredations of the guardacostas led to English demands for compensation and finally to war between England and Spain in 1739. During this war, the British again disrupted the fleet sailings Philip V had attempted to revive. In 1740 they were suspended. Their place was taken by swifter and more economical register ships, which sailed singly, under license from the crown. Ships bound for Peru used the route around Cape Horn; others sailed directly to Buenos Aires. The end of the South American fleet, known as the *galeones,* brought the death of the Portobelo Fair. The New Spain fleet was alternately revived and suspended, but abandoned in 1789. The convoy system, says John H. Parry, "had long outlived its usefulness; in war it had become inadequate, in peace unnecessary."

The introduction of register ships did not, however, end the monopoly of the Cádiz *consulado* (merchant guild), whose members alone could load these vessels. The first breach in the wall of this monopoly came in the 1720s, with the organization of the Caracas Company, which was founded with the aid of capitalists in the Biscay region. In return for the privilege of trade with Venezuela, this company undertook to police the coast against smugglers and develop the

138

resources of the region. Despite the company's claims of success in achieving these objectives, it failed to stop a lively contraband trade with the nearby Dutch colony of Curaçao or overcome the bitter hostility of Venezuelan planters and merchants, who accused the company of paying too little for cocoa, taking too little tobacco and other products, and charging excessive prices for Spanish goods.

Biscayan and Catalan capital organized similar companies for trade with Havana, Hispaniola, and other places the old system of colonial trade had left undeveloped. These enterprises, however, were financial failures, in part because of inadequate capital, in part because of poor management. These breaches of the Cádiz monopoly brought no benefits to creole merchants, who continued to be almost completely excluded from the legal trade between Spain and her colonies.

The first Bourbons made few changes in the administrative structure of colonial government, contenting themselves with efforts to improve the quality of administration by more careful selection of officeholders. One major reorganization was the separation of the northern Andean region (present-day Ecuador, Colombia, and Venezuela) from the viceroyalty of Peru. In 1739 it became a viceroyalty, named New Granada, with its capital at Santa Fe (modern Bogotá). This change had strategic significance, reflecting a desire to provide better protection for the Caribbean coast, especially the fortress of Cartagena. It also reflected the rapid growth of population in the central highlands of Colombia. Within the new viceroyalty, Venezuela was named a captaincy general, with its capital at Caracas, and became virtually independent of Santa Fe.

The movement for colonial reform, like the program of domestic reform, reached a climax in the reign of Charles III. Part of this reform had been foreshadowed in the writings of a remarkable Spanish economist and minister of finance and war under Ferdinand VI, José Campillo. Shortly before his death in 1743, Campillo wrote a memorial on colonial affairs that advocated the abolition of the Cádiz monopoly, a reduction of

duties on goods bound for America, the organization of a frequent mail service to America, the encouragement of trade between the colonies, and the development of colonial agriculture and other economic activities that did not compete with Spanish manufacturers. Most of these recommendations were incorporated in a report made to Charles III by a royal commission in 1765. The shock of Spain's defeat in the Seven Years' War, which cost her the loss of Florida and almost the loss of Cuba, provided impetus for a program of imperial reorganization and reform.

In this period, the trading monopoly of Cádiz was gradually eliminated. In 1765 commerce with the West Indies was thrown open to seven other ports besides Cádiz and Seville; this reform, coming at a time when Cuban sugar production was beginning to expand, gave a sharp stimulus to the island's economy. This privilege was gradually extended to other regions until, by the famous decree of free trade of 1778, commerce was permitted between all qualified Spanish ports and all the American provinces except Mexico and Venezuela. In 1789, New Spain and Venezuela were thrown open to trade on the same terms.[2] The burdensome duties levied on this trade were also replaced by simple ad valorem duties of 6 or 7 percent. Restrictions on intercolonial trade were also progressively lifted, but this trade was largely limited to non-European products. A major beneficiary of this change was the Río de la Plata area, which in 1776 was opened for trade with the rest of the Indies. Meanwhile, the Casa de Contratación, symbol of the old order, steadily declined in importance until it closed its doors in 1789. A similar fate overtook the venerable Council of the Indies. As a consultative body it lasted on into the nineteenth century, but most of its duties were entrusted to a colonial minister appointed by the king.

[2] It must be stressed, however, that these reforms did not seriously weaken the dominant role of the Cádiz monopolists and their American agents in colonial trade. As late as 1790, more than 85 percent of the trade moved through Cádiz, thanks to its superior facilities for shipping, insurance, warehousing, and communication.

The success of the "free trade" policy was reflected in a spectacular increase in the value of Spain's commerce with Spanish America, an increase said to have amounted to about 700 percent between 1778 and 1788. The entrance of new trading centers and merchant groups into the Indies trade and the reduction of duties and the removal of irksome restrictions had the effect of increasing the volume of business, reducing prices, and perhaps diminishing contraband (although one cannot speak with certainty here, for the easing of restrictions inevitably facilitated the activity of smugglers).

But the achievements of the Bourbon commercial reform must not be overestimated. The reform ultimately failed in its aim of reconquering colonial markets for Spain for two basic reasons: first, Spain's industrial weakness, which the best efforts of the Bourbons were unable to overcome, and, second, Spain's closely related inability to keep her sea-lanes to America open in time of war with England, when foreign traders again swarmed into Spanish-American ports. Indeed, the Spanish government openly confessed its inability to supply the colonies with needed goods in time of war by lifting the ban against foreign vessels of neutral origin (which meant United States ships, above all) during the years from 1797 to 1799 and again in the years from 1805 to 1809. This permission to trade with neutrals gave rise to a spirited United States commerce with the Caribbean area and with the Río de la Plata.

Increased Economic Activity

Perhaps the most significant result of the Bourbon commercial reform was the stimulus it gave to economic activity in Spanish America. To what extent this increased economic activity should be ascribed to the beneficial effects of the Bourbon reform and to what degree it resulted from the general economic upsurge in western Europe in the eighteenth century cannot be stated with certainty. What is certain is that the latter part of the century saw a rising level of agricultural, pastoral, and mining production in Spanish America.

Stimulated by the Bourbon reform and by the growing European demand for sugar, tobacco, hides, and other staples, production of these products rose sharply in this period. There developed a marked trend toward regional specialization and monoculture in the production of cash crops. After 1770 coffee, grown in Venezuela and Cuba, joined cacao and sugar as a major export crop of the Caribbean area. The gradual increase in population also stimulated the production of food crops for local markets, notably wheat, preferred over maize by the European population. Tithe collections offer an index of agricultural growth: in the decade from 1779 to 1789, tithe collections in the principal agricultural areas were 40 percent greater than in the previous decade.

It appears, however, that agricultural prosperity was largely limited to areas producing export crops or with easy access to domestic markets. David Brading paints a gloomy picture of the financial condition of the Mexican haciendas in the eighteenth century. Except in the Valley of Mexico, the Bajío,[3] and the Guadalajara region, markets were too small to yield satisfactory returns. Great distances, poor roads, and high freight costs prevented haciendas from developing their productive capacity beyond the requirements of the local market. Private estates were worse off than church haciendas, because they had to pay tithes and sales taxes and bore the double burden of absentee landowners and resident administrators. Great landed families who possessed numerous estates in different regions, producing varied products for multiple markets, were more fortunate; their profits averaged from 6 to 9 percent of capital value in the late eighteenth century. Thanks to cheap labor, however, even a low productivity yielded large revenues, which enabled hacendados to maintain a lavish, seigneurial style of life. Many haciendas were heavily indebted to ecclesiastical institutions, the principal bankers of the time.

[3] A relatively urbanized area with a diversified economy (agriculture, mining, manufacturing) lying within the modern Mexican states of Guanajuato and Querétaro.

140

The increase in agricultural production, it should be noted, resulted from more extensive use of land and labor rather than from the use of improved implements or techniques. The inefficient *latifundio* (great estate), which used poorly paid peon labor, and the slave plantation accounted for the bulk of commercial agricultural production. The Prussian traveler Alexander von Humboldt, commenting on the semifeudal land tenure system of Mexico, observed that "the property of New Spain, like that of Old Spain, is in a great measure in the hands of a few powerful families, who have gradually absorbed the smaller estates. In America, as well as in Europe, large commons are condemned to the pasturage of cattle and to perpetual sterility."

The increasing concentration of landownership in Mexico and the central Andes in the second half of the eighteenth century reflected the desire of hacendados to eliminate the competition of small producers in restricted markets and to maintain prices at a high level. To help achieve this end, great landowners hoarded their harvests in their granaries and sent grain to market at that time of the year when it was scarcest and prices were at their highest. Given the low productivity of colonial agriculture, however, such natural disasters as drought, premature frosts, or excessive rains easily upset the precarious balance between food supplies and population, producing frightful famines like that of 1785–1787 in central Mexico. Thousands died of hunger or diseases induced by that famine.

What sugar, cacao, and coffee were for the Caribbean area, hides were for the Río de la Plata. The rising European demand for leather for footwear and industrial purposes and the permission given in 1735 for direct trade with Spain in register ships sparked an economic upsurge in the Plata area. The unregulated hunting of wild cattle on the open pampa soon gave way to the herding of cattle on established *estancias* (cattle ranches). By the end of the century, these were often of huge size—15 to 20 square leagues— with as many as eighty or a hundred thousand head of cattle. By 1790, Buenos Aires was exporting nearly a million and a half hides annually. The meat of the animal, hitherto almost worth-

less except for the small quantity that could be consumed immediately, now gained in value as a result of the demand for salt beef, processed in large-scale *saladeros* (salting plants). Markets for salt beef were found above all in the Caribbean area, especially Cuba, where it was chiefly used for feeding the slave population. The growth of cattle raising in La Plata, however, was attended by the concentration of land in ever fewer hands and took place at the expense of agriculture, which remained in a very depressed state.

The eighteenth century also saw a marked revival of silver mining in the Spanish colonies. Peru and Mexico shared in this advance, but the Mexican mines forged far ahead of their Peruvian rivals in the Bourbon era. The mine owners included creoles and peninsulars, but the Spanish merchants who financed the mining operations received most of the profits. As in the case of agriculture, the increase in silver production was not due primarily to improved technique; it resulted from the opening of many new as well as old mines and the growth of the labor force. The crown, however, especially under Charles III, contributed materially to the revival by offering new incentives to entrepreneurs and by its efforts to overcome the backwardness of the mining industry. The incentives included reductions in taxes and in the cost of mercury, a government monopoly.

In New Spain the crown promoted the establishment of a mining guild (1777) whose activities included the operation of a bank to finance development. Under this guild's auspices was founded the first school of mines in America (1792). Staffed by able professors and provided with modern equipment, it offered excellent theoretical and practical instruction and represented an important source of Enlightenment thought in Mexico. Foreign and Spanish experts, accompanied by teams of technicians, came to Mexico and Peru to show the mine owners the advantages of new machinery and techniques. These praiseworthy efforts were largely frustrated by the traditionalism of the mine owners, by lack of capital to finance changes, and by mismanagement. Yet the production of silver steadily increased. Supplemented by the gold of Brazil, it helped to spark the Industrial Revolution in northern Europe and to stimulate commercial activity on a worldwide scale. In addition, American silver helped the Bourbons meet the enormous expenses of their chronic wars.

Colonial manufacturing, after a long and fairly consistent growth, began to decline in the last part of the eighteenth century, principally because of the influx of cheap foreign wares with which the domestic products could not compete. The textile and wine industries of western Argentina fell into decay as they lost their markets in Buenos Aires and Montevideo to lower-priced foreign wines and cloth. The textile producers of the province of Quito in Ecuador complained of injury from the same cause. In the Mexican manufacturing center of Puebla, production of chinaware, of which the city had long been a leading center, slumped catastrophically between 1793 and 1802. Puebla and Querétaro, however, continued to be important centers of textile manufacturing.

Although Spain adopted mercantilist legislation designed to restrict colonial manufacturing—especially of fine textiles—this legislation seems to have been only a small deterrent to the growth of large-scale manufacturing. More important deterrents were lack of investment capital, the characteristic preference of Spaniards for land and mining as fields of investment, and a semiservile system of labor that was equally harmful to the workers and to productivity. Humboldt, who visited the woolen workshops of Querétaro in 1803, was disagreeably impressed

not only with the great imperfection of the technical process in the preparation for dyeing, but in a particular manner also with the unhealthiness of the situation, and the bad treatment to which the workers are exposed. Free men, Indians, and people of color are confounded with the criminals distributed by justice among the manufactories, in order to be compelled to work. All appear half naked, covered with rags, meagre, and deformed. Every workshop resembles a dark prison. The doors, which are double, remain constantly shut,

and the workmen are not permitted to quit the house. Those who are married are only allowed to see their families on Sunday. All are unmercifully flogged, if they commit the smallest trespass on the order established in the manufactory.

One of the few large-scale lines of industry was the manufacture of cigars and cigarettes. In the same town of Querétaro, Humboldt visited a tobacco factory that employed three thousand workers, including nineteen hundred women.

Labor Systems in the Eighteenth Century

Humboldt's comments testify to the persistence of servitude and coercion as essential elements of the labor system from the beginning to the end of the colonial period. Despite the Bourbons' theoretical dislike of forced labor, they sought to tighten legal enforcement of debt peonage in the Indies. Concerned with more efficient collection of Indian tribute, José de Gálvez, the reforming minister of Charles III, tried to attach the natives more firmly to their pueblos and haciendas. In 1769 he introduced in New Spain the system of clearance certificates, documents that certified that peons had no outstanding debts and could seek employment with other landowners. The mobility of peons who lacked these papers could be restricted. Debt peonage was authorized by the Mining Ordinances of New Spain and was also practiced in the gold and silver mines of Chile, where a system of clearance certificates like that used in Mexico was employed. A recent study by James D. Riley notes a trend in Bourbon policy to make debts "considerably less coercive" in Mexico after 1785, but also notes that there was little official reluctance to pursue debtors and force them to pay up or work. On Jesuit farms in eighteenth-century Quito (Ecuador), says Nicholas Cushner, "the debt was a mechanism for maintaining a stable work force" whose wages were pitifully low. "It was an Indian analogue of black slavery," adds Cushner.

In practice, as previously noted, the importance of debt peonage and the severity of its enforcement depended on the availability of labor.

142   In New Spain, by the late eighteenth century, the growth of the labor force through population increase and the elimination of small producers had sharply reduced the importance of debt as a means of securing and holding laborers. Eric Van Young, for example, has documented a reduction of the per capita indebtedness of resident peons in the Guadalajara area, suggesting their decreased bargaining power in dealing with employers. The new situation enabled hacendados to retain or discharge workers in line with changing levels of production. Thus in late eighteenth-century Mexico, landowners simply dismissed workers when crop failures occurred in order to save on their rations. These changes were accompanied by a tendency for real wages and rural living standards to decline.

In the Andean area, in provinces subject to the mita, it continued to play an important role in the provision of mining and agricultural labor almost to the end of the colonial period. In other provinces, agricultural labor was theoretically free, but heavy tribute demands and the operations of the repartimiento de mercancías (the forced purchase of goods by the Indians from corregidors) created a need for cash that compelled many natives to seek employment on Spanish haciendas. These yanaconas included a large number of so-called *forasteros* ("outsiders") who had fled their native pueblos to escape the dreaded mita service and tribute burdens. In addition to working the hacendado's land, these laborers or sharecroppers and their families had to render personal service in the master's household. Theoretically free, their dependent status must have sharply limited their mobility.

Early Labor Struggles

Our knowledge of labor struggles in colonial Spanish America is fragmentary, in part because historians took little interest in the subject until recently. The first labor conflicts of a relatively modern type seem to have taken place in late eighteenth-century Mexico, the colony with the most developed and diversified economy. Strikes sometimes took place in artisan shops; in 1784, for example, the workers in the bakery of Basilio Badamler went on strike to protest "horrible working conditions." More commonly, they occurred in a few industries having large concentrations of workers or a division of labor that promoted workers' cooperation and solidarity. One large-scale industry was the manufacture of cigars and cigarettes by the royal tobacco monopoly, whose founding was accompanied by a ruthless suppression (1773–1776) of artisan production of these goods. The immense factory operated by the monopoly in Mexico City employed about 7,000 workers of both sexes. The workers, who included Indians, mixed-bloods, and some Spaniards, were paid in cash, and the annual payroll in the 1780s and 1790s came to about 750,000 pesos. The militancy of these workers was displayed in strikes and protests and worried the authorities. In 1788 the consulado of Mexico City declared that this large assembly of workers presented a threat to public order, and cited a march on the viceroy's palace caused by a "small increase" in the length of the workday. The workers, heedless of the guards, swarmed into the palace and occupied the patios, stairs, and corridors. The viceroy, having heard their complaint, "prudently gave them a note ordering the factory's administrator to rescind that change, and so with God's help that tumult ended, the multitude left, bearing that note as if in triumph, and the viceroy decided to overlook that turbulent action, so likely to cause sedition." In 1794 the workers again marched on the viceregal palace to protest a change in the contractual arrangement that permitted them to take part of their work home to prepare for the next day's tasks.

A more dramatic labor struggle broke out in the 1780s in the Mexican silver mining industry. The scene of the conflict was the mines of Real del Monte in northern Mexico. Here, as in all other Mexican silver mines, the majority of the work force was free, but a minority of the workers were conscripted from the surrounding Indian villages through a repartimiento, or labor draft. Press gangs also picked up men charged with "idleness" or "vagrancy" to relieve the chronic shortage of labor. It was the grievances of the free skilled workers, however, that caused a series of confrontations with an arrogant unyielding employer and ultimately a work stoppage. The extreme division of labor in the silver mining industry—to get the ore out of the vein below and load it on mules above required some thirty different specialized tasks—tended to develop a sense of shared interests and cooperation among the workers.

Work in the mines was dangerous, daily exposing the miners to loss of life and limb through accidents, and even more to debilitating or fatal diseases. According to Francisco de Gamboa, the leading Mexican mining expert of the time, the miners worked "in terror of ladders giving way, rocks sliding, heavy loads breaking their backs, dripping icy waters, diseases, and the damp, hot, suffocating heat." Humboldt, who visited Mexico in the last years of the colony, claimed that Mexican miners seldom lived past the age of thirty-five. But the pay was good by colonial standards; workers who went below received four reales (fifty cents) for each twelve-hour shift (one real would buy a pound of wool or five pounds of beef or veal), more than double the pay of agricultural workers. This customary pay was supplemented by the *partido,* the skilled worker's right to a certain share of his day's haul of silver ore over an assigned quota.

Attempts by mine owner Romero de Terreros to lower wage rates of *peones* (ore carriers) from four to three reales, increase quotas, and gradually eliminate partidos provoked a series of crises culminating in the strike. A sympathetic parish priest advised the workers on legal ways to achieve their objectives and sought to mediate their dispute with the employer. (The priest was later expelled from the pueblo for his activism.) Eventually, the state intervened, aware of the critical importance of silver production to the royal treasury and of the workers' strong bargaining position because of the chronic labor shortage. Francisco de Gamboa, the leading expert on mining and mining law, was sent to arbitrate the conflict. His arbitration satisfied virtually all the workers' demands: abusive bosses

were fired, the pay cuts revoked, and the right to partidos confirmed in writing.[4]

Doris Ladd has written a brilliant, sensitive reconstruction of these events. She interprets the struggle at Real del Monte as a class struggle prior to the existence of a working class—reflecting an emerging class consciousness—and describes the workers' ideas as "radical" and "revolutionary." She cites the strikers' insistence on social and economic justice, expressed in the words of their lawyer: "It is a precept in all systems of divine, natural, and secular law that there should be a just proportion between labor and profit." But this appeal for justice had a limited scope and significance. It applied to a group of relatively privileged, skilled free workers, but did not call into question the forced labor of Indians dragged by press gangs from their homes to the mines. Thanks to a set of favorable conditions, the strikers won a victory, meaning a return to the situation that prevailed before the dispute broke out. But that victory left the conscripted Indian workers in the same intolerable conditions as before. One wonders whether ideas that accepted Indian servitude as normal can be described as truly "radical" or "revolutionary."

Political Reforms

Under Charles III, the work of territorial reorganization of the sprawling empire continued. The viceroyalty of Peru, already diminished by the creation of New Granada, was further curtailed by the creation in 1776 of the viceroyalty of the Río de la Plata, with its capital at Buenos Aires. This act reflected official Spanish concern over the large volume of contraband in the estuary. It also reflected fear of a possible foreign attack on the area by the British, who had recently entrenched themselves in the nearby Malvinas, or

[4] But the workers' victory at the Real del Monte was not the usual outcome of labor conflicts in the mining areas of New Spain in this period. In the late Bourbon era Mexican mine owners displayed a more aggressive attitude toward their workers. Supported by military and paramilitary forces, they often succeeded in eliminating or reducing the partidos that workers were permitted to keep and in reducing wages.

A baroque portrait (1796) of Count Matías de Gálvez, 49th viceroy of New Spain and brother of the more famous José de Gálvez, Charles III's colonial minister.

Falkland, Islands, or by the Portuguese who, advancing southward from Brazil, has established the settlement of Sacramento on the banks of the estuary, a base from which they threatened shipping and the town of Montevideo. To put an end to this danger the Spanish government mounted a major military expedition designed to establish full control of both banks of the river. The commander Pedro de Cevallos came out with the temporary title of viceroy of Buenos Aires. In 1778 the viceroyalty was made permanent with the appointment of the viceroy Juan José de Vér-

tiz y Salcedo, whose rule of over a decade saw a remarkable growth in the prosperity of the area. This prosperity owed much to the decree of "free trade" of 1778, which authorized direct trade between Buenos Aires and Spain and permitted intercolonial trade. In 1783 the establishment of a royal audiencia at Buenos Aires completed the liberation of the Río de la Plata provinces from the distant rule of Lima. The inclusion of Upper Peru in the new viceroyalty, with the resulting redirection of the flow of Potosí silver from Lima to Buenos Aires, signified a stunning victory for the landowners and merchants of Buenos Aires over their mercantile rivals in Lima.

The trend toward decentralization in the administration of Spanish America, combined with a greater stress on supervision and control from Madrid, reflected not only the struggle against foreign military and commercial penetration but an enlightened awareness of the problems of communication and government posed by the great distances between the various provinces, an awareness spurred by advances in cartography and knowledge of the geography of the continent in general. Two indications of this tendency were the greater autonomy enjoyed by the captaincies general in the eighteenth century and the increase in their number. Thus, in 1777 Venezuela was raised to a captaincy general, as previously mentioned. Similarly, in 1778 Chile was raised from the status of a presidency to that of a captaincy general. The increased autonomy enjoyed by the captains general enabled an enlightened ruler like Ambrosio O'Higgins in Chile to attempt major economic reforms, stimulate mining and manufacturing, introduce new crops, and in general try to promote not only the interests of the Spanish crown but the welfare of the Chilean people.

The creation of new viceroyalties and captaincies general went hand in hand with another major political reform, the transfer to the colonies between 1782 and 1790 of the intendant system, already introduced to Spain by France. This reform was made in the interests of greater administrative efficiency and in the hope of increasing royal revenues from the colonies. The intendants, provincial governors who ruled from the capitals of their provinces, were expected to relieve the overburdened viceroys of many of their duties, especially in financial matters. Among their other duties, the intendants were expected to further the economic development of their districts by promoting the cultivation of new crops, the improvement of mining, the building of roads and bridges, and the establishment of consulados and economic societies. Under their prodding, the lethargic cabildos or town councils were in some cases stirred to greater activity. The Ordinance of Intendants also abolished the offices of corregidor and alcalde mayor, notorious vehicles for the oppression of the natives. These officials were replaced as governors of Indian towns by men called *subdelegados,* who were nominated by the intendants and confirmed by the viceroys.

Many of the intendants at the height of the reform era were capable and cultivated men who not only achieved the objectives of increased economic activity and revenue collection but promoted education and cultural progress generally. But the same could not be said of the majority of their subordinates, the subdelegados, who, like their predecessors, soon became notorious for their oppressive practices. A common complaint was that they continued to compel the Indians to trade with them, although the repartimiento had been forbidden by the Ordinance of Intendants. The great popular revolts of the 1780s were fueled in large part by the failure of the Indian and mixed-blood populations to share in the fruits of the eighteenth-century economic advance, whose principal beneficiaries were Spanish and creole landowners, mine owners, and merchants.

Strengthening the Defenses

Increased revenue was a major objective of the Bourbon commercial and political reforms. A major purpose to which that revenue was applied was the strengthening of the sea and land defenses of the empire. Before the eighteenth century, primary dependence for defense had been placed on naval power: convoy escorts and cruiser squadrons. Before the middle of the eighteenth century, standing armed forces in the colonies were negligible, and authorities relied on local forces raised for particular emergencies. The disasters of the Seven Years' War and the loss of Havana and Manila (1762) to the English, in particular, resulted in a decision to correct the shortcomings in the defense system of the colonies. Fortifications of important American ports were strengthened and colonial armies created. These included regular units stationed permanently in the colonies or rotated between

VICEROYALTIES IN LATIN AMERICA IN 1780

peninsular and overseas service and colonial militia whose ranks were filled by volunteers or drafted recruits.

To make military service attractive to the creole upper class, which provided the officer corps of the new force, the crown granted extensive privileges and exemptions to creole youths who accepted commissions. To the lure of prestige and honors, the grant of the *fuero militar* added protection from civil legal jurisdiction and liability, except for certain specified offenses. The special legal and social position thus accorded to the colonial officer class helped to form a tradition, which has survived to the present in Latin America, of the armed forces as a special caste with its own set of interests, not subject to the civil power, that acted as the arbiter of political life, usually in the interests of conservative ruling classes. Under the Bourbons, however, the power of the colonial military was held in check by such competing groups as the church and the civil bureaucracy.

Although the expansion of the colonial military establishment under the Bourbons offered some opportunities and advantages to upper-class creole youth, it did nothing to allay the long-standing resentment of creoles against their virtual exclusion from the higher offices of state and church and from large-scale commerce. Bourbon policy in regard to the problem went through two phases. In the first half of the eighteenth century, wealthy creoles could sometimes purchase high official posts, and for a time they dominated the prestigious audiencias of Mexico City and Lima. But in the second half of the century, an anticreole reaction took place. José de Gálvez, Charles III's colonial minister, was the very embodiment of the spirit of enlightened despotism that characterized his reign. Gálvez distrusted creole capacity and integrity and removed high-ranking creoles from positions in the imperial administration. The new upper bureaucracy, such as the intendants who took over much of the authority of viceroys and governors, was in the great majority Spanish-born.

Other Bourbon policies injured creole vested interests or wounded their sensibilities and traditions. An example was the sudden expulsion of the Jesuits (1767), who enjoyed much favor among the creole aristocracy.

Potentially more explosive was an issue that arose toward the very end of the colonial period. In 1804 the Spanish crown enacted an emergency revenue measure—the *Consolidación de Vales Reales*—that ordered church institutions in the colonies to call in all their outstanding capital, the liens and mortgages whose interest supported the charitable and pious works of the church. The proceeds were to be loaned to the crown, which would pay annual interest to the church to fund its ecclesiastical activities. Although the primary motive of the Consolidation was to relieve the crown's urgent financial needs, it had the secondary reformist aim of freeing the colonial economy from the burden of mortmain and thus promoting a greater circulation of property.

The measure, however, struck hard at two bulwarks of the colonial order, the church and the propertied elite—the numerous hacendados, merchants, and mine owners who had borrowed large sums from church institutions and now had to repay those sums in full or face loss of property or bankruptcy. Many elite families had also assigned part of the value of their estates to the church to found a chaplaincy, paying annual interest to provide the stipend of the chaplain, often a family member. Although the church had not loaned this capital, officials in charge of the Consolidation demanded that the families involved immediately turn over the value of these endowments, in cash. Many small and medium landowners and other middle-class borrowers from the church were also threatened by the Consolidation decree.

The measure caused a storm of protest, and its application was gradually softened by willingness on the part of the officials in charge to negotiate the amounts and other terms of payment. So strong was the opposition of debtors, both creoles and peninsulars, to the decree that little effort was made to implement it outside of New Spain, which provided more than two-thirds of the 15,000,000 pesos collected before it was canceled in 1808 following Napoleon's invasion of Spain. The Consolidation left a heritage of

148 bitterness, especially among individuals like Father Miguel Hidalgo, future torchbearer of the Mexican War for Independence, whose hacienda was embargoed for several years for failure to pay his debts to the Consolidation. Thus, despite and partly because of the reformist spirit of the Bourbon kings, the creoles became progressively alienated from the Spanish crown. Their alienation intensified an incipient creole nationalism that, denied direct political outlets, found its chief expression in culture and religion.

Colonial Culture and the Enlightenment

Colonial culture in all its aspects was a projection of Spanish culture of the time. If we leave aside the very important work done in the study of Indian antiquity and religions, colonial culture only faintly reflected its American milieu in respect to subject matter and treatment. At least until the eighteenth century, a neomedieval climate of opinion, enforced by the authority of church and state, sharply restricted the play of the colonial intellect and imagination. Colonial culture thus suffered from all the infirmities of its parent but inevitably lacked the breadth and vitality of Spanish literature and art, the product of a much older and more mature civilization. Despite these and other difficulties, such as the limited market for books, colonial culture left a remarkably large and valuable heritage.

The Church and Education

The church enjoyed a virtual monopoly of colonial education at all levels. The primary and secondary schools maintained by the clergy, with few exceptions, were open only to children of the white upper class and the Indian nobility. Poverty condemned the overwhelming majority of the natives and mixed castes to illiteracy. Admission to the universities, which numbered about twenty-five at the end of the colonial era, was even more restricted to youths of ample means and pure white blood.

The universities of Lima and Mexico City, both chartered by the crown in 1551, were the first permanent institutions of higher learning. Patterned on similar institutions in Spain, the colonial university faithfully reproduced their medieval organization, curricula, and methods of instruction. Indifference to practical or scientific studies, slavish respect for the authority of the Bible, Aristotle, the church fathers, and certain medieval schoolmen, and a passion for hairsplitting debate of fine points of theological or metaphysical doctrine were among the features of colonial academic life. Theology and law were the chief disciplines; until the eighteenth century, science was a branch of philosophy, taught from the *Physics* of Aristotle.

A strict censorship of books (no book could be published in either Spain or the colonies without the approval of the Royal Council) limited the spread of new doctrines in colonial society. In recent decades it has been shown that the laws prohibiting the entry of works of fiction into the Spanish colonies were completely ineffective, but this tolerance did not extend to heretical or subversive writings. The records of the colonial Inquisition reveal many tragic cases of imprisonment, torture, and even death for individuals who were charged with the possession and reading of such writings. At least until the eighteenth century, when the intellectual iron curtain surrounding Spanish America began to lift, the people of the colonies were effectively shielded from literature of an unorthodox religious or political tendency.

Yet, within the limits imposed by official censorship and their own backgrounds, colonial scholars were able to make impressive contributions, especially in the fields of Indian history, anthropology, linguistics, and natural history. The sixteenth century was the Golden Age of Indian studies in Spanish America. In Mexico a large group of missionaries, especially members of the Franciscan order, carried out long, patient investigations of the native languages, religion, and history. With the aid of native informants, Friar Bernardino de Sahagún compiled a monumental *General History of the Things of New Spain,* a veritable encyclopedia of information on all aspects of Aztec culture; scholars have only begun to mine the extraordinary wealth of ethnographic materials in Sahagún's work. Another Franciscan, usually known by his Indian name of Motolinía (Friar Toribio de Benavente), wrote a *History of the Indians of New Spain* that is an invaluable guide to Indian life before and after the Conquest. Basing his work on Aztec picture writings and a chronicle, now lost, written by an Indian noble in his own language, Father Diego Durán wrote a history of ancient Mexico that preserves both the content and spirit of Aztec tribal epics and legends. The Jesuit José de Acosta sought to satisfy Spanish curiosity about the natural productions of the New World and the history of the Aztecs and Incas in his *Natural and Moral History of the Indies.* His book, simply and pleasantly written, displays a critical spirit rare for its time; it achieved an immediate popularity in Spain and was quickly translated into all the major languages of western Europe.

Not a few historical works were written by Indian or mestizo nobles actuated by a variety of motives: interest and pride in their native heritage joined to a desire to prove the important services rendered by their forebears to the Conquest and the validity of their claims to noble titles and land. Products of convent schools or colegios, they usually combined Christian piety with nostalgic regard for the departed glories of their ancestors. A descendant of the kings of Texcoco, Fernando de Alva Ixtlilxochitl, wrote a number of historical works that show a mastery of European historical method. These works combine a great amount of valuable information with a highly idealized picture of Texcocan civilization. Another writer of the early seventeenth century, the mestizo Garcilaso de la Vega, son of a Spanish conquistador and an Inca princess, gives in his *Royal Commentaries of the Incas,* together with much valuable information on Inca material culture and history, an idyllic picture of Peruvian life under the benevolent rule of the Inca kings. His book, written in a graceful, fluent Spanish, is more than a history; it is a first-class work of art. No other Spanish history was as popular in Europe as Garcilaso's *Royal Commentaries;* its fa-

vorable image of Inca civilization continues to influence our view of ancient Peru down to the present. A precious work, richly informative about social conditions in Peru before and after the Conquest, and illustrated with the author's own delightfully naive drawings, is the *New Chronicle* by the seventeenth-century Indian noble Felipe Waman Puma de Ayala, whose manuscript did not come to light until the early twentieth century. Waman Puma tells that he left his home in order "to know the needs of, and to redeem the poor Indians, for whom there is no justice in this kingdom," and that he hoped that his work would be read by Philip III. Waman Puma's painful effort to express himself in the unfamiliar Castilian tongue, the passionate rush of words interspersed with Quechua terms, the melancholy and disillusioned tone of the work testify to the author's sincerity and the reality of the abuses that he denounces.

Science, Literature, and the Arts

The second half of the seventeenth century saw a decline in the quantity and quality of colonial scholarly production. This was the age of the baroque style in literature, a style that stressed word play, cleverness, and pedantry, that subordinated content to form, meaning to ornate expression. Yet two remarkable men of this period, Carlos Sigüenza y Góngora in Mexico and Pedro de Peralta Barnuevo in Peru, foreshadowed the eighteenth-century Enlightenment by the universality of their interests and their concern with the practical uses of science. Sigüenza—mathematician, archaeologist, and historian—attacked the ancient but still dominant superstition of astrology in his polemic with the Jesuit father Kino over the nature of comets; he also defied prejudice by providing in his will for the dissection of his body in the interests of science. He made careful observations of comets and eclipses of the sun and exchanged his observations with scientists in Europe. Yet the prevailing baroque spirit of fantasy appeared in his speculation that the Greek god Poseidon was the great-grandson of Noah and the forebear of the American Indians.

150

Peralta Barnuevo, cosmographer and mathematician, made astronomical observations that were published in Paris in the *Proceedings* of the French Royal Academy of Sciences, of which he was elected corresponding member; he also superintended the construction of fortifications in Lima. Yet this able and insatiably curious man of science also sought refuge in a baroque mysticism, and in one of his last works concluded that true wisdom, the knowledge of God, was not "subject to human comprehension."

Colonial literature, with some notable exceptions, was a pallid reflection of prevailing literary trends in the mother country. The isolation from foreign influences, the strict censorship of all reading matter, and the limited audience for writing of every kind made literary creation difficult. "A narrow and dwarfed world," the discouraged Mexican poet Bernardo de Balbuena called the province of New Spain. To make matters worse, colonial literature in the seventeenth century succumbed to the Spanish literary fad of *Gongorismo* (so called after the poet Luis de Góngora), the cult of an obscure, involved, and artificial style.

Amid a flock of "jangling magpies," as one literary historian describes the Gongorist versifiers of the seventeenth century, appeared the incomparable songbird, known to her admiring contemporaries as "the tenth muse"—Sor Juana Inés de la Cruz, the remarkable nun and poet who assembled in her convent one of the finest mathematical libraries of the time. But Sor Juana could not escape the pressures of her environment. Rebuked by the bishop of Puebla for her worldly interests, she ultimately gave up her books and scientific interests and devoted the remainder of her brief life to religious devotion and charitable works.

Colonial art drew its principal inspiration from Spanish sources, but, especially in the sixteenth century, Indian influence was sometimes visible in design and ornamentation. Quito in Ecuador and Mexico City were among the chief centers of artistic activity. The first school of fine arts in the New World was established in Mexico City in 1779 under royal auspices. As might be expected,

Sor Juana Inés de la Cruz, sometimes called the greatest Spanish-American poet of the colonial period, entered a convent when she was eighteen years old and died at the age of forty-four. Sor Juana wrote both secular and religious poetry, but it is her love poems for which she was most admired.

religious motifs dominated painting and sculpture. In architecture the colonies followed Spanish examples, with the severe classical style of the sixteenth century giving way in the seventeenth to the highly ornamented baroque and in the eighteenth century to a style that was even more ornate.

The intellectual atmosphere of the Spanish colonies was not conducive to scientific inquiry or achievement. As late as 1773, the Colombian botanist Mutis was charged with heresy for giving lectures in Bogotá on the Copernican system. The prosecutor of the Inquisition asserted that Mutis was "perhaps the only man in Latin America to uphold Copernicus." In the last decades of the eighteenth century, however, the growing volume of economic and intellectual contacts with Europe and the patronage and protection of enlightened governors created more favorable conditions for scientific activity. Science made its greatest strides in the wealthy province of New Spain, where the expansion of the mining industry stimulated interest in geology, chemistry, mathematics, and metallurgy. In Mexico City there arose a school of mines, a botanical garden, and an academy of fine arts. The Mexican scientific renaissance produced a galaxy of brilliant figures that included Antonio de León y Gama, an astronomer of whose writings Humboldt commented that they displayed "a great precision of ideas and accuracy of observation"; Antonio de Alzate, whose *Gaceta de Literatura* brought to creole youth the knowledge of Europe's scientific advances and who championed the intelligence and capacity of the Indian; and Joaquín Velázquez Cárdenas y León, astronomer, geographer, and mathematician, whose services to his country included the founding of the school of mines. These men combined Enlightenment enthusiasm for rationalism, empiricism, and progress with a strict Catholic orthodoxy; Alzate, for example, vehemently denounced in his *Gaceta* the "infidelity" and skepticism of Europe's philosophes.

Spain itself, now under the rule of the enlightened Bourbon kings, contributed to the intellectual renovation of the colonies. A major liberalizing influence, in both Spain and its colonies, was exerted by the early eighteenth-century friar Benito Feijóo, whose numerous essays waged war on folly and superstition of every kind. Feijóo helped to naturalize the Enlightenment in the Spanish-speaking world by his lucid exposition of the ideas of Bacon, Newton, and Descartes. Spanish and foreign scientific expeditions to Spanish America, authorized and sometimes financed by the crown, also stimulated the growth of scientific thought and introduced the colonists to such distinguished representatives of European science as the Frenchman La Condamine and the German Alexander von Humboldt.

Among the clergy, the Jesuits were most skillful and resourceful in the effort to reconcile church dogma with the ideas of the Enlightenment, in bridging the old and the new. In Mexico, Jesuit writers like Andrés de Guevara, Pedro José Marquez, and Francisco Javier Clavigero praised and taught the doctrines of Bacon, Descartes, and Newton. These Jesuits exalted physics above metaphysics and the experimental method over abstract reasoning and speculation, but all of them combined these beliefs with undeviating loyalty to the teachings of the church. Thus, the expulsion of the Jesuits from Spanish America removed from the scene the ablest, most subtle defenders of the traditional Catholic world view. In their Italian exile—for it was in Italy that most of the Jesuit exiles settled—some of them occupied their leisure time writing books designed to make known to the world the history and geography of their American homelands. The most important of these works by Jesuit exiles was the *History of Ancient Mexico* (1780–1781) of Francisco Clavigero, the best work of its kind written to date and an excellent illustration of the characteristic Jesuit blend of Catholic orthodoxy with the critical, rationalist approach of the Enlightenment.

Despite their frequent and sincere professions of loyalty to the crown, the writings of colonial intellectuals revealed a sensitivity to social and political abuses, a discontent with economic backwardness, and a dawning sense of nationality that contained potential dangers for the Spanish regime. Colonial newspapers and journals played a significant part in the development of a critical and reformist spirit among the educated creoles of Spanish America. Subjected to an oppressive censorship by church and state and beset by chronic financial difficulties, they generally had short and precarious lives. More important than the routine news items they carried were the articles on scientific, economic, and social problems they housed and the ideas of social utility, progress, and the conquest of nature they vigorously announced.

The circulation and influence of forbidden books among educated colonials steadily increased in the closing decades of the eighteenth

152 century and the first years of the nineteenth. It would nevertheless be incorrect to conclude, as some writers have done, that the Inquisition became a toothless tiger in the eighteenth century and that radical ideas could be advocated with almost total impunity. It is true that the influence of the Inquisition weakened under the Bourbons, especially Charles III, because of the growth of French influence. But the censorship was never totally relaxed, the Inquisition continued vigilant, and with every turn of the diplomatic wheel that drew Spain and France apart the inquisitorial screws were tightened. Thus, the outbreak of the French Revolution brought a wave of repression against advocates of radical ideas in Mexico, culminating in a major *auto-da-fé* in Mexico City at which long prison sentences and other severe penalties were handed out. How powerless these repressions were to check the movement of new thought is illustrated by the writings of the fathers of Spanish-American independence. Their works reveal a thorough knowledge of the ideas of Locke, Montesquieu, Raynal, and other important figures of the Enlightenment.

Creole Nationalism

The incipient creole nationalism, however, built on other foundations than the ideas of the European Enlightenment, which were alien and suspect to the masses. Increasingly conscious of themselves as a class and of their respective provinces as their *patrias* (fatherlands), creole intellectuals of the eighteenth century assembled an imposing body of data designed to refute the attacks of such eminent European writers as Comte Georges de Buffon and Cornelius de Pauw, who proclaimed the inherent inferiority of the New World and its inhabitants.

In the largest sense, the creole patria was all America. As early as 1696, the Mexican Franciscan Agustín de Vetancurt claimed that the New World was superior to the Old in natural beauty and resources. New Spain and Peru, he wrote in florid prose, were two breasts from which the whole world drew sustenance, drinking blood changed into the milk of gold and silver. In a change of imagery, he compared America to a beautiful woman adorned with pearls, emeralds, sapphires, chrysolites, and topazes, drawn from the jewel boxes of her rich mines.

In the prologue to his *History of Ancient Mexico,* Clavigero stated that his aim was "to restore the truth to its splendor, truth obscured by an incredible multitude of writers on America." The epic, heroic character that Clavigero gave the history of ancient Mexico reflected the creole search for origins, for a classical antiquity other than the European, to which the peninsulars could lay better claim. The annals of the Toltecs and the Aztecs, he insisted, offered as many examples of valor, patriotism, wisdom, and virtue as the histories of Greece and Rome. Mexican antiquity displayed such models of just and benevolent rule as the wise Chichimec king Xolotl and philosopher-kings such as Nezahualcoyotl and Nezahualpilli. In this way, Clavigero provided the nascent Mexican nationality with a suitably dignified and heroic past. The Chilean Jesuit Juan Ignacio Molina developed similar themes in his *History of Chile* (1782).

The creole effort to develop a collective self-consciousness also found expression in religious thought and symbolism. In his *Quetzalcoatl and Guadalupe: The Formation of Mexican National Consciousness* (1976), Jacques Lafaye has shown how creole intellectuals exploited two powerful myths in the attempt to achieve Mexican spiritual autonomy and even superiority vis-à-vis Spain. One was the myth that the Virgin Mary appeared in 1531 on the hill of Tepeyac, near Mexico City, to an Indian called Juan Diego and through him commanded the bishop of Mexico to build a church there. The proof demanded by the bishop came in the form of winter roses from Tepeyac, enfolded in Juan Diego's cloak, which was miraculously painted with the image of the Virgin. From the seventeenth century, the *indita,* the brown-faced Indian Virgin (as opposed to the Virgin of Los Remedios, who had allegedly aided Cortés) was venerated throughout Mexico as the Virgin of Guadalupe. Under her banner, in fact,

Miguel Hidalgo in 1810 was to lead the Indian and mestizo masses in a great revolt against Spanish rule.

The other great myth was that of Quetzalcóatl, the Toltec redeemer-king and god. Successive colonial writers had suggested that Quetzalcóatl was none other than the Christian apostle St. Thomas. On December 12, 1794, the creole Dominican Servando Teresa de Mier arose in his pulpit in the town of Guadalupe to proclaim that Quetzalcóatl was in fact St. Thomas, who long centuries before had come with four disciples to preach the Gospel in the New World. In this the Apostle had succeeded, and at the time of the Conquest, Christianity—somewhat altered, to be sure—reigned in Mexico. If Mier was right, America owed nothing to Spain, not even her Christianity. Spanish officials, quickly recognizing the revolutionary implications of Mier's sermon, arrested him and exiled him to Spain.

The episode illustrates the devious channels through which creole nationalism moved to achieve its ends. One of those ends was creole hegemony over the Indian and mixed-blood masses, based on their awareness of their common patria and their collective adherence to such national cults as that of the Virgin of Guadalupe in Mexico. In the 1780s, however, the accumulated wrath of those people broke out in a series of explosions that threatened the very existence of the colonial social and political order. In this crisis the creole upper class showed that their aristocratic patria did not really include the Indians, mestizos, and blacks among its sons, that their rhetorical sympathy for the dead Indians of Moctezuma's and Atahualpa's time did not extend to the living Indians of their own time.

Colonial Society in Transition, 1750–1810: An Overview

An estimate by the late historian Charles Gibson put the population of Spanish America toward the end of the colonial period at about 17 million people. Gibson supposed that of this total some 7,500,000 were Indians; about 3,200,000, whites; perhaps 750,000, blacks; and the remaining 5,500,000, castas. Those figures point to a continuing steady revival of the Indian population from the low point of its decline in the early seventeenth century, a more rapid increase of the European population, and an even faster increase of the castas.

In the late colonial period the racial categories used to describe and rank the groups composing the colonial population in terms of their "honor" or lack of "honor" became increasingly ambiguous. One reason was the growing mobility of the colonial population, resulting in a more rapid pace of Hispanicization and racial mixture. The laws forbidding Indians to reside in Spanish towns and whites and mixed-bloods to live in Indian towns were now generally disregarded. Large numbers of Indians seeking escape from tribute and repartimiento burdens migrated to the Spanish cities and mining camps, where they learned to speak Spanish, wore European clothes, and adopted other Spanish ways. The many Spaniards and mestizos who settled in Indian communities contributed to the process of race mixture and Hispanicization. Indians who lived in villages remote from the main areas of Spanish economic activity were less likely to be influenced by the presence of Spaniards and mestizos and therefore remained more "Indian." For a variety of reasons connected with the area's history, geography, and economic patterns, the Indian communities in the viceroyalty of Peru seem to have resisted acculturation more tenaciously than those of New Spain. But those Indians who left their pueblos and became assimilated to the white population in dress and language and who achieved even a modest level of prosperity increasingly came to be regarded legally "Spaniards," that is, creoles. The same was true of Hispanicized mestizos and, less frequently perhaps, blacks and mulattos. An individual's race, in short, now tended to be defined not by his color but by such traits as occupation, dress, speech, and how he perceived himself.

The economic advance of the late Bourbon era, featured by the rapid growth of commercial

154

agriculture, mining, and domestic and foreign trade, created opportunities for some fortunate lower-class individuals and contributed to the declining significance of racial labels. A growing number of wealthy mestizo and mulatto families sought to rise in the social scale by marrying their sons and daughters to children of the white elite. Charles III's policy on interracial marriage reflected the dilemmas of this reformer-king, who wished to promote the rise of a progressive middle class but feared to undermine the foundations of the old aristocratic order. Charles, who removed the stigma attached to artisan labor by decreeing that it was no bar to nobility, also issued decrees that empowered colonial parents to refuse consent to interracial marriages of their children that threatened the family's "honor." As interpreted by high colonial courts, however, these decrees as a rule only sanctioned such parental refusal when the parties to a proposed marriage were unequal in wealth, meaning, as previously noted, that a wealthy mulatto was a suitable marriage partner for a member of the white elite. The last Bourbon kings also promoted social mobility by permitting *pardos* (free mulattos), despised for their slave origin, to buy legal whiteness through the purchase of dispensations (*cédulas de gracias al sacar*) that freed them from the status of "infamous." The motives for this liberal policy were not altogether fiscal. The policy, says John Lynch, "was also perhaps part of the economic program of the metropolis and an aspect of its attack on aristocratic power and independence. To increase social mobility would be to reinforce the white elite by an economically motivated and ambitious class; this would simultaneously subvert aristocratic ideals of honor and status and enhance entrepreneurial values."

It would be an error to suppose that these concessions to a small number of wealthy mixed-bloods reflected a crumbling of the caste system and the ideology on which it was based. The very eagerness of mulattos and mestizos to achieve whiteness by purchase of the dispensations mentioned above, the protest of elite groups like the cabildo of Caracas against the more liberal Bourbon racial policy as promoting "the amalgama-

tion of whites and pardos," and the readiness of some parents to litigate against their children to prevent their marriage to dark-skinned individuals testify to the continuing hold of racial prejudice and stereotypes on the colonial mentality.

The partial penetration of elite society, even on its highest levels, by individuals having some traces of Indian or Negro blood, did not alter the rigidity of the class structure, the sharp class distinctions, the vast gulf separating the rich and the poor. Humboldt spoke of "that monstrous inequality of rights and wealth" which characterized late colonial Mexico. But the late colonial period saw some change in the economic base of the elite and some shifts in the relative weight of its various sectors. If the seventeenth century was the golden age of the large landowners, the eighteenth century, especially its last decades, saw their ascendancy challenged by the growing wealth and political and social influence of the export-import merchant class, most of whose members were of Spanish immigrant origin. The merchants provided the capital needed by the mining industry and absorbed much of its profits. They also financed the purchase of the posts of corregidors, officials who monopolized trade with the Indian communities in collusion with the merchants. In order to provide a hedge against commercial losses—not just to secure the prestige identified with landownership—wealthy merchants acquired estates, establishing hacienda complexes producing a variety of crops and situated to supply the major markets. They further diversified by acquiring flour mills, obrajes, and establishing themselves as major retailers, not only in the cities but in the countryside. The wealthiest married into rich and powerful creole extended families, forming an Establishment whose offspring had preference in appointments to important and prestigious positions in the colonial government and church.

The second half of the eighteenth century saw a new wave of immigration from the peninsula. The presence of these newcomers, often of humble origins, who competed with the American-born Spaniards for limited employment opportunities, sharpened the traditional creole resentment of gachupines or chapetones (tenderfoot). Although, according to Humboldt, "the lowest, least educated and uncultivated European believes himself superior to the white born in the New World," most of the new arrivals failed to find the high-status and well-paid employments they expected. The 1753 and 1811 census reports for Mexico City listed some Spaniards working as unskilled laborers and house servants and still others as jobless. The *Diario de México* often carried advertisements by jobless Spanish immigrants willing to accept any kind of low-level supervisory post. Two observant Spanish officials, Jorge Juan and Antonio de Ulloa, who visited the city of Cartagena in New Granada about 1750, found that there the whites, whether creoles or Europeans, disdained any trade below that of commerce. "But it being impossible for all to succeed, great numbers not being able to secure sufficient credit, they become poor and miserable from their aversion to the trades they follow in Europe, and instead of the riches which they flattered themselves with possessing in the Indies, they experience the most complicated wretchedness."

The Revolt of the Masses

A traditional view portrayed the Indian as the more or less passive object of Spanish rule or of an acculturation process. In recent decades, deeper, more careful study of the Indian response to Spanish rule has revealed that the Indians were not mere "passive victims of Spanish colonization" but activists who from the first resisted Spanish rule with a variety of strategies and thereby were able in some degree to modify the colonial environment and shape their own lives and futures. These strategies included revolts, flight, riots, sabotage, and sometimes even using their masters' legal codes for purposes of defense and offense.

Flight, under conditions of intense Spanish competition for Indian labor, effectively evaded Spanish pressures. Historian Jeffrey Cole points out, for example, that Indians' abandonment of pueblos subject to the mita in order to work as yanaconas on farms, ranches, and other enterprises in exempted areas "was their most effective means of opposing the mita, the demands of their curacas and corregidores, and other obligations." Indians also skillfully used Spanish legal codes for purposes of "defense, redress, and even offense." Historian Steve Stern's recent study of the Peruvian province of Huamanga shows that the Indians lightened the burdens of the mita through the defensive strategy of "engaging in aggressive, persistent, often shrewd use of Spanish juridical institutions to lower legal quotas, delay delivery of specific corvées and tributes, disrupt production, and the like." In Mexico there were countless riots—*tumultos*—in the eighteenth century. Indians let Spanish authority know that it could not take them for granted and must heed their complaints.

Revolt was the highest, most dramatic form of resistance to Spanish rule by the Indians and other oppressed groups. Numerous Indian and black slave revolts punctuated the colonial period of Spanish-American history. Before Spanish rule had been firmly established, the Indians rose against their new masters in many regions. In Mexico the Mixton war raged from 1540 to 1542. The Maya of Yucatán staged a great uprising in 1546. A descendant of the Inca kings, Manco II, led a nationwide revolt in 1536 against the Spanish conquerors of Peru. In Chile the indomitable Araucanians began a struggle for independence that continued into the late nineteenth century. In the jungles and mountains of the West Indies, Central America, and northern South America, groups of runaway black slaves established communities that successfully resisted Spanish efforts to destroy them. The revolutionary wave subsided in the seventeenth century but peaked again in the eighteenth when new burdens were imposed on the common people.

The Bourbon reforms helped to enrich colonial landowners, merchants, and mine owners, beautified their cities, and broadened the intellectual horizons of upper-class youths, but the multitude did not share in these benefits. On the contrary, Bourbon efforts to increase the royal revenues by the creation of governmental monopolies and privileged companies and the imposition of new

156

taxes actually made more acute the misery of the lower classes. This circumstance helps to explain the popular character of the revolts of 1780–1781, as distinct from the creole wars of independence of the next generation. With rare exceptions, the privileged creole group either supported the Spaniards against the native uprisings or joined the revolutionary movements under pressure, only to desert them at a later time.

Revolt in Peru

In the eighteenth century, Spanish pressures and demands on the Peruvian Indians increased considerably. A major mechanism for the extraction of surplus from the natives was the previously mentioned repartimiento de mercancías, the mandatory purchase of goods from the corregidor by the Indians of his district. The system functioned as follows: a Lima merchant advanced the sum of money needed by a corregidor to buy his post from the crown. The merchant also outfitted the corregidor with the stock of goods that he would "distribute," that is, force the Indians of his district to buy, sometimes for six or eight times their fair market price. In the Cuzco region typical repartimiento goods were mules and textiles, but sometimes these goods included items for which the Indians had no possible use. The Indians had to pay for their purchases within an allotted time or else go to prison, forcing many to leave their villages in order to obtain the needed cash by work in mines, obrajes, and haciendas. The system thus served to erode the traditional peasant economy and promoted two objectives of the state, the merchants, and other ruling class groups: the expansion of both the internal market for goods and the labor market.

The repartimiento de mercancías was among the most hateful of the exactions to which the Indians were subjected. A recent study finds that it figured as a cause in the great majority of Indian revolts in Peru in the eighteenth century.

In the same period the burdens imposed on the Indians by the mining mita increased. Determined to return the output of Potosí silver to its former high levels, the crown and the mine owners made innovations that greatly intensified the exploitation of Indian labor. The ore quotas that the *mitayos* (drafted workers) were required to produce were doubled between 1740 and 1790 from about fifteen loads per day to thirty, forcing the mitayos to work longer for the same wages and compelling their wives and children to assist them in meeting the quotas. In the same period the wages of both mitayos and mingas (free workers) were reduced. These innovations produced the desired revival of Potosí, with a doubling of silver production, but at a heavy price in Indian health and living standards.

Coupled with increases in alcabalas (sales taxes), the continuing abuses of the repartimiento de mercancías and the mita caused intense discontent. A critical point was reached when visitador José de Areche, sent out by Charles III in 1777 to reform conditions in the colony, tightened up the collection of tribute and sales taxes and broadened the tributary category to include all mestizos. As a result the contribution of the Indians was increased by one million pesos annually. These measures not only caused great hardships to the commoners but created greater difficulties for the native curacas, or chiefs, who were responsible for meeting tribute quotas. Areche himself foretold the storm to come when he wrote: "The lack of righteous judges, the mita of the Indians, and provincial commerce have made a corpse of this America. Corregidores are interested only in themselves. . . . How near everything is to ruin if these terrible abuses are not corrected, for they have been going on a long time."

The discontent of the Indian masses with their intolerable conditions inspired messianic dreams and expectations of a speedy return of the Inca and the Inca empire. The popular imagination transformed this Inca empire into an ideal state, free from hunger and injustice, and free from the presence of oppressive colonial officials and exploitative mines, haciendas, and obrajes. This utopian vision of a restored Inca empire played a part in causing the great revolt of 1780–1781 and determining its direction.

That revolt had its forerunners; between 1730 and 1780 there were 128 rebellions, large and small, in the Andean area. From 1742 to 1755, a

José Gabriel Condorcanqui, an educated and wealthy mestizo, took the name of the last Inca and led the great Peruvian revolt against Spain. Like his predecessor, Tupac Amaru II was defeated, captured, and executed.

native leader called Juan Santos, "the invincible," waged partisan warfare against the Spaniards from his base in the eastern slopes of the Andes. The memory of his exploits was still alive when the revolt of José Gabriel Condorcanqui began. A well-educated, wealthy mestizo descendant of the Inca kings who was strongly influenced by accounts of the Inca splendor in the *Royal Commentaries* of Garcilaso de la Vega, he had made repeated, fruitless efforts to obtain relief for his people through legal channels. In November 1780 he raised the standard of revolt by ambushing the hated corregidor Antonio de Arriaga near the town of Tinta and putting him to death after a summary trial. At this time he also took the name of the last head of the neo-Inca state and became Tupac Amaru II. His actions were preceded by an uprising led by the Catari brothers in the territory of present-day Bolivia. By the first months of 1781, the southern highlands of the viceroyalty of Peru were aflame with revolt. Although the vari-

ous revolutionary movements lacked a unified direction, the rebel leaders generally recognized Tupac Amaru as their chief and continued to invoke his name even after his death.

In the first stage of the revolt, Tupac Amaru did not make his objectives entirely clear. In some public statements he proclaimed his loyalty to the Spanish king and church, limiting his demands to the abolition of the mita, the repartimiento, the alcabala, and other taxes; the suppression of the corregidors; and the appointment of Indian governors for the provinces. But it is difficult to believe that the well-educated Tupac Amaru, who had had years of experience in dealing with Spanish officialdom, seriously believed that he could obtain sweeping reforms from the crown by negotiation, especially after his execution of the corregidor Arriaga. His protestations of loyalty were soon contradicted by certain documents in which he styled himself king of Peru, by the war of fire and blood that he urged against peninsular Spaniards (excepting only the clergy), and by the government that he established for the territory under his control.

More plausible is the view that his professions of loyalty to Spain represented a mask by which he could utilize the still strong faith of many Indians in the mythical benevolence of the Spanish king, attract creole supporters of reform to his cause, and perhaps soften his punishment in case of defeat.

For Tupac Amaru, who had been educated in a Spanish colegio and had thoroughly absorbed the values of Spanish culture, the objective of the revolt was the establishment of an independent Peruvian state that would be essentially European in its political and social organization. His program called for complete independence from Spain, expulsion of peninsular Spaniards, and the abolition of the offices of viceroy, audiencia, and corregidor. The Inca empire would be restored, with himself as king, assisted by a nobility formed from other descendants of the Cuzco noble clans. Caste distinctions would disappear, and creoles, on whose support Tupac Amaru heavily counted, would live in harmony with Indians, blacks, and mestizos. The Catholic church

158

would remain the state church and be supported by tithes. Tupac Amaru's economic program called for suppression of the mita, the repartimiento de mercancías, customshouses and sales taxes, and for elimination of great estates and servitude, but would permit small and medium-sized landholdings and encourage trade. Tupac Amaru's plan, in short, called for an anticolonial, national revolution that would create a unified people and a modern state of European type that could promote economic development.

But the Indian peasantry who responded to his call for revolt had a different conception of its meaning and goal. In an atmosphere of messianic excitement they came to view it as a *pachacuti*, a great cataclysm or "overthrow" that would bring a total inversion of the existing social order and a return to an idealized Inca empire where the humble *runa* or peasant would not be last but first. In their desire to avenge the cruelties of the Conquest and two and a half centuries of brutal exploitation they sacked haciendas and killed their owners without troubling to ascertain whether they were creoles or Europeans; a Spaniard was one who had a white skin and wore European dress. As the revolt spread, the old pagan religion emerged from the underground where it had hidden and flourished for centuries. Tupac Amaru, who sought to maintain good relations with the Catholic church, always went about accompanied by two priests and hoped for support by Bishop Moscoso of Cuzco. But his peasant followers sacked the vestments and ornaments of churches and attacked and killed priests, hanging a number of friars during the siege of Cuzco. In December 1780 Tupac Amaru entered one Indian village and summoned its inhabitants, who greeted him with the words: "You are our God and we ask that there be no priests to pester us." He replied that he could not allow this, for it would mean that there would be no one to attend them "in the moment of death."

These opposed conceptions of the meaning and objectives of the revolt held by Tupac Amaru and his peasant followers spelled defeat for Tupac Amaru's strategy of forming a common proindependence front of all social and racial groups except the peninsular Spaniards. The spontaneous, uncontrollable violence of the peasant rebels ended what little chance existed of attracting the support of the creoles, reformist clergy like Bishop Moscoso, and many Indian nobles. At least twenty Indian caciques, jealous of Tupac Amaru or fearful of losing their privileged status, led their subjects into the Spanish camp. Although the principal base of the revolt was *ayllus* (free peasant communities), the Spaniards were able to mobilize large numbers of yanaconas who helped to break the siege of Cuzco and suppress the revolt.

Tactical errors contributing to the revolt's defeat included failure to attack Cuzco (the ancient Inca capital) and capitalize on the political and psychological significance of its capture before the arrival of Spanish reinforcements. Poor communications between the rebel forces and the vastly superior arms and organization of the royalist armies contributed to the same result. Despite some initial successes, the rebel leader soon suffered a complete rout. Tupac Amaru, members of his family, and his leading captains were captured and put to death, some with ferocious cruelty. In the territory of present-day Bolivia the insurrection continued two years longer, reaching its high point in two prolonged sieges of La Paz (March-October 1781).

The last Inca revolt moved the crown to enact a series of reforms that included the replacement of the hated corregidores by the system of intendants and subdelegados and the establishment of an audiencia or high court in Cuzco, another of Tupac Amaru's goals before the revolt. But these and other reforms proved to be changes in form rather than substance. The miserably paid subdelegados, many of whom were former corregidores, continued the exploitive practices of their predecessors, including the repartimiento de mercancías, which was forbidden by the Ordinance of Intendants. As a result, at the opening of the nineteenth century the Peruvian peasantry continued to be subject to the same or even greater burdens than those that had caused it to rebel in 1780.

Insurrection in New Granada (1781)

The revolt of the Comuneros in New Granada, like that in Peru, had its origin in intolerable economic conditions. Unlike the Peruvian upheaval, however, it was more clearly limited in its aims to the redress of grievances. Increases in the alcabala and a whole series of new taxes, including one on tobacco and a poll tax, provoked an uprising in Socorro, an important agricultural and manufacturing center in the north. The disturbances soon spread to other communities. The reformist spirit of the revolt was reflected in the insurgent slogan: *viva el rey y muera el mal gobierno!* (Long live the king, down with the evil government!)

In view of its organization and its effort to form a common front of all colonial groups with grievances against Spanish authority (excepting the black slaves), the revolt of the Comuneros marked an advance over the rather chaotic course of events to the south. A *común* (central committee), elected in the town of Socorro by thousands of peasants and artisans from adjacent towns, directed the insurrection. Each of the towns in revolt also had its común and a captain chosen by popular election.

Under the command of hesitant or unwilling creole leaders, a multitude of Indian and mestizo peasants and artisans marched on the capital of Bogotá, capturing or putting to flight the small forces sent from the capital. Playing for time until reinforcements could arrive from the coast, the royal audiencia dispatched a commission headed by the archbishop to negotiate with the Comuneros. The popular character of the movement and the unity of oppressed groups that it represented were reflected in the terms that the rebel delegates presented to the Spanish commissioners and that the latter signed and later repudiated; these terms included reduction of Indian and mestizo tribute and sales taxes, return to the Indians of land usurped from them, abolition of the new tax on tobacco, and preference for creoles over Europeans in the filling of official posts.

An agreement reached on June 4, 1781, satisfied virtually all the demands of the rebels and was sanctified by the archbishop in a special religious service. Secretly, however, the Spanish commissioners signed another document declaring the agreement void because it was obtained by force. The jubilant insurgents scattered and returned to their homes. Only José Antonio Galán, a young mestizo peasant leader, maintained his small force intact and sought to keep the revolt alive.

Having achieved their objective of disbanding the rebel army, the Spanish officials prepared to crush the insurrection completely. The viceroy Manuel Antonio Flores openly repudiated the agreement with the Comuneros. Following a pastoral visit to the disaffected region by the archbishop, who combined seductive promises of reform with threats of eternal damnation for confirmed rebels, Spanish troops brought up from the coast moved into the region and took large numbers of prisoners. The creole leaders of the revolt hastened to atone for their political sins by collaborating with the royalists. Galán, who had vainly urged a new march on Bogotá, was seized by a renegade leader and handed over to the Spaniards, who put him to death by hanging on January 30, 1782. The revolt of the Comuneros had ended.

Chapter 8

The Independence of Latin America

The Bourbon reforms, combined with the upsurge of the European economy in the eighteenth century, brought material prosperity and less tangible benefits to many upper-class creoles of Spanish America. Enlightened viceroys and intendants introduced improvements and refinements that made life in colonial cities more healthful and attractive. Educational reforms, the influx of new books and ideas, and increased opportunities to travel and study in Europe widened the intellectual horizons of creole youth.

These gains, however, did not strengthen creole feelings of loyalty to the mother country. Instead, they enlarged their aspirations and sharpened their sense of grievance. The growing wealth of some sections of the creole elite made more galling its virtual exclusion from important posts in administration and the church. Meanwhile, the swelling production of creole haciendas, plantations, and ranches pressed against the trade barriers maintained by Spanish mercantilism. The intendant of Caracas, José Abalos, warned that "if His Majesty does not grant them [the creoles] the freedom of trade which they desire, then he cannot count on their loyalty." At the same time, Bourbon policy denied American manufacturers the protection they needed against crippling European competition.

Background of the Wars of Independence

Creoles and Peninsular Spaniards

The conflict of interest between Spain and its colonies was most sharply expressed in the cleavage between the creoles and the peninsular Spaniards. This quarrel was constantly renewed by the arrival of more Spaniards. In the late eighteenth century, a typical immigrant was a poor but hardworking and thrifty Basque or Navarrese who became an apprentice to a peninsular merchant, often a relative. In the course of time, as his merits won recognition, the immigrant might receive a daughter of the house in marriage and eventually succeed to the ownership of the business. One of the merchant's own creole sons might be given a landed estate; other creole sons might enter the church or the law, both overcrowded professions.

Thus, although there was some elite creole presence in both foreign and domestic trade, peninsular Spaniards continued to dominate the lucrative export-import trade and provincial trade. Spanish-born merchants, organized in powerful consulados, or merchant guilds, also played a key role in financing mining and the repartimiento business carried on among the Indians by Spanish officials. Not unnaturally, some upper-class creoles, excluded from mercantile activity and responsible posts in the government and church, developed the aristocratic manners and idle, spendthrift ways with which the peninsulars reproached them. Many other creoles of the middling sort, vegetating in ill-paid Indian curacies and minor government jobs, bitterly resented the institutionalized discrimination that barred their way to advancement.

As a result, although some wealthy and powerful creoles maintained excellent relations with their peninsular counterparts, fusing their economic interests through marriage and forming a single colonial Establishment, creoles and peninsulars tended to become mutually hostile castes. The peninsulars sometimes justified their privileged position by charging the creoles with innate indolence and incapacity, qualities that some Spanish writers attributed to the noxious effects of the American climate and soil; the creoles retorted by describing the Europeans as mean and grasping parvenus. So intense was the hatred between many members of these groups that a Spanish bishop in New Spain protested against the feeling of some young creoles that "if they could empty their veins of the Spanish part of their blood, they would gladly do so." This inevitably fostered the growth of creole nationalism; Humboldt, who traveled in Spanish America in the twilight years of the colony, reports a common saying: "I am not a Spaniard, I am an American."

The entrance of Enlightenment ideas into Latin America certainly contributed to the growth of creole discontent, but the relative weight of various influences is uncertain. Bourbon Spain itself contributed to the creole awakening by the many-sided effort of reforming officials to improve the quality of colonial life. Typical of this group was the intendant Juan Antonio Riaño, who introduced to the Mexican city of Guanajuato, the capital of his province, a taste for the French language and literature; he was also responsible "for the development of interest in drawing and music, and for the cultivation of mathematics, physics, and chemistry in the school that had been formerly maintained by the Jesuits."

Many educated creoles read the forbidden writings of Raynal, Montesquieu, Voltaire, Rousseau, and other radical philosophes, but another, innocuous-seeming agency for the spread of Enlightenment ideas in Latin America consisted of scientific texts, based on the theories of Descartes, Leibnitz, and Newton, which circulated freely in the colonies. By 1800, the creole elite had become familiar with the most advanced thought of contemporary Europe.

The American Revolution contributed to the growth of "dangerous ideas" in the colonies. Spain was well aware of the ideological as well as political threat the United States posed to its empire. Spain had reluctantly joined its ally France in war against England during the American Revolution, but it kept the rebels at arm's length, refused to recognize American independence, and in the peace negotiations tried unsuccessfully to coop up the United States within the Allegheny Mountains. After 1783 a growing number of United States ships touched legally or illegally at Spanish-American ports. Together with "Yankee notions," these vessels sometimes introduced

162 such subversive documents as the writings of Thomas Paine and Thomas Jefferson.

The French Revolution probably exerted a greater influence on the creole mind. Recalled the Argentine revolutionary Manuel Belgrano,

Since I was in Spain in 1789, and the French Revolution was then causing a change in ideas, especially among the men of letters with whom I associated, the ideals of liberty, equality, security, and property took a firm hold on me, and I saw only tyrants in those who would restrain a man, wherever he might be, from enjoying the rights with which God and Nature had endowed him.

Another cultivated creole, the Colombian Antonio Nariño, incurred Spanish wrath in 1794 by translating and printing on his own press the French Declaration of the Rights of Man of 1789. Sentenced to prison in Africa for ten years, Nariño lived to become leader and patriarch of the independence movement in Colombia and to witness its triumph.

But the French Revolution soon took a radical turn, and the creole aristocracy became disenchanted with it as a model. Scattered conspiracies in some Spanish colonies and Brazil owed their inspiration to the French example, but they were invariably the work of a few radicals, drawing their support almost exclusively from lower-class elements. The most important result directly attributable to the French Revolution was the slave revolt in the French part of Haiti under talented black and mulatto leaders: Toussaint Louverture, Jean Jacques Dessalines, Henri Christophe, and Alexandre Pétion. In 1804, Toussaint's lieutenant, General Dessalines, proclaimed the independence of the new state of Haiti. Black revolutionaries had established the first liberated territory in Latin America. But their achievement dampened rather than aroused support for independence among the creole elite of other colonies. Thus, fear that secession from Spain might touch off a slave revolt helped keep the planter class of neighboring Cuba loyal to Spain during and after the Latin American wars of independence.

Despite the existence of small conspiratorial groups, organized in secret societies, with correspondents in Europe as well as America, the movement for independence might have long remained puny and ineffectual. As late as 1806, when the precursor of revolution, Francisco de Miranda, landed on the coast of his native Venezuela with a force of some two hundred foreign volunteers, his call for revolution evoked no response, and he had to make a hasty retreat. Creole timidity and political inexperience and the apathy of the people might have long postponed the coming of independence if external developments had not hastened its arrival. The revolution Miranda and other forerunners could not set in motion came as a result of decisions by European powers with very different ends in view.

The Causes of Revolution

Among the causes of the revolutionary crisis that matured from 1808 to 1810, the decline of Spain under the inept Charles IV was certainly a major one. The European wars unleashed by the French Revolution glaringly revealed the failure of the Bourbon reforms to correct the structural defects in Spanish economic and social life. In 1793, Spain joined a coalition of England and other states in war against the French republic. The struggle went badly for Spain, and in 1795 the royal favorite and chief minister, Manuel de Godoy, signed the Peace of Basel. The next year, Spain became France's ally. English sea power promptly drove Spanish shipping from the Atlantic, virtually cutting off communication between Spain and its colonies. Hard necessity compelled Spain to permit neutral ships, sailing from Spanish for foreign ports, to trade with its overseas subjects. United States merchants and shipowners were the principal beneficiaries of this departure from the old, restrictive system.

Godoy's disastrous policy of war with England had other results. An English naval officer, Sir Home Popham, undertook on his own initiative to make an attack on Buenos Aires. His fleet sailed from the Cape of Good Hope for La Plata in April 1806 with a regiment of soldiers on board. In its wake followed a great number of English merchant ships eager to pour a mass of goods through a breach in the Spanish colonial system. A swift victory followed the landing of the British troops. The English soldiers entered Buenos Aires, meeting only token resistance. Hoping to obtain the support of the population, the English commander issued a proclamation guaranteeing the right of private property, free trade, and freedom of religion. But Creoles and peninsulars joined to expel their unwanted liberators. A volunteer army, secretly organized, attacked and routed the occupation troops, capturing the English general and twelve hundred of his men. To an English officer who tempted him with ideas of independence under a British protectorate, the creole Manuel Belgrano replied: "Either our old master or none at all."

The British government, meanwhile, had sent strong reinforcements to La Plata. This second invasion force was met with a murderous hail of fire as it tried to advance through the narrow streets of Buenos Aires and was beaten back with heavy losses. Impressed by the tenacity of the defense, the British commander gave up the struggle and agreed to evacuate Buenos Aires and the previously captured town of Montevideo. This defeat of a veteran British army by a people's militia spearheaded by the legion of *patricios* (creoles) was a large step down the road toward Argentine independence. The creoles of Buenos Aires, having tasted power, would not willingly relinquish it again.

In Europe, Spain's distresses now reached a climax. Napoleon, at the helm of France, gradually reduced Spain to a helpless satellite. In 1807, angered by Portugal's refusal to cooperate with his Continental System by closing its ports to English shipping, Napoleon obtained from Charles IV permission to invade Portugal through Spain. French troops swept across the peninsula; as they approached Lisbon, the Portuguese royal family and court escaped to Brazil in a fleet under British convoy. A hundred thousand French troops continued to occupy Spanish towns. Popular resentment at their presence, and at the pro-French policies of the royal favorite Godoy, broke out in stormy riots that compelled Charles IV to abdicate in favor of his son Ferdinand. Napoleon now intervened and offered his services as a mediator in the dispute between father and son.

Foolishly, the trusting pair accepted Napoleon's invitation to confer with him in the French city of Bayonne. There Napoleon forced both to abdicate in favor of his brother Joseph, his candidate for the Spanish throne. Napoleon then summoned a congress of Spanish grandees, which meekly approved his dictate.

The Spanish people had yet to say their word. On May 2, 1808, an insurrection against French occupation troops began in Madrid and spread like wildfire throughout the country. The insurgents established local governing juntas in the regions under their control. Later, a central junta assumed direction of the resistance movement in the name of the captive Ferdinand VII. This junta promptly made peace with England. When the Spanish armies fought the superbly trained French troops in conventional battles in the field, they usually suffered defeat, but guerrilla warfare pinned down large French forces and made Napoleon's control of conquered territory extremely precarious.

By early 1810, however, French victory seemed inevitable, for French armies had overrun Andalusia and were threatening Cádiz, the last city in Spanish hands. The central junta now dissolved itself and appointed a regency to rule Spain; this body in turn yielded its power to a national Cortes, or parliament, which met in Cádiz from 1810 to 1814 under the protection of English naval guns. Since most of the delegates actually came from Cádiz, whose liberal, cosmopolitan atmosphere was hardly typical of Spain, their views were much more liberal than those of the Spanish people as a whole. The constitution the Cortes approved in 1812 provided for a limited monarchy, promised freedom of speech and assembly, and abolished the Inquisition. But the Cortes made few concessions to the Spanish American colonies. It invited Spanish American delegates to join its deliberations but made clear that the system of peninsular domination and commercial monopoly would remain essentially intact.

In Spanish America, creole leaders, anticipating the imminent collapse of Spain, considered how they might turn this dramatic rush of events to their own advantage. Those events had transformed the idea of self-rule or total independence,

164

until lately a remote prospect, into a realistic goal. Confident that the armies of the invincible Napoleon would crush all opposition, some creole leaders prepared to take power into their hands with the pretext of loyalty to the "beloved Ferdinand." They could justify their action by the example of the Spanish regional juntas formed to govern in the name of the captive king. The confusion caused among Spanish officials by the coming of rival emissaries who proclaimed both Ferdinand and Joseph Bonaparte the legitimate king of Spain also played into creole hands.

In the spring of 1810, with the fall of Cádiz apparently imminent, the creole leaders moved into action. Charging viceroys and other royal officials with doubtful loyalty to Ferdinand, they organized popular demonstrations in Caracas, Buenos Aires, Santiago, and Bogotá that compelled those authorities to surrender control to local juntas dominated by creoles. But creole hopes of a peaceful transition to independence were doomed to failure. Their claims of loyalty did not deceive the groups truly loyal to Spain, and fighting broke out between patriots and royalists.

The Liberation of South America

The Latin American struggle for independence suggests comparison with the American Revolution. Some obvious parallels exist between the two upheavals. Both sought to throw off the rule of a mother country whose mercantilist system hindered the further development of a rapidly growing colonial economy. Both were led by well-educated elites who drew their slogans and ideas from the ideological arsenal of the Enlightenment. Both were civil wars in which large elements of the population sided with the mother country. Both owed their final success in part to foreign assistance (although the North American rebels received far more help from their French ally than came to Latin America from outside sources).

The differences between the two revolutions are no less impressive, however. Unlike the American Revolution, the Latin American struggle for independence did not have a unified direction or strategy, due not only to vast distances and other geographical obstacles to unity but to the economic and cultural isolation of the various Latin American regions from each other. Moreover, the Latin American movement for independence lacked the strong popular base provided by the more democratic and fluid society of the English colonies. The creole elite, itself part of an exploitative white minority, feared the oppressed Indians, blacks, and half-castes, and as a rule sought to keep their intervention in the struggle to a minimum. This lack of unity of regions and classes helps explain why Latin America had to struggle so long against a power like Spain, weak and beset by many internal and external problems.

The struggle for independence had four main centers. In Spanish South America there were two principal theaters of military operations, one in the north, another in the south. One stream of liberation flowed southward from Venezuela; another ran northward from Argentina. In Peru, last Spanish bastion on the continent, these two currents joined. Brazil achieved its own swift and relatively peaceful separation from Portugal. Finally, Mexico had to travel a very difficult, circuitous road before gaining its independence.

Simón Bolívar, the Liberator

Simón Bolívar is the symbol and hero of the liberation struggle in northern South America. Born in Caracas, Venezuela, in 1783, he came from an aristocratic creole family rich in land, slaves, and mines. His intellectual formation was greatly influenced by his reading of the rationalist, materialist classics of the Enlightenment. Travel in various European countries between 1803 and 1807 further widened his intellectual horizons. He returned to Caracas and soon became involved in conspiratorial activity directed at the overthrow of the Spanish regime.

In April 1810 the creole party in Caracas organized a demonstration that forced the abdication of the captain general. A creole-dominated junta that pledged to defend the rights of the captive

A portrait of the Liberator, Simón Bolívar, by José Gil de Castro. His appearance conforms closely to descriptions of Bolívar in contemporary accounts.

claimed the country's independence and framed a republican constitution that abolished Indian tribute and special privileges (fueros) but retained black slavery, made Catholicism the state religion, and limited the rights of full citizenship to property owners. This last provision excluded the free pardo (mulatto) population.

Fighting had already broken out between patriots and royalists. In addition to peninsulars, the troops sent from Puerto Rico by the Regency Council, and a section of the creole aristocracy, the royalist cause had the support of some free blacks and mulattos, angered by the republic's denial of full citizenship to them. In many areas the black slaves took advantage of the chaotic situation to rise in revolt, impartially killing creole and peninsular Spanish hacendados. But the majority of the population remained neutral, fleeing from their villages at the approach of royal or republican conscription officers; if conscripted, they often deserted when they could or changed sides if prospects seemed better.

On the patriot side, differences arose between the commander-in-chief, Miranda, and his young officers, especially Bolívar, who were angered by Miranda's military conservatism and indecisiveness. Amid these disputes came the earthquake of March 26, 1812, which caused great loss of life and property in Caracas and other patriot territories but spared the regions under Spanish control. The royalist clergy proclaimed this disaster a divine retribution against the rebels. A series of military defeats completed the discomfiture of the revolutionary cause.

With his forces disintegrating, Miranda attempted to negotiate a treaty with the royalist commander and then tried to flee the country, taking with him part of the republic's treasury. He may have intended to continue working for independence, but the circumstances made it appear as if he wished to save his own skin. Bolívar and some of his comrades, regarding Miranda's act as a form of treachery, seized him before he could embark and turned him over to the Spaniards. He died in a Spanish prison four years later. Bolívar, saved from the Spanish reaction by the influence of a friend of his family, received a safe conduct to leave the country.

Ferdinand took power, but its assurances of loyalty deceived neither local Spaniards nor the Regency Council in Cádiz. A considerable number of wealthy creoles of the planter class also opposed independence, and when it triumphed many emigrated to Cuba or Puerto Rico. The patriots were also divided over what policy to follow; some, like Bolívar, favored an immediate declaration of independence, while others preferred to postpone the issue.

Perhaps to get Bolívar out of the way, the junta sent him to England to solicit British aid. He had no success in this mission but convinced the veteran revolutionary Francisco de Miranda to return to Venezuela and take command of the patriot army. In 1811 a Venezuelan congress pro-

Bolívar departed for New Granada (present-day Colombia), which was still partially under patriot control. Here, as in Venezuela, creole leaders squabbled over forms of government. Two months after his arrival, Bolívar issued a Manifesto to the Citizens of New Granada in which he called for unity, condemned the federalist system as impractical under war conditions, and urged the liberation of Venezuela as necessary for Colombian security. Given command of a small detachment of troops to clear the Magdalena River of enemy troops, he employed a strategy that featured swift movement, aggressive tactics, and the advancement of soldiers for merit without regard to social background or color.

A victory at Cúcuta gained Bolívar the rank of general in the Colombian army and approval of his plan for the liberation of Venezuela. In a forced march of three months, he led five hundred men through Venezuela's Andean region toward Caracas. In Venezuela the Spaniards had unleashed a campaign of terror against all patriots. At Trujillo, midway in his advance on Caracas, Bolívar proclaimed a counterterror, a war to the death against all Spaniards. As Bolívar approached the capital, the Spanish forces withdrew. He entered Caracas in triumph and received from the city council the title of liberator; soon afterward the grateful congress of the restored republic voted to grant him dictatorial powers.

Bolívar's success was short-lived, for developments abroad and at home worked against him. The fall of Napoleon in 1814 brought Ferdinand VII to the Spanish throne, released Spanish troops for use in Spanish America, and gave an important lift to the royal cause. Meanwhile the republic's policies alienated large sectors of the lower classes. The creole aristocrats stubbornly refused to grant freedom to their slaves. As a result, the slaves continued their struggle, independent of Spaniards and creoles, and republican forces had to be diverted for punitive expeditions into areas of slave revolt.

The *llaneros* (cowboys) of the Venezuelan *llanos* (plains) also turned against the republic as a result of agrarian edicts that attempted to end the hunting or rounding up of cattle in the llanos without written permission from the owner of the land in question. These edicts also sought to transform the llaneros into semiservile peons by forcing them to carry an identity card and belong to a ranch. These attacks on their customary rights and freedom angered the llaneros. Under the leadership of the formidable José Tomás Boves, a mass of cowboys, armed with the dreaded lance, invaded the highlands and swept down on Caracas, crushing all resistance. In July 1814 Bolívar hastily abandoned the city and retreated toward Colombia with the remains of his army. Although Boves died in battle in late 1814, he had destroyed the Venezuelan "second republic."

Bolívar reached Cartagena in September to find that Colombia was on the verge of chaos. Despite the imminent threat of a Spanish invasion, the provinces quarreled with each other and defied the authority of the weak central government. Having determined that the situation was hopeless, Bolívar left in May 1815 for the British island of Jamaica. Meanwhile, a strong Spanish army under General Pablo Morillo had landed in Venezuela, completed the reconquest of the colony, and then sailed to lay siege to Cartagena. Cut off by land and sea, the city surrendered in December, and the rest of Colombia was pacified within a few months. Of all the provinces of Spanish America, only Argentina remained in revolt. Had Ferdinand made the concession of granting legal equality with whites to the mixed-bloods who supported his cause, the Spanish Empire in America might have survived much longer. But the reactionary Ferdinand would make no concessions.

Bolívar still had an unshakable faith in the inevitable triumph of independence. From Jamaica he sent a famous letter in which he affirmed that faith and offered a remarkable analysis of the situation and prospects of Spanish America. He scoffed at the ability of Spain, that "aged serpent," to maintain Spanish America forever in subjection. Bolívar also looked into the political future of the continent. Monarchy, he argued, was foreign to the genius of Latin America; only a republican regime would be accepted by its peoples. A single government for the region was impracticable, divided as it was by "climatic differences, geographic diversity, conflicting interests, and dissimilar characteristics." Bolívar boldly forecast the destiny of the different regions, taking account of their economic and social structures. Chile, for example, seemed to him to have a democratic future; Peru, on the other hand, was fated to suffer dictatorship because it contained "two factors that clash with every just and liberal principle: gold and slaves."

From Jamaica, Bolívar went to Haiti, where he received a sympathetic hearing and the offer of some material support from the mulatto president Alexandre Pétion, who asked in return for the freedom of the slaves in the territory that Bolívar should liberate. In March 1816 Bolívar and a small band of followers landed on the island of Margarita off the Venezuelan coast. Two attempts to gain a foothold on the mainland were easily beaten back, and soon Bolívar was back in the West Indies. Reflecting on his failures, he concluded that the effort to invade the well-fortified western coast of Venezuela was a mistake and decided to establish a base in the Orinoco River valley, distant from the centers of Spanish power. Roving patriot bands still operated in this region, and Bolívar hoped to win the allegiance of the llaneros, who were becoming disillusioned with their Spanish allies. In September 1816 Bolívar sailed from Haiti for the Orinoco River delta, which he ascended until he reached the small town of Angostura (modern Ciudad Bolívar), which he made his headquarters.

The tide of war now began to flow in his favor. The patriot guerrilla bands accepted his leadership; even more important, he gained the support of the principal llanero chieftain, José Antonio Páez. European developments also favored Bolívar. The end of the Napoleonic wars idled a large number of British soldiers; many of these veterans came to Venezuela, forming a British Legion that distinguished itself in battle by its valor. English merchants made loans enabling Bolívar to secure men and arms for the coming campaign. Helpful too was the mulish attitude of Ferdinand VII, whose refusal to consider making any concessions to the colonists caused the English government to lose patience and regard with more friendly eyes the prospect of Spanish American independence.

On the eve of the decisive campaign of 1819, Bolívar summoned to Angostura a makeshift congress that vested him with dictatorial powers. To this congress he presented a project for a constitution for Venezuela in which he urged the abolition of slavery and the distribution of land to revolutionary soldiers. But the proposed constitution also had some nondemocratic features. They included a president with virtually royal powers, a hereditary senate, and restriction of the suffrage and officeholding to the propertied and educated elite. The congress disregarded Bolívar's reform proposals but elected him president of the republic and adopted a constitution embodying many of his ideas.

The war, however, still had to be won. Bolívar's bold strategy for the liberation of Venezuela and Colombia envisaged striking a heavy blow at Spanish forces from a completely unexpected direction. While llanero cavalry under Páez distracted and pinned down the main body of Spanish troops in northern Venezuela with swift raids, Bolívar advanced with an army of some twenty-five hundred men along the winding Orinoco and Arauco rivers, across the plains, and then up the towering Colombian Andes until he reached the plateau where lay Bogotá, capital of New Granada. On the field of Boyacá the patriot army surprised and defeated the royalists in a short, sharp battle that netted sixteen hundred prisoners and considerable supplies. Bogotá lay defenseless, and Bolívar entered the capital to the cheers of its people, who had suffered greatly under Spanish rule.

Leaving his aide, Francisco Santander, to organize a government, Bolívar hurried off to Angostura to prepare the liberation of Venezuela. Then thrilling news arrived from Spain; on January 1, 1820, a regiment awaiting embarkation for South America had mutinied, starting a revolt that forced Ferdinand to restore the liberal constitution of 1812 and give up his plans for the reconquest of the colonies. This news caused joy among the patriots, gloom and desertions among the Venezuelan royalists. In July 1821, the troops of Bolívar and Páez crushed the last important Spanish force in Venezuela at Carabobo. Save for some coastal towns and forts still held by beleaguered royalists, Venezuela was free.

Bolívar had already turned his attention southward. The independence of Spanish America remained precarious as long as the Spaniards held the immense mountain bastion of the central Andes. While Bolívar prepared a major offensive from Bogotá against Quito, he sent his able young lieutenant, Antonio José Sucre, by sea from Colombia's Pacific coast to seize the port of Guayaquil. Before Sucre even arrived, the creole party in Guayaquil revolted, proclaimed independence, and placed the port under Bolívar's protection. With his forces swelled by reinforcements sent by the Argentine general José de San Martín, Sucre advanced into the Ecuadoran highlands and defeated a Spanish army on the slopes of Mount Pichincha, near Quito. Bolívar, meanwhile, advancing southward from Bogotá along the Cauca River valley, encountered stiff royalist resistance, but this crumbled on news of Sucre's victory at Pichincha. The provinces composing the former viceroyalty of New Granada—the future republics of Venezuela, Colombia, Ecuador, and Panama—were now free from Spanish control. They were temporarily united into a large state named Colombia or Gran Colombia, established at the initiative of Bolívar by the union of New Granada and Venezuela in 1821.

The Southern Liberation Movement and San Martín

The time had come for the movement of liberation led by Bolívar to merge with that flowing northward from Argentina. Ever since the defeat of the British invasions of 1806–1807, the creole party, although nominally loyal to Spain, had effectively controlled Buenos Aires. The hero of the invasions and the temporary viceroy, Santiago Liniers, cooperated fully with the creole leaders. A new viceroy, sent by the Seville junta to replace

Liniers, joined with the viceroy at Lima to crush abortive creole revolts in Upper Peru (Bolivia). But in Buenos Aires he walked softly, for he recognized the superior power of the creoles. Under their pressure he issued a decree permitting free trade with allied and neutral nations, a measure bitterly opposed by representatives of the Cádiz monopoly. But this concession could not save the Spanish regime. Revolution was in the air, and the creole leaders waited only, in the words of one of their number, for the figs to be ripe.

In May 1810, when word came that French troops had entered Seville and threatened Cádiz, the secret patriot society organized a demonstration that forced the viceroy to summon an open town meeting to decide the future government of the colony. This first Argentine congress voted to depose the viceroy and establish a junta to govern in the name of Ferdinand. The junta promptly attempted to consolidate its control of the vast viceroyalty. The interior provinces were subdued after sharp fighting. Montevideo, across the Río de la Plata on the Eastern Shore (modern Uruguay), remained in Spanish hands until 1814, when it fell to an Argentine siege. The junta met even more tenacious resistance from the gauchos of the Uruguayan pampa, led by José Gervasio Artigas, who demanded Uruguayan autonomy in a loose federal connection with Buenos Aires. The porteños (inhabitants of Buenos Aires) would have nothing to do with Artigas's gaucho democracy, and a new struggle began. It ended when Artigas, caught between the fire of Buenos Aires and that of Portuguese forces claiming Uruguay for Brazil, had to flee to Paraguay. Uruguay did not achieve independence until 1828.

The creole aristocracy in another portion of the old viceroyalty of La Plata, Paraguay, also suspected the designs of the Buenos Aires junta and defeated a porteño force sent to liberate Asunción. This done, the creole party in Asunción rose up, deposed Spanish officials, and proclaimed the independence of Paraguay. A key figure in this uprising was the remarkable Dr. José Rodríguez de Francia, soon to become his country's first president and dictator.

Efforts by the Buenos Aires junta to liberate the mountainous northern province of Upper

Peru also failed. Two thrusts by a patriot army into this area were defeated and the invaders rolled back. The steep terrain, long lines of communication, and the apathy of the Bolivian Indians contributed to these defeats.

The Buenos Aires government also had serious internal problems. A dispute broke out between liberal supporters of the fiery Mariano Moreno, secretary of the junta and champion of social reform, and a conservative faction led by the great landowner Cornelio Saavedra. This dispute foreshadowed the liberal-conservative cleavage that dominated the first decades of Argentine history after independence. In 1813 a national assembly gave the country the name of the United Provinces of La Plata and enacted such reforms as the abolition of mita, encomienda, titles of nobility, and the Inquisition. A declaration of independence, however, was delayed until 1816.

Also 1816 was the year in which the military genius of José de San Martín broke the long-standing military stalemate. San Martín, born in what is now northeastern Argentina, was a colonel in the Spanish army with twenty years of service behind him when revolution broke out in Buenos Aires. He promptly sailed for La Plata to offer his sword to the patriot junta. He was soon raised to the command of the army of Upper Peru, which was recuperating in Tucumán after a sound defeat at royalist hands. Perceiving that a frontal attack on the Spanish position in Upper Peru was doomed to failure, San Martín offered a plan for total victory that gained the support of the director of the United Provinces, Juan Martín de Pueyrredón. San Martín proposed a march over the Andes to liberate Chile, where a Spanish reaction had toppled the revolutionary regime established by Bernardo O'Higgins and other patriot leaders in 1810. This done, the united forces of La Plata and Chile would descend on Peru from the sea.

To mask his plans from Spanish eyes and gain time for a large organizational effort, San Martín obtained an appointment as governor of the province of Cuyo, whose capital, Mendoza, lay at the eastern end of a strategic pass leading across the Andes to Chile. He spent two years recruiting, training, and equipping his Army of the Andes.

Like Bolívar, he used the promise of freedom to secure black and mulatto volunteers, and later declared they were his best soldiers. Chilean refugees fleeing the Spanish reaction in their country also joined his forces.

San Martín, methodical and thorough, demanded of the Buenos Aires government arms, munitions, food, and equipment of every kind. In January 1817 the army began the crossing of the Andes. Its march over the frozen Andean passes equaled in difficulty Bolívar's scaling of the Colombian sierra. Twenty-one days later, the army issued onto Chilean soil. A decisive defeat of the Spanish army at Chacabuco in February opened the gates of Santiago to San Martín. He won another victory at Maipú (1818), in a battle that ended the threat to Chile's independence. Rejecting Chilean invitations to become supreme ruler of the republic, a post assumed by O'Higgins, San Martín began to prepare the attack by sea on Lima, fifteen hundred miles away.

The execution of his plan required the creation of a navy. He secured a number of ships in England and the United States and engaged a competent though eccentric naval officer, Thomas, Lord Cochrane, to organize the patriot navy. In August 1820, the expedition sailed for Peru in a fleet made up of seven ships of war and eighteen transports. San Martín landed his army about a hundred miles south of Lima but delayed moving on the Peruvian capital. He hoped to obtain its surrender by economic blockade, propaganda, and direct negotiation with the Spanish officials. The desire of the Lima aristocracy, creole and peninsular, to avoid an armed struggle that might unleash an Indian and slave revolt worked in favor of San Martín's strategy. In June 1821 the Spanish army evacuated Lima and retreated toward the Andes. San Martín entered the capital and in a festive atmosphere proclaimed the independence of Peru.

But his victory was far from complete. He had to deal with counterrevolutionary plots and the resistance of Lima's corrupt elite to his program of social reform, which included the end of Indian tribute and the grant of freedom to the children of slaves. San Martín's assumption of supreme military and civil power in August 1821 added to the factional opposition. Meanwhile, a large Spanish army maneuvered in front of Lima, challenging San Martín to a battle he dared not join with his much smaller force. Disheartened by the atmosphere of intrigue and hostility that surrounded him, San Martín became convinced that only monarchy could bring stability to Spanish America and sent a secret mission to Europe to search for a prince for the throne of Peru.

Such was the background of San Martín's departure for Guayaquil, where he met in conference with Bolívar on July 26 and 27, 1822. The agenda of the meeting included several points. One concerned the future of Guayaquil. San Martín claimed the port city for Peru; Bolívar, however, had already annexed it to Gran Colombia, confronting San Martín with a fait accompli. Another topic was the political future of all Spanish America. San Martín favored monarchy as the solution for the emergent chaos of the new states; Bolívar believed in a governmental system that would be republican in form, oligarchical in content. But the critical question before the two men was how to complete the liberation of the continent by defeating the Spanish forces in Peru.

San Martín's abrupt retirement from public life after the conference, the reluctance of the two liberators to discuss what was said there, and the meager authentic documentary record of the proceedings have surrounded the meeting with an atmosphere of mystery and produced two opposed and partisan interpretations. A view favored by Argentine historians holds that San Martín came to Guayaquil in search of military aid but was rebuffed by Bolívar, who was unwilling to share with a rival the glory of bringing the struggle for independence to an end; San Martín then magnanimously decided to leave Peru and allow Bolívar to complete the work he had begun. Venezuelan historians, on the other hand, argue that San Martín came to Guayaquil primarily in order to recover Guayaquil for Peru. The historians deny that San Martín asked Bolívar for more troops and insist that he left Peru for personal reasons having nothing to do with the conference.

Both interpretations tend to diminish the stature and sense of realism of the two liberators.

San Martín was no martyr, nor was Bolívar an ambitious schemer who sacrificed San Martín to his passion for power and glory. San Martín must have understood that Bolívar alone combined the military, political, and psychological assets needed to liquidate the factional hornet's nest in Peru and gain final victory over the powerful Spanish army in the sierra. Given the situation in Lima, San Martín's presence there could only hinder the performance of those tasks. In this light, the decision of Bolívar to assume sole direction of the war and of San Martín to withdraw reflected a realistic appraisal of the Peruvian problem and the solution it required.

San Martín returned to Lima to find that in his absence his enemies had rallied and struck at him by driving his reforming chief minister, Bernardo Monteagudo, out of the country. San Martín made no effort to reassert his power. In September 1822, before the first Peruvian congress, he announced his resignation as protector and his impending departure. He returned to Buenos Aires by way of Chile, where the government of his friend O'Higgins was on the verge of collapse. In Buenos Aires the people seemed to have forgotten his existence. Accompanied by his daughter, he sailed for Europe at the end of 1823. He died in France in 1850 in virtual obscurity. His transfiguration into an Argentine national hero began a quarter-century later.

San Martín's departure left Lima and the territory under its control in serious danger of reconquest by the strong Spanish army in the sierra. Bolívar made no move to rescue the squabbling factions in Lima from their predicament; he allowed the situation to deteriorate until May 1823, when the Peruvian congress called on him for help. Then he sent Sucre with only a few thousand men, for he wanted to bring the Lima politicians to their knees. The scare produced by a brief reoccupation of the capital by the Spanish army prepared the creole leaders to accept Bolívar's absolute rule.

Bolívar arrived in Peru in September 1823. He required almost a year to achieve political stability and to weld the army he brought with him and the different national units under his command into a united force. After a month of difficult ascent of the sierra, in an altitude so high that Bolívar and most of his men suffered from mountain sickness, cavalry elements of the patriot and royalist armies clashed near the lake of Junín, and the Spaniards suffered defeat (August 6, 1824). The royalist commander, José de Canterac, retreated toward Cuzco. Leaving Sucre in command, Bolívar returned to Lima to gather reinforcements. To Sucre fell the glory of defeating the Spanish army in the last major engagement of the war, at Ayacucho (December 9, 1824). Only scattered resistance at some points in the highlands and on the coast remained to be mopped up. The work of continental liberation was achieved.

The Achievement of Brazilian Independence

In contrast to the political anarchy, economic dislocation, and military destruction in Spanish America, the drive toward independence of Brazil proceeded as a relatively bloodless transition between 1808 and 1822. The idea of Brazilian independence first arose in the late eighteenth century as a Brazilian reaction to the Portuguese policy of tightening political and economic control over the colony in the interests of the mother country. The first significant conspiracy against Portuguese rule was organized in 1788–1789 in Minas Gerais, where rigid governmental control over the production and prices of gold and diamonds, as well as heavy taxes, caused much discontent, and where there existed a group of intellectuals educated in Europe and familiar with the ideas of the Enlightenment. But this conspiracy never went beyond the stage of discussion and was easily discovered and crushed. Other conspiracies in Río de Janeiro (1794), Bahia (1798), and Pernambuco (1801), and a brief revolt in Pernambuco (1817), reflected the influence of republican ideas over sections of the elite and even the lower strata of urban society. All proved abortive or were soon crushed. The stagnation of Brazilian life and the fear of slave owners that resistance to Portugal might spark slave insurrections effectively inhibited the spirit of revolt. Were it not for an accident of European history, the independence of Brazil might have long been delayed.

The French invasion of Portugal (1807), followed by the flight of the Portuguese court to Rio de Janeiro, brought large benefits to Brazil. Indeed, the transfer of the court in effect signified achievement of Brazilian independence. The Portuguese prince regent João opened Brazil's ports to the trade of friendly nations, permitted the rise of local industries, and founded a Bank of Brazil. In 1815 he elevated Brazil to the legal status of a kingdom co-equal with Portugal. In one sense, however, Brazil's new status signified the substitution of one dependence for another. Freed from Portuguese control, Brazil came under the economic domination of England, which obtained major tariff concessions and other privileges by the Strangford Treaty of 1810. One result was an influx of cheap machine-made goods that swamped the handicrafts industry of the country.

Brazilian elites took satisfaction in Brazil's new role and the growth of educational, cultural, and economic opportunities for their class. But this feeling was mixed with resentment at the thousands of Portuguese courtiers and hangers-on who came with the court and who competed with Brazilians for jobs and favors. Portuguese merchants in Brazil, for their part, were bitter over the passing of the Lisbon monopoly. Thus, the change in the status of Brazil sharpened the conflict between mazombos and reinóis.

The event that precipitated the break with the mother country was the revolution of 1820 in Portugal. The Portuguese revolutionists framed a liberal constitution for the kingdom, but they were conservative or reactionary in relation to Brazil. They demanded the immediate return of Dom João to Lisbon, an end to the system of dual monarchy that he had devised, and the restoration of the Portuguese commercial monopoly. Timid and vacillating, Dom João did not know which way to turn. Under the pressure of his courtiers, who hungered to return to Portugal and their lost estates, he finally approved the new constitution and sailed for Portugal. He left

172   behind him, however, his son and heir, Dom Pedro, as regent of Brazil, and in a private letter advised him, in the event the Brazilians should demand independence, to assume leadership of the movement and set the crown of Brazil on his head. Pedro received the same advice from José Bonifácio de Andrada, a Brazilian scientist whose stay in Portugal had completely disillusioned him about the Portuguese capacity for colonial reform.

Soon it became clear that the Portuguese Côrtes intended to set the clock back by abrogating all the liberties and concessions won by Brazil since 1808. One of its decrees insisted on the immediate return of Dom Pedro from Brazil in order that he might complete his political education. The pace of events moved more rapidly in 1822. On January 9, Dom Pedro, urged on by José Bonifácio de Andrada and other Brazilian advisers who perceived a golden opportunity to make an orderly transition to independence without the intervention of the masses, refused an order from the Côrtes to return to Portugal and issued his famous *fico* ("I remain"). On September 7, regarded by all Brazilians as Independence Day, he issued the even more celebrated Cry of Ipiranga, "Independence or Death!" In December 1822, having overcome slight resistance by Portuguese troops, Dom Pedro was formally proclaimed constitutional emperor of Brazil.

Mexico's Road to Independence

In New Spain, as in other colonies, the crisis of the Bourbon monarchy in 1808–1810 encouraged some creole leaders to strike a blow for self-rule or total independence under "the mask of Ferdinand." But in Mexico the movement for independence took an unexpected turn. Here the masses, instead of remaining aloof, joined the struggle and for a time managed to convert it from a private quarrel between two elites into an incipient social revolution.

In July 1808 news of Napoleon's capture of Charles IV and Ferdinand VI and his invasion of Spain reached Mexico City and provoked intense debates and maneuvers among Mexican elites to take advantage of these dramatic events. Faced with the prospect of an imminent collapse of Spain, creoles and peninsulars alike prepared to seize power and ensure that their group would control New Spain, whatever the outcome of the Spanish crisis. The creoles moved first. The Mexico City cabildo, a creole stronghold, called on the viceroy to summon an assembly to be chosen by the creole-dominated cabildos. This assembly, composed of representatives of various elite groups, would govern Mexico until Ferdinand VII, whose forced abdication was null and void, regained his throne. The viceroy, José de Iturrigaray, supported such a call noting that Spain was in "a state of anarchy."

The conservative landed elite that sponsored the movement for a colonial assembly, it must be stressed, desired free trade and autonomy or home rule within the Spanish empire, not independence. They had no intention of taking up arms in a struggle that might bring a dangerous intervention of the exploited classes and thus endanger their own personal and economic survival. The reforms that the chief creole ideologist, Fray Melchor de Talamantes, recommended to the proposed assembly suggested the limits of creole elite ambitions: abolition of the Inquisition and the ecclesiastical fuero (the clergy's privilege of exemption from civil courts), free trade, and measures to promote the reform of mining, agriculture, and industry.

The creole movement for home rule and free trade, however, posed a threat to the peninsular merchants whose prosperity depended on the continuance of the existing closed commercial system with Seville as its center. On the night of September 15, 1808, the merchants struck back. The wealthy peninsular merchant Gabriel de Yermo led the consulado's militia in a preemptive coup, ousting Viceroy Iturrigaray and arresting leading creole supporters of autonomy. A series of transient peninsular-dominated regimes then held power until a new viceroy, Francisco Javier de Venegas, arrived from Spain in September 1810.

The leaders of the creole aristocracy, mindful of its large property interests, did not respond to the peninsular counteroffensive. The leadership of the movement for creole control of Mexico's destinies now passed to a group consisting predominantly of "marginal elites"—upper-class individuals of relatively modest economic and social standing—in the Bajío, a geographic region roughly corresponding to the intendency of Querétaro.

The special economic and social conditions of this region help explain its decisive role in the first stage of the Mexican struggle for independence. It was the most modern of Mexican regions in its agrarian and industrial structure. There were few Indian communities of the traditional type; the bulk of its population, Indians, free blacks, and castas (mixed-bloods), were partially Europeanized urban workers, miners, and peons or tenants of various types. Agriculture was dominated by large commercial irrigated estates producing wheat and other products for the upper classes; maize, the diet of the masses, was chiefly grown on marginal land by impoverished tenants. There was an important textile industry, which had experienced a shift from large obrajes using slaves and other coerced labor to a putting-out system in which merchant-financiers provided artisan families with cotton and wool, which they turned into cloth on their own looms, "forcing growing numbers of artisan families to exploit themselves by working long hours for little compensation." Mining was the most profitable and capital-intensive industry of the region; in some good years the largest mine at Guanajuato, the Valenciana, netted its owners over 1,000,000 pesos in profits.

The quasi-capitalist structure of the Bajío's economy, based largely on free wage labor, promoted a growth of workers' class consciousness and militancy. The mineworkers at Guanajuato, for example, resisted attempts to end their partidos (shares of the ores they mined over a given quota) by methods that included a production slowdown; the employers responded by calling in the militia to force resumption of full production. The Bajío's labor force experienced a decline of wage and living standards and employment opportunities in the last decades of the eighteenth century. These losses were a result of conditions over which they had no control: rapid population growth that enabled landowners to drive down wages or replace permanent workers by seasonal laborers; competition for domestic textiles from cheap industrially produced imports; and the rising cost of aging mines. These factors caused deep insecurity and resentment. Then in 1808 and 1809 drought and famine again struck the Bajío, aggravating all the existing tensions and grievances. As in the earlier drought and famine in 1785, the great landowners profited from the misery of the poor by holding their reserves of grain off the market until prices reached their peak. It was against this background of profound social unrest and a grave subsistence crisis that the struggle for Mexican independence began. The Bajío was its storm center, and the Bajío's peasantry and working class formed its spearhead.

In 1810 a creole plot for revolt was taking shape in the important political and industrial center of Querétaro. Only two of the conspirators belonged to the highest circle of the creole regional elite, and efforts to draw other prominent creoles into the scheme were rebuffed. The majority were "marginal elites"—struggling landowners, a grocer, an estate administrator, a parish priest. From the first the conspirators seem to have planned to mobilize the Indian and mixed-blood proletariat, probably because they doubted their ability to win over the majority of their class. If the motive of most of the plotters was the hope of raising troops, Miguel Hidalgo y Costilla, a priest in the town of Dolores and one-time rector of the colegio of San Nicolás at Valladolid, was inspired by a genuine sympathy with the natives. The scholarly Hidalgo had already called the attention of Spanish authorities to himself by his freethinking ideas; he was also known for his scientific interests and his efforts to develop new industries in his parish.

Informed that their plot had been denounced to Spanish officials, the conspirators held an urgent council and decided to launch their revolt although arrangements were not complete. On Sunday, September 16, 1810, Hidalgo called on the people of his parish, assembled for Mass, to rise against their Spanish rulers. Here, as elsewhere in Spanish America, the "mask of

174

M. HIDALGO Y.C.

A sympathetic portrait of the Mexican Liberator Miguel Hidalgo, by Juan O'Gorman, well conveys Hidalgo's warm, impulsive character.

Ferdinand" came into play; Hidalgo claimed to be leading an insurrection in support of a beloved king treacherously captured and deposed by godless Frenchmen. In less than two weeks the insurgent leaders had assembled thousands of rebels and began a march on the industrial and mining center of Guanajuato. On the march Hidalgo secured a banner bearing the image of the Virgin of Guadalupe and proclaimed her the patron of his movement, thus appealing to the religious devotion of his followers. All along the route the established elites held back from joining the revolt. They watched with dismay as the rebels looted stores and took the crops provided by the bountiful harvest of 1810, after two years of drought and famine. The capture of Guanajuato on September 28 was accomplished with the aid of several thousand mineworkers, who joined in storming the massive municipal gran-

ary in which Spanish officials, militia, and local elites attempted to hold out. It was followed by the killing of hundreds of Spaniards in the granary and the city. The massacre and sack of Guanajuato was a turning point in the rebellion, for it brought into the open the conflict between the basic objective of Hidalgo and his allies—creole domination of an autonomous or independent Mexico—and the thirst for revenge and social justice of their lower-class followers. Learning of the events at Guanajuato, the great majority of the creole elite recoiled in horror before the elemental violence of a movement that Hidalgo was unable to control.

After his first victories, Hidalgo issued decrees abolishing slavery and tribute, the yearly head tax paid by Indians and mulattos. Three months later, from his headquarters at Guadalajara, in his first and only reference to the land problem, he ordered that the Indian communal lands in the vicinity of the city that had been rented to Spaniards be returned to the Indians; it was his wish that "only the Indians in their respective pueblos should enjoy the use of those lands." Moderate though they were, these reforms gave the Mexican revolution a popular character absent from the movement for independence in South America, but further alienated many creoles who may have desired autonomy or independence—but not social revolution. On the other hand, these reforms did not go far enough to redress the fundamental grievances of Hidalgo's peasant and working-class followers in regions like the Bajío and Jalisco: landlessness, starvation wages and high rents, lack of tenant security, and the monopoly of grain by profiteering landowners. In the absence of a clearly defined program of structural social and economic reform, Hidalgo's followers vented their rage at an intolerable situation by killing Spaniards and plundering the properties of creoles and peninsulars alike.

Hidalgo proved unable to weld his rebel horde into a disciplined army or to capitalize on his early victories. Having defeated a royalist army near Mexico City, he camped outside the city for three days and then, after his demand for its surrender was rejected, inexplicably withdrew from the almost defenseless capital without attacking. It has been suggested that he feared a repetition of the atrocities that followed earlier victories or that he believed that he could not hold the great city without the support of the local population. The peasantry of the central highlands, who still possessed communal lands that satisfied their minimal needs and supplemented their meager crops by wage labor on large haciendas, did not rally to Hidalgo's cause. With his army melting away through desertions, Hidalgo retreated toward the Bajío. Driven out of Guanajuato by royalist forces, Hidalgo and other rebel leaders fled northward, hoping to establish new bases for their movement in Coahuila and Texas. Less than one year after his revolt had begun, Hidalgo was captured as he fled toward the United States border, condemned as a heretic and subversive by an inquisitorial court, and executed by a firing squad.

The defeat and death of Hidalgo did not end the insurrection he had begun. The fires of revolt continued to smolder over vast areas of Mexico. New leaders arose who learned from the failure of Hidalgo's tactics. Many, abandoning the effort to defeat the royalist forces with their superior arms and training in conventional warfare developed a flexible and mobile guerrilla style of fighting. The Spaniards themselves had effectively employed guerrilla warfare—a war of swift movement by small units that strike and flee—in their struggle against Napoleon, taking advantage of a familiar terrain and the support of rural populations to foil pursuit and repression. The new Mexican rebel strategy was not to win a quick victory but to exhaust the enemy and undermine his social and economic base by pillaging the stores and haciendas of his elite allies, disrupting trade, and creating war weariness and hostility toward an increasingly arbitrary colonial regime.

Following Hidalgo's death, a mestizo priest, José María Morelos, assumed supreme command of the revolutionary movement. Morelos had ministered to poor congregations in the hot, humid Pacific lowlands of Michoacán before offering his services to Hidalgo, who asked him to organize insurrection in that area. Economic and social conditions in the coastal lowlands region bore some resemblance to those of the Bajío; its principal industries, sugar, cotton, and indigo, were in decline as a result of competition from regions closer to highland markets and from imported cloth. As a result the position of estate tenants and laborers had become increasingly dependent and insecure. The material conditions of Indian villagers had also deteriorated as a result of the renting of community lands by village leaders to outsiders, a practice that left many families without the minimal land needed for subsistence.

The discontent generated by these conditions provided Morelos and his insurgent movement with a mass base in the coastal lowlands. Morelos was sensitive to the problems and needs of the area's rural folk. Like Hidalgo, he ordered an end to slavery and tribute. He also ended the rental of Indian community lands and abolished the community treasuries (*cajas de comunidad*), whose funds were often misused by village notables or drained off by royal officials; henceforth, the villagers were to keep the proceeds of their labor. Morelos also extended Hidalgo's program of social reform by prohibiting all forced labor and forbidding the use of all racial terms except gachupines, applied to the hated peninsular Spaniards. There seems little doubt that in principle Morelos favored a radical land reform. In a "plan" found among his papers, he proposed the division of all haciendas greater than two leagues into smaller plots, denounced a situation in which "a single individual owns vast extents of uncultivated land and enslaves thousands of people who must work the land as *gañanes* [peons] or slaves," and proclaimed the social benefits of the small landholding. But Morelos' freedom of action was restrained by his links with the creole landowning elite, some of whom were his lieutenants and whose property he promised to respect.

A brilliant guerrilla leader who substituted strict discipline, training, and centralized direction for the loose methods of Hidalgo, Morelos, having established a firm base in the Pacific lowlands, advanced toward the strategic central highlands and the capital. His thrust into the

176   rich sugar-producing area (modern Morelos) just south of Mexico City failed to gain sufficient support from the local Indian communities, which retained substantial landholdings, and he was forced to retreat southward into the rugged mountainous region of Oaxaca. His military efforts were hampered by differences with fractious civilian allies and by his decision to establish a representative government at a time when his military situation was turning precarious. In the fall of 1813 a congress he had convened at Chilpancingo declared Mexico's independence, enacted Morelos' social reforms, and vested him with supreme military and executive power. But in the months that followed, the tide of war turned against the insurgent cause, in part because of tactical mistakes by Morelos that involved abandonment of fluid guerrilla warfare in favor of fixed position warfare, illustrated by his prolonged siege of the fortress of Acapulco. In late 1813 Morelos suffered several defeats at the hands of royalist forces directed by the able and aggressive viceroy Felix Calleja.

The defeat of Napoleon and the return of the ferociously reactionary Ferdinand VII to the throne of Spain in 1814 released thousands of soldiers who could be sent overseas to suppress the Spanish American revolts. The congress of Chilpancingo, put to flight, became a wandering body whose squabbling and need for protection diverted Morelos' attention from the all-important military problem. Hoping to revitalize the rebel cause and gain creole elite support by offering an alternative to Ferdinand's brutal despotism, the congress met at Apatzingan and drafted a liberal constitution (October 1814) that provided for a republican frame of government and included an article proclaiming the equality of citizens before the law and freedom of speech and the press. In the course of the year 1815, unrelenting royalist pressure forced the congress to flee from place to place. In November, fighting a rearguard action that enabled the congress to escape, Morelos was captured by a royalist force and brought to the capital. Like Hidalgo, he was found guilty by an Inquisition court of heresy and treason; he was shot by a firing squad on December 22, 1815.

The great guerrilla leader had died, but the revolutionary movement, although fragmented, continued. Indeed, the struggle between numerous insurgent bands and the Spanish counterinsurgency reached new heights of virulence between 1815 and 1820. Avoiding the mistakes of Hidalgo and even Morelos, the rebel leaders shunned pitched battles and made no effort to capture large population centers. Instead, they conducted a fluid warfare in which small units attacked loyalist haciendas they sacked and destroyed, disrupted or levied tolls on trade, severed communications, and controlled large stretches of the countryside. They fled when pursued by counterinsurgent forces and reappeared when the overextended Spanish troops had departed. The destructive effects of a hopeless war on the economy, the heavy taxes imposed on all inhabitants by regional commanders and local juntas for the support of that war, and the harsh treatment meted out not only to insurgents but to high-ranking creoles who favored compromise and autonomy, alienated even the most loyal elements of the creole elite.

These elements, as well as many conservative Spaniards, sought a way out of the impasse that would avoid radical social change under a republican regime of the kind Morelos proposed. A way out seemed to appear in 1820 when a liberal revolt in Spain forced Ferdinand VII to accept the constitution of 1812. Mexican deputies elected to the Spanish Cortes or parliament proposed a solution that would have retained ties with Spain but granted New Spain and the other American "kingdoms" autonomy within the empire. The Spanish majority in the Cortes rejected the proposal and sealed the doom of the empire.

The radical reforms the Cortes adopted in 1820, including the abolition of the ecclesiastical and military fueros, antagonized conservative landlords, clergy, army officers, and merchants, whether creole or peninsular. Fearing the loss of privileges, they schemed to separate Mexico from the mother country and to establish independence under conservative auspices. Their instrument was the creole officer Agustín de Iturbide, who had waged implacable war against the insurgents. Iturbide offered peace and reconciliation to the principal rebel leader, Vicente Guerrero. His plan combined independence, monarchy, the supremacy of the Roman Catholic church, and the civil equality of creoles and peninsulars. Guerrero was a sincere liberal and republican, Iturbide an unprincipled opportunist who dreamed of placing a crown on his own head. But for the moment Iturbide's program offered advantages to both sides, and Guerrero reluctantly accepted it. The united forces of Iturbide and Guerrero swiftly overcame scattered loyalist resistance. On September 28, 1821, Iturbide proclaimed Mexican independence, and eight months later an elected congress summoned by Iturbide confirmed him as Agustín I, emperor of Mexico.

Despite its tinsel splendor, Iturbide's empire had no popular base. Within a few months, Agustín I had to abdicate, with a warning never to return. Hoping for a comeback, Iturbide returned from England in 1824 and landed on the coast with a small party. He was promptly captured by troops of the new republican regime and shot.

Latin American Independence: A Reckoning

After more than a decade of war, accompanied by immense loss of life and property, most of Latin America had won its political independence. The revolutions were accompanied or quickly followed by a number of social changes. Independence brought the death of the Inquisition, the end of legal discrimination on the basis of race, and the abolition of titles of nobility in

most lands. It also gave an impetus to the abolition of slavery, to the founding of public schools, and to similar reforms. All these changes, however, were marginal; independence left intact the existing economic and social structures. This was natural, for the creole elite that headed the movement had no intention of transforming the existing order. They sought to replace the peninsulars in the seats of power and open their ports to the commerce of the world but desired no change of labor and land systems. Indeed, their interests as producers of raw materials and foodstuffs for sale in the markets of Europe and North America required the maintenance of the system of great estates worked by a semiservile native proletariat. No agrarian reform accompanied independence. The haciendas abandoned by or confiscated from loyalists usually fell into the hands of the creole aristocracy. Some land also passed into the possession of mestizo or mulatto officers, who were assimilated into the creole elite and as a rule promptly forgot the groups from which they had come.

Instead of broadening the base of landownership in Latin America, the revolutions actually helped to narrow it. The liberal, individualist ideology of the revolutionary governments undermined Indian communal land tenure in some cases by requiring the division of community lands among its members. This process facilitated the usurpation of Indian land by creole landlords and hastened the transformation of the Indian peasantry into a class of peons or serfs on white haciendas (see Chapters 9 and 10). Since no structural economic change took place, aristocratic values continued to dominate Latin American society, despite an elaborate façade of republican constitutions and law codes.

Part 2

Latin America in the Nineteenth Century

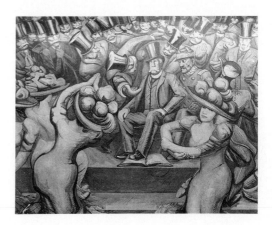

After winning their independence, the new Latin American states began a long, uphill struggle to achieve economic and political stability. They faced immense obstacles, for independence, as previously noted, was not accompanied by economic and social changes that could spur rapid progress—for example, no redistribution of land and income in favor of the lower classes took place. The large estate, generally operated with primitive methods and slave or peon labor, continued to dominate economic life. Far from diminishing, the influence of the landed aristocracy actually increased as a result of the leading military role it played in the wars of independence and of the passing of Spanish authority.

Economic life stagnated, for the anticipated large-scale influx of foreign capital did not materialize, and the European demand for Latin American staples remained far below expectations. Free trade brought increased commercial activity to the coasts, but this increase was offset by the near destruction of some local craft industries by cheap, factory-made European goods. The sluggish pace of economic activity and the relative absence of interregional trade and true national markets encouraged local self-sufficiency, isolation, political instability, and even chaos.

As a result of these adverse factors, the period from about 1820 to about 1870 was for many Latin American countries an age of violence, of alternate dictatorship and revolution. Its symbol was the *caudillo* (strong man), whose power was always based on force, no matter what kind of constitution the country had. Usually, the caudillo ruled with the aid of a coalition of lesser caudillos, each supreme in his region. Whatever their methods, the caudillos generally displayed some regard for republican ideology and institutions. Political parties, bearing such labels as "conservative" and "liberal," "unitarian" and "federalist," were active in most of the new states. Conservatism drew most of its support from the great landowners and their urban allies. Liberalism typically attracted provincial landowners, professional men, and other groups that had enjoyed little power in the past and were dissatisfied with the existing order. As a rule, conservatives sought to retain many of the social arrangements of the colonial era and favored a highly centralized government. Liberals, often inspired by the example of the United States, usually advocated a federal form of government, guarantees of individual rights, lay control of education, and an end to special privileges for the clergy and military. Neither party displayed much interest in the problems of the Indian peasantry and other lower-class groups.

Beginning in about 1870, the accelerating tempo of the Industrial Revolution in Europe stimulated a more rapid change in the Latin American economy and politics. European capital flowed into the area, creating the facilities needed to expand and modernize production and trade. The pace and degree of economic progress of the various countries were very uneven, and depended largely on their geographic position and natural resources.

Extreme one-sidedness was a feature of the new economic order. One or two products became the basis of each country's prosperity, making it highly vulnerable to fluctuations in the world demand and the price of these commodities. Meanwhile, other sectors of the economy remained stagnant or even declined through diversion of labor and land to other industries.

The late nineteenth-century expansion had two other characteristics: in the main, it took place within the framework of the hacienda system of land tenure and labor, and it was accompanied by a steady growth of foreign control over the natural and man-made resources of the region. Thus, by 1900 a new structure of dependency, or colonialism, had arisen, called neocolonialism, with Great Britain and later the United States replacing Spain and Portugal as the dominant power in the area.

The new economic order demanded peace and continuity in government, and after 1870 political conditions in Latin America did, in fact, grow more stable. Old party lines dissolved as conservatives adopted the positivist dogma of science and progress, while liberals abandoned their concern with constitutional methods and civil liberties in favor of an interest in material prosperity. A new type of "progressive" caudillo—Porfirio Díaz in Mexico, Rafael Núñez in Colombia, Antonio Guzmán Blanco in Venezuela—symbolized the politics of acquisition. The cycle of dictatorship and revolution continued in many lands, but the revolutions became less frequent and less devastating.

These are some major trends in the political and economic history of Latin America in the period extending from about 1820 to 1900. Naturally, these trends were accompanied by other changes in the Latin American way of life and culture, notably the development of a powerful literature that often sought not only to mirror Latin American society but to change it. In Part 2, we shall present short histories of four leading Latin American countries—Mexico, Argentina, Chile, and Brazil—in the nineteenth century. All four contain themes and problems common to the area in that period, but each displays variations that reflect the specific backgrounds of the different states.

Chapter 9

Dictators and Revolutions

Independence did not bring Latin America the ordered freedom and prosperity that the liberators had hoped for. In most of the new states, decades of civil strife followed the passing of Spanish and Portuguese rule. Bolívar reflected the disillusionment of many patriot leaders when he wrote in 1829: "There is no good faith in America, nor among the nations of America. Treaties are scraps of paper; constitutions, printed matter; elections, battles; freedom, anarchy; and life, a torment." The contrast between Latin American stagnation and disorder and the meteoric advance of the former English colonies—the United States—intensified the pessimism and self-doubt of some Latin American leaders and intellectuals.

The Fruits of Independence

Frustration of the great hopes with which the struggle for liberation began was inevitable, for independence was not accompanied by economic and social changes that could shatter the colonial mold. Aside from the passing of the Spanish and Portuguese trade monopolies, the colonial economic and social structures remained intact. The hacienda, fazenda, or estancia, employing archaic techniques and a labor force of peons or slaves, continued to dominate agriculture; no significant class of small farmers arose to challenge the economic and political might of the great landowners. Indeed, the revolutions strengthened the power of the landed aristocracy by removing the agencies of Spanish rule—viceroys, audiencias, intendants—and by weakening the ingrained habits of obedience to a central authority. In contrast, all other colonial elites—the merchant class, weakened by the expulsion or emigration of many loyalist merchants; the mine owners, ruined by wartime destruction or confiscation of their properties; and the church hierarchy, often in disgrace for having sided with Spain—emerged from the conflict with diminished weight.

To their other sources of influence the landed aristocracy added the prestige of a military elite crowned with the laurels of victory, for many revolutionary officers had arisen from its ranks. The militarization of the new states as a result of years of destructive warfare and postwar instability assured a large political role for this officer group. Standing armies that often consumed more than half of the national budgets arose. Not content with the role of guardians of order and national security, the military became arbiters of political disputes, as a rule intervening in favor of the conservative landowning interests and the urban elites with whom the great landowners were closely linked.

Economic Stagnation

Revolutionary leaders had expected that a vast expansion of foreign trade, which would aid economic recovery, would follow the passing of Spanish commercial monopoly. In fact, some countries, favored by their natural resources or geographic position, soon recovered from the revolutionary crisis and scored modest to large economic advances; they included Brazil (coffee and sugar), Argentina (hides), and Chile (metals and hides). But others, such as Mexico, Bolivia, and Peru, whose mining economies had suffered shattering blows, failed to recover colonial levels of production.

Several factors accounted for the economic stagnation that plagued many of the new states in the first half of the nineteenth century. Independence was not accompanied by a redistribution of land and income that might have stimulated a growth of internal markets and productive forces. The anticipated large-scale influx of foreign capital did not materialize, partly because political disorder discouraged foreign investment, partly because Europe and the United

States, then financing their own industrial revolutions, had as yet little capital to export. Exports of Latin American staples also remained below expectations, for Europe still viewed Latin America primarily as an outlet for manufactured goods, especially English textiles. The resulting flood of cheap, factory-made European products damaged local craft industries and drained the new states of their stocks of gold and silver, creating a chronic balance-of-trade problem. The British conquest of the Latin American markets further weakened the local merchant class, which was unable to compete with its English rivals. By mid-century the wealthiest and most prestigious merchant houses, from Mexico City to Buenos Aires and Valparaíso, bore English names. Iberian merchants, however, continued to dominate the urban and provincial retail trade in many areas.

In their totality, these developments retarded the development of native capitalism and capitalist relations and reinforced the dominant role of the hacienda in the economic and political life of the new states. The deepening stagnation of the interior of these nations, which was aggravated by lack of roads and by natural obstacles to communication (such as jungles and mountains), intensified tendencies toward regionalism and the domination of regions by caudillos great and small, who were usually local large landowners.[1] The sluggish tempo of economic activity encouraged these caudillos to employ their private followings of peons and retainers as pawns in the game of politics and revolution on a national scale. Indeed, politics and revolution became in some countries a form of economic activity that compensated for the lack of other opportunities, since the victors, having gained control of the all-important customhouse (which collected du-

---

[1] The term *caudillo* is commonly applied to politico-military leaders who held power on the national and regional level in Latin America before more or less stable parliamentary government became the norm in the area beginning about 1870. Military ability and charisma are qualities often associated with caudillos, who came in many guises, but not all possessed the same qualities. Since the semifeudal conditions that gave rise to the caudillo still survive in parts of Latin America, it can be said that caudillos and *caudillismo* still exist.

ties on imports and exports) and other official sources of revenue, could reward themselves and their followers with government jobs, contracts, grants of public land, and other favors. This reliance by members of the elite on political and military activity as a career and on the customhouse as a source of government revenue had two negative results. One was the rise of bloated military and bureaucratic establishments that diverted resources from economic development; the other a stress on foreign trade that intensified the trend toward dependency.

Politics: The Conservative and Liberal Programs

The political systems of the new states made large formal concessions to the liberal bourgeois ideology of the nineteenth century. With the exception of Brazil, all the new states adopted the republican form of government (Mexico had two brief intervals of imperial rule) and paid their respects to the formulas of parliamentary and representative government. Their constitutions provided for presidents, congresses, and courts; often they contained elaborate safeguards of individual rights.

These façades of modernity, however, poorly concealed the dictatorial or oligarchical reality beneath. Typically, the chief executive was a caudillo whose power rested on force, no matter what the constitutional form; usually, he ruled with the support of a coalition of lesser caudillos, each more or less supreme in his own domain. The supposed independence of the judicial and legislative branches was a fiction. As a rule, elections were exercises in futility. Since the party in power generally counted the votes, the opposition had no alternative but revolt.

Literacy and property qualifications disfranchised most Indians and mixed-bloods; where they had the right to vote, the *patrón* (master) often herded them to the polls to vote for him or his candidates. The lack of the secret ballot (voting was usually open, with colored ballots) made coercion of voters easy. Whether liberal or conservative, all sections of the ruling class agreed

on keeping the peasantry, gauchos, and other "lower orders" on the margins of political life, on preventing their emergence as groups with collective philosophies and goals. The very privileges that the new creole constitutions and law codes granted the Indians—equality before the law, the "right" to divide and dispose of their communal lands—weakened the solidarity of the native people and their ability to resist the competitive individualism of the creole world. But especially gifted, ambitious, and fortunate members of these marginal groups were sometimes co-opted into the creole elite and provided some of its most distinguished leaders; two examples are the Zapotec Indian Benito Juárez in Mexico and the mestizo president Andrés Santa Cruz in Bolivia.

At first glance, the political history of Latin America in the first half-century after independence, with its dreary alternation of dictatorship and revolt, seems pointless and trivial. But the political struggles of this period were more than disputes over spoils between sections of a small upper class. Genuine social and ideological cleavages helped produce those struggles and the bitterness with which they were fought. Such labels as "conservative" and "liberal," "unitarian" and "federalist," assigned by the various parties to themselves or each other, were more than masks in a pageant, although opportunism contributed to the ease with which some leaders assumed and discarded these labels.

Generally speaking, conservatism reflected the interests of the traditional holders of power and privilege, men who had a stake in maintaining the existing order. Hence, the great landowners, the upper clergy, the higher ranks of the military and the civil bureaucracy, and monopolistic merchant groups tended to be conservatives. Liberalism, in contrast, appealed to those groups that in colonial times had little or no access to the main structures of economic and political power and were naturally eager to alter the existing order. Thus, liberalism drew much support from provincial landowners, lawyers and other professional men (the groups most receptive to new ideas), shopkeepers, and artisans; it also appealed to ambitious, aspiring Indians and mixed-bloods. But regional conflicts and clan or family loyalties often cut across the lines of social and occupational cleavage, complicating the political picture.

Liberals wanted to break up the hierarchical social structure inherited from the colonial period. They had a vision of their countries remade into dynamic middle-class states on the model of the United States or England. Inspired by the success of the United States, they usually favored a federal form of government, guarantees of individual rights, lay control of education, and an end to a special legal status for the clergy and military. In their modernizing zeal, liberals sometimes called for abolition of entails (which restricted the right to inherit property to a particular descendant or descendants of the owner), dissolution of convents, confiscation of church wealth, and abolition of slavery. The federalism of the liberals had a special appeal for secondary regions of the new states, eager to develop their resources and free themselves from domination by capitals and wealthy primary regions.

Conservatives typically upheld a strong centralized government, the religious and educational monopoly of the Roman Catholic church, and the special privileges of the clergy and military. They distrusted such radical novelties as freedom of speech and the press and religious toleration. Conservatives, in short, sought to salvage as much of the colonial social order as was compatible with the new republican system. Indeed, some conservative leaders ultimately despaired of that system and dreamed of implanting monarchy in their countries.

Neither conservatives nor liberals displayed much interest in the problems of the Indian, black, and mixed-blood masses that formed the majority of people in most Latin American countries. Liberals, impatient with the supposed backwardness of the Indians, regarded their communalism as an impediment to the development of a capitalist spirit of enterprise and initiated legislation providing for the division of communal lands—a policy that favored land grabbing at the expense of Indian villages. Despite their theoretical preference for small landholdings and a rural middle class, liberals recoiled from any program of radical land reform. Conservatives correctly regarded the great estate as the very foundation of their power. As traditionalists, however, the conservatives sometimes claimed to continue the Spanish paternalist policy toward the Indians and enjoyed some support among the natives, who tended to be suspicious of all innovations.

This summary of the conservative and liberal programs for Latin America in the first half-century after independence inevitably overlooks variations from the theoretical liberal and conservative norms, variations that reflected the specific conditions and problems of the different states. An examination of the history of four leading Latin American countries in this period, Mexico, Argentina, Chile, and Brazil, reveals not only certain common themes but a rich diversity of political experience.

Mexico

The struggle for Mexican independence, begun by the radical priests Hidalgo and Morelos, was completed by the creole officer Agustín de Iturbide, who headed a coalition of creole and peninsular conservatives terrified at the prospect of being governed by the liberal Spanish constitution of 1812, which was reestablished in 1820. Independence, achieved under such conservative auspices, meant that Mexico's economic and social patterns underwent little change. The great hacienda continued to dominate the countryside in many areas. Although Indian villages managed to retain substantial community lands until after mid-century and even improved their economic and political position somewhat with the passing of Spanish centralized authority, the trend toward usurpation of Indian lands grew stronger as a result of the lapse of Spanish protective legislation. Peons and tenants on the haciendas often suffered from debt servitude, miserable wages, oppressive rents, and excessive religious fees. At

188 the constitutional convention of 1856–1857, the liberal Ponciano Arriaga declared:

With some honorable exceptions, the rich landowners of Mexico . . . resemble the feudal lords of the Middle Ages. On his seigneurial lands, with more or less formalities, the landowner makes and executes laws, administers justice and exercises civil power, imposes taxes and fines, has his own jails and irons, metes out punishments and tortures, monopolizes commerce, and forbids the conduct without his permission of any business but that of the estate.

The church continued to wield diminished but still considerable economic and spiritual power. An anonymous contemporary writer reflected the disillusionment of the lower classes with the fruits of independence: "Independence is only a name. Previously they ruled us from Spain, now from here. It is always the same priest on a different mule. But as for work, food, and clothing, there is no difference."

The Mexican Economy

The ravages of war had left mineshafts flooded, haciendas deserted, the economy stagnant. The end of the Spanish commercial monopoly, however, brought a large increase in the volume of foreign trade; the number of ships entering Mexican ports jumped from 148 in 1823 to 639 in 1826. But exports did not keep pace with imports, leaving a trade deficit that had to be covered by exporting precious metals. The drain of gold and silver aggravated the problems of the new government, which inherited a bankrupt treasury and had to support a swollen bureaucracy and an officer class ready to revolt against any government that suggested a cut in their numbers or pay. The exodus of Spanish merchants and their capital added to the economic problems of the new state. Complicating those problems was the disorder that was a legacy of the war; bands of robbers made travel on the roads so unsafe that "whether coming or going from Puebla or Veracruz, the Mexico City traveler expected to be robbed."

Foreign loans appeared to be the only way out of the crisis. In 1824–1825, English bankers made loans to Mexico amounting to 32 million pesos, guaranteed by Mexican customs revenues. Of this amount the Mexicans received only a little more than 11 million pesos, as the bankers went bankrupt before all the money due to Mexico from the loan proceeds was paid. By 1843 unpaid interest and principal had raised the nation's foreign debt to more than 54 million pesos. This mounting foreign debt not only created crushing interest burdens but threatened Mexico's independence and territorial integrity, for behind foreign capitalists stood governments that might threaten intervention in case of default.

Foreign investments, mainly from Britain, however, made possible a partial recovery of the decisive mining sector. Old mines, abandoned and flooded during the wars, were reopened, but the available capital proved inadequate, the technical problems of reconstruction were greater than anticipated, and production remained on a relatively low level.

An ambitious effort to revive and modernize Mexican industry also got under way, spurred by the founding in 1830 of the *Banco de Avío,* which provided governmental assistance to industry. Manufacturing, paced by textiles, made some limited progress in the three decades after independence. Leading industrial centers included Mexico City, Puebla, Guadalajara, Durango, and Veracruz. But shortages of capital, lack of a consistent policy of protection for domestic industry, and a socioeconomic structure that sharply limited the internal market hampered the growth of Mexican factory capitalism. By 1843 the Banco de Avío had to close its doors for lack of funds. The Mexican economy, therefore, continued to be based on mining and agriculture. Mexico's principal exports were precious metals, especially silver, and such agricultural products as tobacco, coffee, vanilla, cochineal, and henequen (a plant fiber used in rope and twine). Imports consisted primarily of manufactured goods that Mexican industry could not supply.

Politics: Liberals versus Conservatives

A liberal-conservative cleavage dominated Mexican political life in the half-century after independence. That conflict was latent from the moment that the "liberator" Iturbide, the former scourge of insurgents, rode into Mexico City on September 27, 1821, flanked on either side by two insurgent generals, Vicente Guerrero and Guadalupe Victoria, firm republicans and liberals. The fall of Iturbide in 1823 cleared the way for the establishment of a republic. But it soon became apparent that the republicans were divided into liberals and conservatives, federalists and centralists.

The constitution of 1824 represented a compromise between liberal and conservative interests. It appeased regional economic interests, which were fearful of a too-powerful central government, by creating nineteen states that possessed taxing power; their legislatures, each casting one vote, chose the president and vice president for four-year terms. The national legislature was made bicameral, with an upper house (Senate) and a lower house (Chamber of Deputies). By assuring the creation of local civil bureaucracies, the federalist structure also satisfied the demand of provincial middle classes for greater access to political activity and office. But the constitution had a conservative tinge as well: although the church lost its monopoly of education, Catholicism was proclaimed the official religion, and the fueros of the church and the army were specifically confirmed.

A hero of the war of independence, the liberal general Guadalupe Victoria, was elected first president under the new constitution. Anxious to preserve unity, Victoria brought the conservative Lucas Alamán into his cabinet. But this era of good feeling was very short-lived; by 1825, Alamán was forced out of the government. The liberal-conservative cleavage now assumed the form of a rivalry between two Masonic lodges, the York Rite lodge, founded by the American minister Joel Roberts Poinsett, and the Scottish Rite lodge, sponsored by the British chargé d'affaires Henry Ward. Their rivalry reflected the An-glo-American competition for economic and political influence in Mexico. The old mining and landowning aristocracy, which looked to Great Britain for leadership and assistance in the economic and political reconstruction of Mexico on a sound conservative basis, formed a pro-British faction; the liberals and federalists, who regarded the United States as a model for their own reform program, formed a pro-American *Yorkino* faction.

The fate of the thousands of Spaniards, including many wealthy merchants who remained in Mexico after the fall of the colonial regime, soon became a major political issue. Spain's continued occupation of the fortress of Veracruz until 1825, its refusal (until 1836) to recognize Mexican independence, and the discovery of plots against independence in which Spaniards were implicated created much anti-Spanish feeling. But conservative leaders like Alamán strongly opposed ouster of the Spaniards as being harmful to the economy and to the Mexican upper class, threatened by the ambitions of upstart middle-class politicians. Nonetheless, in 1827 the liberal Yorkinos pushed through Congress a decree of expulsion against the Spaniards. Although not fully enforced, the decree hastened the transformation of the conservative and liberal factions into political parties.

The Conservative party represented the old landed and mining aristocracy, the clerical and military hierarchy, monopolistic merchants, and some manufacturers. Its intellectual spokesman and organizer was Lucas Alamán, statesman, champion of industry, and author of a brilliant history of Mexico from the conservative point of view. The Liberal party represented a creole and mestizo middle class—provincial landowners, professional men, artisans, the lower ranks of the clergy and military—determined to end special privileges and the concentration of political and economic power in the upper class. A priest-economist, José María Luis Mora, presented the liberal position with great force and lucidity. But the Liberal party was divided; its right wing, the *moderados,* wanted to proceed slowly and sometimes joined the conservatives; its left wing, the

ATLANTIC OCEAN

M E X I C O
1821

San Antonio

Rio Grande

GULF OF MEXICO

BAHAMA IS.
(Br.)

PUERTO RICO
(Sp.)

Mexico City
Veracruz

CUBA
(Sp.)

BR. HONDURAS

HAITI
1804

Guatemala

CARIBBEAN SEA

TRINIDAD
(Br.)

UNITED PROVINCES OF
CENTRAL AMERICA
1823–1839

Panama

Caracas

BR. GUIANA
DUTCH GUIANA
FR. GUIANA

Bogotá

GRAN COLOMBIA
1819–1830

Quito

·D₀

GALAPAGOS IS.

Indefinite Boundary

PERU
1821

Lima

EMPIRE OF BRAZIL
1822

BOLIVIA
1825

Bahia

Sucre

PACIFIC OCEAN

PARAGUAY
1813

Asunción

Rio de Janeiro

CHILE
1817

UNITED
PROVINCES
OF
LA PLATA
1816

Santiago

URUGUAY
1828

Buenos Aires

Montevideo

0   500   1000 Miles

0   500   1000 Kilometers

LATIN AMERICA IN 1830

the Americans. By
dalgo (1848), Mexi
ceding Texas, Cali
United States; in
million and the c
against it.

La Reforma, Ci
French Interver

A succession of
mildly conservativ
efficient, struggled
postwar Mexico.
fered by Mexico ur
ated widespread
policies and stimu
ism. In 1846, duri
tions had come tc
and Michoacán. Ir
was Melchor Oca
profoundly influer
utopian socialist
Indian lawyer, Be
As governor, he g
efficiency, and th
manners.

Ocampo and Ju
ovated liberalism
called *La Reform*
the 1830s, the Re
vestiges and imp
ideology, howeve
aristocratic, intel
its puro left wing
ures, such as Poi
mírez, who rose a
ideology by their
fense of labor and
vanced ideas.

The revived lil
for the abolition
church property,
actionary forces.
regime of Marian
in 1850, did not c
radical change.

puros, advocated sweeping antifeudal, anticlerical reforms.

The election of 1828 produced the first political
crisis of the republic. The conservatives united
behind Manuel Gómez Pedraza, a leader of the
moderados; the puro candidate was Vicente
Guerrero, a hero of the war for independence
whose popularity should have assured his election. But Gómez Pedraza was secretary of war,
and army pressure on the state legislatures produced a vote of ten to nine for him and the conservative vice-presidential candidate, Anastasio
Bustamante. Liberal indignation was great, and
General Antonio López de Santa Anna, who had
overthrown Iturbide and saw another opportunity to make political capital by assuming the
role of liberator, rose in revolt against Gómez
Pedraza. By January 1829, the liberals had triumphed and Congress declared Guerrero president of the republic. Hoping to promote unity,
Guerrero asked Bustamante to remain as vice
president, a serious error, as events proved.

An honest but uneducated man who doubted
his own ability to govern, a mestizo scorned by
the aristocratic creole society of the capital,
Guerrero lasted barely one year in office. He
coped successfully with a Spanish effort to reconquer Mexico (1829), but was overthrown the
next year by an army revolt organized by Bustamante. For two years, a conservative dictatorship
dominated by Lucas Alamán used the army to remove liberal governors and legislatures in the
states, suppress newspapers, and jail, shoot, or
exile puro leaders. The climax of this reign of terror was the execution of the veteran revolutionary Guerrero by a firing squad in 1831.

Growing unrest informed Santa Anna that the
political pendulum was swinging toward the liberals, and in 1832 this careerist, a true conservative at heart, led a revolt against Bustamante.
Province after province joined the revolt, and by
the end of the year Bustamante had been forced
into exile. Following congressional elections in
March 1833, a new liberal government, dominated by the puros, was formed. Santa Anna, still
posing as a liberal, was elected president, and
Valentín Gómez Farías, a physician who remained a pillar of the liberal cause for a quarter-

century, was chosen vice president. But Santa
Anna would not assume responsibility for carrying out the liberal program; pleading ill health,
he retired to his hacienda on the Veracruz coast
and turned over to Gómez Farías his office.

The year 1833 was a high-water mark of liberal
achievement. Aided by José María Luis Mora, his
minister of education, Gómez Farías pushed
through Congress a series of radical reforms: abolition of the special privileges and immunities of
the army and church (meaning that officers and
priests would now be subject to the jurisdiction
of civil courts), abolition of tithes, secularization
of the clerical University of Mexico, creation of a
department of public instruction, reduction of
the army, and creation of a civilian militia. These
measures were accompanied by a program of internal improvements designed to increase the
prosperity of the interior by linking it to the capital and the coasts. In their use of the central government to promote education and national economic development, the liberals showed that
they were not doctrinaire adherents of laissez
faire.

The liberal program inevitably provoked clerical and conservative resistance. Army officers
began to organize revolts; priests proclaimed
from their pulpits that the great cholera epidemic
of 1833 was a sign of divine displeasure with the
works of the impious liberals. Santa Anna waited
until the time was ripe. Then, in April 1834, he
placed himself at the head of the conservative rebellion, occupied the capital, and sent Gómez
Farías and Mora into exile. Resuming the presidency, he summoned a hand-picked reactionary
congress that repealed the reform laws of 1833
and suspended the constitution of 1824. Under
the new conservative constitution of 1836, the
states were reduced to departments completely
dominated by the central government, upper-
class control of politics was assured through high
property and income qualifications for holding
office, and the fueros of the church and army
were restored.

Santa Anna and the conservatives ruled Mexico for the greater part of two decades, 1834 to
1854. Politically and economically, the conservative rule subordinated the interests of the re-

gions and the (
densely popula
City, Puebla, a
was reflected ir
stored the alca
customhouses,
nopoly, insurin;
to Mexico City.

War and Ter

Conservative n
border areas li
contributed to
to the loss of Y
of provincial a
nists in Texas,
patriotic federa
tyranny. Santa
contributed to
and mestizo c
cinto (1837), wl
ence of Texas. I
of 1839 comb
against consei
war against fe
ade, Yucatán r

After the de
nexation by th
greater disaste
Its immediate
ico and the U
Texas, but the
nation of the I
only Texas bu
war ended in
cally due to l
tary training, ;
ble, selfish att
and church cc

In 1846, aft
fered a series
turned the pui
constitution c
puros had a |
duced a curio
plan called f

ing many disgruntled moderados and conservatives. In early 1854, the old liberal caudillo from the state of Guerrero, Juan Alvarez, and the moderado general Ignacio Comonfort issued a call for revolt, the Plan of Ayutla, demanding the end of the dictatorship and the election of a convention to draft a new constitution. Within a year, Santa Anna's regime began to disintegrate, and in August 1855, seeing the handwriting on the wall, he went into exile for the last time. Some days later, a puro-dominated provisional government took office in Mexico City. The seventy-five-year-old Juan Alvarez was named provisional president; to his cabinet he named Benito Juárez as minister of justice and Miguel Lerdo de Tejada as treasury minister.

One of Juárez's first official acts was to issue a decree, the *Ley Juárez*, proclaiming the right of the state to limit the clerical and military fueros to matters of internal discipline. The decree raised a storm of conservative wrath, and Comonfort, now minister of war, himself disapproved of the measure. By December, moderado and conservative pressure, wielded through Comonfort, brought a shift to the right in the cabinet. Melchor Ocampo, the most radical of the puros, was forced out, and a few days later Alvarez himself resigned, turning over the presidency to Comonfort, who proposed to steer a cautious middle course that he hoped would satisfy both liberals and conservatives.

The *Ley Lerdo* (Lerdo Law) of June 1856, drafted by Miguel Lerdo de Tejada, was poorly designed to achieve such a reconciliation, for it struck a heavy blow at the material base of the church's power, its landed wealth. The law barred the church from holding land not used for religious purposes and compelled the sale of all such property to tenants, with the rent considered to be 6 percent of the sale value of the property. Real estate not being rented was to be auctioned to the highest bidder, with payment of a large sales tax to the government.

The law's intent was to create a rural middle class, but since it made no provision for division of the church estates, the bulk of the land passed into the hands of great landowners, merchants, and capitalists, both Mexican and foreign. Worse,

the law barred Indian villages from owning land and ordered that such land be sold in the same manner as church property, excepting only land and buildings used exclusively for the "public use" of the inhabitants and for communal pastures (*ejidos*). As a result, land-grabbers descended on the Indian villages, "denounced" their land to the local courts, and proceeded to buy it at auction for paltry sums. The law provided that the Indian owners should have the first opportunity to buy, but few Indians could pay the minimum purchase price. When the Indians responded with protests and revolts, Lerdo explained in a circular that the intent of his law was that Indian community lands should be divided among the natives, not sold to others. But he insisted that "the continued existence of the Indian communities ought not to be tolerated . . . , and this is exactly one of the goals of the law." He was also adamant on the right of those who rented Indian lands to buy them if they chose to do so. So, during the summer and fall of 1856 many Indian pueblos lost crop and pasturelands from which they had derived revenues vitally needed to defray the cost of their religious ceremonies and other communal expenses. Indian resistance and the liberals' need to attract popular support during their struggle with the conservative counterrevolution and French interventionists in the decade 1857–1867 seem to have slowed enforcement of the Lerdo Law as it applied to Indian villages, but the long-range tendency of liberal agrarian policy was to compel division of communal lands, facilitating their acquisition by hacendados and even small and middle-sized farmers. The result was a simultaneous strengthening of the latifundio and some increase in the size of the rural middle class.

While the provisional government was causing consternation among conservatives with the Ley Juárez and the Ley Lerdo, a constitutional convention dominated by moderate liberals had been completing its work. The constitution of 1857 proclaimed freedom of speech, press, and assembly; limited fueros; forbade ecclesiastical and civil corporations to own land; and proclaimed the sanctity of private property. It restored the federalist structure of 1824, with the same division of Mexico into states, but replaced the bicameral national legislature with a single house and eliminated the office of vice president (the chief justice of the Supreme Court should succeed if the office of president became vacant). An effort by the puro minority to incorporate freedom of religion in the constitution failed; the resulting compromise neither mentioned toleration nor explicitly adopted Catholicism as the official faith.

A few voices were raised against the land monopoly, peonage, and the immense inequalities of wealth. "We proclaim ideas and forget realities," complained the radical delegate Ponciano Arriaga. "How can a hungry, naked, miserable people practice popular government? How can we condemn slavery in words, while the lot of most of our fellow citizens is more grievous than that of the black slaves of Cuba or the United States?" Despite his caustic attack on the land monopoly, Arriaga offered a relatively moderate solution: the state should seize and auction off large uncultivated estates. The conservative opposition promptly branded Arriaga's project "communist"; the moderate majority in the convention passed over it in silence.

Having completed its work, the convention disbanded and elections followed for the first Congress and president and the members of the Supreme Court. Comonfort, who had already expressed unhappiness with the constitution, was elected president, and Juárez chief justice of the Supreme Court.

Since the new constitution incorporated the Lerdo Law and the Juárez Law, the church now openly entered the political struggle by excommunicating all public officials who took the required oath of loyalty. Counterrevolution had been gathering its forces for months and found an instrument in the vacillating Comonfort. In December 1857 General Félix Zuloaga "pronounced" in favor of a Comonfort dictatorship, occupied the capital, and arrested Juárez. Pressed by the reactionaries to repeal the Juárez and Lerdo laws, Comonfort refused and finally found the strength to break with his reactionary supporters. He released Juárez, declared the constitution re-established, and himself went into exile, unmolested by the victorious rebels. Meanwhile, the liberals in the provinces had raised an army; proclaiming that Comonfort had violated the constitution and ceased to be president, they declared Juárez president of Mexico. For their part, the conservatives, in control of Mexico City, Puebla, and other major cities, declared the constitution void and the Juárez and Lerdo laws repealed.

The tremendous Three Years' War (1857–1860) had begun. In regional terms, the war pitted the rich central area, dominated by the conservatives, against the liberal south, north, and Veracruz. Controlling extensive regions and enjoying the support of a clear majority of the population, the liberals nevertheless suffered serious defeats in the first stage of the war. The main reason was that most of the permanent army had gone over to the conservatives, while the liberals had to create their own armed forces. The liberal armies, composed of elements of the national guard and guerrilla bands, were at the outset inevitably inferior in discipline and equipment to the conservative troops, which won almost all the pitched battles. In March 1858 conservative troops occupied the important mining center of Guanajuato and approached Querétaro, the seat of Juárez's government. He was forced to move his headquarters, first to Guadalajara and later to Veracruz, which remained the liberal capital until the end of the war.

As the struggle progressed, both sides found themselves in serious financial difficulties. The conservatives, however, had the advantage of generous support from the church. In July 1859, Juárez struck back at the clergy with reform laws that nationalized without compensation all ecclesiastical property except church buildings; the laws also suppressed all monasteries, established freedom of religion, and separated church and state. The reform laws were designed to encourage peasant proprietorship by dividing church estates into small farms, but this goal proved illusory; thanks to the Ley Lerdo, wealthy purchasers had already acquired much of the church land.

By the middle of 1860, the tide of war had turned in favor of the liberals. In August 1860 the

196 best conservative general, Miguel Miramón, was routed at Silao. In October, Guadalajara fell to the liberals. And by the beginning of January 1861 Juárez had re-entered the capital, and the conservative leaders had fled the country. The war was effectively over, although conservative bands in the provinces continued to make devastating raids.

Beaten in the field, the reactionaries looked for help abroad. The conservative governments of England, France, and Spain had no love for the Mexican liberals and Juárez. Moreover, there were ample pretexts for intervention, for both sides had seized or destroyed foreign property without compensation, and foreign bondholders were clamoring for payments from an empty Mexican treasury. The three European powers demanded compensation for damages to their nationals and payment of just debts. Juárez vainly pleaded poverty and noted the dubious nature of some of the claims.

In October 1861 the three powers agreed on a joint intervention in Mexico, and in January 1862 they sent occupation forces to Veracruz. England and Spain, having received assurances of future satisfaction of their claims, soon withdrew, but the French government rejected all Mexican offers, and its troops remained. Napoleon III wanted more than payment of debts. A group of Mexican conservative exiles had convinced the ambitious emperor that the Mexican people would welcome a French army of liberation and the establishment of a monarchy. Napoleon had visions of a French-protected Mexican Empire that would yield him great political and economic advantages. It remained only to find a suitable unemployed prince, and one was found in the person of Archduke Ferdinand Maximilian of Hapsburg, brother of Austrian Emperor Franz Josef.

To prepare the ground for the arrival of the new ruler of Mexico, the French army advanced from Veracruz into the interior toward Puebla. At Puebla, instead of being received as liberators, the interventionists met determined resistance on the part of a poorly armed Mexican garrison and were thrown back with heavy losses. The date—May 5, 1862—is still celebrated as a Mexican national holiday. Reinforced by the arrival of thirty thousand fresh troops, General Elie-Frédéric Forey again besieged Puebla in March 1863, and by May 17 the starving garrison had been forced to surrender. The fall of Puebla and the loss of its garrison of some thirty thousand men left Juárez without an adequate force to defend the capital, and at the end of May his government and the remnants of his army abandoned it and retreated northward. On June 10, the French entered the city to the rejoicing of the clergy; by the end of the year the interventionists had occupied Querétaro, Monterrey, San Luis Potosí, and Saltillo. But the invaders had secure control only of the cities; republican guerrilla detachments controlled most of the national territory.

Meanwhile, in October 1863, a delegation of conservative exiles called on Maximilian to offer him a Mexican crown. As a condition of acceptance, the prince insisted that the Mexican people be consulted, and the French authorities obligingly staged a plebiscite that supposedly gave an overwhelming vote in favor of Maximilian. In April 1864, he accepted the Mexican throne and presently departed with his wife Carlota for their new home.

The conservative conspirators had counted on Maximilian to help them recover their lost wealth and privileges, but the emperor, mindful of realities, would not consent to their demands; the purchase of church lands by native and foreign landlords and capitalists had created new interests that Maximilian refused to antagonize. Confident of conservative support, Maximilian even wooed moderate liberals and won the support of such intellectual lights as the historians José Fernando Ramírez and Manuel Orozco y Berra. These scholars were impressed by Maximilian's good will and they cherished the illusion of a stable and prosperous Mexico ruled by an enlightened monarch.

But the hopes of both conservatives and misguided liberals were built on quicksand. The victories of Maximilian's generals could not destroy the fluid and elusive liberal resistance, firmly grounded in popular hatred for the invaders and aided by Mexico's geography (a rugged terrain with vast, thinly populated territories and few roads). A turning point in the war came in the spring of 1865 in the United States, with the Union triumph over the Confederacy. American demands that the French evacuate Mexico, a region regarded by Secretary of State William Seward as a U.S. zone of economic and political influence, grew more insistent, and American troops were massed along the Rio Grande. Facing serious domestic and diplomatic problems at home, Napoleon decided to cut his losses and liquidate the Mexican adventure.

Marshal Achille François Bazaine, preparing to embark with the remaining French troops, urged Maximilian to abdicate and leave Mexico, but his conservative advisers, who still believed that defeat could be avoided, prevailed on him to stay. With liberal armies converging on Querétaro, the same die-hard conservatives persuaded Maximilian to go there and assume supreme command. Together with the imperialist generals Miguel Miramón and Tomás Mejía, he was captured on May 14, 1867. After a trial by court-martial, all three were found guilty of treason, sentenced to death, and executed by a *Juarista* firing squad.

Postwar Attempts at Reconstruction and the Death of *La Reforma*

Juárez, symbol of the successful Mexican resistance to a foreign usurper, resumed his office of president in August 1867. His government inherited a devastated country. Agriculture and industry were in ruins; as late as 1873, the value of Mexican exports was below the level of 1810. To reduce the state's financial burdens and end the danger of military control, Juárez dismissed two-thirds of the army, an act that produced discontent and uprisings that his generals managed to suppress.

Juárez devoted a considerable part of the state's limited resources to the development of a public school system, especially on the elementary level; by 1874 there were about eight thousand schools with some three hundred and fifty thousand pupils. One of the few material achieve-

ments of his administration was the construction of an important railroad line running from Veracruz through Puebla to Mexico City, completed after his death in 1872.

In his agrarian policy, Juárez continued the liberal program of seeking to implant capitalism in the countryside, at the expense not of the hacienda but of the Indian communities. Indeed, the period of the "Restored Republic" (1868–1876) saw an intensified effort by the federal government to implement the Lerdo Law by compelling dissolution and partition of Indian communal lands, opening the way for a new wave of frauds and seizures by neighboring hacendados and other land-grabbers. The result was a series of nationwide peasant revolts, the most serious occurring in the state of Hidalgo (1869–1870). Proclaiming the rebels to be "communists," the hacendados, aided by state and federal authorities, restored order by the traditional violent methods. A few liberals raised their voices in protest, but were ignored; one was Ignacio Ramírez, who condemned the usurpations and frauds practiced by the hacendados with the complicity of corrupt judges and officials and called for suspension of the law. On the other hand, the period saw the first legislative efforts to improve labor conditions and the formation in the cities of numerous trade unions whose leaders combined liberal and trade unionist principles.

Re-elected president in 1871, Juárez was able to put down a revolt by a hero of the wars of the Reforma, General Porfirio Díaz, who charged Juárez with attempting to become a dictator. But Juárez died the next year of a heart attack and was succeeded as acting president by the chief justice of the Supreme Court, Sebastián Lerdo de Tejada. Lerdo scheduled new elections for October 1872, ran against, and easily defeated Díaz, but in turn faced a growing movement of opposition that accused him of violations of republican legality. When Lerdo announced in 1876 that he intended to seek re-election, Díaz again rose in revolt. Aided by a group of Texas capitalists with strong links to New York banks, he defeated troops loyal to Lerdo and sent him into flight.

198

Díaz had seized power in the name of the ideals of the Reforma. In fact, the year 1876 marked the death of the Reforma and the idealistic principles of natural law that formed its theoretical base. The age of Díaz continued the efforts of the Reforma to construct a bourgeois society, but with new men, new methods, and a new ideology. The libertarian creed to which Juárez subscribed, no matter how often he deviated from it, was replaced by the ideology of positivism as propounded by its French founder, Auguste Comte, ideology that ranked order and progress above freedom.

The Reforma had paved the way for this change by transforming the Mexican bourgeoisie from a revolutionary class into a ruling class that was more predatory and acquisitive than the old creole aristocracy. The remnants of that aristocracy speedily adapted to the ways of the new ruling class and merged with it. The interests of the old and the new rich required political stability, a docile labor force, internal improvements, and a political and economic climate favorable to foreign investments. The mission of the "honorable tyranny" of Porfirio Díaz was to achieve those ends.

Argentina

In 1816 delegates to the congress of Tucumán proclaimed the independence of the United Provinces of the Río de la Plata. "Disunited," however, would have better described the political condition of the area of La Plata, for the creole seizure of power in Buenos Aires in 1810 brought in its train a dissolution of the vast viceroyalty of the Río de la Plata.

The Liberation of Paraguay, Uruguay, and Upper Peru

Paraguay, having repelled efforts by the junta of Buenos Aires to "liberate" it, declared its own independence and fell under the dictatorial rule of the creole lawyer José Gaspar Rodríguez de Fran-

cia, who effectively sealed it off from its neighbors. Francia had his reasons for the system of isolation: the rulers of Buenos Aires controlled Paraguay's river outlets to the sea, and isolation and self-sufficiency were the alternatives to submission and payment of tribute to Buenos Aires. Francia did permit a limited licensed trade with the outside world by way of Brazil, chiefly to satisfy military needs.

Francia's state-controlled economy brought certain benefits: the planned diversification of agriculture, which reduced production of such export crops as yerba maté, tobacco, and sugar, insured a plentiful supply of foodstuffs and the well-being of the Indian and mestizo masses. An interesting feature of Francia's system was the establishment of state farms or ranches—called *estancias de la patria*—that successfully specialized in the raising of livestock and ended Paraguay's dependence on livestock imports from the Argentine province of Entre Ríos. The principal sufferers under Francia's dictatorship were Spaniards, many of whom he expelled or penalized in various ways, and creole aristocrats, who were kept under perpetual surveillance and subjected to severe repression.

The gaucho chieftain José Gervasio Artigas, who resisted the efforts of the junta of Buenos Aires to dominate the area, led Uruguay, then known as the Banda Oriental, toward independence. In 1815 the junta abandoned these efforts, evacuated Montevideo, and turned it over to Artigas. No ordinary caudillo, Artigas not only defended Uruguayan nationality but sought to achieve social reform. In 1815 he issued a plan for distributing royalist lands to the landless, with preference shown to blacks, Indians, zambos, and poor whites. But he was not given the opportunity to implement this radical program. In 1817 a powerful Brazilian army invaded Uruguay and soon had a secure grip on the Banda Oriental. Artigas had to flee across the Paraná River into Paraguay. He received asylum from Francia but was never allowed to leave again; he died in Paraguay thirty years later.

Soon Uruguay again became a battlefield when a small group of Uruguayan exiles, supported by

The gaucho, often a product of racial mixture, was a fearless nomadic horseman. The gaucho wore long, full riding pantaloons that fell in accordion pleats to his ankle, where they fit tightly over the tops of the boots.

Buenos Aires, crossed over the estuary in 1825 and launched a general revolt against Brazilian domination. Brazil retaliated by declaring war against the United Provinces. The three-sided military conflict ended in a stalemate. Uruguay finally achieved independence in 1828 through the mediation of Great Britain, which was unwilling to see Uruguay fall under the control of either of its more powerful neighbors.

Upper Peru, the mountainous northern corner of the old viceroyalty of La Plata, also escaped the grasp of Buenos Aires after 1810. Three expeditions were sent into the high country, won initial victories, then were rolled back by Spanish counteroffensives. Logistical problems, the apathy of the Indian population, and the hostility of the creole aristocracy, which remained loyal to Spain until it became clear that the royalist cause was doomed, contributed to the patriot defeats. Not until 1825 did General Antonio José de Sucre, Bolívar's lieutenant, finally liberate Peru. Renamed Bolivia in honor of the liberator, it began its independent life the next year under a complicated, totally impractical constitution drafted by Bolívar himself.

The Struggle for Progress and National Unity

Even among the provinces that had joined at Tucumán to form the United Provinces of La Plata, discord grew and threatened the dissolution of the new state. The efforts of the wealthy port and province of Buenos Aires to impose its hegemony over the interior met with tenacious resistance. The end of the Spanish trade monopoly brought large gains to Buenos Aires and lesser gains to the littoral provinces of Santa Fe, Entre Ríos, and Corrientes; their exports of meat and hides increased, and the value of their lands rose. But the wine and textile industries of the interior, which had been protected by the colonial monopoly, suffered from the competition of cheaper and superior European wares imported through the port of Buenos Aires.

The interests of the interior provinces required a measure of autonomy or even independence in order to protect their primitive industries, but Buenos Aires preferred a single free-trade zone under a government dominated by the port city. This was one cause of the conflict between Argentine *federales* (federalists) and *unitarios* (unitarians). By 1820 the federalist solution had triumphed; the United Provinces had in effect dissolved into a number of independent republics, with the interior provinces ruled by caudillos, each representing the local ruling class and having a gaucho army behind him.

A new start toward unity came with the appointment in 1821 of Bernardino Rivadavia as chief minister under Martín Rodríguez, governor of the province of Buenos Aires. An ardent liberal, strongly influenced by the English philosopher Jeremy Bentham, Rivadavia launched an ambitious program of educational, social, and economic reform. He promoted primary educa-

tion, founded the University of Buenos Aires, abolished the ecclesiastical fuero and the tithe, and suppressed some monasteries. Rivadavia envisioned a balanced development of industry and agriculture, with a large role assigned to British investment and colonization. But the obstacles in the way of industrialization proved too great, and little came of efforts in this direction. The greatest progress was made in cattle raising, which expanded rapidly southward into former Indian territory. To control the large floating population of gauchos, Rivadavia enacted vagrancy laws requiring them to have passports for travel and to have written permission from the estanciero to leave his ranch.

In 1822, hoping to raise revenue and increase production, Rivadavia introduced the system of emphyteusis, a program of distribution of public lands through long-term leases at fixed rentals. Some writers have seen in this system an effort at agrarian reform, but there were no limits on the size of grants, and the measure actually contributed to the growth of latifundia. The lure of large profits in livestock raising induced many native and foreign merchants, politicians, and members of the military to join the rush for land. The net result was the creation not of a small-farmer class but of a new and more powerful *estanciero* class that was the enemy of Rivadavia's progressive ideals.

Rivadavia's planning went beyond the province of Buenos Aires; he had a vision of a unified Argentina under a strong central government that would promote the rounded economic development of the whole national territory. In 1825 a constituent congress met in Buenos Aires at Rivadavia's call to draft a constitution for the United Provinces of the Río de la Plata. Rivadavia, who was elected president of the new state, made a dramatic proposal to federalize the city and port of Buenos Aires. The former capital of the province would henceforth belong to the whole nation, with the revenues of its customhouse to be used to advance the general welfare.

Rivadavia's proposal reflected his nationalism and the need to mobilize national resources for a war with Brazil (1825–1828) over Uruguay. Congress approved Rivadavia's project, but the federalist caudillos of the interior, fearing that the rise of a strong national government would mean the end of their power, refused to ratify the constitution and even withdrew their delegates from the congress. In Buenos Aires a similar stand was taken by the powerful estancieros, who had no intention of surrendering the privileges of their province and regarded Rivadavia's program of social and economic reform as a costly folly.

Defeated on the issue of the constitution, Rivadavia suffered a further loss of prestige when his agent signed a peace treaty with Brazil recognizing Uruguay as a province of the Brazilian Empire. Rivadavia rejected the treaty, but popular anger at the agreement combined with opposition to his domestic program had sealed his political doom. In July 1827 he resigned the presidency and went into exile. The liberal program for achieving national unity had failed.

After an interval of factional struggles, the federalism espoused by the landed oligarchy of Buenos Aires triumphed in the person of Juan Manuel Rosas, who became governor of the province in 1829. He forged (1831) a federal pact under which Buenos Aires assumed representation for the other provinces in foreign affairs but left them free to run their own affairs in all other respects. Federalism, as defined by Rosas, meant that Buenos Aires retained the revenues of its customhouse for its exclusive use and controlled trade on the Río de la Plata system for the benefit of its merchants. A network of personal alliances between Rosas and provincial caudillos, backed by use of force against recalcitrant leaders, insured for him a large measure of control over the interior.

Rosas' long reign saw a reversal of Rivadavia's policies. For Rosas and the ruling class of estancieros, virtually the only economic concern was the export of hides and salted meat and the import of foreign goods. The dictator also showed some favor to wheat farming, which he protected by tariff laws, but he neglected artisans and machine industry. Rosas himself was a great estanciero and owner of a saladero (salting plant) for the curing of meat and hides. He vigorously pressed the conquest of Indian territory, bringing much new land under the control of the province

of Buenos Aires; this land was sold for low prices to estancieros, and Rivadavia's policy of retaining ownership of land by the state was abandoned. Although he professed to favor the gauchos, Rosas enforced the vagrancy laws against them even more rigorously, seeking to convert so-called idlers into ranch hands or soldiers for his army. Rosas also discarded Rivadavia's policy of promoting immigration and education. Rosas handed over what schools remained to the Jesuits, who were recalled from exile in 1836 (ultimately, Rosas found the order too independent and expelled it).

By degrees the press and all other potential dissidents were cowed or destroyed. To enforce the dictator's will there arose a secret organization known as the *Mazorca* (ear of corn—a reference to the close unity of its members). In collaboration with the police, this terrorist organization beat up or even murdered Rosas' opponents. The masthead of the official journal and all official papers carried the slogan "Death to the savage, filthy unitarians!" Even horses had to display the red ribbon that was the federalist symbol. Those opponents who did not knuckle under and escaped death fled by the thousands to Montevideo, Chile, Brazil, or other places of refuge.

Under Rosas, the merchants of the city and the estancieros of the province of Buenos Aires enjoyed a measure of prosperity, although an Anglo-French blockade of the estuary of La Plata from 1845 to 1848, caused by Rosas' mistreatment of English and French nationals and his efforts to subvert Uruguayan independence, resulted in severe losses to both groups. But this prosperity bore no proportion to the possibilities of economic growth; technical backwardness marked all aspects of livestock raising and agriculture, and port facilities were totally inadequate.

Meanwhile, the littoral provinces, which had experienced some advance of livestock raising and agriculture, became increasingly aware that Rosas' brand of federalism was harmful to their interests and that free navigation of the river system of La Plata was necessary to assure their prosperity. In 1852 the anti-Rosas forces formed a coalition that united the liberal émigrés with the caudillo Justo José de Urquiza of Entre Ríos, who was joined by the great majority of the provincial caudillos, and Brazil and Uruguay. At Monte Caseros, their combined forces defeated Rosas' army and sent him fleeing to an English exile.

Victory over Rosas did not end the dispute between Buenos Aires and the other provinces, between federalism and unitarianism. Only the slower process of economic change would forge the desired unity. A rift soon arose between the liberal exiles who assumed leadership in Buenos Aires and the caudillo Urquiza of Entre Ríos, who was backed by his victorious army. Urquiza, who still sported the red ribbon of federalism, proposed a loose union of the provinces, with all of them sharing the revenues of the Buenos Aires customhouse. But the leaders of Buenos Aires feared the loss of their economic and political predominance to Urquiza, whom they wrongly considered a caudillo of the Rosas type; in fact, Urquiza was a sincere convert to the gospel of modernity and progress.

Within the province of Buenos Aires, opinions were divided. Some favored entry into a new confederation but with very precise guarantees of the interests of their province; others argued for total separation from the other thirteen provinces. After Urquiza had unsuccessfully attempted to make Buenos Aires accept unification by armed force, the two sides agreed to a peaceful separation. As a result, delegates from Buenos Aires were absent from the constitutional convention that met at Santa Fe in Entre Ríos in 1852.

The constitution of 1853 reflected the influence of the ideas of the journalist Juan Bautista Alberdi on the delegates. His forcefully written pamphlet, *Bases and Points of Departure for the Political Organization of the Argentine Republic,* offered the United States as a model for Argentina. The new constitution strongly resembled that of the United States in certain respects. The former United Provinces became a federal republic, presided over by a president with significant power who served a six-year term without the possibility of immediate re-election. Legislative functions were vested in a bicameral legislature,

a senate and a house of representatives. The Catholic religion was proclaimed the official religion of the nation, but freedom of worship for non-Catholics was assured. The states were empowered to elect governors and legislatures and frame their own constitutions, but the federal government had the right of intervention—including armed intervention—to insure respect for the provisions of the constitution. General Urquiza was elected the first president of the Argentine Republic.

The liberal leaders of Buenos Aires, joined by the conservative estancieros who had been Rosas' firmest supporters, refused to accept the constitution of 1853, for they feared the creation of a state they did not control. As a result, two Argentinas arose: the Argentine Confederation, headed by Urquiza, and the province of Buenos Aires. For five years, the two states maintained their separate existence. In Paraná, capital of the confederation, Urquiza struggled to repress gaucho revolts, stimulate economic development, and foster education and immigration. Modest advances were made, but the tempo of growth lagged far behind that of the wealthy city and province of Buenos Aires, which prospered on the base of a steadily increasing trade with Europe in hides, tallow, salted beef, and wool.

Hoping to increase the confederation's scanty revenues, Urquiza began a tariff war with Buenos Aires, levying surcharges on goods landed at the Paraná River port of Rosario if duties had been paid on them at Buenos Aires. Buenos Aires responded with sanctions against ships sailing to Rosario and threatened to close commerce on the Paraná altogether. In 1859 war between the two Argentine states broke out. Defeated at the battle of Cepeda, Bartolomé Mitre, the commander of the Buenos Aires forces, accepted a compromise whereby Buenos Aires would join the confederation after a constitutional reform that protected its special interests. But the peace was short-lived; war broke out again in the presidency of Santiago Derqui, Urquiza's successor and personal rival. In the decisive battle of Pavón (1861), in which Mitre, now governor of the provinces of Buenos Aires, commanded the Buenos

Aires army, the forces of the confederation, led by Urquiza, suffered defeat.

The military and economic superiority of Buenos Aires, the need of the other provinces to use its port, and an awareness on all sides of the urgent need to achieve national unity dictated a compromise. At a congress representing all the provinces, held at Buenos Aires in 1862, it was agreed over the opposition of a die-hard group of Buenos Aires federalists that the city should be the provisional capital of both the Argentine Republic and the province and that the Buenos Aires customhouse should be nationalized, with the proviso that for a period of five years the revenues of the province would not fall below the 1859 level. In conformity with decisions of the congress, elections to choose the first president of a united Argentina were held the same year, and Bartolomé Mitre—distinguished historian, poet, soldier, and statesman—was elected president for a six-year term.

Mitre's term of office saw continued economic progress and consolidation of national unity. The customhouse was nationalized, as had been promised, and plans were made for the federalization of the capital. The construction of railways and telegraph lines that would forge closer links between Buenos Aires and the interior had begun, and European immigrants arrived in growing numbers. Some advances were made in the establishment of a public school system. But great problems remained. The shadow of the provincial caudillo continued to fall on the Argentine Republic; in the north, a revolt by one of Rosas' old allies had to be put down by armed force. The most difficult problem Mitre had to deal with, however, was the long, exhausting Paraguayan War (1865–1870).

The Paraguayan War

On the death of the dictator Francia in 1840, power in Paraguay was assumed by a triumvirate in which Carlos Antonio López soon emerged as the dominant figure. In essence, López continued Francia's dictatorial system but gave it a thin disguise of constitutional, representative government. Since he had inherited a stable, prosperous state, López could afford to rule in a less repressive fashion than his predecessor. More flexible than Francia, too, with a better understanding of the outside world, López made a successful effort to end Paraguay's diplomatic and commercial isolation. After the fall of Rosas, a stubborn enemy of Paraguayan independence, López obtained Argentine recognition of his country's independence, and the Paraná was at last opened to Paraguayan trade. López also established diplomatic relations with a series of countries, including England, France, and the United States. A special diplomatic mission to Europe, headed by his son, Francisco Solano López, also made important economic and cultural contacts, placing orders for ship construction, and inviting specialists to work in Paraguay.

The end of the policy of isolation was accompanied by a major expansion of the Paraguayan economy. Although agriculture (especially the production of such export crops as tobacco and yerba maté) continued to be the principal economic activity, López assigned great importance to the development of industry. One of his proudest achievements in this field was the construction of an iron foundry, the most modern enterprise of its type in Latin America. Transportation was improved with the building of roads and canals, the creation of a fleet of merchant ships, and the construction of a short railroad line.

Continuing Francia's policy, López enlarged the role of the state sector in the national economy. In 1848 he transferred to state ownership forest lands producing yerba maté and other commercial wood products and much arable land. The lucrative export trade in yerba maté and some other products became a government monopoly, and the number of state-owned ranches rose to sixty-four. López promoted education as well as economic growth; by the time of his death, Paraguay had 435 elementary schools with some 25,000 pupils, and a larger proportion of literate inhabitants than any other Latin American country.

At the same time, López took advantage of his position to concentrate ownership of land and various commercial enterprises in his own hands and those of his children, relatives, and associates; thus, there arose a bourgeoisie that profited by its close connection with the state apparatus, which enabled it to promote its own interests. The number of large private estates, however, was small; the private agricultural sector was dominated by small or medium-sized farms cultivated by owners or tenants, sometimes aided by a few hired laborers. By contrast with the situation in other Latin American countries, peonage and debt servitude were rare (slavery had been put in the way of extinction by a gradual manumission law in 1842). The relative absence of peonage and feudal survivals contributed to a rapid growth of Paraguayan capitalism and the well-being of its predominantly Indian and mestizo population. When López died in 1862, Paraguay was one of the most progressive and prosperous states in South America.

His son, Francisco Solano, whom López designated his heir apparent when his death approached, succeeded his father as dictator. The younger López inherited a tradition of border disputes with Brazil that erupted into open war when Brazil sent an army into Uruguay in 1864 to insure the victory of a pro-Brazilian faction in that country's civil strife. López could not be indifferent to this action, which threatened the delicate balance of power in the basin of La Plata. López also feared that Brazilian control over Uruguay would end unrestricted Paraguayan access to the port of Montevideo, which would make Paraguayan trade dependent entirely on the good will of Buenos Aires.

When the Brazilian government disregarded his protests, López sent an army to invade the Brazilian province of Mato Grosso, but this foray into virtually empty territory had no military significance, and he soon withdrew his troops. Hoping to strike a more effective blow at Brazil, López requested President Mitre's permission in January 1865 to cross Argentine territory (the state of Corrientes) en route to Uruguay. López regarded Mitre's refusal as an unfriendly act. In March 1865 the Paraguayan congress declared war on Argentina, and Paraguayan troops occu-

pied the town of Corrientes. On May 1, 1865, Brazil, Argentina, and the Brazilian-sponsored Flores regime in Uruguay concluded a Triple Alliance against Paraguay; a separate secret treaty between Brazil and Argentina provided for the partition of more than half of Paraguay's territory between them. Mitre was named commander in chief of the allied forces. Paraguay thus faced a coalition that included the two largest states in South America, with an immense superiority in manpower and other resources.

Yet the war dragged on for five years, for at its outset Paraguay possessed an army of some 70,000 well-armed and disciplined soldiers that outnumbered the combined forces of its foes. Expelled from the territory they had overrun in Argentina and Brazil, the Paraguayan troops stubbornly defended themselves against the allied forces that crossed the Paraná into Paraguay in mid-April 1866. In August 1868, Fort Humaitá was stormed by Brazilian troops under Marshal Luis Alves de Lima Caxias, at the cost of two thousand men. In January 1869, the allies occupied Asunción. Retreating northward, López attempted to organize a new defense against overwhelming numerical odds. The end came on March 1, 1870. With a few followers, López made his last stand at a point near the Brazilian border. López was slain by a Brazilian soldier. With his death, effective Paraguayan resistance ended.

For Paraguay the war's consequences were tragic. Perhaps as many as 20 percent of the prewar population of some 300,000 perished as a result of military action, famine, disease, and a devastating Brazilian occupation. The peace treaty assigned much Paraguayan territory to the victors and burdened Paraguay with extremely heavy reparations. Brazil, the occupying power, installed a puppet regime composed of former López generals, who began a radical reconstruction of the Paraguayan economy and state. The essence of the new policy was to liquidate the progressive changes made under the Francia and López regimes. Most of the state-owned lands were sold to land speculators and foreign businessmen at bargain prices, with no restriction on the size of holdings. Tenants who could not present the necessary documents were ejected even though they and their forebears had cultivated the land for decades. By the early 1890s, the state-owned lands were almost gone. Foreign penetration of the economy through loans, concessions, and land purchases soon deprived Paraguay of its economic as well as its political independence.

The Paraguayan War caused increased taxes and other hardships; for these reasons, it was unpopular in Argentina. The burdens of the war revived the dying spirit of provincial separatism and compelled Mitre to leave the front to direct the suppression of revolts in different provinces. By 1867 these domestic difficulties had virtually taken Argentina out of the war; when it ended, however, Argentina obtained its share of Paraguayan reparations and territorial concessions (Formosa, Chaco, and Misiones).

Progress and Development Under Sarmiento

At the close of his presidential term, Mitre returned to civilian life. He was succeeded by Domingo Faustino Sarmiento (1868–1874), a gifted essayist, sociologist, and statesman, former Argentine minister to the United States, and an enthusiast for its institutions. Like Mitre, Sarmiento worked for Argentine unity and economic and social progress.

After the Paraguayan War, a flood of technological change began to sweep over Argentina. Railways penetrated the interior, extending the stock-raising and farming area. The gradual introduction of barbed-wire fencing and alfalfa ranges made possible a dramatic improvement in the quality of livestock. In 1876 the arrival of an experimental shipload of chilled carcasses from France prepared the way for the triumph of frozen over salted meat, which led to a vast expansion of European demand for Argentine beef. Labor was needed to exploit the rapidly expanding pasturelands and farmlands; during Sarmiento's administration alone, some three hundred thousand immigrants poured into the country. But Sarmiento taught that it was not enough to build

railroads and expand acreage; it was necessary to change people's minds. Believing in the need for an educated citizenry in a democratic republic, he labored to expand and improve the public school system; to this end he introduced to Argentina teacher-training institutions of the kind his friend Horace Mann had founded in the United States. But there was a darker side to Sarmiento's policies. Regarding Indians and gauchos as obstacles to the advance of "civilization," he waged a war of extermination against the pampa Indians and used vagrancy laws, press gangs, and other repressive measures to break the gaucho's spirit and destroy his free way of life.

When Sarmiento left office, Argentina presented the appearance of a rapidly developing, prosperous state. But there were clouds in the generally bright Argentine sky. The growth of exports and the rise in land values did not benefit the forlorn gauchos, aliens in a land over which they had once freely roamed, or the majority of European immigrants. Little was done to provide these newcomers with homesteads. Immigrants who wished to farm usually found the price of land out of reach; as a result, many preferred to remain in Buenos Aires or other cities of the littoral, where they began to form an urban middle class largely devoted to trade. Meanwhile, foreign economic influence grew as a result of increasing dependence on foreign—chiefly British—capital to finance the construction of railways, telegraph lines, gasworks, and other needed facilities. The growing concentration of landownership reinforced the colonial land tenure pattern; the tightening British control of markets and the country's economic infrastructure reinforced the colonial pattern of dependence on a foreign metropolis, with London replacing Seville as commercial center. But Mitre, Sarmiento, and other builders of the new Argentina were dazzled by their success in nation-building and by a climate of prosperity they believed permanent. These men did not suspect the extent of the problems that were in the making nor did they anticipate what problems future generations of Argentines would have to attempt to solve.

Chile

The victories of José de San Martín's Army of the Andes over royalist forces at Chacabuco and Maipú in 1817 and 1818 gave Chile its definitive independence. From 1818 until 1823 Bernardo O'Higgins, a hero of the struggle for Chilean liberation and a true son of the Enlightenment, ruled the country with the title of supreme director. O'Higgins energetically pushed a program of reform designed to weaken the landed aristocracy and the church and promote a rapid development of the Chilean economy along capitalist lines. His abolition of titles of nobility and entails angered the great landowners of the fertile Central Valley between the Andes and the Pacific; his expulsion of the royalist bishop of Santiago and his restrictions on the number of religious processions and the veneration of images infuriated the church. Dissident liberals who resented his sometimes heavy-handed rule joined the opposition to O'Higgins. In 1823 O'Higgins resigned and went into exile in Lima. There followed seven turbulent years, with presidents and constitutions rising and falling.

Portales and Economic Growth

In Chile, as in other Latin American countries, the political and armed struggle gradually assumed the form of a conflict between conservatives, who usually were also centralists, and liberals, who were generally federalists. The conservative-centralists were the party of the great landowners of the Central Valley and the wealthy merchants of Santiago; the liberal-federalists spoke for the landowners, merchants, and artisans of the northern and southern provinces, who were resentful of political and economic domination by the wealthy central area. The victory of the conservative General Joaquín Prieto over the liberal General Ramón Freire in the decisive battle of Lircay (1830) brought to power a government headed by Prieto as president but dominated by one of his cabinet ministers, Diego Portales.

From 1830 until his death in 1837, Portales, who never held an elective office, placed the enduring stamp of his ideas on Chilean politics and society. A businessman of aristocratic origins, owner of a successful import house, he faithfully served the interests of an oligarchy of great landlords and merchants that dominated the Chilean scene for decades. Although Portales expressed atheist views in private, he supported the authority of the church as an instrument for keeping the lower classes in order. He understood the importance of trade, industry, and mining and promoted their interests. Assisted by his able finance minister, Manuel Rengifo, Portales continued the work of O'Higgins, removing remaining obstacles to internal trade. He introduced income and property taxes to increase the state's revenues and trimmed government spending by dismissing unnecessary employees. Agriculture was protected by high tariffs on agricultural imports. Port facilities were improved, measures were taken to strengthen the Chilean merchant marine, and in 1835 a steamship line began to connect the Chilean ports. Under the fostering care of the conservative regime and in response to a growing European demand for Chilean silver, copper, and hides, the national economy made steady progress in the 1830s.

Measures designed to stimulate economic growth were accompanied by others that fortified the social and political power of the oligarchy. In order to tighten the bond between the conservative government and the church, Portales restored the privileges the church had lost under liberal rule and normalized the troubled relations between Chile and the papacy.

In 1833 a conservative-dominated assembly adopted a constitution that further consolidated the power of the oligarchy. Elections were made indirect, with the suffrage limited to men of twenty-five years or over who could satisfy literacy and property qualifications. Still higher property qualifications were required of members of the lower and upper houses. The constitution restored entails, insuring perpetuation of the latifundio. Catholicism was declared the state religion, and the church was given control over marriage. The president enjoyed an absolute veto over congressional legislation, appointed all high officials, and could proclaim a state of siege.

The process of amending the constitution was made so difficult as to be virtually impossible. Since the president controlled the electoral machinery, the outcome of elections was a foregone conclusion. In 1836 Prieto was re-elected president for a second five-year term.

Realizing the futility of legal opposition to the conservative dictatorship, many liberals boycotted the election and later took to arms. This revolt, led by General Freire, was quickly crushed, and Freire was exiled to Australia. The Freire revolt had been organized in Peru, and this fact added to the tensions created by a tariff war between Peru and Chile. Relations between the two countries deteriorated further in 1836 as a result of the formation of a Peruvian-Bolivian confederation under the auspices of the ambitious Bolivian president, Andrés Santa Cruz. Portales saw in this union a threat to Chile's northern borders and obtained a congressional declaration of war on Peru in November 1836. The war lasted three years; it ended with a Chilean victory and dissolution of the confederation. Meanwhile, however, Portales had caused much resentment at home by his highhanded use of the extraordinary powers vested in him in wartime to arrest and jail all critics of the war. In June 1837 mutinous troops seized Portales and killed him before loyal troops could gain his release.

Recovery Under Bulnes

In 1841, General Manuel Bulnes succeeded Prieto to the presidency; he was re-elected to a second five-year term in 1846. Victorious at home and abroad, the conservative leadership decided it could relax the strict discipline of the Portales period. Chile's economic life quickly recovered from the strains of the war of 1836–1839 and began a renewed advance. Commerce, mining, and agriculture prospered as never before. The Crimean War and the gold rushes to California and Australia of the 1850s created large new markets for Chilean wheat, stimulating a considerable expansion of the cultivated area. In 1840 a North American, William Wheelright, established a steamship line to operate on the Chilean coasts, using coal from newly developed hard

coal mines. Wheelright also founded a company that in 1852 completed Chile's first railroad line, providing an outlet to the sea for the production of the mining district of Copiapó. The major Santiago-Valparaíso line, begun in 1852, was not completed until 1863. Foreign—especially British—capital began to penetrate the Chilean economy; it dominated foreign trade and had a large interest in mining and railroads, but national capitalists constituted an important, vigorous group and displayed much initiative in the formation of joint stock companies and banks.

The great landowners were the principal beneficiaries of this economic upsurge; their lands appreciated in value without any effort on their part. Some great landowners invested their money in railroads, mining, and trade. But the essential conservatism of the landed aristocracy and the urge to preserve a semifeudal control over its peons discouraged the transformation of the great landowners into capitalist farmers. A pattern of small landholdings arose in southern Chile, to which German as well as Chilean colonists came in increasing numbers in the 1840s and 1850s. The rich Central Valley, still dominated by the latifundio, reflected inefficient techniques and reliance on the labor of *inquilinos*—tenants who also had to work the master's fields. Thus, alongside an emerging capitalist sector based on mining, trade, banking, intensive agriculture, and some industry, there existed a semifeudal sector based on the latifundio, peonage, and an aristocracy that hindered the development of Chilean capitalism.

Yet Chile at this period presented a more progressive aspect than most other Latin American states. President Bulnes continued the law-and-order system initiated by Portales but tempered its authoritarian rigor. His minister of justice and instruction, Manuel Montt, established a system of public instruction that included the humanities and technical subjects. In 1842 the University of Chile was founded. Its first rector was the distinguished Venezuelan poet, scholar, and educator Andrés Bello, who helped to train a whole generation of Chilean intellectuals.

One of Bello's disciples was José Victorino Lastarria, historian, sociologist, and a deputy of the

Liberal party, which he helped to revive. Dissatisfied with the modest concessions to modernity of the new conservatives, liberals like Lastarria wanted to accelerate the rate of change. They demanded radical revision of the constitution of 1833 and an end to oligarchical rule.

To the left of Lastarria stood the firebrand Francisco Bilbao, author of a scorching attack on the church and the Hispanic heritage, "The Nature of Chilean Society" (1844). Later, he spent several years in France and was profoundly influenced by utopian socialist and radical republican thought. He returned to Chile in 1850 to found, with Santiago Arcos, the Society of Equality, uniting radical intellectuals and artisans, which advocated these advanced ideas. The society carried on an intensive antigovernmental campaign and within a few months had a membership of four thousand.

Montt's Moderate Reforms

The Society of Equality was founded on the eve of the election of 1850, for which President Bulnes had designated Manuel Montt his heir. Despite Montt's progressive educational policies and patronship of the arts and letters, liberals identified him with the repressive system of Portales and the constitution of 1833. Liberals like Lastarria and radical democrats like Bilbao proclaimed the impending election a fraud and demanded constitutional reforms. The government responded by proclaiming a state of siege and suppressing the Society of Equality. Regarding these acts as a prelude to an attempt to liquidate the opposition, groups of liberals in Santiago and La Serena rose in revolts that were quickly crushed. Lastarria was exiled; Bilbao and Arcos fled to Argentina. The conservatives easily elected their candidate; like his predecessor, he served two terms (1851–1861). In the wake of the election, however, the liberals again rose in a large-scale revolt that Montt crushed with a heavy loss of life. Montt had triumphed but immediately took steps to resolve the crisis by granting amnesty to the insurgents; he went on to make concessions to the spirit of the times

with two important reforms: the abolition of entails and the tithe.

The abolition of entails, which was designed to encourage the breakup of landed estates among the children of the great landowners, affected a dwindling number of great aristocratic clans. Its effects were less drastic than the anguished cries of the affected parties suggested, for the divided estates were almost invariably acquired by other latifundists, and the condition of the inquilinos who worked the land remained the same. The elimination of the tithe, and Montt's refusal to allow the return of the Jesuits, greatly angered the reactionary clergy. Responding to their attacks, Montt promulgated a new civil code in 1857 that placed education under state control, gave the state jurisdiction over the clergy, and granted non-Catholics the right of civil marriage.

The abolition of entails and the tithe represented a compromise between liberals and conservatives, between the new bourgeoisie and the great landowners. In the process, the bourgeoisie gained little, and the landowners lost almost nothing; the chief loser was the church. Montt's reforms alienated the most reactionary elements of the Conservative party; in Congress these elements combined into a conservative-clerical bloc that formed the right-wing opposition to the government. On the other hand, his reforms gained Montt the support of moderate liberals while he retained the loyalty of the majority of moderate conservatives. In the 1850s this coalition of moderate liberals and conservatives took the name of the National party. Its motto was the typically positivist slogan "Freedom in Order."

The radical liberals, however, continued to demand the repeal of the constitution of 1833. A leading spokesman for the left wing of the Liberal party was the brilliant historian Benjamín Vicuña Mackenna, who founded a newspaper in 1858 in which he hammered away at the need for drastic political and social change. The government shut the newspaper down and Vicuña Mackenna was exiled.

In the last years of his second term, President Montt faced severe economic and political problems. The 1857 depression caused a sharp fall in the price of copper and reduced Australian and Californian demand for Chilean wheat. The economic decline fed the fires of political discontent. Montt had designated his energetic and influential cabinet minister, Antonio Varas, to succeed him in 1861. But the radical liberals disliked Varas for his stern suppression of dissidents, while clerical conservatives associated him with Montt's attacks on the church's privileges. Agitation against Varas's candidacy erupted in January 1859 into another large-scale revolt. The rebels included radical intellectuals, northern mining capitalists and their workers, artisans, and small farmers, all groups with grievances against the dominant Central Valley alliance of great merchants and landowners. Their demands included a democratic republic, state support for mining and industry, the splitting up of the great estates, and abolition of the semifeudal *inquilinaje* system of peonage as incompatible with demoncratic principles. Before the revolt was crushed, it had taken 5,000 lives in a population of less than a million and a half. Some of the bourgeois leaders of the revolt were imprisoned, others deported, and others fled into exile, but a large number of miners, artisans, and peasants were executed. Maurice Zeitlin's recent study of the civil war of 1850–1851 regards it as a crucial turning point in Chilean history: "Defeat of the revolutionary bourgeoisie amounted to virtual suppression of an alternative and independent path of capitalist development for Chile—a realm of objective historical possibilities unfulfilled because of the failure of the bourgeois revolution."

Montt had managed to quell the revolt, but his political position had been seriously weakened. Hoping to avoid new storms, Montt allowed Varas to withdraw his candidacy and supported a new candidate, José Joaquín Pérez, who was acceptable to moderate liberals and many conservatives. He easily won election as the candidate of the National party but formed a coalition government composed of Nationals, conservatives, and liberals. He served the customary two terms (1861–1871).

By 1861 the depression had lifted, and another boom began, creating new fortunes and bringing large shifts of regional influence. A growing stream of settlers, including many Germans, flowed into southern Chile, founding cities and transforming woodlands into farms.

But Chile's true center of economic gravity became the desert north, rich in copper, nitrates, and guano; the last two, in particular, were objects of Europe's insatiable demand for fertilizers. The major nitrate deposits, however, lay in the Bolivian province of Antofagasta and the Peruvian province of Tarapacá. Chilean capital, supplemented by English and German capital, began to pour into these regions and soon dominated the Peruvian and Bolivian nitrate industries. In the north there arose an aggressive mining capitalist class that demanded a place in the sun for itself and its region. A rich mine owner, Pedro León Gallo, abandoned the liberals to form a new party, called Radical, that fought more militantly than the liberals for constitutional changes, religious toleration, and an end to repressive policies. Under Pérez, liberals and Radicals combined to secure reforms that included toleration for non-Catholics, a curtailment of presidential powers, and a ban on immediate presidential reelection.

Liberal Control

The transition of Chile's political life to liberal control, begun under Montt, was completed in 1871 with the election of the first liberal president, Federico Errázuriz Zañartú. Between 1873 and 1875 a coalition of liberals and Radicals pushed through Congress a series of constitutional reforms: reduction of senatorial terms from nine to six years; direct election of senators; and freedom of speech, press, and assembly. These victories for enlightenment also represented a victory of new capitalist groups over the old merchant-landowner oligarchy that traced its beginnings back to colonial times. By 1880 of the fifty-nine Chilean personal fortunes of over 1 million pesos, only twenty-four were of colonial origin and only twenty had made their fortunes in agriculture; the rest belonged to coal, nitrate, copper, and silver interests or to merchants

210

whose wealth had been formed only in the nineteenth century. Arnold Bauer has observed that the more interesting point is "not that only twenty made their fortune in agriculture, but that the remaining thirty-nine—designated as miners, bankers, and capitalists—subsequently invested their earnings in rural estates. This would be comparable to Andrew Carnegie sinking his steel income into Scarlett O'Hara's plantation." Bauer's comment points to the "powerful social model" that the Chilean agrarian oligarchy continued to exert. For the rest, the victories of the new bourgeoisie brought no relief to the Chilean masses, the migrant laborers and tenant farmers on the haciendas, and the young working class in Chile's mines and factories.

Brazil

Dom Pedro, Emperor

Brazil took its first major step toward independence in 1808, when the Portuguese crown and court, fleeing before a French invasion of Portugal, arrived in Rio de Janeiro to make it the new capital of the Portuguese Empire. Formal national independence came in 1822, when Dom Pedro, who ruled Brazil as regent for his father, João VI, rejected a demand that he return to Portugal and issued the famous Cry of Ipiranga: "Independence or Death!" Dom Pedro acted with the advice and support of the Brazilian aristocracy, determined to preserve the autonomy Brazil had enjoyed since 1808. It was equally determined to make a transition to independence without the violence that marked the Spanish-American movement of liberation. The Brazilian aristocracy had its wish; Brazil made a transition to independence with comparatively little disruption and bloodshed. But separation from Portugal with a minimum of internal dislocation meant that independent Brazil retained not only monarchy and slavery but the large landed estate and monoculture; a wasteful, inefficient agricultural system; a highly stratified society; and a free population that was 90 percent illiterate and prejudiced against manual labor.

Dom Pedro had promised to give his subjects a constitution, but the constituent assembly that he summoned in 1823 drafted a document that seemed to the emperor to place excessive limits on his power. He responded by dissolving the assembly and assigning to a hand-picked commission the making of a new constitution, which he approved and promulgated by imperial proclamation. This constitution, under which Brazil was governed until the fall of the monarchy in 1889, concentrated great power in the hands of the monarch. In addition to a Council of State, it provided for a two-chamber parliament, a lifetime Senate whose members were chosen by the emperor, and a Chamber of Deputies elected by voters who met property and income requirements. The emperor had the right to appoint and dismiss ministers and summon or dissolve parliament at will. He also appointed the provincial governors or presidents.

Resentment over Dom Pedro's highhanded dissolution of the constituent assembly and the highly centralist character of the constitution of 1824 was particularly strong in Pernambuco, a center of republican and federalist ferment. Here in 1824 a group of rebels, led by the merchant Manoel de Carvalho, proclaimed the creation of a Confederation of the Equator that would unite the six northern provinces under a republican government. A few leaders voiced antislavery sentiments, but nothing was done to abolish slavery, which deprived the movement of the potential support of a large slave population. Within a year, imperial troops had smashed the revolt and executed fifteen of its leaders.

Dom Pedro had won a victory but resentment of his autocratic tendencies continued to smolder, and his popularity steadily waned. The emperor's foreign policies contributed to this growing discontent. In 1826, in return for recognition of Brazilian independence and a trade agreement, Dom Pedro signed a treaty with Great Britain that obligated Brazil to end the slave traffic by 1830. Despite this ban and the efforts of British warships to intercept and seize the slave ships, the trade continued with the full knowledge and approval of the Brazilian government. But British policing practices caused the price of slaves to rise sharply. The prospering coffee growers of Rio de Janeiro, São Paulo, and Minas Gerais could afford to pay high prices for slaves, but the cotton and sugar growers of the depressed north could not compete with them for workers and blamed Dom Pedro for their difficulties.

Another source of discontent was the costly and fruitless war with Argentina (1825–1828) over the Banda Oriental (Uruguay), which the Brazilians called the Cisplatine Province. The war was supported by the ranchers of Rio Grande do Sul, who coveted the rich pasturelands of Uruguay, but it aroused much opposition elsewhere. When it ended in a compromise that guaranteed the independence of Uruguay, its outcome was regarded as a humiliating defeat for Brazil, and Dom Pedro suffered a further loss of prestige. Two other causes of the emperor's growing unpopularity were the favoritism he showed to the corrupt Portuguese courtiers of his entourage and his continued involvement in Portuguese politics, especially his effort in upholding the claims of his daughter Maria to the Portuguese throne.

News of the July Revolution of 1830 in France, a revolution that toppled an unpopular, autocratic king, produced rejoicing and violent demonstrations in Brazilian cities. *Exaltados* (radical liberals) placed themselves at the head of the movement of revolt and called for the abolition of the monarchy and the establishment of a federal republic. In the face of the growing crisis, Dom Pedro vacillated; first he made concessions to anti-Portuguese sentiment by appointing a new cabinet of Brazilian-born ministers, then he dissolved it and named a new cabinet that included the most hated figures in his Brazilian entourage. In April 1831 mass demonstrations in the capital were joined by the local garrison. A delegation of city magistrates demanded that he reinstate the former ministry; Dom Pedro refused. The next day, April 7, he abdicated in favor of his five-year-old son Pedro, and two weeks later he sailed for Portugal, never to return. These developments, eliminating the dominant influence of Portuguese merchants and Portuguese-born courtiers under Emperor Pedro I,

may be regarded as completing the transition to full Brazilian independence.

Regency, Revolt, and a Boy Emperor

The revolution had been the work of radical liberals who viewed Dom Pedro's downfall as the first step toward the establishment of a federal republic, but its fruits were garnered by more moderate men. In effect, the radicals had played the game of the monarchist liberals who guided the movement of secession from Portugal and later lost influence at court as a result of Dom Pedro's shift to the right. Dom Pedro's departure was a victory for these moderates, who hastened to restore their ascendancy over the central government and prevent the revolution from getting out of hand.

As a first step, parliament appointed a three-man regency composed of moderate liberals to govern for the child emperor until he reached the age of eighteen. Another measure created a national guard, recruited from the propertied classes, to repress urban mobs and slave revolts. Simultaneously, the new government began work on a project of constitutional reform designed to appease the strong federalist sentiment. After a three-year debate, parliament approved the Additional Act of 1834, which gave the provinces elective legislative assemblies with broad powers, including control over local budgets and taxes. This provision assured the great landowners of a large measure of control over their regions. The Council of State, identified with Dom Pedro's reactionary rule, was abolished. But centralism was not abandoned, for the national government continued to appoint provincial governors with a partial veto over the acts of the provincial assemblies. Centralism was even strengthened by the replacement of the three-man regency with a single regent. To this post parliament named the moderate liberal Diogo Antônio Feijó.

Almost immediately, Feijó had to struggle against a rash of revolts, most numerous in the northern provinces, whose economy suffered from a loss of markets for their staple crops, sugar and cotton. None occurred in the central southern zone (the provinces of Rio de Janeiro, São Paulo, and Minas Gerais), whose coffee economy prospered and whose planter aristocracy had secure control of the central government. These revolts had a variety of local causes. Some were elemental, popular revolts; such was the so-called *cabanagem* (from the word *cabana,* "cabin") of Pará, which originated in the grievances of small tradesmen, farmers, and lower-class elements against the rich Portuguese merchants who monopolized local trade. Others, like the republican and separatist revolt in Bahia (1837–1838), reflected the frustrations of the planter aristocracy of this once-prosperous area over its loss of economic and political power.

Most serious of all was the revolt that broke out in 1835 in the province of Rio Grande do Sul. Although it was dubbed the *Revolução Farroup-ilha* (Revolution of the Ragamuffins) in contemptuous reference to its supposed lower-class origins, the movement was led by cattle barons who maintained a more or less patriarchal sway over the gauchos who formed the rank-and-file of the rebel armies. An intense regionalism, resentment over taxes and unpopular governors imposed by the central government, and the strength of republican sentiment were major factors in producing the revolt of Rio Grande. The presence of considerable numbers of Italian exiles such as Giuseppe Garibaldi, ardent republicans and antislavery men, gave a special radical tinge to the revolt in Rio Grande. In September 1835 the rebels captured the provincial capital of Pôrto Alegre; one year later they proclaimed Rio Grande an independent republic. For almost a decade, two states—one a republic, the other an empire—existed on Brazilian territory.

The secession of Rio Grande and the inability of imperial troops to quell the revolt further weakened the position of Feijó, whose authoritarian temper and disregard for parliamentary majorities in the choice of ministers had caused much discontent. By now the political struggle had begun to assume an organized form, with the emergence of a Liberal party composed chiefly of moderate liberals who favored concessions to federalism, and a Conservative party, which preferred to strengthen the central government.

However, on such essential issues as the monarchy, slavery, and the maintenance of the status quo in general, liberals and conservatives saw eye to eye.

In September 1837 Feijó resigned and was succeeded as regent by the conservative Pedro de Araújo Lima. Like his predecessor, Araújo Lima concentrated his efforts on putting down the Rio Grande rebellion and other regional revolts in the north. The Rio Grande experiment in republican government and its offer of freedom to all slaves who joined the republic's armed forces posed an especially serious threat to monarchy and slavery. Among both liberals and conservatives, the idea gained favor of calling the young Pedro to rule before his legal majority in order to strengthen the central government in its war against subversive and separatist movements. By the beginning of 1840, the project had won virtual acceptance, liberals and conservatives differing only with respect to timing and other details. On July 22, in what was in effect a parliamentary coup d'état the two chambers of parliament proclaimed the fourteen-year-old Dom Pedro emperor; he was formally crowned a year later, in July 1841.

In March 1841, after forcing a short-lived liberal ministry to resign, the emperor called the conservatives to power. The new government proceeded to dismantle the federalist reforms in the Additional Act of 1834. The powers of the provincial assemblies were sharply curtailed; locally elected judges were stripped of their judicial and police powers, which were vested in a new national police; and the Council of State was restored. Having consolidated their position, the conservatives decided to change the balance of forces in the new Chamber of Deputies, where the liberals had won a majority and, charging corruption in the elections, persuaded the emperor to dissolve it.

The liberals of São Paulo and Minas Gerais responded with a revolt (1842) that had little popular support, for it was dictated solely by the desire for the spoils of office. Troops led by the conservative leader Baron Caxias swiftly crushed the uprising. But the emperor treated the vanquished rebels leniently; indeed, a short time later he called on the liberals to form a new ministry. Once returned to power, the liberals made no effort to repeal the conservative revisions of the constitution and made use of the broad police powers vested in the central government for their own ends.

With the unity of the ruling class restored, the government undertook to settle scores with the rebels of Rio Grande. As a result of internal squabbles and the cessation of aid from friendly Uruguay when that country was invaded by Rosas' troops in February 1843, the situation of the republic became extremely difficult. Meanwhile, Baron Caxias advanced with large forces against the rebels and wrested town after town from their troops. Facing defeat, the republican leaders accepted an offer from Rio de Janeiro to negotiate a peace, which was signed in February 1845. The peace treaty extended amnesty to all rebels but annulled all laws of the republican regime. The cattle barons won certain concessions, including the right to nominate their candidate for the post of provincial governor and retention of their military titles.

The last large-scale revolt in the series that shook Brazil in the 1830s and 1840s was the uprising of 1848 in Pernambuco. Centered in the city of Recife, its causes included hostility toward the Portuguese merchants who monopolized local trade, the appointment of an unpopular governor by the conservative government, and hatred for the greatest landowners of the region, the powerful Cavalcanti family. The rebel program called for the removal from Recife of all Portuguese merchants, expansion of provincial autonomy, work for the unemployed, and division of the Cavalcanti lands. Even this radical program, however, contained no reference to the abolition of slavery. The movement collapsed after the capture of Recife by imperial troops in 1849. Many captured leaders were condemned to prison for life, but all were amnestied in 1852.

Underlying these rebellions and armed conflicts of the 1830s and 1840s was economic stagnation, the weakness of foreign markets for Brazil's traditional exports. The expansion in the center-south of coffee, already important in the 1830s but flourishing after 1850, strengthened the hand of the central government with increased revenues and laid the basis for a new era of cooperation between regional elites and the national government. The new coffee prosperity, confirming the apparent viability and rationality of the neocolonial emphasis on export agriculture, also discouraged any thought of taking the more durable but difficult path of Brazilian autonomous development.

The Game of Politics and the Crisis of Slavery

By 1850, Brazil was at peace. The emperor presided over a pseudoparliamentary regime, exercising his power in the interests of a tiny ruling class. He paid his respects to parliamentary forms by alternately appointing conservative and liberal prime ministers at will; if the new ministry did not command a majority in parliament, one was obtained by holding rigged elections. Since the ruling class was united on essential issues, the only thing at stake in party struggles was patronage, the spoils of office. An admirer of Dom Pedro, Joaquim Nabuco, described the operation of the system in his book *O abolicionismo:*

The president of the council lives at the mercy of the crown, from which he derives his power; even the appearance of power is his only when he is regarded as the emperor's lieutenant and is believed to have in his pocket the decree of dissolution—that is, the right to elect a chamber made up of his own henchmen. Below him are the ministers, who live by the favor of the president of the council; farther down still, on the third plane, are found the deputies, at the mercy of the ministers. The representative system, then, is a graft of parliamentary forms on a patriarchal government, and senators and deputies only take their roles seriously in this parody of democracy because of the personal advantage they derive therefrom. Suppress the subsidies, force them to stop using their positions for personal and family ends, and no one who had anything else to do would waste his time in such shadow boxing.

As noted above, the surface stability of Brazilian political life in the decades after 1850 rested

214 on the prosperity created by a growing demand and good prices for Brazilian coffee. As the sugar-growing northeast and its plantation society continued to decline because of exhausted soil, archaic techniques, and competition from foreign sugars, the coffee-growing zone of Rio de Janeiro, São Paulo, and Minas Gerais gained new importance.

The crisis of the northeast grew more acute as a result of English pressure on Brazil to enforce the Anglo-Brazilian treaty banning the importation of slaves into Brazil after November 7, 1831. Before 1850 this treaty was never effectively enforced; more than fifty thousand slaves a year were brought to Brazil during the 1840s. In 1849 and 1850, however, the British government instructed its warships to enter Brazilian territorial waters if necessary to seize and destroy Brazilian slave ships. Under British pressure, the Brazilian parliament passed the Queiroz anti-slave-trade law, which was effectively enforced. By the middle 1850s, the importation of slaves had virtually ended.

The ending of the slave trade had major consequences. Because of the high mortality among slaves due to poor food, harsh working conditions, and other negative factors, the slave population could not be maintained by natural re-

Anonymous, *Allegory of the Departure of Dom Pedro II for Europe after the Declaration of the Republic,* 1890, oil on canvas. As will be discussed further in Chapter 10, this romantic painting suggests the respect and affection many Brazilians, including supporters of the republic, felt for the ousted emperor.

production, and the eventual doom of the slave system was assured. The passing of the slave trade created a serious labor shortage, with a large flow of slaves from the north to the south because of the coffee planters' greater capacity to compete for slave labor. This movement aggravated the imbalance between the prosperous south central zone and the declining north. The end of the slave trade had another important result: large sums formerly expended for the purchase of slaves were now channeled to other uses, partly into coffee agriculture, partly into the building of an infrastructure for the emerging national economy. The first telegraph lines in Brazil were established in 1852; the first railroad line was begun in 1854. In these years, a pioneer of Brazilian capitalism, Irineu Evangelista de Sousa, later the Baron Mauá, laid the foundations of a veritable industrial and banking empire.

By the 1860s, a growing number of Brazilians had become convinced that slavery brought serious discredit to Brazil and must be ended. The abolition of slavery in the United States as a result of the Civil War, which left Brazil and the Spanish colonies of Cuba and Puerto Rico the only slaveholding areas in the Western Hemisphere, sharpened sensitivity to the problem. The Paraguayan War also promoted the cause of emancipation. In an effort to fill the gaps caused by heavy losses at the front, a decree was issued granting freedom to government-owned slaves who agreed to join the army, and some private slave owners followed the official example. Criticism of slavery was increasingly joined with criticism of the emperor, censured for his cautious posture on slavery. Alongside the antislavery movement there arose a nascent republican movement. In 1869 the left wing of the Liberal party, organized in a Reform Club, issued a manifesto demanding restrictions on the powers of the emperor and the grant of freedom to the newborn children of slaves. The crisis of slavery was fast becoming a crisis of the Brazilian Empire.

Chapter 10

The Triumph of Neocolonialism

Beginning about 1870, the quickening tempo of the Industrial Revolution in Europe stimulated a more rapid pace of change in the Latin American economy and politics. Responding to a mounting demand for raw materials and foodstuffs, Latin American producers increased their output of those commodities. The growing trade with Europe helped stabilize political conditions in Latin America, for the new economic system demanded peace and continuity in government.

Encouraged by the increased stability, European capital flowed into Latin America, creating railroads, docks, processing plants, and other facilities needed to expand and modernize production and trade. Latin America became integrated into an international economic system in which it exchanged raw materials and foodstuffs for the factory-made goods of Europe and North America. Gradual adoption of free-trade policies by many Latin American countries, which marked the abandonment of efforts to create a native factory capitalism, hastened the area's integration into this international division of labor.

The New Colonialism

The new economic system fastened a new dependency on Latin America, with Great Britain and later the United States replacing Spain and Portugal in the dominant role; it may, therefore, be called "neocolonial." Despite its built-in flaws and local breakdowns, the neocolonial order displayed a certain stability until 1914. By disrupting the markets for Latin America's exports and making it difficult to import the manufactured goods that Latin America required, World War I marked the beginning of a general crisis the area has not yet overcome.

Although the period from 1870 to 1914 saw a rapid overall growth of the Latin American economy, the pace and degree of progress were uneven, with some countries (like Bolivia and Paraguay) joining the advance much later than others. A marked feature of the neocolonial order was its one-sidedness (monoculture). One or a few primary products became the basis of each country's prosperity, making it highly vulnerable to fluctuations in the world demand and price of these products. Thus, Argentina and Uruguay depended on wheat and meat; Brazil on coffee, sugar, and briefly on rubber; Chile on copper and nitrates; Honduras on bananas; Cuba on sugar.

In each country, the modern export sector became an enclave largely isolated from the rest of the economy; this enclave actually accentuated the backwardness of other sectors by draining off their labor and capital. The export-oriented nature of the modern sector was reflected in the pattern of the national railway systems, which as a rule were not designed to integrate each country's regions but to satisfy the traffic needs of the export industries. In addition, the modern export sector often rested on extremely precarious foundations. Rapid, feverish growth, punctuated by slumps that sometimes ended in a total collapse, formed part of the neocolonial pattern; such meteoric rise and fall is the story of Peruvian guano, Chilean nitrates, and Brazilian rubber.

The triumph of neocolonialism in Latin America in the late nineteenth century was not inevitable or predetermined by Europe's economic "head start" or the area's past history of dependency. The leap from a feudal or semifeudal economy and society to an autonomous capitalist system, although difficult, is not impossible, as witness the case of Japan. Following independence, the new states had to choose between the alternatives of autonomy or dependency, or in the words of historian Florencia Mallon, "between focusing on internal production and capital formation, on the one hand, and relying increasingly on export production, foreign markets, and ultimately foreign capital, on the other." Given Latin America's history, however, the formation of the dynamic entrepreneurial class and the large internal market required by an autonomous capitalism could not be achieved without such sweeping reforms as the breakup of great estates, the abolition of peonage and other coercive labor systems, and the adoption of a consistent policy of supporting native industry, reforms that most sections of the elite found too costly and threatening. Most Latin American elites, therefore, chose the easier road of continued dependency, with first Great Britain and later the United States replacing Spain as the metropolis.

Latin America in the nineteenth century, however, produced some serious efforts to break with the pattern of dependence. We have already described two such efforts. A remarkable and temporarily successful project for autonomous development was launched in Paraguay under the rule of Dr. Francia and the López, father and son. Their state-directed program of agrarian reform and industrial diversification transformed Paraguay from a backward country into a relatively prosperous and advanced state, but the disastrous Paraguayan war interrupted this progress and returned Paraguay to backwardness and dependency. In Chile, in the 1850s, an alliance of mining capitalists. small farmers, and artisans attempted to overthrow the landed and mercantile oligarchy and implement a radical program of political and social reform; their "frustrated bourgeois revolution" was drowned in blood. In the present chapter we describe a second Chilean effort to achieve autonomous development under the slogan of "Chile for the Chileans"; it too ended in defeat and in the death of the president who led it.

Expansion of the Hacienda System

The neocolonial order evolved within the framework of the traditional system of land tenure and labor relations. Indeed, it led to an expansion of the hacienda system on a scale far greater than the colonial period had known. As the growing European demand for Latin American products and the growth of national markets raised the value of land, the great landowners in country after country launched assaults on the surviving Indian community lands. In part, at least, this drive reflected an effort to eliminate the competition of Indian peasants in the emerging market economy. In Mexico the Reforma laid the legal basis for this attack in the 1850s and 1860s; it reached its climax in the era of Porfirio Díaz. In the Andean region similar legislation turned all communal property into individual holdings, leading to a cycle of Indian revolt and bloody governmental repressions.

Seizure of church lands by liberal governments also contributed to the growth of the latifundio. Mexico again offered a model, with its Lerdo Law and the Juárez anticlerical decrees. Following the Mexican example, Colombian liberal governments confiscated church lands in the 1860s, the liberal dictator Antonio Guzmán Blanco seized many church estates in Venezuela in the 1870s, and Ecuadoran liberals expropriated church lands in 1895.

Expansion of the public domain through railway construction and Indian wars also contributed to the growth of great landed estates. Lands taken from the church or wrested from Indian tribes were usually sold to buyers in vast tracts at nominal prices. Concentration of land, reducing the cultivable area available to Indian and mestizo small landowners, was accompanied by a parallel growth of the *minifundio*—an uneconomical small plot worked with primitive techniques.

The seizure of Indian community lands to use immediately or to hold for a speculative rise in value provided great landowners with another advantage by giving them control of the local labor force at a time of increasing demand for labor. Expropriated Indians rarely became true wage earners paid wholly in cash, for such workers were too expensive and independent in spirit. A more widespread labor system was debt peonage, in which workers were paid wholly or in part with vouchers redeemable at the *tienda de raya* (company store), whose inflated prices and often devious bookkeeping created a debt that was passed on from father to son. The courts enforced the obligation of peons to remain on the estate until they had liquidated their debts.

Peons who protested low wages or the more intensive style of work demanded by the new order were brought to their senses by the landowner's armed retainers or by local police or military authorities.

In some countries, the period saw a revival of the colonial repartimiento system of draft labor for Indians. In Guatemala, this system required able-bodied Indians to work for a specified number of days on haciendas. It was the liberal President Justo Rufino Barrios who issued instructions to local magistrates to see to it "that any Indian who seeks to evade his duty is punished to the full extent of the law, that the farmers are fully protected and that each Indian is forced to do a full day's work while in service."

Slavery survived in some places well beyond mid-century—for example, in Peru until 1855, in Cuba until 1886, in Brazil until 1888. Closely akin to slavery was the system of bondage, under which some ninety thousand Chinese coolies were imported into Peru between 1849 and 1875 to work on the guano islands and in railway construction. The term *slavery* also applies to the system under which political deportees and captured Indian rebels were sent by Mexican authorities to labor in unspeakable conditions on the coffee, tobacco, and henequen plantations of southern Mexico.

More modern systems of agricultural labor and farm tenantry arose only in such regions as southern Brazil and Argentina, whose critical labor shortage required the offer of greater incentives to the millions of European immigrants who poured into those countries between 1870 and 1910.

Labor conditions were little better in the mining industry and in the factories that arose in some countries after 1890. Typical conditions were a workday of twelve to fourteen hours, miserable wages frequently paid in vouchers redeemable only at the company store, and arbitrary, abusive treatment by employers and foremen. Latin American law codes usually prohibited strikes and other organized efforts to improve working conditions, and police and the armed forces were commonly employed to break strikes, sometimes with heavy loss of life.

Foreign Control of Resources

The rise of the neocolonial order was accompanied by a steady growth of foreign corporate control over the natural and man-made resources of the continent. The process went through stages; in 1870 foreign investment was still largely concentrated in trade, shipping, railways, public utilities, and government loans. At that date, British capital enjoyed an undisputed hegemony in the Latin American investment field. By 1914 foreign corporate ownership had expanded to include most of the mining industry and had deeply penetrated real estate, ranching, plantation agriculture, and manufacturing. By that date, too, Great Britain's rivals had effectively challenged its domination in Latin America. Of these rivals, the most spectacular advance was made by the United States, whose Latin American investments had risen from a negligible amount in 1870 to over $1.6 billion by the end of 1914 (still well below the nearly $5 billion investment of Great Britain).

Foreign economic penetration went hand in hand with a growth of political influence and even armed intervention. The youthful U.S. imperialism proved to be the most aggressive of all. In the years after 1898, a combination of "dollar diplomacy" and armed intervention transformed the Caribbean into an "American lake" and reduced Cuba, the Dominican Republic, and several Central American states to the status of dependencies and protectorates of the United States.

The Politics of Acquisition

The new economy demanded a new politics. Conservatives and liberals, fascinated by the atmosphere of prosperity created by the export boom, the rise in land values, the flood of foreign loans, and the growth of government revenues, put aside their ideological differences and joined in the pursuit of wealth. The positivist slogan "Order and Progress" now became the watchword of Latin America's ruling classes. The social Darwinist idea of the struggle for survival of the fittest and Herbert Spencer's doctrine of "inferior races," frequently used to support claims of the inherent inferiority of the Indian, mestizo, and mulatto masses, also entered the upper-class ideological arsenal.

The growing domination of national economies by the export sectors and the development of a consensus between the old landed aristocracy and more capitalist-oriented groups caused political issues like the federalist-centralist conflict and the liberal-conservative cleavage to lose much of their meaning; in some countries, the old party lines dissolved or became extremely tenuous. A new type of "progressive" caudillo—Porfirio Díaz in Mexico, Rafael Núñez in Colombia, Justo Rufino Barrios in Guatemala, Antonio Guzmán Blanco in Venezuela—symbolized the politics of acquisition.

As the century drew to a close, dissatisfied urban middle-class, immigrant, and entrepreneurial groups in some countries combined to form parties, called Radical or Democratic, that challenged the traditional domination of politics by the creole aristocracy. They demanded political, social, and educational reforms that would give more weight to the new middle sectors. But these middle sectors—manufacturers, shopkeepers, professionals, and the like—were in large part a creation of the neocolonial order, depended on it for their livelihood, and as a rule did not question its viability. The small socialist, anarchist, and syndicalist groups that arose in various Latin American countries in the 1890s challenged both capitalism and neocolonialism, but the full significance of these movements lay in the future.

The trends just described lend a certain unity to the history of Mexico, Argentina, Chile, and Brazil in the period from 1870 to 1914. Each country's history, however, presents significant variations on the common theme—variations that reflect that country's specific historical background and conditions.

Mexican Politics and Economy

Dictatorship Under Díaz

General Porfirio Díaz seized power in 1876 from President Lerdo de Tejada with the support of

Beginning in the 1920s, with considerable support from the state, there arose in Mexico a school of socially conscious artists who sought to enlighten the masses about their bitter past and the promise of the revolutionary present. One of the greatest of these artists was David Alfaro Siqueiros, whose painting depicts with satire the former President Porfirio Díaz, who tramples on the Constitution of 1857 as he diverts his wealthy followers with dancing girls.

disgruntled regional caudillos and military personnel, liberals angered by the political manipulations of the entrenched Lerdo machine, and Indian and mestizo small landholders who believed that Díaz would put an end to land seizures. He also owed his success to the open support of American capitalists, army commanders, and great Texas landowners who, regarding Lerdo as "anti-American," supplied Díaz with arms and cash. Having installed himself as president, Díaz paid his respects to the principle of no re-election by allowing a trusted crony, General Manuel González, to succeed him in 1880. However, he returned to the presidential palace in 1884 and continued to occupy it through successive re-elections until his resignation and flight from Mexico in 1911. He got rid of the now-inconvenient issue of no re-election by having the constitution amended in 1887 and 1890 to permit his indefinite re-election; in 1904 he obtained an extension of the president's term from four to six years. Thus, Díaz, who had seized power in the name of republican legality, erected one of the longest personal dictatorships in Latin American history.

But the construction of the dictatorship was a gradual process. During his first presidential term, Congress and the judiciary enjoyed a certain independence, and the press, including a vocal radical labor press, was free. The outlines of Díaz's economic and social policies, however, soon became clear. Confronted with an empty treasury, facing pressures from above and below, Díaz decided in favor of the great landowners, moneylenders, and foreign capitalists, whose assistance could insure his political survival. In return, he assured these groups of protection for their property and other interests. Díaz, who had once proclaimed that in the age-old struggle between the people and the haciendas he was on the side of the people, now sent troops to suppress peasant resistance to land seizures. Before taking power, Díaz had denounced Lerdo for his generous concessions to British capitalists; by 1880, Díaz had granted even more lavish subsidies for railway construction to North American companies. Economic development had become for Díaz the great object, the key to the solution of his own problems and those of the nation.

Economic development required political stability; accordingly, Díaz promoted a policy of conciliation that consisted of offering an olive branch and a share of spoils to all influential opponents, no matter what their political past or persuasion—*Lerdistas,* Juaristas, conservatives, clericals, anticlericals. A dog with a bone in its mouth, Díaz cynically observed, neither kills nor steals. In effect, Díaz invited all sections of the upper class and some members of the middle class, including prominent intellectuals and journalists, to join the great Mexican barbecue, from which only the poor and humble were barred. An important instrument of Díaz's law-and-order policy was a force of mounted police, the *rurales,* distinguished by their picturesque dress. The former bandits and vagrants who had composed a good part of this force were gradually replaced by artisan and peasant recruits, who had been dislocated by the large social changes that took place during the *Porfiriato.* Aside from chasing unrepentant bandits, the major function of the rurales was to suppress peasant unrest and break strikes.

There was another side to the policy of conciliation, however, a side described by the formula *pan o palo* (bread or the club). Opponents who refused Díaz's bribes—political offices, monopolies, and the like—suffered swift reprisal. Dissidents were beaten up, murdered, or arrested and sent to the damp underground dungeons of San Juan de Ulúa or the grim Belén prison, a sort of Mexican Bastille. Designed to hold two hundred prisoners, Belén commonly held four to five thousand inmates.

By such means, Díaz virtually eliminated all effective opposition by the end of his second term (1884–1888). The constitution of 1857 and the liberties it guaranteed existed only on paper. Elections to Congress, in theory the highest organ of government, were a farce; Díaz simply circulated a list of his candidates to local officials, who certified their election. The dictator contemptuously called Congress his *caballada,* his stable of horses. The state governors were appointed by Díaz, usually from the ranks of local great landlords or his generals. In return for their loyalty, he gave them a free hand to enrich themselves and terrorize the local population. Under them were district heads called *jefes políticos,* petty tyrants appointed by the governors with the approval of Díaz; below them were municipal presidents who ran the local administrative units. One feature of the Díaz era was a mushrooming of the administrative and coercive apparatus; government costs during this period soared by 900 percent.

The army, as indispensable to Díaz as it had been to Santa Anna, naturally enjoyed special favor. Higher officers were well paid and enjoyed many opportunities for enrichment at the expense of the regions in which they were quartered. But the Díaz army was pathetically inadequate for purposes of national defense. Generals and other high officers were appointed not for their ability but for their loyalty to the dictator. Discipline, morale, and training were extremely poor. A considerable part of the rank-and-file were recruited from the dregs of society; the remainder were young Indian conscripts. These soldiers, often used for brutal repression of strikes and agrarian unrest, were themselves harshly treated and miserably paid—the wage of ranks below sergeant was fifty cents a month.

222

The church became another pillar of the dictatorship. Early in his second term, Díaz reached an accommodation with the hierarchy. The church agreed to support Díaz; in return he allowed the anticlerical Reforma laws to fall into disuse. In disregard of those laws, monasteries and nunneries were restored, church schools established, and wealth again began to accumulate in the hands of the church. Faithful to its bargain, the church turned a deaf ear to the complaints of the lower classes and taught complete submission to the authorities. As in colonial times, many priests were utterly venal and corrupt. Only in the closing years of the dictatorship did the church, sensing the coming storm, begin to advocate modest social reforms.

The Díaz policy of conciliation was directed at prominent intellectuals as well as more wealthy and powerful figures. A group of such intellectuals, professional men, and businessmen made up a closely knit clique of Díaz's advisers. Known as *Científicos,* they got their name from their insistence on "scientific" administration of the state and were especially influential after 1892. About fifteen men made up the controlling nucleus of the group. Their leader was Díaz's all-powerful father-in-law, Manuel Romero Rubio, and, after his death in 1895, the new minister of finance, José Yves Limantour.

For the Científicos, the economic movement was everything. Most Científicos accepted the thesis of the inherent inferiority of the Indian and mestizo population and the consequent necessity for relying on the native white elite and on foreigners and their capital to lead Mexico out of its backwardness. In the words of the journalist Francisco G. Cosmes, "the Indian has only the passive force of inferior races, is incapable of actively pursuing the goal of civilization."

But there were differences of opinion within the group. The most distinguished intellectual among the Científicos was the old-time liberal Justo Sierra, a biographer of Juárez who wistfully clung to his libertarian ideas, yet served Díaz, believing that he was preparing Mexico to be free. By contrast with such racists as Francisco Bulnes and José Yves Limantour, Sierra rejected the notion of Indians' racial inferiority and argued that education could correct their seeming dullness and apathy.

Some members of the Díaz establishment even harbored doubts about Díaz's policies and methods. Troubled by the immobility of the regime, fearing revolution, some Científicos urged a variety of reforms, including an end to re-election and the introduction of a multiparty system. But their advice was not heeded and, being practical men, most resigned themselves to the more profitable task of enriching themselves.

Thanks to the devoted efforts of educators like Justo Sierra, the Díaz era saw some advances in public education. In 1887, Sierra secured the adoption of a federal law making primary education obligatory. Despite the law, however, it appears that on the average only one out of three children between the ages of six and twelve were enrolled. The vast majority of these children probably went only through the first year and remained functionally illiterate. The principal beneficiaries of the educational progress under Díaz were the sons of the rich: for every student enrolled in the primary schools in 1910, the state spent about 7 pesos; for every student in the college preparatory schools, it spent nearly 100 pesos.

In the last analysis, however, apologists for the dictatorship rested their case on the "economic miracle" that Díaz had allegedly worked in Mexico. A survey of the Mexican economy in 1910 reveals how modest that miracle was.

Concentration of Landownership

At the opening of the twentieth century, Mexico was still predominantly an agrarian country; 77 percent of its population of 15 million still lived on the land. The laws of the Reforma had already given impetus to the concentration of landownership, and under Díaz this trend was greatly accelerated. There is some evidence of a link between the rapid advance of railway construction, which increased the possibilities of production for export and therefore stimulated a rise in land values, and the growth of land-grabbing in the Díaz period.

A major piece of land legislation was a law of 1883 that provided for the survey of so-called vacant public lands, *tierras baldías*. The law authorized real estate companies to survey such lands and retain one-third of the surveyed area; the remainder was sold for low fixed prices in vast tracts, usually to Díaz's favorites and their foreign associates. The 1883 law required the surveying companies and purchasers to settle at least one person for each five hundred acres surveyed, but a second law (1894) removed this obligation and deleted the clause restricting the amount of land that one individual could purchase.

The 1883 and 1894 laws opened the way for vast territorial acquisitions. One individual alone obtained nearly 12 million acres in Baja California and other northern states. But the land companies were not satisfied with the acquisition of true vacant lands. The law of 1894 declared that a parcel of land to which a legal title could not be produced might be declared vacant land, opening the door to expropriation of Indian villages and other small landholders whose forebears had tilled their lands from times immemorial but who could not produce the required titles. If the victims offered armed resistance, troops were sent against them, and the vanquished rebels were sold like slaves to labor on henequen plantations in Yucatán or sugar plantations in Cuba. This was the fate of the Yaqui Indians of the northwest, defeated after a long, valiant struggle.

Another instrument of land seizure was an 1890 law designed to give effect to older Reforma laws requiring the distribution of Indian village lands among the villagers. The law created enormous confusion. In many cases, land speculators and hacendados cajoled the illiterate Indians into selling their titles for paltry sums. Hacendados also used other means, such as cutting off a village's water supply or simply brute force, to achieve their predatory ends. By 1910 the process of land expropriation was largely complete. More than 90 percent of the Indian villages of the central plateau, the most densely populated region of the country, had lost their communal lands. Only the most tenacious resistance enabled villages that still held their lands to survive the assault of the great landowners. Landless peons and their families made up 9.5 million of a rural population of 12 million.

As a rule, the new owners did not use the land seized from Indian villages or small landholders more efficiently. Hacendados let much of the usurped land lie idle. They waited for a speculative rise in value or for an American buyer. By keeping land out of production, they helped keep the price of maize and other staples artificially high. The technical level of hacienda agriculture was generally extremely low, with little use of irrigation, machinery, and commercial fertilizer, although some new landowning groups—such as northern cattle raisers and cotton growers, the coffee and rubber growers of Chiapas, and the henequen producers of Yucatán—employed more modern equipment and techniques.

The production of foodstuffs stagnated, barely keeping pace during most of the period with the growth of population, and per capita production of such basic staples as maize and beans actually declined toward the end of the century. This decline culminated in three years of bad harvests, 1907–1910, due principally to drought. As a result, the importation of maize and other foodstuffs from the United States steadily increased in the last years of the Díaz regime. Despite the growth of pastoral industry, per capita consumption of milk and cheese barely kept pace with the growth of population, for a considerable proportion of the cattle sold was destined for the export market.

The only food products whose increase exceeded the growth of population were alcoholic beverages. Some idea of the increase in their consumption is given by the fact that the number of bars in Mexico City rose from 51 in 1864 to 1,400 in 1900. At the end of the century, the Mexican death rate from alcoholism—a common response to intolerable conditions of life and labor—was estimated to be six times that of France. Meanwhile, inflation, rampant during the

224

last part of the Díaz regime, greatly raised the cost of the staples on which the mass of the population depended. Without a corresponding increase in wages, the situation of agricultural and industrial laborers deteriorated sharply.

The Economic Advance

While food production for the domestic market declined, production of food and industrial raw materials for the foreign market experienced a vigorous growth. By 1910, Mexico had become the largest producer of henequen, source of a fiber in great demand in the world market. Mexican export production became increasingly geared to the needs of the United States, which was the principal market for sugar, bananas, rubber, and tobacco produced on plantations that were largely foreign-owned. American companies dominated the mining industry, whose output of copper, gold, lead, and zinc, rose sharply after 1890. A spectacular late development was shown by the oil industry, which was controlled by American and British interests; by 1911, Mexico was third among the world's oil producers. French and Spanish capitalists virtually monopolized the textile industry and other consumer goods industries that had a relatively rapid growth after 1890. Operating behind the protection of tariff walls that excluded foreign competition in cheap goods, they compelled the masses to pay high prices for articles of inferior quality.

Foreign control of key sectors of the economy and the fawning attitude of the Díaz regime toward foreigners gave rise to a popular saying: "Mexico, mother of foreigners and stepmother of Mexicans." The ruling clique of Científicos justified this favoritism by citing the need for a rapid development of Mexico's natural resources and the creation of a strong country capable of defending its political independence and territorial integrity.

Thanks to an influx of foreign capital, some quickening and modernization of economic life did take place under Díaz. The volume of foreign trade greatly increased, a modern banking system arose, and the country acquired a relatively dense network of railways. But these successes were achieved at a very heavy price: a brutal dictatorship, the pauperization of the mass of the population, the stagnation of food agriculture, the strengthening of the inefficient latifundio, and the survival of many feudal or semifeudal vestiges in Mexican economic and social life.

Labor, Agrarian, and Middle-Class Unrest

The survival of feudal vestiges was especially glaring in the area of labor relations. There was some variation in labor conditions from region to region. In 1910 forced labor and outright slavery, as well as older forms of debt peonage, were characteristic of the south (the states of Yucatán, Tabasco, Chiapas, and parts of Oaxaca and Veracruz). The rubber, coffee, tobacco, henequen, and sugar plantations of this region depended heavily on the forced labor of political deportees, captured Indian rebels, and contract workers kidnaped or lured to work in the tropics by a variety of devices.

In central Mexico, where a massive expropriation of Indian village lands had created a large landless Indian proletariat, tenantry, sharecropping, and the use of migratory labor had increased, and living standards had declined. The large labor surplus of this area diminished the need for hacendados to tie their workers to their estates with debt peonage. In the north the proximity of the United States, with its higher wage scales, and the competition of hacendados with mine owners for labor made wages and sharecropping arrangements somewhat more favorable and weakened debt peonage. In all parts of the country, however, the life of agricultural workers was filled with hardships and abuses of every kind.

Labor conditions in mines and factories were little better than in the countryside. Workers in textile mills labored twelve to fifteen hours daily for a wage ranging from eleven cents for unskilled women and children to seventy-five cents for highly skilled workers. Employers found ways of reducing even these meager wages. Wages were discounted for alleged "carelessness" in the use of tools or machines or for "defective goods";

Striking workers at the Rio Blanco textile works in Mexico in 1909; the business was controlled by French capital. Troops broke up the strike and much blood was shed.

workers were usually paid wholly or in part with vouchers good only in company stores, whose prices were higher than in other stores. Federal and state laws banned trade unions and strikes. Scores of workers, both men and women, were shot down by troops who broke the great textile strike in the Orizaba (Veracruz) area in 1907, and scores were killed or wounded in putting down the strike at the American-owned Consolidated Copper Company mine at Cananea (Sonora) in 1906. Despite such repressions, the trade union movement continued to grow in the last years of the Díaz era, and socialist, anarchist, and syndicalist ideas began to influence the still small working class.

The growing wave of strikes and agrarian unrest in the last, decadent phase of the Díaz era indicated an increasingly rebellious mood among ever broader sections of the Mexican people. Alienation spread among teachers, lawyers, journalists, and other professionals, whose opportunities for advancement were sharply limited by the monolithic control of economic, political, and social life by the Científicos, their foreign allies, and regional oligarchies. In the United States in 1905 a group of middle-class intellectuals, headed by the Flores Magón brothers, organized the Liberal party, which called for the overthrow of Díaz and advanced a platform whose economic and social provisions anticipated many articles of the constitution of 1917.

Even members of the ruling class began to join the chorus of criticism. These upper-class dissidents included liberal hacendados of a more bourgeois type and national capitalists who resented the competitive advantages enjoyed by foreign companies in Mexico. They also feared that the static, reactionary Díaz policies could provoke the masses to overthrow the capitalist system itself. Fearing revolution, these upper-class critics urged Díaz to end his personal rule, shake up the regime, and institute the reforms needed to preserve the existing economic and social order. When their appeals fell on deaf ears, some of these bourgeois reformers reluctantly prepared to take the road of revolution. Typical of these men was the wealthy hacendado and businessman Francisco Madero, soon to become the Apostle of the Mexican Revolution.

The simultaneous advent of an economic recession and a food crisis sharpened this growing discontent. The depression of 1906–1907, which spread from the United States to Mexico, caused a wave of bankruptcies, layoffs, and wage cuts. At the same time the crop failures of 1907–1910 provoked a dramatic rise in the price of staples like maize and beans. By 1910 Mexico's internal conflicts had reached an explosive stage. The workers' strikes, the agrarian unrest, the agitation of middle-class reformers, the disaffection of some great landowners and capitalists all reflected the disintegration of the dictatorship's social base. Despite its superficial stability and posh splendor, the house of Díaz was rotten from top to bottom. Events proved that only a slight push was needed to send it toppling to the ground.

Argentinian Politics and Economy

In the presidential contest of 1874, Nicolás Avellaneda, a lawyer from Tucumán who had the support of Domingo Sarmiento and powerful provincial bosses, defeated former president Bartolomé Mitre. Mitre, who believed that Buenos Aires must retain control of the republic if it were to stay on a progressive course, promptly organized a revolt. He was defeated and captured but was soon released and continued to enjoy for many years the position of Argentina's most honored elder statesman.

Avellaneda, however, did not represent provincial backwardness and caudillismo. A cultured liberal and a disciple of Sarmiento, in whose cabinet he had held office, he continued his predecessor's work of promoting education, immigration, and domestic tranquillity. In 1876 he inaugurated railroad service between Buenos Aires and his native city of Tucumán. The new line forged stronger economic and political links between the port city and the remote northwest, contributing to the end of the long quarrel between Buenos Aires and the interior.

Consolidation of the State

One more sharp confrontation, however, proved necessary before the quarrel between Buenos Aires and the interior could be finally laid to rest. For almost two decades, Buenos Aires had been both capital of the province of the same name and provisional capital of the republic. In 1880 Carlos Tejedor, governor of the province of Buenos Aires and a fanatical champion of the city's predominance, became a candidate for the presidency against another *Tucumano,* Julio Roca. Roca was Avellaneda's secretary of war and protégé and was supported by a powerful group of provincial politicians known as the Córdoba League. Tejedor and his supporters responded to Roca's election with a new revolt that government and provincial forces soon crushed.

The victors proceeded to carry out the long-standing pledge to federalize Buenos Aires, which became the capital of the nation, while the provincial capital was moved to the city of La Plata. The interior seemed to have triumphed over Buenos Aires, but that apparent victory was an illusion; the provincial lawyers and politicians who carried the day in 1880 had absorbed the commercial and cultural values of the great city and wished not to diminish but to share in its power. Far from losing influence, Buenos Aires steadily gained in wealth and power until it achieved an overwhelming ascendancy over the rest of the country.

The federalization of Buenos Aires completed the consolidation of the Argentine state. Simultaneously, however, a certain decline appeared in the quality of Argentina's political leadership. The great architects of Argentine national unity—Mitre, Alberdi, Sarmiento—had ardently promoted material progress, which they regarded as the key to the solution of all other problems, but their ultimate goal was a democratic society based on access to land and education for the broad masses. That is why they had sponsored—unsuccessfully—homestead legislation and promoted public education, believing, in the words of Sarmiento, that education would "make the poor gaucho a useful man."

With President Roca, a new generation of leaders came to the fore, closely identified with and often recruited from the ruling class of great landowners and wealthy merchants. The "generation of 1880," or the oligarchy, as it was also called, shared the faith of Alberdi and Sarmiento in economic development and the value of the North American and European models, but that faith was now deeply tinged with cynicism, egotism, and a profound distrust for the popular classes. These autocratic liberals prized order and progress above freedom. They regarded the gauchos, the Indians, and the mass of illiterate European immigrants flooding Argentina unfit to exercise civic functions. Asked to define universal suffrage, a leading oligarch, Eduardo Wilde, replied, "It is the triumph of universal ignorance."

The new rulers identified the national interest with the interest of the great landowners, wealthy merchants, and foreign capitalists. Regarding the apparatus of state as their personal property or as the property of their class, they used their official connections to enrich themselves. Although they maintained the forms of parliamentary government, they were determined not to let power slip from their hands and organized what came to be called the *unicato* (one-party rule), exercised by the National Autonomist party, which they formed. Extreme concentration of power in the executive branch and systematic use of fraud, violence, and bribery were basic features of the system.

Economic Boom and Inflation

The ominous new trends of the oligarchy emerged in the administration of President Julio Roca (1880–1886) and flowered exuberantly under his political heir and brother-in-law, Miguel Juárez Celman (1886–1890). Roca presided over the beginnings of a great boom that appeared to justify all the optimism of the oligarchy. As secretary of war under Avellaneda, Roca had led a military expedition—the so-called Conquest of the Desert—southward against the pampa Indians in 1879–1880. This conquest added vast new areas to the province of Buenos Aires and to the national public domain. The campaign created a last opportunity for implementing a democratic land policy directed toward the creation of an Argentine small farmer class. Instead, the Roca administration sold off the area in huge tracts for nominal prices to army officers, politicians, and foreign capitalists. The aging Sarmiento, who had seen the defeat of his own effort to acquire and distribute to settlers public land suitable for farming, lamented: "Soon there will not remain a palm of land for distribution to our immigrants."

Coming at a time of steadily mounting European demand for Argentine meat and wheat, the Conquest of the Desert triggered an orgy of land speculation that drove land prices ever higher and caused a prodigious expansion of cattle raising and agriculture. This expansion took place under the sign of the latifundio. Few of the millions of Italian and Spanish immigrants who entered Argentina in this period realized the common dream of becoming independent small landowners.

Some foreign agricultural colonies were founded in the provinces of Santa Fe and Entre Ríos in the 1870s and 1880s. By the mid-1890s, with wheat prices declining and land prices rising, there was a shift from small-scale farming to extensive tenant farming. This was true even in Santa Fe, the heartland of the foreign colonies. Soaring land prices and the traditional unwillingness of the estancieros to sell land forced the majority of would-be independent farmers to become ranch hands, sharecroppers, or tenant

228

farmers. As sharecroppers or tenants, their hold on the land was very precarious; leases were usually limited to one, two, or three years. The immigrant broke the virgin soil, replaced the tough pampa grass with the alfalfa pasturage needed to fatten cattle, and produced the first wheat harvests but then had to move on, leaving the landowner in possession of all improvements.

As a result, the great majority of new arrivals either remained in Buenos Aires or, having spent some years in the countryside, returned with their small savings to the city, where the rise of meat-salting and meat-packing plants, railroads, public utilities, and many small factories created a growing demand for labor. True, the immigrant workers received very low wages, worked long hours, and crowded with their families into one-room apartments in wretched slums. But in the city barrio they lived among their own people, free from the loneliness of the pampa and the arbitrary rule of great landowners, and had some opportunity of rising in the economic and social scale. As a result, the population of Buenos Aires shot up from 500,000 in 1889 to 1,244,000 in 1909. There arose a growing imbalance between the great city and its hinterland, which held the greater portion of the wealth, population, and culture of the nation, and the interior—particularly the northwest—which was impoverished, stagnant, and thinly peopled. Argentina, to use a familiar metaphor, became a giant head set on a dwarf body.

Foreign capital and management played a decisive role in the expansion of the Argentine economy in this period. The creole elite obtained vast profits from the rise in the price of their land and the increasing volume of exports but showed little interest in plowing those gains into industry or the construction of the infrastructure required by the export economy, preferring a lavish and leisurely lifestyle over entrepreneurial activity. Just as they left to English and Irish managers the task of tending their estates, so they left to English capital the financing of meat-packing plants, railroads, public utilities, and docks and other facilities. As a result, most of these resources remained in British hands. Typical of the oligarchy's policy of surrender to foreign interests was the decision of Congress in 1889 to sell the state-owned Ferrocarril Oeste, the most profitable and best-run railroad in Argentina, to a British company. Service on a growing foreign debt claimed an ever larger portion of the government's receipts.

Meanwhile, imports of iron, coal, machinery, and consumer goods grew much faster than exports. Combined with the unfavorable price ratio of raw materials to finished goods, the result was an unfavorable balance of trade and a steady drain of gold. New loans with burdensome terms brought temporary relief but aggravated the long-range problem. Under President Miguel Juárez Celman, the disappearance of gold and the government's determination to keep the boom going at all costs led to the issue of great quantities of unbacked paper currency and a massive inflation.

The great landowners did not mind, for they were paid for their exports in French francs and English pounds, which they could convert into cheap Argentine pesos for the payment of local costs; besides, inflation caused the price of their lands to rise. The sacrificial victims of the inflation were the urban middle class and the workers, whose income declined in real value.

The Formation of the Radical Party

In 1889–1890, just as the boom was turning into a depression, the accumulated resentment of the urban middle class and some alienated sectors of the elite over the catastrophic inflation, one-party rule, and official corruption produced a protest movement that took the name *Unión Cívica* (Civic Union). Although the new organization had a middle-class base, its leadership united such disparate elements as urban politicians like Leandro Além, its first president, who was at odds with the Roca–Juárez Celman machine; new landowners and descendants of old aristocratic families who felt excluded from office and access to patronage by the same clique; and Catholics outraged by the government's anticlerical legislation. Aside from the demand for effective suffrage, the only thing uniting these heterogeneous elements was a common determination to overthrow the government.

The birth of the new party at a mass meeting in Buenos Aires in 1890 coincided with a financial storm: the stock market collapsed, bankruptcies multiplied, and in April the cabinet resigned. Encouraged by this last development, and counting on support from the army, the leaders of the Unión Cívica planned a revolt against Juárez Celman in July. Three days of sharp fighting ended in defeat for the rebels.

The oligarchy now showed its ability to maneuver and divide its enemies. Juárez Celman was forced to resign with an abject confession of his errors; his place was taken by his vice president, Carlos Pellegrini (1890–1892), who moved to appease disgruntled elements of the elite by revising the system of distribution of jobs. Bartolomé Mitre, among other aristocratic dissidents, took the bait and reached an accommodation with the oligarchy that provided for an electoral accord between the National party and his followers. Simultaneously, Pellegrini took steps to improve economic conditions by a policy of retrenchment that reduced inflation, stabilized the peso, and revived Argentine credit abroad. Thanks to these measures and a gradual recovery from the depression, popular discontent began to subside.

The defection of Mitre and other aristocratic leaders of the Unión Cívica isolated Leandro Além and other dissidents who were excluded from Pellegrini's peacemaking scheme. Denouncing the accord between Mitre and Pellegrini as a sellout, Além and his nephew, Hipólito Yrigoyen, formed a new party committed to a "radical" democracy—the *Unión Cívica Radical.* The party named Bernardo de Yrigoyen as its presidential candidate in 1892 but, knowing that rigged elections made his victory impossible, they also prepared for another revolt—a move that Pellegrini effectively squelched by deporting Além and other Radical leaders until after the election of Luis Sáenz Peña (1892–1895).

On his return from exile, Além organized a new revolt, which began in July 1893. The rebels briefly seized Santa Fe and some other towns, but after two and a half months of fighting, the revolt collapsed for lack of significant popular support. Depressed by his failures and the intrigues of his nephew to seize control of the Radical party, Além committed suicide in 1896.

Between 1896 and 1910, the Radical party, now led by Yrigoyen, proved unable to achieve political reform by peaceful or revolutionary means. The reunited oligarchy continued to win election after election by the traditional methods. The architect of the system of corruption and nepotism, Julio Roca, was re-elected president in 1898 and was succeeded by another oligarch, Manuel Quintana, in 1904; on Quintana's death in 1906, Vice President José Figueroa Alcorta served out the rest of his term. A Radical revolt in 1905 proved to be another dismal fiasco.

In Yrigoyen, however, the Radicals possessed a charismatic personality and a masterful organizer who refused to admit defeat. Yrigoyen was a onetime police superintendent in Buenos Aires, a former minor politician who had maneuvered among various factions in the official party, using his political connections to acquire a considerable wealth, which he invested in land and cattle. As a Radical caudillo, Yrigoyen surrounded himself with an aura of mystery, lived in an ostentatiously modest manner, avoided making speeches, and cultivated a literary style that cloaked the poverty of his thought with turgid rhetoric. "Abstention," refusal to participate in rigged elections, and "Revolutionary Intransigence," the determination to resort to revolution until free elections were achieved, were the party's basic slogans.

The vagueness of the Radical program was dictated by the party's need to appeal to very diverse elements and by its wholehearted acceptance of the economic status quo. The Radical party represented the bourgeoisie, but it was a dependent bourgeoisie that did not champion industrialization, economic diversification, or nationalization of foreign-owned industries. Far from attacking the neocolonial order, the Radical

230

party proposed to strengthen it by promoting co-operation between the landed aristocracy and the urban sectors, which were challenging the creole elite's monopoly of political power. In all respects, it was much more conservative than the contemporaneous reformist movement of José Batlle y Ordóñez in Uruguay.[1]

The Radical party went into eclipse after the debacles of 1890 and 1893, but gradually revived after 1900, due in part to Yrigoyen's charismatic personality and organizing talent. The most important factor, however, was the steady growth of an urban and rural middle class largely composed of sons of immigrants. The domination of the export sector, which limited the growth of industry and opportunities for entrepreneurial activity, focused middle-class ambitions more and more on government employment and the professions, two fields dominated by the creole elite. Signs of growing unrest and frustration in the middle class included a series of student strikes in the universities, caused by efforts of creole governing boards to restrict enrollment of students of immigrant descent.

Electoral Reform and the Growth of the Labor Movement

Meanwhile, a section of the oligarchy, headed by Carlos Pellegrini, had begun to advocate electoral reform. These aristocratic reformers argued that the existing situation created a permanent state of tension and instability; they feared that

[1] Under the leadership of José Batlle y Ordóñez (1856–1929), president of Uruguay from 1903 to 1907 and again from 1911 to 1915, Uruguay adopted an advanced program of social reform that made it "the chief laboratory for social experimentation in the Americas and a focal point of world interest." The program included the establishment of the eight-hour day, old-age pensions, minimum wages, and accident insurance; abolition of capital punishment, separation of church and state, education for women, and recognition of divorce; and a system of state capitalism that gradually brought under public ownership banks, railroads, electric systems, telephone and telegraph companies, street railways, and meat-packing plants. Batlle supported labor in its strikes against foreign-owned enterprises. But his advanced welfare legislation was effective only in the port city of Montevideo. Batlle made no effort to challenge the land monopoly of the great estancieros or to apply his social legislation to their peons.

sooner or later the Radical efforts at revolution would succeed. It would be much better, they believed, to make the concessions demanded by the Radicals, open up the political system, and thereby gain for the ruling party—now generally called Conservative—the popular support and legitimacy it needed to remain in power. Moreover, the conservative reformers were aware of a new threat from the left—from the labor movement and especially its vanguard, the socialists, anarchists, and syndicalists—and hoped to make an alliance with the bourgeoisie against the revolutionary working class.

Pellegrini converted President Figueroa Alcorta to his viewpoint, and Figueroa's disciple and political heir, Roque Sáenz Peña, took office as president in 1910 with a promise that he would satisfy the Radical demands. At his urging, Congress passed a series of measures known collectively as the Sáenz Peña Law (1912). The new law established universal and secret male suffrage for citizens when they reached the age of eighteen. This measure, conceding the Radicals' basic demands, compelled them to abandon their revolutionary posture and operate as a regular party through legal channels. In 1912, having abandoned "Abstention," the Radicals made large gains in congressional and local elections, foreshadowing the victory of Hipólito Yrigoyen in the presidential election of 1916.

The Sáenz Peña Law, "an act of calculated retreat by the ruling class," in the words of David Rock, opened the way for a dependent bourgeoisie to share power and the spoils of office with the landed aristocracy. The principal political vehicle for working-class aspirations was the Socialist party, founded in 1894 as a split-off from the Unión Cívica Radical by the Buenos Aires physician and intellectual Juan B. Justo, who led the party until his death in 1928.

Despite its professed Marxism, the party's socialism was of the parliamentary reformist kind, appealing chiefly to highly skilled native-born workers and the lower middle class. The majority of workers, foreign-born noncitizens who still dreamed of returning someday to their homelands, remained aloof from electoral politics but readily joined trade union organizations. Here the Socialist party competed for influence with the anarchists and syndicalists, who in turn competed with each other for leadership of trade unions and strikes. Between 1902 and 1910 wage scales and working conditions deteriorated as surplus immigrant labor accumulated in Buenos Aires; a series of great strikes was broken by the government with brutal repression and the deportation of so-called foreign agitators. Despite these defeats and the negative consequences of discord among socialists, anarchists, and syndicalists, the labor movement continued to grow and struggle, winning such initial victories as the ten-hour workday and the establishment of Sunday as a compulsory day of rest.

Chilean Politics and Economy

Nitrates and War

In 1876 the official Liberal candidate for the presidency, Aníbal Pinto, defeated two rivals, both distinguished historians—Miguel Luis Amunátegui and Benjamin Vicuña Mackenna. From his predecessor, the new president inherited a severe economic crisis (1874–1879). Wheat and copper prices dropped, exports declined, and unemployment grew. The principal offset to these unfavorable developments was the continued growth of nitrate exports from the Atacama Desert as a result of a doubling of nitrate production between 1865 and 1875. But nitrates, the foundation of Chilean material progress, also became the cause of a major war with dramatic consequences for Chile and her two foes, Bolivia and Peru.

The nitrate deposits exploited by the Anglo-Chilean companies lay, it will be recalled, in territories belonging to Bolivia (the province of Antofagasta) and Peru (the province of Tarapacá). In 1866 a treaty between Chile and Bolivia defined their boundary in the Atacama Desert as the twenty-fourth parallel, gave Chilean and Bolivian interests equal rights to exploit the territory between the twenty-third and twenty-fifth parallels, and guaranteed each government half of the tax revenues obtained from the export of minerals

from the whole area. Anglo-Chilean capital soon poured into the region, developing a highly efficient mining-industrial complex. By a second treaty of 1874, Chile's northern border with Bolivia was left at the twenty-fourth parallel. Chile relinquished her rights to a share of the taxes from exports north of that boundary but received in return a twenty-five-year guarantee against increase of taxes on Chilean enterprises operating in the Bolivian province of Antofagasta.

Chile had no boundary dispute with Peru, but aggressive Chilean mining interests, aided by British capital, soon extended their operations from Antofagasta into the Peruvian province of Tarapacá. By 1875, Chilean enterprises in Peruvian nitrate fields employed more than ten thousand workers, engineers, and supervisory personnel. At this point, the Peruvian government, on the brink of bankruptcy as a result of a very expensive program of public works, huge European loans, and the depletion of the guano deposits on which it had counted to service those loans, decided to expropriate the foreign companies in Tarapacá and establish a state monopoly over the production and sale of nitrates. Meanwhile, Peru and Bolivia had negotiated a secret treaty in 1874 providing for a military alliance in the event either power went to war with Chile.

Ejected from Tarapacá, the Anglo-Chilean capitalists intensified their exploitation of the nitrate deposits in Antofagasta. In 1878 Bolivia, counting on her military alliance with Peru, challenged Chile by imposing higher taxes on nitrate exports from Antofagasta, in violation of the treaty of 1874. When the Chilean companies operating in Antofagasta refused to pay the new taxes, the Bolivian government threatened them with confiscation. The agreement of 1874 provided for arbitration of disputes, but the Bolivians twice rejected Chilean offers to submit the dispute to arbitration.

In February 1879, despite Chilean warnings that expropriation of Chilean enterprises would void the treaty of 1874, the Bolivian government ordered the confiscation carried out. On February 14, the day set for the seizure and sale of the Chilean properties, Chilean troops occupied the

232

port of Antofagasta, encountering no resistance, and proceeded to extend Chilean control over the whole province. Totally unprepared for war, Peru made a vain effort to mediate between Chile and Bolivia. Chile, however, having learned of the secret Peruvian-Bolivian alliance, charged Peru with intolerable duplicity and declared war on both Peru and Bolivia on April 5, 1879.

In this war, called the War of the Pacific, Chile faced enemies whose combined population was more than twice its own; one of these powers, Peru, also possessed a respectable naval force. But Chile enjoyed major advantages. By contrast with its neighbors, it possessed a stable central government, a people with a strong sense of national identity, and a disciplined, well-trained army and navy. Although small, the navy included two modern ironclads with revolving turrets and heavy firing power. Chile also enjoyed the advantage of being closer to the theater of operations, since Bolivian troops had to come over the Andes, while the Peruvian army had to cross the Atacama Desert.

All three powers had serious economic problems, but Chile's situation was not as catastrophic as that of its foes. Equally important, Chile had the support of powerful English capitalist interests, who knew that the future of the massive English investment in Chile depended in large part on the outcome of the war. The prospect of Chilean acquisition of the valuable nitrate areas of Antofagasta and Tarapacá naturally pleased the British capitalists. British capital was also invested in Bolivia and Peru, but whereas the Chilean government had maintained service on its debt, Bolivia and Peru had suspended payment on their English loans. Besides, the Peruvian nationalization of the nitrate industry in Tarapacá had seriously injured British interests.

The decisive battle of the war took place on the sea on October 8, 1879, when the two Chilean ironclads, recently acquired from England, forced the surrender of the Peruvian ship *Huáscar,* which had done great damage to Chilean coastal traffic, and severed communications between Santiago and the Chilean forces operating in the Atacama Desert. Having command of the sea, the Chilean forces resumed operations in the Atacama, and in a short time overran the Peruvian provinces of Tarapacá, Tacna, and Arica. By the middle of 1880, Bolivia had effectively been knocked out of the war. In January 1881 a thirty-thousand-man Chilean army under the command of General Manuel Baquedano overcame tenacious Peruvian resistance and occupied the enemy capital of Lima. Meanwhile, the Chilean navy had sunk the last Peruvian warship, the *Atahualpa.* Although scattered fighting between Chilean occupation forces and Peruvian guerrillas continued for over two years, Chile had clearly won the war.

By the Treaty of Ancón (October 20, 1883), Peru ceded the province of Tarapacá to Chile in perpetuity. Tacna and Arica would be Chilean for ten years, after which a plebiscite would decide their ultimate fate. But the plebiscite was never held, and Chile continued to administer the two territories until 1929, when Peru recovered Tacna and Arica went to Chile. An armistice signed in April 1884 by Bolivia and Chile assigned the former Bolivian province of Antofagasta to Chile, but for many years no Bolivian government would sign a formal treaty acknowledging that loss. Meanwhile, Chile remained in de facto possession of the port and province of Antofagasta. Finally, in 1904, Bolivia signed a treaty in which Chile agreed to pay an indemnity and to build a railroad connecting the Bolivian capital of La Paz with the port of Arica. That railroad was completed in 1913.

Aftermath of the War of the Pacific

Chile took advantage of the continued mobilization of its armed forces during the negotiations with Peru to settle scores with the Araucanian Indians, whose struggle in defense of their land against encroaching whites had continued since colonial times. After two years of resistance against very unequal odds, the Araucanians were forced to admit defeat and sign a treaty (1883) that resettled the Indians on reservations but permitted them to retain their tribal government and laws. The Araucanian campaign of 1880–

1882, which extended the Chilean frontier to the south into a region of mountain and forest, sparked a brisk movement of land speculation and colonization in that area.

From the War of the Pacific, which shattered Peru economically and psychologically and left Bolivia more isolated than before from the outside world, Chile emerged the strongest nation on the west coast, in control of vast deposits of nitrates and copper, the mainstays of its economy. But the greater part of these riches would soon pass into foreign hands. In 1881 the Chilean government made an important decision: it decided to return the nitrate properties of Tarapacá to private ownership, that is, to the holders of the certificates issued by the Peruvian government as compensation for the nationalized properties.

During the war, uncertainty as to how Chile would dispose of those properties had caused the Peruvian certificates to depreciate until they fell to a fraction of their face worth. Speculators, mostly British, had bought up large quantities of these depreciated certificates. In 1878 British capital controlled some 13 percent of the nitrate industry of Tarapacá; by 1890 its share had risen to at least 70 percent. British penetration of the nitrate areas proceeded not only through formation of companies for direct exploitation of nitrate deposits but through the establishment of banks that financed entrepreneurial activity in the nitrate area and the creation of railways and other companies more or less closely linked to the central nitrate industry. An English railway company with a monopoly of transport in Tarapacá, the Nitrate Railways Company, controlled by John Thomas North, paid dividends of up to 20 and 25 percent, compared with earnings of from 7 to 14 percent for other railway companies in South America.

The Chilean national bourgeoisie, which had pioneered in the establishment of the mining-industrial-railway complex in the Atacama, offered little resistance to the foreign takeover. Lack of strong support from the state, the relative financial weakness of the Chilean bourgeoisie, and the cozy and profitable relationships maintained throughout the nineteenth century between the Chilean elite and British interests facilitated the rapid transfer of Chilean nitrate and railway properties into British hands and the transformation of the Chilean bourgeoisie into a dependent bourgeoisie content with a share in the profits of British companies.

The presidential election of 1881 pitted a conservative military hero of the War of the Pacific, General Manuel Baquedano, against the candidate of a liberal coalition, Domingo Santa María, who won handily. The religious issue, one of the few still separating the new bourgeoisie from the landed aristocracy, dominated his administration (1881–1886). A dispute with the Vatican over its refusal to approve the government's nomination of an archbishop of liberal views led to the expulsion of the apostolic delegate, followed by congressional passage of a series of religious reforms: civil marriage, civil registration of births and deaths, and lay control of some cemeteries. However, the church continued to own extensive properties and receive subsidies from the state. More radical proposals to divorce church and state failed to win approval. In 1884 an electoral reform was adopted; the property qualification for voting was replaced with a literacy test. Since the great majority of Chilean males were illiterate *rotos* (seasonal farm workers) and inquilinos, this change did not materially add to the number of voters; as late as 1915, out of a population of about 3.5 million, only 150,000 persons voted.

The official liberal candidate for president in the election of 1886, José Manuel Balmaceda, had a distinguished record of public service as a diplomat and cabinet minister. As minister of the interior in Santa María's cabinet, he had piloted through Congress the religious reforms just described. Balmaceda took office with a well-defined program of state-directed economic modernization. By the 1880s, factory capitalism had taken root in Chile. In addition to consumer goods industries—flour mills, breweries, leather factories, furniture factories, and the like—there existed foundries and metal-working enterprises that served the mining industry, railways, and agriculture. Balmaceda proposed to consolidate and expand this native industrial capitalism.

Balmaceda's Nationalistic Policies

Balmaceda came to office when government revenues were at an all-time high (they had risen from about 15 million pesos a year before the War of the Pacific to about 45 million pesos in 1887). The chief source of this government income was the export duty on nitrates. Knowing that the proceeds from this source would taper off as the nitrate deposits diminished, Balmaceda wisely planned to employ those funds for the development of an economic infrastructure that would remain when the nitrate was gone. Hence, public works figured prominently in his program. In 1887 he created a new ministry of industry and public works, which expended large sums on extending and improving the telegraphic and railway systems and on the construction of bridges, roads, and docks. Balmaceda also generously endowed public education, needed to provide skilled workers for Chilean industry. During his presidency, the total enrollment in Chilean schools rose in four years from some 79,000 in 1886 to over 150,000 in 1890. He also favored raising the wages of workers but was inconsistent in his labor policy; yielding to strong pressure from foreign and domestic employers, he sent troops to crush a number of strikes.

Central to Balmaceda's program was his determination to "Chileanize" the nitrate industry. In his inaugural address to Congress, he declared that his government would consider what measures it should take "to nationalize industries which are, at present, chiefly of benefit to foreigners," a clear reference to the nitrate industry. Later, Balmaceda's strategy shifted; he encouraged the entrance of Chilean private capital into nitrate production and exportation to prevent the formation of a foreign-dominated nitrate cartel whose interest in restricting output clashed with the government's interest in maintaining a high level of production in order to collect more export taxes. In November 1888, he scolded the Chilean elite for their lack of entrepreneurial spirit:

Why does the credit and the capital which are brought into play in all kinds of speculations in our great cities hold back and leave the foreigner to establish banks at Iquique and abandon to strangers the exploiting of the nitrate works of Tarapacá? . . . The foreigner exploits these riches and takes the profit of native wealth to give to other lands and unknown people the treasures of our soil, our own property and the riches we require.

Balmaceda waged a determined struggle to end the monopoly of the British-owned Nitrate Railways Company, whose prohibitive freight charges reduced production and export of nitrates. His nationalistic policies inevitably provoked the hostility of English nitrate "kings" like North who had close links with the Chilean elite and employed prominent liberal politicians as their legal advisers.

But Balmaceda had many domestic as well as foreign foes. The clericals remembered his leading role in the religious reforms and noted his plans to further curb the powers of the church. The landed aristocracy resented his public works program because it drew labor from agriculture and pushed up rural wages. The banks, whose uncontrolled emission of notes had fed an inflation whose sole beneficiaries were mortgaged landlords and exporters who received payment in foreign currencies, were angered by his proposal to establish a national bank with a monopoly of note issue. The entire oligarchy, liberals as well as conservatives, opposed his use of the central government as an instrument of progressive economic and social change.

Meanwhile, the government's economic problems multiplied, adding to Balmaceda's political difficulties by narrowing his mass base. By 1890 foreign demand for copper and nitrates had weakened. Prices in an overstocked world market fell, and English nitrate interests responded to the crisis by forming a cartel to reduce production. Reduced production and export of nitrates and copper sharply diminished the flow of export duties into the treasury and caused growing unemployment and wage cuts even as inflation cut into the value of wages. The result was a series of great strikes in Valparaíso and the nitrate zone in 1890. Despite his sympathy with the workers' demands and unwillingness to use force against them, Balmaceda, under pressure from domestic and foreign employers, sent troops to crush the strikes. These repressive measures insured much working-class apathy or even hostility toward the president in the eventual confrontation with his foes.

Indeed, Balmaceda had few firm allies at his side when that crisis came. The industrial capitalist group whose growth he had ardently promoted was still weak. The mining interests, increasingly integrated with or dominated by English capital, joined the bankers, the clericals, and the landed aristocracy in opposition to his nationalist program of economic development and independence.

Since the elections of 1888, Balmaceda had lacked a reliable parliamentary majority, a condition that made for a growing deadlock between president and Congress. In October 1890 Balmaceda dismissed a cabinet imposed upon him by the congressional majority and appointed one acceptable to himself. Instead of summoning Congress, which was dominated by a coalition of anti-Balmaceda forces, to pass the budget for 1891, the president simply announced that the 1890 budget would continue in force for the next year. In effect, Balmaceda abolished the system of parliamentary government and returned to the traditional system of presidential rule established by the constitution of 1833. His rash act, made without any serious effort to mobilize popular forces, played into the hands of his enemies, who were already preparing for civil war.

On January 7, 1891, congressional leaders proclaimed a revolt against the president in the name of legality and the constitution. The navy, then as now led by officers of aristocratic descent, promptly went over to the rebels, while most army units remained loyal to the president. A junta headed by fleet captain Jorge Montt assumed direction of the revolt. With navy support, the congressionalists seized the ports and customhouses in the north and established their capital at Iquique, the chief port of Tarapacá.

English-owned enterprises actively aided the rebels. Indeed, by the admission of the British minister at Santiago, "our naval officers and the British community of Valparaíso and all along the coast rendered material assistance to the opposition and committed many breaches of neutrality." Many nitrate workers, alienated by Balmaceda's repression of their strike, remained neutral or even joined the rebel army, organized by a German army officer, General Emil Korner. Having gained control of the north and its vast revenues, the congressionalist forces moved south. Victories over Balmaceda's army in the battles of Concón and Placilla opened the way for capture of Valparaíso and Santiago, forcing the president to seek refuge in the Argentine embassy. On September 19, 1891, the day on which his legal term of office came to an end, Balmaceda put a bullet through his head.

The death of Chile's first anti-imperialist president restored the reign of the oligarchy, a coalition of landowners, bankers, merchants, and mining interests closely linked to English capital. A new era began, the era of the so-called Parliamentary Republic. Taught by experience, the oligarchy now preferred to rule through a Congress divided into various factions rather than through a strong executive. Such decentralization of government favored the interests of the rural aristocracy and its allies. A new law of 1892, vesting local governments with the right to supervise elections both for local and national offices, reinforced the power of the landowners, priests, and political bosses who had fought Balmaceda's progressive policies. The presidents of this period, beginning with Jorge Montt (1891–1896), were little more than puppets pulled by strings in the hands of congressional leaders. Corruption, cynicism, and factional intrigue characterized the political life of the Parliamentary Republic. Members of Congress, who received no salaries, paid large sums to secure election, which gave them access to the ample opportunities for graft on the national level.

The Parliamentary Republic, Foreign Economic Domination, and the Growth of the Working Class

The era of the Parliamentary Republic was accompanied by a growing subordination of the

236 Chilean economy to foreign capital, which was reflected in a steady increase in the foreign debt and foreign ownership of the nation's resources. English investments in Chile amounted to 24 million pounds in 1890; they rose to 64 million pounds in 1913. Of this total, 34.6 million pounds formed part of the Chilean public debt. In the same period, North American and German capital began to challenge the British hegemony in Chile. England continued to be Chile's principal trade partner, but United States and German trade with Chile grew at a faster rate. German instructors also acquired a strong influence in the Chilean army, and the flow of German immigrants into southern Chile continued, resulting in the formation of compact colonies dominated by a Pan-German ideology.

The revival of the Chilean economy from the depression of the early 1890s brought an increase of nitrate, copper, and agricultural exports and further enriched the ruling classes, but it left inquilinos, miners, and factory workers as desperately poor as before. Meanwhile, the working class grew from 120,000 to 250,000 between 1890 and 1900, and the doctrines of trade unionism, socialism, and anarchism achieved growing popularity in its ranks.

Luis Emilio Recabarren (1876–1924), the father of Chilean socialism and communism, played a decisive role in the social and political awakening of the Chilean proletariat. In 1906 Recabarren was elected to Congress from a mining area but was not allowed to take his seat because he refused to take his oath of office on the Bible. In 1909, he organized the Workers Federation of Chile, the first national trade union movement. Three years later, he led the founding of the Socialist party, a revolutionary Marxist movement, and became its first secretary.

The growing self-consciousness and militancy of the Chilean working class found expression in a mounting wave of strikes. Between 1911 and 1920, almost three hundred strikes, involving more than 300,000 workers, took place. Many were crushed with traditional brutal methods that left hundreds and thousands of workers dead.

Brazilian Politics and Economy

The Antislavery Movement

From the close of the Paraguayan War (1870), the slavery question surged forward, becoming the dominant issue in Brazilian political life. Dom Pedro, personally opposed to slavery, was caught in a crossfire between a growing number of liberal leaders, intellectuals, and urban middle-class groups who demanded emancipation and slave owners determined to postpone the inevitable as long as possible. In 1870 Spain freed all the newborn and aged slaves of Cuba and Puerto Rico, leaving Brazil the only nation in the Americas to retain slavery in its original colonial form. Yielding to pressure, a conservative ministry pushed through parliament the Rio Branco Law in 1871. This measure freed all newborn children of slaves but obligated the masters to care for them until they reached the age of eight. At that time, owners could either release the children to the government in return for an indemnity or retain them as laborers until they reached the age of twenty-one. The law also freed all slaves belonging to the state or crown and created a fund to be used for the manumission of slaves.

The Rio Branco Law was a tactical retreat designed to put off a final solution of the slavery problem. The imperial government applied the law with ponderous slowness, the compensation fund was never large enough to buy the freedom of many slaves, and few slave owners came forward to redeem slave children for money. As late as 1884, when Brazil still had over a million slaves, only 113 had been freed by this means. Given the option of exploiting the labor of these children until they reached the age of twenty-one or exchanging them for government bonds, the great majority of slave owners chose the first course. Regarding them as temporary property, masters often worked these "free" children very hard; even after they reached the age of twenty-one, tradition and lack of education tended to keep them in a condition of semibondage. In effect, the Rio Branco Law gave an indefinite stay of execution to Brazilian slavery.

Slaves drying coffee on a plantation in Terreiros, in the state of Rio de Janeiro, about 1882.

Abolitionist leaders denounced the law as a sham and illusion and advanced ever more vigorously the demand for total and immediate emancipation. From 1880 on, the antislavery movement developed great momentum. Concentrated in the cities, it drew strength from the process of economic, social, and intellectual modernization under way there. To the new urban groups, slavery was an anachronism, glaringly incompatible with modernization. Among the slave owners themselves, divisions of opinion appeared. In the north, where slavery had long been dying as a result of the sale of the best slaves south and where many of those who remained were aged or dying, a growing number of planters converted to the use of free labor, drawing on the pool of freedmen made available by the Rio Branco Law and the *sertanejos* (inhabitants of the interior), poor whites and mixed-bloods who lived on the fringes of the plantation economy. Another factor in the decline of the slave population of the northeast was the great drought of 1877–1879, which caused many of the region's wealthier folk to abandon the area. Some sold their slaves before departing for Rio; others brought slaves with them. In states like Amazonas and Ceará, where black slaves were few and most of the work was done by Indians and mixed-bloods, the move to emancipation was relatively easy; in 1884 both of these states declared the end of slavery within their borders. By contrast, the coffee planters of Rio de Janeiro, São

238   Paulo, and Minas Gerais, joined by northern planters who trafficked in slaves, selling them to the coffee zone, offered the most tenacious resistance to the advance of abolition.

The abolitionist movement produced leaders of remarkable intellectual and moral stature. One was Joaquim Nabuco, son of a distinguished liberal statesman of the empire, whose eloquent dissection and indictment of slavery, *O abolicionismo,* had a profound impact on its readers. Another was a mulatto journalist, José de Patrocinio, a master propagandist noted for his fiery, biting style. Another mulatto, André Rebouças, an engineer and teacher whose intellectual gifts won him the respect and friendship of the emperor, was a leading organizer of the movement. For Nabuco and his comrades-in-arms, the antislavery struggle was the major front in a larger struggle for the transformation of Brazilian society. Abolition, they hoped, would pave the way for the attainment of other goals: land reform, public education, and political democracy.

Yielding to mounting pressure, parliament adopted another measure on September 28, 1885, that liberated all slaves when they reached the age of sixty but required them to continue to serve their masters for three years and forbade them to leave their place of residence for five years. These conditions, added to the fact that few slaves lived beyond the age of sixty-five, implied little change in the status of the vast majority of slaves. The imperial government also promised to purchase the freedom of the remaining slaves in fourteen years—a promise that few took seriously, in the light of experience with the Rio Branco Law. Convinced that the new law was another tactical maneuver, the abolitionists spurned all compromise solutions and demanded immediate, unconditional emancipation.

By the middle 1880s, the antislavery movement had assumed massive proportions and a more militant character. Large numbers of slaves began to vote for freedom with their feet; they were aided by abolitionists who organized an underground railway that ran from São Paulo to Ceará, where slavery had ended. Efforts to secure the return of fugitive slaves encountered growing resistance. Army officers, organized in a *Club Militar,* protested against the use of the army for the pursuit of fugitive slaves.

In February 1887 São Paulo liberated all slaves in the city with funds raised by popular subscription. Many slave owners, seeing the handwriting on the wall, liberated their slaves on condition that they remain at work for some time longer. By the end of 1887, even the die-hard coffee planters of São Paulo were ready to adjust to new conditions by offering to pay wages to their slaves and improve their working and living conditions; they also increased efforts to induce European immigrants to come to São Paulo. These efforts were highly successful; the flow of immigrants into São Paulo rose from 6,600 in 1885 to over 32,000 in 1887 and to 90,000 in 1888. As a result, coffee production reached record levels. With its labor problem solved, São Paulo was ready to abandon its resistance and even join the abolitionist crusade.

When parliament met on May 3, 1888, to deliberate again on the slavery question, the institution was in its last throes. By overwhelming majorities, both houses of parliament approved a measure whose laconic text read: "Article 1. From the date of this law slavery is declared abolished in Brazil. Article 2. All contrary provisions are revoked." Princess Isabel, ruling as regent for Dom Pedro, who was in Europe for medical treatment, signed the bill on May 13. Contrary to a traditional interpretation, however, the decision of May 1888 was not the climax of a gradual process of slavery's decline and the peaceful acceptance of the inevitable by the slave owners. The total slave population dropped sharply only after 1885, as a result of abolitionist agitation, mass flights of slaves, armed clashes, and other upheavals that appeared to many conservatives to threaten anarchy. In effect, abolition had come not through reform but by revolution.

The aftermath of abolition refuted the dire predictions of its foes. Freed from the burdens of slavery and aided by the continuance of very high world coffee prices (until about 1896), Brazil made more economic progress in a few years than it had during the almost seven decades of imperial rule. For the former slaves, however, little had changed. The abolitionist demand for the grant of land to the freedmen was forgotten. Relationships between former masters and slaves in many places remained largely unchanged; tradition and the economic and political power of the fazendeiros gave them almost absolute control over their former slaves. Denied land and education, victims of prejudices inherited from the days of slavery, the freedmen were assigned the hardest, most poorly paid jobs. Fazendeiros replaced freedmen with immigrants in the coffee plantations; in the cities, black artisans lost their jobs to immigrants.

The Fall of the Monarchy

Abolition dragged down slavery's sister institution—the monarchy. The empire had long rested on the support of the planter class, especially the northern planters, who saw in the empire a guarantee of the survival of slavery. Before 1888, the Republican party had its principal base among the coffee interests, who resented the favor shown by the imperial government to the sugar planters and wished to achieve a political power corresponding to their economic power. Now, angered by abolition and embittered by the failure of the crown to indemnify them for their lost slaves, those planters who had not previously shifted to the use of free labor joined the Republican movement. The monarchy that had served the interest of the regional elites for the previous sixty-seven years had lost its reasons for existence.

Republicanism and a closely allied ideology, positivism, also made many converts in the officer class, disgruntled by what it regarded as neglect and mistreatment of the armed forces by the imperial government. Many of the younger officers came from the new urban middle class or, if of aristocratic descent, were discontented with the ways of their fathers. Positivism, it has been said, became "the gospel of the military academy," where it was brilliantly expounded by a popular young professor of mathematics, Benjamin Constant Botelho de Magalhães, a devoted disciple of Auguste Comte, the doctrine's founder. The positivist doctrine, with its stress on science, its ideal of a dictatorial republic, and its distrust of the masses, fitted the needs of urban middle-class groups, progressive officers, and businessmen-fazendeiros who wanted modernization but without drastic changes in land tenure and class relations.

In June 1889 the liberal ministry headed by the Viscount of Ouro Prêto made a last effort to save the monarchy by proposing a reform program that included extension of the suffrage, autonomy for the provinces, and land reform. It was too late. On November 15, a military revolt organized and headed by Benjamin Constant and Marshal Floriano Peixoto overthrew the government and proclaimed a republic with Marshal Deodoro da Fonseca as provisional chief of state. Like the revolution that gave Brazil its independence, the republican revolution came from above; the coup d'état encountered little resistance but also inspired little enthusiasm. Although the provisional government included some sincere reformers like Ruy Barbosa, a champion of public education and civil liberties, the radical wing of the abolitionist movement was excluded. Power was firmly held by representatives of the business and landed elites and the military.

The new rulers promptly promulgated a series of reforms. On November 15, 1889, the same day that Brazil was proclaimed a republic, a decree ended corporal punishment in the army; on November 19, a literacy test replaced property qualifications for voting (since property and literacy usually went together, this measure did not significantly enlarge the electorate); and in January 1891, successive decrees separated church and state and established civil marriage.

The New Republic

In November 1891, two years after the revolt, a constituent assembly met in Rio de Janeiro to draft a constitution for the new republic. The draft offered for approval by the assembly provided for a federal, presidential form of government with the customary three branches—legislative, executive, and judicial. The principal debate was between the partisans of greater autonomy for the states and those who feared the divisive results of an extreme federalism. The coffee interests, which dominated the wealthy south central region, sought to strengthen their position at the expense of the central power. The bourgeois groups, represented in the convention chiefly by lawyers, favored a strong central government that could promote industry, aid the creation of a national market, and offer protection from British competition.

The result was a compromise tilted in favor of federalism. The twenty provinces in effect became self-governing states with popularly elected governors, the exclusive right to tax exports (a profitable privilege for wealthy states like São Paulo and Minas Gerais), and the right to maintain militias. The national government was given control over the tariff and the income from import duties, while the president obtained very large powers: he designated his cabinet ministers and other high officers, he could declare a state of siege, and he could intervene in the states with the federal armed forces in the event of a threat to their political institutions. The constitution proclaimed the sanctity of private property and guaranteed freedom of the press, speech, and assembly.

If these freedoms had some relevance in the cities and hinterlands touched by the movement of modernization, they lacked meaning over the greater part of the national territory. The fazendeiros, former slave owners, virtually monopolized the nation's chief wealth, its land. The land monopoly gave them absolute control over the rural population. Feudal and semifeudal forms of land tenure, accompanied by the obligation of personal and military service on the part of tenants, survived in the backlands, especially in the northeast. Powerful *coronéis* (colonels) maintained armies of *jagunços* (full-time private soldiers) and waged war against each other.[2] Banditry flourished in the interior, the bandits sometimes hiring themselves out to the coronéis,

sometimes operating on their own, and occasionally gaining the reputation of modern Robin Hoods.

In this medieval atmosphere of constant insecurity and social disintegration, there arose messianic movements that reflected the aspirations of the oppressed sertanejos for peace and justice. One of the most important of such movements arose in the interior of Bahia, where the principal activity was cattle raising. In this area appeared a messiah called Antônio Conselheiro (Anthony the Counselor), who established a settlement at the abandoned cattle ranch of Canudos. Rejecting private property, Antônio required all who joined his sacred company to give up their goods, but he promised a future of prosperity in his messianic kingdom through the sharing of the treasure of the "lost Sebastian" (the Portuguese king who had disappeared in Africa in 1478 but would return as a redeemer) or through division of the property of hostile landowners.

Despite its religious coloration, the existence of such a focus of social and political unrest was intolerable to the fazendeiros and the state authorities. When the sertanejos easily defeated state forces sent against them in 1896, the governor called on the federal government for aid. Four campaigns, the last a large-scale operation directed by the minister of war in person, were required to break the epic resistance of the men, women, and children of Canudos, nearly all of whom were killed in the final assault by the national army. A Brazilian literary masterpiece, *Os sertões* (Rebellion in the Backlands) by Euclides da Cunha (1856–1909), immortalized the heroism of the defenders and the crimes of the victors. It also revealed to the urban elite another and unfamiliar side of Brazilian reality.

The Economic Revolution

An enormous historical gulf separated the bleak sertão—in which the tragedy of Canudos was played out—from the cities, the scene of a mushrooming growth of banks, stock exchanges, and corporations. With the economic revolution came a revolution in manners. In Rio de Janeiro, writes Pedro Calmon,

[2] The title *coronel* was often honorary and did not necessarily indicate a military command or landownership; especially after 1870, a coronel might be simply a political boss, a merchant, or even an influential lawyer or priest.

barons with recently acquired titles jostled each other in the corridors of the Stock Exchange or in the Rua da Alfandega, buying and selling stocks; the tilburies [light two-wheeled carriages] that filled the length of São Francisco Street were taken by a multitude of millionaires of recent vintage—commercial agents, bustling lawyers, promoters of all kinds, politicians of the new generation, the men of the day.

A few more years and even the physical appearance of some of Brazil's great urban centers would change. These changes were most marked in the federal capital of Rio de Janeiro, which was made into a beautiful and healthful city between 1902 and 1906 through the initiative and efforts of Prefect Pereira Passos, who mercilessly demolished the narrow old streets to permit the construction of broad, modern avenues, and the distinguished scientist Oswaldo Cruz, who waged a victorious struggle to conquer the endemic malaria and yellow fever by filling in swamps and installing adequate water and sewerage systems.

The economic policies of the new republican regime reflected pressures from different quarters: from the planter class, from urban capitalists, from the military. Many planters, left in a difficult position by the abolition of slavery, required subsidies and credits to enable them to convert to the new wage system. The emerging industrial bourgeoisie, convinced that Brazil must develop an industrial base in order to emerge from backwardness, asked for protective tariffs, the construction of an economic infrastructure, and policies favorable to capital formation. Within the provisional government, these aspirations had a fervent supporter in the minister of finance, Ruy Barbosa, who believed that the factory was the crucible in which an "intelligent and independent democracy" would be forged in Brazil. Finally, the army, whose decisive role in the establishment of the republic had given it great prestige and influence, called for increased appropriations for the armed services. Their demands far exceeded the revenue available to the federal and state governments.

The federal government solved this problem by resorting to the printing press and allowing private banks to issue notes backed by little more than faith in the future of Brazil. In two years, the volume of paper money in circulation doubled, and the foreign exchange value of the Brazilian monetary unit, the *milréis*, plummeted disastrously. Since objective economic conditions (the small internal market and the lack of an adequate technological base, among other factors) limited the real potential for Brazilian growth, much of the newly created capital was used for highly speculative purposes, including the creation of fictitious companies.

The great boom collapsed in 1891, bringing ruin to many investors and unemployment to workers even as inflation continued to cut into the real value of their wages. Disputes over methods of coping with the crisis contributed to a clash between President Deodoro da Fonseca and Congress when it assembled for its first session in November 1891. When da Fonseca attempted to dissolve Congress and assume dictatorial power, the army and navy turned against him. Faced with a threat from the navy to bombard Rio, the president resigned and was succeeded by his vice president, Marshal Floriano Peixoto.

Under Peixoto, the urban middle-class sector gained even greater influence in the government, and inflation continued unchecked. The rise in the cost of many imported items to almost prohibitive levels stimulated the growth of Brazilian manufactures: the number of such enterprises almost doubled between 1890 and 1895. The discontent of the "outs" sparked a new revolt with strong aristocratic and monarchical overtones in 1893. The movement began in Rio Grande do Sul and was soon joined by the navy, a stronghold of aristocratic prejudice and influence. Peixoto's firm refusal to bow to threats of a naval bombardment of the capital brought a collapse of the fleet revolt and allowed the governments to launch an offensive south against the rebels of Rio Grande; by August 1895 the last insurgents had surrendered.

Peixoto's victory, which won him the name of "consolidator of the republic," was largely due to the loyalty and financial and military support of the state of São Paulo. But this support came at

242 a price; the coffee planters were resolved to end the ascendancy of the urban middle classes, whose policies of rapid industrialization they distrusted and held responsible for the financial instability that had plagued the first years of the republic. In 1893 the old planter oligarchies, whose divisions had temporarily enabled the middle classes to gain the upper hand in coalition with the military, reunited to form the Federal Republican party, with a program of support for federalism and fiscal responsibility. Since they controlled the electoral machinery, they easily elected Prudente de Morais president in 1894. Morais, the first civilian president of Brazil (1894–1898), initiated an era marked by the renewed domination of the coffee interests and the relegation of urban capitalist groups to a secondary role in political life.

Morais' successor, Manuel Ferraz de Campos Sales (1898–1902), continued and expanded his program of giving primacy to agriculture. Campos Sales fully endorsed the system of the international economic division of labor as it applied to Brazil. "It is time," he proclaimed, "that we take the correct road; to that end we must strive to export all that we can produce better than other countries, and import all that other countries can produce better than we." This formula confirmed the continuity of neocolonialism from the empire through the early republic. Determined to halt inflation, Campos Sales drastically reduced expenditures on public works, increased taxes, and made every effort to redeem the paper money in order to improve Brazil's international credit and secure new loans to cover shortfalls in government revenues.

Coffee was king. Whereas in the period from 1880 to 1889, Brazil produced only 56 percent of the world's coffee output, in the period from 1900 to 1904 it accounted for 76 percent of the total production. Its closest competitor, rubber, supplied only 28 percent of Brazil's exports in 1901. Sugar, once the ruler of the Brazilian economy, now accounted for barely 5 percent of the nation's exports. Minas Gerais and especially São Paulo became the primary coffee regions, while Rio de Janeiro declined in importance. Enjoying immense advantages—the famous rich, porous *terra roxa* (red soil), an abundance of immigrant labor, and closeness to the major port of Santos—the *Paulistas* harvested 60 percent of the national coffee production.

The coffee boom from the late 1880s through the mid-1890s soon led to overproduction, falling prices, and the accumulation of unsold stocks after 1896. Because coffee trees came into production only four years after planting, the effects of expansion into the western frontier of São Paulo continued to be felt even after prices fell; between 1896 and 1900 the number of producing trees in São Paulo alone went from 150 million to 570 million. Large international coffee-trading firms controlled the world market, and they added to planters' difficulties by paying depressed prices during the height of each season and selling off their reserves in periods of relative shortage when prices edged up.

Responding to the planters' clamor for help, the São Paulo government took the first step for the "defense" of coffee in 1902, forbidding new coffee plantings for five years. Other steps soon proved necessary. Faced with a bumper crop in 1906, São Paulo launched a coffee price-support scheme to protect the state's economic lifeblood. With financing from British, French, German, and North American banks, and the eventual collaboration of the federal government, São Paulo purchased several million bags of coffee and held them off the market in an effort to maintain profitable price levels. Purchases continued into 1907; from that date until World War I the stocks were gradually sold off with little market disruption. The operation's principal gainers were the foreign merchants and bankers who, since they controlled the Coffee Commission formed to liquidate the purchased stocks, gradually disposed of them with a large margin of profit. The problem, temporarily exorcised, was presently to return in even more acute form.

The valorization scheme, which favored the coffee-raising states at the expense of the rest, reflected the coffee planters' political domination. Under President Campos Sales, this ascendancy was institutionalized by the so-called *poli-*

tica dos governadores (politics of the governors). Its essence was a formula that gave the two richest and most populous states (São Paulo and Minas Gerais) a virtual monopoly of federal politics and the choice of presidents. Thus, the first three civilian presidents from 1894 to 1906 came from São Paulo; the next two, from 1906 to 1910, came from Minas Gerais and Rio de Janeiro, respectively.

In return, the oligarchies of the other states were given almost total freedom of action within their jurisdictions, the central government intervening as a rule only when it suited the local oligarchy's interest. Informal discussions among the state governors determined the choice of president, with his election a foregone conclusion. No official candidate for president lost an election before 1930. In 1910 the distinguished statesman and orator Ruy Barbosa ran for president on a platform of democratic reform and antimilitarism against the official candidate, Hermes da Fonseca, a conservative military man. Barbosa was beaten by almost two to one; out of a population of 22 million, about 360,000 voted. Similar reciprocal arrangements existed on the state level between the governors and the coronéis, urban or rural bosses who rounded up the local vote to elect the governors and were rewarded with a free hand in their respective domains.

Despite the official bias in favor of agriculture, industry continued to grow in the period from 1904 to 1914. By 1908 Brazil could boast of more than three thousand industrial enterprises. Foreign firms dominated the fields of banking, public works, utilities, transportation, and the export and import trade. Manufacturing, on the other hand, was carried on almost exclusively by native Brazilians and permanent immigrants. This national industry was concentrated in the four states of São Paulo, Minas Gerais, Rio de Janeiro, and Rio Grande do Sul. Heavy industry did not exist; over half of the enterprises were textile mills and food-processing plants. Many of these "enterprises" were small workshops employing a few artisans or operated with an archaic technology, and Brazilians in the market economy

continued to import most quality products. The quantitative and qualitative development of industry was hampered by the semifeudal conditions prevailing in the countryside, by the extreme poverty of the masses, which sharply limited the internal market, by the lack of a skilled, literate labor force (as late as 1910, Brazil had an enrollment of only 566,000 pupils out of a population of 22 million, and the great majority received less than two years of formal instruction), and by the hostility of most fazendeiros and foreign interests to industry.

Together with industry there arose a working class destined to play a significant role in the life of the country. The Brazilian proletariat was partly recruited from sharecroppers and minifundio peasants fleeing to the cities to escape dismal poverty and the tyranny of coronéis, but above all it was composed of the flood of European immigrants, who arrived at a rate of 100,000 to 150,000 each year. Working and living conditions of the working class were often intolerable. Child labor was common, for children could be legally employed from the age of twelve. The workday ranged from nine hours for some skilled workers to more than sixteen hours for various categories of unskilled workers. Wages were pitifully low and often paid in vouchers redeemable at the company store. There was a total absence of legislation to protect workers against the hazards of unemployment, old age, or industrial accidents.

Among the European immigrants were many militants with socialist, syndicalist, or social-democratic backgrounds who helped to organize the Brazilian labor movement and gave it a radical political orientation. National and religious divisions among workers, widespread illiteracy, and quarrels between socialists and anarcho-syndicalists hampered the rise of a trade union movement and a labor party.

But trade unions grew rapidly after 1900 in response to unsatisfactory working conditions, with immigrant workers often providing the leadership. In 1906 the first national labor congress, representing the majority of the country's trade unions, met and began a struggle for the eight-

244   hour workday. One result of the congress was the formation of the first national trade union organization, the Brazilian Labor Confederation, which conducted a number of strikes. Repression was the typical answer of the authorities and employers to labor's demands. Police conducted periodic roundups of labor leaders. Immigrants were deported, while native-born leaders were imprisoned or sent to forced labor on a railroad under construction in distant Mato Grosso. The phrase "the social question is a question for the police" was often used to sum up the labor policy of the Brazilian state.

Chapter 11

Society and Culture in the Nineteenth Century

Independence left much of the colonial social structure intact. This fact was very apparent to liberal leaders of the postindependence era. "The war against Spain," declared the Colombian liberal Ramón Mercado in 1853, "was not a revolution. . . . Independence only scratched the surface of the social problem, without changing its essential nature." A modern historian, Charles C. Griffin, comes to much the same conclusion. "Only the beginnings of a basic transformation took place," he writes, "and there were many ways in which colonial attitudes and institutions carried over into the life of republican Spanish America."

How New Was the New Society?

We should not minimize, however, the extent and importance of the changes that did take place. Independence produced, if not a major social upheaval, at least a minor one. It opened wide fissures within the elite, dividing aristocratic supporters of the old social order from modernizers who wanted a more democratic, bourgeois order. Their struggle is an integral aspect of the first half-century after the end of Spanish and Portuguese rule. Independence also enabled such formerly submerged groups as artisans and gauchos to enter the political arena, although in subordinate roles, and even allowed a few to climb into the ranks of the elite. The opening of Latin American ports to foreign goods also established a relatively free market in ideas, at least in the capitals and other cities. With almost no time lag, such new European doctrines as utopian socialism, romanticism, and positivism entered Latin America and were applied to the solution of

Part 3

Latin America in the Twentieth Century

262 The complexity of Latin America's political and economic evolution in the twentieth century seems to require an overview of the process that will enable us to comprehend it as a whole. In Part 3, our survey of Latin American history broadens to include three Andean republics with predominantly Indian populations (Peru, Bolivia, and Ecuador); Cuba, the scene of a socialist revolution with continental repercussions; and three Central American countries where social revolutionary movements are in various stages of development (Nicaragua, El Salvador, and Guatemala). In addition we look at Mexico, Argentina, Chile, Brazil, and the Bolivarian lands of Venezuela and Colombia.

The struggle of Latin America's peoples to eliminate neocolonialism and *latifundismo,* the chief obstacles to the achievement of a more just economic and social order, gives meaning and direction to the turbulent flow of modern Latin American history. Viewed in the large, that history, with all its contradictory aspects, its gains and setbacks, appears to form a sequence of stages, each representing a higher level of effort to achieve complete economic and political emancipation. Such an overview inevitably ignores the great differences between the Latin American countries but it helps make clear the general unity of problems and the common direction of movement of all the Latin American states.

1910–1930

The Mexican Revolution of 1910 and the start of World War I offer two points of departure for this period. The Revolution swiftly developed into the first major effort in Latin American history to uproot the system of great estates and peonage and curb foreign control of the area's natural resources. The famous constitution of 1917 spelled out this social content of the revolution. In the leadership struggle between agrarian and bourgeois revolutionaries, the latter emerged victorious and adopted a program that subordinated the interests of peasants and workers to the goals

of rapid capitalist development. Despite the discrepancies between its professed social ideals and its achievements, the Revolution unleashed creative energies in art, literature, and the social sciences that gave Mexico a leading role in the cultural life of Latin America.

World War I seriously disrupted the markets for Latin America's goods and placed difficulties in the way of importing needed manufactured goods. As a result, some local capital and labor were diverted from agriculture to manufacturing in an effort to supply these goods. Although the postwar period saw some revival of the export economy, declines in the price levels of Latin America's exports encouraged a further growth of manufacturing. But at the end of this period, industrialization was still almost completely limited to light consumer goods industries.

The United States, which emerged from World War I as the world's principal industrial and financial power, soon replaced Great Britain as the major source of foreign investments in Latin America. Continuing the "big stick" and "dollar diplomacy" policies of their predecessors, Democratic and Republican administrations used armed intervention and economic pressure to expand United States control over the Caribbean area. By the end of the period, deep Latin American resentment of these strong-arm tactics had forced Republican policy makers to consider a change in dealing with Latin America.

1930–1945

The Great Depression dramatically exposed the vulnerability of a neocolonial, monocultural economy: the area's foreign markets collapsed, and the prices of its raw materials and foodstuffs fell much more sharply than those of the manufactured goods it had to import. Latin America's unfavorable balance of trade made necessary exchange controls and other trade restrictions that encouraged the growth of industries to produce goods formerly supplied through importation. World War II, which caused a virtual suspension of imports of manufactured goods, gave further stimulus to the movement for Latin American industrialization.

The nationalist temper of the times also found expression in the formation of state enterprises in such fields as oil exploitation and in efforts to nationalize some foreign-owned utilities and natural resources. The most dramatic example of this trend was the seizure of foreign oil properties in Mexico by President Lázaro Cárdenas in 1938. The new nationalist regimes also made concessions to labor in the form of social legislation but maintained tight control over working-class organizations.

By 1945 the movement for Latin American industrialization could point to some successes. Consumer goods industries had arisen in all the Latin American republics, and some countries had laid the foundations of heavy industry. Industrial development, however, was everywhere hampered by shortages of capital, lack of advanced technology, and the extremely low purchasing power of the masses. Latin American economists often related these deficiencies to such background conditions as latifundismo and its corollary of wretchedly small farms (minifundismo), widespread disease and illiteracy, and absorption of a large part of the area's economic surplus by foreign investors in the form of dividends, interest, and the like. Meanwhile, aside from the massive assault of Lázaro Cárdenas on the Mexican latifundio, little or nothing was done in the way of agrarian reform.

In the same period, the United States, reacting to the diplomatic and economic losses caused by the old-style imperialism and a wave of "anti-Yanqui" feeling throughout the continent, adopted the Good Neighbor Policy, which proclaimed the principle of nonintervention by one American state in the affairs of another. But the policy represented more of a change in form than in content. Washington's friendly, cooperative relations with such tyrannies as those of Anastasio Somoza in Nicaragua, Rafael Trujillo in the Dominican Republic, and Fulgencio Batista in Cuba insured a continuance of North American hegemony in the Caribbean. For the rest, the immense economic power of the United States in Latin America, exercised through investments and its role as the area's main trading partner, usually sufficed to obtain approval of its policies in most parts of the continent.

1945–1959

In the new postwar era, the Latin American drive to industrialize continued, but after 1950 the pace of advance slowed and the industrialization process underwent a certain deformation. Perceiving the changes taking place in the Latin American society and economy as a result of industrialization and the growth of urban markets, foreign firms began to shift the bulk of their new investments from agricultural and mining activities to manufacturing. This shift allowed them to leap over tariff walls and penetrate the Latin American market. The immensely superior resources of foreign firms and their advanced technology gave them a great advantage over national companies. The result was that many small and middle-sized national companies fell or were swallowed up by subsidiaries of foreign firms.

A favorite device of foreign economic penetration was the mixed company, dominated by foreign capital, with native capitalists reduced to the role of junior partners or directors. The huge sums exported annually by foreign companies in profits, dividends, and other types of income led to a process of "decapitalization" that slowed down the rate of Latin American capital accumulation and industrial growth.

The failure to modernize archaic agrarian structures and improve income distribution also held back industrialization. Indeed, the experience of those countries that had the largest growth of capitalism, such as Brazil and Argentina, suggested that the new industrial and financial oligarchies were as fearful of social change, as prone to come to terms with foreign economic interests, as the old landed aristocracy had been. In the 1950s, a number of leading South American countries moved to the right.

mately $2.20 to their home countries. To cover the deficits in their balance of payments, Latin American countries had to borrow from Western bankers at interest rates that reached double digit figures by 1980.

By 1982, with their national treasuries almost empty of foreign exchange, a number of major Latin American countries faced the prospect of immediate default. This posed immense dangers to the international banking system, for defaults by Mexico and Brazil alone could wipe out 95 percent of the capital of the nine largest U.S. banks. Defaults were averted by emergency aid packages provided by Western governments and bankers in return for agreements by the recipient governments to carry out "austerity" programs that further reduced the living standards of their workers and peasants. Nevertheless the problem had been postponed, not resolved. There was no prospect that even a portion of the huge Latin American debt could be repaid without large write-offs and long delays in payment. Meanwhile the flow of new loans by commercial banks sharply declined.

In the later 1980s, despite populist rhetoric about resisting the tyranny of the International Monetary Fund and the World Bank, which monitored debtor countries' compliance with the "structural adjustment programs"—privatization of state companies, an end to subsidies, opening their economies to foreign investment—imposed as a condition for new loans, Latin American governments did little more than demand reschedulings and lower interest payments. Recent efforts by Latin American governments to reduce their debt burdens under the Brady Plan proposed by the United States include debt-bond swaps, in which foreign debt is exchanged at a discount for new government bonds, and debt-equity swaps, in which foreign debt is exchanged for equity, i.e., shares in local companies. None of this has made a serious dent in the region's foreign debt, which grew between 1990 and 1993 from $439 billion to $487 billion, an increase of 10 percent. In the same period exports grew from $121.8 billion to $132.9 billion, less than 8 percent. The debt problem is complicated by the fact that Latin America's imports are growing more rapidly than its exports, with the area's balance of payments deficit rising from $6,171 billion in 1990 to $42,570 billion in 1993. Without an expansion of exports, a new debt crisis is likely to arise. Meanwhile, major Western banks have reduced their Latin American exposure by selling parts of the debt at a discount, by setting aside huge reserves to cover possible losses on loans to developing countries, and by the debt-bond swaps and debt-equity swaps mentioned above.

The United States under Presidents Reagan and Bush, using debt as a weapon of coercion, played a leading role in imposing the neoliberal or "structural adjustment" system of austerity, privatization, and free trade on Latin America. The logical next step was the incorporation of Latin America into a U.S.-dominated Western Hemisphere common market that would aid the United States in its competition with Japan and the European Community. A major move toward that goal was approval of the North American Free Trade Agreement with Mexico (1993), negotiated by the Bush administration and pushed through Congress by President Bill Clinton. By eliminating remaining tariff restrictions and restrictions on investment, the pact ensured that Mexico would become a cheap-labor preserve for American industry, with a likely loss of better-paying jobs in the United States. The opening of Mexico to U.S. low-cost agricultural products, especially corn, was expected to have a devastating effect on less efficient and less productive Mexican small farmers. Similar pacts were planned with other Latin American countries, beginning with Chile. The fragility of the foundations on which the hemispheric free trade project was based became apparent in December 1994. Hoping to deal with a huge account deficit financed with borrowed money, incoming Mexican President Ernesto Zedillo Ponce de León announced a surprise currency devaluation designed to reduce imports and spur exports. In a replay of the 1982 debt crisis, Mexico faced a new round of inflation and possible debt default, with the prospect of a shrinking economy, large losses to foreign private investors, and more austerity and hardship for Mexico's long-suffering people.

The chapters that follow document in detail the staggering economic and social costs of the neoliberal or structural adjustment program for Latin America. Here we offer a few social indicators of Latin American "underdevelopment": Between 1980 and 1990 the number of poor people in the region increased by 66 million. Nine out of every twenty inhabitants live in conditions of "critical poverty," meaning they do not have the means to acquire a basic family food basket. One hundred fifty million children live in poverty, and 15 percent of children die before the age of five. Out of every 1,000 children born in Central America, 300 are born in homes without safe drinking water, 150 are born underweight, and 56 die before their first birthday.

In order to emerge from underdevelopment, Latin American countries will have to adopt more autonomous, inward-directed strategies of development based on more rational exploitation of human and natural resources. But such strategies cannot be implemented without profound changes in the relations between Latin America and the developed countries and in Latin America's economic and social structures, particularly in land tenure and use, ownership of industry, and income distribution. Nor can such strategies be implemented without a democratization of Latin American political life that would allow popular interests and wishes to influence the direction of economic and social policy.

In the early eighties, in fact, it appeared that a democratic revival had begun as the reactionary tide of the 1970s began to recede and in country after country—Argentina, Brazil, Bolivia, Uruguay—discredited military regimes gave way to popularly elected governments. By 1990 the last military or personal dictatorships, in Chile and Paraguay, had fallen. In part because of the long repression of left-wing parties and trade union movements, the emerging democratic movements of the 1980s and 1990s as a rule had a centrist or conservative complexion. Often they cultivated accommodation with the former military rulers, granting pardons or amnesties for their crimes, and thus perpetuated a climate of impunity for human rights abuses. Sometimes, too, the new democratic regimes displayed a broad authoritarian streak, resorting to free use of rule by decree to bypass Congress and other arbitrary measures. Peruvian President Alberto Fujimori's seizure of power by a "self-coup" (*autogolpe*) (1992) and the overthrow of President Jean-Bertrand Aristide by Haiti's military leaders (1991) revealed the fragility of the recent democratic revival.

None of the new democracies made a clean break with the failed economic policies of the past. This was reflected in their usual acquiescence in payment of the immense foreign debt and their acceptance of the harsh neoliberal remedies prescribed by the International Monetary Fund and the World Bank. In particular, the acceptance by Latin America's old and new democracies of privatization and tariff-reduction policies represented a virtual abandonment of half a century of struggle to achieve independent capitalist development. To date, in countries like Mexico, Brazil, Argentina, Venezuela, Peru, and Bolivia, these policies have resulted in increases in unemployment and declines in living standards, relieved in Peru and Bolivia by a thriving informal or underground economy based on the production of coca and cocaine. The reliance of Peru and Bolivia on the demand for cocaine in the United States and Europe represents a grotesque new kind of Latin American "dependency" on the advanced countries.

Not all political signs pointed to the right. In Uruguay's 1994 general elections a left-wing coalition ended the country's traditional two-party system by winning one-third of the vote and seats in Congress and strengthening its control of Montevideo, with half the country's population. In a 1994 referendum in Argentina, a left-center coalition emerged as the country's third most powerful political force. In Brazil's 1994 general elections the socialist Workers Party's candidate for president lost to a right-wing candidate (who professed to represent the "viable left"), but the party doubled its representation in the lower house of Congress and remained the only significant political opposition. In Haiti, in the first democratic election in the country's history, a left-wing priest was elected president by a landslide in 1990, but was ousted by a military coup in 1991, then returned to power by a U.S.-brokered deal with the military, backed by U.S. troops, in October 1994. Signs of exhaustion and growing rejection of the neoliberal model multiplied in 1993–1994, as candidates who claimed they opposed it, or at least wanted to mitigate its harmful effects, were elected to the presidency in Venezuela, Honduras, Costa Rica, Panama, and Colombia. The dramatic revolt led by the self-styled Zapatista Army of National Liberation in the Mexican state of Chiapas in January 1994 has been called an "armed critique" of Mexico's neoliberal policies.

Central America in the 1980s and early 1990s continued to be the scene of struggles between the forces of revolution and counterrevolution. In 1990 peace came at last to Nicaragua, whose Sandinista government had resisted for almost ten years the implacable efforts of the United States to topple it. Weary of war and hunger, Nicaraguans voted in a conservative president and congress, but the Sandinistas maintained a strong political presence, defended as best they could the structural reforms achieved during their tenure, and prepared to try to return to power in the election of 1996.

In El Salvador, another long struggle continued between a leftist guerrilla army and a repressive regime supported by the United States. In 1989 a formidable guerrilla offensive forced the right-wing government to the bargaining table, and by January 1992 the two sides had reached a U.N.-sponsored agreement that provided for a sweeping reduction and cleansing of the armed forces and full integration of the insurgents into the country's political life. In March 1994, for the first time in the country's history, a leftist coalition took part in general elections that were far from being free and fair but established a substantial presence in the national legislature.

In Guatemala, where a CIA-organized coup had overthrown a democratic reformist government in 1954, another guerrilla movement revived after temporary defeats and waged a struggle against military-dominated civilian governments that tolerated or were powerless to prevent numerous death-squad killings and other human rights abuses. Here too a U.N.-sponsored peace effort was under way, but it moved forward at a snail's pace. More time is needed to tell whether these developments represent the twilight of the tyrants in Central America.

Chapter 12

The Mexican Revolution—and After

On the eve of the presidential election of 1910, signs of unrest multiplied in Mexico. Peasant risings and workers' strikes became more frequent, and the Mexican Liberal party, founded and led by the exiled revolutionary journalist Ricardo Flores Magón, intensified its conspiratorial activities. Divisions appeared within the oligarchy. Bernardo Reyes, a foe of the Científicos and the powerful governor of Nuevo León whose rule combined iron-fisted repression with reformist trends, announced his candidacy for the post of vice president. Reyes saw this office as a steppingstone to the presidency when Díaz, who was eighty years old in 1910, died or retired.

In an unusual atmosphere of political ferment and debate, there appeared a tract for the times, *The Great National Problems* (1909) by the lawyer Andrés Molina Enríquez. Financed by Reyes, the book combined the customary eulogies of Díaz with incisive criticism of his political system and especially of his agrarian policy. Its denunciation of the latifundio and appeal for land reform anticipated the radical slogans of the coming revolution.

Díaz had contributed to this ferment by announcing in 1908 that Mexico was now ready for democracy and he would welcome the emergence of an opposition party. Francisco Madero, a Coahuila hacendado whose extensive family interests included cattle ranches, wheat farms, vineyards, textile factories, and mines, took Díaz at his word. A member of the elite, Madero was no revolutionary, but he feared that continuance of the existing political order would inevitably breed social revolution. Madero made clear, however, that by democracy he meant control by an elite. "The ignorant public," he wrote, "should

270 take no direct part in determining who should be the candidate for public office."

Madero criticized Díaz's social policies—his genocidal Indian wars and violent repression of strikes—as counterproductive; in place of those brutal tactics, he proposed a policy of modest concessions to peasants and workers that would reduce mounting tensions and check the growth of radical ideas. Madero regarded democracy as an instrument of social control that would promote the acceptance of capitalism through the grant of limited political and social reforms, with a large stress on education.

In December 1909 Madero began to tour the country, making speeches in which he explained his reform program. In April 1910, an opposition anti-re-electionist party was formed and announced Madero as its candidate for president. Díaz at first refused to take Madero seriously but soon became alarmed by his growing popularity. In early June he had Madero arrested and charged with preparing an armed insurrection; arrests of many of his supporters followed. On June 21 the election was held, and it was announced that Díaz and his hand-picked vice-presidential candidate, Ramón Corral, had been elected by an almost unanimous vote.

After the election, Díaz no longer considered Madero dangerous and allowed him to be released on bail. Convinced that the dictator could not be removed by peaceful means, Madero prepared to resort to armed struggle. On October 7, he fled across the border to Texas and from there announced the Plan of San Luis Potosí. Declaring the recent elections null and void, Madero assumed the title of provisional president of Mexico but promised to hold general free elections as soon as conditions permitted and turn power over to the elected president. The plan made a vague reference to the return of usurped peasant lands, but most of its articles dealt with political reforms. That Madero was allowed to organize the revolution on U.S. soil with little interference by the authorities suggests the United States government's displeasure with Díaz. Fearing that North American domination of investments in Mexico threatened Mexican economic and polit-

ical independence, the dictator had recently favored British over North American capitalists in the grant of concessions and had given other indications of an anti-U.S. attitude. The administration of President Taft evidently hoped that Madero would display a more positive attitude toward United States interests.

The Great Revolution, 1910–1920

The revolution got off to a shaky start when Madero, having crossed back into Mexico, found only twenty-five supporters waiting for him and hurriedly returned to Texas. But it soon gathered momentum as two major movements of peasant revolt responded to his call. In the huge northern border state of Chihuahua, where peons and small farmers suffered under the iron rule of the Terrazas-Creel clan, masters of a vast landed empire, the rising began under the leadership of Pascual Orozco, a mule driver, and Pancho Villa, a bandit with a reputation for taking from the rich to give to the poor. By the end of 1910, guerrilla armies had seized control of most of the state from federal troops.

Another seat of rebellion was the mountainous southern state of Morelos, where Indian communities had long waged a losing struggle against encroaching sugar haciendas. Here the mestizo insurgent leader Emiliano Zapata, attracted by the promise of land reform in the Plan of San Luis Potosí, proclaimed his loyalty to Madero.

In May 1911 the rebels won two decisive victories. Rather than face an invasion of the poorly defended capital by Zapata's dreaded agrarian rebels, Díaz and his advisers decided to reach an agreement with Madero. Disregarding urgent warnings by the left wing of the revolutionary movement against compromises with the Díaz regime, Madero signed the Treaty of Ciudad Juárez on May 21, which provided for the removal of Díaz but left intact all existing institutions. It was completely silent on the subject of social

The colorful *soldaderas,* women who joined their lovers or husbands and sometimes fought at their side, made their own contribution to the victory of the Mexican Revolution.

change. On May 25, the aged dictator resigned the presidency; a few days later he left for Europe. Francisco León de la Barra, the Mexican ambassador to the United States, assumed the interim presidency.

On June 7, 1911, Madero entered Mexico City in triumph, but the rejoicing of the crowds who thronged into the streets to greet the "apostle of democracy" was premature. The provisional president was closely tied to the old regime and had no sympathy with the revolution. The *Porfirista* aristocracy and its allies had not given up hope of regaining power; they regarded the compromise that made León de la Barra provisional president a tactical retreat, a means of gaining time to allow the revolutionary wave to subside so they could prepare a counterblow. Under the interim president, the huge Díaz bureaucracy remained largely intact. The reactionary officer corps remained in command of the federal army and burned for revenge over the revolutionary peasant armies that had defeated it.

Social conditions throughout the country remained largely unchanged, and the provisional government sought a total restoration of the status quo. Efforts were made to disband the revolutionary troops, and León de la Barra sent federal forces into Morelos to initiate hostilities against the Zapatistas, who had begun to confiscate large estates and distribute land to the villages. Madero's ineffective efforts to halt the fighting and mediate between Zapata and León de la Barra only deepened the hatred of the reactionaries for the visionary meddler who had unleashed anarchy in Mexico. But the revolutionary wave was still running strong, and reaction had to bide its time. In October 1911 Madero and his running mate, José María Pino Suárez, were elected president and vice president by over-whelming majorities.

Madero's Presidency: Inadequacy and Revolt

On November 6, 1911, Madero assumed the presidency from León de la Barra. It soon became evident that the "apostle of democracy" had no fundamental solutions for Mexico's grave social and economic problems. Even on the political plane, Madero's thought was far from advanced. His conception of democracy was a formal democracy that would give the masses the illusion of power and participation in political life but would vest all decision making in the hands of an elite.

In regard to economic and social democracy, his vision was even more limited. Madero allowed workers to organize trade unions and to strike and permitted a national workers' center, the *Casa del Obrero Mundial,* to be formed in Mexico City. But his answer to the agrarian problem was a totally inadequate program of purchase of land from large landowners and recovery of national land for distribution among landless peasants. In fact, Madero, who believed that only large landholdings would permit Mexican agriculture to modernize, was totally opposed to land reform at the expense of the haciendas. Madero's retreat on the land issue led to a break with his most faithful ally, Emiliano Zapata. Zapata urged Madero to carry out the agrarian provisions of the Plan of San Luis Potosí. Madero refused, arguing that the treaties that set up the interim government of León de la Barra obliged him to accept the legality of the legal and administrative decisions of the Díaz regime. Madero also demanded the disarmament of Zapata's peasant troops; in effect, he demanded Zapata's total surrender.

Convinced that Madero did not intend to carry out his pledges to restore land to the villages, Zapata announced his own program on November 28, 1911. The Plan of Ayala proclaimed that "the lands, woods, and waters usurped by the hacendados, Científicos, or caciques through tyr-

anny and venal justice" would be returned to their owners, and Zapata began to put the plan into effect. The Zapatista movement soon spread to other states in central and southern Mexico. Madero sent a series of generals against Zapata but failed to crush Zapata and his armies.

Madero's failure to carry out a genuine agrarian reform lost him the trust and support of the revolutionary peasantry without mollifying the reactionaries, who resented his modest concessions to labor and his efforts to transform Mexico into a bourgeois democracy with freedom of speech and press and the rule of law. They also feared that under pressure from the peasantry and under the influence of urban middle-class reformers like Luis Cabrera, a strong advocate of land reform, Madero might move farther to the left.

The aristocracy, its possessions and influence almost intact, dreamed of restoring the lost paradise of Don Porfirio, when peasants, workers, and Indians knew their place. Almost from the day that Madero took office in November 1911, therefore, counterrevolutionary revolts sprouted in various parts of Mexico. Most serious was a revolt in the north led by Pascual Orozco, who was encouraged and bribed by conservative elements in Chihuahua, especially the Terrazas-Creel clan. Federal troops under General Victoriano Huerta crushed the Orozco revolt in a series of battles, but Huerta's victory, joined with the alienation of Zapata and other of Madero's old revolutionary allies, increased Madero's dependence on an officer corps whose loyalty to his cause was highly dubious.

Abortive revolts followed one after another throughout the rest of 1912. The danger to Madero increased as it became clear that he had lost the support of the United States. Although Madero had made it clear that he favored foreign investments and guaranteed their security, he refused to show special favors to American capitalists and warned foreign investors that the crony system that had operated under Díaz was dead. This independent spirit, plus Madero's legalization of trade unions and strikes and his inability to cope with the peasant revolution and establish stability, alienated the United States.

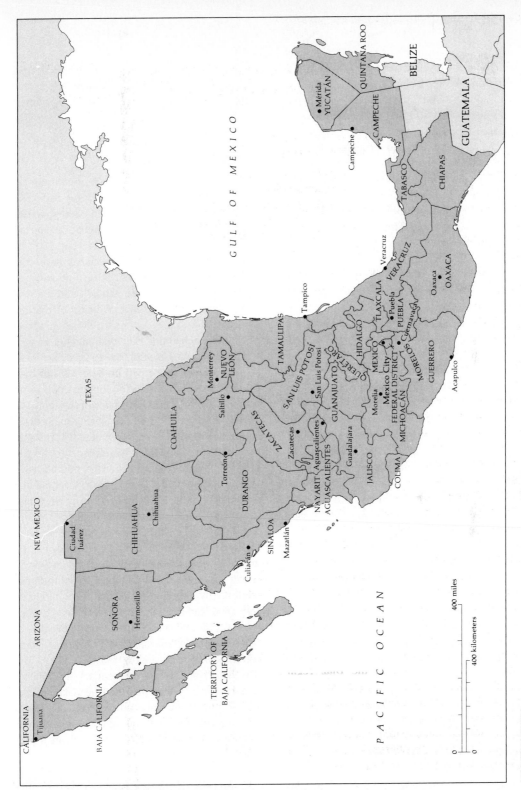

MODERN MEXICO

American foreign policy, originally favorable to Madero, turned against him.

U.S. Ambassador Henry Lane Wilson became increasingly hostile to Madero. In February 1912 a hundred thousand American troops were stationed along the border, and throughout the year Wilson made vehement threats of intervention if the Madero government failed to protect American lives and property.

Meanwhile, preparations for a coup d'état were under way in the capital. Implicated in the conspiracy were General Huerta, the recent conqueror of Orozco; General Miguel Mondragón, former chief of artillery under Díaz; Bernardo and Rodolfo Reyes, father and son; and Félix Díaz, nephew of the old dictator.

The blow fell on February 9, 1913. On that day, the military garrison at Tacubaya "pronounced" against Madero. The rebels marched on the National Palace. Their attack failed, and Bernardo Reyes was killed in an exchange of fire. Díaz then retreated with his troops to the Citadel, a well-fortified army arsenal, and between the rebels and the loyal troops holding the palace there developed a bitter artillery duel. Since the two parties were more than a mile apart, the principal victims of the cannonade were civilians. Meanwhile Huerta, to whom Madero had entrusted command of military operations, only awaited the right moment to dispose of the president.

Meanwhile, the American ambassador, in complete sympathy with the counterrevolutionary revolt, was secretly negotiating with Huerta and Díaz. On February 12 Wilson sent Madero a sharp protest against the conduct of military operations in Mexico City because they threatened American life and property. At his urging, the British, German, and Spanish representatives sent similar demands. As the crisis moved toward a climax, Wilson became feverishly active. On February 14, he demanded that the Mexican government begin negotiations with the other warring parties; otherwise, American marines would be landed in Mexican ports. The same day, Wilson invited other foreign diplomats to a conference at which it was agreed to force Madero to resign. A message to that effect was sent to Madero from the diplomatic corps. Madero firmly rejected the demand. He would rather die, he said, than allow foreign intervention.

Huerta's Dictatorship

Ambassador Wilson's activities were clearly coordinated with those of the conspirators and encouraged Huerta to strike the long-planned blow. On February 18, a detachment of Huerta's troops entered the palace and arrested the president, his vice president, Pino Suárez, and other members of his government. A dispute between Huerta and Díaz over who should head the new regime was settled through Wilson's mediation. At a meeting at the American embassy, agreement was reached that Huerta should head a provisional government, with Díaz to succeed him as soon as an election could be held. Wilson then called a meeting of foreign diplomats to whom he introduced Huerta as the "savior of Mexico."

To give some semblance of legality to his usurpation, Huerta obtained the "voluntary" resignations of Madero and Pino Suárez in return for the promise that they would then be free to leave Mexico. An intimidated Congress accepted the resignations and recognized Huerta as provisional president, almost without dissent. There remained the question of what should be done with Madero. Asked by Huerta for his advice, the American ambassador replied that he should do "what was best for the country." Despite urgent requests by other members of the diplomatic corps and Madero's wife that he intercede to save Madero's life, Wilson refused. On the evening of February 22, Madero and Pino Suárez were murdered as they were being transferred from the National Palace to the penitentiary; the official explanation was that they had been killed during an attempt by armed men to release them. The two assassins, officers of the rurales, were quickly advanced in rank, one being made a general.

Huerta's seizure of power, which was greeted with rejoicing by the landed aristocracy, the big capitalists, and the church, was an effort to set the Mexican clock back, to restore the Díaz system of personal dictatorship. The promise to Félix Díaz that he would succeed Huerta as president was soon broken, and Díaz was shunted aside by sending him off on a diplomatic mission to Japan. On October 10, 1913, preparing for his own election, Huerta arrested 110 congressmen and dissolved both houses. He then installed a new Congress packed with his military followers. The election held on October 26 under these auspices was so fraudulent, the results so obviously falsified, that Huerta's own Congress, with his approval, nullified it and put off a new election until a future date, with Huerta to continue as provisional president. Meanwhile, political assassinations occurred at a rate unknown earlier in Mexican history.

Hoping to broaden the social base of his dictatorship and conceal its reactionary character as long as possible, Huerta for a time continued Madero's labor policies, but as the terrorist nature of the regime became more apparent and labor more and more allied itself with the anti-Huerta movement, he proceeded to arrest its leaders and eventually closed down the Casa del Obrero Mundial.

The Opposition: Zapata, Villa, Carranza, and Obregón

Huerta had counted on a quick victory over the peasant revolutionaries of the south and favorable reception of his coup d'état by conservative economic and political interests in the north. However, the revolutionary wave, still running strong, rose even higher in reaction to Madero's brutal murder and the imposition of Huerta's terrorist regime. Zapata intensified his struggle against local great landowners, Huerta's allies, and federal troops. In the northern border states of Sonora, Chihuahua, and Coahuila, meanwhile, an anti-Huerta coalition of disparate social groups—liberal hacendados, middle classes, miners, industrial workers, vaqueros, and peasants—began to take form.

The successive campaigns launched by Huerta against the Zapatistas failed to achieve decisive victories. In mid-1913 the peasant armies laid siege to Cuernavaca, the capital of the state of Morelos, and cut it off from the national capital. Driven from Morelos in the latter part of 1913, they continued to operate in neighboring states. In April the Zapatistas returned to Morelos and by the end of May had taken all the towns in the state except Cuernavaca. In June they laid siege to Cuernavaca and took it in August 1914.

By forcing Huerta to commit a considerable part of his troops to the campaign in the south, Zapata assured the success of the revolutionary movement that sprang up anew in the north. Pancho Villa assumed leadership of the Constitutionalists, as Huerta's northern opponents called themselves, in Chihuahua (March 1913). Enjoying an immense popularity among the state's vaqueros, he soon recruited an army of three thousand men. By the end of the summer he had won control of almost all Chihuahua except the large cities. In mid-November he captured Ciudad Juárez and went on to capture the state capital, Chihuahua City.

Master of Chihuahua City, Villa imposed a revolutionary new order on the state capital. He employed his soldiers as a civil militia and administrative staff to restore normal life. Villa ordered a reduction of meat prices and distributed money, clothing, and other goods to the poor. Education was a passion with the almost illiterate Villa; according to the U.S. correspondent John Reed, who accompanied him, Villa established some fifty new schools in Chihuahua City.

Clearly, Villa's social policies were more radical than those implemented by the Constitutionalist leaders in the neighboring states of Sonora and Coahuila. In December 1913 he announced the expropriation without compensation of the holdings of the pro-Huerta oligarchy in Chihuahua. His agrarian program, however, differed in significant ways from that of Zapata. Whereas in the area ruled by Zapata confiscated estates were promptly distributed among the peasants, Villa's decree provided that they should remain under state control until the victory of the revolution. The revenues from these estates would be used to finance the revolutionary struggle and support the widows and orphans of the revolutionary soldiers. Once victory had been achieved, they were to be used to pay pensions to such widows and orphans, to compensate veterans of the revolution, to restore village lands that had been usurped by the hacendados, and to pay taxes left unpaid by the hacendados. Meanwhile Villa turned control of some confiscated haciendas over to his lieutenants; the rest were administered by the state. Cattle were sold in the United States to secure arms and ammunition for Villa's army, and meat was distributed on a large scale to the urban unemployed, to public institutions like orphanages and children's homes, and for sale in the markets. The differences between the agrarian programs of Villa and Zapata may be explained in part by the fact that the economy of the north was based not on agriculture but on cattle raising, which required large economic units. These units had to be administered by the state or on a cooperative basis. In addition, the percentage of peasants in the population was much smaller in the north, and the problem of land hunger much less acute.

In the neighboring state of Coahuila, meanwhile, the elderly Venustiano Carranza, a great landowner who had once served Díaz but joined Madero in 1911 and was appointed by him governor of the state, raised the standard of revolt against Huerta. On March 26, 1913, he announced his Plan of Guadalupe, which called for the overthrow of the dictator and the restoration of constitutional government but did not mention social reforms. Carranza assumed the title of first chief of the Constitutionalist Army. By April he commanded some forty thousand men. He was soon joined by Villa, who placed himself under Carranza's command, but retained much autonomy in Chihuahua; Villa's troops were renamed the Northern Division. Carranza gained another important recruit in the young ranchero Alvaro Obregón, who led the anti-Huerta forces in the state of Sonora. Named commander of the Army of the Northwest, he soon proved his large military gifts by driving the federal troops out of almost all Sonora; in April the state legislature recognized Carranza as first chief of the revolution.

Intervention by the United States

By the beginning of 1914, the Constitutionalist revolt had assumed significant proportions and Huerta's fall appeared inevitable. Meanwhile, in March 1913, Wilson had succeeded Taft as president of the United States. Alone among the great powers, Wilson's government refused to recognize the Huerta regime. Wilson justified his nonrecognition policy with moralistic rhetoric, refusing to recognize a government that had come to power illegally. More important, he was convinced that Huerta could not provide the stable political climate U.S. interests required in Mexico.

Wilson's concern with a suitable political climate for American investments emerges from a note sent to British officials in November 1913, in which he assured those officials that the United States government "intends not merely to force Huerta from power, but also to exert every influence it can exert to secure Mexico a better government under which all contracts and business concessions will be safer than they have been." On the other hand, Huerta's policy of favoring British capital gained him support.

By yielding to a British demand for uniform rates for all shipping using the nearly completed Panama Canal, Wilson obtained an end of British support for Huerta by the end of 1913. As a result, Huerta's financial position became increasingly difficult. Seeking to avert a catastrophe, he suspended payment on the interest on the national debt for six months but that extraordinary measure only increased Huerta's difficulties. Foreign creditors began to demand the seizure of Mexican customhouses, and some even clamored for immediate intervention. By February 1914 Wilson decided force must be used. After receiving assurances from Carranza's agent in Washington that the Constitutionalists would respect foreign property rights, including "just and equitable concessions," Wilson lifted the existing embargo on arms shipments to the Carranza forces.

Wilson found a pretext for intervention when a party of U.S. sailors from the cruiser *Dolphin* landed in a restricted area of Tampico and were arrested. They were almost immediately released, with an apology, but the commander of the *Dolphin,* under orders from Washington, demanded a formal disavowal of the action, severe punishment for the responsible Mexican officer, and a twenty-one-gun salute to the American flag. For Huerta to grant these demands might have meant political suicide, and he refused.

President Wilson now sent a fleet into the Gulf of Mexico, and on April 21, 1914, learning that a German merchant ship was bound for Veracruz with munitions, he ordered the seizure of the city. When Mexican batteries at the fortress of San Juan de Ulua attempted to prevent a landing, they were silenced by answering fire from the U.S. ships. Huerta's forces evacuated Veracruz the same day, but the local population and cadets of the naval academy continued a courageous resistance until April 27, when the American flag was raised over Veracruz. The occupation of Veracruz sent a wave of anti-Yankee sentiment rolling through Mexico; protests were also organized in a number of Latin American countries. Meanwhile Carranza, whom Wilson had hoped to control, bitterly denounced the U.S. action and demanded the immediate evacuation of Veracruz.

The rising storm of Mexican anger and Carranza's defiant stand placed Wilson in a quandary. He sought a way out of his difficult situation by obtaining an offer from Argentina, Brazil, and Chile to mediate the dispute between the United States and Mexico. A conference was convened at Niagara Falls, Canada, in May 1914. Wilson hoped to do more than reduce tensions; he intended to use the mediation as a means of eliminating Huerta and establishing a new provisional Mexican government that he could control. The U.S. candidate to head this provisional government was the moderate Carranza, since the revolutionary peasant leaders Zapata and Villa were obviously unacceptable. But Carranza would not rise to Wilson's bait. The conservative but fiercely nationalist first chief sent representatives to the Niagara Falls conference but did not give them official status and refused the conference's mediation. Mexico, his representatives informed the United States delegates, would settle its own problems without interference from foreign sources.

By this time the fall of the Huerta regime was imminent. With the northern tier of states securely in Constitutionalist hands, Pancho Villa's Northern Division drove south in March from Chihuahua City toward Torreón, a major railroad center. On April 2, Torreón fell to Villa after twelve days of bitter fighting; the fall of Monterrey, Saltillo, and Tampico followed soon after. Having taken Saltillo, Villa advanced on Zacatecas and took the city by storm on June 23. Meanwhile, Obregón's Army of the Northwest was advancing down the Pacific coast into Jalisco; on July 9, he seized the important railroad and industrial center of Guadalajara. Recognizing that his situation had become hopeless, Huerta took flight for Europe on July 15. On August 15 Obregón's troops entered Mexico City.

Huerta's fall deprived the United States of any pretext for continuing its armed intervention, but Wilson delayed the evacuation of Veracruz as long as possible in the hope of securing commitments from Carranza that would have effectively prevented any basic changes in Mexico's social and economic structure. Despite hints that "fatal consequences" might follow, Carranza resolutely rejected these demands and continued to insist on the end of the military intervention. U.S. troops finally evacuated Veracruz on November 23, 1914.

Fighting Among the Victors

As the day of complete victory drew near, differences emerged within the Constitutionalist camp, especially between Carranza and Villa. There were personal factors, such as Carranza's jealousy of Villa as a potential rival, but more important was Carranza's failure to define his position on such fundamental issues as the agrarian question, the role of the church, and the new political order. Villa proposed to incorporate in an agreement a clause drawn up by one of his intellectuals that defined "the present conflict as a struggle of the poor against the abuses of the powerful" and committed the Constitutionalists "to implant a democratic regime . . . to secure the well-being of the workers; to emancipate the peasants economically, making an equitable distribution of lands or whatever else is needed to solve the agrarian problem." Under pressure from his generals, who recognized the potential dangers of an open break with Villa, Carranza permitted his representatives to sign the agreement containing this radical clause, which he personally found unacceptable. Villa, however, continued to distrust Carranza, and his distrust was confirmed by various of Carranza's actions, notably his unilateral occupation of the capital.

Relations also deteriorated between Carranza and Zapata. Zapata had waged war against Huerta independently of Carranza's forces and refused to recognize his leadership; a Zapatista manifesto proclaimed that the Plan of Ayala must prevail and all adherents of the old regime must be removed.

In October 1914 a convention of revolutionary leaders and their delegates met at Aguascalientes to settle the conflict between Carranza and Villa. At the insistence of the *Villistas,* Zapata was invited to attend, and presently a delegation from "the Liberating Army of the South" arrived. The convention endorsed the Plan of Ayala, assumed supreme authority, called for the resignation of Carranza as first chief, and appointed General Eulalio Gutiérrez provisional president of the nation. Gutiérrez was a compromise candidate pushed by delegates equally opposed to Carranza and Villa. Since Aguascalientes swarmed with Villa's troops, Gutiérrez had no choice but to name Villa commander in chief of the Conventionist Army, as the Northern Division now came to be called.

But Carranza refused to accept the decisions of the Aguascalientes convention, claiming it had no authority to depose him. When he failed to meet the deadline for his resignation, November 10, the armies of Zapata and Villa advanced on the capital and occupied it. Carranza retreated with his depleted forces to Veracruz, which had been evacuated by the Americans shortly before. There he established his Constitutionalist government, while Obregón, who had remained loyal to Carranza, rebuilt his army with the aid of arms and munitions purchased abroad.

On December 4 Villa and Zapata held their first meeting and came to full agreement. But although the peasant revolutionaries controlled the capital and much of the country, they could not consolidate their successes. Unskilled in politics, they entrusted state power to the unreliable provisional president, Gutiérrez, a former general in Carranza's army, who sabotaged the Conventionist war effort and opened secret negotiations with Obregón. Meanwhile a conservative wing in the convention strongly opposed land reform, expropriation of foreign properties, and other radical social changes. Villa's sympathies on land reform were with the radicals, but he avoided taking sides in the dispute, probably because he believed that unity was necessary to gain both a rapid military victory and recognition by the United States, which he also regarded as essential to his final triumph. For these and other reasons the convention proved unable to forge a clear national program of socioeconomic reforms that could unite the interests of the peasantry, industrial workers, and the middle class. His later attempts to broaden his program to attract labor, the middle class, and even national capitalists were too little and too late.

The Constitutionalists did not make the same mistake. At the insistence of Obregón and intellectuals like Luis Cabrera, who were aware of the need for broadening the social base of the Constitutionalist movement, the conservative Carranza adopted a program of social reforms designed to win the support of peasants and workers. In December 1914, during the darkest days of the Constitutionalist cause, Carranza issued in Veracruz a decree that promised agrarian reform and improved conditions for the industrial workers. Other decrees followed, the most notable being one of January 6, 1915, which provided for the restoration of lands usurped from the villages and the expropriation of additional needed land from haciendas. (Simultaneously, Carranza secretly promised the hacendados that he would return the haciendas that had been confiscated by revolutionary authorities—prom-

In early December 1914 Pancho Villa (left) met with Emiliano Zapata (right) in Mexico City, where both attended the installation of a new president. Earlier, Villa and Zapata had reached agreement on a course of action for the revolution, but the arrangement soon fell apart.

ises that in the end he would keep.) Carranza's agrarian decrees, gained him a certain base among the peasantry. Carranza also courted labor support by the promise of a minimum wage law applying to all branches of industry and by affirming the right of workers to form trade unions and to strike.

After Obregón's troops reoccupied Mexico City in January 1915, an alliance was formed between the Carranza government and the Casa del Obrero Mundial, which was restored after the fall of Huerta. Members of the Casa agreed to join "the struggle against reaction," meaning above all the revolutionary peasantry. Six "red battal-

ions" of workers were formed and made an important contribution to the offensive launched by Obregón against Villa and Zapata in January 1915. Inadequate understanding on the part of the peasant and working-class leaders of their common interests and the skillful opportunism of the middle-class politicians in Carranza's camp contributed to this disastrous division between labor and the peasantry.

As a result, the balance of forces shifted sharply in favor of the Constitutionalists. In early 1915 Carranza's forces won significant victories; having captured Puebla, they threatened the capital. President Gutiérrez, who had long wanted to break with Villa, left the city with a group of his ministers, some troops, and 10 million pesos from the national treasury. Shortly afterward, he submitted his resignation. Following Gutiérrez's flight, the Conventionist government, or what remained of it, designated Roque González Garza as president in his place.

Under pressure from Carranza's troops, Villa was forced on January 19 to evacuate Mexico City, which Obregón soon occupied. A series of complicated movements followed, with Constitutionalists and Conventionists successively occupying and abandoning the city. These maneuvers ended with Obregón in possession of the capital. In April 1915 Obregón advanced toward the important railroad center of Celaya, occupied it, and awaited Villa's attack. Obregón had studied accounts of the great war in progress in Europe and had learned that trenches and barbed wire could stop mass attacks. His army received Villa's furious infantry and cavalry assault with a withering fire from machine-gun emplacements and entrenched infantry. For the first time in his military career, Villa suffered a disastrous defeat, with thousands of men killed or taken prisoner. Fighting a series of battles, he retreated northward. In the hour of his defeat (May 1915), Villa issued a comprehensive, well-thought-out agrarian reform law, providing that all estates above a certain size were to be divided among the peasantry, with some indemnity for the owners, and payment by the peasants in small installments, but the program was never implemented. By the end of 1915, he was back in Chihuahua; here, among his own people, on terrain that he knew perfectly, he was invincible. For three more years he carried on guerrilla warfare but ceased to exist as a major political and military factor. The Constitutionalists had destroyed Villa, whom they regarded as the primary danger.

There remained the Zapatistas, who threatened the capital and who had temporarily occupied it in July. But Zapata's battered forces could not check the advance of General Pablo González's army. In August the Constitutionalists returned to Mexico City to stay, while González, one of Carranza's ablest generals, pursued the

Zapatistas into Morelos in a campaign of devastation and plunder.

In October 1915, after unsuccessful efforts to play off the revolutionary chiefs against each other or to achieve a coalition under United States leadership, President Wilson acknowledged Carranza's ascendancy and extended de facto recognition of his regime; equally important, he placed an arms embargo on Carranza's opponents. But the United States had not abandoned its efforts to influence the course of the Mexican Revolution. A memorandum to Carranza dictated the conditions he must meet before he could obtain de jure recognition. They amounted to a claim to determine Mexican policy not only in the area of foreign economic rights but in such internal matters as the role of the church, elections, and the like. These demands were as unacceptable to Carranza in October 1915 as they had been a year before.

In early 1916 relations between the United States and Mexico deteriorated sharply. In part, this resulted from initial efforts by Mexican federal and state authorities to regulate the operations of foreign oil companies. A crisis arose in March when Villa, angered by the arms embargo and wrongly convinced that Carranza had bought United States recognition by agreeing to a plan to convert Mexico into a United States protectorate, raided Columbus, New Mexico, in an apparent effort to force Carranza to show his hand. The Wilson administration responded by ordering General John Pershing to pursue Villa into Mexico. The United States counted on the enmity between Villa and Carranza to secure the latter's neutrality. Carranza denounced the invasion, demanded the immediate withdrawal of American forces, and began to prepare for war with the United States. In a note to other Latin American nations, the Mexican government declared its belief that the basic reason for U.S. intervention was its opposition to the Mexican policy of eliminating privileged treatment of foreign capital and affirmed that the "foreign invasion" must be repelled and Mexican sovereignty respected.

The United States had anticipated an easy victory, but Pershing's hot pursuit of the elusive

Villa proved a fiasco, and Wilson accepted Carranza's offer to negotiate a settlement. Wilson was unsuccessful in his efforts to link the evacuation of American forces with acceptance of the United States formula for Mexican domestic policy. In January 1917, influenced by the troubled international scene and his conviction that a war with Mexico would involve at least half a million men, Wilson decided to liquidate the Mexican venture. Mexican nationalism had won a major victory over yet another effort to impose U.S. hegemony.

The Constitution of 1917

In the fall of 1916, Carranza issued a call for the election of deputies to a convention that was to frame a new constitution and prepare the way for his election as president. The convention opened in Querétaro on December 1, 1916. Since the call effectively excluded persons who had not sworn loyalty to his 1913 Plan of Guadalupe, it seemed likely that the constitution would be what Carranza wanted. The draft did not contemplate a radical agrarian reform; for labor, it limited itself to proclaiming the "right to work" and the right of workers to form organizations for "lawful purposes" and to hold "peaceful" assemblies.

These abstract proposals were unsatisfactory to a majority of the deputies, who formed the radical wing of the convention. The principal spokesman for this left wing was Francisco J. Múgica, a young general who helped make the first land distribution of the revolution. The radicals obtained majority approval to create a commission to revise Carranza's project. Múgica himself was largely responsible for Article 3, which struck a heavy blow at church control of education by specifically forbidding "religious corporations" and "ministers of any cult" to establish or conduct schools.

A most important article was Article 123, dealing with the rights of labor. Carranza had asked only that the federal government be empowered to enact labor legislation. The convention went much further. The finished article, a true labor code, provided for the eight-hour day; abolished

the tienda de raya, or company store, and debt servitude; guaranteed the right of workers to organize, bargain collectively, and strike; and granted many other rights and privileges, making it the most advanced labor code in the contemporary world.

Article 27, dealing with property rights, had an equally advanced character. It proclaimed the nation the original owner of all lands, waters, and the subsoil; the state could expropriate them, with compensation to the owners. National ownership of water and the subsoil was inalienable, but individuals and companies could obtain concessions for their exploitation. Foreigners to whom that privilege was granted must agree that they would not invoke the protection of their governments in regard to such concessions. Of prime importance were the same article's agrarian provisions. It declared that all measures passed since 1856 alienating ejidos (communal lands) were null and void; if the pueblos needed more land, they could acquire it by expropriation from neighboring haciendas.

These and other provisions of the constitution of 1917 made it the most progressive law code of its time. It laid legal foundations for a massive assault on the latifundio, for weakening the power of the church, and for regulating the operations of foreign capital in Mexico. But the constitution was not anticapitalist. It sanctioned and protected private property; it sought to control rather than eliminate foreign enterprises, creating more favorable conditions for the development of national capitalism.

The convention completed its work on January 31, 1917, and Carranza ordered promulgation of the new constitution on February 5, 1917. Carranza expressed reservations about the new constitution but promised to uphold it. Then he issued a call for an extraordinary presidential election to be held in March. His election was a foregone conclusion, and on May 1, 1917, he was formally installed as president, the first legally elected president since Madero. On inauguration day, Obregón, his secretary of war, resigned and retired to private life. Obregón, who had been moving to the left, distrusted many of the men around Carranza as reactionaries of Porfirista stamp.

Carranza's Presidency

The three remaining years of the Carranza regime were marked by a sharp swing to the right. Carranza soon made it clear that he did not intend to implement the reform articles of the constitution. Only a trifling amount of land was distributed to the villages. Carranza returned many confiscated haciendas to their former owners; others he turned over to his favorite generals. Official corruption existed on a massive scale. The working class suffered severe repression. Carranza shut down the Casa del Obrero Mundial. The constitution's promise of free education was ignored. Only in Carranza's foreign policy, marked by a genuine revolutionary nationalism, did the spirit of the constitution live. Carranza staunchly resisted U.S. pressure to give guarantees that Article 27 of the constitution would not be implemented against foreign interests. He also kept Mexico neutral in World War I and insisted on an independent Mexican diplomatic position in the hemisphere, postures that the United States regarded as unfriendly.

Meanwhile, Carranza continued to battle the tenacious Zapatista movement in the south and Villa in the north. Against the Zapatistas, Carranza's favorite general, Pablo González, launched campaign after campaign. Zapata's forces diminished and the territory under his control shrank to the vanishing point, but he remained unconquerable, supported by the affection and loyalty of the peasantry. His fall came through treachery. Invited to confer with a Carrancista officer who claimed to have gone over to his side, Zapata was ambushed and slain on April 10, 1919. But his people continued their struggle for *tierra y libertad* (land and liberty).

Carranza's legal term was due to end in 1920, but the president had no intention of relinquishing power. Barred from running again by the constitutional rule of no re-election, he picked as his successor the ambassador to Washington, Ignacio Bonillas, generally regarded as a nonentity. Meanwhile, Obregón, supported by a Labor party

formed to further his interests, announced his candidacy for the presidency. As the campaign proceeded, it became clear that Carranza intended to manipulate the electoral machinery to impose Bonillas on the nation. In April 1920 Obregón and the governor of Sonora, Adolfo de la Huerta, issued a call for the removal of Carranza and the appointment of a provisional government until an election could be held. The swift triumph of the revolt revealed the depth of the unpopularity of the distant, aloof Carranza and his policies. In May 1920 Carranza fled from the capital toward Veracruz, taking with him 5 million pesos in gold and silver from the national treasury. On the night of May 21, the mountain village in which he slept was attacked by local guerrillas and Carranza was slain.

On May 24 Adolfo de la Huerta, chief of the Liberal Constitutionalist Army, was chosen president at a special session of Congress. He promptly scheduled a presidential election for September 5, with the candidacy and victory of Obregón a certain outcome. Under the interim president, pacification was the order of the day. The Zapatistas, who had joined the uprising against Carranza, obtained confirmation of the agrarian reform for which they had so long fought. Villa, who also aided the anti-Carranza movement, was rewarded with a hacienda, and other lands were given to his men. Villa did not long enjoy his newfound peace and prosperity; he was assassinated in the summer of 1923 under obscure circumstances.

In November 1920, Obregón assumed the presidency. Peace had come to Mexico, and the work of reconstruction could begin. It would not be an easy task. The great wind that swept Mexico had left a devastated land, with hundreds of thousands dead or missing; the Mexican population had actually declined by 1 million since 1910. The constitution of 1917 offered a blueprint for a new and better social order, but major obstacles to change remained. Not the least were the hundreds of generals thrown up by the great upheaval, men of humble origins who once had nothing and now had an incurable itch for wealth and power. With his characteristic wry humor, Obregón summed up the problem when he said that the days of revolutionary banditry had ended because he had brought all the bandits with him to the capital to keep them out of trouble.

Reconstruction: The Rule of the Millionaire Socialists

Obregón and Reform

With Obregón there came to power a group of northern generals and politicians who began the work of economic and social reconstruction that Madero, Huerta, and Carranza were unable or unwilling to achieve. Of middle-class or even lower-class origins—Obregón had been a mechanic and farmer, his successor Calles, a schoolteacher—both were products of a border region where U.S. cultural influence was strong, where capitalism and capitalist relations were more highly developed than in any other part of Mexico. Obregón and Calles thus possessed a pragmatic business mentality as far removed from the revolutionary agrarian ideology of Zapata as it was from the aristocratic reformism of Carranza. These men deliberately set out to lay the economic, political, and ideological foundations of a Mexican national capitalism.

Aware that the revolution had radicalized the masses, aware of the appeal of socialism and anti-imperialism to the workers on whose support they counted, Obregón and Calles employed a revolutionary rhetoric designed to mobilize popular support and conceal how modest were the social changes that actually took place. In practice, the Obregonian program was revolutionary only by contrast with the reactionary trend that characterized the last years of Carranza's rule. Far from promoting socialism, Obregón sought accommodation with all elements of Mexican society except the most reactionary clergy and landlords. He allowed exiles of the most varied political tendency to return to Mexico, and radical intellectuals rubbed shoulders with former Científicos in his government. Power was held by a ruling class of wealthy generals, capi-

talists, and landlords; elections remained a farce; the president was a dictator who kept power by playing regional warlords and various factions against one another. Labor and the peasantry were the government's obedient clienteles, represented by a Labor party and an Agrarian party whose leaders formed part of the establishment and mediated between their clienteles and the all-powerful president.

Regarding agrarian reform as a useful safety valve for peasant discontent, Obregón distributed some land to the pueblos. But the process proceeded slowly, haltingly, against the intense opposition of the hacendados and the church, which condemned the agrarian reform because it did not take account of the "just rights of the landlords." Litigation by landlords, their use of armed force to resist occupation of expropriated land, and the opposition of the clergy, slowed down the pace of the land reform.

Even after a village had received land, its prospect for success was poor, for the government failed to provide the peasants with seeds, implements, and adequate credit facilities or modern agricultural training. Such credit assistance as they received usually came from government rural banks, which exercised close control over land use, intensifying the client status of the peasantry, or from rural loan sharks. The Obregón land reform was neither swift nor thoroughgoing; by the end of his presidency, only some 3 million acres had been distributed among 624 villages, while 320 million acres remained in private hands.

Obregón also encouraged labor to organize, for he regarded trade unions as useful for stabilizing labor-capitalist relations and as an important bulwark of his regime. The principal trade union organization was the *Confederación Regional Obrera Mexicana* (CROM), formed in 1918. Despite the rhetoric of its leaders about "class struggle" and freedom from the "tyranny of capitalism," CROM was about as radical as the American Federation of Labor, with which it maintained close ties. Its perpetual boss was Luis Morones, known for his flashy dress, diamonds, and limousines. As the only labor organization sponsored and protected by the government,

284 CROM had virtually official status. Despite this official protection, Morones's method of personal negotiation with employers yielded scanty benefits to labor; wages barely kept pace with the rising cost of living.

Perhaps the most solid achievements of the Obregón regime were in the areas of education and culture. The creation of a native Mexican capitalism demanded the development of a national consciousness, which meant the integration of the Indian peoples—still made up of so many small nations—into the national market and the new society. From this point of view, the Indians were the key problem of Mexican reconstruction. Because incorporating them into the modern world required a thorough understanding of the Indians' past and their present conditions of life, the revolutionary regimes encouraged scientific study of the Indians. Under Obregón, Manuel Gamio, appointed director of the first government office of anthropology in the Americas in 1917, fused the methods and goals of archaeology and applied anthropology in his famous pilot study of Teotihuacán. Gamio sought not only to preserve and restore a precious cultural heritage but to amass the data needed for a sound plan of economic and social recovery for this area.

An integral part of *indigenismo* was a reassessment of the Indian cultural heritage. To insist on the greatness of the old Indian arts was one way of asserting the value of one's own, of revolting against the tyranny of the pallid, lifeless French and Spanish academicism over Mexican art during the last decades of the Díaz era.

From Europe returned two future giants of the Mexican artistic renaissance, Diego Rivera and David Alfaro Siqueiros, to join another gifted artist, José Clemente Orozco, in creating a militant new art that drew much of its inspiration from the Indians and their ancient art. Believing that "a heroic art could fortify the will to reconstruction," Obregón's brilliant young secretary of education, José Vasconcelos, offered the walls of public buildings for the painting of murals that glorified the Indians, past and present.

The Indianist cult had great political significance. The foes of the revolution, unregenerate Porfiristas, clericals, and reactionaries of all stripes, looked back to Spain as the sole source of enduring values in Mexican life and regarded Cortés as the creator of Mexican nationality; partisans of the revolution tended to idealize Aztec Mexico (sometimes beyond recognition) and elevated the last Aztec warrior-king, Cuauhtémoc, to the status of a demigod.

Convinced that the school was the most important instrument for unifying the nation, that "to educate was to redeem," Vasconcelos, with ample budgetary support from Obregón, launched an imaginative program of cultural missions designed to bring literacy and health to primitive Indian villages. Hundreds of young, idealistic teachers went out to bring the gospel of sanitation and literacy to remote pueblos. Vasconcelos also founded teacher-training colleges, agricultural schools, and other specialized schools. An achievement in which he took special pride was the publication of hundreds of classic works in cheap editions for free distribution in the schools.

The new secular, nationalist school provoked clerical anger, for it threatened to supplant the priest with the teacher as the guiding force of the Indian community and to replace the religious world outlook taught by the Catholic church with a scientific world outlook. The church fought back with all the means at its disposal. Some priests denounced secular education from their pulpits and threatened parents who sent their children to state schools with excommunication. As a result of this campaign, many teachers were attacked and some killed by fanatical villagers. Despite this campaign, Obregón made no effort to implement Article 3 of the constitution, which banned religious primary schools, for he believed that in the absence of enough resources on the part of the state it was better that Mexican children receive instruction from priests than remain illiterate.

The Catholic issue joined with other issues to cause Obregón difficulties in his relations with the United States. For three years, the United States government withheld diplomatic recognition from Obregón in an effort to force him to recognize that Article 27 of the constitution should not apply to mineral concessions obtained by foreigners before 1917. Like Carranza, Obregón was willing to respect the principle of nonretroactivity but refused to formalize it in a treaty, which he considered humiliating.

However, in 1923, with a growing threat of a counterrevolutionary coup to prevent the victory of Obregón's hand-picked successor, Plutarco Elías Calles, Obregón decided to compromise. Mexican diplomats signed the Bucareli Agreement (not a formal treaty), which confirmed that Article 27 was not retroactive, and agreed to pay compensation for damages to American property during the revolution. The United States promptly extended formal recognition to Obregón in August 1923. When the expected revolt broke out in December, the United States allowed Obregón to procure large quantities of war materiel. Together with the help of the organized labor and peasant movements, this aid enabled Obregón to crush the uprising, which was supported by reactionary landowners, clergy, and military. On November 30, 1924, Calles assumed the presidency of Mexico.

Calles's Regime

In and out of office, as legal president or de facto dictator, Calles dominated the next decade of Mexican politics. Building on the foundations Obregón had laid, he continued his work with much the same methods. His radical phraseology tended to conceal the pragmatic essence of his policy, which was to promote the rapid growth of Mexican national capitalism, whose infrastructure he helped to establish. To strengthen the fiscal and monetary system he created the Bank of Mexico, the only bank permitted to issue money. A national road commission was organized, and a national electricity code was enacted to aid the electric power industry. These measures stimulated the growth of construction and consumer goods industries, in which members of Calles's official family—or the "revolutionary family," as the ruling elite came to be called—were heavily involved. Protective tariffs, subsidies, and other forms of aid were generously extended to industry, both foreign and domestic. In 1925 an assem-

bly plant of the Ford Motor Company began operations in Mexico after Calles and the company negotiated an agreement providing for numerous concessions.

Calles showed more enthusiasm for land reform than Obregón, and the tempo of land distribution increased sharply during his presidency. Like Obregón, Calles regarded land reform as a safety valve for peasant unrest. During the four years of his term, Calles distributed about twice as much land as Obregón.

But less than one-fourth of that amount consisted of arable land, for Calles did not require the hacendados to surrender productive land, and most of the land given up came from pasture or forest lands, or even land that was completely barren. Nor did Calles make a serious effort to provide the peasantry with irrigation, fertilizer, implements, or seed. He established a government bank that was supposed to lend money to the ejidos, promote modern farming techniques, and act as agents for the sale of their produce. But four-fifths of the bank's resources were loaned not to ejidos but to hacendados with much superior credit ratings, and many of the bank's agents took advantage of their position to enrich themselves at the expense of the peasants.

Under these conditions, it is no wonder that the land reform soon appeared to be a failure. By 1930 grain production had fallen below the levels of 1910, and Calles, concluding that peasant proprietorship was economically undesirable, announced the abandonment of land distribution. Meanwhile, on his own large estates Calles introduced machinery and other modern agricultural techniques and advised other large landowners to do the same.

Like Obregón, Calles regarded labor unions as desirable because they helped stabilize labor-capitalist relations and avert radical social change. But by the end of the *Callista* decade, Mexican labor, disillusioned with a corrupt leadership that kept wages at or below the subsistence level, had begun to break away from CROM and form independent unions.

Calles continued the Carranza and Obregón policies of asserting Mexico's right to regulate the conditions under which foreign capital could exploit its natural resources, but he was far from hostile to foreign capital. Indeed, he gave assurances that "the government will do everything in its power to safeguard the interests of foreign capitalists who invest money in Mexico."

But a serious dispute with the United States arose in 1925 when the Mexican Congress passed laws to implement Article 27. The most important of these measures required owners of oil leases to exchange their titles for fifty-year concessions dating from the time of acquisition, to be followed, if necessary, by a thirty-year renewal, with the possibility of yet another extension if needed. No Mexican oil well had ever lasted more than eighty years. Far from injuring the foreign oil companies, the law eliminated the vagueness of their status under Article 27, gave them firm titles emanating from the government, and served to quiet more radical demands for outright nationalization. However, a number of American oil companies denounced the law as confiscatory and threatened to continue drilling operations without confirmatory concessions.

The State Department vigorously protested the restrictive legislation, and the United States ambassador, James R. Sheffield, pursued a hard-line, uncompromising policy. By late 1926 the United States appeared to be moving toward war with Mexico.

Fortunately, the interventionist policy came under severe attack from Progressive Republican senators, the press, church groups, and the academic world. President Calvin Coolidge and Secretary of State Kellogg, realizing that war with Mexico would have little national support, sought a way out of the impasse and were aided by U.S. international bankers, who had a firmer grasp of Mexican policies and intentions. The appointment of Dwight Morrow, a partner in the financial firm of J. P. Morgan, as ambassador to Mexico in September 1927 marked a turning point in the crisis. Morrow managed to persuade Calles that portions of the oil law had the potential for injuring foreign property rights, with the result that the Mexican Supreme Court found unconstitutional that portion of the law setting a time period on concessions. But as rewritten the law still provided for confirmatory concessions and reaffirmed national ownership of the subsoil.

In addition, a serious domestic dispute arose as a result of the growing opposition of the church to the whole modernizing thrust of the revolution. Under Calles this opposition assumed the proportions of a civil war. In January 1926, the church hierarchy signed a letter declaring that the constitution of 1917 "wounds the most sacred rights of the Catholic Church" and disavowed the document. Calles responded by enforcing the anticlerical clauses of the constitution, which had lain dormant. The Calles Law, as it was called, ordered the registration of priests with the civil authorities and the closing of religious primary schools. The church struck back by suspending church services throughout Mexico, a powerful weapon in a country so overwhelmingly Catholic.

But neither this strike nor the boycott organized by the church, which urged the faithful to buy no goods or services except absolute necessities, brought the government to its knees. By the end of 1926, militant Catholics, in frequent alliance with local hacendados, had taken to arms. Guerrilla groups were formed, with the mountainous backcountry of Jalisco the main focus of their activity. Government schools and young teachers sent into remote areas were frequent objects of clerical fury; many teachers were tortured and killed. The total number of Catholic guerrillas, known as *Cristeros* from their slogan, *Viva Cristo Rey* (Long Live Christ the King), was small, but federal commanders helped to keep the insurrection alive by the brutality of their repressions. By the summer of 1927, however, the revolt had largely burned itself out, and Calles could turn his attention to the forthcoming presidential election in July 1928.

In an apparent deal between Calles and Obregón, the latter's supporters in Congress amended the constitution to allow a former president to be re-elected after one term, and the presidential term was extended from four to six years. The plan was for Obregón to succeed Calles and Calles to succeed Obregón. Angered by this arrangement, two frustrated presidential hopefuls,

General Francisco Serrano and Arnulfo Gómez, began to conspire against Obregón and Calles. Calles acted decisively; the plotters were seized and shot, and Obregón remained the only candidate. In July Obregón was duly elected, but three weeks later a fanatical Cristero assassinated him in a Mexico City restaurant.

With the passing of the formidable Obregón, Calles became the *jefe máximo,* the maximum chief of the revolution. The presidents who successively held office during what was to have been Obregón's six-year term—Emilio Portes Gil, Pascual Ortiz Rubio, and Abelardo Rodríguez— were Calles's stooges and obediently resigned when they incurred his displeasure. In 1929, after crushing a rebellion that proved to be almost the last hurrah of the regional military caudillos, Calles organized the National Revolutionary party (PNR) as an instrument for pacifying the country and institutionalizing the rule of the "revolutionary family," the military leaders and politicians who had ruled the country since 1920. Under different names and with leaderships of differing composition, the party formed by Calles has been the ruling party of Mexico since 1929. The official party's candidates for president have not lost an election in six decades.

As the "revolutionary family" consolidated its power and its wealth increased, its members became more conservative. Their humble beginnings disposed the revolutionary generals to become even more corrupt and predatory than the old Porfirista aristocracy. As large landowners, they were naturally hostile to agrarian reform; as owners of construction firms and factories, they were naturally hostile to strikes and unions.

Calles and his cronies had never been committed to a radical reconstruction of Mexican society, but after 1928, they retreated from their own modest reform program. To camouflage their shift to the right and validate their revolutionary credentials they indulged freely in anticlerical demagoguery and excesses. Their acts blew new life into the dying Cristero movement, causing a brief but bitter new conflict that took many lives.

This rightward shift of the Callista regime coincided with the beginning in 1929 of the Great Depression, which exposed the bankruptcy of capitalist economics and added to the misery of Mexican peasants and workers. Their growing unrest created fears of a new revolutionary explosion. Rumblings of protest were heard even within the ruling party. A new generation of young, middle-class reformers demanded vigorous implementation of the constitution of 1917. Some were intellectuals influenced by Marxism and the success of the Soviet example, especially by its concept of economic planning, but their basic message was the need to resume the struggle against the latifundio, peonage, and economic and cultural backwardness, that is, to resume the advance of the bourgeois revolution, stalled by the corruption, cynicism, and conservatism of the Callistas.

By 1933 the growing influence of the progressive wing within the PNR had led to a partial reform of the agrarian laws that transferred land distribution from the states to the federal government and to the beginnings of a school reform under the direction of the brilliant Narciso Bassols during his brief tenure as secretary of education under Abelardo Rodríguez.

The acknowledged leader of the reform group within the PNR was General Lázaro Cárdenas, governor of Michoacán. As governor, Cárdenas had established an enviable record for honesty, compassion, and concern for commoners. He had spent almost 50 percent of his budget on education, doubling the number of schools in the state. Despite his progressive ideas, he was close to the inner circle of the "revolutionary family," and the jefe máximo regarded him as a loyal lieutenant. In October 1930 he was chosen chairman of the PNR, a post that made him one of its most powerful figures.

The 1934 presidential elections approached. Aware of the growing strength of the left wing in the PNR, Calles decided to make concessions to the reformers that would leave him in control of the government. With Calles's blessing, Cárdenas was nominated for president at the PNR convention in 1933. With Calles's approval, the convention also drafted a Six-Year Plan (in obvious imitation of the Soviet model) that would give life to the ideals and promises of the constitution of 1917. Although there was no doubt that he would be elected, Cárdenas campaigned vigorously, visiting the most remote areas of the country, patiently explaining to workers and peasants the Six-Year Plan and the need to strengthen the ejidos, build modern schools, and develop workers' cooperatives. In July 1934 he was elected and took office with a cabinet hand-picked for him by Calles. The jefe máximo was confident that the loyal Cárdenas would carry out his orders as the puppet presidents who preceded him had done.

The Years of Cárdenas

Under Cárdenas, the Mexican Revolution resumed its advance. Land distribution to the villages on a massive scale was accompanied by a many-sided effort to raise agricultural productivity and improve the quality of rural life. Labor was encouraged to replace the old, corrupt leadership with militant leaders and to struggle for improved conditions. A spirit of service began to pervade at least a part of the governmental bureaucracy. Cárdenas set an example to subordinates by the democratic simplicity of his manners, by cutting his own salary in half, and by making himself available to the delegations of Indians and workers who thronged the waiting rooms of the National Palace.

These and other policies of the new president—such as the closing down of illegal gambling houses, most of which were owned by wealthy Callistas—angered the jefe máximo. In June 1935 Calles summoned a number of senators to Cuernavaca, denounced the labor movement and its alleged radicalism, and ominously recalled the brief tenure of President Ortiz Rubio. Cárdenas responded by requesting the resignation of all his cabinet members; then he proceeded to form a new cabinet dominated by the left wing but representing a broad coalition of anti-Callista elements, from right to left. There followed a purge of reactionary state governors, acclaimed by peasants' and workers' demonstra-

tions. By the end of 1935, Cárdenas was the undisputed master of Mexico. In April 1936, amid indications that Calles was planning a coup with the aid of a fascist organization, the Gold Shirts, and other reactionary groups, Cárdenas ordered his immediate deportation to the United States.

Land Reform

Having consolidated his political control, Cárdenas proceeded to implement his reform program. He regarded land distribution as of prime importance. Land was distributed to the peasantry in a variety of ways, according to the climatic and soil conditions of the different regions. The principal form was the ejido, the communal landholding system under which land could not be mortgaged or alienated (except under very special conditions), with each *ejidatario* entitled to use a parcel of community land. The ejido was the focal point of the agrarian reform. But Cárdenas also distributed land in the form of the *rancho,* the individual small holding widely prevalent in the northern Mexican states. Finally, in regions where natural conditions favored large-scale cultivation of such commercial crops as sugar, cotton, coffee, rice, and henequen, large cooperative farms (collective ejidos) were organized on a profit-sharing basis. The government generously endowed these enterprises with seeds, machinery, and credit from the *Banco de Crédito Ejidal.*

During the Cárdenas years, some 45 million acres of land were distributed to almost twelve thousand villages. The Cárdenas distribution program struck a heavy blow at the traditional, semifeudal hacienda and peonage, satisfied the land hunger of the Mexican peasantry for the time being, and promoted a general modernization of Mexican life and society. By 1940, thanks to the land reform, supplemented by the provision of villages with schools, medical care, roads, and other facilities, the standard of living of the peasantry had risen, if only modestly. These progressive changes in turn contributed to the growth of the internal market and therefore of Mexican industry. The land reform also justified itself in terms of productivity; average agricultural production during the three-year period from 1939 to 1941 was higher than it had been at any time since the beginning of the revolution.

Granted these benefits and Cárdenas's excellent intentions, the fact remains that the land reform suffered from the first from certain structural defects. To begin with, it was basically conceived as a means of satisfying land hunger rather than as an instrument of dynamic agricultural development. Seeking to satisfy land hunger by the grant or restitution of land to the villages, government agencies overlooked the need to establish agricultural units that would be viable from an economic point of view. In many cases, the *ejidal* parcel, especially in areas of very dense population, was so small as to form a minifundio. Much of the distributed land was of poor quality (the agrarian law always allowed the landowner to retain a portion of his estate, and naturally he kept the best portion for himself), and aid in the form of seeds, technical assistance, and credit was frequently inadequate.

In addition, the peasant received his land from the government and was tied to it through the operations of the *Departamiento Agrario,* the Banco de Crédito Ejidal, and the officially organized Peasant Leagues; thus, he was increasingly dependent on the public authorities. Under Cárdenas, officials of these agencies often worked in a spirit of disinterested service and sought to develop peasant collective initiative and democracy; under his successors in the presidency, they tended to become corrupt and self-seeking, to enmesh the peasantry and its organizations in a bureaucratic network that manipulated them to satisfy its own interests. After 1940 Mexican governments increasingly favored the large private property and neglected the ejido. In concert with the structural defects of the land reform, this produced a gradual decline of the ejido system and a parallel growth of the large landed property, leading to the emergence of a new latifundio.

Labor Reform

Under Cárdenas the labor movement was revitalized. Aware of the sympathetic attitude of the new regime, workers struck in unprecedented numbers for higher wages and better working conditions; in 1935 there were 642 strikes, more than twice the number in the preceding six years. In 1936 the young radical intellectual Vicente Lombardo Toledano organized a new labor federation, the *Confederación de Trabajadores Mexicanos* (CTM), to replace the dying and discredited CROM. Labor supported and in turn was supported by Cárdenas.

Labor, the peasantry, and the army became the three main pillars of the official party, reorganized in 1938 and renamed the Party of the Mexican Revolution (PRM). The power of the generals was weakened by a policy of raising wages and improving the morale of the rank and file and by the distribution of weapons to the peasantry, formed into a militia. The last important regional caudillo, General Saturnino Cedillo of San Luis Potosi, a foe of Cárdenas's agrarian policy who was linked to the fascist Gold Shirts, launched a revolt in 1938. It was promptly smashed, and Cedillo was killed in a skirmish with federal troops.

Like the land reform, the labor reform had structural flaws that created serious problems for the future. In return for concessions from a paternal government, labor, like the peasantry, was invited to incorporate itself into the official apparatus and to give automatic and obligatory support to a government that in the last analysis represented the interests of the national bourgeoisie. In the domestic and international situation of the 1930s, which was dominated by a struggle between profascist and antifascist forces, the interests of that bourgeoisie and Mexican labor largely coincided, but in the changed conditions after 1940, labor's loss of independence and the meshing of its organizations with the official apparatus led to a revival of corruption and reactionary control of the trade unions.

Economic Reform

Although Cárdenas was sympathetic to labor's demands for better conditions, he was no foe of private enterprise, despite efforts by his foes to link him to socialism and communism. In fact, industrial capitalism made significant strides under Cárdenas. If Cárdenas supported labor's efforts to raise wages where the financial condition of an enterprise warranted it, he also favored Mexican industry with government loans and protective tariffs that insured the creation of a captive market for high-priced consumer goods. In 1934 his government established the *Nacional Financiera,* a government bank and investment corporation that used funds supplied by the federal government and domestic investors to make industrial loans, finance public welfare projects, and issue its own securities. The coming of World War II, which sharply reduced the availability of imports, greatly stimulated the movement toward industrialization and import substitution.

Mexico's struggle for economic sovereignty reached a high point under Cárdenas. In 1937 a dispute between North American and British oil companies and the unions erupted into a strike, followed by legal battles between the contending parties. When the oil companies refused to accept a much-scaled-down arbitration-tribunal wage finding in favor of the workers, Cárdenas intervened. On March 18, 1938—a date celebrated by Mexicans as marking their declaration of economic independence—the president announced in a radio speech that the properties of the oil companies had been expropriated in the public interest. With support from virtually all strata of the population, Cárdenas was able to ride out the storm caused by economic sanctions against Mexico on the part of the United States, England, and the oil companies. The oil nationalization was a major victory for Mexican nationalism. It provided cheap, plentiful fuel for Mexican industry, and the needs of the nationalized oil industries further stimulated industrialization. But the oil nationalization did not set a precedent; some 90 percent of Mexico's mining industry remained in foreign hands.

The Cárdenas government gave firm support to governments resisting the advance of fascism. Mexico and the Soviet Union were the only countries to give significant amounts of aid to the Republicans during the Spanish civil war of 1936–1939. After the Fascist victory in Spain, Mexico opened its doors to Loyalist refugees, including many talented Spanish professionals who made a significant contribution to Mexican culture and economic life. It steadfastly refused to recognize the legality of the Franco regime.

Cárdenas's Growing Moderation and the Election of 1940

Education, especially the rural school system, made considerable progress under Cárdenas, but in the last years of his presidency, in apparent deference to clerical and conservative opposition, he soft-pedaled the so-called socialist character of Mexican education. Of Tarascan Indian origin, Cárdenas displayed much concern for Indian welfare. He created a *Departamiento de Asuntos Indígenas* to serve and protect Indian interests and encouraged the study of Indian culture, past and present, by founding the *Instituto Nacional de Antropología de México.*

Right-wing opposition to Cárdenas's progressive policies grew in the closing years of his presidency. Reactionary groups encouraged and financed by German agents and the Spanish fascist Falange attacked the regime for its supposed communist tendencies. In apparent response to conservative pressure, Cárdenas slowed down the pace of land distribution during the last years of his presidency and displayed a conciliatory attitude toward the entrepreneurial class, assuring its members that he regarded them as part of the *fuerzas vivas* (vital forces) of the country and that they need not fear for the safety of their investments.

On the eve of the presidential election of 1940, right-wingers organized a campaign in favor of General Juan Andreu Almazán, a veteran revolutionary who was now a wealthy industrialist of Monterrey. The left wing of the PRM advanced the candidacy of General Francisco Múgica, author of some of the most advanced provisions of the constitution of 1917 and Cárdenas's close friend and mentor. No man was better qualified to carry out the promises of the second Six-Year Plan, which proposed to continue the rapid pace of agrarian reform; provide the ejidos with cheap credit, irrigation, and roads; and intensify collectivization of ejidos. But the official party was an amalgam of social forces, including increasingly conservative and influential industrialists. Evidently fearing that the nomination of the radical Múgica would be a signal for a rightist revolt, Cárdenas gave him no support, and Múgica soon withdrew. Supported by the powerful CTM, the party gave its nomination to General Manuel Ávila Camacho, who was loyal to Cárdenas. A devout Catholic and a man of generally conservative views, Ávila Camacho was elected with almost 99 percent of the vote.

The defeated Almazán fled to Texas, proclaiming fraud. For a time, it seemed that a revolt would break out, but Almazán soon returned to Mexico and private life. Meanwhile, Ávila Camacho was making statements designed to reassure foreign and domestic capital. He dissociated himself from the radical leadership of the unions, expressed a flexible attitude toward the question of whether the ejido or small private property was the best form of agrarian organization, and assured the Catholics he was a *creyente* (believer). In December 1940 Ávila Camacho assumed the presidency without any serious disturbances.

The Big Bourgeoisie in Power, 1940–1976: Erosion of Reform

The Cárdenas era was the high-water mark of the struggle to achieve the social goals of the revolution. Under his successors, there began an erosion of the social conquests of the Cárdenas years. During those years the material and cultural condition of the masses had improved, if only modestly; peasants and workers managed to secure a somewhat larger share of the total national income. After 1940 these trends were reversed. The new rulers of Mexico favored a development strategy that sharply restricted trade union activity, slowed the tempo of agrarian reform, and reduced the relative share of total income of the bottom two-thirds of the Mexican population.

Ávila Camacho presided over the first phase (1940–1946) of this reversal of policy. Regarding unlimited private profit as the driving force of

economic progress, he proposed to create a favorable climate for private enterprise. In practice, this meant the freezing of wages, the repression of strikes, and the use of a new weapon against dissidents, a vaguely worded law dealing with the "crime of social dissolution."

Meanwhile, World War II stimulated both the export of Mexican raw materials and import substitution through industrialization. Significant advances were made in food processing, textiles, and other consumer goods industries, and the capital goods industry, centering in the north, was considerably expanded. Steel production increased, with Monterrey Steel and other companies producing structural and rolled steel for buildings, hotels, highways, and steel hardware. The Nacional Financiera played a leading role in this process of growth through loans to industry for plant construction and expansion. In view of this spontaneous economic growth, the concept of planning was forgotten; the second Six-Year Plan remained on paper. Indeed, a characteristic of the economic expansion was its unplanned character. No effort was made to produce a balanced development of the Mexican regions; most of the development took place in the Federal District and the surrounding area. Meanwhile, land distribution was sharply reduced, and a conservative spirit began to pervade the educational system.

In 1946 the official party changed its name from PRM to the PRI (*Partido Revolucionario Institucional*), and Ávila Camacho was succeeded as president by the lawyer Miguel Alemán (1946–1952), who continued the policies of his predecessor. Alemán made every effort to encourage private investment through tariff protection, import licensing, subsidies, and government loans. This favorable economic climate attracted domestic and foreign investors looking for outlets for their surplus capital after World War II. A characteristic of the new foreign capital investment was that it flowed primarily into manufacturing rather than the traditional extractive industries.

Under Alemán, land distribution and efforts to increase the productivity of the ejidos were neglected in favor of the large private landholding.

To provide an incentive to capitalist entrepreneurs, Alemán had Article 27 of the constitution amended. This "reform" consisted in the grant of certificates of "inaffectibility" to landowners, which exempted them from further expropriation for holdings up to 100 hectares of irrigated land or 200 hectares of land with seasonal rainfall. For the production of certain specified crops, the size of inaffectible holdings was made even larger.

A massive program of irrigation contributed to the explosion of capitalist agriculture that began in this period. The irrigation projects were concentrated in northern and northwestern Mexico, where much of the land was owned directly or indirectly by prominent Mexican politicians, their friends, and relatives. Alemán presided over a great boom in public works construction, accompanied by an orgy of plunder of the public treasury by entrepreneurs and officials; his was probably the most corrupt administration in modern Mexican history.

Under Alemán's successor, Adolfo Ruiz Cortines (1952–1958), the pace of land distribution was further reduced and the ejidos suffered a neglect that contributed to the low productivity for which they were criticized. Irrigation works continued to be concentrated in areas dominated by large private landholdings. Thanks to the new laws of "inaffectibility" and the varied ruses employed by large landowners to violate the agrarian laws, concentration of landownership continued to grow. There arose a new hacienda, technically efficient and often arrayed in modern corporate guise, that soon accounted for the bulk of Mexico's commercial agricultural production and shared its profits with processing plants that were usually subsidiaries of foreign firms. By 1961, fifty years after the revolution began, less than 1 percent of all farms possessed 50 percent of all agricultural land. Increasing numbers of small landholders meanwhile, starved for credit and lacking machinery, had to abandon their parcels of land and become peons on the new haciendas or emigrate to the cities in search of work in the new factories.

Industry continued to grow but was increasingly penetrated and dominated by foreign capital. A favorite device for foreign penetration of Mexican industry was the mixed, or joint, company, which had a number of advantages. It satisfied the requirement of Mexican law that Mexican nationals hold 51 percent of most companies operating in Mexico; it camouflaged actual domination of such enterprises by the foreign partners through control of patents, licensing agreements, and other sources of technological and financial dependence; and it formed strong ties between foreign capitalists and the native industrial and financial bourgeoisie.

The economic and social policies of President Adolfo López Mateos (1958–1964) and Gustavo Díaz Ordaz (1964–1970), did not differ significantly from those of their predecessors. Under Díaz Ordaz discontent among workers mounted as their real income shrank as a result of chronic inflation, a virtual freeze on wages, and official control of trade union organizations. Student unrest also grew in reaction to police brutality against student protesters and violations of the constitutional autonomy of the national university. The student protest broadened into a nationwide movement demanding democratization of Mexican economic and political life. The government responded with a savage assault by army troops on a peaceful assembly of students and others in the Plaza of Three Cultures in Mexico City (October 2, 1968), leaving a toll of dead and wounded running into the hundreds.

The economic strategy of the Díaz Ordaz administration centered on providing the greatest possible incentives to private investment, foreign and domestic. The foreign debt grew alarmingly under Díaz Ordaz, with the volume of foreign loans reaching a figure four times that of the Ruiz Cortines era. This heavy influx of loans increased the dependent character of the Mexican economy.

In his foreign policies, however, Díaz Ordaz continued the traditional Mexican posture of diplomatic independence. Despite objections from the United States, Mexico maintained diplomatic relations with revolutionary Cuba, expressed disapproval of U.S. intervention in Cuba (the Bay of

Pigs affair), and opposed President Lyndon Johnson's intervention in the Dominican Republic. This independent foreign policy reflected both popular anti-imperialist sentiment and a striving on the part of the Mexican ruling class to achieve a partial independence from Washington.

The official presidential candidate, Luis Echeverría, took office in 1970 amid deepening political, social, and economic storm clouds. Echeverría signaled a tactical shift when he released a large number of students and intellectuals imprisoned after the 1968 student disturbances, promised to struggle against colonialism and corruption, and condemned the unjust distribution of income in Mexico.

Echeverría's foreign policies gave some credibility to his liberal image; he hosted a visit by Marxist President Salvador Allende of Chile, opened Mexico's doors wide to Chilean refugees after the fascist seizure of power in Chile, and urged Cuba's full re-entry into the inter-American community. These actions gave Echeverría a reputation for radicalism in certain quarters, especially in the United States.

There seems little doubt that Echeverría began his administration with a genuine desire to achieve reform, reduce dependency, spread the fruits of development more widely, and create a somewhat more open, democratic political system. Conservative Mexican capitalists, closely linked with foreign capital, struck back by withholding investment funds from the market, setting off a serious recession. Under intense pressure from the right, Echeverría retreated. During his last three years in office he reverted to traditional policies and methods, poorly concealed by a populist rhetoric. He publicly denounced colonialism and multinational corporations, but his government did its utmost to attract foreign investments, especially from the United States. With the investments came growing foreign penetration and domination of Mexican industry, especially of its most strategic sectors. By the mid-seventies, 70 percent of earnings from the capital goods industry went to foreign capital, leaving 20 percent for public firms and 10 percent for national private companies.

As the investments increased, so did Mexico's indebtedness and the drain of its capital in the form of dividends, interest, and other returns on foreign investment. By June 1976 Mexico's foreign debt had reached $25 billion. Mexico and Brazil shared the distinction of having the highest foreign debts among Third World countries. By September of that year the growing trade deficit had forced the government to order a 60 percent devaluation of the peso, causing a sharp rise in inflation and greater hardship for the masses.

When he came to office in 1970, Echeverría promised to provide the ejidos with irrigated land and other aid; in fact, little aid was given. When he left the presidency six years later, the problem of landlessness or inadequate land and rural unemployment and underemployment remained as stubborn as ever. Some 6 million peasants were landless.

Prospects for the solution of Mexico's urgent problems through the electoral process appeared dim because the PRI, dominated by the industrial and financial oligarchy, had an unshakable grip on power. That power rested in the last analysis on a system of institutionalized coercion and fraud. But fraud, force, and threat of force were not the only means used by the government and the ruling party to retain control. Other methods included the co-optation of dissidents into the state apparatus; the provision of greater access to medical services, schools, low-cost housing, and other benefits to such strategic groups as state employees, professionals, and organized workers; the paternalistic distribution of goods and services to the urban poor; and a populist rhetoric that identified the ruling party with the great ideals of the Revolution. These policies did little to reduce mass poverty or the growing inequalities of income in Mexican society, but they provided a precarious popular base and legitimacy for the PRI's monopoly of political power. By the mid-seventies, both popularity and legitimacy were threatened by rampant inflation and a stagnant economy.

In the 1976 election the official party candidate, José López Portillo, ran without opposition other than that of an unregistered (that is, officially unrecognized) Communist party candidate. The PRI rolled up the usual huge majority.

López Portillo continued the long-established policy of favoring the country's elites, making it clear that he was opposed to further large-scale land distribution and would not touch efficiently run large estates even if their size exceeded legal limits. In the words of one Mexican weekly, "the constitution is to protect peasants wearing collars and ties, and not those wearing rope sandals."

On the other hand, López Portillo, like Echeverría, appeared to recognize the need to provide a safety valve for growing political dissent and to modernize the monolithic political structure created by Calles in 1929. In October 1977, he offered a constitutional reform bill that eased the requirements for registration of minority political parties and created a system of partial proportional representation designed to insure the presence of opposition elements in Congress. Under the plan the chamber of deputies was expanded from 300 to 400 seats, with the additional seats apportioned to minority parties on the basis of their vote. Nothing in the so-called reform bill, however, threatened the PRI's control over the electoral machinery and its continued domination of the government.

From Oil Boom to Bust, 1977–1987

López Portillo took office on December 1, 1976, amid growing optimism over Mexico's economic prospects as a result of the recent discovery of vast new oil and gas deposits on Mexico's east coast. Figures for the country's estimated and proven oil reserves steadily rose; by January 1980 they were put at 200 billion barrels, and Mexico ranked among the world's major oil producers. With oil prices increasing steeply, government planners counted on the oil and gas bonanza to alleviate Mexico's balance-of-payments problem and to finance the purchase of the goods needed for further development and

the creation of new jobs. The resulting expansion of production, however, was largely concentrated in capital-intensive industries—petrochemical factories, steel mills, and the like—that generated relatively few jobs. In agriculture, too, the main growth was in capital-intensive, export-oriented agribusiness operations that created little employment and diverted labor and acreage from staple food production. Indeed, staple food production actually declined during the 1970s; by 1980 one-third of the maize consumed in Mexico came from the United States.

The cost of the imported equipment and technology required to expand oil production came very high and had to be covered by new loans. Despite increasing revenues from oil and gas exports, Mexico's trade deficit rose from $1.4 billion in 1977 to over $2 billion in 1978, and $3 billion in 1979. Inflation again moved upward; Mexican workers lost 20 percent of their purchasing power between 1977 and 1979. Despite these troubling signs, the international bankers appeared eager to lend more, advancing Mexico $10 billion in 1980. Who could question the credit of a country that seemed to float on a sea of oil?

The oil boom and the massive infusions of foreign loans gave a new dimension to the familiar problem of corruption in Mexican political life.[1] One of its signs was a wave of monumental private construction. But "the dance of the billions" was drawing to a close. In the first months of 1981, responding to weakening demand and a developing world oil glut, oil prices fell sharply. Mexico's projected earnings in 1982 from oil and gas exports, source of 75 percent of Mexico's foreign exchange, fell from $27 billion to under $14 billion. Many wealthy Mexicans, losing confidence in their currency, hurried to buy dollars and deposit them in U.S. banks. In February 1982, with the government's foreign exchange reserves dwindling at an alarming rate, López Portillo allowed the peso to fall by 60 percent. Fear of further devaluations provoked another flight of dol-

[1] One Mexican news magazine, *Proceso,* estimated that officials of López Portillo's administration had misused or stolen $3 billion of public funds.

lars. The growing shortage of dollars, vitally needed fuel for Mexican industry, caused a widening recession and unemployment.

In July 1982 Mexicans went to the polls to elect a new president. The PRI, operating with its usual efficiency, gave the official candidate, Harvard-trained economist Miguel de la Madrid, some 74 percent of the vote; the main opposition parties, the Christian Democratic *Partido de Acción Nacional* (PAN) and a coalition of leftist forces, the *Partido Socialista Unificado de México* (PSUM), were allotted 14 percent and 6 percent of the vote, respectively. On the local level there was evidence of growing resistance to efforts to impose official candidates. Yielding to popular pressure, the regime accepted the victory of opposition candidates in a number of towns.

President-elect De la Madrid was not to take office until December 1, and López Portillo had to cope with the growing economic crisis. The peso continued its steady decline, falling to the rate of 95 pesos to one dollar by the end of August, while the cost of imported goods rose sharply. Bankruptcies and closings multiplied as more and more businesses lacked the dollars needed to obtain imported parts and raw materials or to pay debts contracted in dollars. With the Banco de México almost drained of reserves, López Portillo took a dramatic step. On September 1, in his last annual message to Congress, he announced the nationalization of all private (but not foreign) banks and the establishment of stringent exchange controls. The bank nationalization, the most radical measure taken by a Mexican president since the "Mexicanization" of the oil industry by Cárdenas in 1938, was greeted with cries of protest from the private banking sector and great demonstrations of support by the PRI and its client organizations, the trade unions, and the parties of the left.

In Washington, usually so allergic to all measures smacking of collectivism or socialism, the bank nationalization did not arouse the hostility that might have been expected, probably because even conservative United States officials regarded it as a necessary step, given the circumstances. The prime concern of the Reagan administration was to save Mexico, the third largest trading partner of the United States, from a default that could wreck the international banking system and bring down the great American banks to which Mexico owed $25.8 billion, almost a third of its foreign debt. Since July, consultations had been taking place between Mexican finance minister Jesús Silva Herzog and United States officials concerning the details of the rescue operation. The final plan provided for United States aid of $2.9 billion for Mexico's current-account problem; a seven-month freeze on the repayment of principal due to American, Western European, and Japanese bankers; and an eventual IMF (International Monetary Fund) loan of $3.9 billion, which could initiate a new cycle of commercial bank loans to Mexico. The IMF loan was, of course, subject to the usual conditions: Mexico must accept certain austerity measures—reduction of subsidies, restraints on wage increases, and other economies that were bound to hit Mexico's poor the hardest.

Even before he took office on December 1, 1982, President-elect De la Madrid had indicated his approval of the strong financial medicine prescribed by the IMF. These politically unpalatable steps included price increases of 100 percent and 50 percent on gasoline and natural gas, respectively, and the lifting of price controls and subsidies for consumer items ranging from shoes to television sets. Another measure was a new devaluation of the peso that was expected to stimulate exports. It would, however, also make imports more costly, increase the burden of foreign debt service, and reduce real wages. Finally, accepting the bank nationalization as "irreversible," De la Madrid clearly indicated that he would not use nationalization to control private credit and investment. He even sent Congress a bill that partially "denationalized" the banks by allowing private investors to purchase 34 percent of their shares.

The solution for the Mexican crisis devised in Washington and accepted by the Mexican political leadership consisted, in essence, of adding new debts to old ones, without the slightest prospect that the huge foreign debt of some $85 billion could ever be paid or even significantly reduced without a large write-off, and of imposing heavy new burdens on already impoverished groups of the Mexican population.

Four years after the rescue operation worked out by Silva Herzog, United States officials, and the banks, the debt problem was more intractable than ever. By the fall of 1986 Mexico's foreign debt had risen to more than $100 billion; the exchange rate of the peso in mid-1987 was about 1,400 to the dollar.

The drain of billions of dollars to service the foreign debt, coupled with the plunge in oil prices and the effects of the IMF-imposed austerity program, had disastrous economic consequences for Mexico. Many businesses, unable to obtain loans from state banks, had to close their doors. High unemployment and inflation (for the first nine months of 1986 the inflation rate stood at about 104 percent) sharply reduced purchasing power and forced many industries to shut down or to cut production, resulting in more unemployment. By the government's own figures, 1986 was the worst year for the Mexican economy since 1982. A major natural disaster, the earthquake of September 19, 1985, caused over 20,000 deaths, changed Mexico City's center forever, and created huge reconstruction problems, adding to the public and official woes.

The economic crisis was intertwined with a growing crisis in U.S.–Mexican relations. The Reagan administration, fanatically devoted to a "free market" economy and committed to the overthrow of the Sandinist government in Nicaragua, sought to use negotiations with Mexico over its foreign debt as a means of reshaping Mexico's economic structures and even its foreign policy. The U.S. economic demands included the opening up of Mexican industry to foreign investments, selling off state-owned enterprises, liberalizing foreign trade, and abandoning regulation of direct foreign investment. Despite the many concessions made by the De la Madrid government in economic policy, the Reagan administration demanded more.

Mexico's independent stance toward Central America also caused great anger in Washington. Especially irksome to the United States was Mexico's leading role in the Contadora group of Latin American nations, which sought settlement of Central American problems through dialogue and political agreements and opposed military intervention by outside powers. The displeasure of right-wing elements in the United States with Mexico's independent stance was reflected in a two-day hearing on Mexico in May 1986 by a U.S. Senate Foreign Relations subcommittee, called by ultraright Republican senator Jesse Helms. Helms attacked Mexico's political system, comparing the PRI to the Communist party of the Soviet Union, while Elliot Abrams, assistant secretary of state for inter-American affairs, criticized the PRI for its domination of Mexican politics and Mexican foreign policy for its alleged support of the Nicaraguan Sandinistas.

Certainly the Mexican political process continued to be tainted by fraud and corruption as was made evident in the 1986 state elections in Chihuahua and Oaxaca. But Helms (a strong supporter of Pinochet's fascist regime in Chile) and Abrams (who was shown in June-July 1987 to have lied to Congress regarding the Iran-Contra scandal) did not attack Mexico's alleged political sins from an attachment to pure democracy. In Mexico the hearings' attack was seen by many as a scheme to destabilize the Mexican government and to destroy the revolutionary nationalist principles the PRI championed.

The Second Conquest of Mexico, 1987–1995

Thus at the opening of 1987 Mexico faced a profound, many-sided crisis. In essence, it was a crisis of the import-substitution model of development institutionalized by Cárdenas and continued, with a pronounced shift to the right, by his successors in the presidency. That model was based on state ownership of key industries, protection and subsidies for private industry, and such redistributive policies as the provision of social services, subsidized food prices, and land reform. It also called for the alternate use of cooptation and repression by the one-party state to keep restive labor, peasants, and intellectuals in line. By the early 1980s, however, that model had exhausted its possibilities for growth. The signs of its failure included a chronic depression and a gigantic, unpayable foreign debt.

Confronted with that failure, a dominant section of the Mexican elite opted for a new, neoliberal model of development that abandoned the internal market in favor of exports of manufactured goods and integration with the world economy, especially with the United States. The economic program of President De la Madrid marked the transition to the new economic order. Two important steps in that direction were Mexico's signing in 1986 of the General Agreement on Tariffs and Trade, designed to lower tariffs and eliminate quotas and other restrictions on trade, and the liberalization under American and Japanese pressure of foreign investment laws. The full implementation of the neoliberal project, however, had to await the outcome of the historic election of 1988.

By mid-1987 a "democratizing faction" within the ruling party had grown dissatisfied with the conduct of policy; this led to an open rift with the official leadership. Heading the pro-democracy group was Cuauhtémoc Cárdenas, son of former president and national hero Lázaro Cárdenas. Cuauhtémoc, a former PRI senator and a former governor of Michoacán, was joined by such PRI notables as Porfirio Muñoz Ledo, former Mexican ambassador to the United Nations and secretary of labor and education in previous administrations, and Carlos Tello, former head of Mexico's Central Bank and widely regarded as the author of the 1982 nationalization of the country's banking system. Calling itself "Democratic Current," the group was critical of certain policies of the De la Madrid administration. Specifically the group opposed payment of the foreign debt at the expense of the living standards of the Mexican people; it also called for more grassroots participation in the choice of the 1988 presidential candidate, traditionally selected by the incumbent president.

But the PRI leadership rejected the calls for reform and put forward as its candidate another Harvard-trained economist, Carlos Salinas de Gortari, politically almost a carbon copy of De la Madrid. Cárdenas and other prominent dissenters then withdrew from the PRI and formed a National Democratic Front (FDN) that ran Cárdenas as its presidential candidate; eventually the Front was joined by the Mexican Socialist party and other left-wing parties. Cárdenas's program called for an end to political corruption and electoral fraud, suspension of foreign debt payments and renegotiation of the debt with creditor banks and governments, a mixed economy, and state assistance to the ejido farming sector. His candidacy inspired a wave of popular enthusiasm and mobilization unknown since the election of 1934 that brought his own father to power.

Most political observers believe that Cárdenas actually won the general election of July 6, 1988. On election night, with the first returns overwhelmingly favorable to Cárdenas, the computerized voting system "crashed," and when it came back, after a two-day news blackout, Salinas had taken the lead. Cárdenas and Manuel Clouthier, presidential candidate of the right-wing National Action Party (PAN), cried fraud, but since the PRI counted the votes, Salinas was declared the winner and assumed office on December 1; the official count gave Salinas 50.1 percent of the 19 million ballots cast, 31.1 percent to Cárdenas, and 17 percent to Clouthier. Still, the election altered Mexican politics in important ways. In the Chamber of Deputies opposition parties now held 240 seats and the PRI 260 seats. In the Senate opposition parties won representation for the first time, with four of the sixty-four seats. Faced with popular anger and the enormous popular mobilization behind Cárdenas, Salinas and the forces he represented within the PRI opted to abandon the traditional practice of winning all legislative seats, known as the *carro completo,* in favor of narrower but more plausible victories. The midterm elections of August 1991, however, were again marked by widespread repression and fraud.[2] The PRI gave itself 61.4 of the vote, gaining

[2] But repression and fraud are not the only methods used by the PRI to retain power. An important new agency serving that end is the National Solidarity Program (PRONASOL), which by 1991 accounted for 35 percent of nondebt government spending. Ostensibly designed to assist Mexico's poorest classes, it gives carefully selected communities supplies and equipment for local development projects.

320 seats in the Chamber of Deputies, 61 seats in the Senate, and all but three of the governorships. Mass protests, including a march of thousands on Mexico City, forced Salinas to order the resignation or removal of some new PRI state governors and allow the seating of some PRD mayors. These retreats, however, seemed primarily designed to placate and disarm public anger; when new elections were held they were marked by the same or more sophisticated forms of fraud, with the same results.

To counter the outcry over the regime's blatant fraud, Salinas promised electoral reform and a democratization of the PRI's structure and methods to make it more responsive to its constituents. More significant was the PRI's strategy of rapprochement with the conservative PAN, whose program, stressing privatization and reduced state intervention, was almost indistinguishable from PRI's own program. One sign of this rapprochement was the PRI's willingness to recognize PAN victories, like its victories in the 1989 gubernatorial election in Baja California and the 1992 gubernatorial election in Chihuahua while using traditional fraudulent methods and violence to impose PRI's candidates in local elections won by the newly formed Democratic Revolutionary Party (PRD) in Michoacán and Guerrero. Cárdenas and the PRD correctly viewed this rapprochement as having, among other ends, the goal of splitting the opposition and isolating the new party. The indisputable fact is that the Mexican government remained a dictatorship, a dictatorship of a special kind, but still a dictatorship.

The PRD, the government's main opposition, was hampered in the growth of its influence by internal divisions, by its difficulty in delivering promised benefits to its supporters (80 percent of municipal revenue is provided by the federal government and can be withheld from local governments under opposition control), and by its failure to develop a comprehensive economic and social program, to project a distinctive vision of a future Mexico. To date its program has not gone far beyond a stress on the suspension of payments on the foreign debt in order to increase spending on social programs and

the rebuilding of national industry and agriculture and opposition to NAFTA (the North American Free Trade Agreement) in its present form. However, Cárdenas and the PRD offered the only genuine alternative to the policies of austerity and privatization pursued even more energetically by Salinas de Gortari than his predecessor.

On coming to office, Salinas slated for privatization almost all of Mexico's remaining 770 state-owned enterprises, presiding over a fire sale of some of Mexico's choicest properties, including mines, sugar mills, a five-star hotel chain, and the national insurance company. Two government airlines, state-owned steel companies, 70 percent of the petrochemical industry, and the Teléfonos de México, have also been sold. Many were sold well below their market value, and only some were operating inefficiently and at a loss. The process was accompanied by widespread layoffs and wage cuts and growing foreign conquest of Mexican industry, aided by repeal of the law that restricted foreign control to 49 percent ownership of Mexican businesses. Observers noted that the state companies were being sold to the same small group of people and their foreign partners who already controlled most of Mexico's economy, with no effort to promote "popular capitalism" through stock offerings in the open market. "Crony capitalism," ran one comment, "seems to be the current government's style."

The denationalization of Mexican industry through privatization was accompanied by the demise of many small and medium-sized domestic businesses as a result of the removal of most tariff barriers. These developments reflected a general tendency on the part of Mexico's recent rulers to abandon the struggle for economic independence that had been a major goal of the Mexican Revolution, of Lázaro Cárdenas, and even of the conservative but nationalistic presidents who followed him. The foreign conquest of the Mexican consumer goods market since 1986 is very evident: "Everything from Italian pasta and Diet Coke to European cookies and Italian loafers is now available. . . . In many cases local manufacturers have closed down because imports are cheaper and better made."

The decision to abandon the struggle for economic independence was reflected in the Mexican government's encouragement of the program that permits U.S. companies to establish plants (called *maquiladoras* or *maquilas*) for production of parts and their assembly on the Mexican side of the border. The program permits duty-free entry of parts and machinery into Mexico and allows total U.S. ownership of the plants. U.S. customs regulations allow the finished products to enter the United States with duty paid only on the value of the labor, not on that of the goods themselves. The lure of low wages has caused an explosive growth of maquiladora plants, whose number has grown from some 455 with 130,000 workers in 1982 to about 2,000 with nearly 600,000 workers in 1993. In these plants workers assemble television sets, radios, computer hardware, and the like for the American market. Many of the plants were unorganized; in others the workers were represented by government-controlled unions who usually offer employers "protection contracts" that do not meet the labor standards mandated by the Mexican Federal Labor Law. These unions cooperate with employers to keep wages low. Mexican officials defend the program by arguing that it relieves the heavy Mexican unemployment. But since many of the plants are true sweatshops, with health and safety problems widespread among the workers, it tends to institutionalize poverty on both sides of the border, for the program inevitably tends to depress wages in the U.S. border zone. In the United States, unions are concerned about the loss of thousands of jobs and the prospect of more to come. Environmentalists and health workers are alarmed by the shockingly poor environmental and health record of the maquiladoras, which have freely released various toxins into the air and water and routinely neglected to treat hazardous wastes. The American Medical Association declared that the maquiladora program had created "a virtual cesspool" on the American-Mexican border.

All these economic and environmental problems were likely to be multiplied by the North American Free Trade Agreement that was approved in November 1993 by the U.S. Congress after a bitter debate during which President Bill Clinton freely offered public works projects, agricultural deals, and miscellaneous swaps to secure the support of wavering members of Congress. This cynical bargaining, it was estimated, would cost American taxpayers as much as $50 billion. American corporations spent $30 million in their lobbying campaign for NAFTA, and the Salinas government spent an estimated $30 to $35 million. Labor unions and grassroots environmental organizations strongly opposed the program.

In Mexico the treaty was denounced by independent labor and peasant unions and organizations and by the PRD. Speaking for the PRD, Cuauhtémoc Cárdenas called for a new trade agreement, providing workers in the three countries with the same workplace conditions, collective bargaining rights, and occupational safety and health standards. But Mexico's PRI-dominated Senate swiftly brushed aside all objections and ratified the treaty on November 22.

NAFTA eliminates tariffs between Canada, the United States, and Mexico over fifteen years and permits the free flow of investment capital across borders. To meet the concerns of labor unions and conservationists, negotiators from Canada, the United States, and Mexico worked out side agreements dealing with labor and the environment. But the commissions created by the accords are simply "watchdog" bodies, with no enforcement powers or minimum standards to enforce. Moreover, the Mexican government routinely manipulates or juggles workplace information.

American labor unions have good reason to fear that free trade between the United States and Mexico, where wages are only one-tenth of the U.S.,[3] will result in the loss of many thousands of jobs. Estimates of the probable job losses in the United States as a result of the implementation of NAFTA range from the estimate of 150,000 by

[3] In October 1993 the Economic Research Institute of Vienna issued a report showing just how low average wages are in Mexico: about $2.35 per hour, compared with $17.02 in the U.S., $16.16 in Japan, and $25.94 in Germany. They are even lower than those of the "Asian Tigers": $3.89 in Hong Kong, $4.93 in South Korea, and $5.19 in Taiwan.

300

President Bush's Secretary of Labor Lynn Martin to the forecast of 550,000 jobs lost over ten years by Jeff Faux, president of the Economic Policy Institute. Aside from the actual job loss, NAFTA will surely put severe pressure on American labor to make wage and other concessions to employers. President Clinton and his Secretary of Labor Robert Reich have argued that the United States might lose low-paid, unskilled jobs to Mexico but will retain the high-tech, high-paid jobs that will be created through their plans for rebuilding America and job-retraining programs. In fact, three-quarters of the new manufacturing jobs created by American companies in Mexico are precisely in the high-tech, capital-intensive fields of auto and electronics, and the productivity of Mexican labor is rising rapidly. The claim that job creation through increased exports to Mexico will more than compensate for any job losses in the United States is equally dubious. The primary targets of NAFTA are the United States and Canada, not the impoverished Mexican market. Over 50 percent of the Mexican population lives below the poverty levels set by the United Nations. It is estimated that only one-third of the population has sufficient income to constitute an effective market for more than basic necessities.

Meanwhile the De la Madrid and Salinas policies have created an unprecedented crisis for the ejido sector of Mexican agriculture. Even before the passage of NAFTA, Mexican small farmers faced increasing competition from foreign agricultural imports as a result of Mexico's entry into the General Agreement on Tariffs and Trade (GATT) and steadily reduced import restrictions. NAFTA, allowing the free entrance of American corn into Mexico, may deal a death blow to Mexican maize producers, since maize costs about two or three times as much to produce per ton in Mexico as in the United States. According to one estimate, as a result of NAFTA's coming into force the number of maize farmers in Mexico will decline from about 2.8 million to 420,000 in a few years.

The very existence of the ejido system was threatened by a February 1992 reform of Article 27 of the Constitution. This constitutional reform allows the division of the ejidos into individual lots and their rental, sale, or joint cultivation with domestic or foreign partners. The provision for rental of ejido land legalized a previously existing practice, but it was predicted that the lure of cash will induce many impoverished ejidatarios to sell their land. Others will lose their land though foreclosure by banks. Increasingly, companies with easier access to credit and capital will buy the most productive areas of the Mexican countryside.

Where will the hundreds of thousands of farmers who abandon the land as a result of NAFTA and the agrarian reform go? Many will leave for the overcrowded cities, swelling the numbers of unemployed or underemployed Mexicans; others will find low-wage jobs in the border maquiladoras or on farms producing fruit or vegetables for the U.S. market. Many will head for the United States to join the pool of Mexican undocumented workers, numbering in the millions and growing between 200,000 and 300,000 a year, who work in agriculture, domestic service, small industry, and food service. From time to time the Immigration and Naturalization Service (INS) rounds up and deports undocumented workers and "tough" new proposals to prevent the smuggling of undocumented immigrants are made, but meantime the influx continues and the hiring of such immigrants continues and even increases. The fact is that the existence of this pool of low-paid, vulnerable workers—vulnerable precisely because they are undocumented and can be deported—represents a source of superprofits to employers and contributes to the weakness of organized labor. In general, U.S. unions have done little to incorporate the migrants into their ranks or protest their abuse by police and border guards. The wave of anti-Mexican, anti-immigrant sentiment, with strong racist overtones, now sweeping through the United States has heightened tension on both sides of the border. This sentiment is reflected in California's 1994 passage of Proposition 187, which denies social services to illegal immigrants.

In Mexico, meanwhile, despite Salinas's reformist airs, the traditional abuses in the area of civil liberties and human rights continued unchecked. In its 1991 report, Americas Watch, a

U.S.-based human rights group, noted that torture "occurs in all parts of the country and is practiced by most if not all branches of the federal and state police, as well as by the armed forces." The Federal Judicial Police (PJF) and its agents, commonly called *madrinas* (godmothers), "remain the most frightening force in the land." Killings and "disappearances" continue; some 250 members of the PRD have been killed since 1988.

Despite widespread poverty, repression, and discontent, as 1993 drew to a close Mexico seemed tranquil and there appeared to be little effective opposition to PRI's monolithic control of Mexican politics and its neoliberal economic program. In late November the PRI held the traditional *destape* or "unveiling" of the party's presidential candidate in the August 1994 elections, Luis Donaldo Colosio. Colosio had managed the fraud-riddled 1988 election in which Salinas was elected president and presided over the vast "Solidarity" public works program used to allay social discontent and insure PRI's continued electoral success.

Then a succession of dramatic events shattered Mexico's surface calm and raised serious doubts about the ruling party's secure grip on power and its internal unity. On New Year's Day 1994, a revolt led by a self-styled "Zapatista Army of National Liberation" (EZLN), believed to number several thousand members, broke out in the southern state of Chiapas, one of the poorest regions of Mexico, with a largely Mayan population. The rebels proclaimed NAFTA and its free-trade program "a death certificate" for the native peoples of Mexico and demanded sweeping political and economic reforms, including self-rule for Mexico's Indian communities, repeal of the reforms to Article 27, and fraud-free elections. The rebels seized and briefly held the highland city of San Cristóbal de las Casas and three other towns before melting back into the Lacandon rainforest after a savage counteroffensive by 14,000 Mexican army troops, accompanied by bombing of Indian villages, summary executions, torture of suspects, and other repressive measures. Then, in apparent response to a wave of domestic and foreign criticism, the Salinas government halted

the offensive, announced an amnesty for all participants in the violence, and appointed Manuel Camacho Solís, believed to belong to the reformist wing of PRI, chief peace commissioner to negotiate with the Zapatistas. The government expressed willingness to negotiate virtually all their thirty-four demands except the demand that Salinas resign as president, and promised major social, economic, and political reforms, including an electoral reform that would ensure the fairness of the elections scheduled for August 21.

On June 11, 1994, casting doubt on the government's sincerity and citing a resounding 97.88 nay vote by the communities in revolt, the Zapatistas rejected a peace settlement that did not contain the political reforms they demanded but offered to renew negotiations for the establishment of democratic institutions throughout Mexico. They also promised not to resume fighting as long as they were not attacked. At the end of 1994 a fragile truce continued between the Zapatistas and government troops who surrounded the area in revolt, with no solution to the conflict in sight.

With some specific features that reflect its tragic history, Chiapas's problems epitomize the problems of rural Mexico. The Mexican Revolution of 1910 never really reached Chiapas, with the result that no agrarian reform took place here. The great landowners own about 40 percent of the land, while 63 percent of the campesinos own plots of less than 2.5 acres. Recently, emboldened by the crisis and the standoff with the government, land-hungry campesinos, not waiting for the government to act, have occupied nearly 100,000 acres of farmland, resulting in armed clashes with paramilitary groups organized by the great landowners.

The problems of the campesinos have been aggravated by severely eroded soils, cutbacks in credits and subsidies by the Salinas administration since 1988, and the collapse of world coffee prices. According to the economist José Luis Calva, the "time bomb" that exploded in Chiapas resulted from the government's structural adjustment plan and the official free trade policy, which is expected to result in a greatly increased importation of cheap corn from the United States. In his view, the recent reforms to Article 27 of the

302 Constitution, threatening what remained of the communal ejido system, "detonated" the crisis.

Whatever the outcome of the Chiapas crisis, it has already deeply wounded the PRI and the Salinas regime, exposing the hollowness of their claims that Mexico is now fully a part of the First World. On March 23 Mexicans were again stunned when PRI's presidential candidate, Colosio, was assassinated while campaigning in the border city of Tijuana. There was widespread disbelief that the assassin, a twenty-three-year-old factory worker, acted alone, a position that the government promulgated. Whatever the motives for the assassination, it revealed deep cleavages within the ruling party. Salinas quickly named another U.S.-trained economist and Colosio's campaign manager, Ernesto Zedillo Ponce de León, as PRI's new presidential candidate to face PRD's Cuauhtémoc Cárdenas and PAN's Diego Fernández de Cevallos in the August elections. Despite official claims that recent changes in the electoral code ensured a fraud-free election, the PRD and a large majority of the Mexican public did not expect honest elections on August 21.

The election took place with the PRI seemingly in trouble as a result of a number of factors: the dramatic Chiapas revolt; the murder of Colosio, which revealed deep fissures within the ruling party; a declining economy; and an unprecedented mobilization of citizen's groups to prevent the heavy-handed corruption that had characterized Mexican elections in past decades. Tens of thousands of Mexican observers, and about one thousand foreign monitors, watched over the votes. Yet two days after the elections, with a record voter turnout of more than 70 percent, the government could claim that Zedillo's margin of victory topped 50.08 percent, the "magic number" needed to retain control of the Congress and ensure a presidential mandate. The "reformed" Federal Electoral Institute (IFE), still a PRI-controlled entity—assigned 27 percent of the vote to Fernández de Cevallos's PAN and 17 percent to Cuauhtémoc Cárdenas's PRD, leaving it with only sixty-nine out of five hundred deputies in the new Congress.

In the United States, the *New York Times* and most other mainstream media claimed that de-spite some irregularities the majority of Mexicans had backed the PRI in an honest, clean election. In Mexico, however, Cuauhtémoc Cárdenas charged "colossal fraud." In Chiapas, where the PRI candidate for governor suddenly came up with 50.04 of the vote in an election marred by numerous irregularities and a severe shortage of ballots, the PRD vowed not to let him take his seat. In the months leading up to the elections security forces had harassed members of Mexican human rights groups, and the army, in particular, detained, searched, and threatened human rights activists, accusing them of being guerrillas. According to the *New York Times,* recent army sweeps in areas where opposition support was strong, "have been understood as an ominous message of what might happen should the PRI lose."

The PRI, meaning the Mexican state, the "perfect dictatorship," as the Peruvian writer Mario Vargas Llosa once called it, brought all its enormous advantages to play in the August 21 election. It outspent the PRD on the order of perhaps two hundred to one and dominated the electronic and news media. In the week before the election, it passed out government aid checks to many poor farmers. The message, observed a *New York Times* correspondent, was clear: "Vote for PRI and continue to cash in."

The government also displayed its mastery of electoral fraud, an art refined through a half century or more of practice. Cárdenas's PRD discovered more than six thousand polling places in which more votes were cast than the number of voters on the voting list. An unknown number of persons was erased from the voting rolls; the independent observer group Civic Alliance (AC) found that 65 percent of the nation's polling stations featured shaved registries. Many thousands of would-be voters found themselves without ballots on election day, causing angry protests in Mexico City, Ciudad Juarez, Querétaro, and other cities. The unexpectedly large final turnout (77 percent) was certainly inflated by PRI "carousels" (motorized multiple-voting operations). Civic Alliance's observers witnessed people voting more than once at 9 percent of the polling places they watched. Meanwhile, in early August, the Zapatistas of Chiapas had convened a National Democratic Convention in the Lacandon forest to which it invited all sectors of "civil society," including all political parties except PRI, "the common enemy to us all." The convention, modeled on the 1914 revolutionary convention summoned by Zapata and Villa, reflected the Zapatista decision to broaden the scope of their movement, to develop electoral activity as an adjunct to armed struggle, leading to the drafting of a new constitution. Some five thousand delegates, representing mostly leftist parties and groups, and including many leading intellectuals, made the difficult journey to the Lacandon jungle. The convention endorsed a one-hundred-member committee proposed by the Zapatistas to guide the movement in the months ahead.

As Zedillo prepared to succeed Salinas in December 1994, he faced a sea of troubles. In Chiapas the military standoff continued, but there was widespread and growing disorder. In October, claiming large-scale fraud in the August election that gave victory to the PRI candidate for governor, supporters of the PRD candidate, a crusading newspaper editor backed by the Zapatista rebels, installed him as governor in an open-air Mayan ceremony in the state capital, Tuxtla Gutiérrez, blocks away from where the official winner was inaugurated. Since October, Indian and mestizo farmers had established four autonomous zones in different regions of Chiapas. They blocked roads, refused to pay taxes and electricity bills to federal and state authorities, and ejected local PRI officials. The Zapatista leadership proclaimed these areas "zones of rebellion." Meanwhile the wave of land take-overs continued, producing the unfamiliar spectacle of over one hundred wealthy landowners staging a hunger strike in Mexico City to call attention to their plight. Zedillo must choose between coming to terms with the rebels or crushing them with armed force. From the PRI's point of view, either option could have dangerous consequences.

Mexican public opinion, as expressed in polls and demonstrations, favored a peaceful solution that took into account the just grievances of the Indian and mestizo peasants of Chiapas. But PRI hardliners, the right-wing PAN, and foreign inves-

tors demanded a military solution of the problem. A January 1995 memorandum written by Chase Manhattan Bank advisor Riordan Roett and leaked to an investigative newsletter, warned that "the government will need to eliminate the Zapatistas to demonstrate [to the investment community] their effective control of the national territory and of security policy." In addition to calling for the Zapatistas's liquidation, the memo warned the Zedillo administration "to consider carefully whether or not to allow opposition victories if fairly won at the ballot box," because "a failure to retain PRI controls runs the risk of splitting the government party." In a related development, in February 1995 elections in the state of Jalisco the right-wing PAN won the governorship and the mayoralty of Guadalajara. This, the worst defeat suffered by PRI in its history, appeared to reflect large defections from the ruling party by hardline elements discontented with, among other things, Zedillo's handling of the Chiapas crisis.

Facing these rival pressures, Zedillo appeared to flounder. On assuming office, he held out an olive branch to the Zapatistas and their supporters, agreeing to hold new fraud-free elections in Chiapas and the neighboring state of Tabasco, pressuring the official winner of the governor's race in Chiapas to resign and promising to Chiapas a program of economic and social reform. But on February 9, 1995, on the pretext that Zapatista arms caches had been found in Mexico City and Veracruz, Zedillo sent thousands of troops, backed by tanks and heavy artillery, into the rebel-held territory, with orders to arrest the Zapatista leadership. The rebels, along with thousands of their supporters, fled into the jungle area near the Guatemalan border. The government's action provoked angry protests, including a march of almost 100,000 people in Mexico City. Then, on February 14, Zedillo made an about-face, halting the military operation, withdrawing the order for the arrest of rebel leaders, and calling for new negotiations. These maneuvers created the impression of a weak, vacillating president without a firm policy.

A more immediate threat to the regime was the prospect of an economic collapse. NAFTA, which was supposed to bring prosperity to Mexico, instead had deepened the recessive tendencies of the Mexican economy. The removal of trade barriers had ruined many small farmers who found themselves unable to compete with the influx of cheaper U.S. grain, milk, and other agricultural products. Mexican national industries like the shoe and textile industries were threatened with destruction by competition from more technologically advanced U.S. and Canadian producers. An overvalued peso—deliberately overvalued to promote confidence in the Mexican economy, ensure the passage of NAFTA, and attract foreign investment—contributed to the flood of imports. This in turn caused a chain of events: a growing trade deficit, a decline in the value of the peso against the dollar, and the flight of domestic and foreign capital out of the country.

Mexico had long financed its account deficits with foreign loans; its total foreign debt was about $160 billion, which cost more than $20 billion in interest and principal in 1994. Of the $80 billion borrowed in recent years, only some $15 billion was invested in plant and equipment, and the rest was used to service previous loans and restore Mexico's exhausted currency reserves. In 1994 the shortfall was $30 billion. In December, with $20 billion in short-term loans coming due in a few months, the peso free-falling, and capital flight accelerating, Mexico faced a replay of the 1982 debacle of inflation and looming default. Mexican stocks fell sharply, sending shock waves through the hemisphere's money markets.

Once again foreign governments, led by the United States, and international lending agencies came to Mexico's rescue with a bailout package of loans and loan guarantees amounting to some $50 billion to pay or renegotiate the huge loans coming due and to stem the peso's collapse. But the price of the February 1995 bailout was high. In return for $20 billion from the United States in loan guarantees, Mexico must put up $7 billion a year in oil-export revenues as collateral, to be deposited at the New York Federal Reserve, and must pay a large fee every time it accesses this money. Another $27.5 billion came from the IMF

and the Bank for International Settlements, with the usual conditions: Mexico must cut social spending, continue the privatization program begun in the 1980s, and keep wage increases low. Many Mexicans viewed the deal not as a bailout but as a sellout. "The gringos have us by the throat again," commented one Mexico City taxi driver.

The cost for ordinary Mexicans will be more austerity and more hardships. With the peso down 40 percent and inflation expected to top 20 percent in 1995, the real minimum wage, according to an economics writer for the national daily *La Jornada,* will drop from $4.00 a day to $2.82. These sacrifices will not restore the Mexican economy to health. The bailout, filling the pockets of bankers and multinationals, will do nothing to promote economic development. "The immediate consequence of the $47.5 billion package," concluded a report in *The Nation,* "is to allow resumption of the speculative merry-go-round, with investment banks swiftly resuming their lucrative practice of underwriting and trading Mexican securities." But some observers wondered how long the bailout could last and the Mexican "game" be kept in play.

At the heart of the continuing Mexican economic, political, and social crisis was the debt problem and the system of dependent capitalism that produced it. North American scholar Peter Evans had presciently written in 1979:

Like Brazil, Mexico has found that dependent development requires a mass of imported outputs even larger than the exports it generates, and that even when the multinationals cooperate in the promotion of local accumulation they still ship more capital back to the center than they bring in. . . . Dependent development does not correct the imbalances in semiperipheral relations with the center; it replaces old imbalances with new ones.

Sooner or later, Mexico has to apply the lessons of its long experience with the model of development that collapsed so ingloriously in 1982 and again in 1994.

Chapter 13

Argentina: The Failure of Democracy

After thirty years of explosive economic growth and sustained political stability, Argentina seemed ready to take a place among the developed nations by the first decade of the twentieth century. Argentines could proudly point out that their nation was the world's greatest exporter of grain and one of the most important exporters of meat; they could boast of a railroad network unsurpassed outside western Europe and the United States and of a capital, Buenos Aires, that ranked among the world's most beautiful and cultured cities. Argentines were seemingly prosperous, relatively well educated, and increasingly urban. The burgeoning population (nearly 8 million in 1910) and transportation system promised to create an internal market that would stimulate the rise of native manufacturing and elevate Argentina to the position of one of the world's modern industrialized countries.

The full flowering of democracy, too, seemed close at hand. With the passage of the Saenz Peña reforms in 1912, providing for universal suffrage and the secret ballot, the landed oligarchy, which had long monopolized Argentine politics, at last appeared ready to recognize the aspirations of other social groups and even to share political power with the middle class.

The appearance of prosperity and emerging democracy, however, proved illusory. Stagnation, interspersed with periods of depression and runaway inflation, marked the Argentine economy during succeeding decades. Military coups, disorder, and brutal repression afflicted the nation's politics. At the base of these problems lay Argentina's structural dependence on foreign markets and capital, a dependence that placed the country's economy at the mercy of foreign events and

306 decisions made abroad and helped perpetuate a deformed social and political system.

The Export Economy

Argentina's dynamic economic development during the last quarter of the nineteenth century and the early twentieth century was due to three factors: the appearance of a large market in Europe for its products—wool, mutton, beef, and wheat; the inflow of millions of immigrants, who provided cheap labor for the expanding agricultural sector; and finally, the influx of large quantities of foreign investment capital, which went to construct railroads, to put more land under cultivation, and to establish food (mainly meat) processing plants. The nation's prosperity depended on its ability to export huge amounts of agricultural commodities, to import the manufactured goods it required, and to attract a steady stream of large-scale foreign investment.

Consequently, Argentina was critically vulnerable to fluctuations in international market and finance conditions. Any reduction in overseas trade reverberated disastrously throughout the economy. Because Argentines usually imported more than they exported—a tendency made worse by the fact that the market price for raw materials remained steady or declined while the prices of manufactured goods rose—the country suffered from large deficits in its balance of payments. To make up the difference, the nation relied heavily on foreign investment.

Foreign investment reached enormous proportions in the first decades of the twentieth century. During the years 1900 to 1929, foreigners came to control between 30 and 40 percent of the nation's fixed investments. Argentina absorbed nearly 10 percent of all foreign investment carried out by capital-exporting nations, one-third of all the foreign investment in Latin America, and more than 40 percent of the total foreign investment of Great Britain, the world's leading capitalist power. Investment was concentrated in railroads and government bonds, the proceeds from which were used to subsidize the construction of railroads and public works.

Although foreign investment unquestionably helped fuel economic development, it simultaneously created immense economic difficulties. Huge interest payments on foreign debts and the profit remittances of foreign-owned companies, often representing between 30 and 50 percent of the value of Argentina's exports, produced serious balance of payments problems. Because government bodies owed much of the foreign debt, a substantial portion of government revenue went to service payments. Rigid interest rates and repayment schedules meant that the burden remained the same, even when state revenues declined because of adverse economic conditions, and that revenues earmarked for debt service could not be diverted to other areas.

Every sector of the Argentine economy depended on exports. Agriculture and livestock raising employed 35 percent of the work force. The nation's greatest agricultural area, the pampas, exported 70 percent of its production. Argentine industry centered on food processing, mainly meat packing. As late as 1935, foodstuff processing accounted for 47 percent of all industrial production, and textiles for another 20 percent. The transportation industry—railroads and coastal shipping—handled mostly export commodities.

Rich and poor alike relied on the export economy for their livelihood. The ruling elite was composed of large landowners, who produced almost entirely for the export trade. Their income and their political power rested squarely on the export economy. In addition to large numbers of farm laborers, many urban and industrial workers depended on exports for their jobs. The major trade and industrial unions in Argentina arose in those industries—coastal shipping, railroads, dock work, and packinghouses—whose workers owed their well-being to overseas trade. Because the government relied on revenues derived from import taxes, significant numbers of white-collar workers and professionals employed by the government also were intimately tied to the export economy.

Foreign control and influence permeated the economy. Most of the large merchant houses, which carried on the all-important export-import trade, were either owned by or closely affiliated with foreign houses. The major shipping lines (both intercoastal and interoceanic), the railroads, and the *frigoríficos* (meat-packing plants) were owned and operated by British or American companies.

The export economy brought indisputable benefits to Argentina, but those benefits were unequally distributed. There were, for example, sharp differences in economic development among regions. While the pampas and Buenos Aires boomed, most of the interior provinces stagnated. Mendoza and Tucumán with their wine and sugar made some headway, but all the other central and northwestern provinces—Jujuy, La Rioja, Santiago del Estero, and Salta—experienced social and economic decline.

The inequalities of property and income between the various classes were equally glaring. The rich were very rich and growing richer; the poor grew poorer. In the countryside, the estancieros, masters of thousands of acres of rich land, built palaces, while the majority of foreign-born immigrant sharecroppers eked out a miserable living. In Buenos Aires, wealthy landowners, merchants, and lawyers gathered at the sumptuous Jockey Club, while laborers struggled to make ends meet as inflation eroded their already insufficient paychecks.

Argentina's greatest treasure was its land, but only a few Argentines owned sizable portions of it. In 1914, farm units larger than 2,500 acres accounted for only 8.2 percent of the total number of farms but held 80 percent of the nation's farm area. Over 40 percent of farms were worked by tenants, most on terms that were less than favorable. In 1937 a mere 1 percent of the active rural population controlled over 70 percent of Argentina's farmland, much of which they left idle. Yet the land was fertile and suitable for intensive agriculture. Thousands of immigrants came to Argentina in search of land only to discover that virtually all had long since been taken up by the estanciero oligarchy.

Income distribution followed the same pattern. Less than 5 percent of the active population garnered 70 percent of the gross income derived from agriculture. Not only did workers and rural laborers receive little benefit from the export system, but the operation of the system's finances and taxation eroded what little return they did receive for their labor. Faced with chronic deficits in the balance of payments and unwilling or unable to tax the land or income of the landed elite, the government had no alternative but to resort to the printing press to finance its costs. The result was inflation. Exporters also demanded a fluctuating currency exchange rate, which had an adverse effect on wage earners. Finally, the tax structure placed its burden squarely on the mass of consumers through such indirect taxes as those on imports.

Argentine Society

Argentine society divided roughly into three classes—upper, middle, and lower. The upper class acquired its wealth and prestige through its ability to capitalize on opportunities presented by the export economy. Large landholders even before the export boom of the last quarter of the nineteenth century, the upper class used the boom to solidify and enhance its power. The most powerful group in the elite was the cattle fatteners, who supplied beef for both the domestic and foreign markets. This inner circle was composed of approximately four hundred families who were closely allied through social clubs and business associations. Geographically, most of the wealth was located in the cattle and cereal regions of the pampas near Buenos Aires. From 1880 to 1912 the elite class that controlled the nation's land and wealth also controlled its politics. It used its control over the government to promote meat and grain exports, guarantee easy credit for members, and provide more favorable taxation and currency policies. The other great institutions of Argentine society, the military and the church, also reflected the views of the elite.

Barranquilla
Cartagena
Puerto Cabello
Caracas
Maracaibo
Orinoco R.
Cd. Guayana
GUYANA
Georgetown
SURINAM
Paramaribo
FRENCH GUIANA
Cayenne
VENEZUELA
Medellín
Bogotá
Buenaventura
Cali
COLOMBIA
Esmeraldas
Popayán
Quito
ECUADOR
Guayaquil
Iquitos
Talara
Manaus
Amazon R.
Belém
Trujillo
PERU
B R A Z I L
Natal
Recife
Cerro de Pasco
Oroya
Callao
Lima
Cuzco
L. Titicaca
Arequipa
Mollendo
Arica
BOLIVIA
La Paz
Oruro
Santa Cruz
Sucre
Potosí
Corumbá
Brasilia
Bahia
Belo Horizonte
Iquique
PARAGUAY
São Paulo
Antofagasta
Asunción
Rio de Janeiro

PACIFIC OCEAN
Florianapolis
Tucumán
Paraná R.
Uruguay R.
Pôrto Alegre
CHILE
Santa Fe
Córdoba
Valparaiso
Mendoza
Rosario
URUGUAY
Santiago
Buenos Aires
Montevideo
ARGENTINA
La Plata
Concepción
Bahia Blanca
Mar del Plata
Valdivia
Puerto Montt
ATLANTIC OCEAN

Comodoro Rivadavia

Falkland/Malvinas Is.

— International Boundaries

0   500 Miles
0   500 Kilometers

MODERN SOUTH AMERICA

As the nation grew more urban, its class structure became more complex. An urban middle class arose. This middle class, heavily concentrated in the bureaucracy and professions, depended on the export economy and attached itself to the Radical party.

The lower class divided into two groups, workers and urban marginals. Most members of the working class lived in Buenos Aires. They labored in small factories, where Argentina's industrial expansion was concentrated until 1914. (The primary exceptions to the predominance of small industries were the frigoríficos.) A considerable number of workers were employed by the railroads and urban tramways and in the Port of Buenos Aires.

Although the Socialist party, born during the 1890s, professed to represent the working class, it failed to achieve a position of leadership because its roots and leaders were mainly middle class. The working class did, nevertheless, organize into unions. The most important unions were those of the railroad workers (*La Fraternidad*) and the dockworkers. Numerous strikes occurred after the turn of the century and throughout the first Radical regime (1916–1922). The labor movement, however, was weakened by diverse viewpoints on political activity and by internecine rivalries among Socialists, Anarchists, and Syndicalists.

The Military

In the first decade of the twentieth century, the Argentine military underwent two important transformations: it was professionalized, and it became a national institution. By 1910 seniority and merit were firmly entrenched as the criteria for promotion. The Superior School was established in 1901 to train officers in modern warfare. Also in 1910 a law of conscription was instituted; this greatly expanded the size of the armed forces and required the expansion of the officer corps. As a result, the social makeup of the officer corps changed. In time, men of the middle class, mostly the sons of immigrants, replaced the old officer groups, and the oligarchy gradually lost its predominance. Military personnel developed considerable pride and independence. They resisted political tampering and demanded modern weapons and better pay from the government. As cohesion grew, the military became an important political force. In 1916 it favored the transfer of power from the oligarchy to the Radical party.

The Radical Era, 1916–1930

The Rise of the Radical Party

Amid growing unrest among the urban middle class, university students, and small groups of junior military officers, the Radicals staged their third unsuccessful attempt to overthrow the oligarchy by force in February 1905. Despite their failure, the Radicals attracted growing popular support in the decade that followed. Local party organizations, formed before the February coup, expanded rapidly, drawing heavily from university-educated sons of immigrants. After the adoption of the Saenz Peña Law in 1912, the Radicals abandoned use of the sterile policy of electoral abstention and began to organize the urban middle class from the grassroots level, especially in Buenos Aires.

Radical party strength rested on twin pillars: its local urban organization, which acted to meet the needs of the middle class, and its leader, Hipólito Yrigoyen, who played a dual role as the titular head of the Radical party. First, he was the great mediator who managed to reconcile the often conflicting interests of the middle class and large landowners who made up his political coalition. Second, although inarticulate and a recluse, Yrigoyen managed to project an austere democratic image that made him the party's charismatic leader. This clever deal maker and manipulator symbolized for the middle class the Radical dedication to democracy. Despite a checkered past that included shady business deals, he furnished the party with much of its moral appeal.

310

The Radical propaganda effectively presented the party as a national party, transcending the narrow regional and class interests that had previously governed Argentine politics. The Radical program was purposely vague. It straddled the line between its two major constituencies, the middle class and the landed elite. The Radicals (reflecting the views of both the landowners and the dependent middle class) never challenged the basic premises of the export economy. The party advocated neither land reform nor industrialization.

From 1912 to 1916, the Conservatives failed to construct the broad-based national political party they had hoped would arise as a result of the passage of the Saenz Peña Law. The Socialist party also failed to become a party of national scope. Like the Radicals, the Socialists suffered from a political split personality. The bulk of the party's support came from the working class, but the leaders of the party were middle-class intellectuals. For the most part, the Socialists could never extend their influence beyond Buenos Aires, nor could they get the group for whom the party had the greatest attraction, the foreign-born workers, to register to vote. The party was, however, strong among skilled workers, particularly those on the railroad.

The Socialists had competition for working-class and union support. Anarchists gained the allegiance of dock workers and of many workers in small industrial and service occupations. They played an important rule in the rise of Argentine unions from the 1890s. After 1906 Syndicalists increasingly influenced the unions. The Syndicalists, who shared the Anarchist ideal of abolishing the state, stressed economic struggle and powerful unions as a means of attaining that goal. They won support among larger workers' groups, such as the coastal shipping workers and railway shop workmen.

Having the advantages of a finely tuned grassroots political organization and a well-known and astute leader as their presidential candidate and untroubled by an ideology or specific program other than the vaguely defined "class harmony," the Radicals won the 1916 presidential elections with 46.5 percent of the vote. Although it was necessary for Yrigoyen to put together a backroom political deal to get a majority of the electoral college, the Radicals had clearly won a great victory. The Progressive Democrats, their nearest rivals, managed to win only 13 percent of the popular vote.

The First Radical Government: Yrigoyen, 1916–1922

The characters of the first and subsequent Radical administrations were determined by the delicate relations between the Radicals and the conservative landowner elite. The elite controlled the military and the major agricultural lobbying groups and had close contacts with the powerful foreign business interests. Yrigoyen continually walked an unsteady tightrope between the middle class, which wanted a piece of the governmental pie, and the oligarchy, which was still wary of the party that had rebelled three times in three decades and that had won an election campaigning against the selfish interests of that oligarchy. He could not push too hard too fast or the oligarchy would surely overthrow him.

The operating mechanism of the Radical government was a conservative fiscal policy and political stability, in return for which the oligarchy was to allow the middle class wider access to the governmental bureaucracy and the professions. Yrigoyen had little room to maneuver, for there were inherent difficulties in the operation of this arrangement. First, expansion of access to government employment meant that government expenditures necessarily had to increase. But this violated the tenet of fiscal conservatism, unless the economy continued to expand at a rapid rate. Second, Yrigoyen had to maintain the fragile alliance of landowners and members of the middle class within his own party. In sum, the key to the Radicals' staying in power was Yrigoyen's ability to distribute the fruits of Argentine economic development to the middle class without antagonizing the oligarchy.

Nonetheless, the most pressing political problem was that the Radicals did not have control over the government. Although they had won the 1916 election for the presidency, they did not control most of the provinces and were a minority in Congress. Not until 1918 did they win a majority in the Chamber of Deputies. Because Senate terms were for nine years, they did not control that body until 1922. Without complete political control, Yrigoyen faced an impossible task in attempting to meet the conflicting requirements of the elite and the middle class. His first cabinet reflected both the makeup of his party and his eagerness to win the goodwill of the ruling elite; it was composed entirely of members of the landed oligarchy.

Yrigoyen's balancing act became even more difficult with the emergence of labor agitation for improved wages and working conditions. Wartime demand for Argentine exports had brought on inflation, and as a result, the purchasing power of wages was seriously eroded. Yrigoyen had to move cautiously in attempting to alleviate labor's plight, for the oligarchy might look upon such moves as interference in their economic domain. The problem was complicated by the fact that much of the labor agitation was directed against foreign-owned companies with close ties to the elite. There was growing discontent on the part of the middle class, too, because the decline in government revenues from imports meant fewer government jobs for its members.

From 1913 to 1917, Argentina experienced a serious depression. The prospect of war dried up foreign investment in 1913 and 1914, and the war itself caused a shortage of shipping for export commodities and of imported goods, both of which were critical in an economy based on the export of foodstuffs (bulk commodities) and the import of manufactured goods. To make matters worse, the 1913 harvest failed.

Between 1917 and 1921, however, Argentina again prospered from an export boom. The distribution of the benefits of the new prosperity were decidedly uneven, however, and Yrigoyen again found himself under pressure from his rival constituencies. Europe's mounting demand for cereals and meat exports forced prices for domestically consumed food to rise rapidly. Food prices rose 40 percent, and the cost of living in the cities rose 65 percent. The Radical government was squeezed between the urban com-

munity's need for lower prices (wages had not kept pace) and the interests of the landed elite, which insisted on keeping the prices of its products high. The best way to satisfy both constituent groups was to expand job opportunities in government, but this expansion required an increase in government spending, which was severely limited because sources of revenue were limited and the oligarchy was opposed to it. In 1918 the Radicals proposed a modest income tax and a tax on exports, but these proposals met defeat at the hands of a conservative Congress. Some relief came in 1919, when revenues again started to increase.

After becoming president, Yrigoyen sought to broaden his support by making some overtures to the working class. But he had little success, for his fear of antagonizing the landed elite severely limited the concessions he could offer the workers. The use of patronage—a tactic eminently successful with the middle class—failed when applied to the working class. When the strategy of attaching the rank-and-file of the workers to the local Radical political machine failed, Yrigoyen sought to form individual links with the leadership of the trade unions, which at this time were under strong Socialist influence.

From 1916 to the early 1920s, however, Yrigoyen's efforts to form an alliance with organized labor clashed with the Radicals' obligations to the oligarchy, which regarded such an alliance as prejudicial to its interests. Confronted with the bitter opposition of the ruling elite, Yrigoyen backed down and abandoned the workers.

From 1916 to 1919, Yrigoyen had to deal with a wave of large, sometimes violent strikes. Radical policy toward these struggles was clearly determined by expediency and, in the last analysis, by the degree of pressure exerted by the landed elite. The major strikes occurred against foreign-owned companies engaged in export-related enterprises. The workers sought higher wages to compensate for the erosion of their wages by wartime inflation.

Since Argentine governments often sent in the police and armed forces to break strikes, the attitude of the Yrigoyen regime was decisive. The Maritime Workers' Federation struck twice, in

312   1916 and 1917, for higher wages. The first strike was timed to coincide with harvest shipments. In both instances the union gained access to Yrigoyen, the government kept out of the dispute, and the union won. But in late 1917, the government abandoned the unions when a general strike began to jeopardize export interests. With the strike threatening the entire harvest, the British government and the elite brought joint pressure on Yrigoyen to intervene, and troops were used. The strike collapsed. The frigorífico strike of 1917–1918 met the same fate when the government sent in marines to subdue the strikers.

The climactic episode came in January 1919 and is known in Argentine history as the *Semana Trágica* (Tragic Week) in reference to the heavy loss of life that followed when Yrigoyen, apparently fearing intervention by the army to topple his government, abandoned his original conciliatory position and sent police and armed forces to break a general strike that had grown out of a strike in a metal works. This violence was accompanied by a wave of brutal pogroms against Russian Jewish immigrants by members of the elite and the middle class, organized in an Argentine Patriotic League. Instead of denouncing the anti-"communist" witch hunt, the Radical government added its voice to the right-wing cry that the strike was a revolutionary conspiracy and even encouraged party members to join the vigilante bands. From that time, the Yrigoyen government gave up efforts to achieve a reconciliation with the workers. Henceforth, it concentrated on catering to its middle-class constituency through the use of patronage and on strengthening Yrigoyen's popular electoral base. The last three years of Yrigoyen's term were a struggle merely to survive.

The Argentine university reform of 1918, which had continental reverberations, reflected Yrigoyen's desire to cater to his middle-class constituency. The series of events leading to this famous reform began with a student strike at the University of Córdoba; the students demanded, among other changes, simplification of the entrance requirements and secularization of the curriculum. When the strike deteriorated into violence, Yrigoyen intervened and acceded to the student demands. But he went further, establishing a series of new universities that increased middle-class access to the professions and the government jobs for which so many middle-class aspirants hungered.

The government also sought to strengthen its electoral position by intervention in the provinces, removing provincial governors on the pretext that they had violated the federal constitution. The government also strove to enhance its popularity by expanding the patronage system.

By 1921 the boom unleashed by the war had ended, and depression followed. The union movement disintegrated. Layoffs eroded union membership, and internal bickering rendered the unions ineffective. The Radicals actually experienced some success in recruiting among the workers during the depression, because their local committees were able to provide charitable services.

The Second Radical Government: Alvear, 1922–1928

Despite adverse economic conditions, the Radicals won the election of 1922. With 48 percent of the vote, Marcelo de Alvear, Yrigoyen's hand-picked successor, became president. Immediately, however, the party began to come apart. Although couched in personal terms—Alvear against Yrigoyen—the division more accurately reflected the growing split between the middle-class and elite sectors of the party.

Alvear cut the payroll to trim expenses and hiked tariff rates to increase revenue. The tariff increase was also aimed at reducing imports and alleviating the balance of payments problem. A balanced budget directly contradicted middle-class demands for even more government employment opportunities. In 1924 the Radicals split into two factions. The Radical party's Anti-Personalist wing separated under the leadership of Alvear.

Yrigoyen's Second Term, 1928–1930

Four years later, Yrigoyen made a smashing comeback, winning his second presidential term with an overwhelming 57 percent of the vote. But in October 1929, the depression hit Argentina. The Radicals, whose strength had been increasing, suffered a mortal blow. Exports dropped 40 percent; foreign investment stopped. Unemployment was widespread. Government efforts to spark a recovery served only to induce inflation. The decline in imports severely undermined the government's fiscal position since it relied on import duties for most of its revenue.

The government incurred a huge deficit, which it tried to cover by borrowing. As a result, it found itself in the position of competing for increasingly scarce credit resources with the landed elite, which desperately needed money to ride out the decline in the export market. Yrigoyen's policy threatened the interests of the landed elite, and he became expendable. Further, his meddling with the military had seriously undercut his standing with that powerful institution. Finally, the depression destroyed his personal popularity in the middle class, his main base.

Yrigoyen became the scapegoat. His enemies pictured him as senile and corrupt, incapable of ruling the nation in a time of crisis. The depression ruined the party apparatus, for there was no patronage to dispense. The political situation continued to disintegrate, and violence increased. Yrigoyen was overthrown by the military on September 6, 1930.

The "Infamous Decade," 1930–1943: The Conservative Restoration

The coup marked the end of Argentina's short experiment with democracy and the entry of the military into the nation's politics; it ushered in a period of harsh repression and corruption, which came to be known as the "infamous decade." Lieutenant General José F. Uriburu, who had led the group of conspirators that overthrew Yrigoyen, became the head of a coalition of widely diverse elements, including traditional Conservatives, right-wing nationalist-fascists, and such center and left parties as the Progressive Democrats, Independent Socialists, and Socialists. These strange bedfellows had agreed on the elimination of Yrigoyen, but little else. Consequently, the loosely built alliance soon fell apart. The military was also divided. One faction, led by Uriburu, sought to establish a regime patterned on the Italian corporate state. A second faction, led by General Agustín P. Justo, desired only a return to the pre-1916 political arrangements. The split was exacerbated by the long-standing and bitter personal rivalry between Uriburu and Justo.

In the months following the coup, Uriburu conducted a campaign of brutal repression against opponents of his provisional government. At the beginning of 1931, he felt the opposition was sufficiently cowed and—in the case of the Yrigoyen Radicals—sufficiently discredited to call elections for Buenos Aires Province. The result of the elections was a tremendous victory for the Yrigoyen Radicals. Uriburu quickly annulled the elections. The Conservatives scrambled to find allies and at last found a partner in the Anti-Personalist wing of the Radicals. They formed a coalition: the *Concordancia*. Their agreement called for the Anti-Personalists to provide a presidential candidate, while the Conservatives would furnish a running mate and control government finances. The alliance soon crumbled when Uriburu refused to permit the ex-president, Alvear, to head the ticket. Alvear took most of his party with him, and the Radicals adopted a policy of electoral abstention until 1935.

What remained of the Concordancia, the conservative National Democratic party and some Anti-Personalists, chose General Justo as their presidential candidate. With the help of fraud, the intimidation tactics of goon squads and gangsters, and the general apathy of an embittered and cynical electorate, Justo won easily. The Concordancia had a very narrow popular base, but its main potential opposition, the Radical party, was deeply fragmented and unable to cooperate with other opposition groups. The regime used its patronage power and benefited from the upturn in the economy after 1934 to consolidate its hold on power.

The Radicals staged several unsuccessful rebellions in the provinces during the early 1930s. Yrigoyen died in 1933, but not before he had been reconciled with Alvear and passed on the mantle of Radical leadership to his old rival. In 1935 Alvear rejoined the main Radical party and led it back into the political arena. In 1937 he opposed the Concordancia ticket composed of the Radical Roberto M. Ortiz for president and the right-wing Conservative Ramón S. Castillo for vice president. With the aid of widespread vote fraud, Ortiz won.

Hoping to broaden the political base of the Concordancia, Ortiz set about restoring some semblance of free and honest elections. Unfortunately for Argentine democracy, however, Ortiz was a diabetic who was rapidly losing his vision. He therefore had to take an extended leave of absence, handing over the reins of government to Castillo in 1940. Castillo was an archconservative who attempted to undo Ortiz's reforms. The two men fought publicly until Ortiz died in 1942, and Castillo became president. For three years, he maintained an almost constant state of siege and ruled by decree.

Despite his narrowing base of support, Castillo insisted on naming as his successor the unpopular Conservative Robustiano Patrón Costas, a millionaire sugar planter from Salta who was notorious for mistreatment of his Indian laborers. On June 4, 1943, a coup organized by the secret officers' lodge known as the Group of United Officers (GOU) overthrew Castillo and established a ruling junta. Its first head, General Arturo Rawson, lasted only two days; he was followed by General Pedro P. Ramírez, who fell in his turn in 1944; his successor, General Edelmiro Farrell, ruled from 1944 until the elections of 1946.

Before leaving the "Infamous Decade," we should take note of the economic policies pursued by the Conservative administrations. Abandoning the free-trade, laissez-faire economic doctrines on which the prewar export economy was based, Conservative economic policy of the 1930s established state intervention as a decisive factor in the economy. The basic aim of their policy was to protect the nation from the effects of the cyclical nature of the world capitalist economy. To accomplish this, they sought to protect their main foreign market, Great Britain, limit production of farm commodities, and restrict imports through indirect methods, such as the establishment of a currency exchange system that discriminated against non-British imports. They also sought to establish new import-substitution industries primarily through foreign investment.

In this period, finding that they could not export manufactured goods to Argentina on a competitive basis because of high tariffs and the discriminatory exchange system, United States manufacturers established plants in Argentina. As a result, foreign capital played an increasingly important role in the economy during the 1930s, accounting for 50 percent of the total capital invested in Argentine industry. Foreign companies virtually monopolized the meat-packing, electric power, cement, automobile, rubber, petroleum, pharmaceutical, and several other industries.

The British market for beef and grain was critical for the Argentine export economy. During the late 1920s and early 1930s, the British government was under constant pressure to reduce Argentine imports in order to protect producers within the empire. The result of Argentine efforts to secure the British market was the controversial Roca-Runciman Treaty of 1933. By this treaty, Britain guaranteed Argentina a fixed, though somewhat reduced, share of the chilled beef market. It also promised to eliminate tariffs on cereals. Argentina, in return, lowered or eliminated tariffs on British manufactures. It also agreed to spend its earnings from the British market on British goods to be imported into Argentina.

The economy improved after 1934, and by 1936 the crisis had passed. Cereal prices rose gradually on the world market until 1937, when they again dropped. Meat prices rose until 1936 and then remained steady. Industrial investment reached predepression levels. Although real wages declined, unemployment fell sharply as a result of public works and industrial investment. In general, Argentines were relatively well off during the 1930s. Consumption of consumer goods and food rose considerably.

The process of industrialization was accompanied by a growth of the native industrialist class and a parallel increase in the size of the working class and its organizations. In 1930 the General Confederation of Labor (CGT) arose from the merger of two large unions. By 1943 the membership of the trade union movement was estimated to be between three hundred and three hundred and fifty thousand.

The growth of the Argentine industrial bourgeoisie, a class profoundly dissatisfied with the economic policies of the landed oligarchy, and of the working class, still relatively small and unorganized but gaining in self-consciousness and developing new social and political aspirations, heightened the tensions within Argentine society. The military coup of 1943 represented an effort to resolve the gathering crisis.

The Perón Era, 1943–1955

Perón's Rise to Power

The military coup that overthrew Castillo in 1943 had deep and tangled roots. The fraud and corruption that tainted both Conservative and Radical politics in the "Infamous Decade" no doubt offended military sensibilities, and Castillo's choice of the pro-Ally Patrón Costas as his successor also angered some of the military, who were divided in their attitude toward the belligerents in World War II. But the coup of 1943 had deeper causes. During the 1930s, the officer corps of the Argentine armed forces, predominantly middle class in its social origins, developed an ardent nationalism that saw the solution for Argentina's problems in industrialization and all-around technical modernization. The interest of the military in industrialization was closely linked to its desire to create a powerful war machine capable of creating a Greater Argentina that could exercise hegemony in a new South American bloc. To industrialize it was necessary to end Argentina's neocolonial status, to free it from dependence on foreign markets. The pro-German attitude of many officers stemmed in part from the German military instruction that they had received and from their admiration for the supposed successes of the Nazi New Order, but even more, perhaps, from the conviction that England and the United States had conspired to keep Argentina a rural economic colony. Their pro-German attitude was not translated into a desire to enter the war on Germany's side but rather into the wish to keep Argentina neutral in the great conflict.

As concerned domestic policy, the military proposed a massive speedup of industrialization and technical modernization, even though it feared the social changes and forces that such transformations might unleash. In particular, it feared the revolutionary potential of the working class. In effect, the military proposed to build Argentine industrial capitalism with a thoroughly cowed, docile working class. As a result, one of the first acts of the military regime was to launch an offensive against organized labor. The government took over the unions, suppressed newspapers, and jailed opposition leaders. This policy of direct confrontation and collision with labor had disastrous results and threatened to wreck the industrialization program. The military was saved from itself by an astute young colonel, Juan Domingo Perón, who took over the Department of Labor in October 1943 and promptly raised it to the status of the Ministry of Labor and Welfare.

Born in 1895, the son of immigrant and creole parents of somewhat marginal economic status (his father was a farmer), Perón entered the military college at sixteen and very slowly rose in rank to captain in 1930. During the next decade, he spent several years in Europe, where he was much impressed by the German and Italian dictatorships. In 1941, Perón joined the Group of United Officers, although only a junior colonel, and quickly rose to its leadership ranks. He was prominent in the colonels' clique that replaced the GOU in power in 1944. Beginning with a sub-cabinet post as secretary of labor and welfare, Perón became the indispensable man in the Ramírez government. He subsequently became

316 vice president and minister of war, in addition to secretary of labor and welfare.

Perón's genius lay in his recognition of the potential of the organized and unorganized working class and the need to broaden the social base of the nationalist revolution. He became the patron of the urban proletariat. Workers were not only encouraged to organize but favored in bargaining negotiations, in which his department participated. As a result, workers' wages not only rose in absolute terms but their share of the national income grew. This, of course, increased mass purchasing power and thereby promoted the process of industrialization. Perón also created a state system of pensions and health benefits, with the result that employers' contributions for pensions, insurance, and other benefits rose steadily until the year of Perón's fall (1955). In return for these real gains, however, the unions lost their independence and became part of a state-controlled apparatus in Perón's hands. Meanwhile, Perón was strengthening his position within the military. In February 1944 he led a group of officers in forcing the resignation of President Ramírez, who was replaced by General Farrell.

Not all of the military was happy with Perón's prolabor policies or with his meteoric rise to power. The end of the war in 1945 also provoked civilian demands for an end to military rule and the restoration of the constitution. In October 1945 Perón's military and civilian foes staged a coup that resulted in his ouster and imprisonment. But the organizers of the coup were divided and unclear about their objectives, and Perón's followers mobilized rapidly. Loyal labor leaders organized the Buenos Aires working class for massive street demonstrations to protest Perón's jailing. The workers virtually took over the city, without opposition from the armed forces. The bewildered conspirators released Perón from prison. Thereupon, he resigned from his various government posts, retired from the army, and began his campaign for the presidency in the 1946 elections.

In preparation for the election of 1946, Perón, taking due account of the defeat of fascism in Europe, cast himself in the role of a democrat ready to abide by the result of a free election. He created a Labor party to mobilize the working class, the principal component in a class alliance whose other major elements were the national industrial bourgeoisie and the army. Perón's chief opponent was José Tamborini, candidate of the *Unión Democrática* (Democratic Union), a heterogeneous coalition of conservative landed elite, the bureaucratic and professional middle class that traditionally supported the Radical party, and even the Socialist and Communist parties. Perón defeated Tamborini, by 300,000 votes out of 2.7 million. He was helped in the election by the blundering foreign policy of the United States, whose State Department issued a Blue Book blasting Perón for his fascist ties. Perón countered by circulating a Blue and White Book (blue and white being Argentina's national colors) that stressed the theme of Yankee imperialism.

Postwar Economics

The postwar boom enabled Perón to keep his coalition together. The export sector produced large surpluses in the balance of payments, making available funds for industrialization, mainly in labor-intensive manufactures. Between 1945 and 1948, real wages for industrial workers rose 20 percent. Personal consumption also rose. Since there was only a slight decline in the share of the national income that went to profits, the redistribution of income to the working class did not come at the expense of any other segment of the alliance. Industrialists kept profits up and benefited from increased domestic consumption, which provided a growing market for their products. The only sector of the economy that was slighted was agriculture.

Perón managed to win over a considerable sector of the dependent middle class through his use of government patronage, just as Yrigoyen had done before. He kept the military happy by his commitment to industrialization, which was an important aspect of the military's desire for national self-sufficiency and by providing it with generous salaries and the latest equipment for modern warfare.

Juan and Evita Perón, 1952.

One of Perón's greatest assets was his beautiful and stylish wife Eva Duarte de Perón, known affectionately by Argentines as "Evita" (little Eva), who acted as his liaison to the working class. Evita, a former dance hall girl and radio and movie star, headed a huge charitable network that dispensed tremendous amounts of money and patronage. So beloved was she that when she died in 1952 at the age of thirty-two, Perón led a movement to get the Catholic church to canonize her. The president's popularity with the working class suffered after her death. Evita strongly advocated women's suffrage, which was granted in 1947. Consequently, women supported Perón in large numbers.

After 1948, however, the economic picture changed drastically. With the exception of a short-lived recovery during the Korean war, Argentina entered a period of severe recession, which included several drought-induced bad harvests. The late 1940s brought the first signs that Argentina would face serious long-term economic difficulties. Its export commodities began to confront increased competition from the United States and from revitalized Western European agriculture. Later, the advent of the Common Market worsened Argentina's position. Balance of payments deficits replaced the large surpluses that had financed the nation's import-substitution industrialization. Industrial production fell, as did per capita income. Real wages dropped 20 percent from the 1949 level in 1952–1953. It was in this decline that Perón's political failure was rooted.

318

Whatever one may think of Perón's economics, the fact remains that he solved none of the country's major economic problems. The main roadblocks remained. Transportation continued to be inadequate and obsolete, and a scarcity of electric power stood in the way of industrial modernization. Argentina did not produce enough fuel to meet domestic needs, and this created an enormous drain on the balance of payments. The nation's industry remained limited for the most part to import-substitution light industry. Despite his anti-imperialist rhetoric, Perón did not nationalize such key foreign-owned industries as meat packing and sugar refining. Most serious of all, Perón did nothing to break the hold of the latifundio on the land. As a result, agriculture was marked by inefficient land use, which impeded long-range development.

Perón's Downfall

After his re-election in 1952 and in response to the economic crisis of the early 1950s, Perón formulated a new plan (the Second Five-Year Plan, 1953–1957) that, to a great extent, reversed his previous strategy. He tried to expand agricultural production by paying higher prices to farmers for their produce and by buying capital equipment for this sector (tractors and reapers). He sought to increase the agricultural production available for export by means of a wage freeze, which he hoped would restrict domestic consumption. Although real wages declined, workers did not suffer proportionately more than other groups. But the industrial bourgeoisie was unhappy, for labor productivity declined while the regime's prolabor policies propped up wages. The industrialists, supported by a considerable portion of the army, wanted deregulation of the economy so they could push down wages. But the major problem of the industrial sector was lack of capital since the agricultural sector no longer generated a large surplus.

In order to solve the capital shortage, Perón abandoned his previously ultranationalistic stand and actively solicited foreign investment. In 1953 the government reached an agreement with a North American company, the Standard Oil Company of California, for exploration, drilling, refining, and distribution rights in Argentina. Perón hoped thereby to reduce the adverse effect oil purchases abroad had on the balance of payments. Foreign capital, however, used the most modern technology and machines, which required fewer workers and tended to create unemployment in the affected industrial sectors.

In order to maintain government expenditures and a bloated bureaucracy in the face of declining revenues, Perón printed more money. The amount in circulation increased from 6 to 45 billion pesos during his two terms. By 1954 he had had some success in stabilizing the economy; he achieved a balance of payments surplus, and capital accumulation showed an upward curve. But his new economic strategy had alienated key elements of his coalition of workers, industrialists, and the armed forces. Perón then sought to divert attention from economic issues—with disastrous results.

Perón adopted two new strategies. First, he attempted to enhance his moral and ideological appeal. Second, he began to employ greater coercion to suppress a growing opposition. The vehicle for his ideological and moral appeal was *justicialismo,* Perón's ideal of justice for all—a third route to development that was neither communist nor capitalist.

Perón's strategy included attacking the church. Starting in 1951, the regime grew more repressive. The government suppressed and took over Argentina's most famous newspaper, *La Prensa* (1951). Further, Perón used his National Liberating Alliance, a private army of thugs, and the thirty-five-thousand-man federal police force to intimidate the political opposition. Torture, imprisonment, censorship, purges, and exile became the order of the day. After 1954, even the General Confederation of Labor became a coercive force, whose prime function seemed to be to suppress opposition within the labor movement.

Perón's reluctance to go along with the industrialists' desire to push down wages and increase productivity alienated that group; the industrial bourgeoisie then joined forces with the agrarian interests, which had long and bitterly opposed Perón. This desertion ended Perón's once highly successful coalition. Inevitably, Perón's hold on the working class loosened as the wage freeze and inflation reduced the value of their wages. The death of Eva Perón in 1952 contributed to the deterioration in the relations between Perón and the working class. She had served as her husband's ambassador to the workers. With Evita no longer at the head of the Social Aid Foundation, a vast philanthropic organization that distributed food, clothing, and money to the needy, Perón's relations with labor did not go so smoothly.

Despite economic adversity, Perón could not have been overthrown had not the military abandoned him. For the better part of a decade, he had masterfully balanced, divided, and bribed the military. Most of the senior officers owed him both their rank and their prosperity. The army was heavily involved in industrial production, and this provided an excellent means to become rich. In addition, to win its allegiance, Perón had showered the military with expensive military hardware and excellent wages. However, his relations with the armed forces began to disintegrate when he altered his economic policy to lessen emphasis on industrialization and self-sufficiency. On this score, his concession to Standard Oil in 1953 was the last straw for the nationalist military. The military was also affronted by the dictator's personal behavior (he had an affair with a teenage girl), and it objected to his virulent attacks on the Catholic church, a pillar of traditionalism, during 1954 and 1955. It also resented Perón's efforts to indoctrinate the military in the tenets of justicialismo.

Thus, in struggling to extricate the nation from an economic quagmire, Perón undermined the multiclass coalition that had brought him to power and sustained him there. When the final successful revolt took place in September 1955, after a failure in June, enough of the working class was alienated to assure the military's success. Perón briefly threatened to arm his working-class supporters, the *descamisados* (the shirtless ones), but instead fled into exile.

The Shadow of Perón, 1955–1973

Economic Stagnation

Chronic, sometimes violent, economic fluctuations characterized the post-1955 period. At the base of these difficulties lay continuous balance of payments deficits, which were caused by the decline in agricultural production. The nation could not earn enough from its exports to pay for the large expenditures necessary to fuel domestic industry. Periods of rapid economic growth were invariably followed by acute depressions, which wiped out all previous gains. Runaway inflation accompanied these cyclical conditions.

The governments of this period, whether military or civilian, tended to promote the inflow of foreign investment as a development strategy. But development initiated by foreign investment had severe drawbacks. Foreign companies tended to monopolize credit opportunities, certain key industries became concentrated in foreign hands, and profits earned by foreign subsidiaries and remitted to the home company added to the balance of payments deficits. Finally, foreign investment was usually technologically intensive and therefore created unemployment. It was during the post-Perón era of development spurred by foreign capital that Argentina saw the emergence of large numbers of underemployed and unemployed urban workers.

At various times during the period, the Argentine government had dealings with the International Monetary Fund (IMF), an agency that was supposed to help nations overcome their economic difficulties through advice and loans. The IMF's main concern was to control inflation. Its recommended stabilization programs invariably led to downturns in the business cycle, and unemployment and business failures ensued at an awesome rate. Such austerity programs were politically unpalatable because they held down real wages and therefore elicited labor opposition. During the presidential term of Arturo Frondizi (1958–1962), the IMF had a great deal of influence, and the result was disastrous. Inflation

320

proved unconquerable, and the fund's economic "medicine" was too bad-tasting for Argentines to tolerate.

The Military in Politics

The politics of the period 1955 to 1973 were as turbulent as its economics. Direct military rule alternated with elected civilian regimes that were ousted when they strayed from the military's Conservative economic policies or proved too conciliatory toward the Peronists. In June 1966, unhappy with Radical President Arturo Illia's failure to crack down on Peronists and left-wingers and frightened by the possibility of a Peronist victory in the presidential election of 1969, the military ousted Illia and installed General Juan Carlos Onganía as president. This time it appeared the military had come to stay. The government abolished political parties and purged the universities of left and center elements. The trade union movement, meanwhile, suffered from internal divisions owing to differences in policy and personal rivalries over the successor to Perón after his anticipated death. This split enabled Onganía to crack down on the militant wing of the labor movement with the cooperation of its moderate wing.

As minister of the economy Onganía appointed Adalbert Krieger Vasena, who presided over a program of spurring foreign investment to revive the lagging economy. To attract foreign capital, Krieger Vasena removed all restrictions on profit remittances; he also stimulated the process of industrial denationalization by devaluating the peso by 40 percent. Devaluation of the peso meant that many local companies could no longer afford expensive capital imports and royalty payments to owners of foreign technology. These local companies disappeared, leaving their share of the market to the remaining firms. In this way, Coca-Cola and Pepsi gained control of 75 percent of the soft-drink market. Bankruptcies grew from 1,647 in 1968 to 2,982 in 1970. In other cases, devaluation encouraged the process of acquisition of national companies by foreign firms, a process that had grown almost uninterruptedly since Frondizi's time. Between 1963 and 1971,

foreign interests bought out fifty-three Argentine companies representing almost every industrial sector, particularly the automotive, chemical, petrochemical, metallurgical, and tobacco industries. Meanwhile, wages were frozen, although prices continued their steady rise.

Growing outrage on the part of workers and students over the government's economic program, especially its policy of industrial denationalization and the wage freeze, erupted into violence in the interior in the spring of 1969. Major riots took place in Rosario, Corrientes, and Córdoba. In Córdoba, the most industrialized city of Argentina, workers and students rose in revolt, occupying major sectors of the city until they were ousted by troops. At the same time, there was an upsurge of urban guerrilla activity by a number of groups, of which the most important was the Montoneros, who represented the left wing of the Peronist movement. Their tactics included raids on police stations, assassinations, and robberies. In May 1970, the Montoneros kidnaped and later killed former President Aramburu.

Onganía's failure to cope with the mounting wave of guerrilla activity precipitated the military coup of June 1970, which deposed him and installed General Roberto M. Levingston as president. An expert in military intelligence and counterinsurgency, Levingston decreed the death penalty for terrorist acts and kidnapings; his repressive decrees were answered with fresh acts of violence by the guerrillas. Meanwhile, to make things worse, the economy, after some recovery under Onganía, turned down again in 1970–1971. Industrial production declined and unemployment increased.

The Return of Perón

Displeased with a resurgence of labor unrest, the military ousted Levingston in March 1971. His replacement, General Alejandro Lanusse, carried out a dual policy combining brutal repression of leftist guerrillas with a general liberalization of the political climate. In effect admitting the military's failure to renovate Argentine politics, Lanusse undertook negotiations that led to the restoration of political activity and the return of the Peronists to full electoral participation for the first time since 1955.

The military briefly held out hope that the moderate political parties would unite to stand against the Peronists, but the latter's superior organization and their leader's unchallenged popularity assured their victory. The Peronists formed the FREJULI party (*Frente Justicialista de Liberación* or Justicialist Liberation Front), which nominated Héctor J. Cámpora, a leader of the Peronist left wing, as its presidential candidate. Cámpora handily won the March 1973 election with 50 percent of the vote against 21 percent for Radical party candidate Ricardo Balbín. In a series of fast-moving events during the spring and summer, Cámpora took office in May, Juan Perón returned from exile in June, and Cámpora resigned in July to pave the way for Perón. Perón, with his wife Isabel Martínez de Perón as his running mate, was overwhelmingly elected president in September.

At the heart of the Peronist program were formal agreements with labor and industry that pledged compliance with a wage and price freeze. (These included the so-called Social Contract, or *Pacto Social,* with the labor unions and the *Acto Compromiso del Campo* with industrialists.) This cooperation lasted for about a year, while the Argentine economy, buoyed by high world market prices for beef and grain, boomed. The agreements disintegrated in mid-1974 with the onset of renewed inflation brought on by a huge increase in international oil prices.

Even before these economic arrangements ended, the Peronist movement had begun to disintegrate, divided between left and right wings. By the time Perón died in July 1974, the regime had already veered rightward. With the rise of Welfare Minister Jóse López Rega during the first months of President Isabel Perón's administration, the shift to the right quickened. The level of violence increased. (In 1975 left- and right-wing thugs reportedly killed 1,100 people.) Rightist "death squads" roamed the streets. Left-wing terrorists staged spectacular kidnapings. In the face of escalating violence and economic chaos, the military stepped in again, overthrowing Isabel in March 1976 and installing General Jorge Rafael Videla as president of a three-man junta composed of the three commanders of the armed forces.

Military Rule

In the ensuing years, the military presided over a roller-coaster economy that tore the guts out of Argentine industry and a reign of terror unprecedented in the nation's history. By the summer of 1982, the annual rate of inflation shot up to a catastrophic 500 percent, the highest in the world. Economic growth fluctuated wildly: the gross domestic product (the total of all the goods and services produced) grew in 1977 and 1979 and fell in 1978 and 1980. During the first six months of 1982, the GDP fell a dismaying 7 percent. Worst of all, the free market policies of finance minister José Alfredo Martínez de Hoz led to record numbers of bankruptcies and bank failures. By eliminating tariffs on imported industrial goods and reducing government involvement in the economy, Martínez de Hoz presided over the destruction of many of Argentina's largest corporations. The real wages of Argentine workers plummeted 40 percent between 1976 and 1979, before recovering in 1980 and falling again in the severe crisis of 1982.

Unlike in its previous coups of 1955 and 1966, the military for the first five years of its dictatorship seemed determined to maintain itself in power in order to effect a "Process of National Reorganization." To this end the junta banned all normal political activity and embarked on a "dirty war" against the left. Under military rule, perhaps as many as 30,000 Argentines disappeared, many victims of illegal rightist death squads. Argentines came to fear the knock on the door at midnight, after which unknown kidnapers would take family and friends, who were never to be heard from again.

Retired Major General Roberto Viola succeeded Videla as president in October 1980. He

322

was unable to manage the growing economic crisis and deepening criticism from landowners and industrialists, who had ranked among the regime's firmest backers. With the "dirty war" won by 1980, the military itself was split into hardliners (*duros*) and moderates (*blandos*) over whether or not to ease repression.

In response to intensifying criticism, Viola opened his cabinet to representatives of critical groups. This came too late, however. The military ousted Viola in November 1981, replacing him with the commander-in-chief of the army, General Leopoldo Galtieri.

The unpopularity of the military widened as the economy continued to deteriorate and the full extent of its butchery was gradually revealed to the Argentine people. The persistent marches of mothers of the *desaparecidos* (the disappeared ones) in Buenos Aires and the revelations of newspaper editor Jacobo Timerman brought the junta international notoriety.[1]

The Malvinas War

In April 1982, Galtieri took a desperate gamble to divert the nation from its economic woes and unite Argentines behind the regime. He sent Argentine forces to capture the Malvinas Islands (known also as the Falklands) in the South Atlantic, three hundred miles off the coast. Argentina and Great Britain had both claimed the islands for 150 years. For the previous seventeen years the two nations had conducted on-and-off negotiations to turn them over to Argentina, but each time agreement seemed imminent talks had broken off. On April 2, Galtieri sent 9,000 troops to settle the matter once and for all.

The invasion was the culmination of a series of colossal miscalculations by the Argentine military. First, Galtieri had not expected Britain to fight to retain the islands. The British, however, sensitive to their position as a declining world power, chose to fight as a matter of national

honor. The Argentines also misjudged the position of the United States. They believed that the United States, which had recently made a number of friendly overtures, would remain neutral in the conflict. Instead, after an initial period during which it tried to mediate a peaceful agreement, the United States actively supported the British.

The war was a disaster for Argentina. Although the air force acquitted itself well, inflicting heavy casualties on the British, the navy stayed in port after the tragic loss of the *Belgrano* (300 men died) and, most important, the army disgraced itself. Poorly trained, atrociously led Argentine troops offered little resistance to the British. Some Argentine commanders actually abandoned their soldiers. In the ten-week war the British recaptured the islands and took the Argentine army prisoner. There were nearly 2,000 casualties in all, about 600 Argentines died.

The military compounded its devastating losses on the battlefield by misleading Argentines with false reports of victory. Thoroughly humiliated and discredited, the military faced an unprecedented political and economic crisis. Inevitably, the generals had to yield power to a civilian government. Galtieri was forced out and replaced in July by another retired general, Reynaldo Benito Antonio Bignone.

Return to Democracy and the Death of Peronismo

Argentina ended nine years of nightmarish military rule in the fall of 1983 with the landslide victory of Radical party candidate Raul Alfonsín. Alfonsín thus became the first democratically elected majority president since Perón in 1946. For the first time, too, Peronism was defeated in an open election.

During Alfonsín's first year and a half in office the Argentine economy deteriorated badly. Inflation soared to 566 percent during 1984 and to 1,200 percent in June 1985. That month, however, Alfonsín instituted the "austral plan." This established wage and price controls, introduced new

---

[1] Timerman was imprisoned and tortured. His memoir, *Prisoner Without a Name, Cell Without a Number*, accused the junta of virulent anti-Semitism.

currency (the austral replaced the peso), and reduced government spending. Almost overnight currency stabilized. Inflation fell to 25 percent.

Though the immediate crisis ended, the nation's economic problems remained manifold and profound. Argentina's industrial base was technologically backward, its foreign debt exceeded $50 billion by the late 1980s, and it was still dependent on primary export markets plagued by low prices. Unemployment in 1985 was the highest in twenty years.

Alfonsín faced the difficult problem of the trials of the military accused of atrocities during the so-called dirty war of the 1970s and failures during the war with Great Britain. When the military refused to try officers in its own courts, the president transferred the cases to civilian jurisdiction. Shortly after taking office in 1983, he appointed a commission headed by Ernesto Sábato, an internationally known author, to investigate military terrorism. The commission's report, aptly titled *Nunca más* (Never Again), revealed the full extent of the horror. The commission found the armed forces responsible for 8,971 disappearances; it documented torture, kidnaping, and other crimes, and labeled the acts as "the greatest and most savage tragedy in our history." In the trials that followed the commission's report, several generals were convicted and awarded long prison sentences. Alfonsín confronted the problem of what to do with lower-ranking officers and enlisted men who actually carried out the crimes. In early 1987, against overwhelming public opposition, Alfonsín ended prosecutions of most lower-rank military for human rights abuses on the grounds that they had simply carried out orders. Despite this lenient attitude, Alfonsín faced a series of mutinies by sections of the divided and disgruntled armed forces. They had no popular support and were quickly crushed by loyal troops, but the light punishments meted out to the ultrarightist leaders of these mutinies by military courts contributed to a continuing atmosphere of indiscipline and turmoil in the armed forces.

Alfonsín had to deal with an economic crisis of unprecedented proportions; by 1989 Argentina's per capita gross product had fallen more than

In this picture, "Mothers of the Square of May" wear white kerchiefs in silent protest against the disappearance of their loved ones and distribute newspapers that report the trials of those held responsible for the "dirty war."

15 percent since 1981. To cope with the crisis he resorted to traditional conservative remedies, seeking to push exports and enacting the austerity measures—cuts in government services and wage restraints—demanded by the IMF as a condition for new foreign loans to keep the Argentine economy afloat. By spring 1989 the foreign debt stood at about $60 billion. Payment on the debt took some $6 billion a year, but the country's earnings in 1988 were below $3 billion. The deficit had to be made up by new loans, which only increased the country's dependency. The policy of austerity and faithful service of the foreign debt meant that little capital was available for development; new austerity measures announced in 1989 included a 50 percent cut in all major development programs. The economy program con-

324   tributed to a deterioration of the infrastructure, with long daily blackouts and energy rationing.

By May 1989, as the country prepared to go to the polls to elect a new president, it had the worst of all economic worlds: a profound recession marked by declining production and rising unemployment and an annual inflation rate of 12,000 percent, with prices rising four times a day. In the last forty-five days real wages had dropped 35 percent. The situation sparked a week of food riots that spread across the country, with desperate thousands of people taking over supermarkets, cleaning out the shelves but usually leaving the cash in the registers. The government responded by declaring a nationwide state of emergency and banning all demonstrations and strikes.

Against this background of economic collapse, the election in mid-May 1989 of the Peronist candidate Carlos Saúl Menem, governor of the La Rioja province, who had campaigned on a program featured by the invitation "Follow me, I will not fail you" and vague promises of a "productive revolution," was a foregone conclusion. With the situation worsening daily, Alfonsín decided to cut short his term and hand power over to Menem in July, five months early. Menem's followers, including the powerful Peronist-controlled unions, naturally expected him to repudiate the conservative policies that had led to an unprecedented economic and social crisis. What followed was a stunning surprise. Convinced that an even more powerful dose of those policies offered the only solution for the crisis, Menem, who professed his admiration for Ronald Reagan, Margaret Thatcher, and Augusto Pinochet, abandoned his party's traditional economic and political positions in favor of a thoroughgoing neoliberal program.

Contrary to all expectations, therefore, Menem included in his cabinet many conservatives, including representatives of big business like the great firm of Bunge and Born, representing one of the most powerful multinational groups, with links to the agricultural oligarchy that Peronists had traditionally distrusted, and announced a program of privatization of state-owned compa-

nies, the dismissal of thousands of state employees, and cuts of billions in government spending over the next year. The program represented a deepening of the policies attempted without much success by the brutal military governments between 1976 and 1983 and by the Alfonsín regime, with equal lack of success.

The process of privatization was carried out with frenzied haste and clearly favored large economic groups. Typical of the process was the "fire-sale" aspect of the privatization of two profitable state firms, Entel (the telephone company) and Aerolineas Argentinas (the national airline). *The Wall Street Journal* commented that these two privatizations "more resemble corporate raids than stockholders' sales. Both Aerolineas Argentinas and Entel are being sold for a fraction of their net worth." In July 1993 bidding began for the jewel of the state properties, the state oil company, Yacimientos Petrolíferos Fiscales, a profitable company with assets calculated at $7.4 billion and projected revenues of $5 billion. Among Latin America's oil producers, Argentina was the only one to sell off its oil state monopoly, usually regarded as a "strategic" asset, lock, stock, and barrel.

Menem's "shock therapy" on his way to the goal of a free market economy provoked resistance. The Peronist trade union movement, once his ardent supporter, split into pro- and anti-Menem wings, followed by a series of strikes to which Menem responded by firing strike leaders and seeking to curtail the right to strike by law or decree. The generally ineffective resistance of the once powerful labor movement to Menem's policies reflected a number of factors: the decline in size of the blue-collar labor force; the increase in the number of unemployed and underemployed, creating a substantial reserve labor force that weakened militancy; labor's traditional loyalty to the Peronist party; and the opportunism and greed of Peronist labor bosses, who were accustomed to live off state money and collaborate with the party, whatever its policies. To these factors one should add the weakness of the Argentine left, divided and decimated by state terrorism during the years of military rule.

To combat inflation, in March 1991 Menem's new finance minister, Domingo Cavallo, unveiled the "ultimate anti-inflation shock," a plan making the Argentine currency convertible in relation to the dollar and forbidding the Central Bank to print money that was not backed by gold or foreign currency. To ensure wage and price stabilization Cavallo pledged government budget cuts of $6 billion, largely at the expense of public-sector jobs. The policy entailed extensive budget cuts in health, education, welfare, and pensions. From the government's point of view, the Cavallo plan was a great success. Prices plummeted, the stock market exploded, and the Buenos Aires financial district hailed the start of the "Argentine miracle." The United States and the IMF rewarded Menem's fiscal orthodoxy by approving a Brady Plan that refinanced $21 billion of Argentina's foreign debt over thirty-five years.

With inflation apparently curbed, in the September 1991 congressional and gubernatorial elections the Peronist (Justicialista) party won a solid victory over Alfonsín's Radicals and repeated that victory two years later in the congressional elections of October 1993. In reality, despite the personal insults hurled by Menem and Alfonsín at each other, little separated the two parties, for they were in agreement on major issues. Apparently moved above all by the need to preserve the neoliberal model that Menem had put in place, in November 1993 Alfonsín, who only a month earlier had called Menem "a traitor to democracy," announced his support for Menem's proposal for a constitutional reform that would allow him to run again and be re-elected in 1995. The proposal was endorsed by U.S. Ambassador James Cheek and Argentine business leaders but opposed by a majority of Argentines in public polls. The distrust of Menem reflected more than the economic pain inflicted by his neoliberal project—in Argentina, which until recently had the highest per capita beef consumption in Latin America, hunger, malnutrition, and diseases like cholera, linked to extreme poverty, had become endemic. Developments like Menem's stacking of the Supreme Court with loyal followers, his bypassing of Congress through free

use of executive decrees, his interior ministry's collection of intelligence on political opponents, and a series of attacks by Peronist thugs on journalists critical of the regime raised questions about the democratic health of the Menem government and the country. Adding to the unease was a wave of corruption scandals involving Menem's appointees and relatives.

As 1993 drew to a close, much of the luster had gone out of the Argentine "success story." True, inflation was down to around 12 percent, foreign debt had been cut to 25 percent of the gross domestic product, and Argentina, with a level of economic growth of almost 9 percent a year, was cited by the IMF as a model for developing nations. But there were signs that all was not well with the country, particularly a combined unemployment and underemployment figure of 25 percent of the economically active population and social indicators pointing to widespread poverty and deprivation. A striking development was the appearance of a class of "new poor," including many members of Argentina's once substantial middle class. It was estimated that nearly 30 percent of Argentina's population over sixty fell into this category.

Other negative economic developments included a crisis of agriculture as a result of low international prices, declining markets, and the high cost of credit, leading to the unusual sight of protest marches by farmers through the streets of Buenos Aires. The removal of tariff barriers had also caused a flood of cheap textiles and other imports, causing many businesses to close and pushing up unemployment, even as exports were shrinking.

On the political front, Menem's bid for re-election in 1995 suffered a check in the elections for a constituent assembly on April 10, 1994. In those elections corruption was a major issue. Nationally, the ruling *Partido Justicialista* (PJ) received 38 percent of the vote (down from the 43 percent it received in the October 1993 legislative elections), failing to gain the majority needed to unilaterally reform the constitution and allow Menem immediate re-election. But Menem's ally, the *Unión Cívica Radical* (UCR), which had sup-

326   ported his constitutional reform proposals, suffered a disastrous decline, its vote falling from 30.9 percent in October's elections to 20.5. The surprise of the elections was the big vote (38 percent) garnered in the capital district of Buenos Aires by the *Frente Grande* (FG), a left-center coalition that based its campaign on the fight against corruption. But Menem had stumbled, not fallen, and Alfonsín's confirmation that his party would support Menem on the core package of constitutional issues assured the outcome of the constituent assembly that opened its sessions in June. A further agreement by the two leaders to submit the agreed reforms as a simple package, with assembly members allowed to cast a "yes" or "no" vote, virtually reduced the assembly to a rubber-stamping role, causing the FG to announce that it would boycott that decisive vote. But Menem's victory in 1995 was far from assured. "The government thought that it was going to win re-election in 1995 in a waltz," ironically commented the Argentine daily *Clarín,* "but it now realizes that there is no dance guaranteed."

Doubts concerning Menem's political future deepened as a result of growing social unrest. On July 6, 1994, thousands of workers, representing unions that had split off from the collaborationist GTC, public workers, teachers, farmers, and representatives of small- and medium-sized business groups, converged on the Government Palace in Buenos Aires to show their opposition to Menem's neoliberal policies. The protests took place against the background of a salary freeze, in place since April 1, 1991, when the government's stabilization plan went into effect, and a return to hyperinflation (56 percent in the last thirty-seven months). The Menem government responded by describing the protests as the acts of "groups of subversive agitators" and considering a proposal to create a security force of some 80,000 agents at an annual cost of $2.4 billion to "control the activities of disintegrative elements." Menem's further movement to the right was reflected in a speech in early November 1994, in which he defended the "dirty war" unleashed against left-wing guerrillas in the 1970s. Critics viewed the speech as opening the way for a new political repression.

Menem, who claimed to assume the mantle of Perón and to continue his work, had dealt a death blow to what remained of Perón's economic and political project. It remained to be seen whether Menem's neoliberal project, based on the sell-off of the national patrimony, the subordination of labor, and an alliance with domestic and foreign ruling classes, was more viable that the one he destroyed.

Chapter 14

The Chilean Way

For a century and a half, Chile set a relatively high standard of political behavior on a continent notorious for its turmoil and dictatorships. Compared to its neighbors, Peru, Bolivia, and Argentina, Chile was a model of domestic tranquility. Chilean democracy appeared so firmly rooted that it permitted the election and installation of a Marxist head of state, President Salvador Allende Gossens, in 1970. Only three years later, however, amid growing economic and political chaos, military rebels overthrew Chile's legitimate government and established a right-wing dictatorship whose rule was characterized by brutal oppression.

How could Chile maintain its parliamentary democracy so long when the rest of Latin America could not? Why, after almost a hundred and fifty years of respect for parliamentary democracy, did it crumble so swiftly? In retrospect, the bounds of Chilean democracy were narrowly drawn; the elite never allowed political freedom and the practice of politics to endanger its basic interests. Instead of seeking to solve the nation's desperate economic and social problems, successive governments merely evaded them. When, finally, a coalition government headed by Chile's working-class parties came to power in 1970 and inaugurated structural reforms that threatened oligarchical privilege, the elite responded by calling in the army, abolishing parliamentary democracy, and establishing a reactionary dictatorship.

328   An Economic History, 1900–1970

The Export Sector in the Twentieth Century

The export sector played a crucial and basically detrimental role in Chilean history. Raw material exports generated enormous profits, but relatively few benefits flowed to the nation as a whole. Instead of stimulating balanced economic growth, the lucrative export sector tended to stunt the country's social and political development. Like the "banana republics" of Central America and the sugar islands of the Caribbean, Chile relied for its revenues on one export commodity, first nitrate and then copper, making it extremely vulnerable to cyclical world market demands for its products. Moreover, the copper industry, which produced the nation's major export in the twentieth century, was operated as an enclave, almost totally isolated from the rest of the economy. Finally, and most important, the presence of an export sector that produced sufficient revenue to operate the government and provide employment for a growing middle class enabled the Chilean oligarchy to retain political power and maintain an obsolete system of land tenure and use; these conditions severely hampered the growth of democracy and economic development.

Until World War I, nitrate was Chile's primary export, but after the war a cheaper, synthetic product displaced it on the world market; copper then became Chile's leading export. Initially, small-scale, low-technology operations mined most of Chile's copper, but shortly after 1900 a downturn in copper prices forced many of these producers to close. At the same time, the introduction of improved methods for the extraction of low-grade ore and the lower transportation costs promised by the opening of the Panama Canal attracted large North American companies, which soon dominated the industry. From 1904 to 1923 giant United States–based corporations such as Guggenheim, Kennecott, Anaconda, and

Braden purchased the largest and most productive copper mines, including the three mines of the *Gran Minería.*

In 1960 the three great mines of the Gran Minería, all owned by the foreign giants Anaconda and Kennecott, accounted for 11 percent of the country's gross national product, 50 percent of its exports, and 20 percent of government revenues. But the millions of dollars in sales, profits, and tax revenues generated by copper mining provided little stimulus for Chilean commerce and industry. Copper extraction was capital-intensive and required relatively few employees. Employment in the mines declined steadily in the post–World War II era, and the surplus of miners made it possible for the companies to pay the largely unskilled labor force relatively low wages. Until the 1950s, machinery, equipment, and technical skills were imported entirely from abroad.

The copper companies earned huge profits, which they remitted to their parent corporations in the United States, adding to the outflow of capital from the country. Chile's modest share in copper's riches took the form of taxes, wages, and other limited economic linkages. The Chilean government did not impose an income tax on profits until 1925, when the levy was set at 6 percent. Subsequently, the tax rate was raised to 18 percent in 1931, to 33 percent in 1938, and to 60 percent in 1953.

A brief history of the copper industry since 1929 illustrates Chile's vulnerability to world market cycles. In 1929 the price of copper dropped precipitously. Since the government relied heavily on copper taxes for revenue, the depression forced it to curtail daily operations severely and default on its large foreign debt. In 1932 the United States, Chile's main market for copper, adopted a high tariff on copper imports, which caused mine closings and severe unemployment.

Copper prices recovered in 1935, however, and by 1937 copper production exceeded the pre-depression level. World War II brought a new copper boom, although profits and revenues were limited by price ceilings imposed by the United States. After the war, with the elimination of controls, prices skyrocketed. The Korean war (1950–1953) brought new price controls by the United States, but on somewhat better terms for Chile. In 1953 world market prices again plummeted, and Chile was rescued only by the United States government's purchase of a hundred thousand tons of copper for its military reserve. By the mid-1950s, copper boomed again, and the boom continued through the 1960s. A new down cycle, however, occurred during the last two years of the Allende administration (1971–1973).

The revenues generated from copper taxes enabled the government to avoid taxing large landholdings. Without the spur of equitable taxes, latifundists continued to leave vast tracts of fertile land uncultivated or underutilized. Although it had the potential to feed its own people, Chile had to import foodstuffs—a policy that drained the nation of foreign exchange that would have been better used to purchase capital goods for industrialization or to build roads and harbors.

An equitable tax on idle or underutilized land might have led to the breakup of the latifundia, the modernization of agriculture, and the emergence of a class of small peasant proprietors. Thanks to government policy in favor of the latifundia, however, none of this happened. Chilean agriculture remained relatively backward and inefficient.

With its coffers swelled by revenue from the export sector, the Chilean government expanded its role in the economy. A large bureaucracy developed, staffed by an emerging middle class. As the government became the major employer of the middle class and the nation's most important venture capitalist, Chile grew ever more dependent for its economic development on factors beyond its control.

Foreign Domination of the Chilean Economy

After World War I, the United States replaced Great Britain as the major foreign investor in Chile. Guggenheim and Anaconda accounted for better than 80 percent of the copper production,

Bethlehem monopolized iron ore, and Guggenheim held 70 percent of the nitrate industry through its *Compánia de Salitres de Chile* (Chilean Nitrate Company, or COSACH).

Although depression and war slowed the inflow, foreign capital surged into Chile in the postwar period, not only into the extractive sector but into manufacturing and commerce as well. From 1954 to 1970, foreigners invested $1.67 billion in Chile. U.S. companies continued to dominate copper, nitrate, and iodine production. Foreign companies conducted approximately half the nation's wholesale trade, monopolized the telephone and telegraph industries, and had important stakes in electric utilities and banking. Even the major advertising agencies were foreign subsidiaries or affiliates.

Chile depended not only on direct investment from abroad but on loans as well. Payment of interest and amortization on the national debt consumed an increasing share of its revenue from the export sector. The country also relied on foreign sources for industrial technology.

Because most foreign investment, like the copper enclave, was capital-intensive, it provided little employment and few linkages to the rest of the economy. The benefits to Chile's long-range economic development were minimal. Without doubt, Chile was not the master of its own economic fate.

The Concentration of Land and Wealth

In 1964, on the eve of the first serious effort in Chile's history to reform its agrarian structure, there was an extreme concentration of landownership, the condition of rural laborers was wretched, and the inefficient great landed estates were clearly incapable of providing enough food to feed Chile's growing urban centers. By contrast with the situation in most underdeveloped nations, Chile's agricultural sector played only a small role in the economy. The inability of agriculture to provide employment, on the one hand, and sufficient food, on the other, resulted in an overurbanized, underemployed, and undernourished population.

The statistics of landholding indicate that there was little change in these patterns between 1930 and 1970. In 1930 holdings of over 2,500 acres composed only 2 percent of the total number of farms but comprised 78 percent of the cultivable land. Eighty-two percent of all farms were under 125 acres but held only 4 percent of the land. By the 1960s, 11,000 units, accounting for 4.2 percent of the farms, composed 79 percent of the land. Farms under 100 acres—77 percent of all farms—held 10.6 percent of the land. Over 700,000 people, the majority of the rural labor force, had no land at all. The living and working conditions of agricultural laborers were appalling—and getting worse. Agricultural wages had consistently declined since the 1940s, falling 23 percent from 1953 to 1964.

Government credit and tax policies before 1964 assured that the maldistribution of land and agricultural income would continue. Small landholders, having no access to bank or government loans, had to rely on moneylenders or store owners, who charged outrageous interest. Smallholders and agricultural laborers also bore a disproportionate burden of taxes. Taxes on land, capital, income, and inheritance, on the other hand, were light. The large estates, especially those that were not farmed, went virtually untaxed.

Despite unused land and plentiful manpower, production of food did not keep pace with population growth from the mid-1930s. The deficit had to be made up by imports, which aggravated the balance of payments problem and contributed to Chile's chronic inflation. As a result, the poor were undernourished, and even large portions of the middle class suffered from inadequate diet.

Land was not the only sector of the Chilean economy concentrated in a very few hands. A few powerful clans controlled a wide variety of industrial and financial enterprises and thus exerted a decisive influence on the national economy as a whole. In 1967, 12 companies out of 2,600 transacted nearly half the total wholesale business in the country. One bank, Banco de Chile, furnished 32 percent of the nation's private bank credit; the five largest banks furnished 57.4 percent.

These facts, however, tell only part of the story, for control of the economy was even more concentrated. Fifteen large economic groups controlled the Chilean economy. The most powerful of the clans, the Edwards family, controlled one commercial bank, seven financial and investment corporations, five insurance companies, thirteen industries, and two publishing houses and was closely associated with North American companies active in the country. The family's newspaper chain accounted for over half the circulation of daily newspapers in Chile; together with another publishing house, it virtually controlled the entire market for periodicals.

A Political History, 1891–1970

The Parliamentary Republic, 1891–1920

The defeat and suicide of President José Manuel Balmaceda during the civil war of 1891 ushered in the era of the so-called Parliamentary Republic. It was a time of political stagnation, in sharp contrast to the rapid social change. The dominant political parties, the Liberal and Conservative, represented the great landowners of the Central Valley and supplied the nation's presidents and congressmen. The six presidents who served during the period of the Parliamentary Republic were little more than puppets manipulated by congressional leaders.

A third major party, the Radicals, founded in 1861 by dissident Liberals, enjoyed the support of low-level professionals, bureaucrats, teachers, artisans, and other middle-class groups, as well as that of large landowners on the southern frontier around Concepción, northern mine owners from the Copiapó region, and businessmen from Santiago, the capital. A fourth party, the Democrats, had some base in the lower middle class and among workers.

The only issue separating the major parties was the role of the church in education. The chief concerns of the parties appeared to be the preservation of the status quo and the distribution of the spoils of office. Corruption and inefficiency pervaded the political life of the era.

While politics stagnated in an atmosphere of fraud and apathy, Chilean society underwent profound transformation. The nation grew increasingly urbanized and industrialized, and new classes emerged from these processes. An industrial working class rose in the mining regions of the north, first in the nitrate fields and then in the copper mines. Although their wages were higher than elsewhere in the country, the miners suffered from low pay, inadequate housing, the tyranny of company stores, and unsafe working conditions. In the cities, where wages were even lower, workers lived in wretched slums and were periodically battered by epidemic disease.

After the turn of the century, workers began to struggle against these dismal conditions. The first major strike broke out in Iquique in the northern mining region in 1901 and lasted for two months. In 1907 the nitrate workers of Iquique again struck against inhuman living and working conditions; the government responded by sending in troops who slaughtered two thousand workers. The wave of strikes continued, with a notable upsurge during World War I. Unrest increased at the war's end, for the nitrate industry collapsed, leaving thousands of miners unemployed and plunging the entire country into a severe depression. In 1919, faced with growing unrest, the government declared a state of siege (suspending civil liberties) in the mining areas.

Labor had meantime begun to organize in the effort to achieve better conditions. Luis Emilio Recabarren played a leading part in establishing the Workers' Federation of Chile (*Federación de Obreros de Chile,* or FOCH) in 1909. Three years later he founded the first workers' party, the Socialist, or Socialist Labor, party. In 1922 it became the Communist party and joined the Third (Communist) International. By contrast with the Argentine Socialist party, with its large middle-class base, Chile's first working-class party grew directly out of the labor movement.

In the same period, the middle class became larger and more diverse. The growth of industry and commerce and the expansion of the state created many new white-collar jobs. This growing middle class displayed few of the entrepreneurial traits commonly associated with the North American and European middle classes. The domination of decisive sectors of the economy by large-scale enterprise effectively barred small and medium-size entrepreneurs from playing an important role in economic life. Aristocratic control of choice government jobs through clientele and kinship ties also restricted the sphere of middle-class activity. As the twentieth century opened, the middle class began to agitate for a place in the sun.

Meanwhile, the composition of the oligarchy was also changing, for it began to incorporate new elements from among industrialists and businessmen. More completely than elsewhere in Latin America, the Chilean landed elite fused with the new urban upper and upper-middle classes. They intermarried, and the urban rich acquired land, adopting the values of the traditional elite. This was a serious impediment to reform. Missing in Chile, too, were the large number of immigrants who in some measure challenged the values and hegemony of the elite in Argentina. The relatively few immigrants who came to Chile preferred to emulate rather than challenge the oligarchy.

Alessandri, the Military Radicals, and Reform

By 1920, even sections of the oligarchy were aware that they could no longer ignore the needs of the rest of Chilean society. In 1918 the Liberal Alliance, which included Radicals, Liberals, Democrats, and *Balmacedistas,* achieved control of the Chamber of Deputies in the election of that year, and in 1920 it offered a possible "savior" of the country, nicknamed the "Lion of Tarapacá," Arturo Alessandri, as its candidate for president.

A former corporation lawyer turned populist politician, Alessandri appealed to the lower and middle classes with promises to reform the constitution and relieve the bleakness of working-class life. He promised a social security system, a labor code, cheap housing, educational reform, women's rights, and state control of banks and insurance companies. With considerable support from sections of the oligarchy, which hoped that he could placate the restless masses with a minimum of effective social change, Alessandri defeated the candidate of the conservative National Union in the election of 1920.

During the first four years of Alessandri's term, he proved unable to make good his campaign pledges. The Liberal Alliance, which had supported his election, split and failed to give him the support he needed in Congress. Congress, representing entrenched oligarchical interests, stood squarely in the way of any meaningful social and political reforms. Accordingly, Alessandri urged the passage of laws that would restore the balance of power between Congress and the executive branch, a balance destroyed after the civil war of 1891. He also sought such social reforms as a shorter workday, labor laws to protect women and children, the right of workers to strike, and health insurance. These modest proposals certainly did not threaten the status quo, but they would require money. In view of the catastrophic decline of the nitrate industry, this money could be raised only by taxing the oligarchy's land and income, a solution the elite found unthinkable. As a result of the parliamentary deadlock, the Chilean government could not cope with the mounting economic and social crisis.

The Liberal Alliance won a majority in both houses of Congress in 1924, but the new Congress, ignoring the pressing need for reform legislation, proceeded to vote themselves salaries for the first time in Chilean history. The innovation was entirely proper, for congressmen no longer came exclusively from the oligarchy and needed salaries to support themselves, but in a time of depression, when many public employees had not been paid for many weeks, it gave great offense.

The Chilean military, predominantly of middle-class origins, had observed the unfolding crisis with growing impatience and resentment. Many junior and middle-grade officers favored the enactment of Alessandri's social and political reform program; they also felt that Congress had neglected the needs of the armed forces. For these officers, the salary episode was the last straw. Organized in a military junta, they staged a coup in September 1924 and compelled Congress to enact in rapid succession all of Alessandri's reform proposals and, in addition, to raise the size of the army and its pay scale. Alessandri, however, refused to share power with the military and left the country.

Growing tension between progressive junior and middle-grade officers on the one hand and conservative generals on the other produced another coup in January 1925, which brought to power a reform-minded group of officers, led by Carlos Ibáñez del Campo and Marmaduke Grove. The new junta promptly invited Alessandri to return, which he did in March.

On his return, Alessandri set about accomplishing the political reforms for which he had campaigned. The result was the constitution of 1925, which ended the Parliamentary Republic and restored the balance of power between Congress and the president. It provided that the president would be elected by direct vote, serve a six-year term, be ineligible for immediate re-election, and have control over his cabinet and government finance. The constitution proclaimed the inviolable right of private property but stated that this right could be limited in the interest of social needs. Other measures included a new and extensive labor code, the grant of the vote to literate males over twenty-one, the establishment of an electoral registry to reduce electoral fraud, a nominal income tax on income over ten thousand pesos a year, and the establishment of a central bank.

In September, a plebiscite approved the constitution. Soon thereafter, Alessandri again resigned, citing unbearable military pressure. The ensuing election brought to the presidency the weak and colorless Emilio Figueroa Larrain. However, Ibáñez, who became interior minister in the new administration, gradually emerged as a strong man. Blaming the country's problems on communism, Congress, and the leadership of all political parties, he proceeded to jail or deport Communists and key members of Congress who dared to challenge his power. In May 1927, placed in an untenable position by Ibáñez's inroads on his authority, Figueroa resigned. Less than two weeks later, Ibáñez, running unopposed, was elected president in a special election.

Ibáñez and the Great Depression

The military reform movement of 1924, which for a time appeared to be forging an alliance with the working and middle classes for the achievement of structural reforms, ended in the military dictatorship of Ibáñez (1927–1931). The only fruits of that movement for social change were the social legislation adopted since 1924 and provided for in the constitution of 1925.

To implement that legislation and secure the position of state employees, which was necessary to maintain political stability, Ibáñez needed substantial amounts of money; his program of welfare, public works, and modernization was based above all on huge loans from foreign bankers. The armed forces were a special beneficiary of government largesse, obtaining generous promotions and salary increases. Meanwhile, all opposition was suppressed, political foes were jailed or deported, and efforts were made to split the Communist-led labor movement by the sponsorship of government-backed unions.

Aided by a temporary revival of copper and nitrate sales and massive foreign loans, the Chilean economy prospered for the first two years of Ibáñez's rule. But the Wall Street crash of 1929 cut off the all-important flow of capital and loans, and by the following year the nitrate and copper markets had both collapsed. Unemployment spread throughout the nation. In a vain effort to find a solution for the economic crisis, the government tried to limit nitrate sales to push up prices. Ibáñez trimmed social services and his public works program and hiked taxes, but the financial situation grew increasingly desperate.

In July 1931, confronted by a general strike that involved not only workers but professionals, white-collar employees, and students and faced with growing doubts about the army's loyalty to him, Ibáñez resigned and went into exile in Argentina. The next seventeen months brought a succession of military coups. One such coup, led by Marmaduke Grove, commander of the air force, led to the proclamation of a Socialist Republic of Chile, which lasted barely twelve days before it was overthrown by a new military revolt. Ironically, the program of the socialist republic was not socialist; it proposed, rather, to create jobs through public works financed by the issue of paper money.

Finally in September 1932, a new coup installed a caretaker regime that presided over new elections and a return to civilian government. In the presidential election, Arturo Alessandri, supported by Radicals, Liberals, Democrats, and even some Conservatives, defeated five rivals, including Grove.

The Return of Alessandri

Alessandri began his second term in the depths of the depression, with a hundred and sixty thousand people unemployed in Santiago alone, while a typhoid epidemic ravaged the country. Income from nitrates was one-twentieth the 1927 figure; public employees, including soldiers and policemen, had not been paid for months. In the succeeding five years, 1932 to 1937, the president and his finance minister, Gustavo Ross, presided over an economic recovery that reflected a partial revival and stabilization of the world market. As the economy revived, government revenues increased and Alessandri had more money to implement social legislation already on the books.

But Alessandri had no greater success in solving Chile's structural problems in the 1930s than he did in the 1920s. Foreign capital controlled the lucrative mining sector of the economy, and the inefficient latifundio continued to dominate Chilean agriculture. Workers' strikes for better wages and living conditions were often brutally suppressed.

Middle-class critics of the regime fared little better. Following the example of Ibáñez, Alessandri closed down hostile newspapers, exiled political critics, and dealt highhandedly with Congress. These conditions produced a major new effort to mobilize workers, peasants, and the ur-

334 ban middle sector to defend democracy and promote social progress. This effort was called the Chilean Popular Front.

The Rise of the Left and the Popular Front

The Chilean left had its roots in the Socialist Labor party, founded by Luis Emilio Recabarren in 1912; ten years later, it joined the Third (Communist) International and became the Communist party. During the 1920s, the Communists won considerable support among organized labor, particularly the railroad workers' union and the Confederation of Chilean Workers (FOCH), which claimed two hundred thousand members. Although they had had a part in framing the constitution of 1925, Communist leaders were imprisoned and exiled during the Ibáñez regime. After the fall of Ibáñez in 1931, however, the party began to revive under the leadership of Carlos Contreras Labarca, and it gained considerable popularity among workers and intellectuals.

The communists' principal rival on the left was the Socialist party. Its predominantly middle-class leadership, though it advocated a leftist program that included revolution, was highly opportunistic. From the first, the party was an uneasy alliance of left and right wings.

Chile in the 1930s was fertile ground for the growth of left-wing parties and ideologies because the working class was excluded from the benefits of economic recovery and Alessandri harshly suppressed working-class dissent. Between 1935 and 1937 the Chilean Communist party, at the urging of the Third International, alarmed at the growing threat of fascism, joined with left and moderate parties to form the Chilean Popular Front. The Communists, Socialists, and Radicals united for the elections of 1938, nominating Radical Pedro Aguirre Cerda as their presidential candidate.

The Popular Front's electoral platform called for the restoration of constitutional rule and civil liberties and basic social reforms, summed up in the slogan *pan, techo, y abrigo* (bread, clothing, and a roof). Despite the advantages enjoyed by Alessandri's candidate, Gustavo Ross, including control of the electoral machinery and the support of the large state bureaucracy, Aguirre Cerda gained a razor-thin victory, receiving 50.3 percent of the vote.

The short, stormy life of the Popular Front—it officially ended in 1941 when first the Socialists and then the Radicals withdrew, but was reformed in 1942 as a "Democratic Alliance" of Communists, Radicals, and miscellaneous groups that lasted until 1947—yielded some achievements. In 1938 the State Development Agency, CORFO, was formed to foster industrialization. Aided by a virtual cessation of imports as a result of World War II and by governmental policies of subsidies, low taxes, and protective tariffs on imported consumer goods, native manufacturing made steady progress between 1940 and 1945.

The policy of state-supported industrialization also promoted the growth of the Chilean industrial working class; between 1940 and 1952, the number of workers employed in manufacturing rose from 15 percent of the work force to 19 percent. The industrialization process was accompanied, at least until 1945, by improvement in workers' real purchasing power—up 20 percent between 1940 and 1945—while that of white-collar workers increased 25 percent. After 1945, as Radical administrations moved to the right and the basis of the Popular Front strategy disintegrated, the working class's relative share of the national income declined.

The Popular Front era produced no structural changes in the Chilean economy or society. Chilean governments were unable to institute basic economic and social reforms because the members of the coalition had irreconcilable differences over domestic and foreign policy.

In the 1946 election, the Socialist party ran its own candidate, but Radical Gabriel González Videla (1946–1952) won with the support of the Communist party. Soon, responding to the pressures of the cold war, González Videla moved to the right, ousted the Communist members of his cabinet, broke a strike of Communist-led coal miners (with Socialist support), and the following year pushed through the Law for the Defense of Democracy, known unofficially as the *Ley Maldita,* or the Accursed Law, which outlawed the Communist party and eliminated Communists from Congress. González Videla also established a concentration camp for Communist party members and other left-wing militants in an abandoned mining camp in the northern desert. The Socialist party split into the Socialist party of Chile, which endorsed González Videla's repressive measures, and the Popular Socialist party, which denounced the president's anti-Communist drive.

Massive discontent with skyrocketing inflation, the freezing of workers' wages, and González Videla's repressive policies paved the way for a comeback by the old ex-dictator Carlos Ibáñez del Campo in 1952. Offering repeal of the Ley Maldita, a minimum salary, a family allowance for workers, and a sympathetic hearing for just wage demands, Ibáñez defeated several rival candidates, including Salvador Allende Gossens of the Socialist party, who had Communist support. But the decline in Chilean copper revenues following the end of the Korean war made it impossible for Ibáñez to make good on his populist promises. To stabilize the economy he sought loans from North American banks and the International Monetary Fund; meanwhile, he sought to force the working class to absorb inflation through cuts in real wages. Threatened with labor unrest, Ibáñez embarked on a course of harsh repression. By the end of his term, he had alienated all sectors of the Chilean people.

New Alignments: The Emergence of Christian Democracy

Between 1953 and the presidential election year of 1958, the parties of the left restored their unity by forming the *Frente de Acción Popular* (Popular Action Front, or FRAP), which included the reunited Socialist party and the Communists. Simultaneously, a new Christian Democratic party emerged, led by Eduardo Frei; it appealed to Catholic workers, especially white-collar sectors, with a vague ideology that claimed to be neither

capitalist nor socialist. In its first try for office in 1958, this party demonstrated its electoral force.

Four major candidates contested the presidency in 1958. They were the Conservative Jorge Alessandri, a son of the former president and a leading industrialist; Eduardo Frei, a Christian Democrat; Salvador Allende, of FRAP; and Luis Bossay, a Radical. Surprisingly Alessandri beat Allende by a threadbare margin of only 33,500 votes. Allende would probably have won if an obscure minor-party candidate had not drawn away some slum and rural poor votes.

Alessandri had no more success than his predecessors in coping with Chile's problems of inflation and economic stagnation. His formula for recovery was to restore the free market, end state intervention in the economy, and employ foreign loans and investment as the basis for economic development. By 1962, however, the injections of foreign capital had lost their capacity to stimulate the nation's economy. A serious balance of payments problem arose, and inflation began to increase again.

Politics in Chile during the early 1960s were profoundly affected by changes in United States policy in response to the Cuban Revolution (1959). The United States sought to bolster reform movements throughout Latin America as an alternative to social revolution. As part of this policy, it covertly financed the Christian Democrats. Combined with the backing of the conservative parties, which were badly scared by Allende's near-election six years earlier, U.S. support enabled Frei to win the 1964 election with 56 percent of the vote.

Frei and Christian Democracy, 1964–1970: A "Revolution in Freedom" Unfulfilled

Eduardo Frei came to the presidency with promises of a "revolution in freedom" that would correct the extreme inequities of Chilean society without a violent class struggle. The problems he faced were familiar ones: inflation and stagnation, a domestic market too narrow to support an efficient mass industry, and an industry and an

336

agriculture incapable of supplying the basic needs of the population. In order to create the market needed for a modern mass industry, Frei proposed agrarian reform, tax reform, and other measures to redistribute income to the lower classes.

Frei's plan for the Chileanization of the copper industry was designed both to appease widespread nationalist sentiment and to obtain new government revenue through increased copper production. The plan required the government to buy 51 percent of the shares in the foreign-owned mines. In return for a promise to increase production and refine more ore in Chile, the foreign companies retained control of management and obtained new concessions with respect to taxation and repatriation of profits. But, the plan failed to expand production significantly or to increase government revenues.

Frei's program of agrarian reform also had mixed results. He began by attempting to improve conditions in rural areas by increasing wages, establishing peasant unions, and instituting a more equitable system of taxation; he also redistributed some land to the peasants, but inflation eroded wage gains and land redistribution fell far short of what was promised. As a gradualist, Frei shied away from precipitous or widespread expropriations. Peasants who received land faced a difficult time, for the government did not provide them with credit needed to start off as independent farmers. Frei lost labor support when he adopted a tough line toward strikes and wage demands and tried to undermine the country's major labor federation. Increased worker militancy made Socialist and Communist union leadership more influential.

As early as 1965, the president had decided on an economic policy that would attract foreign and domestic investors; as a result, he abandoned the redistributive efforts of his first year and froze wages. During 1966 the government reacted harshly to strikes in the copper mines, at one point sending in troops.

The need to appease his political constituency and the economic decline after 1966 defeated Frei's efforts at reform. Upper-class Catholic in-

tellectuals had founded and provided the leadership of the Christian Democratic party. Its membership was overwhelmingly middle class, including urban professionals, white-collar workers—especially from the public sector—skilled workers, and managers—groups that had emerged during the preceding two decades as the Chilean economy diversified. The party did well in the larger towns, among urban slum dwellers, and among women. In 1964 Frei got considerable support from industrialists and bankers who feared the election of Allende. These were hardly the elements of a revolutionary party. Frei's program of reform depended entirely on a healthy, expanding economy that would enable the government to distribute benefits to the lower class without injuring the middle class or altering the basic economic and social structures.

When Frei came to office in 1964, the economy was expanding rapidly, for the Vietnam war kept copper prices high. Frei's moderate reform goals insured good relations with the United States and a resulting flow of loans and private investment. Even Chile's chronic inflation slowed. Two good years, however, were followed by four bad ones. After 1967 the economy stagnated while inflation surged again. Income inequalities increased, and living standards declined sharply. Frei's rhetoric brought hope to Chileans, but he fulfilled few of his promises. During his term, the working class grew increasingly restive. Groups like *pobladores* (urban slum dwellers) and rural workers organized for the first time. As the Christian Democrats proved less and less capable of dealing with Chile's economic woes, these newly organized groups and the trade unions moved further to the left.

This leftward move was reflected within the Christian Democratic party itself. In 1969 disillusioned progressives split off to form the Movement for United Popular Action (MAPU), which later joined the Popular Unity Coalition. This break left Frei the leader of the right wing of the party and Radomiro Tomic the head of what remained of the left wing after the secession of MAPU. Since Frei was ineligible to run again under the constitution, and the party could not risk further erosion of its social base by running a hard-liner, it advanced Tomic as its presidential candidate in 1970. He ran on a platform almost indistinguishable from that of Allende, the candidate of the left coalition, *Unidad Popular* (Popular Unity, or UP), whose main elements were the Socialist, Communist, and Radical parties.

The right backed ex-President Jorge Alessandri, the standard-bearer of the National party (formed in 1966 through the merger of the Conservative and Liberal parties). The right, already alienated by Frei's agrarian reform, found Tomic totally unacceptable and refused to join forces with the Christian Democrats as it had in 1964. Allende won the election with 36 percent of the vote, while Alessandri got 35 percent and Tomic 28 percent. Since Allende failed to receive a majority, the election went to Congress which, after much-publicized maneuvering, approved Allende as president.

The Chilean Road to Socialism

The Opposition

When Allende took office in 1970, political conditions appeared favorable to his program for the achievement of socialism in Chile within a framework of legality and nonviolence. The assassination in October 1970 of General René Schneider, the commander in chief of the army, who had kept the army neutral during the period after the election just before Allende assumed the presidency, had discredited the right. Prospects were excellent that the Popular Unity would receive the cooperation of the left wing of the Christian Democratic party in Congress. For the time being, the UP coalition remained united behind a program that called for the progressive take-over of large foreign companies and monopolies in the fields of commerce, industry, and land distribution and expropriation of all landholdings over 80 hectares.

Nonetheless, the forces against the UP were formidable. It did not have a majority in Congress. Both the judiciary and the *Controlaría*

General (the government's fiscal arm) opposed Allende's policies. The entire domestic economic establishment, foreign interests, much of the officer corps of the military and national police, and the Catholic church were also aligned against the UP. The anti-UP political coalition, the *Confederación Democrática* (Democratic Confederation) controlled virtually all of the nation's media—two of the three television stations, 95 percent of the radio stations, 90 percent of the newspaper circulation, and all of the weekly magazines.

On its side, the UP had 36.3 percent of the voters, who made up the best-organized and most politically active sector of the electorate. However, most of the labor force was unorganized (only 2 percent belonged to unions) and unsympathetic with the left. Wide disparities in the economic conditions of various sectors of the working class made it difficult to construct a program that would satisfy all interests. White-collar workers were much better off than blue-collar workers and therefore tended toward conservatism, seeking to maintain what they had. There were sharp differences among blue-collar workers also. For example, copper miners were among the most highly paid workers, while coal and nitrate miners received very low wages. Similar differentials existed in the various industrial and craft unions. The UP also had trouble organizing in the countryside, for most campesinos were firmly attached to the Christian Democrats, who still controlled the state bureaucracy that dealt with agrarian affairs.

A lack of internal cohesion also hindered the UP. At the moment of victory, its leadership was not fully prepared for the task of governing. Many had doubted that it could win the election. Later, a schism arose within the coalition when the Leftist Revolutionary Movement (*Movimiento Izquierdista Revolucionario,* or MIR) demanded a more radical land program. This split reflected the variety of viewpoints within the UP on the strategy and tactics of the transition to socialism. The old problem of how to satisfy the claims of both the working class—even more militant than during the Popular Front days—and the middle

Salvador Allende, president of Chile, died during the military coup of September 1973.

sectors—who worried that their interests were being threatened by the structural reforms undertaken by the UP—was never fully resolved.

The First Year, 1971

The UP's immediate problems were to better the living standard of the working class and get the economy moving. The government accomplished this goal by bringing about an enormous increase in purchasing power, which in turn stimulated demand and industrial production. During the first year of Allende's term, worker income rose a startling 50 percent. The government instituted a massive program of public spending, especially for labor-intensive projects such as housing, education, sanitation, and health. At the same

time, the government established price controls, which were backed up by local, housewife-operated price and supply committees. The rate of inflation fell to 22.1 percent in 1971 from 34.9 percent in 1970 and, as a result, real income rose 30 percent.

The short-term policies of the UP government, which aimed to stimulate the dormant economy, alleviate unemployment, improve living standards, and increase popular support for a minority regime, were highly successful—a success reflected in the municipal elections of April 1971, in which the Popular Unity won over 50 percent of the vote. In the long run, however, the depletion of stocks, the outflow of foreign exchange to pay for the import of consumer goods, and the fall of profits in what was still basically a market economy proved very damaging to the government's economic program.

For the first year, middle-class businessmen, industrialists, and peasants fared very well and cooperated with the Allende regime. There were scattered cases of larger owners sabotaging their own property but, for the most part, business was not hostile. The government also employed coercion to gain cooperation from industry, threatening companies with intervention if they did not agree to increase production. Coercion and increased demand combined to bring about an expansion of industrial production and employment.

Allende's first problems arose when copper prices declined sharply, leading to an imbalance in terms of trade and the depletion of foreign exchange reserves. In addition, the expropriation of the Gran Minería in July 1971 virtually halted the flow of private investment capital from the United States and put an end to the extensive credit that had been forthcoming from such agencies as Agency for International Development (AID), the Export-Import Bank, the Inter-American Development Bank, and the World Bank. The Soviet bloc, Western European nations, and other Latin American countries provided credit, but not enough to compensate for the loss of U.S. loans. The fall of copper prices and the resulting deficit in the balance of payments led Allende to stop servicing the national debt. He eventually managed to reach satisfactory agreements with all of Chile's creditors except the United States, whose continued opposition posed a serious impediment to economic development.

The Left's Old Dilemma: Caught in the Middle, 1972–1973

The first year's gains gave way to economic stagnation and resurgence of inflation. Although Allende's popularity remained high in 1971, he struggled unsuccessfully to reach a delicate balance between needed structural reform demanded by the working class and special interests of the middle class. The government's policy of expropriating large enterprises benefited few

workers and alienated owners of small and medium-size businesses, who employed 80 percent of the working population. To make matters worse, workers began occupying and operating factories. State enterprises were badly mismanaged.

The socialist government was also unable to solve the agricultural crisis. Chile's inefficiently managed agricultural production was perhaps the biggest economic roadblock, for it neither raised enough to feed the country's inhabitants nor provided employment for the large pool of rural labor. A hostile Congress forced Allende to operate with reform laws inherited from the Frei administration; nonetheless, by the end of 1972, Allende had effectively liquidated the latifundio system. Expropriation and redistribution proceeded, but with considerable cost to production. The amount of land under cultivation decreased by 20 percent, and the harvest of 1972–1973 was poor.

The Allende administration faced a full-fledged economic and political crisis by the fall of 1972. The inevitable disruptions that accompany revolutionary conditions were aggravated by mistakes and shortcomings of the UP government and conflicts within the coalition. Moreover, the Chilean oligarchy and its North American allies were formidable, unrelenting opponents. The United States was deeply involved in Chilean politics. We know from the testimony of William Colby, the director of the Central Intelligence Agency before a U.S. Senate subcommittee that the CIA spent $11 million between 1962 and 1970 to help prevent Allende from being elected president and that the CIA, with authorization from President Richard Nixon and Secretary of State Henry Kissinger, spent $8 million between 1970 and 1973 to "destabilize" the Chilean economy. Nixon told the U.S. ambassador to Chile that he would "smash that son-of-a-bitch Allende."

The Chilean upper class, although it had lost much of its economic base due to the nationalization of large industries and expropriation of large landholdings, retained control over much of the mass media, the judiciary, a majority in Congress, and the armed forces.

The struggle hinged, finally, on the middle sectors. Soaring inflation eroded their economic position. All of Allende's efforts to reassure and win over the middle class failed to overcome its traditional hostility toward socialism and its association with the bourgeoisie. This middle class provided the mass base for the coup that overthrew the Popular Unity.

Allende's opponents took advantage of the growing economic crisis in late 1972 to embark on a program of sabotage and direct action that included an employers' strike in October, a strike of truck drivers (subsidized by the CIA), which developed into a full-scale lockout by a majority of Chilean capitalists.

The strike ended when Allende made major concessions to his opponents, guaranteeing the security of small and medium-size industries. He also agreed to the inclusion of generals in his cabinet to insure law and order and to supervise the congressional election scheduled for March 1973. The opposition hoped to gain a sweeping victory in the election, that would give it the two-thirds majority needed to impeach Allende and legally oust his government. Instead, the UP vote rose from 36 percent (in 1970) to 44 percent, proof that its socialist policies had substantially increased its support among the working class and peasantry. But the opposition still commanded a majority in Congress and it redoubled efforts to create economic and political chaos by disruptive strikes, the organization of terrorist bands, and calls on the armed forces to intervene.

When Popular Unity came to power in 1970, the Chilean officer class was divided into two factions: a sizable conservative wing and a moderate wing sympathetic to reform of the kind advocated by the Christian Democrats. General René Schneider, commander in chief of the Chilean army, who was assassinated by reactionary military in 1970, and General Carlos Prats, who succeeded Schneider and held various cabinet posts in the Allende government, were among the moderates. Unquestionably, the Chilean military was greatly influenced by the United States military. Many Chilean officers had counterinsurgency training either in the United States or in the Panama Canal Zone. Throughout the Allende presidency, even after the United States had cut off all forms of economic aid to Chile and successfully exerted pressure on international banks to cut off loans, U.S. military aid continued. The United States even doubled its usual contribution in 1973. Chile and Venezuela were the principal beneficiaries of U.S. military aid in Latin America. The rigid anti-Communist stance of much of the military was bolstered significantly by material support from the United States, which enabled them to maintain their intransigent opposition to Allende.

By the spring of 1973, the balance of forces within the military had shifted in favor of the conservative wing, and preparations for a coup were well advanced. On June 29 a premature coup was put down by loyal troops under the direction of General Prats. Following the defeat of the coup, workers called for occupation of the factories and distribution of arms among them. Instead, Allende renewed his efforts to achieve a compromise with the Christian Democrats, relying on the armed forces to maintain law and order. The armed forces raided factories in search of illegal weapons, while making no effort to disarm the rightist paramilitary groups. Control of many localities effectively passed from the UP administration to the armed forces. In the face of the growing danger from the right-wing military, the government seemed paralyzed. In August General Prats, under great pressure from his colleagues, resigned from the cabinet and as commander in chief; Allende, acceding to the requests of the generals, appointed General Augusto Pinochet as Prats's successor.

The coup began on September 10, 1973. The next morning, after Allende rejected a demand by the armed forces that he resign, the army and the air force attacked the presidential palace; Allende, who had promised not to leave the palace alive, committed suicide after broadcasting a final message to the Chilean people. Despite scattered resistance, the left was crushed within a week.

The Junta

After the coup, Chileans endured a brutal and large-scale repression. The four-man military junta headed by General Augusto Pinochet set about to "regenerate" Chilean society. To this end they abolished civil liberties, dissolved the national congress, banned union activities, prohibited strikes and collective bargaining, and erased the Allende administration's agrarian and economic reforms. The junta jailed, tortured, and put to death thousands of Chileans. The dreaded secret police, DINA (*Dirección de Inteligencia Nacional*)—with guidance from Colonel Walter Rauff, a former Nazi who supervised the extermination of Jews at Auschwitz—spread its network of terror throughout Chile and carried out assassinations abroad. The junta also set up at least six concentration camps. It is estimated that one of every one hundred Chileans was arrested at least once under the military regime.

The dictatorship outlawed or suspended left and center political parties and suspended dissident labor and peasant leaders and clergymen. Eduardo Frei and other Christian Democratic leaders initially supported the coup. Later, they assumed the role of a loyal opposition to the military rulers, but soon lost most of their influence. Meanwhile, left-wing Christian Democratic leaders like Radomiro Tomic were jailed or forced into exile. The church, which at first expressed its gratitude to the armed forces for saving the country from the danger of a "Marxist dictatorship," became increasingly critical of the regime's social and economic policies.

With Pinochet there came to power in Chile a group of economists known as the Chicago Boys because many of them had studied at the University of Chicago under Milton Friedman and espoused his free-market doctrines. The Chicago Boys made Chile a laboratory for the testing of Friedman's doctrines. Public spending was cut drastically, almost all state companies privatized, the peso devalued, and import duties sharply reduced. The social consequences of the "shock treatment" soon became apparent. Gross domestic product fell 16.6 percent in 1975. Manufacturing suffered particular injury, with some industries, like the textile industry, devastated by foreign imports. Wages had fallen by 1975 to 47.9 percent of their 1970 level. Unemployment stood at 20 percent, or 28 percent if the people working on government emergency programs were included.

A recovery partly based on export products—minerals, timber, and fish—but above all on a speculative spree of immense proportions began in 1977 and turned into a boom that lasted until 1980, with annual growth rates averaging 8 percent. The Chilean "economic miracle," however, was superficial and short-lived. Hoping to attract heavy foreign investment that would turn Chile into a South Korea or Taiwan, the Chicago Boys deliberately kept interest rates high. Foreign capital did pour in, but almost all of it was in the form of loans to Chilean banks, which made enormous profits from interests on loans to the private sector. Chilean banks borrowed abroad for 12 percent and loaned it out at 35 to 40 percent. The borrowing companies, belonging to a few huge conglomerates, did not invest in production, which the high interest rates made unprofitable but used the loans for speculation in real estate or to buy up at fire sale prices the state companies sold under the privatization program. The bubble began to burst in 1980. By the end of 1981 the government, in violation of its own free-market principles, was forced to step in to take over the nation's largest banks in order to forestall economic calamity. Bankruptcies multiplied. Production declined sharply. Between 1982 and 1986 unemployment rose to more than 30 percent and real wages fell by as much as 20 percent. An earthquake in 1985 added to the country's economic woes.

A recovery began in 1986 and turned into another boom, causing some observers to regard the Chilean economy as a showcase for free-market doctrines. But a closer look at Chile's "prosperity" in the last years of the dictatorship reveals how precarious were its foundations and how inequitably its fruits were distributed. The economy was heavily dependent on foreign loans.

In 1983, Chile's four great copper mines were placed under military control. In response, members of the Confederation of Copper Workers voted to strike, leaving the mine shown here at El Teniente and others, deserted.

With a population of 12.5 million, the foreign debt in 1991 stood at $17 billion, in per capita terms one of the heaviest debt burdens in the world. In its last years the Pinochet regime pursued a policy of swapping debt for ownership of Chilean industries and natural resources, with a resulting growth of foreign control of the economy. Moreover, the new boom, like the previous one, was heavily based on such export products as seafood, timber, fruit, and agricultural products.

Exports of fruit and agricultural products sharply increased in those years. But the modernization and expansion of Chilean agriculture did not benefit the mass of the rural population, which lost most of the land and other gains made under the Allende land reform and suffered police repression and chronic unemployment, but the great landowners who controlled the production, commercialization, and export of agricultural products. Farm workers, prevented from forming labor unions and denied welfare benefits, worked no more than three or four months at a time and often lived in intolerable conditions.

Conditions were even worse in urban areas, with high levels of unemployment and underemployment among workers who lived with their families in shantytowns in squalid, overcrowded conditions. Even the middle class suffered a sharp decline in its standard of living. Between

1978 and 1988 the wealthiest 20 percent of the population increased their share of the national income from 51 to 60 percent. The next 60 percent, which includes Chile's large middle class, suffered a substantial drop in income, their share falling from 44 to 35 percent. And the poorest 20 percent continued to receive a meager 4 percent.

In January 1978, the military dictatorship held a plebiscite, which—unsurprisingly—overwhelmingly approved General Pinochet, who subsequently proclaimed that there would be no more elections for ten years. In September 1980, Chileans, again faced with little choice, endorsed a new constitution that would keep Pinochet in power at least until 1989 and perhaps 1997. The military was to choose a new president and to elect a legislature in 1989.

For much of the era of the dictatorship the opposition to Pinochet was fragmented. The left distrusted the Christian Democrats because they had cooperated with the military in 1973. The Christian Democrats remained wary of the left. Nonetheless, Pinochet's harsh repression and unsuccessful economic policies gave rise to mass opposition in 1983 and 1984. Labor and the middle class protested the worsening economic conditions. One poll taken in Santiago in 1985 indicated that only 15 percent of the population supported the government. The first indication that the opposition had begun to close old wounds was in 1983, when the Socialist party joined the Christian Democrats and other center parties to form the Democratic Alliance. Pinochet talked with the AD for a time. But he declared a state of siege in late 1984 that ended only in July 1985. In August 1985 a loose coalition of eleven parties signed an accord for "the transition to full democracy." Even the major rightist parties distanced themselves from Pinochet in 1985, leaving the general with little more than his military in support.

Pinochet's growing isolation reflected changes within Chile and the continent-wide movement away from authoritarian military rule. Even the United States, which had connived the 1973 military coup in Chile and steadfastly supported Pinochet, began to pressure the dictator to make a transition to democracy. The party favored by the United States to guide Chile in the coming democratic era was the moderate Christian Democratic party, led by Patricio Aylwin, who had supported the 1973 military coup but later had a change of heart.

Under growing pressure from the swelling democratic movement, sections of the military, and the United States, Pinochet made limited concessions to the demands for liberalization and amnesty for political prisoners and exiles, even as the repression sometimes intensified. Maneuvering to remain in power, Pinochet called a plebiscite for October 1988, in which Chileans would vote "yes" or "no" on a proposal to grant him eight more years as president. On the eve of the plebiscite, Pinochet permitted a large number of political exiles to return to Chile. On the day of the plebiscite, Chileans voted by a resounding 54.6 percent to 43 percent to deny Pinochet a new term as president. But the old dictator had fallback positions. By the terms of the undemocratic constitution imposed on the country in 1980, even if the "no" vote prevailed Pinochet was to remain in power for one more year and then call general elections. Whatever the outcome of those elections, he would then preside over a military council with broad powers, be able to appoint one-third of the new Senate and become himself a senator for life.

The pro-democratic forces now began to prepare for the general elections for president and the national Congress to be held in December 1989. Eventually, despite their differences, left and center parties agreed on a single presidential candidate, Aylwin, whose principal opponent was Pinochet's finance minister, Hernan Buchi. Despite an electoral law designed to favor the regime and some efforts by security forces to intimidate the voters, the elections gave a clear majority to Aylwin and the congressional list of his Democratic Accord coalition, consisting of seventeen parties headed by the Christian Democratic and Socialist parties. The influential Communist party, although itself banned from running by the regime, had thrown its support to Aylwin.

Mass opposition to the economic policies and repressive tactics of President Augusto Pinochet erupted in 1983 and 1984. In this picture, thousands of Chilean youths march through Santiago calling for democracy and jobs for unemployed copper workers.

Back from Fascism: An Uncertain Course, 1990–1994

The new president assumed office on March 11, 1990, with a cabinet dominated by the Christian Democrats and Socialists. The first democratically elected government since 1970 faced enormous problems. One was the challenge posed by the continued existence of a military junta presided over by Pinochet, in effect creating a dual government. A confrontation between Aylwin and Pinochet ended with the latter's agreement to dissolve the junta, but he remained chief of the armed forces and solidly entrenched in other parts of the state apparatus, including the judiciary and the security forces.

Other problems involved the need to revise or scrap the regime's 1980 constitution, which made it a crime even to think Marxist thoughts, to obtain the release of the remaining political prisoners, to dissolve the security forces and put a final end to torture and other human rights abuses, and to bring to justice the officials who had committed such abuses. Here a major obstacle was the amnesty decreed by Pinochet for acts committed during the so-called internal war between 1973 and 1978, but that amnesty did not cover the many brutal murders committed after that date. The discovery in the first months of 1990 of secret cemeteries, generally located near armed forces bases, containing the remains of numerous victims who had frequently been tortured before being murdered, brought home to all Chileans the full horror of the regime under which they had suffered for seventeen years. One year later, the report of a "Commission of Truth and Reconciliation," released by President Aylwin, provided a partial record of the human rights violations committed under the Pinochet dictatorship between 1973 and the beginning of 1990. The report gave a figure of 2,279 known deaths and disappearances, assigned direct responsibility for these crimes to the armed forces, and charged the courts with negligence for failing to respond properly to such violations of human rights. In releasing the report, Aylwin promised material compensation to the families of the victims and a reform of the court system. Insisting that the amnesty issued by Pinochet in 1978 did not apply to offenses punishable under civil and criminal law, he ordered the supreme court to initiate action to bring to justice the individuals responsible for such crimes.

But the process of settling accounts with the military murderers and torturers proceeded with excruciating slowness, due in part to the grim resistance offered by Pinochet and the army (the other services, not as deeply involved in the atrocities, assumed a less defiant posture) and in part to Aylwin's anxiety to achieve compromise and "reconciliation" with the military. The resulting stalemate between Pinochet and the Aylwin government appeared to create a sort of "dual power." Aylwin's conciliatory attitude toward the military, which included the effort to create what has been called an atmosphere of "gentle accommodation" with them, and his decision to abandon efforts to make Pinochet step down as commander in chief, angered organizations of relatives of the "disappeared" and many other Chileans who claimed that Aylwin's policies tended to institutionalize impunity.

Despite many obstacles, some progress was made in bringing to justice the agents of military repression. An important step in this direction was a partial reform of the judiciary, which had been stacked by Pinochet with his appointees. It is a measure of the strength of reactionary resistance to a settlement of long overdue accounts and the slowness of Chilean justice, however, that as 1993 drew to a close only two convictions

of high-ranking officials of the Pinochet dictatorship had taken place. In November 1993 retired General Manuel Contreras, head of Pinochet's DINA, was sentenced to seven years in prison by a Supreme Court judge as the intellectual author of the 1976 assassination of Allende's former foreign minister Orlando Letelier in Washington. The agency's operations chief, Brigadier General Pedro Espinosa, was sentenced to six years. But these were not ordinary cases. The Chilean Supreme Court had previously refused to allow the extradition of Contreras to the United States, endangering Chilean–United States relations and the hope of securing a free trade agreement with the United States. The passage of a special law in 1991 made possible the transfer of the Letelier case from military to civilian courts, thereby satisfying the grievance of the United States. But such accommodations were not available in the majority of cases involving human rights violations.

A major problem facing the new democratic government was the need to define its attitude toward the economic and social policies of the old regime, which benefited foreign transnationals and their domestic allies at the expense of long-range national interests and the welfare of Chilean workers. The conservative Aylwin had promised to make no major changes in the old regime's free-market policies but also committed himself to improve the living and working conditions of the Chilean masses. In fact, under Aylwin the government considerably increased spending for health care, education, and social services. These increases, combined with more jobs (unemployment averaged 4.6 percent of the economically active population in 1993), resulted in a significant reduction in poverty. Overall poverty fell from 40 percent of the population in 1990 to 33 percent in late 1992, and absolute poverty (defined as insufficient income to buy a basic food basket) fell from 14 percent to 9 percent. But these official figures must be viewed with caution; the figure for unemployment, for example, does not take account of the "hidden" unemployment and underemployment in the so-called informal sector, composing about 50 percent of the work force. Granted some im-

346 provement in living standards since 1990, the structure of Chilean society continues to be marked by great inequity and injustice. The Aylwin government, for example, made little change in the pattern of labor relations inherited from Pinochet, which subordinated the rights of labor to those of the employer. In democratic Chile, for example, farm workers are still prohibited from striking during harvest season—the only time a strike would have any effect.

For its overall economic strategy, the new democratic government implemented even more energetically the export-led model of economic growth, based on foreign loans and investments, that the Chicago Boys had put in place. As before, the stress was on such export products as seafood, lumber, fruit, and agricultural products, with production and commercialization dominated by agribusiness companies, many of them foreign-owned. Typical is the case of wood exports. There has been a veritable explosion of Chilean lumbering, and it is estimated that production will increase 33 percent in the 1990s. In south-central Chile the new tree farms are replacing such traditional crops as wheat, corn, and rice. Environmentalists charge that the new forests are damaging the soil, drying up water sources, and causing a rapid decrease of many species of plants and animals. Chile's export-based economic strategy also had serious health costs. A recent study carried out in the large fruit-growing region around the city of Rancagua, south of the capital of Santiago, revealed an alarming increase in children born with physical deformities to parents whose work exposed them to dangerous pesticides.

The explosive growth of raw-material exports has been accompanied by the collapse of large-scale industry in such areas as textiles and construction. This is reflected in the decline in the number of unionized workers, who by 1985 composed only 13 percent of the total labor force, compared with 41 percent in 1972. Meanwhile the number of Chileans who work alone or own firms with fewer than four employees (the so-called *microempresas*) has greatly increased; these "microenterprises" employed more than 45 percent of the labor force in 1992. Typically, they contract out to or service in a variety of ways the large conglomerates called AFPs (*Asociaciones de Fondos Provisionales*), or Mutual Funds, controlled by the ten richest families in Chile. "Workers in *microempresas,*" writes Cathy Schneider, "are paid salaries barely above subsistence, without fringe benefits or job security. Irregular hours, unstable employment, and low caloric intake have increased levels of physical and mental exhaustion."

By the end of 1993 the recession gripping the capitalist world since 1990 began to make itself felt in Chile, with a sharp drop in exports. With declining demand for its exports and growing competiton among the world's raw-material producers, the "Chilean Miracle" began to show some signs of wear and tear. But there was no suggestion of a change in the economic course; instead Chilean economic planners placed great hopes in expanding export markets through a free trade pact with the United States following the adoption of NAFTA.

In December 1993 Chilean voters went to the polls to elect a new president, 120 members of the Chamber of Deputies, and half of the 36 members of the Senate. Leading the presidential race were Eduardo Frei of the ruling center-left coalition, son of a reformist president of the same name, and Arturo Alessandri, candidate of a coalition of right-wing parties and grandson of another populist politician and former president of the same name. The right was badly divided between Pinochet supporters and those who regarded him as a political albatross. Frei, pledging to eradicate extreme poverty by the year 2000, reform the labor laws and the public health system, and regain civilian control of the military, declared that joining NAFTA would be another of his main goals. He won a decisive victory, gaining 58 percent of the vote to Alessandri's 24 percent. Taking office under darkening economic skies, with a Congress in which he lacked the two-thirds majority needed to change the law that protected Pinochet against removal as commander in chief, Frei faced great difficulty in carrying out his program.

Chapter 15

Republican Brazil

On the eve of World War I, Brazil's economic, political, and social structures showed growing strain and instability. Between 1910 and 1914, the Amazonian rubber boom began to fade as a result of competition from the new and more efficient plantations of the Far East. The approaching end of the rubber cycle revealed the vulnerability of Brazil's monocultural economy to external factors beyond its control and heightened its dependence on coffee. The coffee industry was itself plagued by recurrent crises of overproduction that required periodic resort to valorization—governmental intervention to maintain coffee prices by withholding stocks from the market or restricting plantings.

Violence was endemic over large areas of the country. In the backcountry, feudal coronéis with private armies recruited from dependents and jagunços (hired gunmen) maintained a patriarchal but frequently tyrannical rule over the peasantry. Over large areas of the country, the peasants lived in feudal bondage, obligated to give one or more days per week of free labor as homage to the landowners. Lacking written contracts, they could be evicted at any moment, and could find work elsewhere only on the same conditions. The interior was also the scene of mystical or messianic movements that sometimes assumed the character of peasant revolts. Banditry, especially widespread in the northeast, was another response to the tyranny of rural coronéis and the impotence of officials. A few *cangaceiros* (outlaws) took the part of the peasantry against their oppressors; most, however, served as mercenaries in the coronéis's private wars.

Violence was not confined to the countryside. Even in the growing cities, proud of their European culture and appearance, popular anger at

347

348

the arbitrary rule of local oligarchies, or divisions within those oligarchies, sometimes flared up into civil war. Intervention by the federal government in these armed struggles on the side of its local allies greatly enlarged the scale of violence.

Decline and Fall of the Old Republic, 1914–1930

Economic Impact of World War I

The outbreak of World War I in August 1914 had a negative initial impact on Brazil. Exports of coffee, a nonessential product, declined, and in 1917 the government came to the rescue of the planters with a new valorization (price maintenance) program. However, the growing demand of the Allies for sugar, beans, and other staples had by 1915 sparked a revival that turned into a boom. Brazil's expanding trade with the Allies exposed its shipping to German reprisals, and in October 1917, after German submarines had torpedoed a number of Brazilian merchant ships, Brazil declared war on Germany. Brazil's major contribution to the Allied war effort continued to be the supply of goods, but its navy assisted an English squadron in patrolling south Atlantic waters.

The war accelerated some changes under way in Brazilian economic life. It weakened British capitalism and therefore strengthened the North American challenge to British financial and commercial pre-eminence in Brazil. The virtual cessation of imports of manufactured goods also gave a strong stimulus to Brazilian industrialization. Profits derived from coffee, an industry protected by the state, provided a large part of the resources needed for industrialization. Favored by its wealth, large immigrant population, and rich natural resources, the state of São Paulo led the movement, replacing Rio de Janeiro as the foremost industrial region. Brazil doubled its industrial production during the war, and the number of enterprises (which stood at about 3,000 in 1908) grew by 5,940 between 1915 and 1918. But these increases were concentrated in light industry, especially food processing and textiles, and most of the new enterprises were small shops.

The advance of industry and urbanization enlarged and strengthened both the industrial bourgeoisie and the working class. In response to wartime inflation that eroded the value of workers' wages, the trade union movement grew, and strikes became more frequent. In 1917 a general strike—the first in Brazilian history—gripped the city and state of São Paulo. Although the strike wave of the years 1917–1920 forced many employers to grant higher wages, the living conditions of most workers did not permanently improve. The labor movement, composed largely of foreign-born workers, remained small and weak, without ties with the peasantry, who formed the overwhelming majority of the Brazilian people.

Postwar Industry and Labor

Industrialization and urbanization weakened the foundations of the neocolonial order, which was based on the primacy of agriculture and dependence on foreign markets and loans, but it emerged from the war essentially intact, although its stabilization proved temporary and precarious. A chronically adverse balance of trade and a declining rate of exchange against foreign currencies gave Brazilian industry a competitive advantage in goods of popular consumption. It continued to grow, but it had little support from a central government dominated by the coffee interests. Bitter debates between the friends and foes of tariff protection for industry marked the political life of the 1920s.

As that decade opened, Brazil remained an overwhelmingly rural country. A few export products—coffee, sugar, cotton—dominated Brazilian agriculture; food production was so neglected that the country had to import four-fifths of its grain. There was an extreme concentration of landownership: 461 great landowners held more than 27 million hectares of land, while 464,000 small and medium-sized farms occupied only 15.7 million hectares. Archaic techniques prevailed in agriculture: the hoe was still the principal farming instrument and the wasteful slash-and-burn method the favored way of clearing the land. Even relatively progressive coffee planters gave little attention to care of the soil, selection of varieties, and other improvements. As a result, the productivity of plantations rapidly declined, even in regions of superior soil.

In the cities, most workers toiled and lived under conditions that recalled those of the early Industrial Revolution in Europe. In 1920 the average industrial worker in São Paulo earned about 4 milréis (60 cents) a day; for this wage he or she worked ten to twelve hours, six days a week. Malnutrition, parasitic diseases, and lack of medical facilities limited Brazilians' average life span in 1920 to twenty-eight years. In the same year, more than 64 percent of the population over the age of fifteen was illiterate. Since literacy was a requirement for voting, the general lack of schools kept the people not only ignorant but politically powerless. The peasantry, vegetating in poverty and ignorance, could not initiate a struggle to transform Brazilian society.

Political Unrest

The task of transforming society fell to the rapidly growing urban bourgeois groups, and especially to the middle class, which began to voice ever more strongly its discontent with the rule of corrupt rural oligarchies. In the early 1920s, there arose a many-faceted movement for the renovation of Brazilian society and culture. Intellectuals, artists, junior military officers, professional men, and a small minority of radical workers participated in this movement. But they had no common program and did not comprehend the convergence of their aims and work.

Three seemingly unrelated events of 1922 illustrate the diverse forms that the ferment of the times assumed. First, in February of that year, the intellectuals of São Paulo organized a Modern Art Week to commemorate the centenary of Brazilian independence. The young poets, painters, and composers who presented their works there laid a common stress on independence from old forms and content, on the need to develop an indigenous Brazilian culture. Then, in March, after the appearance of Marxist groups in a number of cities, the Brazilian Communist party was founded at a congress in Rio de Janeiro and began a struggle against the anarcho-syndicalist doctrines that still dominated much of the small labor movement. Last, in July, *tenentes* (junior officers) at the Copacabana garrison in Rio de Janeiro rose to prevent the seating of Artur da Silva Bernardes, who had been elected president according to the agreement between the two dominant states of São Paulo and Minas Gerais. The rebel program denounced the rule of the coffee oligarchy, political corruption, and electoral fraud. Government forces easily crushed the revolt, but it left a legend when a handful of insurgents refused to surrender and fought to the death against overwhelming odds.

The officers' revolt signaled the beginning of a struggle by the Brazilian bourgeoisie to seize power from the rural oligarchy. Given the closed political system, it inevitably assumed the character of an armed struggle; that is why its spearhead was the nationalist young officer group, mostly of middle-class origins, which called for democratic elections, equal justice, and similar political reforms.

President Bernardes (1922–1926) took office amid growing economic and political turmoil. As a result of a massive increase in coffee plantings between 1918 and 1924, the industry again suffered from overproduction and falling prices. In 1924 another military revolt, headed by retired General Isidro Dias Lopes, broke out in São Paulo. It was again organized by junior officers whose program called for the restoration of constitutional liberties and curbs on the executive power but made no reference to economic and social reform. The large working class of São Paulo was sympathetic to the revolt, but its conservative leaders rejected the workers' request for arms.

The rebels held the city for twenty-two days before evacuating it under pressure from greatly superior numbers of government troops. Meanwhile, the revolt had spread to other states. Another group of rebels in Rio Grande do Sul, led by Captain Luís Carlos Prestes, moved north to join the insurgents from São Paulo, and their combined forces, known in history as the Prestes column, began a prodigious march through the interior. The tenentes hoped to enlist the peasantry in their struggle against Bernardes. But they knew little of the peasants' problems and offered no program of agrarian reform. The peasants, for their part, had no interest in fighting the "tyrant" Bernardes in distant Rio de Janeiro. Beating off or eluding attacks by government forces and bands of cangaceiros in the government's employ, the Prestes column covered fourteen thousand miles before reaching Bolivia, where the rebels dispersed.

The long march had much educational value for the officers who took part in it. For the first time in their lives, many of these young men came face to face with the reality of rural Brazil and began to reflect on its problems. As a result, the tenente reform program acquired an economic and social content. It began to speak of the need for economic development and social legislation, including agrarian reform as well as minimum wages and maximum working hours.

Bernardes had survived a second military crisis, but he continued to be plagued by economic problems, with the coffee problem paramount. Bernardes applied the now orthodox remedy of valorization, but gave it a decentralized form. The central government turned over the supervision of the scheme to the individual coffee-producing states. The state of São Paulo established an agency, the Coffee Institute, which undertook to control the export trade in coffee by regulating market offerings to maintain a balance between supply and demand. This was done by withdrawing unlimited stocks of coffee, storing them in warehouses, and releasing them according to the needs of the export trade. The plan required financing the producers whose coffee was withheld from the market. The program appeared to work, for prices rose and remained stable until 1929. But the burdens of valorization steadily grew, for high prices stimulated production, requiring new withdrawals and new loans to finance the unsold output. To make matters worse, Brazil's competitors—especially Colom-

bia—were attracted by the high prices and expanded their own output.

Economic Crisis

In 1926 Bernardes turned over the presidency to the Paulista Washington Luís de Sousa Pereira (1926–1930). He had been elected, without opposition, according to the agreement that usually rotated the presidency between São Paulo and Minas Gerais. During his administration, a series of new loans was made to support the valorization program. As a result, Brazil's foreign debt had risen to $1,181 million by 1930, and debt service in that year amounted to $200 million—one-third of the national budget. By 1930, U.S. investment in Brazil had reached a figure of $400 million, considerably larger than the British total, and the United States had supplanted England as Brazil's chief trading partner.

Brazil's heavy dependence on foreign markets and loans made it extremely vulnerable to the crisis that shook the capitalist world after the New York stock market collapsed in October 1929. Coffee quotations at once fell 30 percent, and the subsequent decline was even sharper; between 1929 and 1931, coffee prices fell from 22.5 to 8 cents a pound, and immense stocks of coffee piled up in the warehouses. By the end of 1930, Brazil's gold reserves had disappeared and the exchange rate plummeted to a new low. As foreign credit dried up, it became impossible to continue the financing of withheld coffee, and the valorization program collapsed, leaving behind a mountain of debt.

The presidential campaign and election of 1930 took place against a background of economic crisis whose principal burdens—unemployment, wage cuts, and inflation—fell chiefly on the working classes. But the crisis sharpened all class and regional antagonisms, especially the conflict between the coffee oligarchy and the urban bourgeois groups, who regarded the depression as proof of the bankruptcy of the old order. A rift even appeared within the coffee oligarchy, and the traditional alliance of São Paulo and Minas Gerais fell apart as a result of the selection by Washington Luís of another Paulista, Júlio Prestes, governor of São Paulo, as his successor. Angered by this violation of the agreement to rotate the presidency between the two states, many politicians from Minas Gerais joined the opposition to the official candidate.

As a result of these alignments and realignments, two coalitions took shape and confronted each other in the election of 1930. One united the coffee planters of São Paulo, their rural allies in other areas, and the commercial bourgeoisie engaged in the export-import trade. The other coalition, called the Liberal Alliance, joined the bulk of the urban groups, groups of great landowners—like the ranchers of Rio Grande do Sul, who resented São Paulo's dominant position—and disaffected politicians from Minas Gerais and other states. The conservative coalition nominated the Paulista Júlio Prestes for president; the Liberal Alliance named Getúlio Vargas, a wealthy rancher and politician from Rio Grande do Sul, as its candidate.

The working class was not a participant in the Liberal Alliance, but many workers sympathized with its program. The most ardent supporters of Vargas were the veterans of the revolt of 1924, but their former leader, Luís Carlos Prestes, an exile in Buenos Aires, would not endorse Vargas or his program. Prestes, now a Marxist, issued a manifesto in May 1930 in which he proclaimed that the chief task before the Brazilian people was to struggle against the latifundio and Anglo-American imperialism. A few years later, he would join the Communist party and become its leader.

During the campaign, both candidates made vague promises and statements, but Júlio Prestes clearly represented the latifundist and neocolonial interests. Vargas, although careful not to give offense to his latifundist supporters, spoke of the need to develop industry, including heavy industry, advocated high tariffs to protect Brazilian industry using local raw materials, and called on Brazilians to "perfect our manufactures to the point where it will become unpatriotic to feed or clothe ourselves with imported goods." Reflecting the influence of the tenentes, he advanced a

program of social welfare legislation and political, judicial, and educational reform. He even made a cautious pledge of "action with a view to the progressive extinction of the latifundio, without violence, and support for the organization of small landed property through the transfer of small parcels of land to agricultural laborers."

In any event, Prestes defeated Vargas in the election of March 1930 by a supposed margin of some three hundred thousand votes. Since both sides cheated on a large scale, the outcome merely proved that the government and its rural allies had control of the electoral machinery in decisive areas. In May, Congress, which was dominated by the administration, refused to seat opposition deputies from Minas Gerais and Paraíba. Political tension ran high and reached the explosive point in July with the murder of Vargas's running mate, João Pessoa, a deed regarded by the opposition as a political assassination.

Vargas's lieutenants now convinced him of the need to overthrow the Washington Luís government. The uprising began simultaneously in Rio Grande do Sul, Minas Gerais, and Paraíba on October 3. Perceiving that the collapse of the discredited regime was probably inevitable, senior army officers deposed Washington Luís on October 24, forming a ruling junta, and ordered the army to lay down its arms; one week later, they turned their power over to Getúlio Vargas as head of the provisional government. The Old Republic, born in 1889 and dominated since 1894 by the coffee oligarchy, was dead. A new era had begun that may with fair accuracy be called the era of the bourgeois revolution. The political career of its chieftain, Getúlio Vargas, faithfully mirrored its advances, retreats, and ultimate defeat.

Vargas and the Bourgeois Revolution, 1930–1954

The liberal revolution of 1930 represented a victory for the urban bourgeois groups who favored industrialization and the modernization of Brazil's economic, political, and social structures.

But the bourgeoisie had gained that victory with the aid of allies whose interests had to be taken into account. Getúlio Vargas presided over a heterogeneous coalition that included conservative fazendeiros—who had joined the revolution from jealousy of the overweening Paulista power but feared radical social change—and intellectuals and tenentes who called for agrarian reform, the formation of cooperatives, and the nationalization of mines. On the sidelines was the working class, vital to the development of Brazilian capitalism but a potential threat to its very existence. Finally, Vargas had to take account of foreign capital interests, temporarily weakened but capable of applying great pressure on the Brazilian economy when the capitalist world emerged from the depths of the Great Depression. Vargas's strategy of attempting to balance and reconcile these conflicting interests helps to explain the contradictions and abrupt shifts of course that marked his career.

Vargas's Economic and Political Measures

The most pressing problem facing the new government was to find some way out of the economic crisis. Vargas did not abandon the coffee industry, the base of his political enemies, to its fate; he attempted to revive it by such classic valorization measures as the restriction of plantings and the purchase of surplus stocks and the more drastic expedient of burning the excess coffee, but the level of coffee exports and prices remained low throughout the 1930s. The government had more success with efforts to diversify agriculture. Production of cotton, in particular, grew with the aid of capital and labor released by the depressed coffee industry, and cotton exports rose steadily until 1940, when the outbreak of war interrupted their advance. But diversification of agriculture could not compensate for the steep decline in Brazil's import capacity. The key to recovery was found in import substitution through industrialization.

The Great Depression did not create Brazilian industrialization, but it created the conditions for a new advance. Beginning as a spontaneous response to the loss of import capacity that resulted from the catastrophic decline of exports and a falling rate of exchange, industrialization received a fresh impetus from Vargas, who encouraged industry through exchange controls, import quotas, tax incentives, lowered duties on imported machinery and raw materials, and long-term loans at low interest rates. Thanks to the combination of favorable background conditions and the Vargas policy of state intervention, Brazilian industrialization, based entirely on production for the home market, made notable strides in a few years: industrial production doubled between 1931 and 1936. As early as 1933, when the United States was still in a deep depression, Brazil's national income had begun to increase, which indicated that for the moment, at least, the economy no longer depended on external factors but on internal ones.

Meanwhile, Vargas pursued an uncertain political course that now appeared to favor the left wing of the revolutionary coalition, the tenentes, and now its conservative fazendeiro wing. The tenentes appeared to have considerable influence over Vargas during the first two years of the provisional government; he used them as his political lieutenants in various capacities, especially as interventors, or temporary administrators, in the states, replacing unreliable elected governors. Believing that a strong centralized government was needed to carry out the necessary structural reforms and fearing that premature elections would enable the oligarchies to frustrate those reforms, the tenentes urged Vargas to remain in power indefinitely.

The political elite of São Paulo had not only lost out when its candidate, Julio Prestes, had been denied the presidency, but Vargas's centralizing policies posed a direct threat to the virtual autonomy São Paulo had enjoyed under the federal system of what soon became known as the Old Republic. Vargas added insult to injury by imposing a leader of the tenente group, João Alberto Lins de Barros, as interventor to govern São Paulo. The Paulistas demanded his removal and a return to constitutional government through immediate elections, preferably under the old federal constitution of 1891, which would most

During a long and complex political career, Getúlio Vargas struggled to create an autonomous Brazilian capitalist state. Here President Vargas is shown watching a military parade on the 116th anniversary of Brazilian independence. To Vargas's right is General Eurico Dutra, who was president from 1946 to 1951, and behind Vargas's left shoulder is General Goes Monteiro, close collaborator and supporter of Vargas from the 1930 revolution to the coup of October 1945. The general to Vargas's left is an Argentine guest.

likely enable them to regain power in their own state. Vargas sought to appease the Paulistas with concessions: he replaced João Alberto with a civilian from São Paulo, appointed a conservative banker from the same state as his first minister of finance, and announced a date for the holding of a constituent assembly.

Emboldened rather than appeased, the Paulistas launched a counterrevolutionary "constitutionalist revolt" in July 1932. Lacking popular support either in São Paulo or in other parts of the country, it collapsed after three months of halfhearted combat. But Vargas neither punished nor humiliated the vanquished rebels. Determined to maintain and strengthen his ties with the São Paulo establishment, he made new concessions: he pardoned 50 percent of the bank debts of the coffee planters and ordered the Bank of Brazil to take over the war bonds issued by the rebel government. After mid-1932 the influence of the tenente group over Vargas rapidly waned, although individual tenentes of moderate tendency continued to hold important positions in the regime.

In February 1932 Vargas had promulgated an electoral code that established the secret ballot, lowered the voting age from twenty-one to eighteen, and extended the vote to working women, but the code still denied the vote to illiterates, who formed the majority of the adult population.

A constituent assembly elected under this code drafted a new constitution, which was promulgated on July 16, 1934. This document retained the federal system but considerably strengthened the powers of the executive. The assembly, constituting itself the first Chamber of Deputies, elected Vargas president for a term extending to January 1938.

The section of the constitution on the "economic and social order" stressed the government's responsibility for economic development. Article 119 declared that "the law will regulate the progressive nationalization of mines, mineral deposits, and waterfalls or other sources of energy, as well as of the industries considered as basic or essential to the economic and military defense of the country."

The section on the rights and duties of labor revealed the importance Vargas attached to the imposition of a tutelage over the working class, a class to be courted through concessions but denied independence of action. The constitution of 1934 established a labor tribunal system, gave the government power to fix minimum wages, and guaranteed the right to strike. Subsequent decrees set the working day at eight hours in commerce and industry, fixed minimum wages throughout the country, and created an elaborate social security system that provided for pensions, paid vacations, safety and health standards, and employment security.

In exchange for these gains, obtained without struggle, the working class lost its freedom of action. The trade unions, formerly subject to harsh repression, but militant and jealous of their autonomy, became official agencies controlled by the Ministry of Labor. The workers had no voice in the drafting of labor legislation. Police and security agencies brutally repressed strikes not approved by the government.

The labor and social legislation, moreover, was unevenly enforced, and employers frequently took advantage of their employees' ignorance of the law. The legislation did not apply to the great majority of agricultural workers, who comprised 85 percent of the labor force. Determined to maintain his alliance with the fazendeiro wing of his coalition, Vargas left intact the system of patrimonial servitude that governed labor relations in the countryside, just as he left intact the latifundio. The promises of agrarian reform made during the campaign of 1930 were forgotten.

Vargas's concessions to the Paulista oligarchy and the ouster of reformist tenentes from positions of power formed part of a rightward shift that grew more pronounced in 1934. This growing conservatism lost Vargas support among liberal tenentes, intellectuals, and radical workers and drew sharp criticism from the Communist party. Founded in 1922, the party gained growing influence after 1930 as a result of its anti-imperialist policies and the prestige of its most famous recruit, Luís Carlos Prestes, who had refused to take advantage of the amnesty for political exiles proclaimed after the revolution but returned in 1934 to join the Communist party and become honorary president of the *Aliança Nacional Libertadora* (National Liberation Alliance, or ANL), a popular front movement that attracted middle-class as well as working-class support with its slogans of liquidation of the latifundio, nationalization of large foreign companies, and cancellation of imperialist debts. The ANL was also sharply critical of the inadequacies of Vargas's labor and social legislation. Meanwhile, on the right there had arisen a fascist movement (*Integralismo,* or Integralism), complete with the trappings of its European models, including colored shirts (green), special salutes, and an ideology that denounced democrats, Communists, Masons, and Jews as "enemies of the state."

While tolerant of the Integralist movement, Vargas and an increasingly conservative Congress harassed the leftist opposition as "subversive." In March 1935 Congress enacted a National Security Act, which gave the government special powers to suppress "subversive" activities. It was clearly directed at the left. In July Prestes made a speech in which he attacked Vargas's failure to implement the tenente ideals and called for the creation of a truly "revolutionary and anti-imperialist government." Vargas responded by banning the ANL and ordering the arrest of many leftist leaders.

With the legal avenues of opposition for the left disappearing, the ANL and one wing of the Communist party began an armed uprising in November. Despite some initial successes, it was quickly crushed by government forces and followed by a savage repression. There were fifteen thousand arrests, and prisoners were tortured, some to death. Prestes and other leaders of the revolt were captured, tried, and sentenced to many years in prison. The Communist party was banned and went underground for a decade.

Vargas as Dictator

The repression of the left paved the way for the establishment of Vargas's personal dictatorship. A presidential election was scheduled for January 1938, but under the new constitution Vargas was barred from succeeding himself. He allowed candidates to emerge and campaign but carefully prepared for the coming coup by strategic "interventions" in the states and transfers in the army that filled key posts with reliable commanders.

On September 29, 1937, armed with the Cohen Plan, a crude forgery concocted by the Integralists that set out a detailed plan for a Communist revolution, War Minister General Eurico Dutra went on the radio and demanded the imposition of a state of siege. He had set the stage for the scrapping of what remained of constitutional processes. On November 10, Vargas made a broadcast in which he canceled the presidential elections, dissolved Congress as an "inadequate and costly apparatus," and assumed dictatorial power under a new constitution patterned on European fascist models. On December 2, all political parties were abolished.

The new regime, baptized the *Estado Novo* (New State), copied not only the constitutional forms of the fascist regimes but their repressive tactics. Strict press censorship was established, and prisons filled with workers, teachers, military officers, and others suspected of subversion. The apparatus of repression included a special police force for hunting down and torturing dissidents. Yet there was little organized resistance to the regime. Labor, its most likely opponent, was neutralized by a paternalist social legislation and doped by populist rhetoric, and it remained passive or even supported Vargas.

The affinity between the Estado Novo and the European police states suggested to some observers that it was merely a Brazilian variant of the Continental fascist model. Brazil's growing trade and increasingly friendly relations with Germany and Italy also led to fears that the country was moving into the fascist orbit. Between 1933 and 1938, Germany became the chief market for Brazilian cotton and the second largest buyer of its coffee and cacao. German penetration of the Brazilian economy also increased, and the German Bank for South America established three hundred branches in Brazil.

But Brazil's economic rapprochement with Germany and Italy did not reflect sympathy with the expansionist goals of the fascist bloc; Vargas, the great realist, sought only to open up new markets for Brazil and to strengthen his hand in bargaining with the United States. Despite its authoritarian, repressive aspects, the Estado Novo continued the struggle against neocolonialism and the effort to achieve economic independence and modernization.

Indeed, under the new regime the state intervened more actively than before to encourage the growth of industry and provide it with the necessary economic infrastructure. Rejecting laissez faire, the Estado Novo pursued a policy of planning and direct investment for the creation of important industrial complexes in the basic sectors of mining, oil, steel, electric power, and chemicals. In 1940 the government announced a Five-Year Plan whose goals included the expansion of heavy industry, the creation of new sources of hydroelectric power, and the expansion of the railway network. In 1942 the government established the *Companhia Vale do Rio Doce* to exploit the rich iron-ore deposits of Itabira; in 1944 it created a company for the production of materials needed by the chemical industry; and in 1946 the National Motor Company began the production of trucks. In the same year, Vargas saw the realization of one of his cherished dreams: the National Steel Company began production at the Volta Redonda plant between Rio de Janeiro and São Paulo. Aware of the need of modern industry for abundant sources of power, Vargas created the National Petroleum Company in 1938 to press the search for oil.

By 1941 Brazil had 44,100 plants employing 944,000 workers; the comparable figure for 1920 was 13,336 plants with about 300,000 workers. Aside from some export of textiles, the manufacturing industries served the domestic market almost exclusively. State and mixed public-private companies dominated the heavy and infrastructural industries and private Brazilian capital predominated in manufacturing, but the 1930s also saw a significant growth of direct foreign investment as foreign corporations sought to enlarge their share of the internal market and overcome tariff barriers and exchange problems by establishing branch plants in Brazil. By 1940 foreign capital represented 44 percent of the total investment in Brazilian stock companies. Vargas made no effort to check the influx of foreign capital, perhaps because he believed that the growth of Brazilian state and private capitalism would keep the foreign sector in a subordinate status.

The Estado Novo banned strikes and lockouts but retained and even expanded the body of protective social and labor legislation. In 1942 the labor laws were consolidated into a labor code, regarded as one of the most advanced in the world. But it was unevenly enforced and brought no benefits to the great mass of agricultural workers. Moreover, spiraling inflation created a growing gap between wages and prices; prices rose 86 percent between 1940 and 1944, whereas between 1929 and 1939, they had risen only 31 percent. In effect, inflation, by transferring income from wages to capitalists, provided much of the financing for the rapid economic growth of the 1940s.

World War II accelerated that growth through the new stimulus it gave to industrialization. Brazil exported vast quantities of foodstuffs and raw materials, but the industrialized countries, whose economies were geared to war, could not pay for their purchases with machinery or consumer goods. As a result, Brazil built up large foreign exchange reserves, $707 million in 1945. Most of the economic advance of the war years was due to expansion and more intensive exploi-

tation of existing plants or the technical contributions of Brazilian engineers and scientists.

However, Vargas adroitly exploited Great Power rivalries to secure financial and technical assistance from the United States for the construction of the huge state-owned integrated iron and steel plant at Volta Redonda. U.S. companies and government agencies were notably cool to requests for aid for establishing heavy industry in Latin America. But Vargas's hints that he might have to turn for help to Germany removed all obstacles. Volta Redonda was a great victory for the Vargas policies of economic nationalism and state intervention in economic life. In return for its assistance, Vargas allowed the United States to lease air bases in northern Brazil even before it entered the war against the Axis. In August 1942, after German submarines had sunk a number of Brazilian merchantmen, Brazil declared war on Germany and Italy.

The paradox of Brazil's participation in an antifascist war under an authoritarian regime was not lost on Brazilians; the demands for an end to the Estado Novo grew stronger as the defeat of the Axis drew near. Ever sensitive to changes in the political climate and the balance of forces, Vargas responded by promising a new postwar era of liberty. In January 1945 he announced an amnesty for political prisoners, promulgated a law allowing political parties to function openly, and set December 2 as the date for presidential and congressional elections.

A number of new parties were formed to fight the coming elections, two by Vargas himself. They were the *Partido Social Democrático* (Social Democratic Party, or PSD) and the *Partido Trabalhista Brasileiro* (Brazilian Labor Party, or PTB). The PSD, the largest of the new parties, united pro-Vargas industrialists and rural machines, above all. The PTB had its base in the government-controlled trade unions and appealed to workers with a populist rhetoric proclaiming Vargas the "Father of the Poor." The *União Democrática Nacional* (National Democratic Party, or UDN) was the most conservative and chiefly represented neocolonial agrarian and commercial interests; it was strongly pro–North

American. Of the other national parties, the most important was the Communist party, led by Prestes, which emerged from the underground with considerable prestige and strength.

A Military Coup

Vargas announced that he would not run for president but set the stage for a well-organized campaign by his supporters, called *queremistas*, (from the Portuguese verb *querer*, "to want"), who wanted Vargas to declare himself a candidate in the forthcoming election. Soon after issuing the decrees restoring political freedom, Vargas moved to the left in economic policy. In June he authorized the expropriation of any organization whose practices were harmful to the national interest.

The authorization decree, which was aimed at keeping down the cost of living, inspired alarm in conservative foreign and domestic circles. Senior military officers regarded Vargas's political maneuvers and leftward move with growing uneasiness. The wartime alliance with the United States had accentuated their inherent conservatism and made them ready to accept the gospel of free enterprise and American leadership in the cold war against the Soviet Union and world communism.

On October 29, 1945, Generals Goes Monteiro and Eurico Dutra staged a coup, forced Vargas to resign, and entrusted the government until after the election to José Linhares, chief justice of the Supreme Court. The new government promptly indicated its tendency by repealing Vargas's antitrust decree and launching a suppression of the Communist party. Ostensibly, the military had acted to defend democracy by preventing Vargas from seizing power as he had done in 1937. But its democratic credentials were more than dubious; Goes Monteiro and Dutra were, after Vargas, the chief architects of Estado Novo and had supported Vargas's most repressive measures.

The military coup insured that Brazil would return to the presidential system of government under conservative auspices, with two generals as the major presidential candidates, Eurico Du-

tra for the PSD and Eduardo Gomes for the UDN. Dutra won, but due to the vagaries of the electoral law candidates could run in more than one constituency and Vargas had the satisfaction of winning election as senator from two states and congressman from six states and the Federal District. The newly elected Congress, sitting as a constituent assembly, framed a new constitution that retained both the federal system and the powerful executive created by Vargas and guaranteed civil liberties and free elections, but it still denied the vote to illiterates and enlisted men in the armed forces—more than half the adult population.

Under the mediocre, colorless President Eurico Dutra (1946–1951), neocolonial interests regained much of the influence they had lost under Vargas. In his foreign and domestic policies, Dutra displayed a blind loyalty to the anticommunist creed propounded by Washington. Alarmed by the growing electoral strength of the Communist party, Dutra outlawed it, and Congress followed by expelling the party's elected representatives. Dutra exploited the resulting witch hunt to smash the independent, left-led labor movement; the Workers' Federation, organized in 1946, was declared illegal, and the government intervened in a large number of unions to eliminate "extremist elements." The imposition of a wage freeze and the failure to raise the officially decreed minimum wage caused the real income of workers to drop sharply.

With respect to economic development, Dutra pursued a laissez-faire policy that meant the virtual abandonment of the Vargas strategy of a state-directed movement toward economic independence. Dutra removed all import and exchange controls and allowed the large foreign exchange reserves accumulated during the war—reserves that Vargas had proposed to use for re-equipping Brazilian industry—to be dissipated on imported consumer goods, luxury goods in large part.

Attracted by the new economic climate, foreign capital flowed into Brazil. Meanwhile, seeking to curb inflation according to the prescription of American advisers, the government pursued a restrictive credit policy harmful to Brazilian entrepreneurs and industrial growth.

Vargas's Return to Power

In 1950, having assured himself of the neutrality of the armed forces, Vargas ran for president with the support of the PTB and a broad coalition of workers, industrialists, and members of the urban middle class. His campaign concentrated on the need to accelerate industrialization and expand and strengthen social welfare legislation. Riding a wave of discontent with the economic and social policies of the Dutra regime, Vargas easily defeated his two opponents.

Vargas inherited a difficult economic situation. After a brief boom in coffee exports and prices in 1949–1951, the balance of trade again turned unfavorable and the inflation rate increased. In the absence of other major sources of financing for his developmental program, Vargas had to rely largely on a massive increase in the money supply, with all its inevitable social consequences. Meanwhile, his national program of state-directed industrialization, using state corporations as its major instrument, encountered increasing hostility from neocolonial interests at home and abroad. In the United States, the Eisenhower administration decided that the Vargas government had not created the proper climate for private investment and terminated the Joint United States–Brazilian Economic Commission. Within Brazil, Vargas's program faced sabotage at the hands of the rural forces that continued to dominate the majority of state governments and Congress. This hardening of attitudes signified that Vargas's options and his capacity for maneuvering between different social groups were greatly reduced.

In December 1951, Vargas asked Congress to approve a bill creating a mixed public-private petroleum corporation to be called *Petrobrás,* which would give the state a monopoly on the drilling of oil and new refineries. Petrobrás illustrated Vargas's belief that the state must own the commanding heights of the economy and represented an attempt to reduce the balance of payments deficit by substituting domestic sources of oil for imported oil. Vargas sought to appease domestic and foreign opponents by leaving the distribution of oil in private hands and allowing existing refineries to remain privately owned. Almost two years passed before Congress, under great popular pressure, passed the law creating Petrobrás in October 1953. However, Vargas's proposal to create a similar agency for electric power—to be called *Electrobrás*—remained bottled up in Congress.

Vargas's labor policy became another political battleground. Under Vargas, labor regained much of the freedom of action it had lost during the Dutra years. In December 1951, the government decreed a new minimum wage that only compensated for the most recent price rises. In 1953 three hundred thousand workers went on strike for higher wages and other benefits. In June of that year, Vargas appointed a young protégé, João Goulart, minister of labor. Goulart, a populist in the Vargas tradition, was sympathetic with labor's demands. In January 1954 Goulart recommended a doubling of the minimum wage. This recommendation evoked a violent "manifesto of the colonels," in which a group of officers charged that the government was penetrated by communism and corruption, that the armed forces were being neglected, and that the recommended new minimum wage would demoralize the badly underpaid officer class. Under military pressure, Vargas dismissed Goulart, but in a May Day speech to workers he announced that the increased minimum wage would be enacted and praised the fallen minister of labor.

The battle lines between Vargas and his foes were being drawn ever more sharply. In speeches to Congress, Vargas attacked foreign investors for aggravating Brazil's balance of payments problem by their massive remittances of profits and claimed that invoicing frauds had cost Brazil at least $250 million over an eighteen-month period. Meanwhile, attacks on him by the conservative-dominated press and radio grew even more bitter; especially vituperative were the editorials of Carlos Lacerda, editor of the ultraconservative *Tribuna da Imprensa.*

An effort to silence Lacerda presented Vargas's enemies with a golden opportunity to destroy him. Unknown to Vargas, the chief of the president's personal guard arranged for a gunman to assassinate Lacerda. The plot miscarried, for Lacerda was only slightly wounded, but one of his bodyguards was killed. An investigation revealed the complicity of palace officials and uncovered the existence of large-scale corruption in the presidential staff. The chorus of demands for Vargas's resignation was joined by the military, which informed him on August 24 that he must resign or be deposed. Isolated, betrayed by the men he had trusted, the seventy-two-year-old Vargas found the way out of his dilemma by suicide. But he left a message that was also his political testament. It ended with the words:

I fought against the looting of Brazil. I fought against the looting of the people. I have fought bare-breasted. Hatred, infamy, and calumny did not beat down my spirit. I gave you my life. Now I offer my death. Nothing remains. Serenely I take the first step on the road to eternity and I leave life to enter history.

Reform and Reaction, 1954–1964

The death of Vargas foreshadowed the demise of the nationalist, populist model of independent capitalist development over which he had presided for the better part of a quarter-century. That model, based on a strategy of maneuver and compromise, of reconciling the clashing interests of the national bourgeoisie, fazendeiros, foreign capitalists, and the working class, of avoiding such structural changes as agrarian reform, had about exhausted its possibilities.

Two options remained. One was for Vargas's political heirs to mobilize the working class and the peasantry for the realization of a program of structural changes, including agrarian reform, that could impart a new dynamic to Brazilian national capitalism. The alternative was for Vargas's political enemies to impose a streamlined neocolonial model based on the denationalization and modernization of Brazilian industry, on

its transformation into an extension of the industrial park of the great capitalist powers, accompanied by a shift in emphasis from the export of raw materials to the export of manufactured goods. Since such a course entailed immense sacrifices for the Brazilian people, it also required the imposition of a dictatorship of the most repressive kind. The balance of forces in 1954 already favored the second option. For a decade, however, Brazil would sway uncertainly between the two alternatives.

The right-wing military and civilian conspirators who spearheaded the movement for Vargas's removal had hoped to use it as a springboard for the establishment of a right-wing dictatorship. But the massive outpouring of grief and protest caused by Vargas's death and suicide message frustrated their plans. Vice president João Café Filho was allowed to serve Vargas's unexpired term. A conservative without sympathy for Vargas's economic nationalist policies, he pursued a course designed to attract foreign capital. One of his decrees exempted foreign firms in Brazil from the need to provide foreign exchange cover for importing machinery. The decree, which discriminated against national companies without foreign links, aroused the anger of nationalists.

The Kubitschek Era

The presidential election of 1955 took place under the watchful gaze of the military. The UDN nominated the conservative General Juarez Távora for president; the PSD and PTB jointly nominated Juscelino Kubitschek, governor of Minas Gerais, with João Goulart as his running mate. Their platform stressed the defense of democracy and the acceleration of economic growth. Kubitschek was not an economic nationalist in the Vargas mold, but the nationalist and reformist groups, knowing the limits of military tolerance, gave him their support. As the campaign progressed, there grew a clamor on the right for a coup to prevent the victory of Kubitschek and Goulart. However, they won the election in October, with the popular Goulart polling more votes than the president-elect.

Kubitschek took office in January 1956 with a promise of "fifty years of progress in five." But this progress was to be achieved with the aid of massive foreign investments, to which Kubitschek offered most generous incentives. Foreign capital flowed into Brazil; the total inflow between 1955 and 1961 amounted to $2.3 billion. The bulk came from the United States, whose investments in Brazil reached the figure of $1.5 billion in 1960.

This influx of capital, which benefited from advantages denied to Brazilian enterprises, promoted a rapid foreign conquest of Brazilian national industry. In the process, the native entrepreneurs were frequently transformed into directors or partners of the foreign-controlled firms. The takeover concentrated on the most modern and fastest-growing industries (chemical, metallurgy, electrical, communications, and automotive). In 1960 foreign investment accounted for 70 percent of the capital invested in the 34 largest companies and more than 30 percent in the 650 corporations with capital of a million dollars or more.

The Kubitschek era was a heady time of unprecedented economic growth, with an average annual growth rate of 7 percent for the period from 1957 to 1961. By 1960, Brazil had been transformed from an agrarian country into an agrarian-industrial country with a base of heavy industry, for it could boast that it produced half its heavy-industry needs. Construction of a series of great dams provided much of the power needed by Brazil's growing industry. Kubitschek's decision to build a new capital, Brasilia, in the state of Goias, six hundred miles from the coast in an area still roamed by Indians, reflected his exuberant optimism about Brazil's future. Completed in three years, the new capital was inaugurated on April 21, 1960. A network of "highways of national unity" was constructed to link Brasilia with the rest of the country, but failed to solve the many difficulties—housing and resettlement problems, cultural isolation, and the like—that faced its inhabitants.

These triumphs of development had to be paid for, and their cost was high. A major source of financing was foreign loans, which swelled Brazil's already large foreign debt from $1.6 billion in 1954 to $2.7 billion in 1961. Service of the foreign debt took an ever-increasing share of the national budget, rising from $180 million to $515 million (more than half the value of Brazil's exports) in the same period. This source of financing had its limits; by 1959 the International Monetary Fund threatened to withhold loans if Brazil did not adopt a stabilization program and live within its means. Kubitschek responded by breaking off negotiations with the IMF and increasing the money supply. The result was an unprecedented inflation rate and a catastrophic decline in the value of the cruzeiro, whose exchange rate for the dollar fell from 70 to 210 between 1955 and 1961. This in turn greatly diminished the value of Brazil's exports. Inflation, like foreign loans, appeared to have reached its limits as a source of financing Brazilian development.

The Quadros Regime

The election of 1960 took place amid growing social unrest and intense debate over domestic and foreign policy. Inflation, corruption, and foreign control of the economy were major campaign issues. The campaign oratory and programs of all the principal candidates reflected the ascendancy that the nationalist, populist ideology had gained over public opinion. Even the conservative UDN recognized this fact by nominating as its candidate the flamboyant Jânio da Silva Quadros, former governor of São Paulo, whose campaign symbol was a broom with which he promised to "sweep out of the government the corrupt elements, the thieves and exploiters of the people." Although Quadros endorsed a balanced budget and stressed the need for a favorable climate for foreign investment, he also opposed the participation of foreign firms in Brazilian oil production, and he showed his independence in foreign policy by paying a visit to revolutionary Cuba at a time when the United States was bringing pressure on Latin American governments to sever diplomatic relations with Cuba.

Quadros's chief opponent was Marshal Henrique Teixeira Lott, who was endorsed by the UDN and the PTB, with Goulart as his running mate. A more authentic economic nationalist than Quadros, Lott favored sharply limiting profit remittances sent abroad by foreign firms and supported giving illiterates the vote. Quadros won the election but Goulart was re-elected vice president.

The short-lived Quadros administration was marked by a mixture of orthodox and unorthodox policies, by an essentially conservative posture in economic affairs and an independent posture in foreign policy. Without breaking with the traditional dependence on the capitalist countries for markets and loans, Quadros sought to reduce that dependence by developing new trade and diplomatic relations with the socialist countries and the Third World. Accordingly, he initiated negotiations for the resumption of diplomatic relations with the Soviet Union, sent a trade mission to the People's Republic of China, and denounced the CIA-backed Bay of Pigs invasion of Cuba in April 1961. Although he stressed the need for foreign investments and guaranteed their security, Quadros proposed to modify the "laws and regulations which place the Brazilian company in an inferior position" and to restrict the remittance of profits abroad.

However moderate, Quadros's foreign and domestic policies aroused the hostility of military and civilian conservatives. Quadros's problems were compounded by an increasingly recalcitrant Congress, in which the eighteen rural states, dominated by conservative fazendeiros, were overrepresented. Determined to break the legislative deadlock by some dramatic act, Quadros submitted his resignation on August 25, 1961, after only seven months of rule. His resignation message recalled Vargas's suicide note in its fervent nationalist tone and its claim that hostile foreign forces had obstructed his program of Brazil for the Brazilians. Convinced that the military would not permit the prolabor Vice President Goulart to succeed him, Quadros evidently believed that public clamor for his return would bring him back to office with the powers he needed to govern.

But he had miscalculated. His resignation caused great public excitement and perplexity, but the clamor that went up was not for his re-

turn but for a constitutional solution to the problem: the elevation of Goulart to the presidency. When the crisis broke out, Goulart was in China on a trade mission. The military cabinet officers, headed by war minister Odílio Denys, regarded Goulart, a wealthy rancher, as a dangerous demagogue and radical and announced that they considered his return to Brazil inadmissible for reasons of "national security."

A grave split developed within the military; in Goulart's home state of Rio Grande do Sul the commander of the Third Army announced his total support for Goulart, and the governor of the state rallied the population to defend the constitution and insure Goulart's elevation to the presidency. The threat of civil war loomed, but the military ministers, facing divisions within the armed forces and feeling the pressure of public opinion, agreed to a compromise. Goulart took office, but a constitutional amendment replaced the presidential system of government with a parliamentary one. Under this system, the president would share power with a council of ministers named by him, but drawn from and responsible to the legislature.

Goulart's Presidency

The right-wing military and its civilian allies had grudgingly accepted Goulart as president, but on probation. Taking office in September 1961, he began by steering a cautious course designed to allay conservative suspicions at home and abroad. In April 1962 he paid a visit to Washington. Addressing a joint session of Congress, he announced his opposition to the Castro regime and promised reasonable treatment of foreign-owned utilities in Brazil. The United States provided $131 million in aid for Brazil's depressed northeast, but the IMF, whose approval was a condition for the cooperation of private bankers, remained skeptical of Goulart's intentions.

At the same time he courted foreign capital, Goulart continued Quadros's independent foreign policy of expanding Brazil's trade and diplomatic contacts with the socialist countries and the Third World. Goulart's refusal to join the United States in imposing sanctions against Castro's Cuba especially angered the right; Congress showed its displeasure with Goulart's able foreign minister, San Tiago Dantas, by refusing to approve his nomination as prime minister.

The first one and a half years of Goulart's rule under the parliamentary system saw few major legislative achievements. One was the passage of a long-delayed law establishing Electrobrás, the national agency proposed by Vargas for the control of the production and distribution of electric power. The other was a law requiring foreign capital to be registered with the Brazilian government and barring profit remittances abroad in excess of 10 percent of invested capital, certainly not a radical measure. Yet it produced a sharp drop in foreign investments, from $91 million in 1961 to $18 million in 1962. Lacking other sources for financing development, Goulart had to resort to the Kubitschek formula of a massive increase of the money supply. The new inflationary spiral brought the collapse of the cruzeiro and a wave of strikes and food riots, and a growing radicalization of labor and sections of the peasantry. But the economic slowdown apparent since 1961 continued. Import substitution as a stimulus to industrialization appeared to have reached its limits, and further advance was blocked by the small domestic market, the inequities of Brazilian income distribution, and the drain of capital through debt repayment and profit remittances (amounting to $564 million, or 45 percent of the value of Brazil's exports, in 1962).

With the advice of the brilliant young economist Celso Furtado, who had directed an ambitious effort to develop Brazil's backward, poverty-ridden northeast, Goulart drafted a program of structural reforms that was intended to impart a new dynamism to Brazil's faltering economy. The major proposed reforms were in the areas of land tenure, tax structure, and voting. Reform of the archaic land tenure system would expand the domestic market and increase agricultural production. Tax reform would reduce the inequities of income distribution and provide funds needed for public education and other social welfare purposes. The grant of votes to the illiterates

would, it was hoped, drastically reduce the power of the rural oligarchy in the national and state legislatures.

To implement these changes, however, the legislative deadlock in Congress had to be broken, so in mid-1962 Goulart launched a campaign for a plebiscite to let the people choose between presidential and parliamentary government. Under great public pressure, Congress agreed to the plebiscite, and on January 1, 1963, more than 12 million voters decided by a three to one majority to restore to Goulart his full presidential powers under the constitution of 1946.

But Goulart's victory did not change the balance of forces in Congress, which repeatedly voted down his reform proposals. Meanwhile, there was a growing polarization of opinion in the country, with the bourgeoisie and the middle class joining the landed oligarchy in opposition to Goulart's domestic program. Goulart's moderate reform proposals in reality favored the industrial bourgeoisie and should have enjoyed its support. But the dynamic industrialist class that had arisen and thrived under Vargas no longer represented a significant social force. The progressive foreign conquest of Brazilian industry had greatly reduced that class's influence as more and more national entrepreneurs gave up an unequal struggle and solved their personal problems by becoming directors or associates of foreign-owned firms. This dependent bourgeoisie shared the fears of social change of its foreign and rural allies. Those fears were also shared by the large urban middle class, battered by inflation and injected by the media with a virulent anticommunist prejudice.

The apprehension of these groups increased as a result of the extravagant rhetoric indulged in by the radical populists and by the spread of radical populism to the countryside. Under the leadership of the lawyer Francisco Julião, peasants in the bleak northeast, afflicted by drought, famine, and oppressive land tenure and labor systems, began to join groups known as Peasant Leagues and agricultural unions and invade fazendas. Their activities seemed to threaten the existence of the latifundio, which was also threatened by

Goulart's proposal to give the vote to illiterates and enact agrarian reform.

By the end of 1963, the forces on the right—the fazendeiros, the big bourgeoisie, the military, and their foreign allies—had begun to mobilize against the threat from the left. The military was especially angered by Goulart's proposal to give the vote and the right to hold office to enlisted men, regarding it as a fatal blow to the principle of hierarchy and discipline. The media launched a powerful attack on Goulart to convince the frustrated middle class that he was an agent of the international communist conspiracy and urging the military to intervene to safeguard "democracy" and "freedom." As 1964 began Governors Adhemar de Barros of São Paulo and Carlos Lacerda of Guanabara announced the imminent military intervention to check what they called the "advance of communism and anarchy."

Defeated in his efforts to secure passage of his legislative program and under strong pressure from the impatient radical populists, Goulart moved to the left. Appearing at a mass rally in Rio de Janeiro in March 1964, he signed two decrees. One nationalized all private oil refineries. The other made liable to expropriation all large and "underutilized" estates close to federal highways or railways and lands of over seventy acres near federal dams, irrigation works, or drainage projects. At the same meeting, Goulart announced that he would shortly issue a decree on rent control. He asked Congress to pass reforms that included tax reform, the vote for illiterates and enlisted men, an amendment to the constitution providing for land expropriation without immediate compensation, and legalization of the Communist party.

By the middle of March, the military-civilian conspiracy for Goulart's overthrow was well advanced. The governors of a number of important states met with a view to transferring Congress to São Paulo, where a "legalist government" would be installed. An emissary returned from the United States with assurances from the State Department that the United States would immediately recognize the new government. Then, if it became necessary, the "legalist government"

would solicit aid from the United States, and the dispatch of American troops would not constitute intervention but a response to a legitimate government's request for aid to suppress communism and subversion.

On March 31, the governor of Minas Gerais announced that he no longer accepted the president's authority. The same day, army units in Minas and São Paulo began to march on Rio de Janeiro. The U.S. ambassador to Brazil, Lincoln Gordon, was well informed of the conspiracy; five days before the coup he cabled Secretary of State Dean Rusk naming General Humberto de Alencar Castelo Branco as the probable head of the new military junta. Published documents also show that the United States was prepared to give military aid, if needed, to the rebels. But Operation Uncle Sam (its code name) proved unnecessary; the Goulart regime fell almost without a struggle on April 1, and the president fled into exile in Uruguay.

The ease with which the Goulart government was overthrown reflected the change in the alignment of forces in Brazil since 1945, and especially the movement of the Brazilian bourgeoisie and middle class into the camp of reaction, but it also revealed the weaknesses and divisions within the camp of Goulart's supporters. The working class, most of which was politically immature and accustomed to passively receiving favors and instructions from populist chieftains, failed to respond to Goulart's appeal for aid. The mass of the peasantry was still under the control of rural coronéis, while the Peasant Leagues and unions were weak and distant from the main theater of events. The left was badly split ideologically; there was little unity of program or coordinated direction of the groups making up the populist coalition.

Another cause of the passivity with which many received the coup was the widespread belief that it was simply another in a long series of military interventions; sooner rather than later the military would return to its barracks and political life would return to normal. Events proved the error of this opinion. As the military regime consolidated its power, it became clear that the

364

generals had come to install the alternative to the nationalist economic model, a neocolonial model based on the thorough integration of a dependent Brazilian economy into the international capitalist economy and the rapid modernization of Brazilian industry and agriculture without regard to its social consequences. Because of the regime's combination of brutally repressive policies with primary economic and political dependence on the United States, the Brazilian scholar Hélio Jaguaribe has aptly called it "colonial fascism."

Brazil's "Colonial Fascism"

The first acts of the military leaders of the self-proclaimed "democratic revolution" on April 1964 revealed their long-range intentions. On April 9, the Supreme Revolutionary Command issued the First Institutional Act, permitting the president to rule by decree, declare a state of siege, and deprive any citizen of civil rights for a period of ten years. A docile Congress approved the military's choice for president, General Humberto de Alencar Castelo Branco. Like many of his colleagues, Castelo Branco was a product of the *Escola Superior de Guerra* (School of Higher Military Studies), dominated in recent years by advocates of a *linha dura* (hard line), whose main tenets were fanatical anticommunism, favorable treatment of foreign capital, and acceptance of the leadership of the United States in foreign affairs.

Encouragement of Foreign Capital and Repression of Labor

It was in the area of economic policy that the new government most clearly defined its character and long-range aims. Roberto Campos, minister of planning, worked out a program for stimulating the entry of foreign capital by incentives that included the free export of profits, reduced taxes on the income of foreign firms, and a special type of exchange for the payment of external financing

in case of devaluation. At the same time, internal credit was severely reduced in compliance with the anti-inflationary prescriptions of the IMF, while the level of consumption of the domestic market fell as a result of a wage freeze and the decline in the real value of wages. These policies, placing Brazilian-owned companies in an unfavorable position, caused many to go under; 440 went bankrupt in 1966, 550 in 1967.

The new government's economic policies accelerated the foreign takeover of Brazilian industry. By 1968 foreign capital controlled 40 percent of the capital market of Brazil, 62 percent of its foreign trade, 82 percent of its maritime transport, 77 percent of its overseas air transport, 100 percent of its motor vehicle production, 100 percent of its tire production, more than 80 percent of its pharmaceutical industry, and 90 percent of its cement industry. The United States led, with about half of the total foreign investment, followed by Germany, Britain, France, and Switzerland.

To ensure foreign and domestic capital of an abundant supply of cheap labor, the government froze wages and banned strikes, with the result that workers' living standards fell sharply. In 1968 the minister of labor estimated that the real value of wages had fallen between 15 and 30 percent in the preceding four years. Labor was further shackled by the appointment of military interventors to oversee more than two thousand of the country's leading industrial unions.

Further, the government suppressed dissent in all areas of Brazilian life and suspended the political rights of thousands of so-called extremists. Thousands of federal employees were fired, and hundreds of nationalist military officers were arbitrarily retired or dismissed. The government shut down the Brazilian Institute of Higher Studies, a major center of nationalist economic theory, suppressed the National Student Union, and outlawed the Peasant Leagues.

Meanwhile, the military government unswervingly followed the lead of the United States in foreign policy. Brazil broke off diplomatic relations with Cuba, opposed the seating of the People's Republic of China in the United Nations, participated in the U.S. military intervention in the Dominican Republic, and actively supported the U.S. military effort in Vietnam.

In October 1965, after the government's candidates had suffered humiliating defeat in a series of local elections, President Castelo Branco issued the Second Institutional Act, which dissolved all political parties and instituted indirect elections of the president and vice president. The Third Institutional Act (February 1966) ended the popular election of governors of states and mayors of state capitals.

Yet for various reasons, probably including the wish to avoid embarrassing their principal patron, the United States, Brazil's military rulers chose to maintain a façade of democracy and representative government. They established two official parties, the *Aliança Renovadora Nacional* (National Renovating Alliance, called Arena) and a legal opposition party, *Movimento Democrático Brasileiro* (Brazilian Democratic Movement, or MDB). Since the ranks of the MDB were carefully screened to exclude subversives and its elected representatives held their mandates at the pleasure of the military, it had little or no impact on policy and legislation. However, it was the only legal channel for expressing and mobilizing dissent, and the vote for the MDB offered a measure of the growing discontent with the dictatorship.

Costa e Silva and a New Constitution

In March 1967, Castelo Branco turned over the presidency to Marshal Artur da Costa e Silva, who had been nominated by the military to succeed him and was duly elected by an obedient, purged Congress. On the day he assumed office, the government gave Brazil a new constitution, the sixth in its history, which incorporated the successive institutional acts. In general, Costa e Silva continued the policies of his predecessor but allowed a certain thaw in the climate of repression; this encouraged a revival of opposition activity and demands for changes in policy. Nationalists inside and outside the armed forces called for a return to the nationalist model of economic develop-

ment, workers for an end to the wage freeze, intellectuals and students for an end to censorship and a return to academic freedom. A portion of the clergy, headed by the courageous archbishop of Recife and Olinda, Helder Câmara, added their voices to the general cry for social, political, and economic reforms.

Heartened by this show of popular resistance to the dictatorship, Congress and the Supreme Court gave signs of wanting to reassert their independence. The Supreme Court defied the military by granting a writ of habeas corpus for three student leaders who had been imprisoned for three months. Congress, after months of heated debate, rejected the government's demand that it lift the immunity of a deputy who had bitterly criticized the military for its brutal treatment of political prisoners and student dissenters.

These acts of defiance precipitated a governmental crisis and brought into the open a struggle within the regime between adherents of the hard line and a group of military officers who proposed to reduce foreign economic influence, pursue a more independent foreign policy, and make some concessions to the clamor for social and political reform. The hard-liners won out; under their pressure, Costa e Silva issued a Fifth Institutional Act in December 1968 that dissolved Congress, imposed censorship, suspended the constitution, and granted the president dictatorial powers.

The "coup within a coup" of December 1968 was accompanied by an increase in the use of terrorist tactics by a variety of police forces, local and national, against real or suspected opponents of the regime. The official security forces were joined by vigilante groups, operating with the covert approval of the government. The systematic use of torture by special units of the military police and the "death squads" reached a level without precedent in Brazilian history. The victims included intellectuals, students, workers and even priests and nuns, as well as common criminals.

This intensified campaign of repression convinced some elements of the Brazilian left that there was no alternative to armed struggle

366

against the dictatorship. There arose some half-dozen guerrilla groups whose activities included attacks on banks and armories, reprisal killings of notorious torturers, and kidnaping of diplomats and other prominent figures to secure the release of political prisoners. But the guerrilla movement never achieved a mass character. The death of the most prominent guerrilla leader, Carlos Marighella, who was slain in an ambush by members of a death squad in November 1969, dealt a heavy blow to the movement, which gradually declined until it ceased to pose a serious problem for the regime.

In August 1969 a stroke incapacitated President Costa e Silva. Disregarding the constitutional provision that made Vice President Pedro Aleixo his successor, the three military ministers seized power in October and formed a triumvirate. When it became apparent that the ailing Costa e Silva could not return to his duties, they designated General Emílio Garrastazú Médici as his successor, and Congress confirmed their choice on October 22. A great landowner and former head of the secret police, Garrastazú Médici was completely identified with the hard line.

At the same time, the military junta presented the country with a new constitution. This document provided that the president would henceforth be chosen indirectly by an electoral college composed of Congress and delegates from state legislatures; it also weakened Congress by stripping its members of immunity against charges of libel or slander and making them liable to prosecution on the vague charge of endangering the public security. The junta also announced that instead of merely serving out the unexpired term of Costa e Silva, the new president was to have a full term of office, serving until March 15, 1974.

President Garrastazú Médici (1969–1974) was succeeded by General Ernesto Geisel (1974–1978), who continued in all essential respects his hard-line policies. Geisel proclaimed his desire for a détente with opposition elements and allegedly attempted to stop torture and arbitrary arrests, but Brazil remained a police state. Torture was routinely used against arrested political dissidents or suspects, who sometimes mysteriously disappeared or committed "suicide," and

Geisel himself freely used the Fifth Institutional Act to strip elected representatives of the MDB of their political rights.

The Economy and Denationalization

Significant changes took place in the Brazilian economy. By 1970 the denationalization of key sectors of Brazilian industry was almost complete. One or a few giant multinational firms dominated each major industry. The automotive industry, which was dominated by three firms—Volkswagen, General Motors, and Ford—typified the concentration of industrial ownership and production. The military champions of free enterprise did not dismantle the state sector, however, as one might expect. Instead they assigned it the function of providing cheap steel, power, and raw materials to the profitable foreign-owned enterprises.

A counterpart of the concentration of production was the concentration of income. Brazil's gross national product grew at an average annual rate of 8 percent, one of the highest in the world, but there was no parallel growth of mass capacity to consume.

The contradiction between a highly productive, technologically advanced industrial plant and an extremely small domestic market had to be resolved somehow. The regime's economic planners found the answer by programming a vast increase in Brazil's exports. Primary products continued to dominate the export trade, but exports of manufactured goods increased at a rate of about 12 percent between 1968 and 1972. Most Brazilians lacked shoes and were poorly clad, but Brazil became a major exporter of shoes and textiles. Increasingly, however, primacy was placed on the export of durable consumer and capital goods, such as cars, electrical products, and machine tools.

Government planners hoped that exports would help to solve the problem of the balance of payments, a problem that grew ever more acute. But even as the volume of exports increased, so did the annual trade deficit. Meanwhile, the foreign debt, which stood at $12.5 billion in 1973, climbed to $17.6 billion in 1974 and stood at about $30 billion by the end of 1976. Service on this foreign debt, an important component of which was the increased cost of imported oil, amounted to nearly the total value of Brazil's exports in 1977. The problem was compounded by the heavy drain of interest and dividends in amounts considerably greater than the foreign investments that generated them. The deficits in the balance of payments contributed to a steep fall in the exchange value of the cruzeiro and an inflationary spiral that reached a rate of about 46 percent in 1976.

The recession that spread throughout the capitalist world in 1973–1974, combined with much higher oil prices, added to Brazil's economic difficulties. The passage of "antidumping" laws[1] in various countries, including the United States, cut into Brazil's exports of manufactured goods, creating overproduction and unemployment in various industries. By the mid-1970s, the bloom was off Brazil's "economic miracle." Official figures showed that the average indebtedness of Brazil's biggest five hundred companies had risen from 50 percent of net assets in 1971 to 63 percent in 1975, suggesting that many of these major companies were dangerously overextended. The contraction in mass purchasing power as a result of the government's wage policies caused concern even in conservative capitalist circles.

The government's own figures documented the devastating effect of the "economic miracle" on the general welfare. By 1974, those figures revealed, the minimum wage was only half the minimum income required to buy food for subsistence. When the costs of rent, clothing, and transportation were added, a worker needed four times the minimum wage. Official data revealed an intolerable situation with respect to public health. Nearly half the population over the age of twenty suffered from tuberculosis and about 150,000 people died every year from the disease; about 42 million suffered from parasitic diseases that caused general debility and reduced working capacity. The great majority of Brazilian houses lacked running water and sanitary facilities, a condition that contributed to the prevalence of parasitic disease. According to the president of the National Institute of Nutrition, 12 million preschool children—70 percent of all children in that category—suffered from malnutrition in 1973.

In February 1969 the government announced a program of agrarian reform. Latifundia that had not been exploited for four years were to be expropriated, with compensation to the owners in cash or government bonds, and divided among the landless. It soon became clear that the "agrarian reform" was primarily directed at prodding and assisting semifeudal great landowners to transform their estates into agribusinesses at the expense of their tenants. The stress on "voluntary" adherence gave landowners time for delay and circumvention of the law by dividing the land among relatives or forming it into commercial enterprises exempt from the law's provisions. Thus, its principal result was to stimulate the development of capitalist large-scale agriculture, accelerating a process that had been under way since the 1930s. Sociologists warned that the "agrarian reform" was spurring a new wave of rural emigration, throwing a new mass of cheap labor on an overstocked urban labor market.

Again, instead of correcting the profound regional contrasts of the Brazilian economy, the government had accentuated them. No serious effort was made to channel investment into the poorer areas of the north and northeast, and private investments naturally flowed into the developed south-central areas, widening the gap between the developed and the "submerged" zones. But official public investment policy also sharpened the tendency toward regional concentration of industry: in 1973 the Council for Industrial Development assigned about 90 percent of its resources to the southeast (of which 77 percent went to São Paulo), and only 3 percent to the northeast.

The Opposition and the Struggle for Rights

Ruled by a brutal military dictatorship, the Brazilian people expressed their dissent and discon-

[1] These laws imposed duties designed to prevent the sale of goods in international trade at below-market prices.

geoisie that proposed to create a modern and relatively independent capitalism. The PFL spoke for more traditional commercial and landed elites. To the left of these majority parties stood the Democratic Labor party (PDT) of Leonel Brizola, populist and reformist in the tradition of Vargas and Goulart; and the leftist Workers' party (PT), which sought to expand from its limited trade union base in São Paulo. The Communist party, legalized by Congress in 1985 after many years in the underground, enjoyed some influence in the labor movement but little on the national political scene. A total control of the mass media by elite interests hindered the development of independent political action and ideological independence on the part of the workers and peasants who form the overwhelming majority of Brazil's population.

This is not to minimize the importance of the return to democracy in Brazil. Following the adoption of a new constitution in 1988, most Brazilians live under a regime that respects civil liberties and human rights (but in the vast interior of the country, where there is little respect for law, great landowners and their hired thugs continue to terrorize peasants and their allies). The new constitution extended the franchise to the illiterate, established direct elections on all levels, permitted parties of all political creeds to operate freely, and allowed workers to form unions, bargain collectively, and strike.

The Sarney administration, however, made little progress in solving Brazil's great social and economic problems, the chief of which was land reform. This was not simply a question of redistributive justice; it was a prerequisite for the creation of a modern national capitalism based on a large domestic market. In November 1985 the Brazilian Congress passed and Sarney signed into law an agrarian reform bill that provided for the distribution of 88 million acres of land to 1.4 million families through 1989. Under a new Ministry of Agrarian Reform and Development, the National Institute of Colonization and Agrarian Reform (INCRA) was to implement the plan on the regional level through mixed commissions of landowners, government officials, and landless

peasants. A decree of May 1986 limited the land available for distribution and expropriation to state-owned lands and to private holdings whose production was below the land-use standards set by government agronomists.

So sluggish was the program's implementation that Minister of Agrarian Reform and Development Nelson Ribeiro resigned in protest. The major obstacle to land reform was the fierce resistance of the landowners. Organized under the Rural Democratic Union (UDR) and the Brazilian Society for the Defense of Tradition, Family, and Property, the landowners hired thousands of former military personnel to staff private militias, paying, it was reported, salaries three times higher than those of the army. The landowners enjoyed the support and protection of local officials and police. Their thugs compiled hit lists of landowners' perceived enemies.

If land reform was the most acute, violence-ridden issue of the "New Republic," Brazil's greatest external problem remained the immense foreign debt, which in 1990 stood at about $120 billion. The continuous drain of foreign exchange had a profoundly negative impact on Brazil's efforts to achieve social reform and economic growth. To many Brazilians, it appeared that the nation must choose between paying the interest and supporting social and economic development.

The new civilian government defined its position on the debt in a speech made by Sarney to the United Nations General Assembly in September 1985: "Brazil will not pay its foreign debt with recession nor with unemployment, nor with hunger . . . a debt paid for with poverty is an account paid with democracy." These were brave words, in sharp contrast to the docility with which military governments had accepted the debt status quo. In the same vein, Dilson Funaro, Sarney's finance minister, said Brazil would no longer accept IMF monitoring of the Brazilian economy as a condition for debt-rescheduling operations, and in February 1987 Brazil announced a suspension of interest payments to private banks. But this revolt by a timid, conservative president did not last long. Under pressure from foreign bankers and right-wing domestic groups, Sarney lifted the moratorium and in February 1988 began negotiations with the banks for a conventional rescheduling.

On taking office the Sarney administration found the economy in recession, racked by galloping inflation and high unemployment. In February 1986 Sarney announced the Plan Cruzado. This program for economic stabilization consisted of measures designed to halt triple-digit inflation through a freeze on wages, prices, and rents, and the replacement of Brazil's monetary unit, the cruzeiro, with a new and strong monetary unit, the cruzado. Workers' resentment at what they regarded as patently unfair policies produced a wave of strikes that were partly successful in achieving the unions' demands, despite government threats and some acts of repression, including the arrest of some union leaders.

Despite fissures in the wage-price structure, the relative success of the Plan Cruzado in halting inflation and a consumer boom fueled by massive government spending inspired confidence and produced large political rewards for the government in the election of November 15, 1986. The PMDB won governorships in twenty of the twenty-three states and gained some 60 percent of the seats in the new congress. These results meant the PMDB majority would have a decisive voice in shaping Brazil's new constitution, the nation's eighth.

Even as voters were going to the polls, the government prepared to announce an abrupt shift in economic policy. Sarney's economic team, alarmed by a recent upsurge in inflation and a sharp decline in Brazil's trade surplus and foreign exchange reserves, put together a package of measures designed to cool down the overheated economy, slow economic growth, and balance the budget by increasing government revenues. Plan Cruzado II, unveiled five days after the 1986 election, provided for a series of devaluations to maintain export effectiveness; the immediate closing or merger of fifteen state companies and of thirty-two more in the coming months; and, most painful of all, large increases in postal rates, the cost of utilities, fuel, and

sugar, and 100 percent increases in taxes on cigarettes and alcoholic beverages.

An explosion of popular wrath followed the announcement of Cruzado II; the fact that the government had concealed its plans until shortly after the November 15 election made it appear like a deliberate act of betrayal. In December the two labor federations, the leftist *Central Unica dos Trabalhadores* (CUT) and its rival, the more conservative *Central Geral dos Trabalhadores* (CGT), joined in a general strike designed to bring about the total repeal of the austerity program; organizers claimed that the strike brought 70 percent of the nation to a standstill. Although shaken by the strike, Sarney rejected the proffered resignation of his finance minister and insisted that what had been done could not be undone.

By this time the economic impact of Sarney's policies had virtually exhausted his reservoir of popular good will, and many called for his resignation. Assured of military support, Sarney responded to such demands in a tough speech by promising to serve out his five-year term. In the same speech he announced a ninety-day freeze on wages to take effect in mid-June 1987. Taken together with other provisions, including a devaluation of the cruzado, the plan was calculated to please foreign creditors by reducing domestic demand and expanding exports, thereby improving Brazil's balance of trade, but it angered Brazilian wage earners, whose purchasing power, already slashed 30 percent since November 1, faced another decline of 29 percent. It was a foregone conclusion that the end of the freeze would see another wave of strikes.

By mid-1987 Sarney's popularity had declined to the vanishing point. The widespread disillusionment with his promises and performance extended to the promise of "The New Republic." The U.S. banker David Rockefeller observed in 1988: "In all my visits to Brazil, I have never before come across such desperate poverty."

In October 1988 the National Congress, acting as a constituent assembly, gave the country a new democratic constitution that represented a sweeping rejection of all the late military regime

Storm over the Andes: The Struggle for Land and Development in the Central Andean Area

In the second half of the twentieth century, reform came at last to three countries whose economic and social structures were among the most archaic in Latin America, the Andean republics of Peru, Bolivia, and Ecuador. Here, as elsewhere on the continent, the movement for reconstruction fused the effort to modernize with the struggle for greater social justice for the masses: economic sovereignty, industrialization, and land reform were the main slogans of the Andean revolutions. But the presence of large, compact Indian-speaking groups, ranging from some 70 percent of the population of Bolivia to about 40 percent of the populations of Peru and Ecuador, gave a distinctive character to the nationalist, reformist movements in these countries.

Three Andean Revolutions

Bolivia, 1952–1995

Landlocked Bolivia, the most Indian of the three lands, a country where as late as 1976 only a minority of the population were monolingual speakers of Spanish, was the scene of the first true Andean social revolution. In 1952 the middle-class National Revolutionary Movement (MNR), led by Victor Paz Estenssoro, overthrew the rule of the great landlords and tin barons with the support of armed Indian miners and peasants. The Bolivian land reform, begun by the spontaneous rising of the peasantry and legitimized by the revolutionary government of President Paz Estenssoro, broke the back of the latifundio system in Bolivia. Like the Mexican land reform, however, the Bolivian reform created some new problems even as it solved some old ones. The former latifundia were usually parceled out into very small farms—true minifundia—and the new peasant proprietors received little aid from the government in the form of credit and technical assistance. Yet despite its shortcomings, the Bolivian land reform brought indisputable benefits: some expansion of the internal market, some rise in peasant living standards and, in the words of Richard W. Patch, "the transformation of a dependent and passive population into an independent and active population."

The new government also nationalized the principal tin mines, most of which were controlled by three large companies, and recognized its debt to the armed miners by placing the mines under joint labor-government management. It also abolished the literacy qualification for voting and thus enfranchised the Indian masses. But the new regime inherited a costly, run-down tin industry, while the initial disruptive effect of the agrarian reform on food production added to its economic problems.

Under strong pressure from the United States, which made vitally needed economic aid to the revolutionary government conditional on the adoption of conservative policies, the MNR leadership gradually moved to the right. The government of Paz Estenssoro offered generous compensation to the former owners of expropriated mines, invited new foreign investment on favorable terms, ended labor participation in the management of the government tin company, and reduced welfare benefits to the miners. Equally important, it agreed to the restoration of a powerful U.S.-trained national army to offset the strength of the peasant and worker militias. These retreats broke up the worker–middle class alliance formed during the revolution and facilitated the seizure of power in 1964 by right-wing generals.

In the violent ebb and flow of Bolivian politics since 1964, governments have risen and fallen, but a persistent theme has been the conflict between radical workers, students, and nationalist military and a coalition uniting a new elite of businessmen and politicians grown wealthy through U.S. aid, and conservative military. The peasantry, neutralized by the land reform that satisfied its land hunger, initially remained passive or even sided with the government in its struggles with labor, but later peasant unrest began to grow as a result of deteriorating economic conditions.

Major factors in Bolivia's continuing political and economic crisis since 1964 have been the collapse in the price of tin, the country's major traditional export, compensated for by the meteoric rise of cocaine as its chief dollar earner; heavy pressure on Bolivia by international lending agencies to adopt neoliberal policies of austerity and privatization; and equally heavy pressure by the United States on Bolivia to take part in a "war on drugs."

The overall rightward direction of Bolivian politics since 1964 was reflected in the important election of July 1985, which turned into a contest between the former dictator, General Hugo Banzer Suárez, candidate of the rightist National Democratic Action party (ADN), and Paz Estenssoro, the 78-year-old leader of the MNR and the revolution of 1952. Disillusioned with politics, two-thirds of the electorate stayed away from the polls; a majority of the votes cast were divided between Banzer and Paz. Since neither candidate commanded more than 50 percent of the vote, the election was thrown into Congress, where leftist deputies and followers of Paz elected him president.

Under pressure from Banzer, who threatened a coup, and from the IMF, which demanded a severe austerity program as a condition for badly needed new loans, Paz veered sharply to the right. Accepting the IMF's terms, he slashed government subsidies for basic services and foods, froze wages, devalued the currency over 1,000 percent, removed all restrictions on foreign imports and investments, and resumed payments on Bolivia's foreign debt. When workers responded with a general strike in September 1985, it was crushed by the military, and more than a thousand labor and peasant leaders were arrested.

As 1986 began, the full dimensions of Paz's turn to the right became clear. In alliance with Banzer, some of whose followers Paz brought into his cabinet, he announced a plan designed to end hyperinflation and stabilize the economy. The plan, drafted by Harvard economist Jeffrey Sachs called for closing down as many as eleven unprofitable state-owned mines, laying off thousands of workers, selling other state enterprises to the private sector, making deep cuts in public services, and increasing taxes. Paz's decision to close down Bolivia's largest tin mine in August brought the conflict between the government and the labor movement to a head. The miners' union called a general strike in the region of Oruro and Potosí, where thousands began a march on the capital of La Paz. The government imposed a state of siege, arresting hundreds of labor and community leaders, and sending troops, tanks, and planes to patrol the mining regions.

The mining crisis added to the tension caused by a July 1986 decision of Paz to invite U.S. troops into the country to work with the Bolivian military on "Operation Blast Furnace" in eradicating the country's cocaine laboratories. Ironically, the most dynamic sector of Bolivia's economy—despite well-publicized anti-narcotic raids and Operation Blast Furnace—was the cocaine trade; this chief source of dollars was compensating for the sharp decline in the country's export earnings. Sale of coca paste generated $600 million annually, one-third more than the nation's legal export earnings of $400 million. The government proclaimed the anti-narcotic Operation Blast Furnace a total success. In fact, however, key figures in the nation's cocaine mafia, obviously forewarned, had fled the country long before the troops' arrival; their raids revealed only a few workers and dismantled laboratories.

The conflict between the miners and the government took a dramatic turn when some one thousand miners protested government mine-closing plans, the state of siege, and other repressive measures by occupying mine shafts and launching a hunger strike. The miners' plight and the stubborn refusal of the government to negotiate a solution to the conflict caused growing public sympathy and demonstrations of support for the miners. Aware of the unpopularity of its position, in September 1986 the Paz government accepted the offer of church mediation in its dispute with the miners. Eleven days of talks produced an agreement providing for the release of a hundred labor, peasant, and community leaders, a halt to government efforts to close mines, new jobs or compensation for miners who lost jobs, a lifting of the blockade on the flow of supplies to the mining regions of Oruro and Potosí, and consultations with the union on further decisions regarding mines.

The miners, the backbone of the *Central Obrera Boliviana* (COB), historically Latin America's strongest labor movement, had beaten off government efforts to destroy their union. But there was no indication of a change in the government's overall economic policy, a neoliberal, free-market policy that sought to eliminate or sell off state-owned industries, remove tariff barriers to foreign imports, and lift all restrictions on foreign investment. The fruits of that policy were apparent in the decline of traditional industries, a drop in consuming power of some 40 percent in 1985–1986, and an unemployment rate of 30 percent. By the end of 1986, 25,000 miners had already lost their jobs and 7,000 more expected layoffs.

Paz and Sachs could point to a drastic decline in the inflation rate as proof of the success of their program. However, free-market theory assumed the tens of thousands of unemployed miners and others who had lost their jobs as a result of the Sachs plan would find work in the private sector. But the only expanding private sector economic activity in Bolivia was coca and cocaine production. Thousands of miners, finding no alternative employment, invested the indemnification money they received from the government in land and began to grow coca. Bolivian coca-leaf production increased 60 percent—from 50,000 metric tons before the Sachs plan to 80,000 afterward—making Bolivia the second largest producer of coca. It is also the second largest producer of cocaine. An estimated 500,000 Bolivians are now dependent on the coca economy, which makes cocaine "like a cushion that is preventing a social explosion."

In July 1986 in a joint Bolivian and U.S. military exercise, Bolivian jungle camps processing cocaine materials were raided. A Bolivian policeman is shown standing in front of a former cocaine-processing camp in the Bolivian jungle.

In August 1989, after the first round of the presidential election had failed to give a plurality to the two leading candidates, a deal struck between the former dictator Banzer and Jaime Paz Zamora, candidate of the social democratic Movement of the Revolutionary Left (MIR), led to Paz Zamora's selection as president by Congress. In office he continued the policies of his predecessor, closing down or privatizing state-owned enterprises and proclaiming states of siege to deal with work stoppages by miners, doctors, and teachers, among others to protest his economic policies.

Although Paz Zamora had initially rejected a United States offer to increase military aid to Bolivia on condition that the Bolivian armed forces be brought into the war on drugs, he eventually yielded to U.S. pressure to reconsider. Joint U.S.-Bolivian sorties were soon regularly occurring in the Chaparé region, where most of Bolivia's coca is cultivated. But there is no evidence that the sorties, the destruction of access roads, and other military measures have won the Bolivian war on drugs. Increasing or declining supplies of coca from the Chaparé region seemed above all to reflect the movement of peasants into and out of coca cultivation according to fluctuations in coca-leaf prices.

Recognition by the new Clinton administration that the highly militarized Andean "drug war" approach—after an expenditure of nearly one billion dollars—had not achieved its goals, resulted

388   those who had voted for him would not do it again and 75 percent of those questioned disapproved of the package. In mid-1993 the unions claimed that living standards had fallen by 50 percent since Durán-Ballén had taken office. The minimum wage is about $30 a month, but unofficial estimates put the cost of a shopping basket of basic goods at about $250.

In October 1993, eight months after Durán-Ballén submitted his project for "modernization of the state" to Congress, it passed a law that made substantial changes in the president's original text. Peremptory dismissals of state employees were struck out, and the privatization of state companies in areas regarded as "strategic," such as oil, telecommunications, and electric power, would require the passage of special laws by Congress. An effective "guerrilla campaign" of strikes and demonstrations by public sector unions combined with the activity of opposition groups in Congress produced this watering down of the "modernization" program.

A nationwide teachers' strike, the longest such strike in Ecuador's history, grew into a major battle in the war between the president and labor. It began October 4, 1993, and ended December 4, and was provoked when Durán-Ballén pushed through Congress changes in the code governing teachers' salary scale and school administration. The strike became a battle of wills; it ended after Congress passed a new package of changes that restored the status quo and assured the National Educators' Union's participation in school policymaking and Durán-Ballén promised not to veto the changes. The union declared that the strike was a turning point in the grassroots struggle against "the IMF-dictated policies that [the government] is implementing."

Another front in Ecuador's social wars opened when a band of Huaorani Indians, who live deep in the Ecuadorian Amazon, traveled to Quito in October 1993 to protest the intrusion of oil companies into their territory. The October protest was aimed at halting the construction of a highway by the Dallas-based company Maxus that would run through the heart of the Huaorani reserves. The Indians complained that the road would bring in thousands of settlers and land speculators, leading to deforestation, loss of animal and plant species, and destruction of the Indian economy and way of life.

President Durán-Ballén met with the Huaorani but made no promises. By the admission of the state oil company (Petroecuador), since 1972, when Ecuador began oil production in large quantities, pipeline failures have dumped 450,000 barrels of oil into the Amazon forest. The polluting process continues; in 1992, reports a 1993 "Letter from the Amazon" in *The New Yorker*, "a spill filled the Napo [River] with a slick that stretched from bank to bank for forty miles." The Huaorani, wrote reporter Joe Kane, "were trapped in the path of an American juggernaut, their fate bound up with a culture whose thirst for oil was second to none." "It is likely," Kane noted sardonically, "that the Huaorani will be wiped out for the sake of enough oil to meet United States energy needs for thirteen days."

The Huaorani have promised to use force if necessary to prevent construction of the highway. In 1993 other Ecuadorian Indian groups filed a billion-dollar class action suit in New York against the Texaco oil conglomerate over massive environmental devastation of the Oriente rain forest. According to the suit, Texaco knowingly dumped millions of gallons of crude oil into open pits and lakes in the region at the rate of 3,000 gallons a day for twenty years. A Harvard University study confirmed that most residents of the area suffered severe health problems as a result of the dumping. The originality of the suit consisted in the fact that these Indians have taken their case to the home of the accused multinational.

To add to Durán-Ballén's troubles, his government was soundly trounced in midterm legislative elections on May 1, 1994. Since taking office, his popularity has declined from more than 70 percent to less than 10 percent because of his neoliberal economic policies, claimed by critics to have led to a drop of more than 50 percent in Ecuador's standard of living. The election results added to Durán-Ballén's problems in implementing the privatization program he had set as his principal goal before presidential elections in 1996.

Peru's "Ambiguous Revolution"

A revolution of a unique kind began in Peru in October 1968. Developments in that country between 1968 and 1975 exposed the fallacy of the common assumption that the Latin American military constitutes one reactionary mass. Moving with greater speed and vigor than any civilian reformist regime in Latin American history, a military junta headed by General Juan Velasco Alvarado decreed the nationalization of key industries and natural resources, a land reform that transferred great estates to peasant and worker cooperatives, and the creation of novel new forms of economic organization that should be "neither capitalist nor communist." In 1975 the Peruvian Revolution halted its advance and began a retreat that threatened even its major conquests—the agrarian reform and the great nationalizations—with erosion and even destruction. Yet it must rank among the more serious recent Latin American efforts to achieve a breakthrough in the struggle against backwardness and dependency. Despite its mistakes and failures, it has already made an indelible mark on Peruvian society. The study of those mistakes and failures should help Peruvians as they search for new approaches to the solution of their country's great national problems.

Peru's "ambiguous revolution" poses some intriguing questions. Why should a group of military officers, a class commonly regarded as the staunchest defenders of the old order in Latin America, launch a major attack on that order in Peru? What economic and social interests did the Peruvian military reformers represent? In the last analysis, was the Peruvian Revolution a "bourgeois revolution" designed to promote the rise of an autonomous native capitalism? If the military reformers failed to make a clean break with the past, with the model of dependent development and the problems it generates, what were the reasons for that failure? An attempt to answer these questions requires an examination not only of

the revolution itself but of its remote origins, going back to the establishment of an independent Peru.

Peru: From Independence to the War of the Pacific

The liberation of Peru from Spanish rule came from without, for the creole aristocracy, whose wealth was derived from the forced labor of Indians and black slaves in mines, workshops, and haciendas, rightly feared that revolution might set fire to this combustible social material. The process of Peruvian liberation began when an army of Argentinians and Chileans under General José de San Martín landed on the coast near Lima in 1820 and occupied the capital. It ended when Bolívar's lieutenant, General Antonio José de Sucre, at the head of a mainly Colombian army, accepted the surrender of José de la Serna, the last Spanish viceroy on the South American continent, on the field of Ayacucho in December 1824.

The liberators, San Martín and Bolívar, attempted to reform the social and economic institutions of the newly created Peruvian state. San Martín decreed a ban on slave importation, the automatic emancipation of all children born of slaves in Peru, and the abolition of Indian tribute, the mita, and all other kinds of Indian forced labor; he also proclaimed that all inhabitants of Peru, whether Indians or creoles, were Peruvians. Since these reforms did not conform to the interests of the creole elite, they were never implemented. When Bolívar assumed power in Peru in 1823, he enacted reforms reflecting the same liberal ideology. Wishing to create a class of independent small-holders, he decreed the dissolution of the Indian communities and ordered the division of the communal lands into parcels of land; each family was to hold its plot as private property, with the surplus to become part of the public domain. While attacking communal property, Bolívar left alone feudal property, the great haciendas serviced by yanaconas, or colonos (Indian sharecroppers or serfs) who had to pay their

390 landlords a rent that amounted to as much as 50 to 90 percent of the value of their crops, in addition to *pongueaje* (free personal service).

The well-intentioned Bolivarian land reform played into the hands of hacendados, public officials, and merchants, who took advantage of Indian weakness and ignorance to build up vast estates at the expense of Indian communal lands; the process began slowly but gathered momentum as the century advanced. Bolívar's efforts to abolish Indian tribute had no greater success. After he left Peru in 1826, the Peruvian government reinstituted the tribute for the Indians of the sierra under the name *contribución de indígenas,* and for good measure reintroduced the *contribución de castas* for the mestizo population of the coast.

The heavy dependence of the new government on Indian tribute as a source of revenue reflected the stagnant condition of the Peruvian economy. The revolution completed the ruin of the mining industry and coastal plantation agriculture, both declining since the close of the eighteenth century, and the scanty volume of exports could not pay for the much greater volume of imports of manufactured goods from Britain. As a result, the new state, already burdened with large wartime debts to English capitalists, developed a massive deficit in trade with Great Britain, its largest trading partner. There was some growth of export of wool after 1836, and in 1840 a new economic era opened on the coast with the beginnings of exploitation of guano, but in its first stage the guano cycle failed to provide the capital accumulation needed to revive the coastal agriculture.

The Military Caudillos

The backward, stagnant state of the Peruvian economy, the profound cleavage between the sierra and the coast, and the absence of a governing class (such as arose in Chile) capable of giving firm and intelligent leadership to the state produced chronic political turbulence and civil wars. Under these conditions, military caudillos, sometimes men of plebeian origin who had risen from the ranks during the wars of independence, came to play a decisive role in the political life of the new state. Some were more than selfish careerists or instruments of aristocratic creole cliques. The ablest and most enlightened of the military caudillos was the mestizo general Ramón Castilla, who served as president of Peru from 1845 to 1851 and again from 1855 to 1862. Castilla presided over an advance of the Peruvian economy based on the rapid growth of guano exports. This export trade was dominated by British capitalists who obtained the right to sell guano to specified regions of the world in return for loans to the Peruvian government (secured by guano shipments). Exorbitant interest and commission rates swelled their profits. Although Castilla gave some thought to direct government exploitation of some guano deposits, to setting controls over the amount and price of guano to be sold, and to plowing guano revenues into development projects, he did nothing to implement these ideas. The guano boom, however, stimulated some growth of native Peruvian commerce and banking and created the nucleus of a national capitalist class. Guano prosperity also financed the beginnings of a modern infrastructure; thus, in 1851 the first railway line began to operate between Lima and its port of Callao.

The rise of guano revenues enabled Castilla to carry out a series of social reforms that also contributed to the process of modernization. In 1854 he abolished the Indian tribute, relieving the natives of a heavy fiscal burden, and that same year he freed the remaining black slaves, numbering some twenty thousand, with compensation to the owners of up to 40 percent of their value. Abolition had an initial disruptive effect on coastal agriculture, but in the long run it was very advantageous to the planter aristocracy. With the indemnities for their freed slaves, planters could buy seeds, plants, and Chinese coolies brought to Peru on a contract basis that made them virtual slaves. Meanwhile, the freed slaves often became sharecroppers who lived on the margins of the hacienda and supplied a convenient unpaid labor force and a source of rent. Stimulated by these developments, cotton, sugar cane, and grain production expanded on the coast. Highland economic life also quickened, though on a smaller scale, with the rise of extensive cattle breeding for the export of wool and leather through Arequipa and Lima.

The general upward movement of the Peruvian economy after 1850 was aided by such favorable factors as the temporary dislocation of the cotton industry of the southern United States and large inflows of foreign capital. As a result, exports of cotton and sugar increased sharply. The coastal latifundia continued to expand at the expense of sharecroppers and tenants, who were expelled from their lands, and of the remaining Indian communal lands. This process was accompanied by the modernization of coastal agriculture by the introduction of cotton gins, boilers, refinery equipment for sugar, and steam-driven tractors.

While profits from the agricultural sector enabled the commercial and landed aristocracy of Lima to live in luxury, the Peruvian state sank even deeper into debt. The guano deposits, Peru's collateral for its foreign borrowings, were being depleted at an ever-accelerating rate, and the bulk of the proceeds from these loans went to pay interest on old and new debts. In 1868, during the administration of the military caudillo José Balta, his minister of the treasury, Nicolás de Piérola, devised a plan for extricating Peru from its difficulties and providing funds for development. The project eliminated the numerous consignees to whom guano had been sold and awarded a monopoly of guano sales in Europe to the French firm of Dreyfus and Company. In return, the Dreyfus firm agreed to make Peru a loan that would tide it over immediate difficulties and in addition to service its foreign debt. The contract initiated a new flow of loans that helped to create a boundless euphoria, an invincible optimism, about the country's future.

U.S. adventurer and entrepreneur Henry Meiggs, who had made a reputation as a railway builder in Chile, easily convinced Balta and Piérola that they should support the construction of a railway system to tap the mineral wealth of the sierra. As a result, much of the money obtained under the Dreyfus contract, and a large part of the proceeds of the dwindling guano reserves, were poured into railway projects that could not show a profit in the foreseeable future.

Pardo and the Civilianist Party

The good fortune of Dreyfus and Company displeased the native commercial and banking bourgeoisie that had arisen in Lima. A group of these men—including former guano consignees who had been eliminated by the Dreyfus contracts—headed by the millionaire businessman Manuel Pardo, challenged the legality of the contract before the Supreme Court, arguing that assignment of guano sales to a corporation of native consignees that they proposed to form would be more beneficial to Peru's economic development. The native bourgeoisie suffered defeat, but in 1871 they organized the *Civilista,* or Civilianist party (in reference to their opposition to military caudillos), which ran Manuel Pardo as its candidate for president. An amalgam of "an old aristocracy and a newly emerging capitalist class," the Civilianist party opposed clerical and military influence in politics and advocated a large directing role for the state in economic development. Pardo won handily over two rivals and took office in 1872.

Pardo presided over a continuing agricultural boom, with exports reaching a peak in 1876. Foreign capital poured into the country. In those years, an Irish immigrant, W. R. Grace, began to establish an industrial empire that included textile mills, a shipping line, vast sugar estates, and Peru's first large-scale sugar-refining plants. While private industry prospered, the government sank ever deeper into a quagmire of debts and deficits. The guano cycle was nearing its end, with revenues steadily declining as a result of falling prices, depletion of guano beds, and competition from an important new source of fertilizer, nitrates, being exploited by Anglo-Chilean capitalists in the southern Peruvian province of Tarapacá. In 1875, wishing to control the nitrate industry and make it a dependable source of government income, Pardo expropriated the foreign companies in Tarapacá and established a state monopoly over the production and sale of nitrates. This measure angered the Anglo-Chilean entrepreneurs whose holdings had been nationalized and who were indemnified with bonds of dubious value. Meanwhile, due to unsatisfactory

Chapter 17

The Cuban Revolution

In 1959 the island of Cuba—ninety miles from Key West, permeated by North American capital and culture, and long ruled by one of the region's most firmly entrenched dictatorships—became the scene of perhaps the first and certainly the most successful social revolution in Latin America during the twentieth century. Under the banner of Marxism and with the military, economic, and political support of the Soviet Union, until recently the government led by Fidel Castro made great progress toward the elimination of such problems as illiteracy, mass unemployment, and unequal distribution of income and wealth. But the collapse of the Soviet Union and Cuba's other trading partners in the socialist bloc, combined with an intensified effort by the United States to bring about its downfall, produced the most serious crisis in socialist Cuba's history, a crisis that it is now struggling to overcome.

Cuba under Spanish Rule

Cuba's development differed markedly from that of most other Latin American countries. For three centuries after its discovery by Christopher Columbus in 1492, the island served primarily as a strategic stopover for the Spanish treasure fleet. Without precious metals or a large indigenous population to exploit, Cuba remained a neglected, sparsely populated outpost of the empire. The island's inhabitants engaged, for the most part, in small-scale farming for domestic consumption. Unlike the other sugar-producing islands of the Caribbean, at the end of the seventeenth century, Cuba had few slaves (its colored population of 40,000 was only one-tenth that of Haiti), many of whom worked in nonagricultural occupations, often as skilled craftsmen.

Economic and Social Change

The second half of the eighteenth century, however, brought profound economic and social change. Spurred by the short-lived British occupation of Havana in 1762 and further stimulated by United States independence in 1783, the island experienced a commercial awakening. Most important, Cuba developed into a major sugar producer and slave importer in the aftermath of the Haitian Revolution of the 1790s, which ruined that island as a sugar producer. During the next half-century, sugar production in Cuba skyrocketed, and nearly 600,000 African slaves arrived on its shores. From 1774 to 1861, the island's population leaped from 171,620 to 1,396,530. Havana and Santiago de Cuba became large, busy urban centers and ports, and no fewer than eight other cities attained populations exceeding 10,000.

The expansion and diversification of trade and the introduction of large-scale sugar production created a fantastic economic boom and delayed the development of the spirit of rebellion against Spanish rule that swept the rest of Spanish America. Cuba stayed loyal to Spain during the Spanish-American wars of independence, for its creole leaders saw no reason to tamper with their new-found prosperity. Discontent grew among the slaves and free blacks, however, as a result of tensions caused by the rise of an increasingly harsh plantation system; major slave rebellions, led by free blacks, erupted in 1810, 1812, and 1844. Meanwhile, the wealthy creoles became increasingly resentful of the arbitrary ways of the corrupt Spanish officialdom, which was determined to enforce continued obedience by Spain's last and richest colony in the New World.

As the colony grew increasingly dissatisfied with repressive Spanish rule, it became less dependent economically on the mother country. By 1776 the British colonies already provided one-third of the island's imports and purchased about one-half of its exports; after the United States achieved independence, Cuba turned more and more toward it as a market for its products and a source of needed imports. As a result of these growing economic ties, schemes for the annexation of Cuba to the United States emerged both in the island and in some North American circles. In Cuba, conservative creole planters saw in annexation an insurance policy against the abolition of slavery; in the United States, some proslavery groups regarded annexation as a means of gaining a vast new area for the expansion of plantation slavery. Some of these groups even dreamed of carving Cuba up into three or five states that would give the South increased power in the national government. The Civil War put an end to these projects.

During the 1860s, creole discontent grew, heightened by a developing national and class consciousness. The creole elite rejected various reform proposals offered by a weak Spanish government that was battered by internal dissension and economic difficulties. It became increasingly clear to the creoles that Spanish economic and political policies were severely restricting Cuban development—a feeling sharpened by a serious economic downturn in the 1860s. On October 10, 1868, in the small town of Yara in Oriente Province, a group of landowners proclaimed Cuban independence and initiated a struggle that was to continue for ten years.

The Ten Years' War

The Ten Years' War, a long, bitter, devastating guerrilla struggle, ended in 1878, when the Cubans accepted a peace that granted them some concessions but withheld independence. The Pact of Zanjón ended hostilities, but some rebel leaders, like the black revolutionary Antonio Maceo, the "Bronze Titan," rejected the settlement because it did not achieve the main goals of the revolution—independence and the abolition of slavery. Ironically, the Spanish government, hoping to win the loyalty of the black population, abolished slavery in 1880, with provision for an eight-year patronato, or period of apprenticeship for the liberated slaves. The abolition of slavery removed the last major factor tending to keep creole planters loyal to Spain. Thereafter, the prospect of independence, offering free,

412 unlimited trade with the United States, became increasingly attractive.

The Ten Years' War had a far-reaching impact on the development of Cuban society. It decimated the creole landowning class, hindering the formation of a traditional Latin American landed elite on the island. Entrepreneurs from the United States came to fill the vacuum created by the ruin of the creole aristocracy and the bankruptcy of Spanish interests by the war. Thousands of North Americans accompanied their investment dollars to the island to run the sugar mills and merchant houses. The McKinley Tariff Act of 1890, which abolished import duties on raw sugar and molasses, greatly increased American trade with and economic influence in Cuba; by 1896, U.S. interests had invested $50 million in Cuba and controlled the sugar industry. The United States purchased 87 percent of Cuba's exports. The growth of United States investment in Cuba also brought about an increasing concentration of sugar production, a trend signaled by the entry of the "Sugar Trust" (the American Sugar Refining Company of Henry Q. Havemeyer) into the island in 1888.

José Martí, father of Cuban independence and a brilliant writer and thinker, is a towering figure in Latin American history.

Independence and the Spanish-Cuban-American War

The Revolutionary Movement

By the early 1890s, the movement for independence had revived, partly as a result of a worldwide depression that struck heavy blows at the Cuban economy. The spiritual, intellectual, and organizational leader of the revolutionary movement was José Martí (1853–1895). As a lad of sixteen, Martí was arrested on a charge of supporting the 1868 revolt and sentenced to six years in prison at hard labor, but in 1871 he was sent into exile. In 1880, Martí came to New York, his home for the next fourteen years. In the United States, he earned his living in brilliant journalistic and literary activity that won him fame throughout Latin America.

Meanwhile, Martí worked tirelessly to establish and unite Cuban émigré revolutionary groups. In 1892 he founded *El Partido Revolucionario Cubano* (the Cuban Revolutionary party), which proposed to obtain, "with the united effort of all men of good will, the absolute independence of the island of Cuba, and to foment and aid that of Puerto Rico." He then set about recruiting such military veterans of 1868 as Máximo Gómez and Antonio Maceo, in preparation for an invasion of the island. In April 1895 Martí himself landed on a Cuban beach with a group of insurgents; a little more than a month later, he was killed in a skirmish with a Spanish patrol.

Despite the loss of its ablest, most charismatic leader, the revolution spread and achieved major successes with the aid of time-proven guerrilla

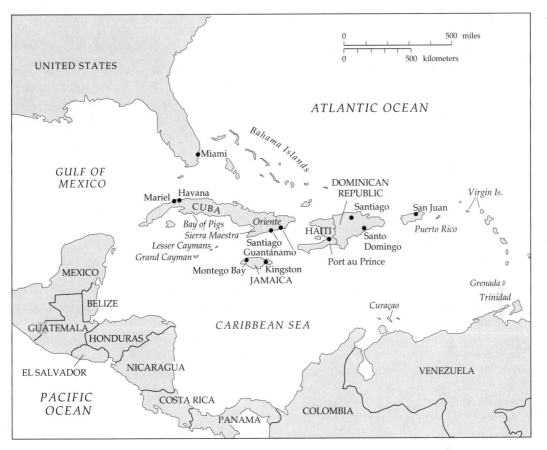

MODERN CARIBBEAN NATIONS

tactics. At the beginning of 1896, a new Spanish commander, General Valeriano Weyler, instituted counterinsurgency measures of the type that would later be employed against twentieth-century rebels in the Philippines, Algeria, and Vietnam. He set up population concentration centers and free-fire zones, which resulted in enormous hardships and losses to the peasantry. But his successes were transient and counterproductive, serving mostly to intensify popular hatred for Spanish rule, and whole provinces remained under the absolute control of the liberating army. The failure of Weyler's military policies and growing pressure from the United States led Spain to make a promise of autonomy to Cuba in late 1897.

Involvement by the United States

As the rebellion spread over the land, it became an increasingly volatile issue in the United States. Inevitably, property was destroyed or damaged in the fighting, and this brought complaints from powerful U.S. businessmen and financiers with interests in Cuba. In addition, the Cuban struggle for independence struck a sympathetic chord with the American people, particularly among the working class. William Randolph Hearst and Joseph Pulitzer, then engaged in a newspaper circulation war in New York City, helped to keep popular interest high by running lurid stories of Spanish brutality.

Meanwhile, within the McKinley administration as well as among enthusiastic expansionists like

414 Theodore Roosevelt there was a growing feeling that the Cuban situation was getting out of control, that the autonomy proposal sponsored by the United States was failing, and that if the United States did not intervene an unmanageable Cuban revolutionary government might take over from the collapsing Spanish regime. In the midst of this ferment, the U.S.S. *Maine* blew up in Havana Harbor on February 15, 1898, with a heavy loss of life. This incident helped spur McKinley to a more belligerent stance; he demanded that Spain terminate the concentration camp policy, offer an armistice to the rebels, and accept the United States as a final arbiter between the parties. There was no mention of Cuban independence. When Spain delayed its response to U.S. demands, McKinley sent a message to Congress asking it to authorize military intervention by the United States in Cuba. Congress, after considerable debate, adopted a joint resolution to that effect. It should be noted in passing that almost every major Cuban revolutionary figure—Martí, Maceo, Gómez—opposed American entry into the war, fearing that it would result in direct or indirect U.S. political and economic control of Cuba. All they sought from the United States was recognition of Cuban belligerency and the right to purchase arms in the United States.

The ensuing war was short and nasty. United States commanders ignored their Cuban counterparts, excluding Cuban generals from decision making and relegating Cuban soldiers to sentry and cleanup duties. Incompetence was the key feature of both Spanish and American war efforts. United States military actions were ill prepared and badly led. Thus, in a bizarre little war, the United States Army—wretchedly led, scandalously provisioned, and ravaged by tropical disease—swiftly defeated a demoralized, dispirited Spanish army and snatched the fruits of victory from the *mambises,* the Cuban guerrilla fighters who had fought gallantly in a struggle of three years' duration. The exclusion of Cuban leaders from both war councils and peace negotiations foreshadowed the course of Cuban-American relations for the next sixty years.

The First United States Occupation, 1899–1902

The United States Army occupied Cuba from January 1899 to May 1902. The occupation had three basic goals. First, the United States sought to make Cuba into a self-governing protectorate, an arrangement designed to achieve political stability without the administrative burdens and costs of an outright colonial occupation. To this end, the American military sought to pacify the island without serious conflict with the Cuban army, which was still intact and in control of much of rural Cuba. The revolutionary army, however, did not resist the American takeover, as did Emilio Aguinaldo and his insurgent forces in the Philippines at the same time. Cuban passivity in part reflected the fact that the years of struggle had taken their toll—the leading Cuban generals, such as Calixto García and Máximo Gómez, were tired old men, and many of the younger men who could have led a resistance movement had died in battle. In addition, the Americans bought off the army by offering to purchase its arms, an offer that hungry, unemployed soldiers found difficult to refuse. They also offered key rebel leaders well-paid positions. At the same time, the occupation government established a Rural Guard, not only to eradicate banditry but, in the words of General Leonard Wood, to put down the "agitators who began to grow restive at the presence of the Americans."

After political stability, necessary to attract American capital, the second major American goal was to repair the destruction wrought by the war and provide the sanitation and other services needed for economic recovery. General Leonard Wood, appointed governor general in 1899, launched a program of public works and sanitation that led to a major achievement of the occupation—the conquest of yellow fever. Taking its lead from a Cuban doctor, Carlos Finlay, whose theory correctly attributed the transmission of the dread disease to the mosquito, the American Sanitary Commission succeeded in eliminating it. Another major accomplishment of the Wood administration was the creation of a Cuban national education system, vastly superior to what had existed under Spain but designed to inculcate American principles; even the textbooks were translations of American textbooks. All these programs and reforms, as well as the expenses of the United States troops, were paid for from the Cuban treasury.

Ruling with arbitrary methods and largely ignoring the former revolutionaries in favor of Spaniards and conservative planters who had opposed independence, Wood presided over the election of a convention to frame a constitution for Cuba. The convention, elected in June 1899, began its work in November and after several months of bitter debate adopted a document that, under intense American pressure, included the so-called Platt Amendment. This amendment limited the ability of independent Cuba to conduct foreign policy and to borrow money abroad, gave the United States the right to maintain a naval base at Guantánamo Bay and, most important, gave the United States the right to intervene in Cuba for the "preservation of Cuban independence" and for the "maintenance of a government adequate for the protection of life, property, and individual liberty."

The third goal of the occupation was to absorb Cuba into the economic sphere of influence of the United States. Since the Platt Amendment assured American businessmen of protection and a generally favorable investment climate on the island, capital poured into sugar and railroad construction. A reciprocal trade agreement signed by the two nations in 1903 was the final step in bringing Cuba under American hegemony. This treaty cut by 20 percent the tariff on Cuban sugar exported to the United States; in return, Cuba reduced the duties on imported American goods.

The Politics of Corruption, 1902–1953

Instability and Intervention, 1902–1924

Cuba's political life, afflicted by its status as a United States protectorate and suffering from in-

terventions, had a weak and stunted growth. At the end of 1901, Tomás Estrada Palma was elected the first president of Cuba, and the Americans left the following May. Although he had not lived in Cuba for twenty-five years, Estrada, who headed the Cuban government-in-exile after the Ten Years' War, began his presidency with considerable popularity. However, his administration produced only scandals.

The 1904 elections to Congress were fraudulent and marked by sporadic violence. Local government was even more turbulent and corruption-ridden. The Estrada presidency established the pattern of Cuban politics for the next fifty years.

In 1905, Estrada, with his adherents in control of the electoral machinery and the opposition boycotting the election, ran for re-election and won. In the summer of 1906, the Liberal party, led by José Miguel Gómez, rose in revolt against the Estrada regime. Unable to suppress the rebellion, the president called for American intervention and left Cuba.

President William Howard Taft responded by sending in the marines, and shortly afterward appointed Charles Magoon, a judge from Minnesota, to preside over an American provisional government. Magoon's solution for the problem of factional violence was to divide the patronage among contending Cuban groups. During the second occupation, Cuban resistance to American domination virtually disappeared. The decline of national consciousness and protest against foreign control was due in large part to the workings of the system of institutionalized corruption, which united all sections of the elite in the eager pursuit of American favor and protection.

In 1920, Alfredo Zayas, a former Liberal who had participated in the unsuccessful revolt of 1917, won the presidency with Conservative support. Troubled over the crash of sugar prices in the second half of 1920 and the resulting political unrest in Cuba, President Warren Harding sent General Enoch Crowder to Cuba in January 1921 as his special representative. In effect, Crowder ruled Cuba from his headquarters on board the battleship *Minnesota* until 1923, when he became United States ambassador.

The sad pattern of corruption dominated Cuban politics from 1902 to 1924. Control of graft and patronage was the goal of all factions; party labels meant nothing. Four times during this period, the losers of presidential elections staged or threatened revolts, alleging fraud (with good reason). In each instance, and in 1912 when there was a minor black rebellion in Oriente Province, United States troops landed to restore order and prevent property damage.

In the last two years of the Zayas administration, Cuban nationalism revived. Crowder's blatant meddling in Cuban politics and the postwar collapse of Cuban sugar revealed the disastrous consequences of foreign domination and monoculture. Searching for solutions for these problems, Cuban university students entered the political arena in the postwar period. Believing that to change society they must change the university, they directed their first attacks against inept and corrupt professors and administrators; in 1922 students at the University of Havana demonstrated for reforms along the lines of the recent university reform in Argentina. Students would henceforth play an important role in Cuban politics until the fall of Batista in 1959.

Machado, 1925–1933

Taking advantage of growing nationalistic sentiment, Gerardo Machado y Morales emerged as the Liberal candidate in the presidential election of 1924. Running against the corruption of Zayas, on a platform of national regeneration, he defeated ex-president Menocal. Despite his nationalistic declarations, Machado had very close links to American economic interests, for he had been until his election vice president of an American-owned utility in Havana. Even before he took office, Machado visited the United States to assure President Calvin Coolidge of his government's good intentions.

Machado began his term auspiciously. He embarked on an ambitious program of public works and attempted to institute a system of controls for sugar production designed to protect small and medium-size producers against severe price declines. Thanks to these and similar efforts, Machado enjoyed unparalleled popularity and faced virtually no opposition for two years.

Already, however, there were disturbing signs of tyranny. The number of political assassinations increased alarmingly. A wave of strikes during 1925 was broken by police shooting down strikers. The nation's most prominent Communist leader, Juan Antonio Mella, was murdered in his Mexican exile by a Machado gunman in 1929. Machado's secret police routinely eliminated his opponents by throwing them to the sharks in Havana Harbor.

Machado secured his re-election in 1928 by the simple expedient of outlawing the party of his main rival, Carlos Mendieta. Until the onset of the world depression in 1930, Machado maintained an iron grip on Cuba, despite mounting opposition from university students, the Communists, labor unions, and many old-line politicians led by Mendieta. The economic crisis had particularly catastrophic consequences for Cuba because of its heavy reliance on exports. Machado responded to the growing political unrest engendered by the economic conditions with increasingly harsh repression. A general strike failed in May 1930. In September, after the killing of a student leader, students at the University of Havana organized a large demonstration, which was followed by the firing of hundreds of teachers and the closing of the university.

In August 1931, Mendieta led a group of old-line politicians in an unsuccessful revolt, a last effort to revive the old strategies and leadership of Cuban politics. Late in 1931, a new secret organization, the ABC, sprang up among young members of the middle class and intellectuals as a moderate alternative to the more radical university students' group, the Student Directory. Machado answered these challenges with tightened censorship and stepped-up terror tactics on the part of his secret police, the *Porra*.

By the beginning of 1933, the United States government had become seriously concerned by the spreading violence, which appeared to threaten U.S. economic interests. In April, incoming President Franklin Roosevelt dispatched

Sumner Welles as ambassador to attempt to negotiate some sort of understanding between Machado and his opponents. For several months, Welles unsuccessfully tried to mediate between Machado and the opposition, but Machado would not compromise, while the opposition was disunited and unable to agree on a course of action.

In the summer, a bus drivers' strike in Havana mushroomed into a general strike that nearly paralyzed the city. After the police massacred several demonstrators in August, Machado's position seriously deteriorated, for he had lost the support of Welles and the army. On August 12, Machado resigned and fled into exile.

The Revolution of 1933

For the next three weeks, a provisional government headed by Carlos Manuel de Cespedes struggled unsuccessfully to end the escalating violence. On September 4, a group of army sergeants, one of whom was Fulgencio Batista, overthrew the government. The Student Directory immediately allied itself with the sergeants, and together they formed a revolutionary junta.

The new junta had no organized political backing, and its two main components, the noncommissioned officers and the Student Directory, had sharply divergent aims. The sergeants were concerned only with defending their newly won dominant position against any challenge, while the students sought genuine reforms but were unsure just how to achieve them. Within a week, the junta turned over the reins of government to Dr. Ramón Grau San Martín, a well-known physician and longtime opponent of Machado. Grau, Antonio Guiteras Holmes, a leader of the Student Directory, and Batista were dominant figures in the new alignment.

The first move of the new government was to abrogate the onerous Platt Amendment. A flurry of decrees produced more social legislation than all the previous history of independent Cuba: an eight-hour day for labor, a labor department, an end to the importation of cheap labor from other islands in the Caribbean, and greater access for children from lower-income groups to the university. There were also measures to redistribute land to peasants, eliminate usury, and give women the vote.

Ultimately, the Grau government was caught in the classic bind of the reformer: the left was dissatisfied because the reforms were not of sufficient scope, and the right opposed all reform. Grau also alienated American financial and agricultural interests when he suspended repayment of several loans owed to the Chase National Bank of New York and seized two mills of the Cuban-American Sugar Company. The United States government adamantly refused to recognize the Grau government.

The revolutionary coalition disintegrated. The ABC would not cooperate with Grau because his program had become too radical. He had earlier lost the support of the more radical elements of the Student Directory, and the Communists attacked him as a "petty bourgeois."

The behavior of Sumner Welles throughout the Grau interregnum was extraordinarily similar to the conduct of U.S. Ambassador Henry Lane Wilson in Mexico during the Madero administration. Welles persistently falsified reports and misrepresented the Cuban government to Secretary of State Cordell Hull and President Roosevelt. As Wilson had befriended Huerta and helped him to power, so Welles allied himself with Batista. Eventually (in November 1933), Welles was recalled, but he had seriously undermined the provisional government. As the economic and political situation worsened, Welles's successor, Jefferson Caffery, maneuvered with Batista to form a new government acceptable to the United States. In January 1934, Grau, unable to rule effectively in the face of American opposition, went into exile and was replaced by Carlos Mendieta.

The Batista Era, 1934–1944

Fulgencio Batista y Zaldivar, the sergeant-stenographer mulatto son of a sugar worker, dominated Cuban politics for the next decade, ruling the island through puppet presidents from 1934 to 1940 and as elected president from 1940 to 1944. Although Batista alienated many of the "respectable" elements of the middle and upper classes, he was extremely popular among the masses. During the first two years after his successful coup, he presided over a mild reform program with some effort at land redistribution. In 1937 he moved leftward and openly courted the support of labor unions and the Communists.

The Auténtico Interlude, 1944–1952

At the end of 1939, Batista permitted the election of a constituent assembly to draft the constitution of 1940. Grau and his Cuban Revolutionary, or *Auténtico* party (founded in 1934) and other moderate parties won the election and produced a liberal document with provisions for the protection of labor and limitations on the right of property when it conflicted with the public good. It was Batista, however, who won the presidential election of 1940.

Choosing to observe the constitutional provision that the president should not succeed himself, Batista, to the general surprise, allowed honest elections to take place in 1944. As a result, Grau defeated Batista's hand-picked choice. Grau, who earlier had been the symbol of Cuban regeneration and democracy, presided over an unparalleled reign of corruption. Violence accompanied the corruption, and the University of Havana became a nest of political gangsterism. True, the Grau government initiated some minor reforms, but it made no attack on such key problems as agrarian reform and monoculture.

In 1947 a charismatic populist leader, Eddie Chibás, launched a new campaign against government oppression and corruption. A former ardent supporter of the Auténticos, Chibás had become disillusioned and formed his own Cuban People's, or *Ortodoxo,* party, which featured a mild program of social reform and clean politics, in the spring of 1947. Extremely popular, he posed a serious threat to the Auténticos. In 1948, Chibás opposed the Auténtico presidential candidate, Carlos Prío Socorrás, former leader of the Student Directory. Prío, who won easily because he controlled the election machinery and had the advantage of four years of economic prosperity, became another in a long line of Cuban country club presidents. He spent much of his time serving his guests daiquiris at his opulent farm in the suburbs of Havana. There was no letup in the corruption, gangsterism, and spoils system characteristic of his predecessor's regime. As under Grau, the prosperity brought on by high sugar prices concealed the mismanagement of the Prío administration.

Chibás was the leading candidate for the presidency for the upcoming election when Batista reappeared in Cuba after a long retirement to announce that he would be a candidate for president in 1952. Cuban politics were thrown into complete disarray when Chibás, in an apparent effort to awake the Cuban public to the extent of political corruption, killed himself on a nationwide radio broadcast in August 1951. In any event, in March 1952, before the election could take place, Batista headed a conspiracy of low-ranking army officers that overthrew Prío. Thoroughly disillusioned with politics, the Cuban people offered little protest.

The Return of Batista as Dictator, 1952–1959

Batista ruled Cuba for the second time until he was overthrown by Fidel Castro in 1959. Like his contemporaries, Carlos Ibañez in Chile, Getúlio Vargas in Brazil, and Juan Perón in Argentina, Batista found the second time around more difficult than the first. A new generation of revolutionaries rose to replace the discredited leaders of 1933. Unlike Grau or Prío, they would not be bought off or collaborate with the dictator. Several groups opposed Batista, including the Auténticos, who plotted from their havens in Florida; the 26th of July Movement led by Fidel Castro, which unsuccessfully tried to overthrow the government in 1953 by assaulting the Moncada army barracks; and the Federation of University Students (FEU). Despite the activities of the students and Castro's guerrilla group, the dictator seemed to be firmly entrenched. The instability and corruption of the Cuban political system was matched in its ill effects by the structural weakness of the economy, produced by reliance on a single crop, sugar.

The Export Economy: Sugar as King

Cuba is a classic case of monoculture—a nation dependent on the production and export of a single crop for its economic livelihood. Like the other Latin American nations we have examined (Argentina, Brazil, Chile, and Mexico), Cuba has suffered from the cyclical nature of world market demand for its product. Moreover, Cuba suffered the additional burden of almost total economic domination by the United States.

The Early History of Sugar

The Cuban sugar industry dates from the early 1790s, when revolution wrecked the sugar production of Haiti, then the world's leading sugar exporter. At the same time, the United States won its independence from Great Britain, thereby furnishing a ready nearby market for Cuban sugar. Cuban agriculturalists took advantage of their opportunity to shift to sugar and to import cheap slave labor from Africa.

Initially, the transfer to sugar did not stimulate the creation of the latifundio; first, because much of the land converted to sugar was the underused acreage of large cattle haciendas, and second, because many farmers did not change over to sugar, preferring instead to produce coffee and tobacco, which then enjoyed high prices resulting from the abolition of the royal monopoly on these commodities. Furthermore, the sugar mills themselves stimulated demand for livestock (to turn the mills) and food crops for the slaves. During the first decades of the nineteenth century, the number of farm proprietors increased markedly, and from their ranks came the leaders of Cuban society for the next century.

The boom that followed the destruction of Haitian sugar production ended by the turn of the century because other Caribbean islands expanded and initiated production in response to the same stimuli, thereby creating an enormous glut on the market. Just as the industry recovered from this setback, diplomatic maneuvering during the Napoleonic wars closed U.S. ports. Shortly thereafter, two new challenges to the Cuban economy arose: the introduction of beet sugar in Europe and the British campaign to end the slave trade. (England forced Spain to end the trade in 1821.) Further impediments resulted from the restrictions imposed by Spanish hegemony: high tariffs, scarce and expensive credit, and the disruptions brought on by the Spanish-American wars of independence.

By 1820 the first of a series of technological innovations began to transform the character of the sugar industry in Cuba. Mill owners had to invest heavily in steam-operated machinery in order to compete with beet sugar. Modern machinery allowed the mills to expand in size, but they could do so only gradually because of the limited transportation facilities that were available. Since railroads were enormously expensive, and in any case there was not sufficient capital on the island or in Spain for large projects of this type, they did not become important until much later.[1] The mills also carried a huge overhead because they were largely unused during the off season. Slaves and livestock had to be fed and sheltered even when the harvest was completed. The problem of fuel for the mills also slowed their expansion. The forests close to the mills were quickly consumed, and transport of wood to the mills proved prohibitively costly. As a result, sugar production was expanded in the first half of the century by increasing the number of mills. In 1827 there were 1,000 mills, by 1846 there were 1,442, and by 1860 there were 2,000.

The Development of the Latifundio

Large plantations developed in Cuba in response to the necessity of building bigger and bigger mills (*centrales*). Sugar technology was continually improving, and Cuban mills had to expend huge sums to remain competitive. The larger the mill the more sugar it could process, the more fuel it consumed, and the more employees it needed. Smaller and less efficient mills were at a severe competitive disadvantage.

Sugar production was set up in one of two ways: the land might be cultivated by resident or temporary labor, or the land might be parceled

[1] The first railroad in Cuba was built in 1836.

Cutting sugar cane, Cuba, 1920. The end of Spanish rule in 1898 and the onset of the American occupation hastened the transformation of the island into a "large sugar plantation producing sugar for the benefit of foreign customers."

out to farmers, known as *colonos,* who would work the land for a salary or a share of the crop. The landowners, in either situation, might or might not also be the mill owners. As the number of mills grew smaller, the colonos became the main suppliers of sugar to the mills. They planted and harvested the cane and brought it to the mill to be processed. They paid for the processing in sugar. By the 1870s, production was specialized into these components, colonos and centrales. The number of large plantations did not increase; instead, the number of colonos gradually rose.

The shake-out of mills during the war, the financial crisis of 1885–1890, and the expansion of the island's railroad network combined to stimulate the spread of the latifundio. As the mills grew, they required more cane and sought it over a wider geographic area than previously. At the same time, the introduction of cheap rails spurred railroad construction in Cuba (and all over the world). In their quest for more cane,

centrales began to lay their own track in an effort to draw it from a greater area. Competition between centrales for cane, a condition previously unknown because of transportation limitations, resulted.

The centrales confronted the necessity of guaranteeing enough cane at the lowest possible prices for the *zafra* (harvest). They could do this either by reducing the independence of the colonos or by acquiring their own cane land. The first method transformed the once-free farmers into satellites of the giant mills. The second led to the creation of latifundia. Small and medium-size growers fell by the way, to be replaced by tenants or day labor. The colonos managed to hold their own until independence, after which time the massive influx of foreign capital into the sugar mills overwhelmed them. With their lesser financial resources, they were doomed.

The end of Spanish rule and the American occupation removed the final obstacles to the development of the latifundio in Cuba. The island, at peace at last, could repair the damage done by forty years of guerrilla warfare. The United States military and the new Cuban Rural Guard would prevent new revolutionary outbreaks, and the Platt Amendment guaranteed a favorable climate for investment. The elimination of yellow fever allowed foreigners to live on the island without fear for their health. The successive occupation governments and their Cuban successors furnished subsidies and other inducements for railroad construction and utilities. At a time when antitrust laws began to restrict industry in the United States, Cuba had no such inhibitions. Finally, Cuban sugar was an attractive investment because the United States was a close and growing market in which it had a competitive advantage because of the reciprocal trade treaty of 1903, which cut the tariff on Cuban sugar by 20 percent.

Two processes worked hand in hand in the following decades: the concentration of land and mills and the proletarianization of the sugar workers. The two wars of independence had devastated small mills: the total number fell from 2,000 in 1860 to 1,000 in 1877 to only 200 in 1899. The rapid and huge influx of foreign—mostly American—investment into sugar enabled the larger mills to buy up surrounding cane land. The colono was reduced to circumstances close to slavery. Ramiro Guerra y Sánchez has estimated that the great mills owned perhaps 20 percent of the island's area in 1927.

The expansion of the latifundio impoverished the rural masses of the island. The colonos were kept at subsistence levels, deeply indebted to the mill and in constant fear of eviction. The wages of rural workers were kept low because the mills imported cheap labor from other Caribbean islands. As a result, a considerable reserve pool of labor was available; even those lucky enough to get work worked only four months of the year during the harvest period. Displaced farmers had two choices. They could remain and work for small wages on a seasonal basis for the centrales, or they could emigrate to the cities, where jobs were also scarce. Small independent growers

were at a severe disadvantage, for the mills squeezed the price paid for their cane to a minimum. In addition, the mills controlled the transportation network.

The ruin of the small mills and farmers and the low wages paid rural labor, which reduced the purchasing power of the masses, sharply limited the domestic market for manufactured goods and commercial services. There was thus little Cuban industrialization. Sugar companies monopolized the railroads and operated them solely for their own benefit, often without regard to the public interest. Although Cuba's railroad network exceeded that of most Latin American nations, it was inadequate to develop an internal market.

American companies poured money into Cuban sugar during the first occupation. By 1913 Americans had invested $200 million in Cuba, predominantly in sugar. This accounted for nearly one-fifth the total U.S. investment in all of Latin America.

World War I and the Dance of the Millions

Cuba's greatest sugar boom and bust occurred as a consequence of World War I. The fighting in Europe, which disrupted sugar production on the Continent, from the first caused large price increases: prices nearly doubled in the first two months alone. Eventually, the Allies became totally dependent on Cuban sugar production, since they were fighting their major former supplier, Austria-Hungary. This demand spurred further expansion of Cuban sugar production, with planters moving into previously uncultivated land. The last great surge of mill construction also occurred. As production spread into virgin land, centrales were built and new towns sprang up.

The Allies attempted to keep commodity prices from skyrocketing by establishing purchasing committees to handle the acquisition of raw materials and food. Nonetheless, Cuban production rose in 1916 to 3 million tons at an average price of 4 cents a pound. Expansion created a severe labor shortage on the island, and laborers were imported from Jamaica and other

430   depersonalize government and make it more responsive to the people, provided for a pyramid of elected bodies. At the bottom were popularly elected members of municipal assemblies, who elected delegates to provincial assemblies and to the National Assembly of People's Power. Most of these representatives were Communist party members. Castro remained entrenched at the top as president of the Council of State (elected from the National Assembly), First Secretary of the Communist Party, and Head of Government. The second congress of the Communist party reaffirmed him in these offices. In 1992 the National Assembly adopted sweeping changes in the constitution and electoral law recommended by the fourth congress of the Communist party. They included strengthening constitutional protection for all religious faiths, amending the constitution to authorize joint venture enterprises with foreign capital, and a new electoral law that provided for direct, secret election by voters of deputies of the National Assembly and provincial assemblies. The first elections under this new law were held in December 1992. More than 97 percent of the eligible voters went to the polls to choose 13,865 members of the municipal councils from over 28,000 candidates, nominated in public assemblies in each precinct. The first direct, competitive elections for deputies of the National Assembly took place in February 1993. They resulted in re-election of 80 percent of the deputies and a lowering of their average age to forty-three—a reflection of the generational change of guard taking place in Cuba, illustrated by the recent appointment of thirty-seven-year-old Roberto Robaina as foreign minister. In another sign of the new political atmosphere, candidates for office no longer need approval by the Communist party, and formal practices borrowed from the former Soviet Union, like the pressure for unanimous votes, have been abandoned as part of the reforms designed to make the National Assembly "a more independent and effective body for legislation, governmental monitoring and oversight, and economic planning."

Political institutionalization has been accompanied by efforts to reorganize and rationalize the economy. Inefficiency and low productivity proved intractable problems and Cuba continued to be heavily dependent on sugar for its economic well-being. From 1976 to 1980 the economic growth rate averaged a disappointing 4 percent a year. At the root of the problem were the lack of professional management, quality control, and labor discipline, all of which added up to poor productivity. Many goods, from shoes to televisions, were poorly manufactured.

Persistent economic problems led to a massive emigration of Cubans, primarily to the United States, from April to September 1980. The so-called Mariel exodus began when Fidel Castro, angered at the Peruvian Embassy's refusal to turn over six Cubans who had taken refuge there, declared that anyone who wanted to leave the island was free to go. He ordered the Cuban guards from the embassy. Within days, 10,000 people crowded into its grounds. Various nations in the region, including the United States, offered to take the refugees. More than 125,000 Cubans left, mostly through the port of Mariel, many aboard dangerously overcrowded, leaky boats. Before drawing certain conclusions from this exodus, it should be remembered that all great political and social upheavals cause similar flights of disaffected people; it is estimated that after the American Revolution 10 percent of the population left for Canada or England rather than live under the new republican rule.

Between 1981 and 1985 Cuba seriously attacked its chronic economic problems and there was a significant quantitative and qualitative improvement of the economy, with an average annual growth rate for the period of 7.6 percent. Export diversification grew in this period, with re-exports of Soviet oil accounting for over 40 percent of Cuba's hard-currency earnings in 1985, but in 1988 this share fell to 17 percent because of lower prices on the world market. The collapse of the Soviet Union and the socialist common market since 1989 deprived Cuba of its major trading partners and dealt a devastating blow to the Cuban economy, resulting in a drop of national income of approximately 45 percent between 1889 and 1992. The crisis was aggra-

The tug boat shown here is filled with more than 800 Cubans headed for Key West. During the "Mariel exodus," more than 125,000 Cubans sought refuge in the United States and other nations in the region.

vated by an intensified effort by the United States to strangle socialist Cuba through passage of the 1992 Torricelli Act, which extends the U.S. trade embargo or boycott against Cuba to U.S. subsidiaries in third countries and bars any ship that docks in Cuba from entering a U.S. port for 180 days. The law drew angry protests from the European Community, which felt the United States had no right to apply its laws extraterritorially. In 1992, 1993, and 1994, the U.N. General Assembly voted by overwhelming majorities to condemn the embargo, and in July 1993 a summit of the leaders of Latin America, Spain, and Portugal unanimously called for an end to the thirty-one-year-old embargo against Cuba. But the Clinton administration, which accepted substantial finan-

cial backing in the 1992 election from a fanatically anti-Castro section of the Cuban-American community, has resisted growing domestic and international pressure for a change in its Cuban policy, which bars even the export of food and medicines to Cuba.

Cuba depends on sugar to as great an extent in the 1990s as at any time in its history. The government has invested heavily in modernizing the industry. Most sugar cane is now harvested by machine—although the recent lack of energy supplies has led to increased use of oxen-drawn tractors—and many new mills have been built. Although the sugar harvests have usually produced over 8 million tons in each year since 1982, in 1992 the harvest fell to a dismal 4.28

432 million tons—the lowest in twenty-five years. The causes ranged from lack of fuel (due to a sharp decline in oil imports from the former Soviet Union) and spare parts to torrential rains. Such shortfalls drastically affect the balance of trade and the foreign exchange earnings that Cuba desperately needs for development and for health care and education. The disappearance of the socialist common market, which provided prices for Cuban sugar that were much higher than prices in the capitalist world market, is a major problem.

Achievements

Despite its mixed economic record, the revolution's achievements in the areas of employment, equitable distribution of income, public health, and education are remarkable. Until the onset of the current economic crisis, which caused many factories to shut down due to lack of fuel, Cuba had the lowest rate of joblessness in Latin America. Workers who have been laid off because of plant closings continue to receive 60 percent of their wages. Inequalities in the standard of living have been dramatically reduced from the days of Batista. The working classes in particular have benefited from government policies; rents are controlled, limited to no more than 10 percent of income, as are rationed food prices (but an open market in farm products exists and is tolerated by the government). Agricultural workers on state farms and cooperatives get furnished houses with televisions and community recreational centers. Cuban city streets have virtually no beggars and sidewalk vendors, which sets them apart from their Latin American counterparts.

The extremely difficult economic situation produced by the collapse of the socialist economic community and the tightened U.S. embargo has reversed the trend of steadily improving social conditions and produced a decline in living standards. Most Cubans today live on a drab diet of white rice and red beans, supplemented by some vegetables and fruit, an occasional chicken, and what they can purchase on the open market. The food rationing system, however, has prevented the emergence of the massive hunger and malnutrition so common in the rest of Latin America. Children continue to be the special objects of the government's solicitude. Children aged seven and under and pregnant women receive a daily distribution of milk. Cuba's infant mortality in 1993, 9.4 per 1,000 live births, was among the lowest in the world and almost equal with that (9.1) of the United States. Despite the recent growth of hardships and resulting slippage in living standards, Cuba continues to lead all other Latin American countries in the quality of life it provides its children. A 1993 study by the United Nations Children's Fund (UNICEF) noted that, among other things, Cuban children have a greater chance at survival, with 12 deaths per 1,000 children up to the age of five. The average for Central America and the Caribbean is forty-seven and for South America fifty-four. The most recent estimate of life expectancy in Cuba, 75.9 years, compares to average life expectancy of 58.2 years in the underdeveloped world. The government provides free medical care and education. Cuba has the lowest doctor-to-patient ratio in Latin America and by 1995 expects to provide comprehensive family practice medical coverage for 100 percent of its population. A recent (1990) study in the *Latin American Research Review* concludes that Cuba "has transformed itself into a world-class health-care provider, an extraordinary achievement." Sophisticated medical procedures now performed in Cuba include heart transplants, heart-lung transplants, and microsurgery. The educational budget amounts to 7 percent of the nation's GNP, the highest in Latin America. The population has an average of a ninth-grade education, and illiteracy has been wiped out. Undoubtedly, most Cubans have benefited from the revolution.

Cuba and the World

From its early years, the Cuban revolutionary government sent military aid to other Third World countries. It helped the Algerian independence movement and guerrilla groups in Zaire, the Portuguese African colonies, and Tanzania during the 1960s. In the same period, facing the bit-

This witty cartoon reminds Americans, who still lack universal health care, that socialist Cuba, against all odds, has transformed itself into a world-class health-care provider.

ter hostility of most Latin American governments, Castro virtually declared war on them (with the exception of Mexico) in the Second Declaration of Havana (1962), vowing to turn the Andes into the Sierra Maestra of South America.

With the murder of Che Guevara and the economic disasters of the late 1960s, Cuba changed course and sought to re-establish normal diplomatic and trade relations with the other governments of the hemisphere. During the 1970s, as the danger of U.S. invasion diminished and the economy improved, Cuba again took an important role in Africa. Eleven thousand Cuban troops assisted Ethiopia in repelling the 1978 invasion of the Ogaden region by Somalia, and fifty thousand Cuban soldiers helped Angolan forces in their four-

teen-year struggle against counterrevolutionary rebels supported by the United States and South Africa and in thwarting a South African invasion of Angola across its southern border. At Cuito Cuanavale, in one of the decisive battles of modern African history, a joint Cuban-Angolan army inflicted a crushing defeat on the South African invaders, which led to the signing of an agreement in 1988 between Angola, Cuba, and South Africa for the mutual withdrawal of Cuban and South African troops and for the independence of Namibia.

Cuba still sponsors what the *New York Times* called "perhaps the largest Peace Corps style program of civilian aid in the world," with some 16,000 doctors, teachers, construction engineers,

434
agronomists, economists, and other specialists serving in twenty-two Third World countries. The Cuban international aid program includes free education in Cuba. In addition to the motive of "international solidarity," Cuban international aid has the objective of providing the country with much-needed hard currency. Fees are charged on the basis of ability to pay, and poor countries receive aid free. Cuba's foreign construction projects have been a major income producer.

Cuba's international relations have steadily expanded in recent years. In 1989 it was elected for a two-year term to the United Nations Security Council by the largest majority ever obtained by a candidate country. Despite past hostilities and rancors, it now maintains good relations with virtually all other Latin American states. In 1994, as in 1993, the annual summit meeting of the Ibero-American heads of state called for the lifting of the U.S. embargo of Cuba. Despite the continuing American trade embargo and other indications of the fixed hostility with which the U.S. government has long regarded Cuba, the Castro regime has persistently sought to normalize its relations with the United States, but its efforts have not been reciprocated. The Guantánamo Naval Base—one of the last vestiges of ninteenth-century-style imperialism—stands as an ever-present reminder of the continuing U.S. military threat to socialist Cuba.

What Lies Ahead?

The chain of events set in motion by Mikhail Gorbachev's launching of *perestroika* (reconstruction) in the Soviet Union—the rapid collapse of Communist-led governments in central and eastern Europe, the dissolution of the Soviet Union itself, and the headlong slide of some of the new democratic regimes toward capitalism—created major political, economic, and ideological problems for Cuba. Castro, speaking on a visit to Brazil in 1990, expressed his profound concern about these developments. Noting that even before perestroika Cuba had begun an effort to improve its own socialism and correct past mistakes in a process of *rectificación* (rectification),

Castro made plain his belief that Gorbachev's reforms had led to a dismantling of socialism in a number of east European countries. According to Castro, these developments and the Soviet Union's striving for peace and good relations with the United States had only encouraged American imperialism. He claimed that the U.S. government interpreted peace as meaning its right to intervene and wage war anywhere in the Third World.

Ideological questions aside, the dramatic changes in eastern Europe have created economic difficulties for Cuba of the kind mentioned above. As part of their transition toward a market economy, some of the eastern European countries with which Cuba has had the bulk of its trade have demanded that that trade be based on international prices and conducted in hard currency. But Cuba needs its limited stock of hard currency to pay interest on its foreign debt and purchase certain vital products from the West. Anticipating increased difficulties with some of its former socialist trading partners, Cuba recently began to diversify its trade links, doubling its trade with China and increasing its trade with Latin America by 20 percent. Despite recent and, it is hoped temporary shortfalls in its sugar harvests, Cuba remains the world's number one sugar exporter and sugar sales comprise about 80 percent of Cuba's exports. Although Cuba has sharp ideological differences with Russia, the main successor state to the former Soviet Union, trade between the two countries, based on the exchange of sugar for oil, continues, but on a greatly reduced scale. Until the end of 1989 Cuba received 13 million tons of oil annually from the Soviet Union; in 1992 oil imports from the former Soviet republics fell to 1.8 million tons. In addition to routine blackouts and factory shutdowns, the resulting energy crunch led to a revival of horse-drawn carriages, the use of oxen-drawn tractors, and wholesale replacement of cars in transport by bicycles—good for the environment and health, but economically inefficient and uncomfortable.

The shortfall in oil dealt a heavy blow to another of Cuba's major hard currency earners, the nickel industry. Currently the industry is limping along, but extraction is predicted to top 80,000 tons by 1996. Cuba holds one-third of the world's reserves of nickel, believed to be good for two hundred years of exploitation. The state-owned nickel company currently trades with twenty-five countries, with 80 percent of exports going to the West.

Cuba has hopes for overcoming its energy crisis through the discovery of large oil reserves off its shoreline. In June 1994 two Canadian firms announced that they had found commercial quantities of oil at wells offshore in Manzanas province. Foreign firms have been eager to engage in other joint ventures in fields ranging from nickel production to a new overseas telephone system and tourism. In June 1994 a Mexican company signed a $1.5 billion deal to rehabilitate Cuba's telephone system. New hotels built by joint ventures with Spanish companies are rapidly springing up on Cuban beachfronts, with the number of foreign tourists topping 500,000 in 1992 and expected to rise to one million annually. Cuba's earnings from tourism were expected to reach $700 million in 1993. The Cuban state views the booming tourist industry, largely segregated from Cuban socialist society but with a clear potential for corrupting that society, as an unhappy necessity.

In addition to promoting such traditional exports as sugar and nickel, and the expansion of tourism, the Castro government has made the development of biotechnology and medical exports an essential part of its economic survival strategy. In the 1980s Havana's center for genetic engineering produced interferon, an important drug in the treatment of cancer. Since then Cuban scientists have gone on to work on a variety of products, including vaccines, most of which are at the forefront of pharmaceutical biotechnology research. Cuban scientists, for example, have developed the best vaccine for meningitis B, and in 1990 Cuba signed a $140 million contract to supply Brazil with the vaccine. Because of the embargo, this vaccine is not available in the United States. If Cuba can find sufficient markets for its biotechnological and medicinal products, the exports could be worth $1 billion a year.

In response to the continuing economic crisis, in 1993 the Cuban government instituted a number of major reforms. Most important is a reorganization of agriculture that replaces large state farms by autonomous cooperatives in land "ceded for an indefinite period by the state." These "Basic Units of Cooperative Production" will operate on a profit-sharing basis and administer their own resources. They will receive from the state credits for purchasing farm equipment, seeds, and other inputs, but must sell their crop to the state once the harvest is in. (In September 1994 this policy was modified to allow farmers to sell in the open market after selling to the government a fixed amount of their harvest.) It is expected that this decentralization of agriculture, appealing to the workers' self-interest, will lead to more efficient use of resources. A second general reform authorizes self-employment in a long list of trades and occupations ranging from carpenters, masons, and plumbers to taxi drivers, barbers, photographers, cooks, and typists. In reality these new rules simply legalize long-existing activities, but they also provide regulatory controls, inspections, and licenses. Finally, in an obvious move to encourage the inflow of dollars through family remittances from the United States, the government announced in July 1993 that it would no longer penalize the holding of foreign currencies and would authorize Cubans to spend U.S. dollars in a network of government stores. The measure would ease the government's cash crisis and put a dent in the flourishing black market, but it has its negative side, dividing Cuban society by creating a privileged class of people with access to U.S. currency.

Cuba has also launched a vast technological experiment in agriculture that it hopes will end dependence on costly foreign agricultural inputs and help solve the current food shortage. In 1994 Cuba was in the third year of the largest conversion of any nation in history from conventional modern agriculture to large-scale organic farming. The "Alternative Model," as the Cubans call it, seeks "to promote ecologically sustainable production by replacing the dependence on heavy farm machinery and chemical inputs with animal traction, crop and pasture rotations, soil

436 conservation, organic soil inputs, and what the Cubans call biofertilizers and biopesticides— microbial pesticides and fertilizers that are nontoxic to humans." Two agricultural scientists, Peter Rosset and Shea Cunningham, who have studied the program, stress its "potentially enormous implications for other countries suffering from the declining sustainability of conventional agricultural production."

As a result of these reforms and Cuba's growing insertion into the world economy, as 1995 opened Cuban officials expressed guarded optimism that Cuba had turned the corner, that the worst was over. Cuba's recovery from its present slump would of course be greatly facilitated and hastened by a change in U.S. policy that would result in economic advantages for both countries. Unfortunately, the United States continues to harbor cold war prejudices and illusions about Cuba that it abandoned long ago about a much more powerful communist state, the People's Republic of China. The collapse of socialism in a number of east European states, the success of the U.S. invasion of Panama in December 1989, and the victory of the U.S.-supported opposition in the Nicaraguan elections of February 1990 produced gloating in Washington and predictions that Cuba, whose economic collapse was considered imminent, was next. But reports of the early demise of the Cuban Revolution were and are greatly exaggerated. Short of a massive U.S. invasion, there is very little prospect that Cuba's socialist regime can be overthrown from within or without. In Cuba, unlike eastern Europe, socialism did not arrive in the wake of a victorious Red Army; it was created by an indigenous popular revolution that linked the ideals of socialism and independence, and it enjoys overwhelming popular support. Despite many economic problems, the Cuban Revolution has a record of social achievement without parallel in Latin American history that presents a vivid contrast to the economic and social crises gripping most of the capitalist societies of Latin America.

The process of "rectification" has been accompanied by efforts to democratize still further Cuba's political and economic structures and widen popular participation in decision making and by greater tolerance for expressions of dissidence in various fields. In recent years the great majority of the "prisoners of conscience" in Cuba's prisons have been freed and those who chose to emigrate and could obtain visas were permitted to do so. Since 1991 Cuba has had a policy of allowing people who wish to leave to do so. (U.S. official denunciations of Cuban restrictions on the right to travel come with poor grace from a government that denied travel visas to Pablo Picasso, Gabriel García Márquez, Julio Cortazar, and Graham Greene, to name only a few well-known intellectuals and artists, and continues to ban travel to Cuba by most Americans.)

The explosive potential of the unrelenting U.S. policy of seeking to create hunger and tension in Cuba through an economic blockade, tightened with the passage of the Torricelli Bill, became evident in summer 1994. Increasingly difficult living conditions caused a growing number of Cubans, many of whom have relatives in the United States, to want to leave their country. But U.S. policy on the subject was contradictory. In 1984 the United States and Cuba signed an immigration accord that permitted up to 20,000 Cubans, plus 3,000 political prisoners, to enter the United States each year. But the United States has never granted that many entry visas to Cubans; it is estimated that somewhere between 1,000 and 3,000 were actually given out each year. But the United States also had a law, the Cuban Adjustment Act of 1978—the only law of its kind on the books— that granted Cubans arriving in the United States immediate legal status. This law encouraged Cubans to leave their country and arrive in the United States by extralegal means, often in dangerous, makeshift boats or rafts; they were encouraged to do so by U.S. radio broadcasts that also called on Cubans to protest and commit acts of sabotage. The United States has never prosecuted any Cuban who hijacked a boat or plane on arrival in the United States. By contrast, in the 1960s, when several planes were hijacked to Cuba, the Cuban government arrested and convicted the hijackers for their crimes.

The problem of illegal emigration came to a head in July-August 1994, when a number of ferry boats in the port of Havana were hijacked by armed groups of people. In the course of these actions two Cuban officers who tried to resist the hijackers were killed. On August 5, apparently drawn by rumors that boats were coming to take them to the United States, several thousand people began to circulate in the port area. But no boats appeared, and the frustrated crowds moved back into the streets of Havana, where rock throwing and some looting began, but order was quickly restored by police and mostly unarmed volunteers. It was the largest protest in the history of the Revolution.

On the evening of August 5 President Fidel Castro went on national TV to discuss these events and their causes, laying the blame for what happened on the United States. He singled out, first and foremost, the economic blockade against Cuba, which created the economic difficulties that impelled Cubans to leave their country. He stressed the contradictions of U.S. immigration policy with respect to Cuba, claiming that the United States was deliberately blocking legal immigration and stimulating illegal immigration for its own propaganda and subversive ends. He declared that any Cuban who wished to leave could do so and called on the United States to take quick and effective measures to solve this problem. If the United States failed to do so, the Cuban government would feel compelled to issue instructions to its coast guard not to stop any boat that wanted to leave Cuba as long as it was not stolen and not to obstruct the entry of boats that came from the United States to pick up Cubans wishing to go to the United States.

The initial response of the Clinton administration was that it would not allow Cuba to determine its immigration policy. But in the ensuing days and weeks, some 28,000 refugees, braving sharks, bad weather, hunger, and thirst, took to the sea in makeshift rafts and boats for their Promised Land, without interference by the Cuban coast guard and police; they were picked up by the U.S. Coast Guard in international waters and brought to Florida. The exodus, threatening to become a second Mariel, created a dilemma for the Clinton administration. The racist impli-

cations of a policy of receiving Cuban economic refugees with open arms, while denying admission to Haitians fleeing the terrorist Haitian dictatorship, angered the Congressional Black Caucus and troubled many other Americans. The governments of Florida and Miami, in particular, already struggling with their own problems of unemployment and homelessness, worried about their lack of resources to deal with a new influx of refugees. In the end, the administration capitulated to Castro's demands. On September 9, 1994, the United States and Cuba signed an agreement under whose terms the United States promised to admit at least 20,000 legal immigrants from Cuba, not counting immediate family relatives of Cubans already in the United States and Cubans on the current visa waiting list. The agreement was tacit recognition that the United States had not complied with the terms of the 1984 immigration pact. For its part, Cuba promised to try to stop the exodus, relying mainly on persuasion. Five days later the Cuban newspaper *Granma* reported that the objective had been achieved "without a single incident, without a single death or injury, without a single drop of blood spilled."

The immigration pact had a significance that went beyond its immediate results. It was the first time in ten years that the two countries had been able to negotiate a substantial diplomatic agreement. Although the Clinton administration had adamantly refused to link the immigration problem to the economic embargo, the linkage was plain to all and strengthened demands for more dialogue and a decisive change in U.S. Cuban policy. Influential newspapers have called for rolling back the embargo. The *New York Times* complained that U.S. policy toward Cuba remained frozen in the past and appeared to be dictated by the most radical factions of the anti-Castro Cuban exile community. Removal of the embargo would bring substantial economic benefits to both the United States and Cuba, and undoubtedly contribute to the further liberalization of Cuban life that the Clinton administration claims to desire.

poverty. Even by the low Latin American standards, the dimensions of those problems are
staggering; according to 1991 official information, the share of national income received by the
poorest 10 percent of the population dropped
from 2.4 percent in 1980 to 0.5 percent in 1991.
The problems are especially acute for the indigenous people (55 to 60 percent of the population). According to official statistics, the indigenous infant mortality rate is 134 per 1,000 live
births, twice that of the nonindigenous population. Only 10 percent of the indigenous population is literate; three out of four indigenous children suffer to some degree from malnutrition;
and the average life expectancy of forty-five years
represents a sixteen-year gap separating them
from other Guatemalans. The root cause of indigenous poverty is lack of access to land. According to a U.S. Agency for International Development (AID) study, 2 percent of the country's
farms hold two-thirds of the farmland, while 70
percent of the farms possess 17 percent of the
land. As noted above, the army's rural counterinsurgency program, designed to eliminate the
guerrillas' social base of support, led to the raz-
ing of hundred of villages and the flight of over a
million peasants to other parts of the country or
to Mexico. Government efforts to promote the
growing of winter vegetables and other nontraditional export crops in the highlands have contributed to the replacement of grain production
for local consumption with the planting of export
crops, promoted concentration of landownership, and spurred the flight of the indigenous
population to the cities.

Many indigenous (and nonindigenous) people
have found employment in the free trade zone
factories or *maquilas,* the fastest-growing sector
of the Guatemalan economy. A 1984 law exempted these factories from import duties and
(for ten years) from taxes. A majority are owned
by Koreans. The maquilas account for 36 percent
of Guatemala's exports to the United States. Seventy percent of the workers are women, and they
earn about $2.50 a day. "I work from 7:30 in the
morning to 10:00 o'clock at night," said one machine operator, "and what I earn doesn't cover

what I need to eat." To date, employers have successfully resisted demands for higher wages,
shorter hours, and better working conditions.

These bleak facts and figures, and the relative
powerlessness of Guatemalan peasants and
workers, are directly connected to the climate of
violence and repression that continues to reign
in the country. A recent victim of the violence
was the president's own cousin, Jorge Carpio Ni-
colle, a former presidential candidate of the National Centrist Union party, killed in July 1993
with three others in an ambush in the department of Quiché. The murder, observed *Latinamerica Press,* was seen as a message to the new
president "as to who was really in control."

The repression continues, but it meets with
growing resistance. One of its signs was the recent return, with United Nations assistance, of
thousands of Guatemalan refugees from exile in
Mexico to their hometowns from which they had
been forced out by the army. Other thousands of
indigenous people, the so-called communities in
resistance, have lived for ten years in the northern regions of Quiché, exposed to bombing from
the air by government planes, refugees in their
own country. But they have survived and developed their own system of organization. The
award of the Nobel Peace Prize to Rigoberta Menchú has given the indigenous people new hope
and courage. In November 1993 thousands of indigenous Guatemalans held a protest march in
the capital to demand total abolition of the civil
defense patrols imposed by the army. The social
ferment has been accompanied by a renaissance
of Maya culture, with the formation of centers for
the study of Maya culture, an association of Maya
writers, and a publishing house devoted to the
publication of books in the Maya languages.

The centerpiece of León Carpio's domestic
program was an anticorruption crusade to purge
a Congress riddled with corruption and despised
by the public. In November, after months of
wrangling, he reached a compromise on constitutional reform with Congress that allowed its
members to remain in office for at least nine
more months and provided for the election of a
new Congress in August 1994, with future mem-

bers and the president to have four-year terms in office instead of five, and for the future Supreme Court to be chosen from a list drawn up by university rectors and legal associations instead of by Congress. A national referendum on the reform was scheduled for January 1994, with new elections to be held in September.

The failure of this puny constitutional reform to tackle such social issues as land, labor, and tax reform angered grassroots organizations, which had high hopes in León Carpio because of his record as human rights ombudsman, and many leaders urged people to abstain from voting in the referendum. In the event, although the reforms were technically approved, the high abstention rate (84 percent of the electorate) represented a rejection of León Carpio and the peculiar democracy, Guatemalan style, put in place in 1985.

Meanwhile, in apparent response to international pressure, in January 1994 the long-stalled talks between the government and the insurgents had revived, and in late March, in a major breakthrough, the URNG and the government signed a human rights accord in which the government agreed to international verification, something to which the Guatemalan army had always objected. By the terms of the accord, a United Nations mission would spend at least one year in Guatemala and could move freely about the country, entering any military base or guerrilla camp without prior notification. A backlash by military hard-liners was not slow in coming. On the heels of the human rights accord, bowing to army pressure, León Carpio dismissed his interior minister and national police chief, who had worked together to remove military influence on the national police, retrain it along European police lines, and replace repression with dialogue, appointing officials linked to army hard-liners. In April *Latinamerica Press* described the move as a blow to the demilitarization of civilian society required by "any transition towards civilian society."

Thus the signs of Guatemala, in mid-1994, were contradictory. On the one hand, violence and repression continued almost unchecked. The number of political murders and other human rights abuses in the first half of 1994 actually increased sharply over the same period in 1993. The León Carpio government appeared to be little more than a façade for the real power, the army, closely linked to a small landed and corporate oligarchy. An ominous development was the victory in the August 1994 congressional elections of a right-wing party headed by the infamous former dictator Efraín Ríos Montt, but his victory was flawed by an abstention rate of 79 percent, the highest in the country's history, reflecting the disgust and apathy of the electorate. On the other hand, there was growing resistance to repression, aided by changes in the international scene, such as the end of the cold war and the growing self-consciousness and mobilization of the Indian peoples of Guatemala and the rest of Latin America. Guatemala's insurgency, the URNG, having survived all efforts to destroy it, remained a guarantor of the popular struggle for democracy and social justice. And the peace process, despite all obstacles, also survived and continued to move forward, if only at a snail's pace.

Nicaragua

Modernization, American Intervention, and Sandino, 1857–1934

The history of Nicaragua for two decades after the collapse of the Central American federation in 1838 was dominated by a struggle between liberals and conservatives. Their responsibility for inviting William Walker to assist them, followed by Walker's attempt to establish his personal empire in Central America, so discredited the liberals that the conservatives were able to rule Nicaragua with very little opposition for more than three decades (1857–1893).

Although coffee was grown commercially as early as 1848, the principal economic activities in Nicaragua until about 1870 were cattle ranching and subsistence agriculture. Indian communities still owned much land, there existed a class

458   Committees. It was completed with such speed that visitors to Nicaragua in the fall of 1979 marveled at the relatively normal appearance of the country. Food shortages were another serious problem and required the importation of great quantities of foodstuffs, mostly financed with foreign donations. Meanwhile emergency food crops were sown so that domestic supplies of food would be available by the middle of 1980. The work of repair was combined with food-for-work schemes to provide a temporary solution for the vast unemployment that was a legacy of the war.

What to do about the national debt was a vexing question for the new government, for it knew well that many of the more recent loans had served only to swell the bank accounts of Somoza and his cronies. But it decided to agree to pay all the loans, even the corrupt ones, for both economic and political reasons. The Sandinistas wanted to retain access to Western loans and technology; they also wished to disprove the charge that the new Nicaragua was a Soviet or Cuban "puppet," solely dependent on the socialist bloc for economic and political support. The socialist countries, particularly the Soviet Union and Cuba, in fact gave considerable aid in the form of food shipments and other supplies. Cuba also sent large numbers of teachers and doctors to assist in the work of reconstruction.

The international lending agencies and Western governments hoped financial aid to Nicaragua would enable the private sector of the country to survive and keep the economy pluralistic. The principal difficulty in renegotiation arose with the United States. The Carter administration agreed to make a new loan of $75 million, chiefly for aid to the private sector. When Ronald Reagan came to the presidency, however, he froze the remaining $15 million of the loan, alleging that Nicaragua was sending arms to the rebels in El Salvador. Thereafter Nicaragua had to rely for aid on the socialist countries, friendly social democratic governments of Western Europe, and Third World countries, including Brazil.

Although some Sandinista leaders viewed socialism as a more or less distant goal, the regime pursued a mixed-economy strategy of national development and recognized that private enterprise had a vital role to play in the reconstruction of the national economy. The state, however, became the most decisive and the most dynamic element in the economy and in the provision of social services, particularly health, education, and housing. The strengthening of the state sector was a direct result of the takeover of the enormous properties of the Somoza dynasty and its allies. These properties became the basis of the People's Property Area, including half the large farms over 500 hectares, a quarter of all industry, large construction firms, hotels, real estate, an airline, a fishing fleet, and more. The expropriation of the holdings of Somoza and his supporters placed approximately 40 percent of the gross national product in the hands of the state. The banking system and foreign trade were completely nationalized.

These expropriations, however, left 60 percent of the GNP in the hands of the Nicaraguan capitalist class, which continued to control 80 percent of agricultural production and 75 percent of manufacturing. Thus, the country remained capitalist, with the state sector no larger than that of France, Mexico, and Peru in the 1970s. The policy of the Sandinista government was to avoid radical changes that might cause a rupture with the "patriotic bourgeoisie," the results of which would be disastrous for the economy. Accordingly, it courted and maintained an alliance with some of the country's largest entrepreneurs. At the same time the government insisted on safeguards with respect to working conditions, wages, hours, and the like that would at least modestly improve the life of Nicaraguan workers. It also encouraged the trade unions to watch over the proper functioning of factories so as to prevent decapitalization, slowdowns in production, and other sabotage by capitalists hostile to the revolution. The result was a built-in tension between the government and a section of the bourgeoisie. Partly because of this tension, partly because of objective conditions—lack of foreign exchange to buy inputs, obsolete machinery, and other problems—private businessmen began dropping out of manufacturing or failing to invest.

The growth of the public sector was most marked in agriculture. Land reform was placed under the *Instituto de Reforma Agraria* (INRA), which by the end of 1979 had confiscated without compensation over one-fifth of Nicaragua's cultivable land that belonged to persons or corporations affiliated with the Somoza regime, land that "was almost universally held to be little more than stolen property." The government proposed to maintain these estates as productive units rather than to divide them into small parcels. Most of these lands were large farms that had been operated as capital-intensive enterprises, so parcelization would have resulted in heavy production losses. The decision was made to convert many of these estates into state farms, combined into 170 productive complexes, which in turn formed 27 agricultural enterprises. Others were organized as production cooperatives, called Sandinist Agricultural Communes. In late 1980 there were about 1,327 of these cooperatives. INRA simultaneously tried to improve the living conditions of state-sector workers through the establishment of clinics, schools, and housing projects. In 1980 more than fifty thousand workers worked full time in the state sector.

Although the government favored state farms and production cooperatives as basic agricultural units, small independent farmers were not neglected. Agricultural credit for small producers was greatly expanded, and they were encouraged to form credit and service cooperatives. In 1979–1980, there were 1,200 of these co-ops organized; they received over 50 percent of the agricultural credit extended by the government in the same period.

Even after the confiscation of the estates of the Somozas and their supporters, large commercial farms producing such crops as cotton, coffee, cattle, and sugar still held 66.5 percent of Nicaragua's cultivable land. The relationship between this private agricultural sector and the revolutionary government was an uneasy one. Most of the large landowners despised the Somozas, resented their hoggish propensities, and welcomed their overthrow. But the rules of the game had changed, and the new rules were not always to their liking. Landowners could no longer mistreat

their workers; they must comply with reform legislation defining the rights of tenants and workers. Despite the government's assurances that it wanted to preserve a private sector, large landowners were understandably nervous about their future. The commercial farmers and cattle ranchers defended their interests through their own associations, which negotiated with the government over prices, acreage quotas, and the like. The commercial farmers had access to credit at low interest rates, and a coffee stabilization fund was established to protect growers against fluctuations in the world market. The economic importance of this sector is evident from the fact that in 1979–1980 it accounted for 62 percent of the production of cotton and 55 percent of the production of coffee.

The difficulties of Nicaraguan agriculture were not due primarily to inadequate volume of production but stemmed above all from falling world prices for its major export crops. Sugar, which sold for 24 cents a pound in 1981, sold for 9 cents in 1983. Natural disasters also hurt production of staple foods in 1982. In May flooding destroyed 20,000 acres of just-planted basic grain crops, destroyed $3.6 million in stored grains, and caused $350 million in damage to the national economic infrastructure according to a United Nations survey. A drought in July and August caused estimated losses of $47 million. Finally, the greatly increased scale of CIA-organized counterrevolutionary activity that began in 1981, diverting manpower and resources to military purposes, caused serious damage to Nicaraguan agriculture and to the economy in general—probably a major aim of the U.S. destabilization program.

The implacable pressure of the Reagan administration on Nicaragua represented a threat not only to its economy but to the existence of the revolutionary government. Although the Carter administration's policy was "more than a little schizophrenic," once the FSLN was firmly in power it made a serious effort to come to terms with the revolution, hoping thereby to enable capitalism to survive in Nicaragua. With the election of Reagan, the U.S. attitude changed drastically. *Newsweek* (November 1982), quoted an insider as reporting that the driving forces behind

1856 declared that if two-thirds of a pueblo's communal lands were not planted in coffee, ownership would pass into the hands of the state. This pressure was replaced by a more direct attack on Indian landholdings: an 1881 law ordered that all communal lands be divided among the co-owners (which opened the way for their acquisition by legal or illegal means by the expanding coffee growers); and thirteen months later a decree abolished all communal land tenure. The new legislation harmed not only the Indian communities but *ladino* (mestizo) small farmers as well. These farmers often relied on municipal *tierras comunes* (the free pasture and woodlot where they could graze their stock) for an important part of their subsistence.

The result of this new legislation was a rapid concentration of landownership in the hands of a landed oligarchy often referred to as "the Fourteen Families." The number, while not an exact figure, expresses symbolically the reality of the tiny elite that dominated the Salvadoran economy and state. As late as September 1979, 0.85 percent of the landowners held 77.3 percent of the cultivable land, while 99.15 percent of the landowners owned 22.7 percent of the land.

Throughout most of the nineteenth century the great landowners used their own private armies to deal with the problem of recalcitrant peasants. Governmental decrees of 1884 and 1889 made these private armed forces the basis of the public Rural Police, later renamed the National Police. In 1912 the *Guardia Nacional* (National Guard), modeled after the Spanish National Guard, was established. Like the National Police, the National Guard patrolled the countryside and offered police protection to haciendas. The national army, created in the 1850s, did not become an instrument of repression until the late twentieth century.

For the rural poor, the social consequences of the coffee boom were disastrous. A few of the dispossessed peasants were permitted to remain on the fincas, or new estates, as colonos—peons who were given a place to live and a milpa, or garden plot, where they could raise subsistence crops. Unlike the old indigo or sugar latifundia,

however, which required a large permanent labor force, the need for labor on the coffee plantations was so seasonal that for the most part planters relied on hired hands. This circumstance determined the pattern of life of the typical Salvadoran campesino. He might farm a small plot as a squatter or a colono on a plantation, but his tiny plot did not as a rule provide subsistence for his family. He would therefore tend to follow the harvests, working on coffee fincas during the harvest season, moving on to cut sugar cane or harvest cotton during August and September, and finally returning to his milpa, hopeful that the maize had ripened. This unstable migratory pattern created many social problems.

The economic and social problems generated by the coffee monoculture became more acute with the advent of the Great Depression in 1929. Campesinos who made 50 cents a day before the depression had their wages reduced to 20 cents a day. The price of coffee was cut in half between July 1929 and the end of the year, ruining many small producers who were forced to go out of business and sell their lands. High unemployment and below-subsistence-level wages added to the discontent caused by harsh treatment by overseers and frauds practiced by company stores.

Even before the depression, there had been scattered peasant revolts in the twentieth century; they were always put down by the National Guard. In the 1920s urban workers and some of the peasantry began to form unions. In 1925 a small Communist party began to operate underground; its leader was Agustín Farabundo Martí, who had been introduced to Marxism at the national university. Expelled from El Salvador in 1927 for his radical activities, Martí joined Augusto César Sandino, who was fighting the United States Marines in Nicaragua. Martí returned to El Salvador in 1930 and again plunged into political activity. Aided by a small group of youths, mostly university students, he carried on propaganda and organizational activity among peasants in the central and western parts of the country. He was soon jailed but was released after going on a hunger strike.

Against this background of depression and growing left-wing agitation, a presidential election, perhaps the first free election in Salvadoran history, was held. The winner was the wealthy reformer Arturo Araujo, who had formed his own Labor party (he was a great admirer of the British Labour party and its policies). This event caused much disquiet among the coffee planters and the military. The new president immediately ran into storms: teachers and other public servants clamored for back pay, peasants demanded land and other reforms, while the coffee oligarchy and the military pressed him to make no concessions. On December 21, 1931, a military coup ousted Araujo and installed his vice president, General Maximiliano Hernández Martínez, as president. The coup signified the end of direct rule by the oligarchy and the beginning of a long era of military domination.

The fall of the liberal Araujo and the rise of Hernández Martínez to power closed the door to popular participation in politics. Convinced that the new regime had no intention of allowing reforms or free elections, Martí and other radical leaders decided on insurrection. Simultaneous uprisings were set to take place in several towns on January 22, 1932. But the authorities got wind of the plot several days in advance, and Martí and two of his aides were seized. Other rebel leaders then tried to call off the revolt, but communications had broken down, and the revolt began without its leadership.

In town after town, the campesinos, including many full-blooded Indians, rose up, often armed only with machetes. Having taken over much of the western area of the country, they attacked the regional center of Sonsonate. The unequal combat between peasants armed with machetes and the garrison, supported by the Guard and other police units, all armed with modern weapons, ended in total defeat for the insurgents. In a few days the captured towns were retaken. Then the oligarchy began to take its revenge, relentlessly hunting down the "communists," defined as any peasant who was not vouched for by a landowner as not having taken part in the revolt. Estimates as to the number of killed range from ten thousand to forty thousand. The commonly accepted figure is thirty thousand. Ferocious repression was the oligarchy's way of teaching the peasantry a lesson, of ensuring that there would be no repetition of the revolt. The history of El Salvador since 1932 shows how vain was that expectation.

Oligarchs and Generals, 1932–1979

The coup that installed General Hernández Martínez in the presidency marked a turning point in modern Salvadoran history. Terrified by the peasant uprising of 1932, the oligarchy struck a bargain with the military that allowed the military to hold the reins of government while the oligarchy directed the economic life of the country. A network of corruption that permitted the officer class to share in the oligarchy's wealth cemented the alliance between the two groups. Nevertheless, the persistence of reformist tendencies among junior officers periodically produced strains and tensions within the alliance that threatened its existence.

General Hernández Martínez, known as *El Brujo* (the Witch Doctor) because of his dabbling in the occult, maintained a tight rule over the country through his control of the army and the National Guard until 1944. In addition, power and access to wealth were concentrated in a clique of Hernández Martínez's cronies. The discontent that this engendered in many junior officers, combined with the political and ideological ferment of the war years, led to his overthrow in 1944. Between that year and 1961, governments came and went. Juntas of reformist junior military and liberal civilians, alternated with governments dominated by conservative military and oligarchs. In 1961 the friendly posture of the military-civilian junta toward the Cuban Revolution as well as its reformist program earned it the distrust of the oligarchy, the conservative military, and the U.S. embassy. The coup that ousted the junta was led by Colonel Julio Adalberto Rivera, who promptly announced that his revolution was anticommunist and anti-Cuban.

Rivera established a system, patterned on the Mexican idea of a single dominant party that would perpetuate itself in power, holding elections every five years and employing fraud, coercion, and co-optation to maintain control. While maintaining his control of the political system, Rivera allowed a number of opposition parties to exist. The most important were the Christian Democratic party, *Partido Demócrata Cristiano* (PDC), headed by José Napoleon Duarte, mayor of San Salvador from 1964 to 1970; a Social Democratic party, *Movimiento Nacional Revolucionario* (MNR), led by Guillermo Manuel Ungo; and the *Unión Democrática Nacionalista* (UDN), a front for the Communist party, which had been illegal since 1932. In the first phase of the system, opposition parties were allowed to win some mayoral contests and even a number of seats in the National Assembly.

As the economic difficulties of the country multiplied during the 1960s and 1970s, however, the strains within the system grew and it became increasingly unworkable. The roots of the problem lay in the monoculture that made the country dependent on a world market over which it had no control and a system of land tenure and use that progressively reduced the land area available to small landowners and staple food production.

Land monopoly and the prevailing system of land use led to population pressure on land, a problem that was greatly aggravated by the population explosion. Thanks to the eradication of yellow fever and malaria and to the successes of preventive medicine, the population shot up from 1,443,000 in 1930 to 2,500,000 in 1961 and 3,549,000 in 1969. By 1970 the population density was about 400 per square mile. The swelling population put great pressure on wage levels: the average daily wage for a field hand in the early 1960s was about 62 cents a day, for an overseer or *mayordomo,* a little over a dollar a day. Since labor on coffee plantations was seasonal and a peon was lucky to get 150 days of work a year, the labor of an entire family for that period might yield a total yearly cash income of $300.

With land reform ruled out as a solution for land hunger and population pressure, Rivera attempted another remedy: industrialization and economic integration through the creation of the Central American Common Market (CACM) in 1961. The underlying reasoning was that the unrestricted flow of goods and capital throughout the area would stimulate an expansion of markets and industrialization, relieving population pressure and unemployment. Unfortunately this industrial expansion took place without a corresponding growth in employment, for the new industries were capital-intensive and required relatively few workers. Also, much of the new industry was foreign-owned and geared to exports; much of it was designed to assemble imported components.

The problem of population pressure on the land grew much more acute as a result of a bitter dispute between El Salvador and Honduras that culminated in the so-called Soccer War between the two countries in 1969—a war that took several thousand lives and left at least 100,000 Salvadorans homeless. Called the Soccer War because it followed a series of hotly contested games between teams representing the two countries in the qualifying rounds of the 1969 World Cup, the conflict had more pragmatic causes. One was a border dispute of long standing. Another was Honduran resentment over the marked imbalance of trade between the two countries as a result of the operations of CACM, to which both countries belonged. Honduras, an extremely underdeveloped country whose economy was largely based on bananas, lumber, and cattle, felt that it was subsidizing the industrial development of El Salvador. The third and decisive cause of the war was the presence in Honduras of some three hundred thousand illegal Salvadoran settlers. In April 1969, following adoption of an agrarian reform law, Honduras ordered the departure of some of the settlers within thirty days; eventually about eighty thousand were expelled. El Salvador retaliated in July 1969 by invading Honduras and destroying most of its air force on the ground. The war was over in five days, largely due to U.S. pressure on El Salvador in the form of threatened economic sanctions. The war, which was very popular in El Salvador, momentarily diverted popular attention from its great problems, but the effects on the country were entirely negative: El Salvador lost the Honduran market for its manufacturers for over a decade, and the return of Salvadorans from Honduras swelled the number of landless and homeless peasants.

These developments contributed to the ever-growing economic and social crisis of the 1970s. Population growth continued to outstrip the food supply; among the Latin American countries, only Haiti's people had a lower caloric intake than El Salvador's. By the early 1970s, unemployment was running at 20 percent and underemployment at 40 percent; in 1974 the annual inflation rate reached 60 percent. The proportion of landless peasantry rose from 11.8 percent in 1950 to 41 percent in 1975. The calamitous economic situation gave the opposition parties hope for victory in the presidential election of 1972; in September of that year the Christian Democratic party, the *Movimiento Nacional Revolucionario,* and the Communist UDN formed a united front, the *Unión Nacional Opositora* (UNO). Its candidate for president was José Napoleon Duarte. Although Duarte had clearly won the election by some 72,000 votes, the electoral commission found that the official candidate, Colonel Molina, had won by about 100,000 votes. The flagrant electoral fraud provoked a revolt by reformist junior military, and for a few days it appeared to have succeeded. But the National Guard and the air force remained loyal to the regime, and by the end of March the rebels had been forced to surrender. Duarte, the candidate of the united opposition, was arrested, tortured, and exiled to Venezuela.

The Molina government continued the oscillation between concession and repression that had characterized military rule since 1932. In 1975, hoping to promote the emerging tourist industry, Molina decided that El Salvador should play host to the 1975 "Miss Universe" pageant and spent about $30 million on the show. In a country with so many unfilled social needs, this impressed many Salvadorans as a scandalous extravagance. Units of the National Guard—without any provocation—fired on students attending a protest rally in San Salvador. At least thirty-seven

died and an unknown number of others "disappeared." The massacre was part of a pattern of growing violence—from the right and from the left. With increasing frequency, guerrilla organizations that had sprung up since 1970 kidnapped and held members of the oligarchy for ransom. In the countryside, the National Guard, aided by right-wing paramilitary organizations like ORDEN (*Organización Democrática Nacionalista*), conducted sweeps against "subversive" peasants, surrounding and destroying villages, killing many villagers, and abducting others who "disappeared."

Although convinced that the familiar pattern of fraud would be repeated in the 1977 presidential election, the UNO decided to run a symbolic candidate, a hero of the Honduran war, Colonel Ernesto Claramount Rozeville. The election was in fact marked by widespread fraud, with rampant stuffing of the ballot boxes for Romero and armed ORDEN thugs on hand to discourage close scrutiny by the opposition at the polls. The outcome was never in doubt. A massive protest demonstration held on February 15 in the main square of San Salvador and addressed by Claramount and other speakers was attacked by army and police units and by members of ORDEN. More than two hundred people were killed by machine-gun fire. Claramount and other leaders sought sanctuary in the cathedral; later Claramount was permitted to go into exile. As he departed for the airport he uttered a prophetic comment: "This is not the end, it is only the beginning."

The fraudulent election of 1977, ending all hope of reform via the electoral process, and the spiral of violence that followed it marked the opening of a new phase that may be called the prerevolutionary stage of development in Salvadoran politics. On the left, the revolutionary organizations that had sprung up since 1970 began to mobilize their forces and attempted to overcome their ideological and tactical differences. All these groups robbed banks, seized radio stations in order to broadcast propaganda, kidnapped oligarchs for ransom, and assassinated persons identified with official or unofficial repression. There was a rapid growth of labor and peasant unions and other mass movements,

472   known collectively as *Fuerzas Populares* (Popular Forces), and of umbrella organizations, such as FAPU (Front for United Popular Action), which united many groups for joint action against the government. On the right, meanwhile, there was increased repressive activity by the National Guard, the National Police, and other security forces as well as by the death squads of ORDEN and another terrorist organization, the White Warrior Union.

A major development of this period was the changing posture of the church toward the Salvadoran crisis. Prior to the Second Vatican Council (1962) and the Medellín Bishops' Conference, the church in El Salvador—as elsewhere in Latin America—supported the regime and the oligarchy. Although most of the hierarchy maintained that position, Archbishop Luis Chávez y González and his successor Oscar Romero, with Vatican II and Medellín as their guides, committed themselves to what Romero called "the preferential option for the poor." One result of this ferment in the church was the formation in a few short years of hundreds of comunidades de base, which combined Bible study with attention to the economic and social problems of their localities. The message the priests brought to their parishioners was that God is "a God of justice and love who acts on the side of the poor and oppressed," that the people "have a basic human right to organize in order to begin taking control of their own lives." Their social activism inevitably marked the priests as targets of right-wing death squads and security forces. The Jesuit Father Rutilio Grande was murdered by a death squad of the White Warrior Union in March 1977, and three other Jesuits who had been working with him were expelled from the country. By May 1977, leaflets urging Salvadorans to "Be a Patriot! Kill a Priest!" were circulating in San Salvador. Altogether, seven priests were killed by death squads or security forces between 1977 and 1979. The death of Father Grande, three weeks after Romero was installed as archbishop, contributed to what the archbishop referred to as his "transformation." From then on, during his three years and one month as archbishop, Romero used his position

to denounce the regime's human rights violations and to plead for social justice. His sermons, transmitted via radio to almost every part of the country, "became the single most listened-to program in the nation."

As the crisis deepened month after month, a differentiation also began to take place within the military. A group of reformist junior military watched with profound anxiety the revolutionary course of events in Nicaragua in July–August 1979; they became convinced that a coup offered the only alternative to a solution of the Nicaraguan type. Planning for a coup began in July 1979, with regular consultations with Archbishop Romero and representatives of the Christian Democratic party as well as contacts with the U.S. embassy, which indicated it would not oppose such an action. On October 15 the coup went off almost without a hitch, with virtually no resistance from any garrison, and incumbent President Carlos Humberto Romero meekly accepted exile. A military-civilian junta was formed. The civilians included two moderate leftists, Román Mayorga Quiroz, rector of the Central American University, and the Social Democrat Guillermo Ungo; the military representatives were the authentically democratic Colonel Adolfo Majano and the rightist Colonel Jaime Abdul Gutiérrez, head of the Military School, who owed his inclusion to U.S. pressure. The junta's program called for dissolution of the terrorist ORDEN organization, respect for human rights, agrarian reform, freedom for the Popular Forces to operate, and improvement of relations with Nicaragua.

Although Gutiérrez gave his nominal approval to the program, he decided, without consulting his colleagues, to change the balance of forces in the government by appointing another conservative, Colonel José Guillermo García, as defense minister in the cabinet that was to assist the junta. It was a fateful decision.

The left and the Popular Forces, meanwhile, regarded the junta with an intense suspicion that time was to justify. On October 28, a demonstration by several organizations demanding to know the fate of the many persons who had "disappeared" was met with gunfire by the National

Guard, leaving twenty-five people dead. In fact, the October 15 coup did not end repression by the security forces; more people were killed by them in the three weeks after the coup than had died in any similar period under Romero. Efforts by civilian junta members Mayorga and Ungo to restrain the official violence were totally ineffective, for the armed forces listened to no one but García.

These events led to the resignation of the civilian members of the junta, followed by the formation of a new government, the product of a secret deal between the military and the Christian Democratic party. Two Christian Democrats replaced Mayorga and Ungo. The military committed itself to a program of agrarian reform and nationalization of the banks; all repression would cease; and the armed forces would open a dialogue with the Popular Forces. Barely one week after accepting these conditions, the security forces fired on a massive demonstration of the Popular Forces, the largest in Salvadoran history, killing about twenty persons. This and similar repressive acts, demonstrating the bad faith of the military, caused a split in the Christian Democratic party. One of its representatives, Héctor Dada, resigned from the junta and was replaced by José Napoleón Duarte. At least 60 percent of its membership resigned from the party by November 1981. To add to the junta's problems, a rightist coup led by Roberto d'Aubuisson, head of the White Warrior Union, was barely averted by Defense Minister García and other high military officers. The agrarian reform promulgated with dramatic suddenness by the junta in March 1980 resulted from intense pressure by the United States, eager to give a reformist face to its protégé, even as James Cheek, the American chargé d'affaires, advised the junta to conduct a "clean counter-insurgency war." Typical of its strategy of reform and repression, the junta announced a state of siege on the same day that it promulgated the agrarian reform.

The agrarian reform was to be implemented in three stages. Phase I, promulgated in March 1980, nationalized 376 estates of more than 500 hectares, belonging to 244 owners and largely con-

sisting of pasture and cotton land. The owners were to be compensated with thirty-year bonds, and the estates were to be converted into cooperatives with 29,755 peasant members. As of January 1, 1983, only 22 cooperatives had received final title, although 130 of the owners had been paid for their farms. Phase II, which would have affected about 200 farms of between 100 and 500 hectares, including most of the coffee fincas, "died before it was born," postponed for an indefinite period.

Phase III, called "land to the tiller," promulgated in April 1980, allowed peasants who rented up to 42 hectares of land to buy it from the owner. As of January 1983, 58,152 applications had been received, roughly half of the number that were possible under Phase III provisions. By June 1982, no permanent titles had been issued to applicants; the number rose to 251 in August of that year, and to 1,050 by January 1983. The Salvadoran Peasants' Union charged that the increase resulted from the need to provide the Reagan administration with proof for certifying to the U.S. Congress that El Salvador was making progress in essential economic reform and had therefore fulfilled the requirements for continued economic and military aid.

This curious land reform was accompanied by a wave of repression directed above all against the peasantry. Responsibility for seizure and distribution of land was assigned to the army and the security forces, who used their authority in several ways. Often they distributed land to members of the terrorist ORDEN organization whether or not they were entitled to it. They also used ORDEN members to identify peasants who belonged to the Popular Forces or to the guerrilla movements; these peasants were then killed by the military. Sometimes they collaborated with landowners who evicted tenants from lands they had recently acquired under land reform provisions. In December 1981 the Peasants' Union reported to junta President José Napoleón Duarte (he had been named president in a leadership reshuffle in November 1980) that the "failure of the agrarian reform is an immediate and imminent danger." The union claimed that at least ninety of its officials and "a large number of beneficiaries" of the agrarian reform had died during 1981 at the hands of ex-landlords and their allies, who were often members of the local security forces. The report also charged that twenty-five thousand former *aparceros,* or sharecroppers, had been evicted from their plots before they could obtain provisional titles. Duarte's inability to carry out the agrarian reform or to check the terror in the countryside proved that the junta was in fact "a rightist military regime with a civilian façade"; it also showed that Duarte himself was an "ornament," in the words of one observer, needed by the United States to maintain the reformist image of the junta, and accepted by the military in order to pacify the U.S. State Department.

The most prominent victim of the terror that accompanied the promulgation of the agrarian reform was Monsignor Oscar Romero, archbishop of San Salvador. For years his attacks on the military and the security forces for their violations of human rights had been a thorn in the government's side. Increasingly disillusioned with the role of the Christian Democratic party in the junta, he gradually moved toward supporting armed struggle as the only remaining resort. In a sermon on February 2, 1980, he proclaimed: "When all peaceful means have been exhausted, the church considers insurrection moral and justified." On March 23, responding to the repression that accompanied the land reform, he appealed to soldiers not to turn their guns on unarmed civilians. The next day, as he celebrated mass in a chapel in San Salvador, he was gunned down, probably by a military officer. The National Guard celebrated his death with a savage attack on his hometown of Ciudad Barrios that left ten dead. According to the judge appointed to investigate his death—who made these revelations after he had fled for his life to Costa Rica—the assassination was planned by General José Alberto Medrano, founder of ORDEN, and Major Roberto d'Aubuisson. Robert White, former U.S. ambassador to El Salvador, informed a congressional committee that there was "compelling" evidence that d'Aubuisson was involved

in the killing. Romero's martyrdom was to have profound political and military repercussions.

The Salvadoran Revolution, 1980–1995

"If I am killed," Archbishop Romero had prophesied shortly before his death, "I shall rise again in the struggle of the Salvadoran people." His death, in fact, served as a powerful catalyst for the growth of that struggle. In particular, it hastened the breakup of the Christian Democratic party and the unification of its center and left wings with Social Democratic and Marxist-led groups in opposition to the junta. In April 1980, a broad coalition of political parties, professional associations, trade unions, and revolutionary groups formed the *Frente Democrático Revolucionario* (Democratic Revolutionary Front, FDR). In January 1981, the FDR set up a kind of government-in-exile, called a "political commission," headed by the Social Democratic leader Guillermo Ungo.

As important as achieving the political unity of the opposition was the unification of the various guerrilla movements. By mid-summer of 1980 the five major guerrilla groups had united in a single command, which was given the name *Frente Farabundo Martí de Liberación Nacional* (FMLN), in honor of the leader of the abortive 1932 revolt. In January 1981, the FMLN launched its first general offensive and achieved significant successes. Eventually, however, the offensive ran out of steam and the guerrillas were forced to retreat to their bases in the thinly populated northern part of El Salvador.

The ensuing military stalemate ended in the middle of 1982, when the scales began to tip in favor of the insurgents. An almost uninterrupted series of government defeats provided an answer to the much disputed question of the source of the FMLN's arms. Contrary to the Reagan administration's claim, based largely on fabricated or dubious data, that the bulk of these arms came from Cuba, Nicaragua, or other external sources, the evidence seems overwhelming that the most important source of weapons was the capture of U.S.-supplied government arms. This explains why the U.S.-supplied M16s virtually became the

Many women, like the Salvadoran guerrilla shown here, took part in recent Central American revolutionary struggles, and some held high positions in the guerrilla commands.

increasingly a lost cause, continued to decline. Desertions became more frequent, and more and more government soldiers surrendered as soon as the first shots were fired.

The rebel successes sowed dissension within the officers' ranks and spurred demands for the removal of Defense Minister García by critics who wanted a more aggressive conduct of the war. In April 1983 García agreed to step down, and Provisional President Alvaro Magaña immediately appointed General Carlos Vides Casanova, former head of the National Guard, as his successor. The move pleased hard-liners and U.S. military advisers, impatient with García's inept direction of the war.

Increased military aid was one pillar of Reagan's Salvadoran policy; the other was a plan to improve the image of the regime by holding elections that would legitimize it, giving it a "democratic" face. The elections, it was assumed, would give victory to the Christian Democratic party and its leader, José Napoleón Duarte. He would then preside over a modest reform and civic action program that would win "hearts and minds" for the government; Duarte's reforms, combined with expanded military aid, should lead to a speedy pacification of the country. In compliance with U.S. wishes, elections for a sixty-member Constituent Assembly were held in El Salvador in March 1982. Boycotted by the left and the guerrillas, who pointed out that there was no possibility of fair elections under existing conditions (the army had recently published a hit list marking leaders of the FDR and the FMLN for death), the elections were largely organized and dominated by the right-wing parties and the military.

In any event, the outcome of the elections did not conform to the expectations of the Reagan administration. With only 35 percent of the vote, Duarte and the Christian Democrats proved unable to form a majority government. The fascist Nationalist Republic Alliance (ARENA) of Roberto d'Aubuisson garnered one-fourth of the vote and pressed for a coalition with other right-wing parties that would leave the Christian Democrats out in the cold. Thus, instead of

FMLN's standard weapon. Between June and October 1982 alone the rebels captured six hundred fifty firearms, over twenty guns, mortars, and heavy machine guns, and about eighty thousand rounds of ammunition.

Although the guerrillas invariably evacuated the large population centers captured in their offensives, by the spring of 1983 they had considerably expanded the zones of their control. They dominated areas inhabited by some two hundred thousand people; in these areas, political power was based on a self-governing system called the *Poder Popular Local* (PPL). While guerrilla self-assurance and confidence in victory grew, the morale of government troops, poorly led and lacking conviction in the justice of what seemed

476

legitimating Duarte and the Christian Democrats, as projected in the Reagan administration scenario, the elections appeared to legitimate D'Aubuisson and ARENA. The chagrin of the Washington policy makers can be imagined. Finally, by applying immense pressure, in August 1982 the United States managed to convince the three major parties—ARENA, the right-wing Party of National Conciliation, and the Christian Democrats—to sign a pact for cooperation in the transition to a new constitutional government. As part of the deal, the U.S.-supported "moderate" banker Alvaro Magaña was elected provisional president of the republic and D'Aubuisson president of the Constituent Assembly.

The Reagan administration's policy in El Salvador had one overriding purpose: at all costs to prevent the FMLN-FDR from coming to power. To ensure congressional support for the large infusions of military and economic aid needed to achieve this objective, the Reagan administration strongly supported the 1984 presidential candidacy of Duarte, who was identified by many in El Salvador and the United States with social reform. At the same time that it backed this supposed reformer, Washington demanded a more aggressive strategy in the war against the rebels, with massive use of air power and large-scale sweeps into rebel territory to force out the civilian population, to isolate the insurgents, and thus deny them the material and logistical support they needed to survive. This more aggressive strategy was to be combined with civic action programs designed to win the rural population's support.

Duarte promised peace through negotiations with the rebels, expansion of agrarian reform, and improved conditions for urban workers (his main political base). In May 1984 he defeated d'Aubuisson, the candidate of the extreme right, in a runoff election. Following the election it was revealed that the CIA had spent several million dollars to promote the Salvadoran electoral process; a large part of the funds went to Duarte's campaign. Duarte consolidated his victory in the congressional and mayoral elections of March 1985, which gave the Christian Democrats a clear majority of seats in Congress.

Soon it became evident that Duarte lacked the power, the resources, and perhaps the will to carry out his promises. He initiated peace talks with the FMLN in late 1984, but broke them off; the talks were probably intended above all to prove his goodwill regarding peace to his domestic supporters and his congressional backers in Washington. Duarte's promises of social and economic reform proved equally illusory. He presided over a moribund economy that survived only due to the immense largesse of the United States. (Between 1981 and 1987 U.S. government military and economic aid to El Salvador totaled $2.7 billion.) Duarte faced a dilemma. His promises and election had encouraged the labor movement to organize, call strikes, and engage in political activity; the right responded with repression, including a revival of death-squad killings and disappearances. Even if he had the means, Duarte could not satisfy labor's economic and social demands over the opposition of the oligarchy, the army, and even the Reagan administration. On the other hand, he could not openly support repression without losing his base in the labor movement. Duarte solved the problem by denouncing repression in words, while tolerating and even sanctioning it in practice.

In January 1986 the Duarte government announced an economic austerity program to help pay the costs of the war against the FMLN-FDR; the program included a 100 percent devaluation of the currency and large increases in fuel prices, measures that hit workers the hardest. Thousands of angry workers responded by leaving the trade union federation, controlled by the Christian Democrats, and joining a newly organized leftist federation, the National Union of Salvadoran Workers (UNTS). In October 1986, Duarte introduced another economic austerity package that levied steep taxes on basic goods and services and reduced already minimal social services. The package, described as an act of "political suicide" by a rebel leader, set off a fresh wave of strikes and demonstrations that drew ever-larger numbers of workers. By the end of 1986, Duarte's labor base had virtually collapsed. He could not even count on the support of the business sector, which organized a twenty-four-hour strike on January 22, 1987, that was said to be 90 percent successful in San Salvador. Of great significance, the strikes and demonstrations increasingly linked economic demands to calls for an end to the civil war through negotiations; these calls were strongly supported by the head of the Salvadoran church, Archbishop Arturo Rivera y Damas.

As if to give a coup de grâce to the battered Salvadoran economy, a powerful earthquake hit San Salvador on October 10, 1986, killing about 1,000 people, leaving 400,000 homeless, and destroying large sectors of the nation's infrastructure. Nearly 50 percent of all buildings within a twenty-block radius of the center were leveled or heavily damaged. The destruction of the capital's major hospitals left 4 million Salvadorans without medical care. A proposal of the FMLN for an indefinite truce during the period of reconstruction was rejected by the Salvadoran army.

Washington's 1984 strategy of depopulating areas of the countryside under guerrilla control by saturation bombing created a large population of internal refugees living in relocation camps at government expense, an added strain on the country's threadbare economy. Under prodding from the United States, the Salvadoran army also stepped up use of a sophisticated pacification program that incorporated civil action and psychological warfare operations. U.S. military advisers assisted with planning, procurement of materials, and training of the Salvadoran personnel. Evidence gathered from different parts of El Salvador suggested that this effort to win "hearts and minds" was less than a brilliant success. "In a country that suffers from deep structural problems for generations," one government development worker remarked, "it won't work to offer a bit of food when three years ago you perhaps killed the [family's] grandmother."

The massive influx of new U.S. military aid, including gunships and helicopters, and a considerable increase in the size of the Salvadoran army undoubtedly changed the balance of forces in the civil war. U.S. reconnaisance flights from Honduras and the Panama Canal Zone helped pinpoint rebel columns and command posts, using infrared tracking systems. Unable to compete with the army in numbers and firepower, the FMLN developed a new strategy. The large battalion-size units were broken up into small units of classic guerrilla warfare; these moved out of the way of the army's sweeps and returned after the army had left. The rebels, however, were still capable of launching major surprise attacks. Other new FMLN tactics included using mines, which caused perhaps as much as 70 percent of the army's casualties; another was economic sabotage through efforts to destroy the country's electrical grid by downing power lines and blowing up installations and dams, and through the destruction of coffee-processing plants. U.S. sources estimated the 1979–1985 loss through economic sabotage at $1.2 billion.

Of particular importance to the promise of victory, the insurgents believed, were the upsurge of the labor movement in the cities, Duarte's increasing isolation, and the growing movement for peace that embraces more strata of the population. These developments, the FMLN-FDR claimed, had given a new dimension to the civil war that strongly favored their cause.

By the beginning of 1988 the failure of the U.S. counterinsurgency strategy in El Salvador was apparent to all. The economy was in ruins, with industry operating at 40 percent of capacity. Riddled with corruption, the Duarte administration had proved unable to end the war, implement serious reforms, or check the repression. The results of the congressional and local elections of March 1988, carried out under the guns of the military, represented a repudiation of both Duarte and his American sponsors. Most of El Salvador's eligible voters stayed away from the polls; a majority of those who voted cast their ballots for D'Aubuisson's ARENA, which gained control of parliament and most of the country's local governments.

One year later, in elections marked by a massive abstention of voters and charges of widespread fraud by the Christian Democrats and other opposition parties, ARENA completed its sweep of political offices with the election of Alfredo Cristiani as president. The FMLN, which had called for a boycott of the elections, paralyzed traffic across the country with a transport stoppage and waged battles with government troops throughout the country.

Cristiani, a big coffee grower, was a man in the Duarte mold: a graduate of an American university, who spoke perfect English and presented an appearance of moderation, claiming he wanted to negotiate with the rebels. But his apparent moderation, which convinced some liberal U.S. senators like Christopher Dodd and John Kerry to vote more money for El Salvador, was another case of window-dressing. Behind Cristiani stood D'Aubuisson, widely suspected of being the author of the murder of Archbishop Romero and four American nuns in 1980. This alliance did not deter Vice President Dan Quayle from making a ceremonial call on D'Aubuisson when he attended Cristiani's inauguration in June 1989.

Cristiani complied with his campaign promise to initiate talks with the FMLN guerrillas following his inauguration but demanded their virtual surrender by insisting they lay down their arms as a condition for a cease-fire. As a result the peace talks were suspended and fighting resumed, accompanied by an escalation of death squad killings and torture of civilians. Cristiani's intransigent attitude, it was widely believed, reflected the decisive influence of the so-called *Tandona,* an elite group of extreme right-wing military from the cadet class of 1966 that included the defense minister, the army's chief of staff, and the chiefs of the air force, the national police, and the national guard. This tight-knit group regarded d'Aubuisson as its leader.

Prospects of peace suffered a shattering blow on October 31, 1989, when bombings of the headquarters of the National Federation of Salvadoran Workers (FENESTRAS) killed ten persons and wounded many others. In response to the bombings, the FMLN announced that it would not resume talks with the government as long as "guarantees for the labor movement are not achieved"; then, on November 11, 1989, it launched its most powerful offensive since 1981, striking at a number of cities, including San Salvador. Its main objectives were the working-class quarters in the city's densely populated northern outskirts. The government responded with a ferocious aerial bombing of the working-class barrios. The FMLN held sections of the city for up to two weeks before withdrawing.

The concentrated bombardment of densely populated working-class barrios, causing many civilian casualties, provoked an international outcry. The bombardment was accompanied by a new wave of repression directed against church and labor critics of the government. Six Jesuit priests and professors at San Salvador's Central American University, whom the military regarded as the "brains" of the uprising, together with their housekeeper and her daughter, were shot in cold blood. One year later, thanks to stonewalling by President Cristiani and the military, the "investigation" of the crime had reached a dead end.

The FMLN's offensive was designed to prove to the Cristiani government and to the United States that after nine years of war the FMLN was stronger than ever and could not be defeated militarily, and thereby to bring the ARENA regime to the bargaining table for serious negotiations.

Moved by this demonstration of rebel power, and even more, perhaps, by the threat of a congressional halt to U.S. aid to El Salvador in reaction to the murder of the six Jesuits and other human rights abuses (in the fall of 1990 Congress voted to freeze half of the allocated aid), the Cristiani government agreed to resume negotiations with the FMLN, without preconditions, with the United Nations as mediator. By mid-May 1990 the two sides had agreed to a timetable that called for a cease-fire by September. The FMLN also agreed to take part in elections if certain conditions were met, including a purge of the army by removal of officers who had been guilty of torture and assassination and a gradual process of demilitarization that would ultimately dismantle both armies and replace them with a civilian police force. Finally, on December 31, 1991, at the United Nations Plaza in New York City, President Cristiani and delegates of the ruling ARENA party and the FMLN announced that they had removed the last obstacles to settlement of the decade-long civil war.

Under the peace accords, signed January 16, 1992, the parties agreed that the National Guard and Treasury Police were to be disbanded and a new professionally trained National Civil Police, open to both former national police and FMLN guerrillas, would be formed and phased in over a two-year period. The size of the armed forces would be reduced by about 50 percent, and the U.S.-trained Immediate Reaction Infantry Battalions, charged with commission of numerous atrocities, were to be disbanded. FMLN military structures were to be dismantled under U.N. supervision and their members integrated into the political and institutional life of the country, but the FMLN could form its own party and set up its own radio and TV facilities.

The accords also dealt with economic and social issues. The government agreed to implement the existing agrarian code and respect the de facto land tenancy in "conflictive zones" (zones under FMLN control during the war) while it sought to purchase land from absentee owners. The FMLN conceded the right of the government to press on with its neoliberal "structural adjustment" policies; the government in turn agreed to take measures to alleviate the social cost of those policies. With the support of the U.N. Development Program, the government agreed to develop a National Reconstruction Plan for the conflictive zones, involving infrastructural development as well as employment, education, housing, and health programs. Finally, the accords provided for the creation of a "Truth Commission," to be composed of three foreigners, which would investigate human rights abuses during the war and could recommend prosecutions or other punishment for the responsible parties.

What was the significance of these peace accords? To begin with, they represented a recognition by the two sides—a very grudging, reluctant recognition on the government side—that neither could win a decisive victory over the other. For the rest, everything depended on the willingness of the Salvadoran government and military to respect the agreements that had been made and the amount of pressure exerted by the popular sectors to make them comply with the agreements. Much, of course, also depended on continuing pressure on the Salvadoran elite from the United States, which, having wasted $6 billion to prop up a genocidal regime, had neither the means nor the inclination to continue on that course.

The accords provided a timetable for the implementation of the various measures, with the cease-fire to go into effect on February 1, 1992. But the process of implementation proceeded with painful slowness and delays, reflecting the desire of the military, the Cristiani administration, and the corrupt judicial system to put as many roadblocks in its way as possible. Gradually and imperfectly, however, some of the promised reforms began to take shape. The infamous U.S.-trained Atlacatl battalion was dissolved, a new police force organized, and preparations began for a general election in March 1994 in which the FMLN, now a political party, would take part.

On March 15, 1993, the U.N.-sponsored Truth Commission released a long-awaited report on its investigation into human rights abuses during the civil war. The report was based on the testimony of 2,000 persons who had come forward, under promises of confidentiality, to testify as witnesses about the fate of 7,000 victims and on secondary information about the fate of more than 18,000 victims. The report found that 85 percent of the 9,000 human rights abuses investigated, and 95 percent of the killings, were committed by government-supported death squads and the military. Government atrocities included the massacre of nearly 1,000 civilians, men, women, and children, in the village of El Mozote and nearby hamlets by the Atlacatl battalion, the 1980 assassination of Archbishop Romero, and the 1989 murder of the six Jesuit priests, their housekeeper, and her daughter. The report found that the FMLN had also committed human rights violations, such as the killing of right-wing mayors, but on a much smaller scale. The report implicitly pointed a finger of blame at the United States by noting that the majority of the human rights abuses were directly attributable to graduates of the School of the Americas at Fort Benning, Georgia, where many of El Salvador's death squad leaders received their training in counterinsurgency methods.

The initial reaction of the Cristiani government was to try to repress and discredit the report. When this failed, on March 20 the right-wing majority in the General Assembly hurriedly rammed through, over minority opposition, a general amnesty that allowed the release of two officers sentenced to thirty years in prison for the Jesuit murders and barred the prosecution of other officials named in the report's documents.

As part of the U.N.-sponsored peace plan, a special commission had recommended the purge of 102 officers guilty of human rights abuses by December 31, 1992. But most of those removed by that deadline were junior officers; the fifteen who resisted the purge included the Minister of Defense, General René Emilio Ponce, General Juan Orlando Zepeda, vice minister of defense, and General Gilberto Rubio, chair of the joint chiefs of staff. Pressure for their removal grew after the Truth Commission implicated all three in ordering the assassination of the six Jesuits, and the United States threatened to withhold $11 million in military aid until the recommendations were complied with in full. Bowing to pressure, the remaining holdouts resigned but were rewarded by a grateful General Assembly with golden parachutes in the form of special legislation providing salaries and other benefits that ensured they would enjoy an affluent lifestyle. As new Minister of Defense, President Cristiani appointed Colonel Humberto Corado Figueroa, reportedly involved in a massacre of forty-five peasants in September 1982.

The Truth Commmission's report and newly declassified documents, published in November 1993, cast a vivid light, among other things, on the deliberate policy of deception practiced by the Reagan and Bush administrations to persuade Congress to provide continued military assistance to the Salvadoran armed forces. In 1981, for example, the CIA called ARENA party leader D'Aubuisson "the principal henchman for wealthy landowners and a coordinator of right-wing death squads that have murdered several thousand suspected leftists and leftist sympathizers" and described him as "egocentric, reckless, and perhaps mentally unstable." The CIA also reported that D'Aubuisson trafficked in drugs,

smuggled arms, and directed the meeting that planned Romero's assassination. But William Walker, Bush's special envoy to San Salvador and Reagan's deputy Assistant Secretary of State for Inter-American Affairs, confronted with the documents, displayed no compunction and responded: "We had to deal with D'Aubuisson."

On the eve of the March 1994 elections, with offices from that of the president down to the mayors up for election, there was a dramatic escalation of violence against candidates and other leading members of the FMLN. Since the cease-fire there have been some two hundred unresolved cases of former guerrillas who have been killed after they laid down their weapons. Despite these troubling signs, the Clinton administration continued to send both military and economic aid ($140 million a year) to El Salvador and maintained 450 military advisers in the country.

Despite serious disadvantages, including the entrenched ARENA machine, a lack of electoral funds, and the ever-present possibility of electoral fraud, the left was openly running in elections for the first time in fifty years. In the interests of "bridge-building," the five groups making up the FMLN endorsed the presidential candidacy of the veteran politician Rubén Zamora, candidate of the Democratic Convergence, a coalition of two left-of-center parties. The Christian Democratic candidate was Fidel Chávez Mena, former foreign minister under Napoleón Duarte.

Despite the presence of some nine hundred international observers, El Salvador's first postwar elections were seriously flawed. The *New York Times,* commenting on El Salvador's "messed-up elections," charitably attributed most of the flaws to "bureaucratic bungling"; others attributed them to fraud organized by El Salvador's Supreme Electoral Tribunal, dominated by the extreme right parties. One flagrant example of fraud or incompetence was the failure to send 340,000 voting cards to voters who were on the voting rolls but were not allowed to vote. In the event, ARENA's presidential candidate, Armando Calderón Sol, having failed to get 50 percent of the vote in the first round on March 20, won the presidency with almost 70 percent of the vote in the second round in late April. ARENA took about half the seats in the 84-member Legislative Assembly and over 200 of the country's 262 mayoralties. The FMLN, with 25 percent of the vote despite all the irregularities, made a respectable showing, gaining twenty-one seats in the legislative assembly, followed by the Christian Democrats with eighteen.

The "messed-up elections" did not augur well for the fulfillment of the peace accords' other terms, including the transfer of land in the former conflict zones, the development of reinsertion programs for former combatants in the civil war, and the demilitarization of the national police force. By the beginning of April 1994, only 25 percent of former FMNL fighters had received the land they were promised in the peace accords. The deployment of the new National Police Force (PNC) was behind schedule; more ominous was the infiltration into the PNC, with the government's consent, of many members of the old security services who were known to be torturers and death squad members.

What lies ahead for the FMLN? Most likely, a long and tortuous struggle. Most of its leadership remain committed to socialism but have adjusted their strategy to the new times and conditions. They have no illusions that the wealthy coffee growers and businessmen who dominate the Salvadoran state will lose their power tomorrow. But they are convinced that dependent capitalism and its neoliberal economic program, which have failed to achieve balanced development and social progress in other countries of the hemisphere, cannot solve El Salvador's problems. They envision a long political and socioeconomic struggle, based on mobilization and growing involvement of grassroots popular organizations, and they believe that in the long run that that struggle will lead to the achievement of a democratic socialist society.

Meanwhile, however, a stagnant economy and the right-wing government's "structural adjustment" policies of austerity and privatization sharpened the country's problems of unemployment, housing, health, and education. Export earnings from the sale of coffee for all of 1994 were expected to come to about $600 million, while remittances from the million or so Salvadorans living and working in the United States were expected to reach $1 billion. "Poor Salvadorans," commented the Jesuit economist Father Javier Ibisate, "are rescuing the economic model created by the rich for the benefit of the rich." In these conditions, the threat of possible deportation of hundreds of thousands of undocumented Salvadorans from the United States as a result of the federal cutoff of Temporary Protected Status (TSP) on January 1, 1995, and the denial of basic social services to all undocumented aliens by Proposition 187 approved by California voters in November 1994, created an atmosphere bordering on panic in El Salvador.

Chapter 19

Lands of Bolívar: Venezuela and Colombia in the Twentieth Century

Modern Venezuela and Colombia have often been cited as oases of democratic and economic stability in a turbulent, poverty-ridden continent. A closer look at their recent history, however, suggests they have not escaped the general crisis of Latin American dependent capitalism. Its effects are clearly evident in the devastating impact of Venezuela's foreign debt on a country whose oil wealth once made it the envy of the continent. In February 1989, after Venezuelan President Carlos Andrés Pérez announced drastic increases in the prices of basic goods and services in order to satisfy the requirements of the International Monetary Fund for loans to his government, the country exploded into riots that were crushed with the loss of hundreds of lives. Between 1981 and 1987 the number of Venezuelans living in poverty had risen from 22 to 54 percent of the population.

Neighboring Colombia presented an even darker picture. Colombia was the home of the Medellín and Cali drug cartels, which accounted for an estimated 76 percent of the refined cocaine smuggled into the United States. Under an ostensibly democratic and moderate regime, death squads linked to the army, security forces, and the drug mafia operated with impunity against leftists, trade union activitists, and even against conservative elite opponents of the drug cartels. In the decade ending in 1989 the mafia's death squads had murdered scores of judges attempting to investigate the activities of the Medellín cartel. Meanwhile, a twenty-five-year guerrilla war—the longest continuing insurgency in Latin America, reflecting the vast accumulation of unsolved social problems in this oligarchical democracy—raged in Colombia's jungles and mountains.

Bolívar and the State of Colombia

The early history of Venezuela and Colombia is inseparably linked to the name of the Liberator Simón Bolívar. Venezuela was his homeland; Colombia (then called New Granada) and Venezuela the theaters of his first decisive victories in the war for Latin American independence. Bolívar sought to unite Venezuela and New Granada into a single large and powerful state and looked toward the creation of a vast federation of all the Spanish-American republics, extending from Mexico to Cape Horn. In 1819 the Congress of Angostura (in Venezuela) approved the formation of the state of Colombia (later called Gran Colombia or Greater Colombia) that would combine Venezuela, New Granada, and Ecuador (then still in Spanish hands). In 1821, at Cúcuta on the Venezuelan-Colombian border, the union was formalized with the adoption of a centralized constitution drafted according to Bolívar's wishes, and he was elected provisional president of the new state. But he soon went off to launch a campaign for the liberation of Peru and Bolivia and entrusted the administration of the new state, with its capital at Bogotá, to his vice president, Francisco de Paula Santander, a veteran revolutionary leader whose policies in general conformed to Bolívar's.

Santander presided over the implementation of a liberal reform program that included the gradual abolition of slavery, the abolition of Indian tribute and the division of Indian communal lands into private parcels (a "reform" that opened the door to landgrabbing at the Indians' expense), the suppression of smaller male convents and the seizure of their property for the support of public secondary education, and a general expansion of education.

The major threat to Gran Colombia's survival came from its geographic, economic, and social realities. Immense distances separated its component parts, and a mountainous terrain made communication very difficult; it took about a month for a letter to reach Bogotá from Caracas. These conditions also hindered the development of economic ties between Venezuela and New Granada, and also Ecuador; Caracas and other Venezuelan coastal cities communicated more easily with Europe than overland via the Andes with Bogotá. Finally, the Venezuelan elite of cacao planters and merchants, joined by a new elite of military leaders or caudillos, had little sympathy for Bolívar's idea of fusing several independent Spanish-American republics into one and even less for his vision of a confederation that would unite all the Spanish-American states.

The latent conflict broke out into the open in 1826, when José Antonio Páez, the principal Venezuelan military commander, refused to appear before Congress in Bogotá to answer charges that he had violated the rights of citizens by sending soldiers to round them up for militia service. Supported by his army of *llaneros* and other caudillos, Páez proclaimed a revolt against the Bogotá government. Bolívar finally returned to deal with Páez's rebellion and the growing unrest.

But Bolívar's efforts to keep the union alive were in vain. In 1829 in Venezuela, "popular assemblies," carefully organized by the caudillos, voted overwhelmingly in favor of independence, for Páez against Bolívar. In mid-1830 Ecuador followed the example of Venezuela and seceded from the union. Gran Colombia was dead. Months before, Bolívar, filled with despair, terminally ill with tuberculosis, had resigned from office. Attended by a retinue of faithful officers and soldiers, he left Bogotá and made his way to the coast, planning to go into self-imposed exile in Europe, but died near Santa Marta in 1830.

Venezuela: The Nineteenth-Century Background

The Reign of Páez, the Conservative-Liberal Cleavage, and the Federal War, 1830–1863

On May 6, 1830, a congress assembled in Valencia to provide the independent state of Venezuela with a constitution, the third in the country's short history. The document limited the suffrage

484   to males who were twenty-one, literate, and had a high income. These requirements excluded most of the population, numbering under 900,000, from participation in political life. Of that number about half were *pardos* (free mulattos) and free blacks; slaves numbered about forty to fifty thousand, and over a quarter were whites. A tiny minority of whites, about ten thousand, composed the ruling class of wealthy merchants, great landowners, and high office holders and military officers, who usually were also landowners. The members of this class, often linked through family networks, dominated politics.

Military hero, longtime champion of Venezuelan independence, and former ranch hand José Antonio Páez was elected president, a post he combined with supreme army commander. His rise illustrates the renewal of the old colonial ruling class through the admission of a new elite of military caudillos, frequently of very humble origins.

The Venezuelan society and economy over which Páez presided essentially resembled the colonial social and economic order. The latifundio continued as the basic unit of economic activity; concentration of landownership increased after independence because of the rapid acquisition of royalist estates and public lands by a small group of military caudillos. A decree of October 15, 1830, compelling the sale of so-called uncultivated lands of Indian communities gave the latifundists more opportunities to expand their landholdings.

Labor relations in the countryside continued to be based on slavery, peonage, and various forms of tenancy, including sharecropping and obligatory personal service. Slavery in Venezuela, as in other parts of Latin America, had long been in decline. The Constituent Congress of 1830 adopted a manumission law freeing the children of slaves but requiring them to work for their masters until the age of twenty-one. Continuing a tendency that began in the late colonial period, however, many slave owners found it more profitable to free their slaves voluntarily since they generally remained on their former masters' land as tenants or peons bound by debts

and other obligations. By 1841, 14,000 had been freed this way and only 150 because they had reached the age of manumission.

The long revolutionary war had caused immense material damage and loss of life—the population had been reduced by 262,000—and destroyed the fragile economic links between the country's different regions. By the time Páez became president, however, a partial recovery had taken place, leading to a boom based on the switch from cacao to coffee as Venezuela's principal export and the country's integration into the capitalist world market, which henceforth absorbed about 80 percent of Venezuela's exports of coffee, cacao, indigo, tobacco, and hides.

The high coffee prices that accompanied the 1830s boom made planters hungry for credit to expand production by obtaining new land. Foreign merchant capitalists, the Venezuelan export-import merchants who were their agents, and native moneylenders obliged on the security of coffee crops and the planters' estates, but there was the obstacle of colonial legislation that regulated interest rates and punished usury. The Venezuelan congress removed this impediment by passing a credit law in 1834 that abolished all traditional Spanish controls on contracts, so the state would enforce a legally executed contract, no matter how exorbitant the interest rate. By the late 1830s, with the world price of coffee in decline, the Venezuelan economy was in serious trouble. Creditors refused to refinance their debtors, and by the 1840s Venezuela was in a severe depression.

The economic crisis caused a rift in the elite, with the emergence of factions that turned into political parties in the 1840s. One called itself Conservative, but opponents dubbed its members *godos* (Goths) to identify them with the unpopular Spanish colonial rule. Páez was its acknowledged leader, and it represented the views and interests of the export-import merchants and their foreign partners, the moneylenders, the high civil and military bureaucracy, and some great landowners. The Liberal party was led by Antonio Leocadio Guzmán and was a loose coalition of debt-ridden planters, the urban middle class, artisans, intellectuals seeking reform, and disaffected caudillos resentful of Páez's long reign.

Guzmán's rhetorical press attacks on Conservative economic policies and on the elections of 1842 and 1846 as fraudulent contributed to a growing social tension. A series of popular uprisings, which Páez described as open warfare against private property, terrified the Conservatives, who raised the specter of a general social race war, waged by pardos and slaves, which they blamed on Guzmán's inflammatory propaganda. In fact, Guzmán and most Liberals feared social revolution as much as their opponents and had no links to the popular revolts of 1846–1847. But the government of President Carlos Soublette, who succeeded Páez, determined to crush these revolts at their supposed source, brought Guzmán to trial, found him guilty of instigating the revolutionary movements, and sentenced him to death. The sentence, breaking with the tradition of exiling aristocratic troublemakers rather than executing them, caused great shock and focused attention on Páez's choice for president to succeed Soublette since it would be up to him to carry it out. In 1848, war hero General José Tadeo Monagas, an eastern caudillo, became the Conservative president through the customary controlled election.

If Páez had expected to find a pliant executor of Conservative policies, he was disappointed. Monagas, determined to free himself from Páez's control and establish his own dynasty, favored moderate Liberals for posts in his cabinet and other government positions. His commutation of Guzmán's death sentence to exile was a virtual declaration of independence from Páez and the Conservatives.

Those Liberals who expected substantial social and political reforms from Monagas were also disillusioned. He paid his political debt to his planter allies by supporting congressional passage of several laws designed to give relief to distressed planters. Under his brother José Gregorio, slavery was abolished in Venezuela (March 23, 1854), with compensation to the slave owners. Slavery had been increasingly unprofitable

as a result of falling coffee prices; even as Congress was discussing emancipation, some planters were voluntarily freeing their slaves to avoid paying their support.

Emancipation brought little change in the lives of most freedmen. In the absence of a modern factory system to provide alternative employment or any program for distributing land to them, most were doomed to remain on their former owners' estates as tenants burdened with heavy obligations or peons whose scanty wages were paid in *vales* (tokens) redeemable only for goods purchased in the estate store (*tienda de raya*) at inflated monopoly prices.

Hard times continued in the late 1850s: depressed coffee prices, the unwillingness of foreign capital to invest in Venezuela because the debt-relief legislation increased the risk of investment, elite fears of a social explosion, and general resentment of the greed and nepotism of the Monagas dynasty persuaded Conservatives and Liberals to join forces in March 1858 in a revolution that overthrew the hated regime. But the coalition soon fell apart when a group of extreme Conservatives seized power and installed a government even more repressive than the Monagas regime, imprisoning or deporting many Liberals, who responded with an uprising that began the Federal War (1858–1863).

The term "Federal" here had different meanings for the Liberal elite and its rank-and-file followers. After their victory the Liberals gave the country a new constitution (1864) with many reforms, including universal male suffrage and increased autonomy for the twenty states. But without substantive social reform, these rights were virtually meaningless. "Federalism" under these conditions simply meant the continued supremacy of the local caudillo, who often was a great landowner as well, and whose arbitrary rule was tolerated by the Caracas government as long as he remained its loyal proconsul.

For the peasants and artisans who rose in spontaneous revolt against the reactionary Conservative regime and accepted Liberal leadership and their slogan of Federalism, the term had a different meaning. Their vague hopes were expressed in a manifesto of Ezequiel Zamora, the veteran guerrilla fighter who had been freed by the Revolution of 1858, then exiled by the Conservative regime, and who returned to Venezuela in February 1859 to open in Coro province another front of a rapidly expanding peasant war.

The advance of Zamora's troops was accompanied by the occupation of large estates by their former peons and tenants, the creation of federal states, and the election of local governments by the citizenry. Zamora's death by an assassin's bullet in 1860 cut short the life of a leader who represented a genuinely democratic, social revolutionary tendency in the Federal War. Conservatives rejoiced, and some moderate Liberals heaved sighs of relief. The war continued, but the Liberal leadership, although favored by the military balance of forces, preferred a negotiated peace to a fight to the finish. The 1863 Treaty of Coche, negotiated by Antonio Guzmán Blanco, son of the famous Liberal caudillo, ended the war. It had cost some 50,000 lives and inflicted immense damage on the economy. Many haciendas had been destroyed, and the cattle herds of the llanos had virtually disappeared as a result of wartime depredations and neglect.

Like the War of Independence, the Federal War produced some social changes. One loser of the conflict was the old Conservative oligarchy: a considerable part of this group had fled or died in battle, and their estates often fell into the hands of victorious Liberal military, some of plebeian background. But for the rank-and-file of the revolutionary armies, the war's end spelled disillusionment and betrayal. They had to surrender the parcels of land they had occupied and return as peons to the great estates. Instead of reversing the trend toward concentration of landownership, the war accelerated it.

Antonio Guzmán Blanco and the Maturing of Neocolonial Venezuela, 1870–1908

The government of Juan Crisóstomo Falcón, who became president in 1863, could not cope with the Federal War's legacy of economic bankruptcy and political instability. He was overthrown in 1868, and the ensuing turmoil ended in 1870 when Antonio Guzmán Blanco, the ablest of Venezuela's nineteenth-century rulers, seized power.

Like his father, Guzmán Blanco was a master of demagogic rhetoric. He was a self-proclaimed Liberal and foe of the oligarchy, an anticlerical and devout believer in the positivist creed of science and progress whose ambition was to create a "Practical Republic," a "civilized people" by means of peace and money. To secure them he forged pacts with the conservative merchant class of Caracas, which viewed him with suspicion when he came to power; with the regional caudillos, traditionally identified with the principle of local autonomy; and with foreign economic interests, whose support he needed for his ambitious program to construct roads, railroads, and telegraph systems. In the end Guzmán Blanco's dream of a developed capitalist Venezuela proved to be a mirage; after two decades of his rule, Venezuela remained rural, monocultural, and dependent, a country in which caudillos again ran rampant as they struggled for power.

His system has been called "a national alliance of caudillos," but over this alliance "The Illustrious American," as he came to be called by his sycophantic Congress and press, presided as the supreme caudillo. The Constitution of 1864 was periodically replaced by new constitutions that reinforced the centralization of power. Although Guzmán's dictatorship was mild by comparison with some others in Venezuelan history, he did not hesitate to use repressive measures against his foes.

By his pact with the caudillos Guzmán secured a relatively stable peace (though there were several large-scale revolts against him between 1870 and 1888 and local uprisings were common throughout the period). Soon after coming to power he established a *Compañía de Crédito* with a powerful group of Caracas merchants. This gave him the resources needed to initiate a program of public works designed to improve transportation and communication. Between 1870 and 1874 fifty-one road-building projects were begun. But local funding did not suffice; Guzmán needed the cooperation of foreign capital, hesitant to invest in a country whose recent history had been marked by recurrent episodes of civil war. In 1879 he secured his first foreign contract, with a group of British investors for the construction of a railroad connecting Caracas with its major port, La Guaira. By the time he left office Venezuela had eleven railroad lines completed or under construction, all designed to serve the export-import trade by connecting Caracas and the major agricultural and mining areas with the ports. Given Venezuela's unfavorable terms of trade—the long-term tendency for the prices of its exports to decline and those of its manufactured imports to rise—the net result was to reinforce Venezuela's economic dependency, promote decapitalization, and leave the country a legacy of large unpaid foreign debt that in time posed a threat of foreign intervention and loss of sovereignty.

Guzmán Blanco's anticlerical policies led to a further weakening of the church. Tithing had already been abolished as "an excessive tax burden" on the citizenry. Under Guzmán Blanco the priestly fuero was ended, civil marriage and civil registration of birth and deaths established, and convents and seminaries closed. The church was also forbidden to inherit real estate, and many church estates were seized by the government.

For the rest, Guzmán Blanco's development programs caused little change in the country's economic and social structures. In 1894 the population, numbering some two and a half million, was overwhelmingly rural; only three cities had a population of more than 10,000. Most of the working population was employed in agriculture; what little modern industry existed was limited to light industry such as food processing and textiles. The artisan shop, employing some 50,000 workers, was economically much more important.

In 1888 The Illustrious American, whose interest in modernizing Venezuela appeared to flag, departed for Europe, leaving a hand-picked successor in charge. After a chaotic decade during which governments rose and fell, in 1899 Cipriano Castro, an energetic young caudillo from the Andean state of Táchira, seized power with his *compadre* (buddy) Juan Vicente Gómez, a prosperous cattle raiser and coffee grower. Castro's seizure of power reflected the growing economic importance of the Andean coffee-growing region. Announcing a program of "new men, new ideals, new methods," Castro formed a provisional government of national unity that included all political factions. In 1901 a constituent assembly elected him president and framed a constitution that extended the executive's term of office to six years.

Castro continued Guzmán Blanco's policy of centralization, appointing or confirming local officials and state governors, and sought to establish a strong national armed force that would replace the old-time personal armies and state militias. His program of military reform was handicapped by declining coffee prices that reduced state revenues, by a series of caudillo revolts repressed at heavy cost, and by a major conflict with foreign powers whose blockade of Venezuelan ports deprived the government of a vital source of income, custom duties.

Castro presided over a country in ruin due to devastating civil wars and a prolonged depression. Hard-pressed for funds, in December 1900 he demanded that Manuel Antonio Matos, Guzmán Blanco's brother-in-law and the country's wealthiest man, and his fellow financiers loan the government money. When they refused he paraded them through the streets of Caracas on the way to jail. The loan was made, but Matos took his revenge, organizing a large-scale revolt that brought together Caracas financiers, foreign investors, and regional caudillos. This *Revolución Libertadora* received considerable aid from foreign firms. Despite this assistance and Matos's own resources, Castro, leading the government forces in person, inflicted a decisive defeat on the rebels at La Victoria in November 1902.

The German and British governments chose this time to demand immediate settlement of their nationals' claims for unpaid debts and damages suffered in various civil wars. The government, having thrown all its resources into the struggle against the Matos revolt, could not pay these claims. In December 1902, despite Castro's offer to negotiate, the two powers sent an Anglo-German squadron of twelve warships into Venezuelan waters with orders to seize or destroy

488

Venezuela's tiny fleet and blockade its ports. The powerful guns of the Anglo-German squadron soon silenced the answering fire of Venezuelan coastal batteries, and the aggressors occupied several Venezuelan ports. The unequal nature of the struggle, the catastrophic economic impact of the Anglo-German blockade, and the continuing Matos revolt in some areas of the country made a settlement necessary. Accordingly, Castro asked the U.S. ambassador to serve as mediator in negotiating a settlement. The terms required Venezuela to allocate 30 percent of its customs duties to the payment of claims and provided for an end to the blockade and re-establishment of diplomatic relations between the parties but denied Venezuela the right to demand compensation for its losses.

Castro's last years in power were troubled by new clashes with foreign states—France, Holland, the United States—usually caused by his insistence that foreign nationals were subject to Venezuelan courts and laws. As Castro's health declined, Juan Vicente Gómez conspired to take power. The regime divided into two bands, one supporting Castro, the other Gómez. Gómez also had the support of foreign powers, notably the United States, eager to get rid of Castro. On November 24, 1908, on the advice of his physicians, Castro left for Europe to seek medical aid. Gómez, assuming the duties of president, staged a coup d'état. Castro attempted to return but was blocked by U.S. warships off the Venezuelan coast and by French authorities on Martinique, who put him on board a ship sailing for Europe. He spent the rest of his life in exile, dying in Puerto Rico in 1924.

Venezuela in the Early Twentieth Century, 1908–1958

The Tyranny of Juan Vicente Gómez, 1908–1935

On taking power, Gómez tried to placate his foreign patrons and promote a flow of investments into Venezuela by nullifying Castro's nationalistic policies. In 1909 he signed agreements with the United States and France restoring to foreign companies the concessionary rights Castro had abrogated. In another move designed to reassure foreign investors, Gómez issued an executive decree allowing foreign nationals who did not like the arbitration of Venezuelan courts to appeal to their own national courts or to international tribunals.

Foreign oil companies were especially favored by Gómez. The explosive growth of the oil industry eventually transformed Venezuelan economy and society, but the process began slowly. The transformation of the economy by "black gold" did not reduce its dependence or broaden its base; the monoculture of coffee and cacao was replaced by the monoculture of oil. The oil industry pumped vast wealth into the hands of the foreign concessionaires—in 1928 three companies, Dutch Shell, Standard Oil, and Gulf, controlled 89 percent of the market—and of Gómez and the small native elite linked to the foreign oil interests, but little of this wealth trickled down to the masses nor did it generate significant industrial progress. Government subsidies failed to stem the decline of agriculture, a sector that traditionally resisted modernization. The agricultural crisis contributed to a wave of rural migration to the oil fields of the Maracaibo Basin and other petroleum areas and to the growing cities.

In the 1920s nationalist resentment of foreign economic domination and hostility toward Gómez began to pervade the growing middle class. Venezuelan professionals and would-be entrepreneurs chafed at the difficulties of operating in an economic climate dominated by monopoly, nepotism, and corruption. In 1928 a celebration of the "Week of the Student" turned into a protest against the dictatorship, as the students were joined by trade unionists and other *Caraqueños* (inhabitants of Caracas). The protest marked the public emergence of an anti-Gómez movement with future importance.

The student protest inspired the military revolt of April 1928, led by young officers of the Caracas garrison and joined by the majority of cadets of the *Escuela Militar* and a number of students. Grievances over the favoritism shown in pay and promotions to officers of unquestioned loyalty to Gómez, and awareness that the army had become a repressive force designed to maintain internal order, fueled their discontent. An informer revealed the conspiracy to the military authorities, and government troops easily crushed the revolt before it had well begun. One group of students, including Rómulo Betancourt, future president of Venezuela, managed to escape and make their way abroad.

In 1931 Gómez was at the peak of his power. But in the next few years his health began to decline and in 1935 the prospect of his early demise led to intense factional maneuvering in his inner circle. The principal contenders for Gómez's throne were two generals, Minister of War López Contreras and the dictator's cousin, Eustoquio Gómez, each supported by his own faction. Eustoquio Gómez's candidacy was supported by the most barbarous followers of the old dictator. López was a more ambiguous figure. Like Gómez, he was an *Andino* (from one of the Andean provinces) and seemed absolutely loyal to the dictator, in whose service he had steadily risen, marrying his daughter and becoming his most trusted aide and heir apparent.

In 1935, amid growing signs that Gómez's illness was terminal, López Contreras wove a network of alliances designed to isolate Eustoquio and ensure his own peaceful coming to power without a civil war or dangerous risings of the masses. López already had the solid support of most army commanders, so by the time of Gómez's death on December 17, 1935, López appeared to have established the necessary conditions for a relatively peaceful transfer of state power into his own hands.

The jubilation and the demands for vengeance and social and political reform that the news of Gómez's death provoked in the long-silent Venezuelan nation not only made a mockery of López's eulogy of the dead dictator but foreclosed the possibility of an easy transition to a social order resembling that of the old regime. The entrance of the Venezuelan middle classes and

workers on the political scene opened two decades of complicated struggle, culminating in the victory of a new capitalist model of development and its associated political form of representative democracy.

Liquidating the Gómez Legacy, 1936–1945

Announcing Gómez's death, López proclaimed two weeks of public mourning. Venezuelans, however, responded to the announcement with rejoicing; in Caracas, angry crowds sacked the palaces of Gómez's most prominent supporters. When police fired on crowds of demonstrators in the Plaza Bolívar, killing many, López Contreras removed the governor of the federal district who was held responsible for the massacre but replaced him with another member of Gómez's inner circle. On December 21 Eustoquio Gómez, who regarded himself as the late dictator's rightful heir and Venezuela as his family estate, attacked the presidential palace in a desperate bid for power and was killed. Nine days later López Contreras was chosen by the dead dictator's hand-picked Congress to fill his unexpired term.

In an atmosphere of great social and political effervescence, many exiles with different ideologies returned home and joined activists emerging from the underground in organizing trade unions, political parties, and professional organizations. López found himself under siege from the right and the left. He sometimes yielded to pressures for reform, then stubbornly resisted demands for change in the undemocratic Gómez political system. Under that system Gómez's hand-picked Congress elected López for a new term as president in April 1936.

In 1936 the country also received a new constitution, but López, as rabidly anticommunist as Gómez, insisted on retaining the Gómez clause that defined communism and anarchism as treason. With the major opposition parties (the reformist *Partido Democrático Nacional* [PDN] led by Rómulo Betancourt and the Venezuelan Communist party of Gustavo Machado) outlawed and their leaders in exile, the outcome of the 1941

490 presidential election was never in doubt. López's hand-picked candidate, General Isaias Medina Angarita, won easily over novelist Rómulo Gallegos, the unofficial candidate of the PDN, whom López had dropped from his cabinet.

World War II, having created an insatiable demand for Venezuela's oil, enabled Medina's government to wrest more favorable terms from the oil companies than were in the old inequitable contracts. Other achievements of his administration included the passage of Venezuela's first social security and income-tax legislation. The government also encouraged the formation of trade unions, which gained considerable strength, particularly in the oil industry. Medina viewed favorably a movement toward a more democratic system, with direct popular election of the president and a broader suffrage, and discussed these reforms with the civilian politicians, but left their implementation to the president who would succeed him in 1946.

Medina also tackled the country's urgent agrarian problem. Near the end of his administration he asked his minister of agriculture, Angel Biaggini, to draft an agrarian reform bill that would distribute the extensive state landholdings to landless peasants. Congress passed the law, but one month after passage it died stillborn as a result of the overthrow of the Medina administration by a military-civilian revolt headed by two men who would dominate Venezuelan politics for the next two decades, Marcos Pérez Jiménez and Rómulo Betancourt.

Betancourt was the most influential personality among that famous generation of student leaders who in 1928 electrified Caracas by leading a public demonstration against Gómez. Of middle-class background, during his years of exile Betancourt had read widely in the classics of Marxist literature. But the most decisive influence on his thought was a nationalist, reformist ideological current best represented in Latin America by the Peruvian Victor Raúl Haya de la Torre, who argued that in Latin America's specific conditions, characterized by economic backwardness and a small, weak working class, the immediate historical task of social revolutionaries was to complete the unfinished bourgeois revolution.

Betancourt thus appears as the standard-bearer of the Venezuelan bourgeois revolution, which sought to end dependency on oil by diversifying the economy through industrialization, to expand the internal market by improving living standards, and to initiate land reform that would increase the productivity of agriculture. All these goals he hoped to achieve within the framework of parliamentary democracy. Betancourt assigned a decisive role in this process to the state, which should plan, regulate, and assist economic development.

The political instrument Betancourt and his colleagues created to achieve Venezuela's bourgeois, democratic revolution was *Acción Democrática* (AD), a multiclass party and a mass organization that enjoyed a large growth from 1941 to 1945, gaining a clear superiority in numbers and influence among workers, peasants, and the middle class over its closest rival, the Communist party.

A Strange Alliance: Betancourt and the Military in Power, 1945–1948

On October 18, 1945, a military-civilian coup overthrew the Medina regime as it was approaching its legal end and established a provisional government headed by Betancourt as president. The motives for this coup, born of an alliance between conservative young military officers and the AD's liberal leadership, continue to provoke historical debate. The fact that Medina's record was on the whole consistently progressive and that he had supported sweeping constitutional reforms, including universal suffrage, raises serious questions as to why AD supported the coup against him.

The dominant motive of the young officers, organized in the *Unión Patriótica Militar* (UPM), who planned the coup and obtained AD's support for it, appears to have been discontent over promotion, salary, and appointment policies within the military. The fighting to achieve the triumph of the less than lofty aims of these allies caused some 2,500 casualties. Once the fighting had ended, the military displayed little interest in governmental affairs and appeared content to leave policy making and its implementation to the AD. Of the seven members of the ruling Revolutionary Junta, headed by Betancourt, only two were military men.

However dubious the motives that inspired the coup of October 18, 1945, it proved a milestone in Venezuelan history. The three years of government by the AD (between October 1945 and November 1948)—a period Venezuelans call the *Trienio*—represented the first serious effort to transform the country's archaic economic and social structures.

Betancourt, acting as the junta's provisional president, ruled by decree from October 1945 until the election of Rómulo Gallegos in December 1947. In March 1946 Betancourt issued two decrees that constituted a new electoral law and provided for universal suffrage. Since Acción Democrática was, in effect, the government and had a large nationwide network of party organizations to mobilize the population, it had a distinct advantage over its political rivals, the conservative Social Christian party, usually called COPEI, led by Rafael Caldera; the liberal, reformist Democratic Republican Union (URD), led by Jovito Villalba; and the Communist party, led by Gustavo Machado.

The AD won an overwhelming victory in the election for the Constituent Assembly, with almost 79 percent of the vote. The Constituent Assembly empowered the Revolutionary Junta to govern until a new constitution had been approved and a congress and president elected.

This period of whirlwind political activity was also marked by a major campaign to organize trade and peasant unions in which the AD played a leading role. AD control of the distribution of land and agricultural credits under the agrarian reform enabled it to build a clientele of peasant union leaders that gave it a commanding majority of the peasant vote. AD established a similar relationship of influence and leadership over most of the more than 500 trade unions organ-

ized in this period and affiliated with the Venezuelan Confederation of Workers, which included both trade and peasant unions.

The Constituent Assembly proclaimed the new constitution on July 5, 1947. The document guaranteed many civil and social rights, including labor's right to organize and strike and the principle that land should belong "to him who works it." The constitution established universal, secret voting for all persons over eighteen, with direct election of the president and both houses of Congress.

On December 14, 1947, presidential and congressional elections were held and the AD candidate for president, Rómulo Gallegos, was elected with almost 75 percent of the popular vote.

Among the economic issues with which the AD government had to deal, oil policy was most important, for it involved fundamental questions of dependency, economic sovereignty, and the revenues needed for economic diversification and modernization. In December 1946 the government had imposed a supertax of 26 percent on all company profits over 28 million bolivars; the law was aimed primarily at the oil companies. This tax alone increased government income in 1947 by 230 percent over its income in 1938.

In view of the great importance the AD program attached to agrarian reform, the junta's approach was timid. Evidently fearing the political and economic repercussions of a frontal attack on the latifundio, the government preferred to distribute land to the peasants from the extensive state holdings taken over on Gómez's death, Venezuela's premier latifundist. Out of a landless peasant population estimated at about 330,000, only between 55,000 and 80,000 received land during the Trienio. Since the average peasant received only 2.2 hectares of land to cultivate, "the problem," as Judith Ewell points out, "then changed from *latifundia* to *minifundia.*"

The creation of an independent national economy through industrialization was a major government goal. The *Corporación Venezolana de Fomento* (CVF) (Venezuelan Development Corporation) was formed in 1946 to promote this

492   process through loans to private entrepreneurs and direct investment in state corporations. Between January 1946 and December 1948 it lent nearly 50 million bolivars to industrial enterprises.

By the Trienio's end, the program of "sowing the petroleum" to diversify and modernize the economy had achieved only modest results. More impressive progress was made in health and education. Under Gallegos the budget for the ministry of education for 1948 tripled and that for the ministry of health quadrupled by comparison to 1945. Important advances were also made in eliminating the country's principal health scourge, malaria, by spraying with DDT the breeding grounds of mosquitos, which carried the disease.

The principal danger to the regime came from the military. The conservative officers, headed by Colonel Pérez Jiménez, gradually became disenchanted with what they regarded as the radical excesses of their civilian partners. On November 24 the government was overthrown by a virtually bloodless coup, and Minister of Defense Carlos Delgado Chalbaud took power as president of a military junta. Many of the leading members of the AD regime were arrested and imprisoned. Betancourt escaped and took refuge in the Colombian Embassy; later he, Gallegos, and other prominent AD leaders were permitted to go into exile.

The Military Dictatorship, 1948–1958

In a proclamation issued on November 25, Delgado Chalbaud, who had personal and political differences with Pérez Jiménez, declared that the junta was a provisional government and did not intend to destroy Venezuelan democracy or prohibit the activities of political parties. But the junta's actions contradicted its claims of democratic intentions. Soon after the coup it dissolved Congress, annulled the 1947 Constitution, and voided the petroleum law and other progressive measures of the Gallegos administration. The agrarian reform program and the school construction program initiated by the AD regime were abandoned or suspended. The junta also imposed a strict censorship, forbidding any criticism of the regime. In January 1949 the junta launched an offensive against the unions, arresting leaders of the Venezuelan labor confederation, forbidding union meetings, and freezing the funds of most of the unions.

Initially resistance to the junta and its repressive policies was largely limited to student protests and the activities of the illegal Communist party, whose members played a leading role in the organization of the resistance movement. In 1949 AD leaders who remained in the country formed an underground organization. Against the objections of the strongly anticommunist Betancourt and other AD leaders in exile, the AD underground cooperated with the Communists and other groups of the resistance movement in the struggle against the dictatorship.

The assassination of Delgado Chalbaud, kidnapped in November 1950 in a Caracas street in full daylight and taken to the outskirts of the city where he was murdered, ended the first phase of the military dictatorship. A civilian puppet of Pérez Jiménez, Germán Suárez Flamerich, now became president of the military junta, and announced that elections would be held and the constitutional order restored as soon as possible.

Simultaneously, however, the military regime intensified its repressive activity. By the fall of 1952, the regime, evidently convinced that the repression had intimidated the Venezuelan people into accepting its rule, decided it would be safe to hold elections for a Constituent Assembly.

Despite the repressive conditions and the call issued by the exiled AD leadership to abstain from voting—a position it reversed at the last moment—Venezuelans gave a two-thirds majority of the popular vote to the opposition parties. Furious at this outcome, Pérez Jiménez nullified the election and announced he was taking office as provisional president in the name of the armed forces. Presently a recount of the vote, made at his orders, showed an "overwhelming victory" for the government party. An obedient Constituent Assembly gave the dictator the constitution he wanted and named him "Constitutional President."

For the next five years (1953–1958) Pérez Jiménez was the absolute ruler of Venezuela. A brutally efficient repression, whose principal instrument was *Seguridad Nacional,* the secret police, made antigovernment activities very difficult. A resistance movement, however, uniting persons of all political tendencies survived and continued its struggle against the dictatorship.

The social and economic policies of the regime generated discontent among ever wider sections of the population. Its limitations on the right to organize and strike contributed to a decline of labor's share of the national income. In place of the AD's focus on education, health, agrarian reform, and balanced economic development, the Pérez Jiménez regime emphasized grand works of infrastructure—highways, urban freeways, and port improvements, and urban constructions, some of little or no social utility, like the Officers Club in Caracas or the many-storied shopping center built on the side of one of Caracas's hills.

Signs of defection from the regime multiplied in 1957. Especially significant was the increasingly critical attitude of the conservative Catholic hierarchy, which issued statements deploring the government's disregard for the interests of the poor. Disaffection also grew among national capitalists, who complained of the government's neglect. With the end of the oil export boom in the late 1950s, the regime's capacity to generate business activity and employment through public works programs began to run out of steam. Within the armed forces there was growing resentment of Pérez Jiménez's arbitrary ways and his reliance on the secret police to watch over the loyalty of officers.

By mid-1957, an underground organization called the *Junta Patriótica* had been formed to unite the principal political parties—AD, COPEI, URD, and the Venezuelan Communist party. This group became the principal motor of the resistance movement and its preparation for a popular revolt. In October Pérez Jiménez, approaching the end of his constitutional term as president and fearing the results of an election, announced that a plebiscite would be held instead to determine whether the people wished him to continue in power. This brazen announcement and the

farcical plebiscite that followed caused an explosion of mingled ridicule and wrath. On January 21 the Junta Patriótica proclaimed a general strike that was overwhelmingly effective and was accompanied by clashes between the people and the regime's security forces. Barricades appeared in the streets of Caracas. The next day the insurgents seized key strategic points in the capital. The majority of military units refused to obey Pérez Jiménez and fraternized with the rebels. On January 23 a military junta headed by Admiral Wolfgang Larrazábal met with Pérez Jiménez and demanded that he resign; within a few hours the dictator had fled the country for the Dominican Republic.

The military junta, enlarged by the addition of two prominent businessmen, became a provisional government: its first decrees proclaimed the restoration of all democratic freedoms, amnesty for all political prisoners and exiles, and legalization of all political parties. Almost ten years of rule by a repressive military dictatorship had ended.

Venezuela's Representative Democracy, 1958–1995

The military-civilian junta headed by the popular Larrazábal presided over the transition to democratic elections, set for December 1958. Larrazábal defeated a number of conspiracies by reactionary military and he was supported by most of the armed forces and thousands of workers and students, who took to the streets in protest.

Chastened by experience, the Betancourt who returning from exile was politically more moderate than the aggressive leader who presided over the reforms of the Trienio. Betancourt's efforts to reassure Venezuela's economic elite about his intentions and his decision to choose the right-leaning COPEI as his principal political ally reflected his new caution.

On October 31, 1958, the three centrist parties—AD, COPEI, and URD—formally endorsed the Pact of Punto Fijo which provided that whatever the election results, the three parties would

494

form a coalition government to carry out a program of democratic socioeconomic and political reforms.

The Pact of Punto Fijo was important far beyond its impact on the 1958 elections because it created a unique Venezuelan model of representative democracy. The Venezuelan government was consciously tailored to isolate the Marxist left, making it virtually impossible for Marxists to wield political power. Secondly, although the Pact of Punto Fijo provided for a three-party coalition, the system evolved toward hegemonic control of political life by two parties, the social democratic AD and the social Christian COPEI, whose reformist programs were broadly similar.

A third distinctive feature of the Venezuelan model of representative democracy was the major role that it assigned to the state as regulator and arbiter of relations between the classes and interest groups. The massive influx of petroleum revenues over most of the past three decades strengthened the state and endowed it with the financial resources to perform this role, which required it to balance and mediate the conflicting demands and interests of all the major classes and pressure groups—labor, the peasantry, capitalists, the middle class, the armed forces, the church, the political parties.

Finally, the architect of the Venezuelan model of representative democracy, Rómulo Betancourt, viewed the state as an instrument for the gradual recapture of the nation's natural resources from foreign control, the reform of its socioeconomic structures, and the promotion of a balanced economic development. Betancourt hoped that, in time, economic development would lead to the rise of an autonomous Venezuelan capitalism capable of providing Venezuelans with a high standard of living and culture. Indeed, over the last three decades Venezuela has made large advances in such problem areas as health and literacy. But the vast sums expended in "sowing the petroleum" over those decades have not achieved Betancourt's main goals; poverty has not declined but increased, income distribution is as inequitable as in Mexico

and Brazil, and today's Venezuela, burdened with an unpayable foreign debt, is more deeply dependent than it was in the time of Juan Vicente Gómez.

A Decade of AD Rule, 1959–1969

Although the three centrist parties had approved a common program of economic, social, and political reform broadly similar to the one carried out during the Trienio, they could not agree on a presidential candidate acceptable to all, and so each ran its own in the December 1958 election. AD's candidate, Betancourt, won with 49 percent of the popular vote and formed a coalition government that included cabinet positions for URD, AD, COPEI, and independents but excluded the Communist party.

Differences within and between the parties over domestic and foreign policy, aggravated by the continuing economic crisis and Betancourt's own contentious nature, soon placed serious strains on the coalition. The victory of the Cuban Revolution in January 1959 and Cuba's gradual turn toward socialism created an especially divisive issue. Younger AD and URD activists hailed the revolution as a model that Venezuela could well emulate. But Betancourt, virulently anticommunist, regarded the Cuban socialist regime as a direct challenge to his own reformist philosophy and program and fully supported U.S. efforts to isolate Castro's regime economically and politically. As a result of Betancourt's position, AD's left wing broke away in April 1960 and formed the Movement of the Revolutionary Left (MIR), which soon proclaimed itself a Marxist-Leninist party. A few months later Betancourt's decision to break off diplomatic relations with Cuba led to the departure of the URD from his government. He responded to these defections by strengthening his ties with the conservative COPEI, the armed forces, with the church, and with the economic elite.

The new constitution promulgated in February 1961 proclaimed the government's responsibility for its citizens' social well-being, provided for proportional minority representation in Congress, and prohibited the president from succeeding himself, but gave him significant powers to suspend constitutional guarantees of personal and civil liberties.

Betancourt's tactics in his struggle against the left strongly suggest a calculated effort to goad the leftist opposition into resorting to violence that would discredit it and that the armed forces could easily repress. The MIR and the Communist party played into Betancourt's hands and initiated an insurgency movement in 1961. At first primarily an urban movement whose participants were recruited from MIR and PCV youth, by April 1962 the insurgency included rural guerrilla bands operating in at least eight of the country's twenty states. Poorly organized and unskilled militarily, most of the bands were soon wiped out by the government's counterinsurgency operations.

During his 1958 election campaign Betancourt laid heavy stress on the need for agrarian reform, and his promise to give land to the landless helped him gain an overwhelming majority of the peasant vote. But the results of the agrarian reform were mixed, at best, and fell far short of solving Venezuela's acute agrarian problem.

By 1969 only some 150,000 out of the 350,000 peasant families without land in 1960 had received plots. Combined with the estimated 200,000 new families formed in those eight years, there remained 400,000 families without land. Government investments in irrigation, roads, and credit and technical assistance primarily benefited large and medium-sized commercial farms, which produced the lion's share of profitable crops and accounted for most of the 150 percent increase in agricultural production during the years between 1959 and 1968.

More significant, perhaps, were the large advances made in health and public education during the Betancourt administration. Nearly 9 percent of the national budget was assigned to the Ministry of Health and Social Assistance. A concerted attack on the problems of endemic disease, infant mortality, and malnutrition resulted in a decline of infant mortality from 64 per 1,000 live births in the 1955–1959 period to 46.5 in

1966. The Betancourt years also saw a significant growth of public education.

A major objective of the Betancourt regime was to increase its share of oil profits in order to make more funds available for development. A tax law of December 1958 raised the tax rate on oil profits to 65 percent.

Agrarian reform and industrialization were the two keystones of the new Venezuela Betancourt wished to build. The slogan "Venezuela must industrialize or die" expressed the militant spirit of the new campaign to industrialize that began in 1958. The AD government transferred large resources generated by oil exports to the industrialization process in the form of loans and direct subsidies.

The campaign for "economic independence," however, had a peculiar outcome; it fastened more firmly the chains of dependence on Venezuela. Confronted with high tariff walls, unwilling to lose the large consumer market created by oil wealth, a growing number of U.S. and other foreign firms chose to establish branches in Venezuela, frequently in association with local capital. The label "Made in Venezuela" increasingly came to mean an article made with raw materials and intermediate materials imported from the United States and finished or assembled in Venezuela.

Between 1958 and 1970 the number of plants producing such items as cans, foodstuffs, clothing, automobiles, auto tires, paint, and cigarettes mushroomed. The alliance of foreign and native capital achieved the goal of import substitution, but since the dominant partner in the alliance was foreign capital, most of the profits flowed back to the home offices of foreign firms. By 1971 Venezuela had the largest gross accumulated foreign investment in any Third World country: $5.57 billion.

The drive for import-substitution industrialization was accompanied by the incorporation of labor as a less-than-equal partner in an alliance with the state and industry. In 1958 labor leaders signed a pact with management that committed the unions to seek conciliation of conflicts with employers. The subordination of labor was completed during the following decade of AD rule.

496

Raul Leoni, AD's nominee for president, won over COPEI's Rafael Caldera and five other candidates in the December 1963 election. Although Leoni continued Betancourt's policy of state-supported import-substitution industrialization, the outcome was a dependent industrialization dominated by foreign-based multinationals. During Leoni's presidency the export of profits reached an annual average of $672 million. Venezuela, observes one economist, had become "a fiscal paradise of foreign monopoly capital."

Caldera in Power, 1969–1973

Internal division contributed to the loss of the AD candidate to Caldera in 1968. Responding to growing nationalist sentiment and charges that the foreign oil companies were withholding further investment in Venezuela in reprisal for higher taxes and increased government control, Caldera had called for the reversion to the nation of all existing oil concessions after 1983. A law passed in 1971 provided for the reversion to the state of all existing oil concessions beginning in 1983 and stipulated that unexploited concessions be ceded to the CVP in 1974. In addition, the oil companies were required to post bonds guaranteeing that their plant and machinery would be turned over in good condition. Also enacted in 1971 were bills nationalizing the foreign-owned natural gas industry and giving the government power to control oil production levels. Finally, during his last months in office, Caldera issued a decree that forbade foreign interest in radio and television stations and electric companies.

Despite the establishment of representative democracy in 1958 and the reforms initiated by Caldera in 1969 a survey of Venezuela's economic and social conditions made in 1973 gave no cause for satisfaction with either of the country's two ruling parties. No basic change in economic structure had occurred; the government remained heavily dependent on oil income. True, import-substitution industrialization had achieved some economic diversification, but it was a dependent industrialization largely based on foreign capital, inputs, and technology. Despite the agrarian reform, agriculture remained the most backward branch of the national economy. In 1971 Venezuela still imported 46 percent of its basic foodstuffs. The failure of the agrarian reform to correct fundamental problems was also reflected in the continuing high concentration of landownership; 1.4 percent of the large estates held 67 percent of all privately owned land in 1973.

Thanks to the eradication of such scourges as malaria and improved health care, the Venezuelan population had grown rapidly, increasing from 7,524,000 in 1958 to 10,722,000 in 1971. But it is doubtful whether the quality of life for the majority of Venezuelans had improved after fifteen years of democratic rule. In 1974, 30 percent of all Venezuelan children suffered from malnutrition; 12 percent of all adults suffered from mental retardation from the same cause, combined with other difficult living conditions. In the early 1960s a United Nations study described Venezuela's income distribution as one of the most unequal in the world. A decade later the situation had not improved.

The Dilemmas of a Petroleum Republic, 1974–1995

From the election of December 1973 the AD candidate, Carlos Andrés Pérez, a Betancourt protégé, emerged an easy winner over the COPEI nominee. The flamboyant Pérez, a master of populist rhetoric, had promised a "war on poverty" and against "privilege." Despite his rhetoric, his program did not differ substantially from those of his predecessors.

Pérez took office under the most favorable auspices: the Arab oil embargo of 1973 had brought a rapid rise in the price of oil, going from $2.01 a barrel in 1970 to $14.26 in January 1974. The resulting vast increase in state revenues appeared to give Venezuela the means to solve all its major social and economic problems. Pérez promised to "manage abundance with the mentality of scarcity," but the flood of oil riches and the irresistible drive to modernize overwhelmed his administration and frustrated his good intentions.

On August 29, 1975, Pérez signed a law nationalizing the Venezuelan oil industry, taking effect January 1, 1976. A state oil company, *Petroven,* was created to control a sector of the economy whose annual sales volume exceeded $10 billion. In addition to a generous compensation of $1 billion to the foreign companies, the nationalization agreement authorized the state to enter into contracts with those companies for the provision of technological assistance and equipment, as well as marketing agreements for the international transshipment of Venezuelan oil exports.

Pérez's economic program called for the creation and expansion of heavy industries, especially petrochemicals, steel, and shipbuilding, that would supply the needs of Venezuela's consumer goods industry. Gradually other projects—a fishery industry, a national rail system, the Caracas metro, and modernized port facilities—were added to this list.

During his campaign Pérez had pledged he would direct "priority attention to the needs of Venezuelan agriculture as the essential motor of economic development." But like his predecessors, Pérez understood those "needs" as the needs of large commercial farmers. Although Pérez claimed in 1975 to have achieved an "agricultural miracle," the reality was very different. Domestic food production increased, but imports of the country's basic foodstuffs rose from 46 percent in 1971 to almost 70 percent by the close of his administration. The rapid growth of the urban population contributed to this increased food dependence.

The immense revenues that flowed to the state from 1974 to 1979 proved inadequate to cover the costs of the government's ambitious development program. Increasingly Pérez had to resort to foreign loans; between 1974 and 1978 Venezuela's foreign debt grew by almost $10 billion.

In foreign policy, Pérez continued an initiative begun by Caldera and resumed diplomatic relations with Castro's government in December 1974. Pérez also supported Panama's efforts to gain control of the Panama Canal and the Sandi-

nista struggle against the dictatorship of Anastasio Somoza.

Pérez cultivated a populist image that did not correspond to his social policies. As a result of the orgy of state spending in the Pérez years, the economy heated up and inflation cut deeply into workers' living standards. For the business, financial, and political elites, however, the boom created vast opportunities for enrichment resulting in an explosion of conspicuous consumption by these classes as the standard of living for peasants and workers deteriorated. The intimate ties between the state, the ruling party, and the economic elites generated corruption on an unheard-of scale.

Finally, the Pérez economic program had clearly failed to solve the dilemma of dependency that continued to plague Venezuela. Measured by the yardsticks of foreign indebtedness and the degree of its reliance for revenue on a single resource—oil—Venezuela was more dependent in 1980 than it had been in 1974.

Pérez's successors in the presidency—the COPEI leader Luis Herrera Campins, elected in 1978, and the AD leader Jaime Lusinchi, elected in 1983—had to struggle with the devastating combined effects of recurrent drops in oil prices and the massive overflow of funds to service the foreign debt. In a New Year's Eve 1989 address to the nation Lusinchi, proclaiming that the debt "is strangling our country's social and economic development and that of the majority of the world's people," announced a payment moratorium on the principal of all debts accumulated with foreign banks before 1983.

The 1988 election saw the return of AD candidate Carlos Andrés Pérez to the presidency. Pérez, who had denounced Lusinchi's subservience to the foreign bankers, inaugurated an economic austerity program in response to the conditions demanded by the IMF in exchange for a $4.5 billion loan over a three-year period. The program included a massive currency devaluation, the lifting of controls and subsidies on a wide range of products and services, such as gasoline, bread, and electricity, and a rise in interest rates. The price increases were announced in

498

advance of their application; as a result goods vanished from the shelves as shopkeepers prepared to take advantage of the higher prices.

On February 27 and 28, 1989, a popular explosion rocked Caracas when a significant rise in bus fares was announced. For many Venezuelans, whose wage increases were cut in half by this measure alone, it was the last straw. Tens of thousands of people took to the streets, rioting and looting shops; from Caracas the rioting spread to the poor barrios surrounding the city, then to the nearby port of La Guaira, and later to more distant cities and towns.

The Pérez government responded with a display of force that many observers found excessive; in contrast to the officially admitted death toll of around 300, unofficial estimates placed the number of dead at between 400 and 1000. The shock waves of the explosion soon reached Washington, where the U.S. Treasury hastened to make a $453 million "bridging loan" to the Pérez government in advance of the signing of an economic adjustment program by Venezuela and the IMF. In another apparent reaction to events in Venezuela U.S. Treasury Secretary Nicholas Brady announced a plan providing for a partial reduction of the Latin American debt. Pérez continued to insist that his "six-month shock" economic program was correct in its essentials and would in time create "a new Venezuela."

In the meantime, however, that program was deepening the recession Pérez had inherited from Lusinchi and causing a growing amount of economic pain. As a result of the currency devaluation and the lifting of price controls and subsidies, by May prices for many basic foods and household items, transport, and electricity had risen between 50 and 100 percent. Real wages had fallen between 20 and 50 percent. In March alone the inflation rate reached 21.3 percent.

Pérez faced a dilemma. He was caught between the demands of the IMF, the World Bank, and the foreign bankers that he continue his austerity program as a condition for obtaining the new loans needed to reactivate the economy and the counterdemands of labor and the middle class that he change course and relieve the suffering

When an increase in bus fares was announced in Caracas during February 1989, tens of thousands of angry Venezuelans took to the streets in protest.

caused by his economic adjustment program and a deepening recession. He decided to continue with his economic adjustment plan, which included the privatization of a large number of state-owned enterprises. Not the least irony was that it was Pérez himself who had nationalized the iron and steel industries and proclaimed "evolutionary socialism" his long-term goal. Pérez himself called his IMF-style austerity program *el gran viraje* ("the great turnabout"). For many suffering Venezuelans, however, it was "the great betrayal."

In December Venezuela held its first direct elections of 269 mayors and 20 state governors. The elections showed the highest rate of abstention in Venezuelan history, reflecting widespread cynicism about the ruling AD and COPEI parties. Also significant was the election of left-wing candidates for governor in two important industrial states, Bolívar and Aragua, where opposition to privatization was very strong.

Critics of Pérez's program for selling off publicly owned enterprises to the private sector in the name of "industrial reconversion" and "rationalization" warned that it would cause significant loss of employment in a country already burdened with large unemployment and that ownership of those enterprises would most likely pass into the hands of foreign multinationals. Despite the opposition within and without his own party López pressed ahead with the program. The first privatizations resulted in the sale of 40 percent of the state-owned telephone company to the U.S. telecommunications giant GTE, the national airline to the Spanish Iberia, and several large hotels to various international private interests. Opponents charged that the privatization sales grossly undervalued these assets and that public officials made questionable deals in order to line their own pockets.

A onetime bonanza of $2 billion in government revenues from the sale of state companies and a boom in the import-led commercial sector as a result of a reduction in import duties helped spur a partial revival of the economy from its deep recession. But the recovery was mainly in the realm of stock market speculation; industry and agriculture continued to stagnate. Some economic and social indicators reflected the failure of neoliberal economic policy to improve the life of most Venezuelans. The real minimum wage in 1991 was only 44 percent of its 1987 value; the number of people living below the poverty line jumped from 15 percent at the end of 1988 to 41 percent in 1991; and inflation, reaching a record high of 80 percent in 1989, has not fallen below 30 percent since then.

Mounting anger over Pérez's austerity program, the growing gap between rich and poor, and revelations of corruption in official circles sparked a series of strikes and protests demanding Pérez's resignation. The growing discontent reached into the middle and lower echelons of the military, whose members were unhappy with their own deteriorating living conditions and with Pérez's privatization program; in February 1992 a coup attempt, led by Lieutenant Colonel Hugo Chávez Frías, involved 10 percent of the nation's armed forces and came perilously close to overthrowing the regime and seizing power. Its program included putting all those engaged in corruption on trial; a reversal of Pérez's neolib-

eral policies; an emergency program to combat misery and poverty; and a dissolution of government and election of a constitutional assembly. Although defeated, overnight Chávez became a folk hero among the poor in Caracas's "belt of misery." A second abortive coup, also stressing the corruption issue, took place in November 1992.

Despite their defeat, the foiled coups combined with the unending wave of strikes, protests, and other expressions of seething unrest to place Pérez and his corrupt practices in the dock of Venezuelan public opinion. Responding to this pressure, on May 20, 1993, the Supreme Court indicted Pérez, and the next day the Senate unanimously voted to lift his presidential immunity. On August 31, after more incriminating evidence had come to light, a special session of Congress voted to make the suspension permanent and confirmed acting President Ramón J. Velásquez in office until his successor, elected in December, should take over in February 1994. The indictment of Pérez charged him with misappropriating $17 million from a secret fund earmarked for national security.

These dramatic events took place against a background of political upheaval. Despite massive fraud, the December 1992 elections for governors, mayors, and city councils produced heavy losses for Pérez's AD party. Only four AD candidates won clear victories in the races for the twenty governorships. A particularly stinging defeat was the victory in Caracas of the mayoral candidate of a small left-wing party, *Causa Radical,* over the AD's candidate, a prominent politician expected to head the party's ticket in the upcoming presidential elections.

As Venezuelan voters prepared to go to the polls again in the December 5, 1993, general election, the economic indicators gave no comfort to the ruling AD party. In the first seven months of 1993 more than 1,000 small and medium-size companies closed, with the loss of 59,000 jobs. High interest rates, inflation approaching 40 percent, an influx of imports, and weak demand caused by low purchasing power were blamed for the increasingly severe recession. Foreign investments, on which the Pérez administration had

500

heavily counted to reactivate the economy, fell by more than 40 percent in the first eight months of 1993.

The results of the general election represented a crushing repudiation, not only of Pérez and his neoliberal policies but of the two-party rule that had prevailed since the fall of General Marcos Pérez Jiménez in 1958. In a four-way race, Rafael Caldera, the seventy-seven-year-old populist who had been rejected by his own COPEI party for his opposition to neoliberal policies—during the campaign he had dismissed AD's and COPEI's candidates as "IMF-package candidates"—ran as the candidate of a coalition of smaller parties and was elected president with 30 percent of the vote. Caldera had the support of most left parties, but Andrés Velásquez, a former steelworker, candidate of the left-wing *Causa R,* received 21 percent of the vote. COPEI's Oswaldo Álvarez Paz received 22 percent and AD's Claudio Fermín 23 percent of the vote. The election also changed the composition of Congress, replacing the traditional two-party dominance by three power blocs: Caldera's coalition (*Convergencia*) and its socialist ally (*Movimiento al Socialismo*, MAS) forming one bloc, *Causa R* the second, and the traditional parties, COPEI and AD, the third. But the traditional parties, which owed many of their seats to fraud, continued to have a majority in Congress, and in February 1994 they inflicted a major setback on Caldera by assigning the most important permanent commissions, including defense and finance, to their own members.

Caldera's victory and the large gains made by left-wing parties in the general election despite expensive advertising campaigns by the traditional parties and efforts to alter the results by the customary frauds—in some states as much as 50 percent of the votes was reportedly nullified by COPEI and AD counters—testified to the strength of the movement for social and economic change. But the stubborn, no-holds-barred resistance of the entrenched COPEI and AD machines gave a foretaste of the obstacles that Caldera and his allies would encounter. They faced not only domestic but foreign opposition. In the United States, where some regarded the neoliberal economic model as the only possible model for Latin America, Caldera's rise was greeted with cries of alarm. During the campaign the *New York Times* had attacked him for "demagoguery" and after his election hinted at the possibility of a military coup if he should stumble; President Clinton had earlier sent an emissary to Caracas to warn against the deviation of protectionism.

In reality, the reform program of Caldera and his allies was quite modest. They agreed on the need for a new labor law—strongly opposed by big business—whose provisions would discourage layoffs in a time of deep recession. Other goals of the Caldera-MAS alliance included increase of the monthly minimum wage, repeal of an IMF-inspired value added tax that had led to sharp price increases on items of popular consumption, new taxes on luxury items, and a reform of the income tax system that would improve tax collection by imposing heavy fines on evaders (tax evasion is estimated at 70 percent). Caldera also had a plan—not unlike one proposed by Fidel Castro—for Latin American debtor countries to work out a common approach in their negotiations with international banks.

A thorough economic reform was vital, but much more was needed to restore Venezuelan society to health. Like other Latin American countries, Venezuela has long had a problem of police and security forces that routinely engage in torture and other human rights abuses against political dissidents and others. According to Amnesty International and the Caracas-based Support Network (quoted in *Latinamerica Press*), Venezuela is "a world at clandestine torture cells." Even the U.S. State Department, which holds Venezuela up as a "model democracy," acknowledged in a recent report on human rights violations in Venezuela that "physical abuse of those detained and of prisoners is widespread and includes the use of electrical shocks, physical assaults, and rape." It remained to be seen how quickly and vigorously the Caldera team would act to end these repressive practices and to cleanse the country's corrupt judicial system.

The conditions under which Caldera took office on February 2, 1994, made for a transition that was anything but smooth. His first crisis occurred even before he officially became president. Four days before his inauguration, he summoned the military high command to his home in Caracas and informed them they were fired. It was alleged that Defense Minister Radames Múñoz and other right-wing officers were plotting to prevent Caldera from taking office; according to the prominent journalist José Vicente Rangel, the CIA was involved in the plot.

Then, on January 16, 1994, government officials shut down the Banco Latino, the nation's second largest bank, amid claims that bank executives had stolen millions of dollars in fraudulent operations, including the laundering of drug money. In early March arrest warrants were issued for eighty-three of the bank's executives, but by then most had fled overseas. The bank was reopened in early April under official supervision after the government had injected $3 billion, but this massive bailout (condemned by one Venezuelan economist as "taking from the poor and giving to the rich") failed to prevent the worst economic crisis in the country's history, with a sharp increase in inflation, a plunge in the value of the nation's currency, and an accelerating capital flight. Annual economic growth was expected to fall to a dismal negative 2.5 percent in 1994.

Former President Carlos Andrés Pérez—who went to jail on May 18 awaiting trial on corruption charges—was deeply implicated in the banking debacle. During his 1989–1993 administration he had invested vast amounts of government money in Banco Latino, enabling it to rise from being the nation's fourteenth to the second largest bank. One of Pérez's cronies, Pedro Tinoco, head of the Central Bank, "helped to engineer Banco Latino's phenomenal growth, which benefited Pérez's friends who worked at or invested in the bank." Pérez, who managed to turn a modest government salary into a fortune estimated in billions of dollars, "is only the most visible symbol of the corruption that has become a way of life here, according to analysts and average Venezuelans," observed *Latinamerica Press* in June 1994.

As his program evolved, Caldera's response to the desperate economic crisis deviated more and more from the expectations of many of his supporters, who had expected him to make a sharp break with the discredited neoliberal policies. By June 1 what the *Latin American Weekly Report* called "the first, idealistic phase of the second Caldera presidency" had ended with the resignation of reform-minded ministers in his government and the formation of a new Cabinet with the predominantly neoliberal outlook demanded by business pressure groups. The government's more conservative complexion was reflected in indications that it would soon renew the drive to privatize practically all state companies and that a rescue operation at public expense of eight banks affected by the Banco Latino collapse was under way. The few offsetting concessions to Caldera's social democratic partner, MAS, included currency controls, price controls on food staples, and placing the former guerrilla and leading MAS member, Pompeyo Márquez, in charge of all social policies. But the currency controls would likely lead to a black market in dollars; price controls could cause merchants to withhold products, resulting in food shortages; and without a drastic change in tax policies and spending priorities Márquez could not even begin to tackle the country's stupendous social problems. Six months into the Caldera administration, 80 percent of the population lived below the poverty line and such public services as schools, hospitals, and roads were falling apart. Children were the most vulnerable victims of the economic and social debacle; according to a Venezuelan research center, only 20 percent of the country's children grew up in acceptable conditions, 36 percent grew up in poverty, and 44 percent were raised in absolute poverty. The same research center reported, not surprisingly, that poor children grew less than wealthier children and that the learning ability of poor children was stunted.

Caldera's return to economic orthodoxy was hailed by the business sector but damaged his

502

image as a crusading populist president among workers and shantytown dwellers. Apparently fearing uprisings like the failed military coups of 1992 and the food riots of 1989, in June 1994 Caldera suspended constitutional guarantees, including the rights to liberty, personal security, and free travel, and to protection against unreasonable search. Security forces searched the homes of activists, former military officials, and politicians both on the left and right; they rounded up hundreds of persons in Caracas's slums. Human rights activists and church leaders condemned the suspensions of constitutional guarantees, comparing Caldera's acts to similar measures by former President Andrés Pérez that Caldera had denounced during last year's presidential campaign. Increasingly, it appeared that the Caldera phenomenon represented another example of the sadly familiar tendency of populist politicians to make promises of sweeping social and political change that they did not intend to keep, simply in order to keep the neoliberal boat afloat.

Colombia: The Nineteenth-Century Background

The Santander Regime and the Birth of a Two-Party System, 1830–1850

Following the secession of Venezuela and Ecuador from Gran Colombia in 1830, the remaining territory went its separate way under the name of the Republic of New Granada (present-day Colombia plus Panama). Struggles for control of the governmental apparatus in Bogotá between followers of Bolívar and Santander ended in the latter's victory. He returned from exile in 1832 to become the first president of an independent New Granada under a constitution that provided for a president elected for four years, a bicameral Congress, and provincial legislatures. The constitution granted suffrage to all free males who were married or aged twenty-one and were not domestic servants or day laborers. In practice,

political life was dominated by a small aristocratic ruling class.

The geographic, economic, and social conditions of the new state posed even greater obstacles to the creation of a true national society than those facing Venezuela. The country's difficult geography, dominated by the towering Andean cordillera whose ranges, valleys, and plateaus were the home of the overwhelming majority of a population numbering less than one and a half million, offered formidable barriers to communication and transport; as late as the end of the nineteenth century it was cheaper to transport goods from Liverpool to Medellín than from Medellín to Bogotá.

This geography contributed to the formation of an economic structure that has been called an "economic archipelago," consisting of a number of isolated regions having little contact with each other. The economy of some of these regions was characterized by traditional haciendas mainly dedicated to growing wheat, barley, potatoes, and raising cattle. Their labor force usually consisted of mestizo peons or tenants who paid rent in labor or in kind for the privilege of cultivating their own small parcels of land; their freedom of movement could be restricted by debts, and sometimes they owed personal service to their patrón.

Alongside these haciendas and on marginal lands and mountain slopes lived other peasants whose precarious independence came from subsistence farming and supplying food to nearby towns. The northwest region of Antioquia, with its rugged terrain and low population, had few haciendas and numerous small and medium landholdings; a more independent peasantry had also arisen in neighboring Santander. Slave labor was chiefly employed on plantations and gold-mining districts in the western states and on the Caribbean coast, but the institution, greatly weakened by the revolutionary wars and legislation providing for the freedom of the children of slaves, was in decline.

The 1821 Congress of Cúcuta had ordered the division of *resguardos* (Indian communal lands) to conform with the prevailing liberal ideology, but the natives resisted. In 1839, however, dissolution of the resguardos was again ordered and a large part of the remaining Indian lands was divided; much of it was acquired for low prices by white landowners and merchants. Some of the former Indian owners became peons or tenants on haciendas; others became minifundio farmers.

New Granadan industry in 1830, like agriculture, displayed many precapitalist features. Most industrial activity (weaving and spinning, the making of pottery, shoeware) was done in the home, chiefly by women. The 1830s saw numerous state-sponsored efforts to establish factories making soap, glassware, textiles, and iron in Bogotá, but most ended in failure. By the 1840s sizable artisan groups had arisen in larger towns like Bogotá, Medellín, and Cali, but despite moderate tariff protection for local industries they had difficulty in competing with imported foreign goods.

The backwardness of economic life was most apparent in transportation; in parts of the country porters and pack mules were used for transport well into the twentieth century. Even after steamboat navigation became regular on the Magdalena River in the 1840s, it took between four and six weeks to make the voyage from Atlantic ports to Bogotá. The low development of productive forces and the sluggish tempo of economic activity were reflected in the modest wealth of even the upper classes. In the first half of the nineteenth century the income of Bogotá's upper class came to about $5,000 per capita and the number of persons whose capital exceeded $100,000 could be counted on one hand.

The lack of a dynamic export base to stimulate the economy and provide resources for a strong nation-state was a major factor in the economic and political difficulties of Colombia in its first half-century. Efforts to replace gold production—which had been in decline even before independence—with tobacco, cotton, cinchona bark, and other products as export staples produced a series of short booms that soon collapsed because of declining markets and prices, competition from foreign producers whose prices or quality Colombia could not match, or exhaustion of resources. The absence of an export base and a nationally dominant elite helps explain the "economic archipelago" or regional isolation and self-sufficiency that developed. A corollary of this economic autarchy was political autarchy, an almost permanent instability punctuated by frequent civil wars or threats of war and even secession by hacendado-generals, who could mobilize private armies of peons to settle scores with rival caudillos or the weak central government.

President Santander was more successful than some of his successors in keeping the peace during his term (1832–1837). A stern, inflexible figure mindful of constitutional legalities, he moved swiftly to crush a number of conspiracies, but generally reined in his Enlightenment passion for liberal economic and social reform.

Under Santander's successor, José Ignacio de Márquez (1837–1841), whose policies continued Santander's brand of moderate liberalism, the political climate turned stormy. Responding to a measure of Congress that closed some small convents in the fervently Catholic province of Pasto in the far South, the population rose up in arms. By 1841 the revolt had been defeated, but it had one lasting effect; its contribution to the formation of the classic Colombian two-party system: liberals versus conservatives.

Until the late 1840s the difference between the ideologies and programs of the two groups was far from absolute. Actually both had more in common with the moderate liberalism of Santander than Bolívar's late conservatism. Both represented upper-class interests but accepted the formal democracy of representative, republican government; both had faith in social and technological progress, believed in freedom of speech and the press and other civil liberties, and in economic policy accepted laissez-faire and liberal economics. Neither party cared about the agrarian problem or other problems of the rural and urban masses. The only genuine issue separating them was the relation between church and state and the church's role in education. The emergent Liberal party was distinctly anticlerical, regarding the church as hostile to progress; they did, however, favor freedom of worship and

504 separation of church and state. The nascent Conservative party endorsed religious toleration but favored cooperation between church and state, believing that religion promoted morality and social peace.

As the Liberal and Conservative parties prepared for the 1849 election, their ideological gap widened and a coalition of three liberal groups emerged. One cause of this was a partial quickening of the economy due to the rapid expansion of tobacco cultivation, the beginnings of the coffee cycle, internal improvements of the Conservative administrations, and a resulting growth of foreign and domestic trade. The economic change was accompanied by important social and intellectual changes.

As the population increased, reaching two million in 1850, the merchant class grew in numbers and self-consciousness. The sons of this class and of some landowners, well educated and influenced by French romanticism, utopian socialism, and the 1848 French Revolution, developed a peculiar sentimental brand of liberalism based on a romantic interpretation of Christianity in which Christ appeared as a forerunner of nineteenth-century secular reformism. Because of their frequent references to Christ as the "Martyr of Golgotha," they came to be known as the Gólgotas. This ideology's practical essence was its demand for the abolition of slavery, the ecclesiastical and military fuero and compulsory tithing, and the removal of all restraints on free enterprise.

The second element in the Liberal coalition that took shape in 1849 was the urban artisan group, whose numbers had increased in the past decade. Competition with foreign imported manufactures had caused serious unemployment among the artisans, who attributed their distress to the lower tariffs enacted under Mosquera; perhaps an equally important cause was the recent establishment of permanent steam navigation on the Magdalena River, which ended the protective isolation of their markets from the outside world. The artisans created a network of "Democratic Societies," beginning with the Democratic Society of Bogotá (1847), which had almost 4,000

members. These clubs were mutual aid societies and carried on educational and philanthropic activities, but they also served as important political vehicles for the Liberal leadership in the 1849 election.

A third faction in the Liberal coalition was the "*Draconianos*," military from the lower officer ranks, who would later align themselves with the artisans.

In the election of 1849 the Conservatives were seriously handicapped by divisions within the party. With the help of the artisans, the Liberal candidate and wealthy landowner General José Hilario López, won the presidency. His election opened one of the strangest chapters in the history of Latin American nineteenth-century political history, featured by "a veritable frenzy of reform activity" as the new merchant elite, with large support from regional landed oligarchies, sought to achieve the triumph of laissez-faire and modernity. This noisy revolution, although full of drama, produced little change in the basic structures of the Colombian economy and society.

The Liberal Hegemony, 1850–1885

Dominating the presidency and Congress, the Liberals began to establish the reign of liberty and reason in New Granada. The new constitution of 1853 provided for universal male suffrage, a provision that troubled some Liberals who knew that illiterate pro-clerical peasants were most likely to vote Conservative. As a matter of fact, since in most areas voters continued to vote the wishes of the local gamonales, or bosses, the new electoral law did not significantly change anything.

In economics the Liberals sought a decisive break with the colonial tradition of restriction and monopoly. The abolition of the state tobacco monopoly, enacted during the Mosquera administration, finally took effect in 1850. An 1850 law ceded to the provinces revenues from tithes (hitherto collected by the state but used for support of the church), the *quinto* tax on gold and other precious metals, and other traditional sources of state revenue. The provinces were also empowered to abolish these taxes. To compensate for the resulting loss of state revenues, Congress adopted a tax on individuals.

Slavery was completely abolished in 1851, and slave owners were compensated. The measure, freeing about twenty-five thousand individuals, had its most severe impact on gold-mining areas, which generally relied heavily on slave labor. Some of the freedmen became peons on haciendas; others turned to subsistence farming.

The Liberals also intensified the attack on resguardos, and land "liberated" by forced division often passed into the hands of neighboring hacendados by legal or illegal means. Indians made landless by such means often became peons serving the hacendados.

The abolition of compulsory tithes and of ecclesiastical fuero formed part of a larger campaign waged by the Liberals against the church, regarded as a state within the state that must be stripped of its economic and ideological power. The Jesuits, recalled to New Granada by the Conservatives in the 1840s, were again expelled in 1850. The 1853 constitution formally established freedom of worship and the separation of church and state. Still to come was the seizure and sale of church wealth and the outlawing of all religious orders.

The alliance between the Gólgotas and the artisans was now coming apart; the Liberal elite, having achieved their ends with artisan support, ignored their allies' demands for tariff protection. The Draconianos were disgruntled over the dismantling of the army under Liberal rule and resented the Gólgotas' wealth and intellectual pretensions. A crisis arose under López's successor, José María Obando. In April 1854 a group of Draconianos staged a coup, overthrew Obando, and installed General José María Melo. Melo, promising to raise tariff rates, received the full support of the artisans, who formed workers' battalions to defend the revolution. But Liberal and Conservative generals, putting aside their differences, raised private armies and defeated Melo in a brief campaign. His artisan allies were imprisoned and 300 were deported to Panama. The economic,

political, and military rout of the artisans was complete.

In 1857 a Conservative, Mariano Ospina Rodríguez, was elected president but held office only long enough to bring back the Jesuits and preside over the adoption of a new constitution (1858) that was more explicitly federalist than the old one. In 1860 a Liberal revolt ousted Ospina and the victors carried their religious and political reforms to their extreme and logical conclusions. Not only the Jesuits but all other religious orders were suppressed, all convents and monasteries closed, and all church wealth was seized by the government and sold. The transfer of massive amounts of church land into private hands produced little or no change in the land tenure system; clerical latifundia simply became lay latifundia, contributing to a further concentration of landownership. The principal buyers were Liberal merchants, landowners, and politicians, but Conservatives also participated in the plunder of church land.

In 1863 Liberal political reform reached its climax when a new constitution changed the country's name to the United States of Colombia and carried the principle of federalism to great lengths. The nine sovereign states became, in effect, independent nations, each with its own armed forces, possessing all the legislative powers not explicitly granted to the central government, which was made as weak as possible.

The Liberals remained in power from 1863 to 1885 in a political climate that approximated institutionalized anarchy, as the central government was powerless to intervene against the local revolutions that toppled and set up state governments.

The economic movement and its quest for the export base that could firmly integrate Colombia into the capitalist world economy continued. By the 1870s tobacco exports were down sharply, but this decline was made up by exporting coffee, quinine, and other products. Coffee was emerging as the country's major export product, but its development lagged behind that of Brazil, which relied increasingly on European immigrant free labor. In Colombia coffee production

506 in its principal centers of Santander and Cundinamarca, was based on traditional haciendas worked by peons and tenants who lived and labored under oppressive conditions. A more satisfactory situation existed in Antioquia and Caldas, characterized by a mix of haciendas with more enlightened forms of sharecropping and smallholdings, operations marked by high productivity. It was in these states that the twentieth-century takeoff of the Colombian coffee industry occurred.

The development of coffee as the major export, the growing ties between foreign and domestic merchants and coffee planters, and the stimulus given to trade and speculation by the expropriation of church lands created economic interests that required a new political model—a strong state capable of imposing order and creating the railroads and the financial infrastructure needed for the expansion of the coffee industry. The Liberal reform had removed many obstacles to capitalist development but had created others by its federalist excesses. By the early 1880s not only Conservatives but many moderate Liberals were convinced that political and social stability required making peace with the church and restoring its traditional role. The unlikely instrument for the creation of this new conservative, unitary order was the poet and intellectual Rafael Núñez, whom his party elected president in 1879.

Rafael Núñez, the "Regeneration," and the War of a Thousand Days, 1880–1903

Núñez began political life as a radical Liberal and had spent thirteen years in the consular service in Europe. He returned home in 1875 and was elected president in 1879, governing with a coalition of right-leaning elements from both the Liberal and Conservative parties. Elected again, in 1884, he swiftly crushed a radical Liberal revolt and announced that the 1863 constitution had "ceased to exist." In 1886 he presented the country with a new constitution that replaced the sovereign states with departments headed by governors appointed by the president, extended the presidential term to six years, established literacy and property qualifications for voting for representatives, and provided for indirect election of senators. Under that constitution, personally or through surrogates, Núñez ruled Colombia until his death in 1894.

Like another religious skeptic, Bolívar, Núñez believed the authority of religion and the church was the foundation of the social order and must be fully supported by the state. The 1886 constitution made Catholicism the official religion and entrusted education to the clergy. The other foundations of Núñez's authoritarian republic were a strong standing army and a national police force. The Liberal regimes had virtually dismantled the regular army; the revolts and civil wars of the federal period had been fought by private armies formed by the great landowners with their tenants and peons. The existence of these regional private armies and militias was incompatible with Núñez's unitary project. The 1886 constitution created a permanent army and reserved to the central government the right to possess arms and ammunition. The national police, organized in 1891, kept under vigilance political suspects and disrupted most plots against the government.

Núñez is credited with two major economic innovations. Claiming that the Liberal policy of free trade or low tariffs was the cause of economic decadence and poverty, which had caused the civil war, he proposed to use tariff protection to stimulate the growth of certain industries. He believed that this would create a new middle class that would form a buffer between the governing social class and the unlettered multitude. But his implementation of this program was timid and inconsistent. The new policy succeeded, however, in providing a modest level of protection for domestic industry.

Núñez's other innovation was the creation in 1881 of a National Bank designed to relieve the financial distress of a government always on the verge of bankruptcy. The bank had the exclusive right to issue money; this monopoly enabled the state to provide for its needs and was managed prudently until 1890. Then its uncontrolled emissions of paper money caused a galloping inflation. The expensive civil war of 1899 provoked the emission of paper money on such a scale that the printers could not keep up with the demand, and the country was flooded with millions of pesos of depreciated currency.

The "Regeneration," as the Núñez era is known, represented an effort to achieve national unification from above, under reactionary auspices; it has been compared with Bismarck's project for German national unification, a compound of feudal and capitalist elements. Under Núñez the conditions for the rise of a modern, capitalist state began. An important step in this direction was his creation of a permanent army and the assumption of a monopoly of the use of force by the state. His removal of internal barriers to trade and his policy of tariff protection, however modest, contributed to the formation of an internal market; his national bank, despite its later scandalous mismanagement, represented an initial effort to create a national system of credit; and he gave impulse to the construction of internal improvements, especially railroads. These policies, combined with the coffee boom, contributed to a growth of capitalism in Colombia. But other policies had profoundly negative effects. By entrusting control of education and civil society to the church Núñez created an environment inimical to technical and scientific progress and strengthened the hold of clericalism over the peasant masses and their subjection to the great landowners.

When he died, Núñez's leadership was assumed by Conservative politicians who lacked his intelligence and iron will. Their corruption, flagrant rigging of elections, and division over freedom of the press and electoral reform collided with Liberal anger at their long exclusion from power and an economic slump caused by a sharp decline of coffee prices. The result was a political crisis followed by a resort to arms. Confident of victory over a thoroughly unpopular government, the Liberals launched a revolt in 1899 that ushered in the disastrous War of a Thousand Days. It raged for three years, caused an estimated loss of 100,000 lives, and immense material damage but ended in a government victory.

Colombia in the Twentieth Century

The Conservative Republic, 1903–1930

The War of a Thousand Days and the loss of Panama dealt a profound psychological shock to Colombians. At the war's end both parties asked the government to reform the political system. The Conservative government disregarded these appeals. New elections, attended by the customary frauds, gave victory to the Conservative General Rafael Reyes (1904–1909), and produced a Congress in which the Liberals had only two seats. But Reyes proved more conciliatory than the party traditionalists, invited Liberals to join his cabinet, and proposed reforms. When Congress balked at his reforms, Reyes dissolved it and established his personal dictatorship, ruling by decree through a puppet national assembly in which one-third of the seats were occupied by Liberals. Despite his dictatorial methods, Reyes's policies of enforcing peace and order, construction of railroads and highways, encouragement of export agriculture, and protection and subsidies for industry initially attracted much elite support.

Reyes's downfall came when he attempted to conclude a treaty with the United States under which Colombia was to receive an indemnity of $2,500,000 in return for its recognition of Panama's independence. Colombia's governing class, aware of the growing importance of the North American market for its coffee and hopeful of attracting North American capital, accepted the new relations. But the wound of Panama was still too fresh, and news of the treaty aroused a public fury of which Reyes's enemies took advantage to force his resignation.

Both parties now organized a constituent assembly to reform the constitution of 1886. The problem for Conservatives was how to create more political space for the Liberals without jeopardizing the supremacy they had just consolidated in the War of a Thousand Days. The reforms included weakening the executive, increasing the powers of Congress, and ensuring

508

minority representation in elective bodies. Other changes included direct election of the president, establishment of elected departmental assemblies, and abolition of the death penalty. These reforms left intact, however, property and literacy qualifications for voting that excluded 90 percent of the adult male population from the suffrage, and the privileged position of the church as the state church.

Although the constitutional reforms made the total hegemony of one party more difficult, control of the electoral process remained in government hands. The constitutional changes also left intact the *gamonal* system under which landowners, public officials, and priests exerted influence on rural voters, and that usually favored the Conservatives.

The characteristic blandness of Colombian politics between 1910 and 1930 contrasted sharply with the sometimes stormy developments in economic and social life. These developments, reflecting the rapid overall growth of Colombian capitalism, included the upsurge of coffee exports, centered in Antioquia, with its system of free labor; the accumulation of capital and its transfer from commerce to industry, with the formation of many new companies; a partial shift from the old semiservile forms of rural labor to free, capitalist wage labor, accompanied by a wave of strikes, land invasions, and clashes between landowners and peasants; and the emergence in cities and plantation areas of the first true trade union movements, left-wing parties, and struggles between workers and employers.

In this period U.S. capital began to flow into Colombia, facilitated by the 1914 treaty by which the United States paid Colombia for its loss of Panama. The "dance of the millions" began in 1921–1922 and was fueled initially by the first installment of a $25 million U.S. indemnity. Between 1922 and 1928 the U.S. government and private investors poured $280 million into Colombia, most of which was expended for a vast, chaotic program of public construction. The boom, luring workers from agriculture into the cities, reduced food production and raised living costs, leaving workers worse off than before.

The golden shower ended in 1929 with the New York stock market crash and the start of a great depression that soon spread to Colombia. Growing unemployment, food shortages, and the government's severe fiscal problems completed the discredit of a regime weakened by political scandals, public outrage over a massacre of banana workers in the tropical Santa Marta zone by government troops, and its own internal divisions. Alarmed by an upsurge of peasant and worker unrest, urban strikes, land invasions by peasants organized in leagues and unions,[1] and the rise of new radical ideologies moderate Conservatives decided the best hope for avoiding revolutions was to support the candidacy of the moderate Liberal Enrique Olaya Herrera, a man of their own kind, close to the oligarchs of both parties, in the election of February 1930.

The New Liberalism: "The Revolution on the March," 1934–1946

Olaya's term was spent waiting for the Depression to end and the infusions of United States loans and investments to resume. His failure to respond to popular expectations for change caused growing tension. In departments where the problem of latifundismo and landlessness was particularly severe, such as Cundinamarca, Tolima, and Cauca, clashes between peasants and landowners and police were frequent. The 1934 election occurred against this troubled background. The divided and demoralized Conservatives abstained from putting up a candidate, and the left-wing Liberal Alfonso López won. He promptly announced a program called *La Revolución en Marcha* (The Revolution on the March). In 1936 he obtained the congressional majority needed to implement his policies.

López and other Liberal reformers knew that social justice and national economic interest required land reform. The advance of Colombian

---

[1] The land invasions were spurred by a 1926 Supreme Court ruling that the only proof of ownership was the original title stating the government had ceded title to the land. Many peasants knew that the estates on which they worked had no such titles and had been formed through illegal acquisition of public lands.

capitalism was blocked by the backwardness of agriculture, especially the food-producing sector, which could not even provide enough food for the growing urban population. The 1936 agrarian reform law provided for reversion to the state of lands not rationally exploited by their owners but gave the latifundists ten years to make the transition to efficient land exploitation based on wage labor. The law also prohibited payment of rent in labor or in kind; this had the effect of speeding up the spread of wage labor and the rise of a land market. The law annulled the 1926 Supreme Court decision and thus confirmed the property titles of the great landowners, but it also gave peasants "squatters' rights" on unused public and private lands that they had improved. The eviction of squatters thus became more difficult and dropped sharply.

Other legislation adopted during López's administration defined the rights of labor. To implement these rights Congress passed a law that established a minimum wage and paid vacations and holidays, forbade the use of strikebreakers, set up the eight-hour day and the forty-eight-hour week, and created a special tribunal to provide arbitration in labor disputes. With López's support, the number of organized workers quadrupled between 1935 and 1947. Equally important was the formation in 1936 of the Colombian Confederation of Labor (CTC), headed by syndicalists, Communists, and liberals.

One of the most revolutionary innovations of the López reform era was a new progressive tax law. Before 1936 tax laws had been ineffectually enforced. The new tax law, effectively enforced, almost doubled the state's revenue-raising capacity.

Despite the moderate character of the reforms, they came under bitter attack from all reactionary elements, and López began to retreat. He announced in December 1936 a "pause" in reform. This "pause" was accentuated by López's successor, the moderate Liberal Eduardo Santos (1938–1942), editor of the influential journal *El Tiempo.* Santos had been chosen by the Liberal nominating convention in 1937 against López's wishes. Santos's selection created a bitter division within

the Liberal ranks between moderates and reformers. In office, Santos failed to implement many of the López reforms. López responded by founding his own newspaper, *El Liberal,* in which he assailed Santos's conservative views and announced his intention of resuming the presidency in 1942.

These Liberal divisions infused new life into the demoralized Conservative party, now under the direction of the right-wing ideologue and admirer of Hitler, Mussolini, and Franco, Laureano Gómez, who fanned the flames of Liberal discord. If López returned to power, Gómez announced, he would personally lead an armed revolution against him.

López won the Liberal nomination for president and easily defeated a candidate of the moderate Liberal faction, but Lopez's second term brought his Revolution on the March to an inglorious close. He began with immense popular support but faced a hostile legislature in which moderate Liberals banded together with Conservatives to defeat his proposals. The world was at war, and Colombia felt the impact in shortages, loss of its coffee markets, and growing unemployment. Meanwhile, Laureano Gómez's mouthpiece, *El Siglo,* poured a steady stream of vituperative attacks on López. Behind Gómez was an array of reactionary forces, including great landowners, the church hierarchy, and industrialists angered by López's concessions to labor, who sought a counterrevolutionary *Reconquista.*

In 1943, weary and discouraged, with one year of his term remaining, López resigned. Congress appointed Alberto Lleras Camargo to head a one-year interim government. He ruled with a coalition cabinet composed of moderate Liberals and Conservatives.

With López's departure the leadership of the Liberal party's left wing passed to Jorge Eliécer Gaitán, who had held various political posts. As mayor of Bogotá, he had been regarded as the best the capital ever had.

Conservatives and many moderate Liberals denounced Gaitán as a demogogue. He was in fact a magnetic speaker of burning sincerity, capable

510

of presenting his economic and social ideas to audiences of peasants and workers in a clear way, but there was nothing exotic or extravagant about those ideas. Although he used socialist terminology, the essence of Gaitán's program was the need for state intervention in the economy in order to democratize capitalism, control the great private monopolies, and ensure that peasants owned the land they cultivated. In 1945 he proposed limiting landownership to a maximum of 1,000 hectares and suggested a minimum size of four hectares for landholdings to avoid the low productivity of minifundios.

As the 1946 elections approached, party leaders met to decide on their strategy and candidates. The Liberal nominating convention, with moderates in firm control, nominated Gabriel Turbay, a wealthy, conservative follower of Santos. Angered by the rejection of their champion, the party's left wing advanced Gaitán. In view of the split in the Liberal party, it was widely believed the Conservatives would not field their own candidate, but would throw their support to Turbay. Instead, the party convention chose Mariano Ospina Pérez as its nominee. With only 42 percent of the vote, he was elected president. The Conservative reconquest of power had begun.

Counterrevolution on the March, 1946–1958

After his inauguration, in a conciliatory gesture to the Liberal party, Ospina Pérez invited six Liberals into his cabinet, thus establishing parity in the twelve ministries and implementing his campaign promise to form a National Union government. He made no effort to consult Gaitán. The snubbing of Gaitán suggests a design on the part of Ospina Pérez to isolate him politically, deepen the rift between Liberal moderates and reformists, and form a bipartisan coalition of conservative elements to barricade against Gaitán's program of radical social and economic change. High inflation, static wages, and growing unemployment in the postwar period added to the anger and frustration of workers as they saw their hopes for change crushed by what they perceived

as a conspiracy of the "double oligarchy"—Liberal and Conservative—that controlled the government.

The Conservative leadership in 1946 presented two faces. Ospina Pérez represented its conciliatory aspect, the desire for a peaceful coexistence of the two traditional parties and their collaboration in a National Union government of sound conservative views. But this aspect was contradicted by the supreme chief of the Conservative party, Laureano Gómez. Gómez, soon to be appointed Ospina's foreign minister, emerged as the new government's Gray Eminence, the power behind the throne and made no effort to conceal his scorn for the National Union policy.

Gómez quickly had the Liberal general who commanded the national police force dismissed and then followed with a wholesale purge of Liberal police officers, who were replaced by officers known for their fanatical conservatism. The pace of events quickened in 1947. In an evident effort to gain the advantage in the March congressional elections armed bands organized by Conservative landowners and officials began to attack and persecute Liberals in many rural areas. The outcome of the elections, however, was a clear victory for the Liberals; equally significant was the predominance of radicals over moderates on the Liberal slate. Claiming the need to restore law and order, Ospina organized a new security force, the *policía política,* or political police, that soon became an extension of the Conservative party and an additional instrument of terror against Liberals; it was widely known as the "creole Gestapo." Beatings, killings, and outrages of every kind spread throughout the countryside provoking a growing polarization and armed responses by the Liberal peasantry, middle class, and landowners.

As 1948 opened the violence in some areas began to assume the proportions of a civil war, with battles taking place between Conservative and Liberal towns. The church, with its immense power, also instigated violence and persecution of Liberals. In March the Liberal convention called on party members to resign from every public office under the Conservative administration. The Conservatives rejoiced; one of their journals exulted: "At last we are alone."

In an atmosphere of growing tension the government prepared to host the Ninth Inter-American Conference in April. On April 9, 1948, as Gaitán was on his way to lunch, he was approached by a stranger who fired four bullets into him. Mortally wounded, Gaitán collapsed on the sidewalk. The man regarded by the masses as the sole hope for their liberation, generally expected to run and win the election for president in 1950, died the same day he was shot. The assassin was an obscure figure with a history of mental trouble.

Gaitán's murder was the signal for a formidable popular insurrection that tore Bogotá apart and spread to the provinces before it was put down by the army at the cost of thousands of lives. The spontaneous rising of the masses, accompanied by peasant expropriation of haciendas, establishment of revolutionary committees and workers' control over foreign-owned oil installations, and other radical measures, frightened Conservative and Liberal elites. Liberal leaders, faced with the choice of joining the insurrection or accepting Ospina's offer to reconstitute a National Union coalition, chose the latter. In the Liberal party, the dominant influence now shifted from the Gaitán to the Santos, or moderate, wing.

During 1949 the coalition government began to come apart as the official and unofficial violence in the countryside, directed above all at Liberals of all classes, continued and widened; it had become a persistent, widespread phenomenon generically called *la Violencia.* In May Liberal leader Carlos Lleras Restrepo announced the irrevocable end of his party's collaboration with the Ospina government. In June a crucial election again gave victory to the Liberals on the municipal, departmental, and congressional levels. That month Laureano Gómez, Conservative candidate for president, returned from Spain to greet the assembled Conservatives with the Fascist salute and announce that it was "incumbent upon the Conservative party to save the republic."

As the presidential election drew nearer, the threatening, repressive atmosphere visibly deepened. In the countryside goon squads, backed by the military, compelled Liberal peasants to turn in their voting cards and register as Conservatives. In some areas landowners took revenge for the land invasions of the 1930s, using hired thugs to kill or expel peasant occupants. In this stage of the Violencia, however, the conflict had primarily a political character and was based on the peasants' loyalty to political bosses on each side. Finally, in response to a move by the Liberal congressional majority to impeach him, Ospina issued a series of decrees providing for a state of siege, the dissolution of Congress and all departmental legislatures and municipal councils, the grant of extraordinary powers for the governors, and national censorship of the press and radio.

In the face of these dictatorial measures the Liberals caved in completely, withdrawing their presidential candidate and leaving the field to Laureano Gómez, who received all but 14 of the 1,140,034 votes supposedly cast. He was inaugurated as president in August 1950.

Ideologically, the Gómez regime (1950–1953) appears "feudal" in its effort to restore the intellectual atmosphere of sixteenth-century Spain. In its economic policies, however, the regime showed itself quite favorable to modern corporate capitalism. In the spirit of economic liberalism, all import and export restrictions were removed and foreign investment was encouraged in all possible ways. But for labor it was the worst of times. Wages lagged behind prices, and the state regularly intervened in labor struggles in favor of employers, permitting the use of strikebreakers and blacklists and annulling the López law that barred parallel unions. This made it possible for employers to form so-called confessional or church-dominated unions that were in effect company unions.

In foreign policy Gómez made a complete volte-face from his shrill denunciations of the United States during World War II. He now proclaimed his friendship for the United States, praised its involvement in the Korean war, and "gave Colombia the dubious honor of having been the only Latin American country to have veterans of the Korean war" by sending a battalion of 3,200 men to participate in that struggle. The United States in turn saw Gómez as a worthy

512

ally in the anticommunist struggle and gave him its full support.

In the Colombian countryside, meanwhile, the Violencia gained in intensity and expanded into new regions. But the conflict now increasingly assumed the nature of a class struggle as peasants resisted the efforts of landowners and their hired thugs to eject them from their parcels and Communist party activists as well as peasant leaders loyal to the Liberal party became active in organizing strongholds of self-defense among uprooted peasants. Thus the period between 1949 and 1953, in addition to a growth of landowner and official terrorism and banditry, saw the rise of an extensive, well-organized resistance in guerrilla zones inhabited by peasants and other fugitives from regions marked by anarchy or terror. Some of these zones had an elaborate political, economic, and social organization. These guerrilla enclaves may have held 20,000 armed men, of whom about half were based in the Llanos. Each zone had its own commander or commanders, some of whom soon became legends.

The failure of the Conservative dictatorship to achieve a military solution to the guerrilla problem contributed to its gradual weakening and eventual collapse. In late 1951 a heart attack forced President Gómez to retire and name Roberto Urdaneta Arbeláez, his minister of war, who had directed the struggle against the so-called bandits, as acting president. The illness of the old lion brought to the surface all the contradictions and clashing personal ambitions within the ruling party.

Many members of both parties found especially disturbing a Gómez project to give Colombia a new reactionary corporate constitution that would ensure the indefinite extension of Conservative rule. This project, clearly influenced by the Falangist ideology and political system of Franco's Spain, widened the breach between the Gómez group and more traditional Conservatives of the Ospina type. Thus a series of factors led to Gómez's isolation and created conditions for a "Bonapartist" solution for the developing political crisis. General Gustavo Rojas Pinilla, who formed part of an officer group sympathetic to

the Ospina faction, became the instrument of the coup d'état. A countermove by Gómez to arrest Rojas backfired; the old caudillo was placed under arrest and sent into exile. Amid general rejoicing, on June 13, 1953 the national radio announced that Rojas Pinilla had assumed the presidency with the support of the armed forces and representatives of both parties.

Rojas Pinilla assumed power on June 13, 1953, in a social and political crisis: a reign of terror prevailed over a large area, and the peasant insurgency dominated another extensive area. Thus his slogan of "Peace, Justice, Liberty" evoked a warm response among the population. One of his first initiatives was to proclaim an unconditional amnesty to all guerrillas who would return to civilian life. Several thousand accepted the amnesty, surrendered their weapons, and returned to their old homes, but the leaders of some guerrilla fronts, especially the Communist leadership in southern Tolima and the Sumapaz region of southern Cundinamarca, distrusted Rojas Pinilla's sincerity, recalled his role as army commander in a famous massacre of Liberals in Cali in 1949, and warned their comrades not to "believe the false promises of propaganda thrown from planes of the dictatorship." These guerrilla fronts preferred to maintain an armed truce and await further developments.

Events proved the skeptics right. The honeymoon between Rojas Pinilla and the elites and the nation as a whole began to wane as it became evident that instead of restoring the traditional political arrangements he was moving toward the establishment of a personal dictatorship with some populist features, not unlike Argentina's Peronist system. One of his reformist measures was giving women the vote in 1954.

Despite some reforms, the essence of Rojas Pinilla's policies was reactionary. One sign of this was the revival of the Violencia as the president gave a free hand to notorious *pájaros* (hired assassins), Conservative vigilante gangs, and army-police forces to wreak vengeance on veterans of the guerrilla war who had accepted amnesty. As a result many former guerrillas left their farms and rejoined the surviving guerrilla fronts.

The renewal of the civil war combined with other repressive measures and with the effects of a deepening depression to unify all elite elements against Rojas Pinilla. In July 1956 the Liberal leader Alberto Lleras Camargo met Conservative Laureano Gómez in the little Spanish town of Benidorm and signed a pact to form a coalition of their parties for joint action in the "reestablishment of liberty and constitutional guarantees." On May 7, 1957, a commercial strike, supported by the middle classes, entrepreneurial class, and the student movement, was followed by a denunciation of the dictatorship by Cardinal Luque, who condemned the regime for "murder" and "sacrilegious profanation" of churches. The next day Rojas Pinilla's military colleagues prevailed on him to resign and power passed to a five-man caretaker military junta.

In July 1957 Lleras Camargo and Laureano Gómez again met and signed an agreement creating a National Front coalition, which in effect provided for a monopoly of shared power for sixteen years by the two parties. There would be parity in legislative positions on both national and local levels and alternation of the presidency between the two parties. A plebiscite held on December 1, with all citizens of twenty-one or over eligible to vote, approved the agreement. In March 1958 congressional elections were held and the Liberals outpolled the Conservatives by 58 to 42 percent; Lleras Camargo was elected president in May and inaugurated in August, with the oath of office given by Laureano Gómez. The Colombian experiment in bipartisan rule and "controlled democracy" had begun.

The National Front: Reform and Repression, 1958–1974

The constitutional pact creating the Colombian National Front in 1958 bears an obvious resemblance to the pact signed between Venezuela's centrist parties the same year. In both cases the intent was the same: to prevent interparty rivalry from reaching a level of conflict that might create situations—like the Violencia and the Rojas Pinilla dictatorship in Colombia or the Pérez Jiménez dictatorship in Venezuela—that the dominant elites could not control and to marginalize or isolate political movements that might pose such threats. Both may therefore be called variants of a type of representative democracy that has been called "controlled democracy" or, more correctly, "restricted democracy." The Colombian power-sharing pact, providing for a monopoly of political power (and a corresponding division of political spoils) for the Conservative and Liberal parties, excluded existing parties like the Communist and the Christian Democratic or new parties that might be formed later. Thus the electorate was denied the opportunity to reject the policies of the National Front coalition or exercise its sovereign right to change the government. The relative absence of issues between the parties promoted voter apathy and alienation, reflected in low turnout rates; participation in congressional elections fell from a high of 68.9 in 1958 to a low of 36.4 percent in 1972.

The rules of the political game established by the National Front, designed to prevent the hegemony of either party, tended to immobilize its governments. Their social policies reflected their fundamentally conservative orientation and did nothing to alter the great inequalities in income distribution. Although the unions gained legal recognition, the government repeatedly intervened in labor conflicts on the employers' side.

In 1958 President Lleras Camargo issued an amnesty—to expire in 1959—for all guerrillas who would return to peaceful life. The establishment of the National Front coalition is usually regarded as marking the end—or at least the beginning of the end—of the Violencia, a conflict estimated to have taken between 200,000 and 300,000 lives. Between 1958 and 1965 the army and police hunted down the remaining outlaw bands. But the continued existence of the latifundio, an estimated one million landless peasants, and landowner and official repression of land-hungry peasants continued and continues to generate violence in the Colombian countryside.

In 1961, evidently fearing that failure to act might produce a Cuban-style revolution, Con-

514 gress adopted an agrarian reform law. Inaugurated with much fanfare, the law vested apparently limitless power to expropriate and redistribute inefficiently exploited land in a new state agency (INCORA). In Tolima, the site of the first program, only 1,115 out of 90,000 landless agricultural workers had received titles to land by 1969.

This innocuous agrarian reform coincided with the launching of a large-scale military effort to destroy the guerrilla zones established under Communist party leadership in eastern and southern Tolima. Like the agrarian law, this offensive seems to have been inspired by the anticommunist strategy of the Kennedy administration's Alliance for Progress, a program combining reform and repression. The success of this and many other later offensives can be gauged by the fact that twenty years later the few guerrilla bases had grown into a network of thirty guerrilla fronts in the Colombian backcountry, with their own military organization, the Communist-led Revolutionary Armed Forces of Colombia (FARC). In addition to the FARC, the largest of the guerrilla groups, created in 1966, whose membership and leadership were primarily peasant, the 1960s and 1970s saw the emergence of other revolutionary organizations, such as the National Liberation Army (ELN), inspired by the Cuban example, and the April 19 Movement (M-19), both largely composed of radical students and other urban elements.

In summary, the National Front's political, economic, and social policies produced basically negative results. Its economic policies successfully promoted the accumulation of foreign and domestic capital, but neglected the interests of workers and peasants, whose living standards sharply declined. In 1964, 25 percent of the total labor force, 24.6 percent of the urban labor force, and 25.4 percent of the rural labor force lived below the absolute poverty line. By 1973 those percentages had risen to 50.7 percent, 43.4 percent, and 67.5 percent. Clearly, instead of contributing to the solution of grave socioeconomic problems, the sixteen years of National Front rule sharpened them.

Drug Lords, Guerrillas, and the Quest for Peace, 1974–1995

The end of the National Front period ushered in a general crisis of Colombian society that it is still struggling to overcome.

Beginning with the 1974 elections, Colombia returned to the political system of electoral competition, except for vestiges of the power-sharing system. Despite the renewal of competition, the political system remained a restricted, oligarchical democracy designed to limit the level of conflict between elites and to "keep the masses in their place," with a system of electoral mobilization based on machine politics and payoffs, known as *clientelismo.*

In addition to their loss of credibility, post–National Front governments faced economic problems of unprecedented proportions. The quadrupling of oil prices in 1974, coming at a time when Colombia ceased to be self-sufficient in oil production, dealt a very heavy shock to the economy. By 1982 Colombia had not only severe inflation but its worst recession in fifty years.

In this time of economic gloom, some relief came from an unexpected quarter: the drug traffic with the United States. Until recently that traffic was negligible, mostly confined to the export of marihuana. It began to mushroom in the 1970s, most likely as a result of antidrug campaigns in Turkey and the Middle East. Skyrocketing prices as a result of effective antidrug efforts and high transportation costs forced the international drug cartels to seek closer sources of supply for the U.S. market. Colombia, with its access to both U.S. coasts, and cocaine, lower in price than heroin or opium, and easier to carry in short plane trips to the Florida coast, provided a solution. An efficient distribution system made the new drug available to the ever-swelling U.S. market. A division of labor and profits emerged between the Colombian producers and exporters, centered in Medellín and Cali, and North American domestic wholesalers, bankers, and money launderers. Contrary to a common misconception, Colombia is not a large grower of coca but processes the substance that comes from Peru, Bolivia, Ecuador, and Brazil. By the mid-1980s, with cocaine prices dropping, a new product—crack—known as *bazuco* in Colombia and packaged in small quantities costing only a fraction of cocaine powder, created a large new class of consumers.

Colombia's Medellín and Cali cartels, it was estimated, made $4 to $6 billion annually in cocaine traffic. Of this amount, according to the economist Salomón Kalmanovitz, between $1 and $1.5 billion entered the Colombian black market. Without this "cushion" for the country's balance of payments, he suggests, an exchange crisis would have broken out in 1983 or 1984 at the latest. This contribution of Colombian narco-capitalism to the country's financial stability and the close ties established between the drug lords and landowners, businessmen, government officials, and members of the police and the armed forces help explain the singular immunity that the drug mafias enjoyed until recently.

This situation changed as a result of two developments. One was increased U.S. pressure on the government of Liberal President Virgilio Barco (1986–1990) to wage a more effective war on drug trafficking. This pressure was accompanied by the offer of financial aid that was difficult to refuse.

The second reason was a growing concern on the part of sectors of the elite that the drug traffickers had gotten out of control and their violence was threatening the monopoly of power the elite had enjoyed since Colombia achieved independence from Spain. For years death squads (the government acknowledged the existence of 149 paramilitary groups) recruited and trained by the drug mafia, in alliance with the police and the armed forces, had murdered, with complete impunity, thousands of trade union and peasant union leaders, left-wing activists, judges, and others who opposed their activities or sought to make Colombia a functioning democracy.

In the course of 1989, however, the mafia went too far and began killing prominent members of the elite who were their known enemies. The victims included the governor of Antioquia, the country's attorney general, Medellín's police chief, and, on August 18, Liberal party senator and presidential candidate Luis Carlos Galán. The murder of the popular Galán, identified with the reformist wing of his party, shocked the Bogotanos. Tens of thousands marched through the streets on the day of his funeral, shouting "Death to the drug traffickers."

Within hours after Galán's death the Barco government had already ordered the searches and seizures of dozens of mansions, hundreds of cars, and more than a hundred airplanes and helicopters claimed to belong to the drug traffickers. A few days later Barco ordered the confiscation of a chain of drugstores and other businesses belonging to the drug cartels. To give these confiscations a firm legal basis Barco issued a decree making "illicit enrichment" a crime punishable by five to ten years in prison. He also reinstated, by decree, the extradition of drug traffickers to the United States—declared unconstitutional by the Colombian Supreme Court in 1987 and opposed by many Colombians as a surrender of the state's autonomy and an admission of the impotence of its judicial system.

The drug lords promptly responded to Barco's offensive. *Los Extraditables,* as they called themselves, issued a communiqué announcing total war on Barco's government and all their other foes and promising that their retaliation would include the destruction of the elite's estates, homes, and businesses. In December a leading Medellín drug lord, José González Rodriguez Gacha, his son, and some followers were killed in a clash with security forces. As 1989 drew to a close the drug war heated up, with a string of selective killings of judges, trade union leaders, and other foes of the drug mafia, leading observers to conclude that the government's offensive against the cartels had only made a temporary impact and that the basic structure of the paramilitary groups remained intact. Support for a negotiated solution began to grow in some political quarters.

There is reason to believe, in fact, that without major social and economic reforms in Latin America, the principal supplier of cocaine, and in the United States, its principal consumer, the drug wars cannot be won. Without new policies that provide Latin American peasants with a

516

Luis Carlos Galán, shown here, was a popular political figure and presidential candidate when he was murdered by the Colombian drug mafia in 1989. His death fueled a massive government response against the drug cartels.

viable alternative to growing coca as a cash crop, its cultivation will continue, no matter how many fields are burned or sprayed with defoliants. If the laboratories that process the coca are destroyed in one part of the region, they will be moved to another. In both the United States and Latin America, where the cocaine epidemic is growing dangerously, its principal social roots are mass poverty, despair, and frustration. Neither the supply side nor the demand side of the problem, in the last analysis, can be solved by military means alone.

The Colombian war against the cartels coincided with the first serious effort to end the thirty-year-old guerrilla war by peaceful means. The drug and guerrilla problems were indissolubly linked, for it had long been common knowl-

edge that there exists a network linking government agencies, elements of the armed forces and police, landowners, industrialists, and the drug lords. The primary target of this alliance is Colombia's left-wing movement, the guerrillas first but also trade unions, peasant unions, and the opposition parties.

In 1984, after the forced resignation of Defense Minister Fernando Landazábal Reyes, who had strenuously opposed a cease-fire with the guerrillas, Conservative President Belisario Betancur (1982–1986) negotiated a series of historic truce agreements with three of the four major guerrilla movements that did not require them to surrender their arms. The accord with the FARC, the largest of the insurgent groups, stipulated that the government would recommend to Congress adoption of an agrarian reform, legislation for improvements in public health, education, and housing, and a law permitting local elections of mayors and city councils in order to broaden popular participation in government, but only legislation permitting local elections was passed by Congress. Despite a boycott of the agreements by the armed forces, which repeatedly attacked guerrilla zones, and the refusal of some smaller guerrilla groups to negotiate a truce, the peace process somehow survived. Barco, Betancur's successor, had little sympathy for the peace project, which came under greater strain as military attacks on the guerrillas and death squad killings multiplied.

In 1985 the FARC decided to form a political movement called the Patriotic Union (UP), a coalition of leftist parties including the Communist party and the Workers Socialist party, and announced it would participate in the 1986 elections. In those elections the UP received over 400,000 votes, won 14 seats in Congress and representatives on 187 city councils, often in coalitions with Conservative and Liberal leaders. It had become a major political force in Colombia, but at a fearful price; over 2,000 of its members, including its first presidential candidate, Jaime Pardo León, have been killed by death squads. Its presidential candidate in the 1990 election, Bernardo Jaramillo, was gunned down in Bogotá's international airport on March 22. Carlos Pizarro, the candidate of a party formed by the small guerrilla April 19th Movement (M-19)—named for the date the presidential election was brazenly stolen from a progressive candidate in 1970—after it had signed a peace pact with the government and surrendered its weapons, was murdered one month later. The elaborate precautions taken by the Liberal party candidate and winner of the May presidential election, César Gaviria—in public appearances he was accompanied by hundreds of bodyguards and a physician carrying several pints of blood, and he always wore a bulletproof vest—tell much about the political and social climate of contemporary Colombia. The abstention rate in the election—67.8 percent of the eligible voters—also revealed the precarious state of Colombian democracy.

The country's greatest writer, Gabriel García Márquez, says, "The Constitution, the laws . . . everything in Colombia is magnificent, everything on paper. It has no connection with reality."

Part of that reality was that Colombia was the scene of two wars. One was the drug war. From the official U.S. point of view this was being waged to stem the tide of cocaine flowing into the United States. For the Colombian elite, however, it was a private quarrel with that section of the "cocaine nouveau riche," centered in Medellín, that sought too aggressively to join it in the seats of power. It is noteworthy that the Cali cartel, which prefers "bribes over bullets" and was more discreet in its dealings with the traditional oligarchy, experienced less interference from the government.

The other war is the "dirty war" waged by an alliance of the military, the security services, drug lords, great landowners, and businessmen against Colombia's left-wing movement, trade unions, and peasant leagues. The military has made no secret that it is far more interested in fighting guerrillas than in fighting drugs. It repeatedly thwarted Betancur's sincere efforts to achieve a cease-fire with the guerrilla movements and continued its repressive activity—bombardments, disappearances, torture, and murder—under Barco, who appeared unable or unwilling to control his armed forces. The majority of the victims have not been guerrillas but peasants, workers, and left-wing activists. In the May 1990 elections, the presidential ballot included a proposal for a national constituent assembly that was overwhelmingly ratified. The assembly was charged with reforming the Colombian political system by ending the Liberal-Conservative "duopoly" of power and the emergency "state of siege" that has been in place for over forty years, providing a cover for countless human rights abuses. The assembly was also expected to revamp the electoral and judicial systems and public administration. Elections of delegates to the assembly were held in December 1990, and the body convened in April 1991. A decree issued by Gaviria limited guerrilla participation in the constituent assembly to delegates of insurgent groups that had disbanded and surrendered their

518

arms. M-19 and two other small guerrilla groups complied, and one of the surprises of the December elections was the strong showing of the socialist-oriented Democratic Alliance (the disbanded M-19), which emerged as the second strongest national party, with nineteen of the seventy-three delegates making up the assembly. But the two largest guerrilla groups, the Revolutionary Armed Forces (FARC) and the National Liberation Army (ELN), while declaring their support for the peace process and the constituent assembly, said they would not negotiate with the government unless there were "positive signs of changes" in the country.

Since then the signs have at best been mixed and contradictory. President Gaviria appeared to show his good will toward the left by appointing the former M-19 leader Antonio Navarro Wolf (who replaced his slain comrade Carlos Pizarro as presidential candidate in the May election and made a remarkably strong showing) as minister of health. On the other hand, the period before, during, and after the election was marked by a stepped-up counterinsurgency campaign by the military, with a marked increase in aerial bombardments by U.S.-supplied planes and helicopters of rural communities throughout the Santander region and other areas. Ostensibly launched to protect the electoral process from "narco-terrorism," the operation actually targeted rural areas where the guerrilla forces were active. There was widespread belief that the offensive represented an effort by an alliance of military hard-liners and drug traffickers to disrupt the peace process and damage Gaviria's prestige. The guerrillas responded with a counteroffensive that included a campaign of economic sabotage, blowing up sections of oil and gas pipelines and destroying communications and energy towers. Under pressure from assembly delegates to negotiate with the guerrillas, Gaviria softened his stand that he would not talk to them until they stopped military actions, and in February 1991 his interior minister said he would meet with them at any time.

For nine months in 1991–1992, first in Caracas and then in Tlaxcala, Mexico, the government held talks with the remaining guerilla organizations, now united in the *Coordinadora Guerrillera Simón Bolívar* (CGSB), over the terms of a cease-fire and a negotiating agreement. But in March 1992 the negotiations broke down. Since then the war has continued without letup. Despite claims of large guerrilla losses and desertions and assurances by Colombia's defense minister that the "subversives" would be defeated by September 1994—assurances that provoked a general Colombian reaction of surprise and ridicule—there is no realistic prospect that either side could defeat the other in the foreseeable future. In fact, attacks by the guerrillas, who number an estimated 10,000 to 15,000 fighters, have increased despite intensive efforts by the army to root out their strongholds. The "state of emergency" (*estado de excepción*) and total war have provided a cover for a stepped-up repression of labor unions, peasants, and real or suspected leftists and collaborators with the guerrillas. Using the emergency decree, the government has arrested and charged with terrorism trade unionists who protest the privatization of state companies and resulting unemployment. The state of emergency and the government's antisubversive ideology have also contributed to a resurgence of death squad activity by the "triple alliance" of security forces, drug cartels, and wealthy landowners, with a large increase in the number of disappearances, massacres, and displaced people.

The leading role of the Colombian military, generously armed by the United States, in this repression has been well documented. The report "State Terrorism in Colombia," published in Belgium in 1993 by a group of eleven human rights organizations, noted that between 1988 and the first six months of 1992, 9,501 persons were assassinated "for motives explicitly or presumably political" and in two years alone, between 1988 and 1990, 313 massacres were committed against farmers. The report provided thumbnail sketches of 350 top-ranking army and police officers who have been accused of human rights violations. In March 1994 Amnesty International released its own report on the subject. Summarizing the report, *Latinamerica Press* described "a picture of abuses committed primarily during army counterinsurgency campaigns that remind the public of El Salvador in the 1980s." The report also showed that civilian and military authorities routinely covered up for the security forces, allowing them to "literally get away with murder." The AI report pointedly criticized the United States for remaining "silent when aid destined to combat drug trafficking was diverted to counterinsurgency operations and thence the killing of unarmed peasants."

The complicity of the drug cartels in death squad and other repressive activities has also been well documented. In the process of money laundering, many wealthy drug traffickers have become large landowners, and their rapacious thirst for more land brings them into conflict with peasant and Indian groups and the guerrillas who defend them, especially in the new frontier zones of peasant colonization. In the departments of Valle and Cauca, for example, the new narco-landowners, who want more land for cultivation of opium poppies and heroin production, have been occupying huge tracts in an area that is the home of most of Colombia's 100,000 Paez Indians. Natives who resist the intrusion have often been killed by hired gunmen.

The government blames the guerrillas for most of the continuing violence in Colombia. This overlooks the fact that the main guerrilla movement, the FARC, was born during the Liberal-Conservative struggle of the 1940s as a defensive reaction to massive right-wing violence that drove an estimated 100,000 peasants from their land. Today the guerrillas, mostly operating in isolated rural areas, continue to protect workers and farmers from the violence of security forces and right-wing paramilitary groups. In the last analysis, the "guerrilla problem" is not the guerrillas but the social problems that gave rise to them.

The government has been more successful in its struggle with the upstart Medellín drug cartel, but not in solving the larger problem of drug trafficking. In December 1990 truce talks began between the new Gaviria government and the major drug traffickers, centering on a proposal that the traffickers should surrender in return for lenient treatment, immunity from extradition, and security for their wealth. The new extradition policy was a serious blow to Washington's "war on drugs." Colombians appeared to give overwhelming approval to the peace plan. By mid-February 1991 members of the major Ochoa clan had turned themselves in, but Pablo Escobar, head of the Medellín cartel, reportedly held out for better terms. But in July 1991, hours after a constitutional convention had adopted a ban on extradition, Escobar and his principal associates surrendered for trial and were lodged in a comfortable jail. One year later, however, fearing, it has been alleged, that the Gaviria government would allow American agents to kidnap him for trial in the United States, he escaped from the prison that he himself had chosen and remained at large until December 1993, when he died in a shoot-out with a special strike force called the Search Block. By that time the Medellín cartel was only a shadow of its former self, with most of its leaders dead or in prison, and the rival Cali cartel had taken over most of the cocaine and heroin trade to the United States and Europe. In December 1993 the *New York Times* quoted an American drug expert in Bogotá as saying, "The Cali cartel is bigger than anyone gives it credit. Their political and economic influence is unprecedented. They have complete control of the city. They have bought most of the cops. There isn't a politician in the Valle del Cauca who isn't on the payroll or intimidated."

But government officials and drug experts alike agreed that Escobar's death would have no effect on the flow of drugs. This pessimism about the possibility of eradicating the drug trade has made decriminalization of cocaine, formerly taboo, a respectable subject for discussion in Colombia; its advocates include Attorney General de Greiff, the Democratic Alliance party leader Antonio Navarro Wolff, and Gabriel García Márquez. The left and the guerrillas, for their part, have offered a program for the eradication of coca, poppy, and marihuana plantations by the substitution of other crops, with government aid to farmers in land, seeds, and equipment. To date the government has given no indication of support either for decriminalization of cocaine or for the crop-substitution plan.

In July 1991, meanwhile, the constitutional convention had completed its work. The new charter, replacing the constitution of 1886, was designed to open up Colombia's political system, ending the monopoly of power long held by a handful of Liberal and Conservative clans. The document provided for the dissolution of Congress three years early, with new elections to be held in October 1991. Until the new Congress was installed in December 1991, President Gaviria would govern with the aid of a multiparty legislative commission with veto powers. The new constitution provided for the popular election of state governors, limited the president to one term, granted Congress the right to veto cabinet members, established the office of a "people's" defender to investigate human rights abuses, recognized the authority of traditional courts on Indian *resguardos,* ensured representation for minorities in Congress, and barred the extradition of native-born Colombians.

The constitution provides a splendid façade for a corrupt, arbitrary social order, but it is still a façade. It does away with the "state of siege" in force in Colombia for most of the past four decades but conveniently replaces it with the estado de excepción, utilized by Gaviria to put the country on a war footing and ride roughshod over the rights of workers and others. Popular cynicism concerning the new Colombian democracy was reflected in the abstention rate of 70 percent in the first election under the new constitution, in October 1991, which gave the Liberal party solid control of Congress, and in the congressional election of March 1994, which again gave victory to the Liberals.

How thin the democratic veneer over a lawless state and society is is reflected in Colombia's murder rate, with 86 murders per 100,000 inhabitants, probably the highest in the world. "Colombia," commented the *Latin American Weekly Report* in May 1993, "even makes the US, with nine per 100,000, seem like a relatively peaceful place." By the admission of Gaviria's own presidential adviser on human rights, Carlos Vicente de Roux, only about 15 percent of the violent deaths were linked to guerrilla actions, and of those half were caused by state agents.

The militarization of the state under cover of the state of emergency has facilitated the imposition of a neoliberal economic policy featured by the privatization of state enterprises, elimination of subsidies, and other austerity measures promoted by the IMF and the World Bank. These measures, added to the immense costs of the guerrilla war, have sharpened all of Colombia's economic and social problems; more than half of Colombia's 33 million people live below the poverty line. In Colombia, as in other Latin American countries, there has been growing protest by labor and other popular organizations against the neoliberal program and its disastrous impact on living standards. This trend found some reflection in the 1994 presidential elections, pitting the Liberal candidate Daniel Samper against the Conservative Andrés Pastrana. Samper's campaign combined promises to continue the free market policies of his predecessor with pledges that he would give those policies a more "human face," making health, social security, housing, and job creation his main priorities. He gained a narrow victory in the second, runoff round of the presidential election in June 1994. Despite the reformist tinge of his platform, there was no evidence that Samper was prepared to initiate the profound economic and social changes needed to turn the promises of the constitution of 1991 into reality. Still, in early 1995 President Samper startled his military and won praise from human rights groups by admitting the government's guilt for the slaughter of 107 peasants in the town of Trujillo between 1989 and 1990; they had been killed at the request of drug traffickers by paramilitary groups with the complicity of police and army forces. A sign of progress? Perhaps. But the army commander in charge was given an honorable retirement, and on technical legal grounds no sanctions were taken against the other military and police involved in the massacre.

Chapter 20

The Two Americas: United States–Latin American Relations

Two consistent themes appear when the relations of the United States with Latin America over nearly two centuries are examined. First and foremost, the United States has sought to protect and expand its economic and political interests in the region. Ever since the administration of James Monroe, the United States has attempted to establish and maintain Latin America as an economic appendage. U.S. policy makers have displayed resourcefulness and flexibility in pursuit of this goal, adapting their methods to meet the varying domestic political pressures, the changing requirements of American economic enterprise, and the shifting conditions in Latin America. Second, the United States has generally subordinated Latin America to its other concerns abroad. Consequently, American policy makers have tended to deal with Latin America either by employing frameworks formed for other regions or by grouping the nations of the area under one heading and ignoring their individual problems and needs.

United States Policy

American policy toward Latin America has changed over time to accommodate burgeoning American economic activities in the region. During the early years of the nineteenth century, U.S. commerce with its southern neighbors demanded little more than policing the Caribbean for marauding pirates. As the United States grew into a commercial, industrial, and, eventually, financial power, its foreign policy broadened in scope. The hunt for new markets brought it into competition with European nations, especially Great Britain. As a result, it became one of the

522   major aims of American policy to check the further penetration of European commerce and capital into Latin America.

By the turn of the century, Latin America had become not only a substantial market for American products but an important source of raw materials and a major area for capital investment as well. Having recently built a powerful navy, the United States assumed the responsibility of protecting American commerce and investment by forcibly maintaining order in the region. Uninvited, it assumed the role of policeman of the Western Hemisphere. In this capacity, the United States focused its attention on the weak and chaotic nations of the Caribbean and Central America, where American economic activity was concentrated.

At mid-century, South America replaced the Caribbean as the focus of American economic expansion. Geography, logistics, and the anti-imperialist temper of the times required the United States to abandon the old policies of military intervention in favor of more subtle and sophisticated ways of achieving its ends; these new methods included the lure of grants and loans, the threat of economic sanctions, and subversion. When these methods failed, however, as they did in Guatemala in 1954, in Cuba in 1959, and in the Dominican Republic in 1965, the United States did not hesitate to resort to the open or covert use of force.

Ideology has always figured in United States policy toward Latin America. Thus, Theodore Roosevelt vowed to "civilize," Woodrow Wilson to "democratize," and John F. Kennedy to "reform" Latin America. But ideology has always been subordinated to the material needs of United States–Latin American policy, and the presidents who made these pious professions were ready to use force in defense of the U.S. empire in Latin America. They were also ready to support the most oppressive regimes in the area as long as they cooperated with the United States.

The two Americas, both born in wars of national liberation, have followed very different historical paths. In two centuries, the United States

has risen to become the industrial and financial giant of the capitalist world; despite its many economic and social problems, it provides the majority of its people with a satisfactory material standard of living. Latin America has fallen far behind the other America and belongs to the underdeveloped world.

Many Latin Americans are convinced that these divergent trends are not unrelated, that Latin American underdevelopment is the other side of North American development, that Latin American poverty and misery have accumulated as the economic and political power of foreign (chiefly North American) multinational corporations has grown.

Prelude to Empire, 1810–1897

Manifest Destiny, 1810–1865

During the early decades of the nineteenth century, westward expansion and nascent commerce brought the United States into its first contact with its southern neighbors. However, American military weakness, lack of information, and British predominance in the area limited U.S. activities in Latin America. U.S. trade with Latin America began in earnest in 1797, when Spain opened the ports of its New World colonies to foreign trade. By 1811 the Spanish colonies accounted for 16 percent of all U.S. trade. A dozen years later, despite the disruptions of the War of 1812, the figure had increased to 20 percent.

With only a small navy and few funds at its disposal, the U.S. government could offer little aid or comfort to the Spanish-American nations during their wars of independence (1810–1826). During the first stage of these wars, the War of 1812 consumed the attention and resources of the United States. From 1817 to 1821, it undertook delicate negotiations with Spain for the purchase of Florida and did not choose to jeopardize these dealings by helping the Spanish-American insurgents.

When it was clear that the Latin American independence movements had succeeded, the

United States acted to prevent other European nations from acquiring colonies or undue influence in the region, developments that could shut off U.S. access to potentially lucrative markets. In his message to Congress on December 2, 1823, President James Monroe declared that as a matter of principle, "the American continents, by the free and independent condition they have assumed and maintain, are henceforth not to be considered subjects for future colonization by any European powers.... We should consider any attempt on their [the European powers'] part to extend their system to any portion of this hemisphere as dangerous to our peace and safety." Monroe went on to say that the United States would not interfere with existing colonies, nor would it meddle in European affairs.

The Monroe Doctrine was ineffective for much of the nineteenth century because the United States had neither the resources nor the inclination to back it up. The doctrine, furthermore, failed to prevent repeated European interventions in Latin America. Following the accepted practice of the time, French and British gunboats regularly bombarded or blockaded Latin American ports to force payment of debts or reparations. The United States, too, adopted this practice, landing troops in the Falkland Islands, Argentina, and Peru during the 1830s, in Argentina, Nicaragua, Uruguay, Panama, Paraguay, and Mexico during the 1850s, and in Panama, Uruguay, Mexico, and Colombia during the 1860s.

Westward territorial expansion involved the United States in two wars during the nineteenth century. After the purchase of Louisiana (1803) and Florida (1821), the country began to cast covetous looks toward the northern provinces of Mexico, where U.S. citizens had begun to conduct flourishing commerce. In 1825 President John Quincy Adams authorized the United States minister to Mexico to negotiate the purchase of Texas. The Mexican government rejected the proposal. During the early 1830s, American settlers poured into Texas and quickly found themselves at odds with Mexican authorities over the issues of local autonomy and the illegal introduction of slavery into the area. In 1836 the settlers

rebelled, defeated Mexico in a short war, and won their independence. Texas remained an independent nation for ten years, for the bitter debate over the extension of slavery prevented its annexation to the United States until 1845.

In 1845 President James Polk sent an emissary, James Slidell, to Mexico to arrange the acquisition of California. Outraged at the annexation of Texas, the Mexicans refused to cede any of their territory. Consequently, Polk trumped up a border incident along the Rio Grande, provoking a military clash that led to the Mexican-American War (1846–1848). The victorious United States took the territories of Arizona, New Mexico, and California. Barely some seventy years old, the United States had successfully waged a war of territorial acquisition.

Commerce and the Canal

From 1815 to 1860, U.S. foreign commerce increased dramatically; exports grew by nearly 400 percent and imports by 300 percent. The nature of U.S. trade was transformed, for instead of re-exporting foreign-made goods, U.S. merchants exported agricultural commodities and manufactured goods produced in the United States. Because of the increased economic activity in the Caribbean, especially Cuba and Central America, the United States began to pay close attention to the region. Cuba became one of the most important U.S. overseas markets, ranking third behind Great Britain and France in total American trade. Throughout the 1850s, there was a strong sentiment, particularly among southerners, to annex the island. President Millard Fillmore tried unsuccessfully to purchase Cuba from Spain in 1852.

Central America became important because of the prospect of a canal through the region. Americans had talked of a canal through the Central American isthmus as early as 1825. In 1846 the United States signed an agreement with New Granada (Colombia) that guaranteed American access to any canal built in Panama, then a province of New Granada. This concern over a canal and its commercial interests in Central America

524

brought the United States into direct confrontation with Great Britain, which had colonies in the region. Each nation sought to keep the other from dominating the area or controlling any canal that would be built. As a result, in 1850 they agreed to the Clayton-Bulwer Treaty, which provided that neither would try to dominate Central America or any part of it or would acquire exclusive rights to a canal. Thus, they eliminated a potential cause of hostilities.

The gold rush to California in 1849 increased the importance of transportation across the isthmus. American entrepreneurs invested heavily in steamships and railroad construction in the region to satisfy the demand for cheap and fast transport across the isthmus to California. Despite the treaty with Britain and these heavy investments in transportation, U.S. interest in a canal continued.

The Awakening Giant, 1865–1887

In the two decades after the Civil War (1861–1865), U.S. policy makers focused their concerns on territorial expansion and increased trade in Latin America, finding little success in either. The major diplomatic triumph of the era came in 1866 when Secretary of State William H. Seward, belatedly invoking the Monroe Doctrine, demanded that France remove its troops from Mexico, where they propped up the rule of the Emperor Maximilian, the Austrian Archduke. Emperor Napoleon III of France complied the following year, more because of growing tensions with Prussia in Europe than because of fear of the United States.

A succession of U.S. presidents and secretaries of state attempted to acquire new territories, but they were inevitably thwarted by Congress. There were also major efforts to expand U.S. trade to Latin America through the negotiation of reciprocal trade treaties and establishment of inter-American diplomatic conferences. The United States signed bilateral reciprocal trade agreements with six Latin American nations during the 1880s but no real benefits accrued. The first Inter-American Conference met in Washington, D.C., in

1889. It resulted in little more than the airing of long-simmering grievances and mistrust.

Adventures in Latin America, 1888–1896

U.S. adventurism in Latin America in the last years of the nineteenth century stemmed from severe domestic economic and social problems and from the country's growing stake in commerce and investment in the region. The United States experienced a deep depression from 1893 to 1898, the third such downturn in twenty-five years (the others occurred in 1873–1878 and 1882–1885). It became evident that the domestic market could not absorb the rapidly growing output of U.S. agriculture and industry. American leaders unanimously agreed that the answer to the problem was to expand foreign markets. The depression of 1893 created deep-seated social unrest as well, resulting in a series of bitter and bloody strikes. Businessmen and politicians alike feared that continued depression would lead to class warfare.

At the same time, U.S. capitalists increased their investment in Latin America. Paradoxically, despite the depression, U.S. banks had surplus funds to invest. Because investments in the United States were unattractive, the bankers turned to potentially more lucrative foreign enterprises. These investors poured millions of dollars into Cuban sugar and Mexican mining and railroads. By 1900 the U.S. stake in Mexico alone had reached $500 million.

American interest, however, was not limited to areas like Mexico and Cuba, where the United States already had large investments. The United States was willing to go to great lengths, even at the risk of war, both to protect potential markets and to reinforce its political dominance in the region. This was particularly true of the Caribbean, which leaders tended to view as an "American lake." Thus, in 1888 the United States intervened in a civil war in Haiti to secure a favorable commercial agreement and a naval base at Môle St. Nicolas. The U.S. fleet actually broke a blockade to bring about the victory of the faction it favored. Once entrenched in power, however, this group reneged on its promises to the Harrison administration (1887–1893). Then Secretary of State James G. Blaine also tried unsuccessfully to obtain Samaná Bay from Santo Domingo.

As the depression of 1893 deepened, U.S. leaders looked southward with growing anxiety. President Grover Cleveland declared in his annual message to Congress in 1893 that unrest and European meddling had threatened American interests in Nicaragua, Guatemala, Costa Rica, Honduras, and Brazil in 1892; the United States fleet was finding it difficult to keep up with its "responsibilities." Markets desperately needed by the United States were threatened by disorders and competition from European nations, particularly Britain.

In 1894 the United States became involved in another revolution when it intervened in Brazil to protect a potentially important market and to check British influence there. The United States had signed a reciprocal trade agreement with the newly proclaimed republic of Brazil in 1891, but the rebels who rose up in 1893 opposed the pact. The main strategy of the rebel forces was to blockade the harbor of Rio de Janeiro, the nation's principal city; they hoped to strangle the government by denying it the all-important customs revenue. The United States helped undermine this strategy by refusing to recognize the blockade. U.S. vessels unloaded their cargoes without interference.

Late in 1894, however, with clandestine aid from the British, the rebellion regained momentum. At this time, important mercantile and oil (Rockefeller) interests, fearing the loss of their Brazilian market, brought pressure on the State Department to intervene. The United States responded by sending most of the Atlantic fleet to the harbor of Rio de Janeiro. By maneuvering to prevent rebel bombardment of the capital, the American warships played a crucial part in the defeat of the revolt.

Shortly thereafter, the United States intervened in Nicaragua to protect American rights to an isthmian canal and the substantial holdings of American investors. In 1893 a nationalist government, headed by General José S. Zelaya, took power in Nicaragua; it threatened to cancel a concession granted by a previous administration to the Maritime Canal Company to build a canal through Nicaraguan territory. Later, Zelaya also threatened the prosperous U.S.-run banana plantations in the Miskito Indian reservation (an area claimed by Nicaragua but controlled by the British) by invading the reservation in 1894. In response, British troops landed and quickly subdued the Nicaraguan force. U.S. interests, with a $2 million stake in the Miskito region, were unwilling to accept either British or Nicaraguan rule. To protect American property, the United States stationed two warships off the coast and in July dispatched marines to restore order. United States troops landed three more times, in 1896, 1898, and 1899, to protect American lives and property.

The Turning Point: Venezuela, 1895–1896

The Venezuelan crisis of 1895–1896 ended in full British recognition of U.S. hegemony in the Western Hemisphere. The United States intervened in a boundary dispute between Venezuela and Great Britain that had festered for over half a century. The controversy concerned the region at the mouth of the Orinoco River, the major artery for northern South America, which was claimed by both Venezuela and the British colony of Guiana (present-day Guyana). In the 1880s, Britain extended its claims, causing Venezuela to break off diplomatic relations.

During 1893 and 1894, the Venezuelan government, confronted with mounting economic difficulties and political unrest, appealed to the United States to help settle the controversy. President Cleveland's entrance into the dispute reflected his deep concern about the apparent resurgence of European intervention in Latin America. Between 1891 and 1895, the British had actively intervened in Chile, Brazil, and Nicaragua. The French had become involved in a dispute with Brazil over the boundary of their colony of Guiana and had threatened intervention in

Santo Domingo to obtain satisfaction for the killing of a French citizen. The simultaneous scramble for territories in Africa magnified the threat; what the European rivals did on one continent, they could do on another. Specifically, President Cleveland feared that British control of the mouth of the Orinoco would exclude American commerce from northern South American markets.

In 1895, in an obvious effort to intensify U.S. support, the Venezuelan government granted a lucrative concession to an American syndicate for the exploitation of rich mineral resources located in the disputed zone. In July 1895 Secretary of State Richard Olney spelled out the American attitude toward European meddling in Latin America. Citing the Monroe Doctrine, he declared that the United States would intervene whenever the actions of a European power in the Western Hemisphere posed a "serious and direct menace to its own integrity and welfare." In effect, Olney claimed hegemony for the United States in Latin America.

The British initially responded to Olney's claims with disdain; the English foreign secretary denied the validity of the Monroe Doctrine in international law and brushed aside the American assertion of supremacy in the Western Hemisphere. President Cleveland, however, firmly supported Olney's position and made it clear that the United States was willing to go to war to uphold it. Meanwhile, international developments worked to soften the British stand; the threat of a war with Germany and British problems in South Africa took precedence. Accordingly, in late 1896, the British agreed to submit the dispute to arbitration. The government of Venezuela neither participated in nor was informed of this agreement.

The Venezuelan affair marked the end of British military predominance in Latin America. Its attention now focused on the growing German power and the competition for territory in Africa, Britain could no longer commit substantial resources to the region. With the growing threat of a general war in Europe, British leaders could also not afford to alienate the United States, a powerful potential ally. Thus, the British formally

recognized U.S. hegemony in Latin America with the signing of the Hay-Pauncefote Treaty of 1901, which allowed the United States unilaterally to build, control, and fortify an isthmian canal. In 1906, Britain withdrew its fleet from the Caribbean. Great Britain retained its predominant economic position in southern South America but was fated to lose that also to the United States after World War I.

An Imperial Power, 1898–1933

By 1898 the United States had emerged as an industrial, financial, and naval power. It surpassed Great Britain as the world's leading manufacturing state. Giant U.S. banks and corporations invested heavily overseas. Increasingly, the nation looked abroad for markets, raw materials, and profits. Recurring economic difficulties and mounting social unrest spurred American leaders to seek solutions in overseas economic expansion and foreign adventures.

The War with Spain

The war with Spain in 1898 established the United States as a full-fledged imperial power. The primary goal of its Cuban policy during the 1890s was to protect the very large (over $50 million) U.S. investment in the island by stopping the chronic political disorder there. When Spain proved unable to end the turmoil, and it appeared that ungovernable native rebels might take over, the United States intervened. In declaring war against Spain, the United States Congress pledged to free Cuba from Spanish tyranny and in the Teller Resolution disavowed any intention to annex the island. But the U.S. government proceeded to conduct the war and negotiate the peace without consulting the Cubans.

The United States occupied and ruled the island from 1898 to 1902, departing only after the Cubans agreed to include in their constitution the notorious Platt Amendment, which made the country a virtual American protectorate. American forces occupied the island three more times, 1906 to 1909, 1912, and 1917 to 1922. As noted in

Chapter 17, instead of bringing the Cubans liberty and economic progress, U.S. intervention promoted and perpetuated corruption, violence, and economic stagnation.

An "American Lake": The "Big Stick" and "Dollar Diplomacy" in the Caribbean

From 1898 to 1932, the United States intervened militarily in nine Caribbean nations[1] a total of thirty-four times. Its occupation forces ran the governments of the Dominican Republic, Cuba, Nicaragua, Haiti, and Panama for long periods; Honduras, Mexico, Guatemala, and Costa Rica experienced shorter invasions. Military intervention was not the only method employed by the United States to control the region; other effective means included threats, nonrecognition, and economic sanctions.

The U.S. economic stake in the Caribbean was substantial. Moreover, the nature of this investment, which was concentrated primarily in agricultural commodities, mineral extraction, oil production, and government securities, made it particularly vulnerable to political disorders. From 1887 to 1914, U.S. investment in Cuba and the West Indies rose almost sevenfold, from $50 million to $336 million. Investment in Central America more than quadrupled, from $21 million to $93 million. By 1914, U.S. investment in Mexico had risen to over $1 billion. In 1914, 43 percent of this investment was in mining, 18.7 percent in agriculture, and 10 percent in oil. An additional 13 percent was invested in railroads, which were built to transport the export products to market. The owners of these enterprises often had considerable influence on American policy.

The United States justified its actions in the Caribbean by the so-called Roosevelt Corollary (1904) to the Monroe Doctrine, so named because President Theodore Roosevelt maintained that the United States, as a "civilized" nation, had the right to end "chronic wrongdoing" and thus could intervene in the Caribbean to maintain order. The Roosevelt Corollary was a logical out-

[1] The Caribbean nations include the West Indies, Cuba, Central America, and Mexico.

growth of the increasingly aggressive policies successively advanced by Seward, Grant, Cleveland, and Olney.

The Panama Canal

United States interest in a canal across Central America to join the Atlantic and Pacific oceans intensified as the nation filled out its continental boundaries and expanded its commercial activities throughout the Western Hemisphere. A group of New York businessmen initiated a project to build a canal in 1825 but failed to obtain financial support. In 1846 the United States signed a treaty with New Granada to assure American access to any future canal constructed in the province of Panama. The California gold rush three years later created a large demand for transportation across the isthmus en route to the West Coast gold fields. In response, a group of New York capitalists constructed a railroad across the 48-mile width of Panama between 1851 and 1855. No sooner was the railway finished than U.S. troops landed to protect American interests from Panamanian insurgents rebelling against Colombian rule. In 1865, U.S. troops again landed to protect American lives and property during another rebellion.

Americans were not the first to attempt to build a canal. Ferdinand de Lesseps, the Frenchman who had constructed the Suez Canal, began a project to dig a sea-level canal across Panama in 1878. After eleven years of effort, de Lesseps, thwarted by tropical disease and engineering problems, gave up the project. Throughout this period, the United States pressured France to abandon the undertaking; it asserted its "rightful and long-established claim to priority on the American continent." The growth of a large United States Navy, which had two coasts to defend, added to the urgency of constructing an isthmian passageway.

In the 1880s and 1890s, support grew for building a canal through Nicaragua. In 1901 a presidential commission endorsed the Nicaraguan route, despite the more favorable engineering and logistical characteristics of the Panamanian alternative, because the French company

528

that controlled the canal concession in Panama wanted the fantastic sum of $109 million for its rights. At this point, two extraordinary entrepreneurs, William N. Cromwell, an influential New York attorney, and Philippe Bunau-Varilla, chief engineer of the de Lesseps project and an organizer of the New Panama Canal Company (the French company that had rights to the canal) acted to change the course of U.S. policy. Cromwell, as lawyer for the canal company, bribed the Republican party to end its support of the Nicaraguan route. He and Bunau-Varilla then convinced the company to lower the price for its concession to a more reasonable $40 million.

The two men were faced with the problem of convincing the United States to purchase their company's concession before it expired in 1904. In 1902, Bunau-Varilla and Cromwell managed to push through Congress the Spooner Amendment, which authorized President Roosevelt to buy the New Panama Canal Company's rights for the asking price of $40 million if he could negotiate a treaty with Colombia. In 1903, Secretary of State John Hay pressured the Colombian ambassador to the United States to sign a pact that gave the United States a 99-year lease on a strip of land across the isthmus in return for $10 million and an annual payment of $250,000. The Colombian Senate, demanding more money, rejected the proposal.

In the meantime, Bunau-Varilla undertook to exploit the long tradition of Panamanian nationalism and rebelliousness for his own end. From the time that Colombia won its independence from Spain in 1821, it had never been able to establish its rule in Panama. During the nineteenth century, the Panamanians revolted fifty times against their Colombian masters. On two occasions, when the Panamanian rebels seemed near success (1855–1856 and 1885), the United States intervened militarily to protect American interests and end the revolts. After a terrible civil war (1899–1902) had severely weakened Colombia, Panamanian nationalists again prepared to rise in revolt. Working closely with the U.S. State Department and the Panamanians, Bunau-Varilla triggered a successful uprising in early November

1903. With the help of the United States Navy and bribes paid to the Colombian officers who were supposed to crush the revolt, Panama won its independence.

The Panamanians, to their own undoing, entrusted to Bunau-Varilla the subsequent negotiations with the United States over the canal concession. Feverishly working to complete the arrangements before the New Panama Canal Company's rights expired, he produced a treaty that gave the United States control over a ten-mile-wide canal zone "as if it were a sovereign of the territory." The United States was to have "in perpetuity the use, occupation, and control" of the zone. In return, the United States was to pay Panama $10 million and assume a virtual protectorate over the new nation. The Panamanian government indignantly protested the terms of the agreement but eventually accepted the pact, fearing that the United States might either seize the canal with no compensation or build one in Nicaragua instead.

United States Marines were stationed in Panama from late 1903 until 1914 to protect American interests while the canal was built. During this period, the United States disbanded the Panamanian army and assumed the responsibility of defending Panama against any external threat. The United States established its own postal system, custom houses, and commissaries in the Canal Zone, privileges that seriously undermined the Panamanian economy and badly injured Panamanian pride. The canal was completed in 1914.

The Dominican Republic, Haiti, and Nicaragua

The United States occupied and administered the governments of the Dominican Republic (1916–1924), Haiti (1915–1934), and Nicaragua (1912–1925 and 1926–1933) to the detriment of these nations' long-range political and economic development.

President Ulysses S. Grant had sought to annex the Dominican Republic (then known as Santo Domingo) in 1869; only rejection of the agreement by the United States Senate prevented him

The construction of the Panama Canal.

from acquiring the nation, which shares the island of Hispaniola with Haiti. In the decades that followed, a series of venal and brutal dictators, often supported by loans from American banks, produced a debilitating cycle of repression and rebellion. In 1893 the Santo Domingo Improvement Company, a U.S. firm, purchased the country's heavy foreign debt in return for the right to collect its customs revenue. In both 1903 and 1904, the United States dispatched marines to protect the interests of the influential New York financiers who were principals in the company. In 1905 the United States government assumed the administration of Dominican customs.

But unrest persisted. In 1916 President Woodrow Wilson sent in marines after the Domin-

ican government refused to accept broader U.S. control over the nation's internal affairs, and the United States Navy maintained a military dictatorship until 1924. The marines brutally repressed guerrilla activities, which threatened American-owned sugar plantations, and in addition, several American officers were subsequently court-martialed for the commission of atrocities.

The U.S. occupation forces attempted administrative and fiscal reforms and built some roads, but these projects were abandoned when the soldiers departed. One institution that remained intact after the occupation ended was the *Guardia Nacional,* the national police force. Rafael Trujillo, with U.S. support, rose through the ranks of the Guardia to become dictator of the Dominican Republic in 1928. His rapacious rule, extending over three decades (he was assassinated in 1961) was the bitter legacy of intervention by the United States.

Events in Haiti followed a similar course. For a century after winning independence from France in 1804, Haiti experienced ruinous political turmoil. Seizing the opportunity presented by the brutal murder of the Haitian president in 1915, Woodrow Wilson sent in the marines, ostensibly to prevent Germany from taking advantage of the chaos to establish a base on the island, which would endanger U.S. commerce and the access routes to the Panama Canal. A treaty signed the next year placed the United States in full control of the country. Although Haitians held public office, they served only at the pleasure of the American authorities. Here, too, American troops committed atrocities while engaged in the suppression of rural guerrillas, and civil liberties were ignored. U.S. control lasted until 1934.

The United States also intervened in Nicaragua to protect the interests of American companies operating there. The U.S. investment totaled only $2.5 million, but the largest American company, the United States–Nicaraguan Concession, had considerable influence in the Taft administration (1909–1913); Secretary of State Philander C. Knox had been the company's legal counsel. In 1909, General José Zelaya, an old nemesis of the United States, canceled a concession to one American company and threatened the Nicaraguan Concession. The same year, the United States backed a revolution that overthrew Zelaya. In 1912, at the request of the Nicaraguan government, U.S. President William Howard Taft sent in the marines to crush a new rebellion; the marines remained for thirteen years. In 1916 the United States and Nicaragua agreed to the Bryan-Chamorro Treaty, which gave the United States sole rights to build a canal through Nicaragua in return for payment of $3 million.[2] President Calvin Coolidge with-

drew American troops for a short period in 1925, but dispatched them again to subdue yet another revolution the following year; the soldiers stayed until 1933.

Puerto Rico

The United States became a colonial power with the conquest and acquisition of the island of Puerto Rico in 1898 during the Spanish-American-Cuban War. From December 1898 until May 1900, U.S. military governors ruled the island. In 1900 the United States Congress passed the Foraker Act, which established a new civilian government for the island with a governor and an executive council appointed by the U.S. president. In 1917 this government was modified by replacing the executive council with an elected Senate. But the president maintained the power to veto legislation passed by the Puerto Rican Congress. The same year the U.S. Congress granted Puerto Ricans United States citizenship in time to make them eligible for the military draft for World War I.

United States occupation cost Puerto Ricans dearly politically. At the time of the Spanish-American War, the island had won a large degree of autonomy from Spain. The new colonial regime stripped that from them and ruled Puerto Rico with tactless, condescending mainlanders, who had no experience in dealing with different cultures. When Puerto Ricans protested against unresponsive government, U.S. authorities reacted harshly. In 1909, for example, members of the Puerto Rican House of Delegates refused to pass the year's appropriation bill because of their objections to the indifference shown in the court system to struggling coffee growers. President William H. Taft angrily demanded that the right of appropriations be taken from the House of Delegates, and the United States Congress enacted this legislation in the so-called Olmstead Amendment. Puerto Rico did not have a native-born governor until 1947 or an elected governor until 1948.

Puerto Rico also underwent drastic economic changes as a result of the United States occupa-

---

[2] This treaty gave the United States control over the two best routes for a canal in Central America.

tion. In 1898 its leading crop, coffee, was exported to Europe. United States policies transformed the island into a monocrop sugar economy with landownership concentrated in very few hands, mostly absentee foreign corporations. Puerto Ricans became dependent on the U.S. sugar quota. The decline of sugar prices during the 1920s and their collapse during the depression of the 1930s brought chronic economic problems. By 1929 near starvation prevailed in many parts of the island. New Deal agencies, such as the Puerto Rican Emergency Relief Administration and the Puerto Rican Reconstruction Administration, poured some $230 million into the island from 1933 to 1941.

During the 1930s and for decades thereafter, the influence of two Puerto Ricans, Pedro Albizu Campos and Luis Muñoz Marín, dominated Puerto Rican politics. Harvard-educated Albizu became the foremost spokesman for independence. He formed the Nationalist party and took an ardently anti-U.S. stand. He spent many years in prison for supporting violent confrontation with the island's colonial master. Muñoz Marín, whose father had led the Unionists in the early years of United States rule, was also educated in the United States. He did not live in Puerto Rico permanently until 1931. During the dark depression days of the 1930s, Muñoz Marín became the star protégé of the New Deal.

The terrible plight of Puerto Rico during the depression led to a re-evaluation of its status by policy makers in the United States in the late 1930s. It was, as historian Arturo Morales Carrión has said, "a crisis of the whole colonial system." North Americanization had brought the "rise of absentee landownership, the collapse of coffee culture, the migration to growing slums, and shocking poverty in rural areas." United States rule had been a "mixture of paternalism and neglect, self-righteousness and condescension." The U.S. administrators of the island reacted harshly to such criticism and to nationalist protests. In March 1937 during a parade of the Nationalist party in San Juan, police killed seventeen protesters in an unprovoked attack. In the crisis that followed in the aftermath of the mas-

sacre, old political coalitions realigned and Muñoz Marín emerged as the leading political figure. Based on his grassroots organization in the countryside, Muñoz Marín's Popular Democratic party (PPD) rose meteorically, sweeping elections from 1944 until 1968. With help from Washington, he was able to lead Puerto Rico into a new era of industrialization and economic development.

The first substantial change in Puerto Rico's status took place after World War II. When Tugwell left office in 1947, President Harry S Truman appointed Jesús T. Pinero, the first native governor. A year later Muñoz Marín became the first elected governor of the island. This did not satisfy all Puerto Ricans' desire for self-rule, however. In November 1950, two Puerto Rican nationalists invaded Blair House in Washington, D.C., Truman's temporary home, in an assassination attempt on the president. In March 1954 three Puerto Rican men and a woman entered the U.S. House of Representatives with guns and wounded five congressmen. But self-rule was not desired by the majority of Puerto Ricans. In June 1950, the island held its first plebiscite on its status, voting by 70 percent for commonwealth status; the Constitution of Puerto Rico, establishing the commonwealth, took effect in 1952. In 1967 another plebiscite showed 60 percent in favor of remaining a commonwealth.

Tugwell and Muñoz Marín engineered the diversification of the Puerto Rican economy under the auspices of Operation Bootstrap. The plan attracted mainland manufacturing companies to the island with special tax inducements and low labor costs. Thus, Puerto Rico enjoyed an economic boom during the 1950s and 1960s; unemployment was also reduced in part by the migration of hundreds of thousands of Puerto Ricans to the mainland, particularly to New York City. By the 1970s, however, Operation Bootstrap had broken down; companies left the island for the Far East or other regions that offered even cheaper labor and lower taxes, leaving many islanders without jobs. Puerto Ricans became almost totally reliant on federal help, much of it in the form of food stamps and other assistance

532   programs. By 1980 over half of the island's population was eligible for food stamps. In 1990 about 60 percent of the island's population and 40 percent of the Puerto Rican population on the mainland lived below or near the poverty line. Unemployment was officially estimated at 18 percent. The inflow of American capital brought more rather than less unemployment, and, instead of declining, the flight of Puerto Ricans to the mainland has increased.

Characteristic of Puerto Rican development is its dependence on the U.S. economy. North American corporations effectively monopolize the key sectors of banking, transport, tourism, and high-tech industrialization. This has discouraged native capital formation. The dependent character of the Puerto Rican economy is reflected in the fact that by the mid-1980s 85 percent of Puerto Rico's production was for export while 45 percent of its food needs was imported from the continental United States. For North American corporations, however, the combination of low wages and tax breaks has proved a bonanza, with profits in the range of $10 billion a year.

The combination of economic, political, and legal dependency—the U.S. Congress controls the Puerto Rican political and legislative systems, and the U.S. Supreme Court can review and revoke decisions of the Puerto Rican Supreme Court—has adversely affected Puerto Rican political culture, breeding a colonial psychology that makes dependency appear a natural condition and independence an impossible dream. Political life moves within the narrow orbits of a two-party system, not unlike that of the United States. Since 1968 the Popular Democratic Party (PPD), which favors continuance of the present status of union with the United States as a "Free Associated State" or commonwealth, and the New Progressive Party, which favors statehood, have alternated in power, with two small pro-independence parties far down in the polls. In November 1993 a plebiscite on the subject, called by New Progressive Governor Pedro Rosselló, gave 48.4 percent of the votes for the commonwealth option, 46.2 for statehood, and 4.4 percent

for independence.[3] In any case, a pro-statehood vote was not binding on the U.S. Congress, which would decide whether to admit Puerto Rico as a state.

The 1993 passage of the North American Trade Agreement (NAFTA) by the U.S. Congress portended more economic difficulties for Puerto Rico. In effect, the pact placed Puerto Rico in competition with Mexico and other Caribbean countries in labor-intensive industries like apparel, footwear, and electronics assembly. The competition will be over which country can offer absentee employers the lowest wages and the fewest labor and environmental regulations. It is likely that as a result Puerto Rican unemployment will increase and already low living and labor standards will further decline.

U.S. economic policy has tied Puerto Rico ever more firmly to the mainland, first as the primary market for its monocrop, sugar, then as the major investor in its industrialization, and finally as the main supporter of the welfare state.

The Mexican Revolution

We have already discussed some aspects of United States policy toward the Mexican Revolution (1910–1920) in Chapter 12. That policy was directed above all at safeguarding the vast U.S. investment below the border and securing the favorable political and economic climate required by American interests in Mexico. The specific policies and tactics employed by the administrations of Presidents Taft and Wilson varied with the shifting conditions in Mexico, political pressures in the United States, and the changing international background. The United States twice resorted to military intervention in Mexico. In 1914 United States Marines occupied the gulf ports of Veracruz and Tampico in an effort to

[3] The reality as opposed to the theory of the relationship of Puerto Rico to the United States was stated very clearly and frankly by Attorney General Richard Thornburg in 1991: "The Congress of the United States holds full powers over Puerto Rico, a relationship that Puerto Ricans are incapable of altering. . . ." He went on to say that this relationship remained inalterable until changed by an amendment to the U.S. Constitution.

bring down General Victoriano Huerta by denying his government the use of customs revenues and arms imports from Europe. The second intervention, General John J. Pershing's incursion into northern Mexico in 1916 in pursuit of Pancho Villa, served only to unite the Mexican nation behind the regime of Venustiano Carranza.

The United States exerted more decisive influence on the military course of the revolution by regulating the flow of arms and munitions across the United States–Mexican border. Through selective application of its neutrality laws, the U.S. government prevented "undesirable" factions from instigating disruptive activities on the American side of the border. Woodrow Wilson introduced a new tactic in United States relations with Mexico by announcing that he would withhold recognition of governments that did not measure up to his standard of "morality." Wilson used this ploy against Huerta, Carranza, and Obregón. Another United States tactic to influence the course of the revolution was the threat of invasion. President Taft's shift of American troops to the border area in Texas, a veiled threat of intervention, may have helped to convince Porfirio Díaz to abdicate in 1911.

United States efforts to control the course of the revolution were diluted by stubborn resistance on the part of nationalist Mexican leaders like Carranza, divisions among U.S. investors in Mexico—some favoring and others opposing military intervention—and, finally, America's growing involvement in World War I. America's entry into the war in 1917 sharply limited policy alternatives, since the country lacked the military resources to fight in both Mexico and Europe. The threat of a Mexican alliance with Germany—a threat strongly posed by the famous Zimmerman telegram[4]—forced the United States to adopt a more moderate policy toward its neighbor.

[4] In this dispatch the German government, not yet at war with the United States, offered to return to Mexico the southwestern part of the United States (lost during the Mexican War, 1846–1848) if Mexico would invade the United States. This telegram was a major factor in President Woodrow Wilson's decision to go to war in 1917.

Wilson and Latin America

In the presidential election campaign of 1912, Woodrow Wilson disavowed the Republican policies of "gunboat" and "dollar" diplomacy. Yet he surpassed his predecessors in the use of military force to impose U.S. hegemony in Latin America. Under the banner of "morality" and "democracy," Wilson occupied most of the Caribbean, maintaining a harsh U.S. rule over five major Caribbean republics (Panama, Nicaragua, Haiti, Cuba, and the Dominican Republic).

Wilson's Secretary of State, William Jennings Bryan, who had railed against "corporate interests," appointed as his main adviser on Latin America a former vice president of the New York City Bank, one of the biggest lenders to the governments of the Caribbean. Bryan, who later resigned in protest against Wilson's aggressive policy toward Germany, was the most ardent supporter of the U.S. intervention in Haiti in 1915.

Quiet Imperialism: The Post–World War I Years

United States investment in Latin America grew rapidly in the period between 1914 and 1929. The world war enabled American entrepreneurs to buy up much of the large British and German investment in the region. Total U.S. investment in Cuba and the West Indies, for example, rose from $336 million in 1914 to $1.2 billion in 1929, nearly four times the amount. United States capital in Central America more than tripled, while investment in South America skyrocketed to about an eightfold increase; investment in South America doubled every five years. In 1929 total U.S. investment in Latin America had reached the staggering sum of $5.4 billion, or 35 percent of all U.S. foreign investment.

Much of the new investment went into oil: U.S. companies channeled $235 million to Venezuela, $134 million to Colombia, $120 million to Mexico, and $50 million to Peru for oil exploration and production. Another $163 million went to manufacturing enterprises in South America. U.S. companies also invested heavily in Chilean copper

534

and nitrate, in Argentine beef, and in Cuban sugar.

This period marked the full-fledged involvement of large U.S. corporations, later called multinationals, in Latin America. Such giants as Standard Oil of New Jersey, the American Smelting and Refining Company, International Telephone and Telegraph, American Foreign Power, and Armour established or added to their vast stake in the region.

The basic goal of United States policy in Latin America did not change during the postwar period; it remained the protection of American economic interests. But, public opinion and realism dictated modifications. Americans were weary of overseas adventures and crusades. The United States remained dominant in the Caribbean, exerting decisive influence in the affairs of Mexico and Cuba and continuing to occupy the Dominican Republic, Haiti, and Nicaragua during the 1920s, but there was growing opposition to the old-style imperialism.

Foreign policy makers in the U.S. also realized that growing anti-American feeling in Latin America, primarily a response to U.S. actions in the Caribbean, posed a serious long-term danger to American economic interests. An early sign of a shift in United States policy came in 1921, when the Colombian government threatened to cancel the concessions of American companies to explore and drill for oil. The United States responded by paying Colombia $25 million to compensate for the loss of Panama. This had a dual meaning: it served to protect U.S. economic interests, and it symbolized a less aggressive policy toward Latin America. The shift in American tactics became even clearer when the United States removed its troops from Cuba in 1922, from the Dominican Republic in 1924, and from Nicaragua in 1925. Despite these actions, the United States encountered bitter criticism of its role in the hemisphere at the Pan-American conferences in Santiago in 1923 and Havana in 1928.

The most important indication that the United States had largely abandoned military intervention as a major tactic was its restraint in dealing with Mexico, the biggest trouble spot in the hemisphere during the 1920s. The Mexican con-

stitution of 1917 was a most radical document by contemporary standards. The constitution's provisions on landownership and ownership of subsoil rights seriously endangered U.S. investments. American oil companies, in particular, objected to the new laws, which sought to reclaim Mexico's rich natural resources from foreign control.

Throughout the 1920s, the United States and Mexico haggled over application of the constitution. Several times they reached temporary compromises, but the basic disagreement inflamed relations until World War II. The United States did not intervene militarily to protect the very large U.S. investments in Mexico because three circumstances discouraged such action. First, public opinion opposed further foreign adventures. Second, a military invasion would have been prohibitively costly in terms of both manpower and finances. Finally, American entrepreneurs with interests in Mexico disagreed sharply over the proper course of action. The oil companies, who were most threatened by the constitution, favored intervention. The banks and the mining companies, whose interests would have been in greater danger in the event of war between the United States and Mexico, opposed intervention. The controversy abated during the late 1920s, when the Calles regime made significant concessions with regard to American oil interests in Mexico.

President Herbert Hoover and Secretary of State Henry L. Stimson continued to shift toward moderation and stepped up U.S. efforts to win goodwill in Latin America. During the interim between his election and inauguration, Hoover toured Latin America. On taking office, he abandoned Wilson's policy of denying recognition to "unworthy" governments. The Clark memorandum, published in 1930, was a milestone in Hoover's efforts. It declared that the Roosevelt Corollary had no support in the Monroe Doctrine; consequently, the United States would no longer interfere in the internal affairs of Latin American nations under the provisions of the doctrine. But the president carefully refrained from rejecting intervention outright. In 1933 he withdrew United States troops from Nicaragua and would have removed them from Haiti as well had the Haitians not objected to the withdrawal terms.

A New Era: The Good Neighbor in Depression and War, 1933–1945

Franklin D. Roosevelt assumed the presidency in 1933 amid a severe economic depression. Rejecting "interference in the internal affairs of other nations" and proclaiming the United States to be a "good neighbor" to the rest of the world, Roosevelt built his relations with Latin America on the foundations laid by his predecessor. First, expanding Hoover's initiative, Roosevelt renounced the right to intervene in Latin American affairs. The following year, the United States reached an agreement with Cuba to abrogate the Platt Amendment, thus abandoning its protectorate over the island; the same year, it withdrew its occupation troops from Haiti. In 1937 the United States gave up its right to intervene militarily to protect transit across the Isthmus of Tehuantepec in Mexico.

The nonintervention policy was soon put to the test in Cuba. In 1933 political unrest there threatened the substantial American investment on the island. Roosevelt dispatched Sumner Welles to Havana to try to arrange an accommodation between dictator Gerardo Machado and his opponents. After several months of unsuccessful negotiations, Machado fled, and power fell into the hands of a disorganized and disunited junta. Eventually, Dr. Ramón Grau San Martín emerged as leader of the government. He quickly fell into disfavor with the United States when he suspended loan repayments to a large New York bank and seized two American-owned sugar mills. As a result, the United States refused to recognize the Grau government. With U.S. warships lingering in Havana harbor, Grau was forced to relinquish his leadership. Supported by the United States, Fulgencio Batista emerged as the strongman of Cuba. Despite the protestations of the United States to the contrary, it was evident that it had not entirely abandoned the "big stick."

Nonintervention was put to another severe test in Mexico in 1938. The long dispute between the Mexican government and the oil companies culminated in the expropriation of foreign oil holdings when the oil companies defied an order of the Mexican Supreme Court in a labor dispute. While the oil companies clamored for reprisal, Roosevelt tried to settle matters peacefully. In the face of isolationist sentiment in the United States, intervention was unthinkable. Moreover, with war in Europe on the horizon, the United States did not want to endanger an important source of oil. A settlement was eventually reached during the 1940s.

Another aspect of Roosevelt's "good neighbor" policy toward Latin America was the effort to achieve reciprocal trade agreements as a means of increasing U.S. trade with the area. Secretary of State Cordell Hull ardently supported such agreements, believing they would help the United States emerge from the Great Depression. From 1934 to 1941, Hull succeeded in signing reciprocal trade treaties with fifteen Latin American nations. Had these treaties succeeded in significantly increasing U.S. trade, which they did not, they would have adversely affected Latin America's nascent industrialization, which was critically dependent on protective tariffs for its survival. In this area, therefore, United States policy was in direct conflict with the goal of Latin American economic development.

In the 1930s, the United States grew increasingly concerned over the spread of German economic and political influence in Latin America. In response to this growing German economic and political activity, the United States pushed for closer cooperation among the nations of the Western Hemisphere by promoting a series of meetings to consider common problems. In December 1936, the participants in the Inter-American Conference for the Maintenance of Peace agreed to consult in the event of war among themselves or outside the hemisphere. Two years later, the eighth Pan-American Conference met in Lima, Peru; the conferees decided that the mechanism for consultation would be foreign ministers' meetings. In September 1939, shortly after the German invasion of Poland, the First Meeting

536 of Foreign Ministers of the American Republics approved a joint declaration of neutrality and established the Inter-American Financial and Advisory Committee to consider common problems brought on by the war. The foreign ministers proclaimed the existence of a safety zone around the hemisphere and warned belligerents not to wage war within it. In July 1940, after the fall of France, the Second Meeting of Foreign Ministers was held in Havana; the representatives agreed to administer French and Dutch colonies in the Western Hemisphere in the event they were in danger of Nazi takeover. They also proclaimed that an attack on any of the conferring nations would be construed as an attack on all.

The Third Meeting of Foreign Ministers was held shortly after the Japanese attack on Pearl Harbor in early 1942. The ministers agreed to cooperate against the Axis; most Latin American nations severed diplomatic relations with the Axis powers. Every Latin American country but Argentina contributed to the Allied war effort.

The war strengthened the economic links between the United States and Latin America. The United States served as the sole market for the region's exports and the only supplier of its requirements of arms, munitions, industrial equipment, and manufactured goods. North American investment diversified geographically, going increasingly into South America whereas it had previously focused on the Caribbean. A growing proportion of U.S. capital went into manufacturing enterprises instead of raw material extraction. By the end of the war, Argentina accounted for 16 percent of U.S. investment in Latin America, Chile 16 percent, Brazil 13 percent, and Peru 4 percent. For the first time, South America accounted for over half the total U.S. investment in Latin America.

Defending the Empire and Capitalism, 1945–1981

In the postwar era, three factors determined United States–Latin American relations: the need for the United States to protect large investments in the region, the desire of Latin American nations to industrialize and diversify their economies, and the rivalry between the United States and the Soviet Union.

American Investment and Trade

Several important trends characterized U.S. investment in and trade with Latin America after World War II. First, the amount of investment increased enormously. Furthermore, the type of investment changed from mostly extractive industries, such as mining and oil, to manufacturing. Also, this investment became concentrated in the hands of a few large corporations and banks. Last, although the amount of U.S. trade with Latin America grew substantially, the relative importance of this trade to the economies of the United States and individual Latin American nations decreased.

All these trends did not mean that the United States had changed its policies. Its policy makers continued to base their decisions on U.S. economic interests in the region, as trade and investment represented huge sums, despite declining importance. Thus, every overt or covert U.S. intervention in Latin America during this period—in Guatemala, Cuba, the Dominican Republic, and Chile, for example—took place in countries where the security of large American investments appeared to have been endangered.

Post–World War II Adjustments

Despite the high degree of wartime cooperation, sharp differences between the United States and Latin America surfaced in the immediate postwar years. These disagreements emerged initially at the Chapultepec Conference (Inter-American Conference on the Problems of War and Peace) in February 1945. Latin American leaders felt they should be rewarded for their contributions and sacrifices during the war. The United States, however, regarded European recovery as its first priority. There were also major disagreements over trade, industrialization, the overall direction of Latin American economic development, and the role of the United States in this development. The United States insisted on an open door to Latin American markets and investment opportunities but was unwilling to make any concessions that might injure its own producers. Latin Americans, however, feared that such free access to Latin American markets would destroy much of the industrial progress the region had made in the preceding two decades.

United States and Latin American interests were clearly opposed. The United States wanted to protect and maintain its markets and investment in Latin America, whereas Latin American nations sought to industrialize and diversify their economies. Whereas U.S. leaders regarded private capital investment and free trade as the best routes to development, Latin American nations favored a massive government role in industrialization and restrictions on foreign trade and investment as the only means of modernizing and regaining control over their economies.

After the war, Latin America vainly sought help from the United States to finance industrialization and access to American manufactured goods, especially capital equipment in order to further industrialization. These efforts were hindered further in the next few years as high prices for manufactured products dissipated the dollar reserves Latin American nations had accumulated during the war, while declining prices for raw materials eroded Latin America's terms of trade even further.

There was increasing evidence, moreover, that the United States had reverted to its traditional disregard for Latin American sensitivities and to intervention in the internal affairs of nations of the region. In 1946 the United States interfered in the internal political affairs of three South American nations. It meddled disastrously in the Argentine presidential campaign of that year, assuring the election of Juan Perón; it forced the González Videla government in Chile to oust the Communist members of its coalition cabinet; and it helped to undermine a revolutionary regime in Bolivia that had been accused of fascist tendencies.

The Cold War

Alarm in the United States over the vast expansion of Communist influence in Eastern and Central Europe as a result of World War II, the Communist victory in the Chinese civil war, and the gains of Communist parties in Western Europe as a result of their leading role in wartime resistance movements had the effect of pushing Latin America to the back burner. In this initial stage of the cold war, which lasted into the 1950s, the United States focused its attention on checking the further spread of communism in Western Europe by aiding the revival of the shattered capitalist economy of that region through the Marshall Plan. From 1950 to 1953, the United States fought in the Korean war, designed to stem the invasion of the Communist North Koreans.

During this first stage of the cold war, U.S. leaders tended to view the world as two camps, one committed to the United States and its free enterprise system, the other loyal to communism. Since it regarded the world in such black and white terms, the United States viewed with implacable hostility governments and movements that disagreed with its policy or attempted to institute structural social and economic reforms. On two occasions, in Guatemala and Iran, the United States helped topple such governments through the subversive activities of the CIA.

A second stage of the cold war began in the mid-1950s, when a "third world" emerged, made up of the many newly independent states of Africa and Asia, which proclaimed themselves unaligned in the struggle between the blocs led by the Soviet Union and the United States. The two superpowers, faced with the unacceptable consequences of nuclear war, fought out the cold war in the Third World. In this second stage, the United States became intensely concerned with Latin America only after the 1959 Cuban Revolution led to the establishment of the first socialist state in the Americas. U.S. preoccupation with the threat of more Cubas in the hemisphere produced the Alliance for Progress as an alternative to the Cuban model.

The third stage of the cold war followed the disastrous U.S. experience in Vietnam and lasted

538   until Ronald Reagan took office as president of the United States in 1981. Losing the Vietnam war and its tragic cost brought home to the U.S. government and its people the limitations of U.S. power and the dangers involved in trying to prevent social revolutions. Nonetheless, the United States remained determined to maintain its hegemony in the Western Hemisphere and in order to achieve its goals adapted its methods to suit new conditions.

A fourth stage of the cold war brought to the late 1980s the renewal of provocative, anticommunist rhetoric, the simplistic 1950s division of the world into "them" and "us," the return to using force as a policy tool, and a revival of illegal, covert activities. The rise of perestroika under Mikhail Gorbachev in the Soviet Union, the collapse of the Stalinist-type communist regimes in eastern and central Europe, and the resulting demise of the cold war created a problem for the military-industrial complex that had flourished in the cold war's protective shadow and for United States Latin American policy by depriving it of its traditional enemy, "international communism." In the 1990s, the drug trafficker has replaced that traditional enemy as a convenient pretext for intervention in Latin America.

The Latin American Policies of Truman and Eisenhower

The Truman administration (1945–1953) focused its attention on fighting communism in Europe and the Far East. But, as we have seen, it meddled with mixed success in the political affairs of Chile, Bolivia, and Argentina in 1946. Under Truman, the movement for hemispheric cooperation continued, at least outwardly. The Rio Treaty of 1947 brought Central and South America into a military alliance with the United States. The ninth International Conference of American States, held in Bogotá the following year, resulted in the formation of the Organization of American States (OAS). The OAS was to provide collective security, with an attack against one member being viewed as an attack on all. OAS also was to be a mediator in disputes between members. Truman

and his chief advisers were primarily concerned with maintaining the status quo in the region.

The Eisenhower presidency (1953–1961) marked a revival of strong corporate influence in U.S. foreign policy. Eisenhower took office in the middle of the Korean war and at the height of the McCarthy "Red Scare." His administration, particularly the fanatical anticommunist Secretary of State John Foster Dulles, divided the world into two categories: nations that supported the United States and those that did not. Any foreign government that restricted the activities of U.S. corporations under its jurisdiction was adjudged to be communist and a threat to the security of the United States. During his two terms, Eisenhower faced four challenges of this kind in Latin America: Bolivia, British Guiana, Guatemala, and Cuba. In each case, his administration reacted according to the scale of the American economic interests involved and the prevailing domestic and international conditions.

In Bolivia in 1952, a successful revolution headed by Victor Paz Estenssoro and the National Revolutionary Movement (MNR) ushered in sweeping economic and political reforms. In its first year, the new government nationalized the nation's tin mines, wiped out the latifundio system, replaced the old army with workers' and peasants' militias, and greatly increased the number of eligible voters. The MNR, however, encountered serious economic difficulties that arose from the obsolescence of the tin industry, the disruption to agricultural production caused by the land reform, and massive inflation. The outgoing Truman administration, anxious over the radicalism of the regime, withheld recognition and aid from Bolivia. The middle-class leadership of the MNR eventually managed to convince the Eisenhower administration that it was not communist; as a result, Bolivia received millions of dollars in grants and loans and substantial technical assistance over the next decade. U.S. aid had a significant moderating influence on the MNR reform program. Indeed, U.S. assistance decisively altered the whole course of Bolivian development; the United States re-established, equipped, and trained the Bolivian army, which overthrew Paz Estenssoro in 1964, ushering in a period of conservative rule that continued almost uninterruptedly until 1981.

The United States employed different tactics to achieve the same general results under the differing conditions of another Latin American country. In 1953 Marxist Cheddi Jagan was elected on a program of structural reform to head the government of the British colony of Guiana. Guiana, however, was an important source of bauxite and other metals; several large U.S. companies, including Reynolds Metals and Kennecott Copper, had substantial holdings in the colony. Alarmed at the prospect of nationalization of these holdings by a Marxist regime, the United States urged the British to nullify the election; the British government duly sent troops to Guiana and deposed the new government.

The Eisenhower administration employed yet other tactics in Guatemala in 1954; conspiring to overthrow a democratically elected government whose reforms threatened the interests of a large and influential American corporation. In 1944 a revolution toppled the oppressive regime of Jorge Ubico, who had ruled Guatemala since 1931. The victorious middle-class revolutionaries favored a capitalist course of development and were friendly to the United States. However, the reform programs of Presidents Juan José Arévalo (1945–1951) and Jacobo Arbenz (1951–1954) provoked the hostility of the United Fruit Company (UFCO) and Dulles. UFCO had operated in Guatemala since the 1890s, when it acquired a virtual monopoly on banana production and distribution. It was Guatemala's largest employer, with ten thousand workers, and its largest landowner. The company also controlled the nation's main transportation artery, the International Railways of Central America (IRCA), and major port facilities on the Gulf of Mexico.

The Guatemalan government clashed with UFCO over labor and land reform. Arévalo enacted a new labor code in 1947. The company, charging that it was being discriminated against, protested sharply. The ensuing labor agitation severely hampered banana production for several years. In 1952 the Guatemalan Congress en-

acted a land reform program, expropriating large tracts of uncultivated land for distribution among landless peasants. Again, UFCO charged the government with discrimination.

Unfortunately for the Guatemalan government, UFCO enjoyed great influence with the United States government. It was a client of Dulles's law firm. Also, the company's headquarters were in Boston, which made it a constituent of three of the most powerful men in the United States Congress: Senator Henry Cabot Lodge, Speaker of the House Joseph Martin, and Democratic party leader John McCormack. What was more, the family of the assistant secretary of state in charge of Guatemalan relations, John Moors Lodge, was a major stockholder in United Fruit.

Guatemala's independent foreign policy sharpened its differences with the United States. The Guatemalan labor movement, closely linked to the Arévalo and Arbenz administrations, refused to cooperate with the American Federation of Labor's anticommunist international labor organization. Guatemala was critical of the United States at both the Rio (1947) and Bogotá (1948) conferences; the United States responded by cutting off arms supplies to Guatemala in 1948. In both the United Nations and the Organization of American States, Arbenz resisted American efforts to make it mandatory for members to send troops to Korea.

Seizing on allegations of communist participation in the Arbenz government to justify its actions, the United States trained and outfitted a rebel group under the command of Carlos Castillo Armas. Castillo Armas invaded Guatemala through UFCO property and overthrew Arbenz in June 1954. His repressive regime, which lasted until his assassination in 1957, erased all of the postwar reforms and restored UFCO's privileges.

The Cuban Revolution and United States–Latin American Relations

Eisenhower's successful interventions in Bolivia, British Guiana, and Guatemala produced bitter criticism of the United States in Latin America and contributed to the hostile and violent

544   Kirkpatrick, an expert on Latin America, Reagan sought to repair relations with both military regimes in the southern cone, Argentina and Chile. Argentina became an important ally in Central America, providing military advisers to the government of El Salvador.

Misinterpreting the Reagan administration's friendly overtures as a blank check, the shaky military junta in Argentina (see Chapter 13) sought to divert attention from its domestic woes by settling an old dispute with Britain over possession of the Malvinas. A last-minute telephone call from President Reagan to President Galtieri failed to deter the Argentines, who believed the United States would remain neutral in the conflict. On April 2, 1982, the Argentines invaded the islands. Secretary of State Alexander Haig vainly tried to mediate as the British fleet made its way 8,000 miles south to retake the islands. When he failed to bring an end to the war, the United States, after displaying some indecision, shifted to full support of the British. In a short, bloody war the British recaptured the Falklands. The Malvinas war badly undermined Latin American trust in the United States as a reliable ally.

Grenada

On October 25, 1983, the United States invaded the tiny island nation of Grenada in the southern Caribbean in order to oust its allegedly Communist, pro-Cuban government. The Reagan administration proclaimed the invasion its greatest triumph in Latin American policy. It took place hard on the heels of disastrous foreign-policy blunders in the Malvinas war and amid tragic events in Lebanon, where more than 200 U.S. Marines were killed in a terrorist attack.

In March 1979 the New Jewel Movement, led by Maurice Bishop, had overthrown the British and U.S.-backed government of Eric Gairy, who had dominated Grenadan politics since the early 1950s. After Grenada obtained its independence in 1974, Gairy had grown increasingly dictatorial and eccentric. Bishop proclaimed a revolution and set about establishing close ties with Cuba.

Bishop's program included a massive literacy campaign, the institution of free medical care, free secondary education, and an extensive rehabilitation of housing. He stressed agricultural independence, reducing Grenadan food imports. Bishop began to expand tourism, mainly by building a modern airport. But in 1983, he was murdered during a coup led by Bernard Coard's radical faction in Bishop's own party.

The United States invaded Grenada on the pretext of rescuing U.S. medical students on the island and at the invitation of the Association of East Caribbean states whose members claimed to be threatened by their neighbor. The military operation was later revealed to have been marred by poor planning and faulty intelligence. Elections were held in Grenada in December 1984 that brought to power a middle-road coalition headed by Herbert Blaize. United States aid was $57 million until 1985 but declined considerably thereafter. Hoped-for private investment, widely ballyhooed after the invasion, never materialized. The economy has badly deteriorated and unemployment is rampant.

The invasion of Grenada showed clearly that the United States was as willing as ever to use force to protect its perceived interests in the Caribbean. The action also conveyed the message—as did U.S. policies in Central America—that the United States opposed far-reaching economic and social reform in its "backyard." Moreover, Grenada, like so many other "crises" in the region, was not seen as a nation struggling to overcome impoverishment, but as part of a worldwide communist threat or at the very least as "another Cuba."

Haiti

The United States has played a decisive role in the history of Haiti, the poorest country in Latin America and one of the poorest in the world. As we noted earlier, Haiti's black revolutionary leaders established the first liberated territory in Latin America. Those leaders and their immediate successors sought to restore the plantation system with a system of forced labor not unlike slavery; they hoped to use the export of sugar and coffee—the country's main crop since the early nineteenth century—as a means of promoting the country's development. But this plan was frustrated by the resistance of the former slaves, who hated plantation labor and preferred to settle as small peasants on land acquired from the state or abandoned by the large landowners. There also arose a class of large landowners, drawn from the military and political elite, who parceled out their estates to peasants who paid rent with a part of the crop. The country's elites, largely mulatto, also developed a fiscal system that siphoned off the peasants' surplus through export duties on coffee and import duties on food and other necessities; the export-import merchant class, dominated by foreign nationals, and the large landowners passed on these large costs to the peasant producers in a variety of ways.

Independent Haiti, born into a world where slavery was still taken for granted, was long regarded as a pariah state by the great powers. The United States did not even recognize Haiti until 1862, when the Civil War had ended Southern influence in Washington. The United States first seriously turned its attention to Haiti in 1915, when President Wilson, claiming that Germany was planning to establish a base on Haiti, sent the marines to occupy the country. The long U.S. occupation, 1915–1934, marked by brutal suppression of rural guerrillas, left the country, writes Michel Rolph Trouillot, "with two poisoned gifts: a weaker civil society and a solidified state apparatus." The occupiers made no serious effort to change the country's economic structure. Haiti's dependence on coffee and export duties actually increased during this period, but some improvement of the country's material infrastructure, especially through road construction, was achieved by the forced labor of peasants, sometimes bound in ropes. But the occupation strengthened the Haitian state by "pacifying" the countryside, modernizing the rural police, and creating a new centralized U.S.-trained army that, unlike the old one, "was created specifically to fight Haitians" and that "became the final arbiter of Haitian politics."

That new American-trained army imposed the rule of the sinister François "Papa Doc" Duvalier on Haiti through fradulent elections in 1957. Duvalier in turn used the army to centralize power in his own hands to an unprecedented degree. He could not tolerate the existence of any independent institution; "at one point," Trouillot notes, "he even outlawed the Boy Scouts." Distrusting his own army, he organized two parallel paramilitary organizations, a much-feared militia and the overlapping secret police, the even more dreaded Tontons Macoutes. The United States may not have approved of his methods, but it supported him, and when he died in 1971 U.S. Ambassador Clinton Knox personally supervised the transition to the rule of the dictator's son, eighteen-year-old Jean-Claude Duvalier.

The predatory, repressive rule of the Duvaliers aggravated all of Haiti's economic and social problems. The ruin of Haitian agriculture as a result of long misuse of the land and the exactions of the regime caused many thousands of impoverished peasants to flock into the urban centers, especially the shantytowns of Port-au-Prince and its environs. Today Port-au-Prince and its suburbs hold between 1.2 and 1.8 million people. The great majority of these people live in unspeakable conditions, in "miles and miles of broken-down shacks made of rough concrete, mud, straw, cardboard, and scrap sheet metal. . . . Open sewers flow down the dirt streets, which are deeply rutted by erosion. When it rains, the sewage overflows into people's homes. There are no bathrooms, no running water." Workers' families usually eat only one meal a day, consisting of cornmeal with onions or boiled plantains with beans.

Acting on U.S. advice, Jean-Claude Duvalier tried to launch an economic revolution by using this vast underclass to establish export-assembly industries, subcontracted to U.S. firms. But this program did not diminish the immense inequalities of Haitian society or the growing anger of the masses. In 1986, an explosion of urban rioting forced Jean-Claude to depart from Haiti; he was whisked away to a luxurious exile in a jet provided by the Reagan administration. The U.S.

546

Agency for International Development (U.S. AID), meanwhile, continued to promote Haiti as a low-wage haven for U.S. firms, expending $100 million in the effort. A delegation of U.S. trade union leaders, visiting a "model" apparel factory in Haiti's export-assembly sector in 1991, found that the highest-paid workers received the equivalent of $1.47 a day. After paying for transportation and a meager breakfast and lunch they had 71 cents to take home.

The departure of Jean-Paul Duvalier opened a period of stormy political and social struggle, with eleven governments and three coups since 1986. It culminated in the presidential election of December 1990, which pitted the populist priest Jean-Bertrand Aristide, a follower of liberation theology, against the Duvalierist Roger Lafontant, former head of the Tontons Macoutes, supported by the landed oligarchy, and the U.S.-backed Marc Bazin, linked to export-assembly industries and agribusinesses. Aristide represented above all a powerful popular movement, uniting many grassroots worker, peasant, and student organizations. Aristide's campaign stressed the need for a massive literacy campaign, land reform, defense of national industries, and an end to Duvalierist violence and corruption. His program included a massive literacy campaign, price controls on basic foodstuffs, and raising the minimum hourly wage to fifty cents. Despite the $36 million spent on his campaign by Bazin, his chief rival, Aristide won the election with 67 percent of the vote. But he held power for only eight months; in September 1991 a military coup headed by Lieutenant General Raoul Cédras forced him into exile. The coup unleashed a reign of terror in Haiti, claiming thousands of lives and causing a flood of refugees.

The Bush administration's response to the coup was marked by an ambiguity reflecting the contradictions of U.S. foreign policy. The United States claimed to support constitutionally elected civilian regimes like Aristide's, but Aristide's anti-imperialism and opposition to neoliberalism contradicted basic U.S. foreign policy objectives. President Bush denounced the coup and said he wanted Aristide's return to power. But this pro-Aristide stance was contradicted by a policy of limiting sanctions against the coup leaders to a "porous" embargo easily breached by exporters and importers, permitting open attacks against Aristide by a State Department–driven media campaign and CIA leaks casting doubt on his mental stability, and putting immense pressure on him to moderate his positions and strike a deal with the coup leaders. "Underestimating the chasm between the U.S. government's official rhetoric and its true intent," writes Kim Ives, "Aristide took his first step down the slippery slope of negotiations."

President Clinton continued Bush's Haitian policy, virtually unchanged, when he took office in January 1993. During his election campaign Clinton had vigorously denounced Bush's "immoral and illegal policy" of intercepting on the high seas and repatriating Haitian refugees fleeing the military junta's reign of terror. On the eve of his inauguration, however, he announced a strengthened naval blockade of the sailboats bringing refugees from Haiti. The effort to subvert Aristide, to force him into direct negotiations with the coup leaders and impose conditions on his return that would leave him powerless to carry out his program, also continued under Clinton. This was the essence of the deal known as the Governors Island Accord, signed in July 1993, which called for the military rulers to resign, with the promise of an amnesty, and for Aristide to return to power under the control of UN monitors and Somali-style "peacekeeping" forces, an arrangement vehemently opposed by Haitian popular organizations. In this process the UN special envoy Dante Caputo and UN Secretary General Boutros Boutros-Ghali acted as "enforcers" of U.S. and U.N. proposals. In the event, the whole accord "derailed" in October 1993 when a U.S. troop carrier, carrying the first major deployment of U.S. and Canadian troops to Haiti, turned back when about 100 armed anti-Aristide thugs demonstrated at the port and threatened foreign diplomats. The quick pull-back suggested Penatagon and CIA reluctance to be involved in restoring Aristide to power on any terms. Aside from validating the Haitian military ruler Cédras as a negotiating partner, forcing Aristide to bargain with him, and thus helping to entrench the coup leaders in power, the Governors Island Accord had no substantive results.

Under growing pressure from the Congressional Black Caucus and from Aristide himself, who branded his policy "racist," in May 1994 Clinton appeared to be changing his refugee policy and stiffening his resolve to restore democracy in Haiti. But the changes in refugee policy turned out to be largely cosmetic, with the percentage of asylum claims by Haitian refugees accepted remaining about the same. This was also the fate of Clinton's proposal to tighten the embargo against the military regime by securing Dominican President Joaquín Balaguer's cooperation in closing the border with Haiti in return for U.S. promises to overlook massive fraud in his recent re-election. In the absence of any economic penalties for embargo violations by the Dominican Republic, the border was not effectively sealed, and the Haitian military, which controlled most of the black market, continued to profit vastly from smuggling.

As part of Clinton's new "tough" policy toward the military junta, he now talked openly of a military intervention if the embargo failed—a prospect opposed by most Haitians, who, the *New York Times* noted, "remember with anger and shame the U.S. occupation of Haiti, 1915–1934." President Aristide, after some vacillation, gave his support to an armed intervention. *The Nation,* however, warned that "Clinton & Co. have made it distressingly clear that Haitian independence is not on their minds, and that if exiled President Jean-Bertrand Aristide is returned at the head of an American expeditionary force, the result will be continued clienthood, not freedom."

In the event, after a barrage of publicity about an impending invasion to oust Haiti's military rulers if they did not leave peacefully, a carefully staged "solution" of the Haitian problem came with startling suddenness. On the evening of September 18, 1994 a U.S. delegation led by ex-President Jimmy Carter held an amicable meeting with the men whom President Clinton had shortly before described as "thugs and murderers" and signed an accord with them. That accord provided that "certain military officers" would agree to "an early and honorable retirement" once Parliament had voted into law an amnesty, or by October 15, 1994, whichever was earlier. The accord also provided for the eventual return of President Aristide to serve out his term, which ends in 1996, and to preside over the election of a new president in December 1995. The accord envisioned that a U.S. occupation force of some 15,000 troops would remain for an indefinite period to retrain the Haitian army and police and to assist them in maintaining law and order. Despite his initial misgivings, on September 21 Aristide profusely thanked Clinton, Carter, and the Pentagon for their good services.

Aristide's return to Haiti in October 1994 was greeted with joyful demonstrations by his adoring followers. It soon became clear, however, that he was not his own man; on issue after issue his American military and political advisers forced him to back down. Aristide wanted to fire the entire army high command and supervise the formation of a new army and police within his government, but the U.S. military vetoed his plan. The new "professionalized" army and police would be "retrained" by current and former agents of the FBI, the Drug Enforcement Administration, Secret Service, and U.S. police departments, and "candidates" for "professionalization" would be drawn largely from the old armed forces, many of whose officers and specialists had been trained at the notorious School of the Americas at Ft. Benning, Georgia.

Aristide's candidate for prime minister, who had served as foreign minister in his previous government, was turned down by the Haitian business sector and U.S. officials, and the president was forced to accept businessman Smarck Michel to head the new 20-member cabinet. Virtually none of its members represented the grassroots movement that had brought Aristide to power, but the cabinet was full of people who supported and benefited from the coup d'état, including a new Public Works Minister who has been accused of corruption and embezzlement in the past and a new Minister of Defense who had served under former dictator Jean Claude Duvalier. U.S. advisors were working in key offices and ministries to advise Haiti in its return to

The role of former President Jimmy Carter, shown here with the Haitian President Jean-Bertrand Aristide, in negotiating the accord with the military junta that restored Aristide to office in October 1994, displeased many Haitians who believed the accord was too favorable to the military and seriously abrogated Aristide's power.

democracy. Critics complained that in addition to pro-coup politicians and U.S. advisors, Aristide's chief allies appeared to be the Haitian business sector (whom he once described as "patriots of the pocketbook") and U.S. Ambassador William Swing, who almost always accompanied him when he left the palace.

Under U.S. pressure, Aristide scrapped his nationalist program for reviving Haiti's state industries and accepted a program of neoliberal "structural readjustment" of the economy, by which those industries would be sold to private capitalists, both Haitian and U.S. As summarized by Allan Nairn, the plan included, among other features, commitments from Haiti "to eliminate the jobs of half of its civil servants, massively privatize public services, 'drastically' slash tariffs and import restrictions, eschew price and foreign exchange controls, grant 'emergency' aid to the export sector, enforce an 'open foreign investment policy' . . . 'limit the scope of state activity' and regulation . . . and diminish the power of Aristide's executive branch in favor of the more conservative Parliament." In return Haiti would receive $700 million in financial aid, but $80 million of this would immediately go to pay the debt accrued to foreign bankers in the three years since the coup.

Four days after Aristide resumed the presidency, Haitians had a foretaste of the new policy when the subsidy on fuel was removed, doubling its price overnight. Aristide's Commerce Minister, Louis Dejoie, explained that the decision was not his or Aristide's: "Someone just gave me a piece of paper and said, 'This is the price.' Everything was agreed on in Paris and Madrid. I had nothing to do with it."

Ordinary Haitians are attempting to understand what has happened to their idol. The Aristide they elected came to power as the representative of a massive grassroots movement, calling itself the *lavalas* (flood), that proposed to attack the country's fundamental social problems and end the traditional monopoly of power by a repressive military allied with a corrupt merchant bourgeoisie and U.S. economic interests. The new Aristide appeared to have cut a deal with the World Bank and the IMF that sacrificed the popular welfare in exchange for $700 million in aid. Chevannes Jean-Baptiste, leader of Haiti's largest peasant organization, had already warned against premature celebration of Aristide's return in the wake of the U.S. invasion: "Don't celebrate and think that the U.S. army is here to liberate us. Only Haitians can free Haiti!"

Reagan, Bush, and Central America

Ronald Reagan's campaigns against the leftist Sandinista regime in Nicaragua and the leftist Farabundo Martí Front for National Liberation (FMLN) guerrillas in El Salvador took on all the characteristics of a holy crusade against communist forces in Central America. From the beginning of his first term, President Reagan sought to overthrow the Sandinistas, employing tactics that included economic sanctions, a campaign of public misinformation, support of rightist counterrevolutionary armies (the contras), and covert terrorist operations aided by the CIA.

One of Reagan's first official acts in 1981 was to cut off the last $15 million in aid of the $75 million Congress had appropriated for Nicaragua at President Carter's request. More severe economic sanctions followed. By the end of 1985, the United States, by threatening to end its financial support, had effectively foreclosed any possibility of the Sandinistas obtaining loans from any of the major international lending agencies, such as the World Bank or the Inter-American Development Bank. The U.S. government closed Nicaragua's consulates and even forbade the Nicaraguan airline from landing in the United States. The misinformation campaign included unproven allegations against the Sandinistas of running arms to El Salvador, smuggling illegal drugs, and training terrorists.

By far the most damaging U.S. strategy against the Sandinistas was support of the armed opposition to the Nicaraguan government. Predominantly led by ex-Somocista National Guardsmen, the contras were the 1979 creation of the CIA, which recruited ex-guardsman Enrique Bermúdez as their leader. In Reagan's first year in office, he secretly funneled $40 million to support these counterrevolutionaries. The CIA forged the Nicaraguan Democratic Force in late 1981, unifying, temporarily, the contra factions.

Frustrated with Reagan's policy, the United States Congress passed the so-called Boland Amendment, which forbade the use of funds to overthrow the Sandinistas; this legislation was in effect from December 1982 until December 1983. Congress subsequently voted the contras $24 million for 1984. In early 1984 the CIA mined Nicaraguan harbors and staged several helicopter attacks inside Nicaragua. Later that year a CIA manual became public that advised the contras to employ terrorist tactics, including assassinations. The ensuing furor led the Congress to cut off aid to the contras in October. During the next several months White House aides found private sources for supporting them. Eventually, the Congress gave in to White House pressure and approved $27 million in "humanitarian" aid. In June 1986 Congress appropriated $100 million for the contras.

The Sandinistas drove the contras out of Nicaragua in 1985, reducing their activity to hit-and-run raids across the border from Honduras, which the United States transformed into an enormous military base. By 1987 the United States had invested $200 million in support of the contras and had little to show for it. The counterrevolutionaries were corrupt and quarrelsome, their civilian and military leaders hopelessly divided, and they had made no military headway in overthrowing the Nicaraguan government.

Evidently fearing that the Sandinistas would win a free and fair election in Nicaragua, the Reagan and Bush administrations placed obstacles in the way of the peace process initiated by the Guatemala City accords of August 1987 and continued to provide "humanitarian" aid to the contras in Honduras up to February 25, 1990, the date of the elections. The United States gave millions of dollars in aid to the anti-Sandinista coalition (UNO). Exhausted by almost ten years of U.S.-supported contra war and the U.S. economic blockade, Nicaraguans by a large majority voted in the UNO candidate for president, Violeta Chamorro, and a UNO-dominated congress. But the UNO suffered from serious divisions, and the Sandinistas remained the strongest, best-organized political force in the country.

In the process of taking over the counterinsurgency war in El Salvador, the United States took over the nation's economy and politics as well. The United States consistently interfered in Salvadoran politics, successfully keeping the far right, led by Roberto D'Aubuisson, from taking power in 1989 and shoring up the tottering centrist government of President José Napoleon Duarte, from 1984.

The United States poured some $4.5 billion from 1979 to 1990 into a futile effort to defeat the FMLN guerrillas. This included massive military assistance in the form of equipment and training. Between 50 and 100 U.S. advisers planned the counterinsurgency campaign, sometimes accompanying Salvadoran government troops in antiguerrilla forays. For a time, during 1984 and 1985, the Salvadoran army kept the guerrillas at bay because of its advantages in equipment. By early 1987, however, the FMLN was again striking at government forces and installations in almost every part of the country at will. Under domestic and U.S. pressure, both Duarte and his successor, Alfredo Cristiani, initiated peace talks with the guerrillas but appeared to believe their purpose was to negotiate an FMLN surrender. The formidable November 1989 offensive by the FMLN shattered that delusion and forced the government back to the bargaining table without preconditions. By the spring of 1991, despite continuing efforts by hard-line military to obstruct the peace talks, some progress toward agreement had been made and both President Cristiani and the FMLN leadership declared the peace process was "irreversible." Finally, in January 1992, the two sides signed peace accords providing for the reform of the armed forces and security services, the dismantling of FMLN military structures, and the holding of elections in which leftist parties, for the first time in El Salvador's history, could take part.

The Invasion of Panama

On his election as president in 1988, George Bush vigorously continued Reagan's Latin American policy of maintaining and reinforcing U.S. dominance over the region. The new noninterventionist course pursued by the Soviet Union, which withdrew its troops from Afghanistan and made no effort to prevent the collapse of Stalinist-type regimes in eastern and central Europe, was interpreted by Washington to mean that its freedom of action was no longer hampered by the possibility of a Soviet response. Most Latin American countries, mired in the greatest depression in the continent's history and heavily indebted to U.S. banks, were unlikely to make more than token protests against U.S. interventionist actions. If the end of the cold war deprived American imperialism of its stock in trade, the bogeyman of "international communism," a new villain, the Latin American *narcotraficante,* the drug trafficker, provided a convenient pretext for an armed intervention that could also distract attention from the failure of the United States to cope with its drug problem at home.

Bush justified the December 1989 invasion of Panama by the need to protect U.S. citizens (a U.S. marine had been killed in a shooting incident), defend democracy, seize dictator Manuel Antonio Noriega on drug charges, and protect the canal. These arguments convinced few foreign governments; the great majority denounced or deplored the invasion as a violation of the UN charter, the Organization of American States treaty, and the Panama Canal Treaty. But they were accepted without questioning by the U.S. press, which "did little more than parrot the Bush administration's transparent legal justifications for the invasion." The press ignored the fact that until he began to display an inconvenient nationalist independence and stopped being "our man in Panama," Noriega was a prized ally of the United States, receiving, by conservative estimates, more than $1.2 million in payoffs from the CIA just during the last ten years of his thirty-year connection with the agency. As regards his drug connections, as recently as February 1987 Noriega received a letter from the U.S. Drug Enforcement Administration (DEA), expressing its gratitude for his traditional position of support for the DEA and the cooperation of his army. The notion that Bush, the former CIA director, did not know of Noriega's drug links strains one's credulity.

The press overlooked, too, long-standing Republican objections to the Carter-Torrijos canal treaties, which provided that in the year 2000 the canal will become Panamanian territory and the U.S. military bases will be dismantled. A document titled "Santa Fe II: A Strategy for Latin America in the Nineties," issued during the 1988 campaign and reflecting the views of the Republican right, in effect provided a blueprint for the invasion, stressing the need for the replacement of Noriega by a "democratic regime" with which the United States would hold talks concerning "the United States' retention of limited facilities in Panama . . . for proper force projection throughout the Western Hemisphere." These and other recommendations in the Santa Fe document closely conform to the Bush administration's Panama policies.

The administration, echoed by the media and the overwhelming majority of the public, which knew only what it read in the papers or saw on television, proclaimed "Operation Just Cause" a huge success. Panamanian Defense Forces resistance was soon broken by intense bombardment;

Noriega escaped death (the U.S. government had placed a bounty of $1 million on his head) but eventually surrendered and was taken off in triumph to be displayed on U.S. television and then imprisoned to await trial on drug charges. Twenty-four American soldiers were killed; estimates of the Panamanian death toll ranged from Washington's figure of 516 to the figure given by an Independent Commission of Inquiry of between 3,000 and 4,000, the great majority being civilians. The areas hardest hit by the invasion were the poorest neighborhoods of Panama City, inhabited primarily by black and mixed-blood people. Thousands were made homeless and resettled in refugee camps that often lacked medical care, sanitary facilities, and food. In the wake of the invasion the Panamanian Defense Forces were disbanded and replaced by a *Fuerza Pública* (police force), auxiliary to and under the control of the U.S. military command. Hundreds of members of the former ruling Revolutionary Democratic party, of the PDF, and of the volunteer Dignity Battalions organized by Noriega were arrested, and thousands of state employees were dismissed. It was estimated that the invasion had cost $2 billion in damages and reduced the country's economic life, already moribund as a result of U.S. economic sanctions, to paralysis.

In the midst of the invasion, a new president and two vice presidents were sworn in, fittingly enough at a military base of the U.S. Southern Command. The new president, Guillermo Endara, had been leading in the presidential elections of May 1989 (the United States had contributed at least $10 million to his race) when Noriega annulled the election. Endara and his vice presidents represented the traditional oligarchy of very wealthy white families (90 percent of Panama's 2,200,000 population is black, mulatto, or mestizo) who lost their political but not their economic power as a result of the reformist, nationalist revolution of 1968, led by Omar Torrijos. This handful of families, linked by intermarriage and corporate boards, control some 150 of Panama's principal businesses.

The economic and political state of Panama has improved little since the December 1989 invasion. Massive layoffs of government employees by the Endara regime (the government bureaucracy had more than doubled under Noriega) aggravated the country's economic and social problems. Pleas that the United States compensate victims of the invasion for loss of property and family were rejected by the Bush administration. Meanwhile, the fragile coalition supporting Endara's government disintegrated as a result of growing tensions and rivalries between the parties. In February 1990 the *New York Times* attributed the regime's growing unpopularity to resentment "among the poor and lower middle class who made up two-thirds of the population" against "the lawyers and bankers who hold the top posts in the government as descendants of the oligarchy overthrown in 1968 by Mr. Torrijos, then a colonel in the National Guard." Reflecting widespread cynicism, the Panamanian law professor Miguel Antonio Bernal described the post-invasion situation thusly: "The Americans took Ali Baba and left the forty thieves—and they keep working with the forty thieves." Meanwhile, according to law enforcement sources, more drug money now passes through Panama than ever.

This widespread disenchantment with the fruits of the U.S. invasion enabled the *Partido Revolucionario Democrático* (PRD), the party of Torrijos and Noriega, to revive and again become a major political force within a few short years. In May 1994, the party's new leader and presidential candidate, Ernesto Pérez Balladares, won the first national elections since the U.S. invasion of December 1989, defeating the candidates of Endara's *Partido Arnulfista* and several minor parties. A founding member of the PRD who had served in Torrijos's military government and left it after his death, Pérez Balladares repudiated the Noriega heritage of violence and corruption and ran a populist campaign focusing on the social and economic gains achieved by Panama's workers and peasants under the Torrijos regime and its success in negotiating the return of the Panama Canal. Despite the popular perception of the PRD as a party of the working class and of the traditional parties as linked to the elite, Pérez Balladares and his party associates are in no sense leftists. Pérez Balladares himself is a former Citibank executive, a member of the Panamanian ruling class, and a member of the Union Club, the most exclusive club in Panama. He will likely pay more attention to the country's social problems and make some concessions to his popular following, but not deviate seriously from Endara's neoliberal course.

Because the PRD failed to win a majority in Panama's Legislative Assembly, Pérez Balladares would have to form a political alliance with other parties to implement his populist program. Important issues with which the new government would have to deal when it took office on September 1 included the large continuing unemployment, soaring crime rates and a severe shortage of low-income housing, and the return of the canal and eleven U.S. military bases to Panama, scheduled to be turned over to the country by December 31, 1999, in accord with the Carter-Torrijos treaties.

Latin America and the Gulf War

Latin America felt the impact of the crisis that began with the Iraqi invasion of Kuwait in August 1990 and erupted into the short but destructive Gulf War in February 1991. For most countries of the region, heavily dependent on oil imports, the economic effects of the dramatic rise in oil prices were profoundly negative. Brazil, the largest oil importer, was particularly hard hit, for it had a barter arrangement with Iraq whereby it paid for oil with manufactured goods, and U.N. sanctions against Iraq forced Brazil to use its limited hard currency to buy oil from other sources at world market prices. The region's oil exporters—Venezuela, Mexico, Ecuador, Colombia, and Trinidad and Tobago—profited by increasing their oil exports to compensate for the loss of Iraqi and Kuwaiti supplies and by the sharp rise in crude oil prices. But even they stood to lose in the long run—the unexpectedly quick ending of the war left them with large oil surpluses, forcing prices down to much lower levels.

Although most Latin Americans condemned Iraq's invasion of Kuwait, polls showed that they opposed the war option by equal or even greater majorities. In Argentina, whose government was the only one to give military aid to the coalition led by the United States, 91 percent of those questioned opposed Argentina's participation in the war and demanded the return of the two warships sent to join the multinational force. In general, editorial opinion was strongly critical of President Bush's haste to abandon reliance on sanctions against Iraq in favor of war, his rejection of various peace proposals, and the massive destruction of life and material resources caused by the war. There was widespread skepticism, too, regarding Bush's professions of concern for self-determination by critics who recalled the U.S. invasions of Panama and Grenada and the covert war against Nicaragua. Many regarded Bush's call for a "new world order" as a thin disguise for the vision of a unipolar world dominated by the United States, the only superpower.

Bill Clinton's Latin American Policy: More of the Same?

Liberal critics of the Reagan-Bush Latin American policies who anticipated that Clinton's victory in the 1992 elections would bring significant changes in our relations with the region have clearly been proven wrong. The changes have been so minimal that one may properly speak of a single Bush-Clinton Latin American policy. The stand of the Clinton administration on a series of issues—economic policy toward Latin America, Cuba, Haiti, human rights, and the drug problem—reflected this essential continuity in foreign policy.

The greatest triumph of the Reagan-Bush Latin American policy was to impose upon the area, using debt as a powerful weapon of coercion with the IMF and World Bank as "enforcers," a neoliberal economic system based on free trade and privatization. That system required the Latin American countries to nullify past advances toward economic independence, to sell at bargain sale prices or exchange for depreciated debt valuable national enterprises, and to enact aus-

terity programs that helped increase the number of people living in poverty by 39 percent in the course of the 1980s. The imposition of this system prepared the way for the logical next step, the incorporation of the area into a U.S.-dominated Western Hemisphere common market that would aid the United States in its growing competition with Japan and the European Community. The continuity of the Reagan-Bush-Clinton policies in this area is illustrated by the North American Free Trade Agreement with Mexico, negotiated by Bush and pushed through Congress by Clinton over the virtually unanimous opposition of the labor movement that had ensured his election. Similar free trade agreements are projected with other Latin American countries, beginning with Chile.

Given the absence of strong trade union movements in many Latin American countries, including some, like Mexico, where democracy is little more than a façade, NAFTA-type agreements in effect place North American workers in competition with Latin American workers to see who will produce goods for the U.S. and Canadian consumer markets for the lowest possible wages. In conjunction with provisions of the recently completed Uruguay round of the General Agreement on Tariffs and Trade (GATT), they also pose a major threat to environmental standards. The agreements with Canada and Mexico, for example, set up unelected trinational boards, made up of trade experts, as secret and final arbiters in all decisions relating to commerce and trade. Any federal, state, or local law or regulation, no matter how democratically arrived at, can be set aside by a NAFTA disputation board that finds it might be an impediment to trade. The "side agreements" added to Clinton's version of the NAFTA package make the process of challenging a labor rights or environmental violation so difficult and involved that a Mexican government official could "assure concerned industrialists that they should never worry about repercussions from NAFTA's labor and environmental enforcement boards."

The dangers of environmental pollution posed by NAFTA and GATT are of course much greater

554

to Latin America than to the United States or Canada. The Third World has already become what Eduardo Galeano calls "a kingdom of impunity" for environmental polluters. In the absence of strong grassroots opposition, NAFTA and GATT are likely to enhance the trend to make the South "the garbage dump of the North."

Cuba provided another test of Clinton's willingness to rethink old and discredited Reagan-Bush policies. The United Nations Assembly has three times voted overwhelmingly to condemn the U.S. embargo against Cuba; two summits of Latin American heads of state unanimously voted the same way; and a growing number of Cuban-Americans oppose a policy that inflicts hardships on their relatives on the island and obstructs further liberalization of the Cuban regime. The United States has long maintained normal relations with one great communist power, China, and in early 1994, in apparent response to pressure from U.S. business circles, President Clinton lifted economic sanctions against communist Vietnam, with which the United States once fought a long and bloody war. As regards Cuba, however, Clinton appeared frozen in the most hard-line cold war attitude. In part this may reflect his political debt to the most powerful and ultra-right Cuban-American leader, Jorge Más Canosa, son of a Batista official, who controls a Miami-based Cuban American National Foundation and numerous lobbying groups and Political Action committees whose sole reason for existence is to bring about Fidel Castro's downfall. In what has been called "a shameless piece of pandering for the votes of extremist elements of Florida's Cuban exile community," during the election campaign Clinton threatened "to drop the hammer on Cuba." He lost Florida anyway but reportedly received millions of dollars in campaign contributions from Más Canosa's Foundation.

Clinton's response to the overthrow of Haiti's constitutionally elected President Jean-Bertrand Aristide by a military coup in October 1991 also illustrates the essential continuity in the Latin American policies of Reagan, Bush, and Clinton, as discussed above.

On the subject of human rights, the Clinton Administration displays the opportunism of its predecessors. Clinton claims to favor civilian regimes and oppose dictatorships and military coups. In practice, however, that position is applied selectively, pragmatically, taking account of the relationship of the country in question to the United States and its acceptance or rejection of U.S.-sponsored economic policies. Thus the Clinton administration remained silent when the Mexican army ran amuck during the January 1994 uprising in Chiapas, carrying out summary executions, torture of prisoners, and aerial attacks on civil populations. Mexico, of course, is a favored U.S. junior partner. The Clinton Administration took the same benign attitude toward Peru's President Fujimori's *autogolpe* ("self-coup"), after he proved his firm loyalty to the neoliberal economic doctrine and program. In general, in the words of the *Washington Report on the Hemisphere,* "the Administration seems prepared to wink at moderate human rights violations provided they occur in a 'good cause,' like fighting leftist guerrillas."

Still unclear is the future of the Latin American "war on drugs" under Clinton. He inherited from Bush a vast antidrug operation with a heavy stress on military involvement. Bush's 1990 Andean Initiative pledged $2.2 billion in military, law, and economic assistance over five years to be used in the antidrug campaign. Much of the military assistance was openly employed by the Colombian and Peruvian governments for counterinsurgency campaigns that killed more peasants than insurgents. The United States offered no objection to this misuse of its aid. By Bush's last year in office the United States Southern Command was involved in dozens of operations throughout Latin America. That "messy and unsuccessful engagement" continues under Clinton and involves thousands of soldiers and police and billions of dollars of U.S. taxpayers' money. Yet experts agree that the war has failed to reduce the availability or use of drugs in the United States. In September 1993 a report produced jointly by the Senate Judiciary Committee and International Narcotics Control Caucus concluded:

Children walk by an armored vehicle, part of a Mexican invasion force that drove into rebel-held territory in Chiapas in February 1995. Although the offensive was soon halted and Mexican President Zedilio called for renewed peace talks, the Zapatista leadership declared the army must withdraw from captured territory before talks could proceed.

"Regrettably, America's drug epidemic is worse today than it was three years ago."

During and after their campaign Clinton and Gore promised that the emphasis of their drug-control program would change from federal enforcement strategies to community-based treatment and education. Such a change would encounter large obstacles, including the opposition of entrenched bureaucracies like the Drug Enforcement Administration and the Department of Defense. Most difficult of all, such a shift would require recognition that the roots of the drug problem are not in Latin America but at home, in the economic and social decay of communities and the despair and alienation such decay generates. In the current atmosphere in the United States, however, marked by demands for more repression, more prisons, more police—demands Clinton supports—such a shift in thinking about the drug problem is not likely to take place.

Clinton's drug war budget for the 1995 fiscal year requests $13.2 billion—the highest antidrug budget in U.S. history. Of this sum, $7.8 billion is to be used in reducing the supply and $5.4 billion in reducing the demand. Despite the increased funding for treatment and rehabilitation, the Clinton program continues to stress repression and the Latin American source of the problem. In Clinton's view, writes a Peruvian commentator, "the drug trafficking organizations are foreign, and international drug trafficking is responsible for the crime in the streets of the United States. There are only U.S. victims."

Chapter 21

Latin American Society in Transition

Crises in the Twentieth Century

By the early 1990s, Latin America's economic, social, and political problems had reached explosive proportions. The neoliberal economic model imposed on the area by the International Monetary Fund and the World Bank sharpened all the old problems of dependency and created new ones. Those lending agencies used the area's gigantic foreign debt as a weapon to pressure the countries of the region into accepting neoliberal policies—privatization, lower tariffs, cuts in social programs, and emphasis on exports instead of production for internal consumption and development—in return for easier repayment terms and new loans. Agreements under the much ballyhooed Brady Plan, which was supposed to ease the burden of the debtor nations, had failed to provide significant or lasting relief. From 1980 to 1992 Latin America had a net negative transfer of capital of $220 billion, meaning that $220 more billion left the region than came in. Most of this exported capital was in the form of debt payments. Despite this immense drain, the foreign debt did not decrease; from $250 billion in 1980 it rose to $425 billion in 1990 and $478 billion in 1993 and was projected by the World Bank to reach $547 billion in 1994. Deals made with debtor countries under the Brady Plan continued to siphon off enormous sums in interest, while their debt-swap provisions enabled foreign corporations and their domestic partners to acquire profitable Latin American state enterprises in exchange for depreciated debt for a fraction of their worth.

Latin America's unequal terms of trade also caused immense losses to the region. Latin

America exported cheap primary goods that suffered from declining demand and prices but had to pay exorbitantly high prices for imported technology, machinery, and other finished products. The volume of Latin American exports in 1992 was 86 percent more than in 1980, but the value of the exports was only 24 percent higher because of a 42 percent decline in export prices. Latin America, in other words, had to export much more in order to earn as much as before.

These and other economic and social indicators suggested that the nineties might become another "lost" decade, like the eighties. The per capita Gross Domestic Product (GDP), for example, dropped from a base of 100 in 1980 to 92.7 in 1992. Unemployment hovers about 10 percent in most countries, and if the underemployment of the "informal sector" is included, the figure could reach 50 percent or more. Inflation, averaging 1,185 percent in 1990, still registered 410 percent in 1992. Between 1980 and 1992 wages lost 40 percent of their purchasing power. After a decade of neoliberal "structural adjustment," poverty has increased, with 41 percent of the population, or 183 million, living below the poverty line, and 21 percent, or 88 million, described as living in extreme poverty.

The harmful effects of the neoliberal economic program reached into every area of Latin American life, including its political institutions. Politicians like Menem in Argentina, Fujimori in Peru, and Collor in Brazil have resorted to populist demagoguery to gain power and conceal the antipopular essence of their neoliberal projects. This politics of deceit served to discredit democracy and promote cynicism and abstentionism.

Economic Problems

By 1990 the population of Latin America was estimated to be 433 million. It was growing at a rate of about 2 percent a year and was projected to reach 515 million by the end of the century. In order to achieve even a modest improvement in Latin American living standards, per capita staple food production should grow considerably faster than population. In fact, Latin American agricultural production has greatly increased in recent decades due to the expansion of acreage and the "green revolution," which has dramatically raised crop yields through increased use of tractors, fertilizers, and new hybrids. But the bulk of this increase is accounted for by increased production of such export crops as sugar, coffee, and soybeans. Meanwhile, there has been a sharp increase in the importation of grains. Countries that once were self-sufficient now suffer from food shortages. Mexico, which as late as 1969–1971 was a net exporter of grain, had to import one-third of its food needs in 1992. In 1988–1989 Mexican food imports consumed more than half of the foreign exchange obtained from oil exports. The dependence on food imports is reflected in the price of staple foods, which has risen more rapidly than wages in most Latin American countries. The consumption of foods of high nutritive content has declined in recent decades in some of the most favored countries of the area, such as Argentina and Uruguay. The growing dependency in Latin America on imports of basic grains, purchased at international market prices, means that large sectors of the population find these imports prohibitively expensive. Approval by the United States, Canada, and Mexico of the North American Free Trade Agreement (NAFTA) foreshadows similar agreements with other Latin American countries that would open their markets to imports of U.S. grain. Recent changes in the General Agreement on Tariffs and Trade (GATT) that would reduce or eliminate tariffs within five to ten years, opening Latin American markets to unlimited imports, also increase the likelihood of increased Latin American dependence on grain imports. The dangers of such extreme dependency on foreign grain producers are obvious.

Population pressure on limited land resources is not a major cause of the food problem. In 1980, of the total area of 570 million hectares suitable for cultivation, only 143 million hectares, or 28 percent, were actually worked. A major cause of the food crisis is an agricultural strategy, vigorously promoted by the IMF, the World Bank, and the U.S. Agency for International Development,

558 that emphasizes export crops at the expense of internal consumption. A closely related cause of the problem is an unjust system of land tenure and use, the latifundio. The new capitalist, highly mechanized type of latifundio in particular sharply limits employment and absorbs by legal or illegal means many small plots previously devoted to staple food productions, forcing many small farmers to move into rugged hillsides, rain forests, or other land of poor agricultural quality or to migrate to the cities and plantations in search of employment.

Along with Latin America's food crisis there has arisen an ecological crisis of unprecedented proportions caused by reckless, profit-driven exploitation of the area's natural and human resources. Central America again provides a prime example. More than two-thirds of the region's rain forests have been destroyed, resulting in the loss of many valuable plants and animal species. Deforestation and watershed destruction cause massive soil erosion, undermining the basis for continued subsistence farming. Dangerous pesticides, banned in the United States, poison thousands of workers. About 50 percent of all Central Americans lack access to safe drinking water. As a result, infant diarrhea, malaria, and chronic parasitosis remain among the leading causes of death in the region.

There is a direct link between the food and ecological crises and the debt crisis. In Central America, for example, the debt crisis pressures governments to exploit their reserves of natural resources as quickly as possible to pay principal, interest, and interest-on-interest to the international lending agencies. Moreover, in Central America, as in other parts of Latin America, the international banks dictate to debtor governments certain changes in economic policy, innocuously called "structural adjustments," that are designed to make more foreign exchange available to service the foreign debt. In addition to "austerity" measures—meaning reductions in government spending, especially in the realm of social services, education, health, and the like— the debtor states are required to increase production of traditional and nontraditional exports in order to boost foreign exchange earnings. The

immense, unpayable foreign debt weighs like a nightmare on Latin America, draining resources that should be used for sustainable development, imposing economic and social policies that make impossible sound development. Recognition that the debt is unpayable should lead to negotiations between debtors and creditors that result in forgiveness of all or the greater part of the debt. Liberation from the debt is a prior condition for the solution of the food and ecological crises of the area.

Freed from the burdens of the debt and the associated corporate control of economic policy, Latin Americans can adopt a new agricultural strategy based on different priorities that would place meeting the area's nutritional needs ahead of generating foreign exchange to make interest payments or extracting wealth for agribusinesses from the production of industrial crops, livestock feed crops, and luxury fruits and vegetables. Such a shift would have to take place within the context of thorough, democratically controlled agrarian reforms. It would be naive, however, to expect that most Latin American governments, currently controlled by and representing elite interests, will willingly adopt such new policies, which should include strict monitoring and control of the activities of foreign corporations that in the past have practiced "garbage imperialism," using Latin America as a dumping ground for toxic waste, freely polluting its soil and rivers as they have done in the Mexican-U.S. border zone. Sound environmental policies must also recognize the relation between poverty and environmental degradation. Much of the deforestation taking place in the Amazonian rain forest, for example, is the result of the exodus of landless peasants to the region, where they make clearings for planting, firewood, and other uses. That is why agrarian reform must occupy a central place in the solution of both the food and ecological crises.

The obstacles in the path of realizing such reforms are very great since they run counter to the current trend of "globalization" of the world economy, favored by the United States and other major capitalist powers and reflected in the recently approved NAFTA and the amended GATT.

The leading international environmental organization Greenpeace claimed, "Many of NAFTA's provisions . . . are simply impossible to reconcile with the principles of environmental protection and resource conservation." What makes these agreements especially dangerous is that they create organisms with supranational powers, including the right to nullify or make changes in domestic laws. "They augur," observed *Latinamerica Press,* "an Orwellian world ruled by commerce, with secret tribunals guaranteeing the right to trade freely, to exploit natural resources and to produce products at the lowest possible cost regardless of the environmental consequences."

Social Problems

The area's social problems have reached gigantic proportions in recent years. The main causes are growing poverty and reductions in social programs (social-sector spending has declined by more than 50 percent over the last decade). Both developments are directly linked to the ongoing debt crisis and the neoliberal "structural adjustment" programs adopted by most Latin American governments in response to that crisis.

Housing is one of the area's worst social problems. Throughout the area, much of it is improvised, ranging from thatched huts and caves to tin and plywood shacks, and lacks proper sanitary facilities. The absence of adequate drinking water and sewage services contributes to a high incidence of parasitic and infectious diseases.

Rising health problems are clearly related to the present economic crisis, the worst since the Great Depression of the 1930s. Purchasing power has declined by 40 percent or more in many nations in recent years; in some countries half the working force is unemployed or underemployed. Many Latin American governments have sharply reduced health services as part of austerity programs designed to meet interest payments on foreign debt. These cutbacks are reflected in the deterioration of hospital care, fewer pharmaceutical imports, and reduced government support for medical schools.

The reappearance of diseases that had apparently been eradicated in the area provides other evidence that the health situation in Latin America is deteriorating. In 1991 Peru had its first cholera epidemic in more than 100 years. In its first three months the epidemic took over 1,000 lives and infected 150,000 others. From Peru it spread to Colombia, Brazil, Chile, and Ecuador and soon reached the suburbs of Buenos Aires. Like the upsurge in the incidence of malaria that accompanied it, the cholera epidemic was linked to the absence of clean drinking water, inadequate sanitation, and poor health facilities, conditions that are also major causes of such infections as typhoid, hepatitis, and the great killer diarrhea.

Children are the principal victims of malnutrition, the greatest health problem. Recent UNICEF statistics indicate that in Latin America, 3,000 children under the age of five die every day; malnutrition is believed to account for half of these deaths. Commercial infant formulas, aggressively promoted in Latin America by such transnational corporations as Nestlé and Bristol Myers, have contributed to infant malnutrition because poor women have been persuaded to substitute bottled formula for breast milk. In areas without clean water, the mothers' frequent practice of watering the milk to save money on formula makes bottle feeding especially dangerous for newborns, resulting in repeated epidemics of diarrhea and a vicious cycle of diarrhea-malnutrition that brings early death. Latin American infant mortality rates declined in the 1970s but increased in the 1980s as a result of deteriorating economic conditions.

Hunger, neglect, and disease are not the only threats millions of Latin American children and young adults face. There is a frightening indifference on the part of the authorities to the killing of thousands of street urchins by death squads, often composed of off-duty policemen. These "children of chaos" have been forced into the streets to fend for themselves or as street vendors to help out their parents. Some become petty criminals and a source of annoyance to businessmen and conservative middle-class groups who wish to "cleanse" the streets by any means and hire off-duty policemen to assassinate the offending children. A study by the human rights group Americas Watch and the University of São Paulo

The killing of homeless street children by death squads, sometimes hired by businessmen and conservative middle-class groups to "cleanse" the streets, is a fairly common Latin American phenomenon, especially in Brazil and Guatemala. Here a group of Brazilian street urchins organize their own protest against the killing of some of their number.

confirmed that 5,644 teenagers between the ages of fifteen and seventeen were murdered in Brazil between 1988 and 1991. Violence against children is most common in Brazil and Guatemala but occurs elsewhere.

Latin America suffers from a tremendous shortage of educational facilities. In Brazil, for example, a majority of school-age children do not attend school because there are not enough schools and teachers or because the poverty of their parents forces them to join the work force. Almost everywhere the dropout rate is very high. Only socialist Cuba and more recently Nicaragua (until the effects of the contra war and the rightist electoral victory in 1990 reversed that trend)

showed dramatic improvement in this area. Cuba's nationwide campaign to wipe out illiteracy had achieved its goal by 1982.

An accelerated urbanization, caused by a massive migration of rural dwellers to the city, has sharpened all social problems. The rural exodus results from the interplay of two forces: the "pull" of the city, which attracts rural people with the frequently illusory prospect of factory work and a better life, and the "push" of the countryside, where concentration of land and the mechanization of agriculture are expelling millions of peasants from their farms and jobs. "Poverty and despair," writes Jorge E. Hardoy, a leading student of urban problems, "are behind many of these massive displacements." The urban population is increasing at more than twice the rate of the population as a whole. A United Nations estimate foresaw that by the year 2000 the urban population (*urban* here refers to a settlement of more than 2,000) would form some 80 percent of the total population of the area.

Most striking, however, has been the growth in the number of cities with over 1 million inhabitants. Between 1950 and 1970 the number of such cities rose from six to seventeen, and their total population increased from 15 to 55 million. If these trends continue, in the year 2000 the cities will contain about 220 million inhabitants, or about 37 percent of the total Latin American population at that time. In the same period the number of people living below the poverty line is expected to increase from 40 percent in 1985 to 66 percent in 2000.

Industrialization and the rural exodus have produced the phenomenon of hyperurbanization—the rise of vast urban agglomerations or zones of urban sprawl. About 80 percent of Brazil's industrial production is located in the metropolitan zones of São Paulo, Rio de Janeiro, and Belo Horizonte. Two-thirds of Argentine production is concentrated in the area between Buenos Aires and Rosario. More than half of the industrial production of Chile and Peru is located in the metropolitan zones of Santiago and Lima-Callao, respectively. Caracas accounts for 40 percent of the industrial production of Venezuela. Between 25 and 50 percent of the populations of Uruguay, Mexico, and Argentina now live in the capitals of these countries.

As these vast urban concentrations increase, life becomes more and more difficult for their inhabitants. All the urban problems—food, housing, transportation, schools, drinking water, and sanitation—are immensely aggravated. Mexico City is a case in point. At the present rate of growth, the population will reach 30 million by the end of the century. The pollution caused by toxic agents generated by the city's 35,000 industrial establishments and 3 million cars has been denounced by medical specialists as a major danger to health and life; half of all infants have unacceptable toxic levels in their blood, which,

specialists warn, could reduce IQs by as much as 10 percent. Shantytowns cover almost 40 percent of the urban area and house approximately 4 million people, a large proportion of whom are unemployed or underemployed; in 1978, 1.2 million persons lacked potable water. "The Latin American metropolis," writes city planner Thomas Angotti, "is characterized by mass poverty and severe environmental pollution on a scale generally unparalleled in the North."

In Europe and North America, urbanization, industry, and the demand for labor grew at a fairly even pace, but in Latin America, industrial growth and demand for labor lag far behind the explosive growth of the urban population. Much of the new industry, especially its foreign-owned sector, is highly mechanized and automated; it therefore generates relatively little new employment. In such a traditional Latin American industry as textiles, mechanization has actually produced a net loss of jobs. The low purchasing power of the masses also hinders the creation of new jobs, for the market for goods is quickly saturated and industry chronically operates below capacity. Finally, many of the rural migrants are illiterate and lack the skills required by modern industry. Perhaps as many as 50 percent of the area's labor force are completely or partly unemployed.

Industry's inability to absorb the supply of labor has produced an exaggerated growth of the so-called service or informal sector. The growth of this sector considerably exceeds that of the industrial labor force, which grew from 20 to 24 percent of the labor force from 1960 to 1980, while the service sector rose from 33 to 45 percent in the same period. The service sector includes a great number of poorly paid domestic servants and a mass of individuals who eke out a precarious living as lottery ticket vendors, car watchers and washers, shoeshiners, and street peddlers of all kinds. As a result of the economic crisis of the 1980s and 1990s, this informal sector of the economy has grown considerably in the past decade.

Cuba alone has made a serious effort to check and reverse the hypertrophy of the city. Almost from the day it took power, the revolutionary

562 government undertook to redress the balance by shifting the bulk of its investments to the countryside and by raising rural living standards through the provision of adequate medical, educational, and social services; a more rational geographic distribution of the economic infrastructure; and the creation of the planned new cities. Thanks to these policies, aided by the departure of thousands of middle-class dissidents for the United States, the growth of Havana's population had begun to decline by 1965 and a reverse current of migration began from the capital to a countryside that was itself becoming urbanized.

The New Class Structure

In the middle decades of the twentieth century, industrialization, urbanization, and the commercialization of agriculture significantly altered the Latin American social structure and the relative weight of the various classes. These changes included the transformation of the old landed elite into a new latifundista class with a capitalist character, the emergence of a big industrial and financial bourgeoisie with close ties to foreign capital, an enormous growth of the so-called urban middle sectors, and the rise of a small but militant industrial working class. More recently, the neoliberal economic policies adopted by most Latin American governments, favoring multinationals and their local allies, have caused a sharp decline in the number and influence of small and medium national manufacturers; they have also caused growing impoverishment and unemployment among the middle class and the working class as a result of the privatization or dismantling of many state enterprises, reduction of social services, and a general downsizing of the state as part of "structural adjustment" programs demanded by the IMF and the World Bank. A survey of these and other developments suggests the complexity of modern Latin American class alignments and the possible direction of future social and political change.

The Great Landowners

Although they have had to yield first place economically and politically to the big bourgeoisie, with which they maintain close links, the great landowners, Latin America's oldest ruling class, retain immense power, thanks to their control over the land and water resources of the area. Over the last few decades, as earlier chapters have shown, there has been a major expansion of the latifundio, especially of the new agribusiness type, which produces industrial and export crops with the aid of improved technology and wage labor. More recently, the dominant policies of free trade and open doors to foreign investment have further spurred the trend toward concentration of landownership and penetration of Latin American agriculture by foreign capital. Chile, whose civilian government has made no effort to restore the agrarian reform destroyed by the Pinochet dictatorship, and Mexico, where Congress recently approved an agrarian law that ends land redistribution and legalizes the sale or rental of communally owned ejido land, illustrate the shift toward policies favoring the rise of a new latifundio.

The traditional hacendado is a vanishing breed. His successor is often a cosmopolitan, university-trained type who combines agribusiness with industrial and financial interests. But the arbitrary and predatory spirit of the old hacendados survives in the new latifundistas. The great landowners continue to be the most reactionary class in Latin American society.

The New Bourgeoisie

A native commercial bourgeoisie arose in Latin America after independence and consolidated its position with the rise of the neocolonial order after mid-century. In the second half of the nineteenth century, an industrialist class, largely of immigrant stock, appeared in response to the demand of a growing urban population for consumer goods. World War I further stimulated the movement for export-import substitution industrialization. But the day of the industrial entrepreneur did not arrive until the great economic crisis of 1930 disrupted the trading patterns of the area. Aided by favorable international and domestic background conditions and massive state intervention, the native industrial bourgeoisie quickly gained strength and in many countries displaced the landed elite as the dominant social and economic force. As a rule, however, the new bourgeoisie avoided frontal collision with the latifundistas, preferring to form bonds of kinship and interest with the landed elite.

Meanwhile, foreign capital, attracted by the potential of the growing Latin American market, began to pour into the area, particularly after 1945. Possessing immensely superior capital and technological resources, foreign firms absorbed many small- and middle-sized national companies and came to dominate key sectors of the economy of the host countries. Aware, however, that the survival of a national bourgeoisie was essential to their own security, foreign capitalists endeavored to form close ties with the largest, most powerful national firms through the formation of mixed companies and other devices. This dependence on and linkage with foreign corporations explains why the Latin American big bourgeoisie lacks nationalist sentiment.

In its youth, some sections of the Latin American national bourgeoisie supported the efforts of such nationalist, populist chieftains as Cardenas, Perón, and Vargas to restrict foreign economic influence and accepted, though with misgivings, their concessions to labor. But soon the big bourgeoisie adopted the hostility of its foreign allies to restrictions on foreign capital and independent trade unionism. With rare exceptions, the big capitalists supported repressive military regimes in such countries as Brazil, Argentina, Uruguay, and Chile until, convinced that the policies of those regimes threatened the stability of capitalism itself, they became converts to democracy.

The neoliberal policies currently in vogue have given an immense stimulus to the alliance of foreign multinationals and local big capitalists, an alliance in which foreign capital plays the dominant role. The process has been under way in many countries, but particularly in Brazil, Argentina, Mexico, Chile, and Venezuela. Privatization has become a major instrument for denationalizing the Latin American economy through auctions and debt-equity swaps that virtually donate valuable state companies to foreign firms. The privatization and liberalization programs under way enjoy the overwhelming support of the big Latin American industrial bourgeoisie. This surrender of the Latin American state and economic elite to foreign capital represents a transition to a new, more completely dependent relationship.

The Urban Middle Sectors

The urban middle sectors are that great mass of urban dwellers who occupy an intermediate position between the bourgeoisie and the landed elite, on the one hand, and the peasantry and the industrial working class, on the other. The boundaries of this intermediate group with other classes are vague and overlapping. At one end, for example, the group includes highly paid business managers whose lifestyle and attitudes identify them with the big bourgeoisie; at the other, it takes in store clerks and lower-echelon government servants whose incomes are often lower than those of skilled workers.

The oldest urban middle sector consists of self-employed craftsmen, shopkeepers, and owners of innumerable small enterprises. The great number of small workshops in which the owner both works and employs other workers suggests the importance of this sector.

White-collar employees form another large urban intermediate sector. Urbanization, the growth of commercial capitalism, and the vast expansion of the state in the middle decades of the century contributed to an inflation of both public and private bureaucracies. Until recently, public employees made up about one-fifth of the economically active population of the area.

University students compose a sizable urban middle sector. Between 1960 and 1970 their number rose from 250,000 to over 1 million. The great majority come from middle-class backgrounds, and many must combine work and study. Student discontent with inadequate curricula and teaching methods and the injustices of the social and political order have made the university a focal point of dissidence and protest. But the students are in the end transients, in Latin America as elsewhere; their radical or reformist zeal often subsides after they enter a professional career.

Because of their great size, the ideology of the urban middle sectors and their actual and potential role in social change are issues of crucial importance. Following World War II, many foreign experts on Latin America, especially in the United States, pinned great hopes on the "emerging middle sectors" (to which they assigned the new industrialist class), as agents of progressive social and economic change. The history of the following decades did not confirm these expectations. The urban middle sectors mushroomed, but with the exception of many students and intellectual workers—teachers, writers, scientists—they were not a force for social change.

The error of the foreign experts consisted in confusing the Latin American middle sectors with their counterparts in Europe and North America. Unlike the European and North American middle classes, the Latin American middle sectors did not arise from a process of dynamic industrial development. They arose in the protective shadow of a neocolonial export-import economy that was gradually transformed into a dependent, deformed capitalism with strong ties to the latifundia. Very few self-made men came from their ranks. Their ideology mirrored that of the ruling class, whose lifestyle they tried to copy by keeping one or two servants and in other ways. They regarded manual labor as degrading, resented forced contact with the lower orders in buses and trolleys, and looked down on Indians and blacks. Confused and misinformed on economic and political issues, they were easy prey to rightist demagogy and anticommunist propaganda. These groups provided the mass base for the right-wing military coups in Brazil and Chile. But, the urban middle sectors should not be written off as hopeless reactionaries. By their very intermediate nature, they are capable of strong political oscillations, especially in response to the movement of the economy. The "savage

capitalism" implanted in many Latin American countries in recent decades by both military and civilian governments is playing havoc with middle-class living standards and expectations. In the process it is also transforming the traditionally conservative, complacent thought patterns of the urban middle sectors.

The Peasantry

The term *peasantry* refers here to all small landowners, tenants, and landless rural laborers. As documented in previous chapters, the current expansion of the new type of latifundio is creating an unparalleled crisis for the Latin American peasantry. The increased use of tractors and other kinds of mechanized farm equipment has already displaced millions of farmworkers and the process is accelerating. The current movement toward the removal of trade barriers, opening national markets to the competition of foreign grain producers with immensely superior resources, threatens the existence of large groups of small farmers. Meanwhile, the trend is not to adopt land reforms but to reverse them; in Mexico, for example, the recent passage of legislation making communally owned ejido land alienable is removing the last obstacles to the concentration of land in a few hands. Contrary to some earlier assumptions, however, despite the exodus to the cities the countryside is not becoming depopulated; the number of small farmers is actually growing, but in most areas they are becoming increasingly marginalized and pauperized, reduced to subsistence farming or compelled to combine farming with wage labor.

The Industrial Working Class

The rapid growth of capitalism in Latin America since about 1930 has been accompanied by a parallel growth of the industrial working class. Although miners and factory workers form the best-organized and most class-conscious detachments of the army of labor, they are a minority of the labor force. Artisans, self-employed or working in shops employing less than five persons, constitute the largest group. The predominance of the artisan shop, whose labor relations are marked by paternalism and individual bargaining, hinders the development of workers' class consciousness and solidarity.

Despite its small size, the industrial working class has played a key role in major recent movements for social and political democracy in Latin America. Armed Bolivian tin miners helped achieve the victory of the 1952 revolution and its program of land reform and nationalization of mines. Cuban workers gave decisive support to the guerrilla struggle against the Batista dictatorship, and their general strike in 1959 helped topple it. The working class of Buenos Aires intervened at a critical moment (October 1945) to save Juan Perón from being overthrown by a reactionary coup, and its pressure broadened his reform program. In Chile the working class led the Popular Unity coalition that brought Salvador Allende to the presidency, ushering in a three-year effort (1970–1973) to achieve socialism by peaceful means.

These advances—particularly the Cuban and Chilean revolutions—provoked a counterrevolutionary reaction that until recently was still ascendant. In many countries under personal or military dictatorships, all working-class parties were banned, trade unions were abolished or placed under strict government control, and many labor leaders were murdered or forced into exile. The effects of this repression of the Latin American labor movement continue to be felt today.

The gradual restoration of formal democracy in the region did not bring full recognition of labor's right to organize and other basic rights. In Chile, for example, the new civilian government retained major features of the Pinochet labor code. In Mexico, workers may not freely join unions of their choice, and most union members have been forced to join unions affiliated with the ruling PRI. In the export-processing or free trade zones, like Mexico's *maquila* sector, union rights are routinely ignored. A major threat to trade unionism, particularly in Central America and the Caribbean, is the spread of *Solidarismo*—an ideology promoting company unions that withdraw

growing numbers of workers from the collective bargaining process.

Today there are about 40 million union members in Latin America, comprising about 20 percent of the labor force. Despite continuing repression and restrictive legislation, labor is waging increasingly effective strike battles, like the 1993 general strike in Ecuador against the neoliberal economic policies of President Durán-Ballén, and in some countries it is forming coalitions with various grassroots organizations for joint struggle against the devastating social consequences of the "structural adjustment" programs. It is increasingly turning, too, to political action to achieve its goals. The large advances of the Workers' party in Brazil and the December 1993 election of Rafael Caldera to the presidency of Venezuela with the support of a coalition that included socialist and workers' parties illustrate the potential of this approach for changing the direction of economic and social policy in Latin America.

The Service or Informal Sector

Earlier in this chapter we noted that this sector, the largest of all,[1] arose as a result of industry's inability to absorb the supply of labor; we also said that it included "a great number of poorly paid domestic servants and a mass of individuals who eke out a precarious living as lottery ticket vendors, car watchers and washers, shoeshiners and street peddlers." But the meaning of "informal sector" is extremely elastic and the list of occupations that fit the category almost endless. It includes, for example, workers for manufacturing and repair operations who subcontract work they do in their own homes or small workshops, prostitutes, beggars, and garbage pickers who sell various types of wastepaper, bottles, and the like. Its main defining elements are self-employment and the irregular and precarious nature of the work. "Informal sector," observes sociologist Tessa Cubitt, "implies a dualist interpretation

[1] According to the International Labor Organization, from 1980 to 1992 employment in the informal sector rose from 40.2 percent to 54.4 percent of the total.

578 ancient city of Cartagena de las Indias, dreaming behind her great walls. Pirates disturb her sleep, but she awakes serene, then softly closes her eyes; fanned by her palm trees and rocked in the hammock of the waves, she falls asleep again. But Santos Chocano could also sound a note of social protest:

Indian who toils without rest
on the lands that others own,
Do you not know that they are yours
by right of your blood and sweat?[3]

The intensely personal poems of Ramón López Velarde celebrated the provincial scenes of his youth in verse free from sentimentality. His most famous poem, however, is "Suave Patria" (1921), a poem in two tender, teasing "acts" in which the poet expresses his love for Mexico with complete freedom from rhetoric. In the "intermezzo" between the acts, the poet invokes the Indian hero Cuauhtemoc, an early illustration of the indigenismo that is a major aspect of twentieth-century Mexican culture. The intermezzo opens: "Young forebear: hear me praise you, the only hero of artistic stature." But there are no heroics: the mood is subdued, tragic, compassionate. Upon the poet's spirit weigh the terrible losses and sufferings of the Mexican Revolution. His Cuauhtemoc is a Man of Sorrows; he is also an instrument for the fusion of Spanish and Indian elements into a Mexican synthesis.

The Mexican Revolution, which subtly colors "Suave Patria," also pervades the somber novels of Mariano Azuela (1873–1952). Their main theme is the betrayal by middle-class leaders and cynical intellectuals of the peasants and workers whose ignorance and valor they exploit. Azuela's best novel, *The Underdogs* (1916), tells the story of a peasant, Demetrio Macías, who organizes a guerrilla band, rises to the rank of general, and is killed fighting for Villa. He is the victim of blind forces he does not understand, over which he has no control. His simplicity and naiveté contrast with the cunning of the demagogic medical stu-

dent Luis Cervantes, who carefully keeps out of harm's way and uses looted diamonds to lay the foundation of his future professional career.

The new cultural nationalism also found expression in the novels of the Colombian José Eustasio Rivera (1888–1928) and the Venezuelan Rómulo Gallegos (1884–1969). In Rivera's best work, *The Vortex* (1924), a violent tale of rubber collectors in the Amazonian jungle, the implacable wilderness joins the "rubber lords" in debasing men, in shattering their hopes and bodies. A novel of protest against the barbarism of his country, it is also a truly national novel, the first Colombian novel to depict the difficult lives of the cowboys of the plains and the rubber collectors of the jungle.

The novels of Rómulo Gallegos, an active opponent of long-time dictator Juan Vicente Gómez, depict the hitherto neglected life of Venezuela's *llanos* (plains and jungles) and suggest that the country's destructive regional conflicts can be solved by the fusion of the antagonistic elements: whites and blacks, indigenous and European cultures, barbarism and civilization. In *Doña Bárbara* (1929), the mulatta heroine whose name the novel bears embodies the barbaric vigor and lawless spirit of the people of the plains. Santos Luzardo, on whose land she has encroached, is a city-educated lawyer who finds that he himself must resort to violence to defeat her. Their duel is finally ended by Santos Luzardo's marriage to Doña Bárbara's daughter, a child of nature whom he carefully educates, with particular care that she drop the plebeian dialect of the llanos and learn to speak and act like the "exquisite young ladies of Caracas." The patent artificiality of the civilization-barbarism dichotomy, reflecting Gallegos's middle-class liberalism, weakens his works.

A different viewpoint on the quarrel between civilization and barbarism emerges in the gaucho novel *Don Segundo Sombra* (1926) by Ricardo Guiraldes (1886–1927). One of the most perfect of Latin American novels, it evokes with incomparable skill a regional type rapidly receding into the past, but the portrait is clearly touched with nostalgia. The gaucho hero emerges as a digni-

[3] "Quién sabe," quoted in Jean Franco, *The Modern Culture of Latin America* (New York: Praeger, 1967), p. 49.

fied and rounded individual, perfectly adapted to his milieu; he needs no transformation from without, for he is already a completely civilized human being.

Literature and Society, 1930–1995: A Social Consciousness

In the 1930s, a time of growing economic difficulties accompanied by the sharpening of class struggles in mines, factories, and plantations, the radicalization of Latin American writers gave rise to the novel of social protest, frequently influenced by Marxist ideology. Since the principal victims of capitalist exploitation in Latin America were Indians, the new novels of social protest were usually Indianist novels as well. Leading representatives of this genre were Jorge Icaza (b. 1906) in Ecuador, Ciro Alegría (1909–1967) and José M. Arguedas (1901–1969) in Peru, and Miguel A. Asturias (1899–1974) in Guatemala.

The early Indianist novels, like *Birds Without a Nest* (1889) by Clorinda Matto de Turner or *Race of Bronze* (1919) by Alcides Arguedas, had found the roots of Indian misery and exploitation in the personal vices or weaknesses of the ruling classes or of the Indians themselves. In the new Indianist novel, the destruction of the Indians flows inexorably from the operation of blind economic forces, of which the grasping landlord or exploitive foreign company (the Indianist novel is often an anti-imperialist novel as well) are mere instruments. The new Indianist novelists also made a more serious effort to enter the Indian mind and sometimes prepared themselves for their task by living with the Indians to learn their speech and customs.

Icaza's *Huasipungo* (1934) reports with blazing anger the brutal exploitation of a group of Ecuadorian Indians, which culminates in an effort to expel them from their parcels of land (*huasipungos*) to make way for the exploitation of the area by foreign oil companies. But the Indians are shown as so degraded by their servitude, so brutish even in dealing with one another, that it is difficult to sympathize with them. More successful in this respect is Ciro Alegría's *Broad and Alien Is the World* (1941), which also relates the destruction of an Indian community by a landowner bent on acquiring its lands. Alegría's idealized portrayal of Indian life and virtues borders on the sentimental, yet he convincingly portrays a communal society whose driving force is mutual aid and, therefore, engages the reader's sympathy with the Indians.

Land and labor struggles also characterize the Indianist novels of José M. Arguedas, who knew Quechua before he knew Spanish and had a profound mastery of Indian culture and customs. His novels achieve an unusual penetration of the Indian mentality through his effort to reproduce the rhythm and syntax of Quechua and evoke the religious world view of the Indians.

The Guatemalan writer Miguel A. Asturias is one of the founders of the school of magical realism, which attempts to depict Indian life as the Indians themselves might experience it, in terms of myth. In *Men of Maize* (1949), he records from this mythic perspective the losing struggle of the Indians to retain their land and way of life, using a style whose language and rhythms resemble those of the Maya language. The blend of fantasy and reality in Asturias's Indianist novels is far removed from the documentary tone of such regional novelists as Rivera, Gallegos, and Icaza.

In Brazil in the 1920s and 1930s, there arose a "northeastern school" that portrayed the varied social types and struggles of the drought-ridden sertão and the coastal sugar plantations. This group included Graciliano Ramos (1892–1953), José Lins do Rego (1901–1957), and Jorge Amado (b. 1912). In *Barren Lives* (1938), Ramos deals with the struggle of a cowherder against drought and starvation and his eventual flight to the city. The "sugar cane cycle" of Lins do Rego (1932–1943) chronicles the decline and fall of the old sugar aristocracy—the rise of the great *usina* (sugar mill) and the impact of economic change on planters, slaves, and their descendants. Partly based on Lins do Rego's own childhood and adult experiences, these novels reconstruct the social history of Brazilian sugar. In his *Cacao* (1933), Amado describes the life of the workers on the cacao plantations south of Bahia; in *The Violent*

580   *Land* (1943), he records the bloody struggles for economic and political power of the cacao planters.

Cuban novelist Alejo Carpentier applies the method of magical realism to West Indian blacks in *The Kingdom of This World* (1949); set in Haiti in the time of the French Revolution, it presents the rise and fall of the black dictator Henri Christophe and the emergence of a new mulatto ruling class as seen through the eyes of a house slave. Revolution and the corruption of revolutionaries are major themes of Carpentier's *The Age of Enlightenment* (1962), which is also set in the period of the French Revolution but deals with the Caribbean as a whole.

Poetry, like prose, revealed a new social consciousness. At the same time, Latin American poets struggled to free their verse from rhetoric and the tyranny of old forms. The difficult poetry of Peruvian Cesar Vallejo (1892–1938), though concerned from first to last with human anguish, with the inherently tragic human condition, reveals in its later phase a compassion for the victims of war and exploitation, a vision of a possible better life, that reflects his new socialist ideology. For the Chilean poet Pablo Neruda (1904–1973), as for Vallejo, the Spanish Civil War was a turning point; in a poem written at the beginning of the war he declares that henceforth he will unite his "lone wolf's walk" to the "walk of man." At the end of the war, he joined the Communist party and combined his poetic career with political activism until his death in 1973. His major work is *Canto general* (1950), an epic attempt to tell the history of the Latin American continent from the point of view of figures neglected by textbooks—workers, peasants, and fighters for freedom. Another major poet of left-wing tendencies, the Cuban Nicolás Guillen (b. 1902), founded the Afro-Cuban poetry movement, based on the rhythms and images of Cuban black folk poetry. With the passage of time, his poetry acquired strong social revolutionary and anti-imperialist tones.

The period since 1940 has seen a continuing revolution in the technique of the novel. This technical revolution is marked by intensive use of such devices as stream of consciousness,

Gabriel García Márquez, shown here accepting the Nobel literature award in 1982, uses magical imagery and fantasy to depict the violence and horror he sees in Colombian society.

flashbacks, symbolism, and fantasy. Some writers, like Argentina's Jorge Luis Borges in his *Ficciones* (1944), employ fantasy and other avant-garde techniques to demonstrate the absurdity and senselessness of life. Others, however, employ them to heighten awareness of an abhorrent social and political order. To one degree or another, these writers continue the Latin American tradition of employing literature as an instrument of social protest and change. Typical of such novelists is Mario Vargas Llosa, author of *Conversations in the Cathedral* (1970), whose structural and verbal disorder appears to re-enact the disorder of Peruvian life and geography.

We noted Asturias's use of magical realism in such Indianist novels as *Men of Maize*. His powerful *Mr. President* (1941), deals with a sinister dictator who rules with a vast apparatus of repression. In it dreams, memories, and imaginings replace the truth the characters cannot speak. Fantasy and reality blend in Asturias's anti-imperialist trilogy, *Strong Wind* (1950), *The Green Pope* (1954), and *The Eyes of the Buried* (1960), which deal with the formation of a monopolistic banana company and the struggles of small farmers and workers against it. In *Strong Wind*, when those struggles fail, a hurricane summoned by an Indian witch doctor destroys the company's plantations.

Fantasy is the means employed by Gabriel García Márquez to attack a monstrous social and political order in *One Hundred Years of Solitude* (1967), which records the history of an imaginary town set in the remote Colombian *ciénaga* (swampland) where García Márquez grew up. The book describes extraordinary people and events in deadpan fashion; in this magical world, miracles occur in the most natural way. But many of the fantastic situations "are absurd but logical exaggerations of real situations." The fantasies are a parody of Colombian history itself. Indeed, no event depicted in the book is as fantastic as history's la Violencia, the civil war unleashed in the Colombian countryside by conservative repression in 1949, a war that took perhaps 300,000 lives in the course of a few years.

Accelerated urbanization and industrialization have placed their stamp on the new novel; frequently, it is set in the great city and deals with the psychological problems of the urban middle class. In the urban novels of the Mexican Carlos Fuentes (b. 1929), a major theme is the betrayal of revolutionary ideals by the men who made the revolution. In *Where the Air Is Clearer* (1958), *The Clear Consciences* (1959), and *The Death of Artemio Cruz* (1962), Fuentes skillfully depicts the life of a cynical, cosmopolitan society. Alienation and the emptiness of middle- and upper-class life are also common themes in the Argentine urban novel; a good example is *A November Party* (1938) by Eduardo Mallea (b. 1903).

A significant recent development is the emergence of a "testimonial literature" that depicts the struggle of lower-class Latin American women and their families to survive under the most difficult, intolerable conditions. In her diary, *Child of the Dark* (1962), Carolina Maria de Jesus, a black *favela* (shantytown) dweller, records the violence and squalor of favela life. Its publication in Brazil brought Carolina immediate fame, and the book was later translated into many languages. In *Let me Speak! Testimony of Domitila, A Woman of the Bolivian Mines* (1978), Domitila Barrios de Chungara portrays the bleak lives of a Bolivian miner and his family. In *I, Rigoberta Menchú: An Indian Woman in Guatemala* (1982), the Nobel Peace Prize Winner and pro-Indian activist records the cruelties inflicted by the Guatemalan military on her own family and community. These books testify to the intellectual maturity and talent for self-expression of some Latin American peasant and working-class women with little or no formal education.

Although the beginnings of the Latin American film go back to the first decades of this century, its emergence as a major art form dates from the 1960s, when a group of Latin American filmmakers initiated a reaction against the dominant commercial Hollywood model. Revolutionary Cuba took the lead in this process, producing a large number of excellent films in a variety of styles and relatively free from political constraints. Two such works were Tomás Gutiérrez Alea's *Memories of Underdevelopment* and Humberto Solas's *Lucía* (1968). Working under difficult, sometimes clandestine or semiclandestine conditions, Argentine, Bolivian, Brazilian, and Central American filmmakers have produced first-class films that explore the history and the social and political problems of their nations. A number of recent Latin American films have won international awards and distinctions. Particularly valuable for an understanding of some episodes of Latin American history are the Argentine filmmaker María Luisa Bemberg's *I, The Worst of All* (1991), a sensitive reconstruction of the life of the poetess Sor Juana de la Cruz, and two Mexican films, Nicolás Echevarría's *Cabeza de Vaca* (1991), which captures the essence of the conquistador's pro-Indian message, and Alfonso Arau's delightful mix of Mexican twentieth-century history and fantasy, *Like Water for Chocolate* (1992), which broke all foreign-film records for popularity in the United States.

Continuing a tradition established by the founders of Latin American culture, modern Latin American scholars, writers, and artists have often tended to view their work not only as a means of self-expression but as an act of social protest, an instrument of social and political protest. To be sure, in Latin America as elsewhere, there are poets who write very private verse, novelists who deal with intensely personal themes, and painters whose abstract or surrealist art conveys no explicit social message. But to a greater extent than elsewhere, perhaps, the Latin American poet, novelist, painter, and filmmaker have also been the voice and the conscience of the people.

Glossary

Adelantado* Commander of a conquering expedition with governing powers in a frontier or newly conquered province.

Alcabala Spanish sales tax imposed by the crown.

Alcalde Member of a *cabildo* who in addition to administrative duties served as a judge of first instance.

Alcalde mayor Royal governor of a district. See *Corregidor.*

Audiencia A colonial high court and council of state under a viceroy or captain general, or the area of its jurisdiction.

Auto-da-fé or **auto-de-fé** The church's public ceremony of pronouncing judgment during the Inquisition, followed by execution of the sentence by secular authorities.

Ayllu A kinship and territorial unit of social organization, originally Inca, in the Andean region.

Cabildo A municipal council in the Spanish colonies.

Cacique (1) An Indian chief or local ruler. (2) A tyrannical local boss.

Calpulli A kinship and territorial unit of social organization in ancient and colonial Mexico.

Capitão mor The commander-in-chief of the military forces of a province in colonial Brazil.

Capitulación The contract between the Spanish monarch and the leader of an expedition of conquest or discovery.

Chinampa A garden or piece of arable land reclaimed from a lake or pond by dredging up soil from the bottom and piling it on a bed of wickerwork (Mexico).

* Terms repeatedly defined or glossed in the text are not included in the Glossary.

Credits